Communication Theories
for Everyday Life

John R. Baldwin

Stephen D. Perry

Mary Anne Moffitt

Illinois State University

PEARSON

Boston • New York • San Francisco
Mexico City • Montreal • Toronto • London • Madrid • Munich • Paris
Hong Kong • Singapore • Tokyo • Cape Town • Sydney

Executive Editor: *Karon Bowers*
Series Editorial Assistant: *Jennifer Trebby*
Marketing Manager: *Mandee Eckersley*
Senior Editorial-Production Administrator: *Beth Houston*
Editorial-Production Service: *Walsh & Associates, Inc.*
Composition and Prepress Buyer: *Linda Cox*
Manufacturing Buyer: *JoAnne Sweeney*
Cover Administrator: *Linda Knowles*
Electronic Composition: *Omegatype Typography, Inc.*

For related titles and support materials, visit our online catalog at www.ablongman.com

Between the time web site information is gathered and then published, it is not unusual for some sites to have closed. Also, the transcription of URLs can result in typographical errors. The publishers would appreciate notification where these errors occur so that they may be corrected in subsequent editions.

Library of Congress Cataloging-in-Publication Data

Communication theories for everyday life / edited by John R. Baldwin, Stephen D. Perry, Mary Anne Moffitt.
    p. cm.
    Includes bibliographical references and index.
    ISBN 0-205-34806-8
    1. Communication—Philosophy.   I. Baldwin, John R., 1960–. II. Perry, Stephen D. III. Moffitt, Mary Anne, 1944–

P90.C6326 2003
302.2'01—dc22

                                          2003054455

John dedicates this book to

*my wife Kim and
our children
Christopher and Katherine*

Stephen dedicates this book to

*my wife Kay Lynn and
our children
Alex, Grace, and Myles*

Mary Anne dedicates this book to

*my husband Terry and
our children
Alan and Jana, Mary and Greg, and Joseph*

Contents

23 *Building Organizational Relationships
and Integrated Marketing*   361

YUNGWOOK KIM AND DEAN KAZOLEAS

24 *The Bridgestone/Firestone Recall
Image Crisis: A Case Study*   380

KELLY BERG NELLIS

Preface

Communication is a new discipline relative to other, established social science and humanities areas such as psychology, sociology, English, art, or music. Many trace the origin of the study of communication to the early 1900s, when professors of English who focused on public speaking felt disenfranchised by that discipline and formed the new discipline of communication. Since the focus of communication studies is on messages, the field necessarily has a strong interdisciplinary element, receiving influences from linguistics, anthropology, English/literary studies, sociology, psychology, political science, and, recently, even such fields as biology. Communication scholars research personal messages (face-to-face, group, telephone, chatroom, e-mail) and mediated messages (newspapers, radio, television, electronic/Internet). Further, communication research examines the sending and receiving of such messages, the structure of the messages themselves, the causes and effects of messages, and the interpretation of texts and their meanings.

Many communication textbooks have been written that explain this historical development of the field and detail the accepted theories that best explain the process of sending, receiving, and understanding messages in personal settings or through the media. However, these books vary in their level of understanding and practicality. Some privilege theory from the earliest work in speech communication while neglecting the more recent developments in mass media research and in related areas such as organizational communication and public relations. Some texts cite primarily social scientific, or causal, theories; others focus on theories drawn from the humanities and do not include recent models of message meaning drawn from critical and interpretive theories.

And, finally, communication theory books vary in their level of practicality. Advanced texts are appropriately geared to the advanced or graduate student who will use these theories for research. At the opposite end of the spectrum are the very practical books, some of which read more like workbooks in presenting practical skills but give little theoretical background. What is missing from even many of the middle-of-the-road texts are case studies and questions that show the student the practicality of the theories in their everyday lives. We believe strongly, as does seminal theorist and sociologist Kurt Lewin, that there is nothing as practical as a good theory.

This book, *Communication Theories for Everyday Life,* seeks to address both the complexities and the recent changes in the discipline. We see the discipline as one that is always growing and shifting in ways that many texts do not validate. Thus, a text that will adequately introduce the student to the discipline should include, first, clear explanations of and focus on humanistic, social scientific, and critical theories. Second, it should provide language appropriate to introductory learners, with appropriate examples and tools for this group of students. Third, it should contain prominent inclusion of new content areas in the communication field, such as research and findings in the media and new "technologies," intercultural communication, organizations, health communication, and public relations. And, finally, a good introductory communication theory book should present a practical application of these theories to the everyday lives of the students.

Our goal in *Communication Theories for Everyday Life* is to accomplish all of these goals in a way that recognizes interconnections between all the various content areas. Unlike many communication theory books that take a "theory a day" approach, our book attempts to demonstrate the interconnections of theories within and across multiple subject areas. That is, one theory, like selective perception, actually informs our understanding of interpersonal communication, mass media communication, and campaign message design in public relations.

In sum, *Communication Theories for Everyday Life* will include scientific, humanistic, and critical theories, will include a strong component of public relations theories (one of the strongest areas of growth in communication studies), will detail **groups** or **clusters** of theories rather than a "theory a day" approach, and will aim the text to the introductory university student of communication. The chapters are written by a variety of authors, each a specialist in his or her field, but with a collaboration in order to provide consistency in approach, tone, and writing style.

As an introductory text for the undergraduate communication student, this book will include introductory materials, content-focused chapters, and case study applications. The book is organized around the three broad content areas of speech communication, mass communication, and public relations. The introductory information is represented by an introduction to the entire book, in Chapters 1 and 2, which includes definitions and approaches to communication and communication theory and research in general and which previews the three broad content areas. In addition, each of the three subject areas—speech communication, mass communication, and organizational communication/public relations— is introduced by an introductory or overview chapter that summarizes the content areas in the respective section and their historical development, noting how the various approaches respond to the types of theories presented in the introduction and representing a **topic**-based rather than a **theory**-based organization.

Following the overview chapter for each of the three subdisciplinary sections are several content-focused chapters, each presenting several specific theories that have explanatory power for the area/chapter under study. **Communication studies** chapters include content areas on information processing and public speaking, classical rhetoric, cultural communication, interpersonal communication, and group process communication. **Mass communication** chapters discuss the use of the media by the consumer, the effects of media on public opinion and culture at large, and the influence of new technological developments on social change. **Organizational communication/public relations** chapters examine organizational communication theory, conceptualization and execution of a campaign, campaign message design, building relationships between the organization and its audiences, and the new move in business theory of integrated marketing.

Finally, supplementary information is represented by case study applications at the end of each of the three subdisciplinary sections; these allow the student to work with the various theories that appear in the respective section. At various places in the book you will also see an icon like the one at left that refers you "beyond the book." This means that more information or resources are available on the text web site: www.ablongman.com/baldwin.

Our efforts in organizing the content of an introductory textbook in communication theory in this way are to avoid a "boring" listing of theories then explaining each one. Rather, we hope to engage the student of communication theory by demonstrating the application and explanatory power of many theories across many subject areas. Hopefully, the student will appreciate that certain theories can explain and predict meanings and behaviors in many communication settings, while at the same time recognizing that each broad subject area in the communication field, nevertheless, contains theories that pertain to its study and understanding.

Acknowledgments

The editors wish to thank Dylan Simonds for his designs of the original illustrations that are presented in the book. We would also like to thank Amaury da Erastro Moura (Cadastro Internacional de Colecionadores) and Silva Rego, Brazilian numismatists, for their kind help in securing the Brazilian note for Figure 17.2. We deeply appreciate our colleagues in the Department of Communication at Illinois State for their contributions to the project and to our office staff for their support.

We would also like to thank the following reviewers for their time and input: Ferald J. Bryan, Northern Illinois University; Robert C. Chandler, Pepperdine University; Marianne Dainton, La Salle University; Douglas Ferguson, College of Charleston; Suzanne Hagen, University of Wisconsin-River Falls; Amy Hermodson, Winona State University; Linda Godbold Kean, East Carolina University; Randall J. Koper, University of the Pacific; Alfred J. Mueller II, Penn State Mont Alto; Ken Waters, Pepperdine University; Gerald L. Wilson, University of Southern Alabama; and Gust A. Yep, San Francisco State University.

Finally, we express our deep appreciation to the people at Allyn and Bacon/Pearson Publishing, especially Karon Bowers, Jennifer Trebby, and Beth Houston, for their tireless work and encouragement.

About the Editors

John Baldwin (Ph.D., Arizona State University, 1994) is an Associate Professor at Illinois State University. He teaches undergraduate and graduate courses in intercultural/interethnic communication, communication, nonverbal communication, qualitative and critical research methods, and communication theory. Baldwin is an award-winning teacher, receiving recognition for his teaching during graduate work at Arizona State and as a teacher at Illinois State. His work as advisor to the honors student organization has won national awards. Baldwin's research interests are in intercultural, interethnic, and intergroup communication. He has published numerous journal articles and book chapters in these areas. He has a book on defining culture coming out soon.

Stephen Perry (Ph.D., University of Alabama, 1995) is an Associate Professor at Illinois State University. He teaches courses in the field of mass communication, including the introductory mass media course, theories and effects of mass communication, and graduate seminars in media effects. Perry is an award-winning researcher whose publications include over a dozen journal articles and book chapters in the *Journal of Broadcasting & Electronic Media, Journal of Communication, Journalism & Mass Communication Quarterly, Mass Communication & Society,* and the *Journal of Broadcast Studies.* He has also published many other essays, encyclopedia articles, textbook supplements, and video trade magazine articles. His research interests include media effects on public opinion, religion and media, and radio history.

Mary Anne Moffitt (Ph.D., University of Illinois, 1990) is an Associate Professor at Illinois State University. She teaches undergraduate and graduate courses in public relations management, campaign communication, and campaign message design. At the undergraduate level, she also teaches courses in gender and in religion and culture; at the graduate level, she teaches seminars in contemporary rhetorical criticism and qualitative research methods. Moffitt's research interests are in public relations campaign strategy, public relations campaign message design, and corporate images as received in audiences as they relate to organizations. She has published numerous articles in these areas and a book, *Campaign Strategies and Message Design* (1999), published by Praeger Press.

Part I

Introduction

Welcome to the exciting world of communication theory! Okay, so you are probably not thinking as you read this that theory can be an especially exciting topic; you may even be in a communication theory class only because it is required in your major. But we hope as you read these chapters that you will see theory as a tool that can help you have a better life by improving your understanding of how you send or receive media messages, how you communicate in your relationships, how you persuade, or how you manage your own image or that of a company. Later sections will get down to the specific theories for various contexts and areas of your life. There are, of course, a variety of ways we could have organized the book as a whole, such as major theoretical traditions (Craig, 1999). However, we live our lives in a variety of contexts, so we have chosen a "contextual" approach.

The book as a whole is divided into four sections. After this introduction, you will find sections on communication studies, mass communication, and organizational communication/public relations. Public relations is included because it is a growing focus in communication departments, and now most public relations programs are housed within communication programs, often offering majors specifically in PR. Each main section begins with a historical chapter, then moves to consider specific contexts of practical life and work situations within each section. Your instructor may not have you cover all major sections of the book, nor all areas of context in a given section, nor even all theories within a single chapter, depending on the purposes of your major and department.

Before we get to the specific contexts, however, some words of introduction are in order—so we provided lots of them! The first three chapters will introduce you to the key concepts that will guide you throughout this book and, perhaps, your major and your career as a communication professional. Chapter 1 introduces you to the notion of communication (from a theoretical point of view, of course!). Then it presents the idea of theory, describing some types of theories and detailing how theory is built. It will close with a discussion of how you can determine the strengths and limitations of a specific theory. We have chosen in this book not to provide critiques of each theory, opting instead to try to include more theories and practical examples of theories so that they might better help you to be a more effective, responsible, and ethical consumer and producer of messages. However, you can often find evaluations of these theories in summary form in other introduction to theory books (e.g., Griffin, 2000; West & Turner, 2000). Also, the Internet frequently offers many sources on a given theory. Finally, you can consult journals such as *Communication Theory* and *Communication Monographs* to find a wealth of articles on the current status of a specific theory. (Chapter 4 on the web site presents a table of many other journals you might consider.)

In Chapter 2, you will read about the foundation that supports the theories we make and use. This foundation consists of the underlying assumptions that any researcher must make (though we may not always be aware that we are making them)—assumptions about the nature of the social world, about knowledge and what counts as data, and about if and when we should allow our values to influence our theory building. After presenting the issues surrounding each of these areas of assumption, the chapter will summarize three main **paradigms** of communication research that guide the authors in this book: the scientific, humanistic, and critical paradigms. *(Note: Words set in bold throughout the book appear in the glossary on the book's web site.)* The chapter closes with a summary of two major debates that have stretched the field of communication concerning these issues and assumptions.

The last chapter in this introductory section will move to theory's primary companion, research. Without research, our theories would remain uninformed guesses. They might make sense in our own lives (see *lay theories* in Chapter 1), but we would have no way of knowing if they apply to other people in general, nor would they be informed by rigorous research and thought. For this reason, Chapter 3 presents the basic principles of communication research, including the relationship between theory and research and between theory and the data that researchers study. It will then cover the basic terms and methods for two main types of communication inquiry, quantitative and qualitative research, with examples of each. Keep in mind as you read that the "Beyond the Book" (BTB) web site icon indicates that more resources are available online.

We hope these chapters will provide a solid foundation for you as you read the rest of the book. Although this section may seem the least practical of the book, you will likely find yourself returning repeatedly to the terms and ideas in this chapter over your next years as a communication student.

References

Craig, R. T. (1999). Communication theory as a field. *Communication Theory, 9,* 119–161.

Griffin, E. (2000). *A first look at communication theory* (4th ed.). Boston: McGraw-Hill.

West, R., & Turner, L. H. (2000). *Introducing communication theory: Analysis and application.* Mountain View, CA: Mayfield.

1

Introduction to Communication Theory

Sandra Metts

If you stopped a typical student on the way to class and asked if he or she was a "theorist," you would probably get a look of confusion and a more or less polite response of "Uh, I don't think so." However, consider for a moment how you feel when you have no idea what is likely to happen in a certain circumstance, or you are not able to understand why something turned out the way it did. You no doubt feel anxious and uncomfortable. The desire to avoid this uncertainty and feel in control of our environment seems to be fundamental to human nature and motivates ordinary people as well as scholars to build theories. Theories help us feel in control of our environment because they guide our behavioral choices (including the types of messages we send), tell us what other people are likely to do or say in a particular situation, and help us interpret outcomes that are consistent with our expectations as well as those that are not. Our theories might be wrong or misguided, but without some organizing framework, we would be producing random behaviors and would be unable to interpret or explain patterns in the behaviors of other people or events. In short, theories are the organizing frameworks that allow situations to be "meaningful" rather than chaotic; they provide an initial foundation of understanding but are subject to change and elaboration as we encounter inconsistencies and new information.

What distinguishes scientific theories from our own everyday, or lay, theories is that they are tested with research and extended or refined systematically. This process might include applications to different contexts, different types of people, different mediums of expression, manipulation of different variables, or comparison of the observations of different scholars in the same context. Whatever the method used, the goal of theory construction is to increase our confidence that a particular theory has validity or accuracy when it is offered to the public as an explanation for how communication works in a given situation.

This chapter will explore the definition of communication, how communication functions for societies and individuals, and the nature of communication theory. It will also cover different approaches to building theory, closing with a discussion of how we can know a good theory when we see one.

In this chapter, you will read about the following concepts:

- The dialectical relationship between communication and individual and social change
- Communication as strategic and consequential
- The definition of a theory
- Theoretical "concepts" and the different types of relationships between them
  - Temporal
  - Correlational
  - Causal
- Two ways of constructing communication theory
  - Inductively
  - Deductively
- Criteria to determine the quality of theories
  - Utility
  - Scope
  - Parsimony
  - Heurism
  - Falsifiability

Many students will look at a book focused entirely on theories of communication and react with some degree of surprise. Why do we need so many different theories to describe a process that is so ordinary and commonplace? After all, communication occurs countless times a day with little conscious attention. It occurs in every context where human beings come together in social units as friends, romantic couples, families, and social/professional groups. It occurs in any context where people work on tasks—in organizations, in the classroom, at the checkout line, or when ordering a meal in a restaurant. Communication occurs in face-to-face settings, over the telephone, via the computer, and when listening to the radio, watching television, reading a newspaper, reading a magazine, or writing a letter.

Indeed, communication is so pervasive and so commonplace in human societies that we tend to take it for granted. We swim in it effortlessly like fish swim in water. We may forget how essential and complex communication is—well, we forget perhaps until communication breaks down and we lose a valued friend or partner over a misunderstanding, we fail to get the job we want because of a bad interview, or we leave a group meeting frustrated with the lack of progress and with the persistent level of conflict. We also become aware of communication when we fall for a sales pitch that encouraged us to waste our money, try to figure out where a politician stands on an issue to no avail, or watch a friend become sick with anorexia or depression because media images tell us that thin is beautiful. In these cases, we become very aware of how essential, pervasive, and complex communication is.

Unfortunately, of course, no book and no amount of knowledge about communication theories can prevent you from occasionally experiencing poorly managed communication challenges and unfortunate consequences. However, the ability to avoid these situations, to minimize the damage, and to repair it successfully when it does occur increases greatly if you understand the essentials of the communication process. Theories are our window into this process. They not only describe what typically happens; they explain why things happen, and enable us to predict what will likely happen in the future if similar circumstances arise. The goal of this book is to provide the theories that will help you understand the communication process, make better communicative choices of your own, and understand the choices of others.

This first chapter is intended to introduce you more fully to the concept of communication theory so that subsequent chapters on particular theories have a common framework. In order to meet this goal, the chapter begins with a discussion of what communication is and how it functions at both the broad *societal level* and at the *individual level*. You will later see that the theories covered in this book fit into one, and sometimes both, of these general areas. Second, it will offer a more formal definition of theory and its components. Third, this chapter will present a discussion of the two general approaches to theory construction and acknowledge the limitations and advantages of each. Fourth, the chapter closes with a list of the criteria that are typically used for evaluating a theory, giving extended attention to the criterion of utility.

What Is Communication?

Given the pervasive and integral role of communication in human existence, it is perhaps no surprise that scholars offer different definitions of communication. Some scholars take what is referred to as a "receiver perspective" on communication (e.g., Andersen, 1991). These scholars argue that when an individual perceives the behavior of another person, whether verbal or nonverbal, and assigns meaning to it, communication has occurred. From this perspective, a message can be sent unintentionally (e.g., the blush of embarrassment or the growl of a hungry stomach) and unconsciously (e.g., a frowning face when talking to a disliked other), but still count as communication because the receiver interprets it as meaningful and responds to it in some way. Other scholars take what is referred to as a "sender perspective" on communication (e.g., Motley, 1990, 1991). These scholars argue that communication occurs when a sender intentionally encodes a message and sends it to another person or persons. The encoding process involves transformation of some thought (cognition) into a symbolic code. This symbolic code is usually language, although some forms of nonverbal behavior are also symbolic (e.g., a wave or "thumbs up" sign).

Both of these perspectives in their extreme form can be problematic. If interpretation of any attribute or behavior constitutes communication, then everything is a message and communication is simply perception. By contrast, if only messages encoded through a symbol system and intentionally sent to a receiver constitute communication, then much of the broader process of unintentional but informative communication is lost. In actual practice, both definitions have utility when they fit the goals of theory development for certain phenomena. For example, interest in nonverbal behavior or in media effects might benefit from a receiver perspective; interest in compliance gaining, persuasion, or political rhetoric might benefit from a sender perspective. Thus, a definition of communication is not necessarily right or wrong, but more or less useful and appropriate for the concerns of the scholar (Miller, 2002). For the purposes of this chapter and in order to be inclusive of the wide spectrum of theories that follow in subsequent chapters, we opt for a broad definition of **communication** as the process through which messages, both intentional and unintentional, create meaning. This definition allows us to discuss the functions of communication for societies and individuals. We turn to that discussion in the following section.

What Does Communication Do?

At the broadest level, communication is the reason that societies can and do exist. Communication is the mechanism by which culture is constructed, shaped, and sustained over time and across generations. It is the mechanism by which cultural values, norms, rituals, social roles, hierarchies, organizations, and so forth are manifested, understood, and shared by members of a culture. Without communication there would, quite literally, be no social organizing. Paradoxically, however, communication is also shaped and constrained by the very culture it creates (Berger & Luckman, 1967). That is, the cultural values, norms, rituals, social roles, and hierarchies that communication enables also constrain communication because they determine how communication can (or should) be manifested. These **social structures** tell us what types of actions are to be considered appropriate, supportive, rude, hateful, constructive, typical, or friendly, and how to enact the various roles we assume in our personal, social, and professional lives. The interplay between communication and social structures is often referred to as a "dialectical process."

Communication and Social Reality as a Circular (Dialectical) Process

Societies and their communication practices change through a **dialectical process**—that is, where each influences the other in a constant tension. For example, changes in society might include changes in the material world (e.g., discoveries, inventions, technological advances), in the political arena (e.g., revolutions, wars, and new leadership), in the definitions of social groupings (e.g., sex role expectations, increased numbers of healthy elderly persons, and minority positions), and in the patterns of employment (e.g., agricultural to industrial economies, and manual labor to "home officing"). These changes are all interrelated and together necessitate changes in how communication is conducted, as noted in the comic strip in Figure 1.1.

At the same time, the way we communicate influences the nature and extent of change in social structures. For example, the glass ceiling, sexual harassment, and date rape have existed for generations, but now that words have been incorporated into our collective vocabularies to define these phenomena, we can talk about them and implement strategies to recognize and eradicate them.

Communication as Strategic and Consequential: Goals and Effects

At a more individual level, communication is the means by which individual persons link their goals and intentions to other people, groups, or larger audiences. Communication functions in much the same way at this level as at the social level, although the terms used to describe it differ slightly. At this level, we refer to communication as both *strategic* and as *consequential* (Burleson, Metts, & Kirch, 2000). When we refer to communication as

FIGURE 1.1   Both the way we do politics and the way media cover it are influenced by communication and, themselves, influence communication, demonstrating the circular nature of communication and society.

Reprinted with special permission of King Features Syndicate.

strategic, we recognize that sometimes we construct messages with particular motivations or goals in mind. For example, we might approach a teacher with a request for information about an assignment or to let us turn in a paper late; we might approach an attractive person with the hopes of getting acquainted or getting a date; or we might write a news release with the goal of shaping readers' perceptions about some crisis in our organization. Sometimes we have multiple goals in mind, at various levels of awareness. For example, we may want to study for an exam with someone in the class who seems to be doing well; however, we don't want to appear to be incompetent, nor do we want to make the other person feel obligated. Thus, we face the challenge of multiple goals: organizing a study session, protecting our own image or *face,* and not threatening the other person's need for autonomy.

When we have a goal or goals in mind for a particular context and a particular person or audience, scholars suggest that the collection of appropriate actions we have at our disposal, or our communication skills, enable us to convert a mental plan into an action sequence (Dillard, 1990). Much of the research you will read about in this book and other communication texts is concerned with theories that explain why some messages are more effective (i.e., represent more skillful plans) than others in certain contexts and what factors make some people better at constructing these messages (i.e., make them more skillful communicators) than other people.

Much of the time, however, our communication is not strategic in the sense of being goal directed, but it is nevertheless **consequential,** in that it has an unanticipated or at least unintended effects. These consequences can be *perceptual, behavioral,* or *relational.* **Perceptual consequences** include all of the assumptions we make about people's competence, attitudes, disposition, education, social class, and so forth, and of course their assumptions about us. For example, do you sometimes see a person dressed a certain way or hear a certain type of dialect and assume, perhaps unconsciously, that the speaker is probably not very bright or well educated? If so, you have perceived their appearance or their dialect to be a *message,* and it has thereby been consequential. You might also find yourself beginning to enjoy a certain course at school that you did not expect to like or find yourself believing in a certain political position that you had not previously endorsed. You might be aware that your opinions are changing, but no one is specifically trying to persuade you or alter your beliefs. The change has emerged naturally as a consequence of the communication to which you have been exposed.

Behavioral consequences occur when people change their behavior without any particular effort from others to influence that change. Such a consequence might be evident when you actively seek certain people out because you enjoy their company or when you avoid other people because you find their company uncomfortable. Behavioral consequences also occur at the level of *conversational synchrony,* where you find yourself matching the communication patterns of another person during conversation (Giles, Coupland, & Coupland, 1991). For example, you might find yourself becoming more animated and speaking faster when you are with an enthusiastic and lively speaker or, alternatively, becoming slower and more restrained when talking to a less fluent and more plodding speaker. You might even find yourself avoiding slang when talking to a supervisor or professor, or you might speak louder and slower when talking with someone who appears to be elderly. In these cases, you probably do not think to yourself, "I will speaker faster" or "I will try to use proper English with my boss." Instead, your speech patterns converge to those of the other speaker (or in the case of the elderly person, to a stereotype of the elderly) somewhat automatically and probably below the level of a conscious decision. The theory that explains this phenomenon is called communication accommodation theory, and you will learn more about it in Chapter 10.

Finally, consequences can be **relational** in the sense that they create and sustain interaction patterns and expectations within personal, social, and professional relationships. Repeated interaction with the same people over time results in the emergence of a "culture" not unlike what happens at the broader level of society, complete with values, norms, rituals, role expectations, and so forth. How, for example, does your family handle conflict? Does it always seem to occur at dinnertime? Do people raise their voices, remain calm, or simply withdraw? Are there "hot button" topics that you all realize will be problematic? Does one member of the family always have the "last word" no matter what others might think? How much explicit discontent are you (or other family members) allowed to voice and how strongly? It is not likely that anyone sat your family down and said, "This is how we will do conflict." More likely, these patterns simply developed over time and became normative for your family. The same processes occur in groups, committees, workplaces, classrooms, friendships, and romantic couples. Interestingly, although these norms may not be very salient to relational members, a change in the structure of the group will foreground the interaction patterns at the relational level, as, for example, when two people with children remarry and form a blended family, or when a work group gets a new leader or new members.

Whether we are interested in the role of communication at the social or at the individual level, we will be in a better position to understand it if we are familiar with the theories that can explain it to us. The next section offers a working definition of theory to guide your reading through the remaining chapters of this book.

What Is a Theory?

In common terms, a theory is a speculation, a conjecture, or an informed guess about how things work, or why certain events happen, or why certain events follow other events. You no doubt have a theory about why your roommate is so messy or why you may not do well in math. You probably have a theory about why your computer only acts up when you have a paper due or a theory that people who like dogs are more open and trustworthy than people who like cats. These **lay theories** are speculations that you have formulated in order to organize and make sense of the events in your world. Like scholarly theories, they are more than just a belief or opinion about a single cause, but usually involve several aspects of explanation—aspects that a scholar might call variables. For example, you might explain your math success (or lack of success) as a function of natural talent, high school experiences with math, hours of study, whether the teacher likes you, the fact that your math class meets at 8:00 in the morning, or any combination of these elements (see Figure 1.2).

Communication theories written by scholars are also speculations and conjectures. The main difference is that scholars must be able to argue for the **validity** (truth or correctness) of their theories in such a way that other scholars find the ideas convincing based on accepted methods of analysis, logical reasoning, and argument. Still, these theories function for scholars much the same way your own theories function for you. They help scholars *organize* information, *describe* phenomena, and *explain* how communication processes and practices work. Some theories can also be used to *predict* future occurrences by specifying what will likely happen when certain circumstances emerge spontaneously or are generated by communicators. If events can be predicted, we can use theories to *control* future outcomes, for example, reducing teenage violence. More specifically, the formal or traditional definition of **theory** is *a description of concepts and specification of the relationships between or among these concepts.*

FIGURE 1.2 "Lay theories" may tell us that amount of study, among other things, predicts that we will perform well on an exam.

© Image Source

The Building Blocks of Theories: Concepts

When used in a formal definition of theory, the term **concept** does not refer simply to an idea but refers more specifically to a feature, a characteristic, or some quality that is shared by the elements in a category. For example, the number of senses that can be carried through a mediated communication channel is called *media richness,* and certain types of messages that help a person cope with distress are conceptualized as *emotional support.* In these cases, media richness and emotional support would be concepts in a theory.

It is important to remember that concepts are not tangible objects but definitions that allow scholars to investigate a particular phenomenon. To illustrate, consider the two concepts of persuasion and compliance gaining. *Persuasion* is typically defined as message strategies designed to change a receiver's attitudes, values, or beliefs (i.e., cognitions), whether or not any change in behavior follows. *Compliance gaining* is typically defined as message strategies designed to change a receiver's behavior, with or without a corresponding change in attitudes, values, or beliefs. (When a professor tells you to write a paper, you will probably comply with the request whether you believe it is a useful assignment or not.) However, if we move up one level, we see that both persuasion and compliance gaining are similar in that they are intended to influence people in some way; at this level, they both belong to a concept category known as *social influence.* Depending on a scholar's purpose, she or he may use persuasion and compliance gaining as two manifestations of the concept *influence* or may isolate just one of them as the concept of interest.

Relationships between the Concepts: Propositions and Other Statements

In addition to concepts, theories include assumptions about the *associations between or among concepts.* In many cases, these associations are expressed as types of **propositions,** which like concepts are speculations offered by scholars (Hoover, 1984). These propositions tend to reflect one of three types of associations. First, a theory might specify or imply a **temporal relationship,** suggesting that certain concepts precede other concepts in time. For example, according to linguists, cognition precedes speech rather than the reverse (although it might not seem so at times). Likewise, certain types of *conversational turns* precede other types (e.g., a question typically precedes an answer and an assertion typically precedes agreement or disagreement). Second, a theory might specify a **correlational association,** stating that two or more concepts tend to co-occur or change together in patterned ways. For example, the expression of positive emotions in a relationship is correlated with relational satisfaction, but the expression of negative emotion is correlated with relationship dissatisfaction. And being male or female tends to co-occur with the presence of certain communication practices such as men saying "I love you" first in a developing romantic relationship, and women nodding and smiling more in conversations.

For both a temporal and correlational association, no claim is made that one concept causes or necessitates the other. Having a thought does not cause you to speak (we often withhold irrelevant or inappropriate comments), expressing positive emotion does not cause you to be satisfied in your relationship (it may be that other features of the relationship make you happy so you express your positive feelings), and being male or female does not cause you to produce certain types of messages.

A third and more complex association found in some theories is a **causal** ("**cause and effect**" or "**if-then**") **proposition.** To establish this type of linkage between concepts, a theorist must find evidence that one concept precedes another concept, that the concepts are related, and that the first concept causes or motivates the second. For example, according to Berger's uncertainty reduction theory (Berger & Calabrese, 1975; Berger, 1987; see Chapter 7), when we first interact with a stranger, we feel uncomfortable because we cannot predict what he or she will say or do. This discomfort motivates us to reduce our uncertainty by observing the person, asking questions, or disclosing information in order to see what he or she discloses in return. Thus our uncertainty (and corresponding discomfort) leads to or motivates our attempts to reduce uncertainty through certain types of communication strategies.

Although cause-effect and if-then propositions are common in physiological studies of communication, they are more difficult to establish in social scientific research. For example, it is relatively easy to establish (using brain scan analysis) that physiological damage to particular areas of the brain from strokes or trauma is the cause of characteristic difficulties in producing and comprehending speech. It is also relatively easy to determine that the experience of strong negative emotion was caused by a spouse's comment during marital conflict if heart rate and body temperature measures are taken before and after the comment during a laboratory experiment.

However, it is somewhat more difficult to establish claims about causation in everyday social life. As noted previously, communication is shaped by social structures and individuals' goals. Returning to emotion, for example, it may be true that hearing a negative comment causes strong emotion (manifested as physiological arousal), but finding evidence to establish causal links by observing communication episodes can be difficult because people often control the extent to which they visibly display their emotions. According to Ekman and Friesen (1975), society has *display rules* for emotions telling us when we should moderate or intensify the expression of an emotion, when we should not express it at all, and even when we should express an emotion that we are not actually feeling. This suggests that many communication practices conform to situational and relational norms or *rules* rather being a direct result of *natural laws* of the type that we might find in biology. For this reason, when communication theorists present cause-effect and if-then propositions, they typically do so in the form of statistical probabilities (or statistical laws) and remain open to the possibility that the concepts under investigation may not present a full picture of the processes they hope to explain. You will read more about statistical laws and the assumptions that underlie questions of validity in Chapter 3.

Before leaving this discussion of theory, it is important to note that some theorists treat human behavior as even less predictable than is suggested by temporal, correlational, or if-then propositions. They might feel that all three types of propositions imply some sort of predictability of human behavior, even if only probable predictions. These theorists might instead create descriptive frameworks of terms and statements about human nature, typically that can be applied to interpret a single situation. For example, semiotics (the study of signs and meanings; see Chapter 17) is a theory of textual meaning. In different versions of this approach to studying face-to-face behavior or media images, writers develop frameworks of terms (signifiers, signified, codes, and so on). The explanation still has concepts (e.g., *ideology, code*), and there are still relationships among these concepts (e.g., *codes, discourses,* or *sets of signs* that work to reinforce *ideology*). However, such statements are not propositions in the formal sense. Thus, such theories are sometimes referred to as **descriptive/sensitizing schemes** that are designed to sensitize and orient researchers to certain features of a process or context rather than to explain, predict, and control (Turner, 1986).

There is much debate in the communication field as to whether such frameworks, without explicit propositions, should be considered "theory" as such. Settling this debate is beyond the scope of this chapter. For our purposes, it is sufficient to know that communication theories are constructions that represent a scholar's best understanding, at that point, of how some phenomenon should be described, represented, explained, or analyzed. Theories are necessarily subject to extension and refinement as new concepts are identified, and hypothesized relationships are supported or called into question. We turn now to a discussion of the process by which theories are generated and tested.

How Do Scholars Construct Theories?

Scholars construct theories both *inductively* and *deductively,* often moving back and forth between the two approaches. When scholars build theory **inductively,** they try to avoid letting preexisting concepts determine what they look for; instead, they try to observe without discriminating (at least initially) between what data are relevant and what are not. They might observe how people from different cultures talk to one another, how gossip moves through an organization, how groups function, how relationships change, how companies use the media to present their image, how presidential candidates respond to questions during televised debates, or any other phenomenon that intrigues them. They may do extensive interviews or even become part of a group or analyze their own life experiences to fully understand the meanings and patterns in their observations.

When presenting a theory that has been derived inductively, some scholars use their observations with minimal alteration (e.g., portions of interviews or snippets of recorded conversations) to illustrate their conclusions. Other scholars organize their observations into categories or **typologies.** For example, nonverbal researchers have found five general categories of body motions: emblems, illustrators, affect displays, regulators, and adaptors (Ekman & Friesen, 1969). On occasion, scholars might arrange the categories they observe into a hierarchy because more specific categories cluster within higher-order categories. As you will see in Chapter 9 on persuasive communication, Marwell and Schmitt (1967) propose five primary categories of ways that people choose to persuade others to do something (promising a reward, promising a punishment, exhibiting their own expertise, appeal to the other's internalized [impersonal] commitments, or appeal to personal commitments). Each main category contains a number of more specific types of compliance-gaining strategy. Finally, some scholars count the frequency with which observations occur within these categories or count how frequently these categories appear in certain contexts or for certain types of communicators.

When scholars build theory **deductively,** they begin with preformulated expectations (often in the form of hypotheses) about how a process works or what concepts are related to other concepts, and then use observations (often in the form of statistical values) to test these assumptions (see Chapter 3). Such theories are often called *hypothetico-deductive theories* for this reason. In this type of theory building, theorists may do some initial observations or read previous inductive studies, but their goal is to test and confirm their assumptions rather than to "discover" patterns or associations.

In a sense, deductive approaches might be considered "top down" procedures (using theoretical assumptions to guide observation). By contrast, inductive approaches might be considered "bottom up" procedures (using observation to guide theoretical assumptions). These two theory-building approaches are diagrammed in Figure 1.3.

Both approaches are valuable to communication theorists. Inductive approaches have the advantage of avoiding the blinders that preconceived assumptions can create. If we expect to see a certain concept or association, we often see it—sometimes at the expense of overlooking other concepts or relationships.

For example, inductively derived theories based on observations now cause us to question the long-held assumption that the friendships of men are not as close or intimate as those of women. Observations and interviews reveal that men simply enact their closeness differently than women do; they participate in activities together, for example, rather than spending time engaged in intimate conversations. When intimacy and closeness were measured by amount of verbal self-disclosure, it appeared that men's friendships were not very close (Wood, 1996).

On the other hand, deductive approaches afford scholars the advantage of systematically testing and refining their speculations. Although preexiting speculations can act as blinders, they can also act as a guide to lead scholars toward the most defensible and generalizable claims about communication processes and practices. Scholars can test their assumptions or hypotheses to see if they are supported by the observations (data) they collect (for more detail on hypotheses and data, see Chapter 3). If their assumptions are not supported, they can: (1) return to the original concepts and reassess their validity (e.g., maybe the defining characteristic didn't capture the true nature of a set of behaviors or attitudes), or (2) they can return to the associations among the concepts to see if they linked the concepts inappropriately (e.g., it was assumed that X causes Y, but X and Y are only correlated). In other words, they can be systematic in their logic when testing a theory.

One of the most vivid examples is the tradition of deductive work in public speaking and political discourse. Over 2,000 years ago, Aristotle proposed the concepts of logos, ethos, and pathos to describe a good orator. In the last 50 years, numerous deductive investigations have explored these concepts, assessing their role in source credibility, persuasive public

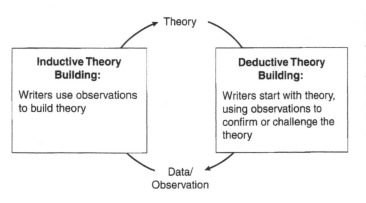

FIGURE 1.3 *Two Approaches to Building Theory: Inductive and Deductive.* Scholars tend to use one of two approaches to building theory, sometimes combining both.

speaking, fear appeals, and so forth (see Chapters 5 and 9). Some of Aristotle's assumptions have been confirmed, and some have not.

Although it might appear that inductive and deductive approaches to theory building are largely scientific jargon, they are actually the ways that all of us build our own personal theories of communication and the social world. If you think about it for a moment, you might recognize that sometimes you meet someone or join a group and tend to sit back and observe. Eventually you formulate conclusions about how these people are likely to act, what seems important to them, whether they are liberal or conservative, and so forth. You then begin to act toward them based on your assumptions. In these situations, you are using induction. At other times, you already have some idea about people you are just meeting or people who will be in your group because someone has given you information about them or because you have been in similar situations before. Needless to say, many students walk into a classroom on the first day of a semester with preconceptions about a professor passed on to them by other students. In such cases, you might informally test your preexisting assumptions, verifying some of them but not supporting others. This would be a deductive approach. If you are like most theorists, you will move back and forth between these two approaches until you reach a "theory" that functions sufficiently to meet your needs to organize, describe, explain, predict, and possibly even control the elements within this environment. Figure 1.4 describes these functions, noting that explanation, prediction,

FIGURE 1.4   *Functions of Theory.*   Theories serve each of these functions, with some theories focusing more on some functions than others.

Function of Theory	What the Theory Does
Organize	Theory helps to take complex phenomenon and put into words or categories that can be easily understood. For example, a theory might organize the various causes and effects of exposure to violent media or organize the reasons people might choose to use violent media.
Describe	Theory describes *what* happens in a given situation or context. Often this is conceived of as *providing understanding,* even deep understanding. For example, a theory might try to classify and make sense of the ways that oppressed groups communicate in a dominant society or describe the way a culture makes requests.
Explain	Theory helps to explain *why* things happen, often in sense of the underlying causes of human behavior (more typically a function of scientific theory). For example, a theory might explain why some types of messages to restore the image of a scandalized politician or company work better than other types.
Predict	Theory helps to predict outcomes (more typically a function of a scientific theory). For example, a theory might predict what types of communication between dating partners will lead to increased intimacy.
Control	Theory can be used to control events or outcomes when relationships among the variables have been established (more typically a function of scientific theory). For example, public service announcements informing women that smoking will be harmful to an unborn child can be used to reduce smoking among women during pregnancy.

and control are more typical of *scientific* theories. The next section of this chapter examines how scholars determine whether their theories are sufficient by applying evaluative criteria.

How Can I Know If a Theory Is "Good"?

Because theories differ a good deal in how they are formulated and in the types of phenomena they are intended to explain, a list of criteria to evaluate them is necessarily tentative. Some theories are more fairly judged on some criteria than are other theories. In addition, it is essential to keep in mind the fact that applications of a theory should be assessed independently of the theory itself. It is not uncommon to see theories misrepresented in secondary sources and/or misrepresented in deductive studies. This chapter is not the place to detail these misrepresentations, but as you apply the criteria below to the theories you encounter in the remaining chapters, try to evaluate them on their own merit and when you have questions, seek out the initial publication of the theory to read it as originally formulated. With that caveat in mind, consider the following criteria when you evaluate a theory.

Utility

The principal criterion used by scholars to evaluate a theory is its **utility.** In fact, as you will be able to see shortly, utility is often tied to three of the other criteria discussed below: scope, parsimony, and heurism. However, in order to clarify utility as a distinct criterion, think about it in terms of its cumulative contributions to the goals of communication scholars over time.

Clearly, a theory that has proven useful over time for understanding the forms, functions, and consequences of communication is a more useful theory than one that has not done so. An early theory of media effects, for example, called the *magic bullet theory,* failed to account for the complex process and intervening variables that determine whether and how media portrayals influence viewer behaviors and attitudes. As with any abstraction, such as a street map or a photograph, a theory's utility can be time-bound if its concepts or propositions are not capable of adaptation. That is, just as changing configurations of a city make some maps obsolete, changes in the configurations of societies make some theories obsolete unless they are adaptable to emerging circumstances. Never before have viewers been able to send e-mails to news commentators expressing their opinions or watch world events unfold in real-time sequence. Whether existing theories of broadcast news will be able to accommodate these technological advances remains to be seen. If not, then their utility will be questioned.

On the other hand, we already have evidence that theories of persuasion that emerged during World War II continue to be useful in explaining the effectiveness of advertising, political campaigns, religious movements, and so forth. Likewise, Goffman's original theory of *face* and *facework,* presented in 1959, continues to provide a useful explanation for social behavior, such as why people feel embarrassment and shame and why people offer apologies or accounts to others when they have committed an inappropriate act. Goffman's theory has been adapted by other scholars to explain such diverse phenomena as a company's public relations announcements in response to crisis (Benoit, 1997), a woman's use of "token resistance" to sexual advances (Cupach & Metts, 1994), and the breakup strategies couples use to terminate their relationship (Metts, 1992).

Unfortunately, scholars are in some (generally polite) disagreement over the precise nature of utility. One point of disagreement is where to locate the audience who evaluates utility. Some scholars believe that theories have no necessary obligation to explain the "real" world or to help ordinary persons conduct their daily affairs. For these scholars, a theory has utility when it promotes dialogue among scholars interested in understanding some phenomenon in its own right, independent of its relevance to the immediate concerns of ordinary people. Other scholars suggest that a theory demonstrates greater utility when it can be used to describe and, more importantly, improve the competence of ordinary people or remedy social problems. In actual practice, most scholars respect both positions; even scholars who prefer to do "pure" research usually support those who attempt to apply theory to the so-called real world or attempt to propose ways it might be relevant in textbooks like this one.

A second, and somewhat more vexing, point of disagreement is whether a theory that organizes and describes some phenomenon is as useful as one that explains and predicts future occurrences. As noted previously, the debate about this issue in the communication discipline is persistent and unresolved. Those who take a conservative position argue that no matter how thick or rich a description might be, if it does not formulate propositions about relationships among concepts it does not constitute a theory at all. That is, they seek a theory that can, by its propositions, predict outcomes in certain situations (called the **predictive validity** of a theory). Those who take a more liberal position argue that the goal of theory is to promote understanding of a phenomenon and if detailed description meets this goal, then it is a theory and a useful theory. In actual fact, what this debate probably reflects is a blurring of the lines between criteria for what constitutes a theory versus criteria for what constitutes utility.

The authors of this book take a liberal view and present to you both descriptive theories and formal predictive theories. Some of the descriptive theories that you will read about are more accurately called "models." A **model** is a representation of a process or complex pattern of phenomena. You might remember from grade school having a model of the universe in your classroom. In Chapter 8, you will read about Tuckman's (1965) model of the stages that task groups pass through when attempting to reach a decision. In Chapter 7, you will read about a model of relationship development and dissolution (the Staircase Model) offered by Mark Knapp (Knapp & Vangelisti, 2000). Models are necessarily descriptive, rather than prescriptive, but their utility lies in their ability to organize and integrate existing information. Specific concepts and even other theories can be incorporated within them to describe the characteristics of phases or steps, without losing the integrity of the larger picture.

Scope

In some ways, **scope** is a subset of utility but is often used independently to evaluate a theory. The scope of a theory refers to its focus—whether it throws a wide net to encompass communication across contexts and/or cultures or whether it has a more limited focus on aspects of communication relevant to specific contexts. Given the fact that certain types of communication episodes are embedded in many contexts, scope typically is conceived of as a continuum, rather than a simple dichotomy. For example, attribution theory is a theory that is relatively narrow in its focus on cognitive processes, but it explains in detail how people make sense of their own and other people's actions by attributing them to personality or to circumstances. Groupthink is also a relatively narrow theory that explains why groups sometimes make poor decisions when group cohesiveness becomes constraining rather than productive (Janis, 1982; see chapter 8). Theories of conflict management styles (Katz & Lawyer, 1985) tend to have a broader scope in that they can be applied to conflict occurring in couples, friendships, families, groups, and the workplace. Brown and Levinson's (1987) theory of politeness is an even broader theory that accounts for the presence of certain linguistic markers used by all speakers, across language families and cultures, to show deference to and regard for the face needs of others during ordinary conversation, when making a request, when offering criticism, when terminating a relationships, when seeking or giving emotional support, and even when requesting the use of a condom during sexual encounters.

Parsimony

Parsimony refers to the manner in which the theory is written. When a theory is presented parsimoniously, it presents complex or abstract ideas in the simplest possible manner. Parsimony might be reflected in the number of concepts and the simplicity of the interconnections between them, or in the way the authors write the theory. Generally speaking, theories should seek to be as simple as possible while still explaining the phenomena with accuracy and an appropriate degree of detail. Some theories that have great utility and broad scope are not necessarily parsimonious. For example, Goffman's facework theory is a highly regarded theory for its utility and scope; however, one must read hundreds of pages of text (several times) to fully understand the theory.

Heurism

Heurism refers to the ability of a theory to stimulate new ways of thinking about an issue, process, or phenomenon and to promote additional research. Theories that offer well-defined concepts and clearly articulated associations among concepts are more likely to have heurism. For example, the media effects theory known as cultivation theory (Gerbner, Gross, Morgan, & Signorielli, 1986) has prompted an extensive line of research focused on understanding cumulative media effects and clarifying the concepts described in the original theory. Likewise, communication accommodation theory (Giles, Coupland, & Coupland, 1991) has led to extensive research, both qualitative and quantitative, on how and why people converge, diverge, or maintain their style of speech in such diverse settings as ordinary conversation and conversations in nursing homes. On the other hand, although muted group theory (Kramarae, 1981) and the spiral of silence theory (Noelle-Neumann, 1993) offer scholars a useful way of explaining how dominant groups maintain their power in a society, they have been difficult to test empirically and thus prompted a comparatively smaller number of studies to refine and extend the original formulations.

Falsifiability

The criterion of **falsifiability** is probably more appropriate for traditional social science theories than for what was identified above as descriptive or inductive theories. This criterion asks whether a theory's claims can ever be proven false. This might strike a reader as an odd criterion, given that we want to confirm theories. However, if a theory's claims cannot be proven false, then they cannot be proven correct either. Consider, for example, the popular theory in social psychology known as social exchange theory. Based on economic principles, the theory as initially formulated by Thibaut and Kelley (1959) stated that people will stay in voluntary groups, associations, or relationships only as long as their rewards exceed their costs. You might assume that it would be easy to test this claim and determine if it holds true by measuring costs and rewards. However, as researchers began to test the theory deductively, they encountered anomalies, such as people leaving relationships in which rewards exceeded costs or staying in relationships where costs exceeded rewards (e.g., abusive relationships). Exchange theorists were forced to argue that what counts as a cost, and what counts as a reward, must be idiosyncratic to individuals and not directly measurable. This position then led to the criticism that if this were the case, the theory could never be proven false. In response, alternative theories have emerged (e.g., investment theory) to account for this problem.

Before leaving this section on criteria, it is worth reiterating the point that the utility of a theory to scholars and ordinary people is a fundamental criterion for judging the worth of a theory. We used this criterion to guide the selection of theories to be included in this book. In addition, we selected theories that had a scope broad enough to be of use in readers' personal and social lives as well as in the variety of professional areas that communication students are most likely to experience. Although parsimony was not used as a standard when selecting theories, we hope the theories we chose are presented to you in a parsimonious manner.

Summary

This chapter has presented a preliminary overview of theory and acquainted you with key terms and issues that will be relevant as you read subsequent chapters. It covered four important areas: the role of communication in society and individuals' lives, informal and formal definitions of theory, two methods of constructing and refining theory, and several criteria that are commonly used to evaluate theory. Hopefully, this information will make you a more informed consumer of the theories that follow.

It is always the case that a theory is an abstraction of or a representation for actual experience. As noted earlier, a theory is like a map, and while a map can guide one's travels, the map is not the territory. However, we believe that the knowledge to be found in theories will empower you to be a more informed and competent communicator, both in your social life and in your professional career. We certainly recognize that knowing theories of communication will not guarantee flawless performance. Not every aspect of communication can be controlled, and we cannot always predict changing circumstances or what another person might say or do. However, knowledge of communication theories will make the ordinary intriguing and demystify the confusing; it will illuminate the processes that we take for granted, and guide you toward better communicative choices.

Discussion Questions

1. Provide an example of some way in which you have used strategic communication within the last 24 hours. Then provide an example of some time when your communication had unintended consequences. Can communication be both "intentional" and "consequential" at the same time? Why or why not?

2. Develop a "model" with different "concepts" that relate to video game usage. Provide at least one concept each that has a temporal, a correlational, and a causal relationship with video game usage. For example, what are some things that might cause video game usage (or that usage might cause)? What are some things that might increase with video game usage (but not be caused by it)?

3. Explain the relationship between inductive and deductive processes of theory building. What would each look like by itself? How might the two work together?

4. Think of some aspect of communication (face-to-face or mediated) that you would like to explain. If you could come up with a theory to describe it, how wide or narrow would you want the "scope" of your theory be, and why?

References

Andersen, P. A. (1991). When one cannot not communicate: A challenge to Motley's traditional communication postulates. *Communication Studies, 42,* 309–325.

Benoit, W. L. (1997). Image repair discourse and crisis communication. *Public Relations Review, 23,* 177–186.

Berger, C. R. (1987). Communicating under uncertainty. In M. E. Roloff & G. R. Miller (Eds.), *Interpersonal processes: New directions in communication research* (pp. 39–62). Newbury Park, CA: Sage.

Berger, C. R., & Calabrese, R. J. (1975). Some exploration in initial interaction and beyond: Toward a developmental theory of interpersonal communication. *Human Communication Research, 1,* 99–112.

Berger, P. L., & Luckman, T. (1967). *The social construction of reality.* Garden City, NY: Doubleday.

Brown, P., & Levinson, S. C. (1987). *Politeness: Some universals in language usage.* Cambridge: Cambridge University Press.

Burleson, B. R., Metts, S., & Kirch, M. J. (2000). Communication in close relationships. In C. Hendrick & S. Hendrick (Eds.), *Close relationships: A sourcebook* (pp. 245–258). Thousand Oaks, CA: Sage.

Cupach, W. R., & Metts, S. (1994). *Facework.* Thousand Oaks, CA: Sage.

Dillard, J. P. (1990). The nature and substance of goals in tactical communication. In M. J. Cody & M. L. McLaughlin (Eds.), *The psychology of tactical communication* (pp. 70–90). Clevedon, UK: Multilingual Matters.

Ekman, P,. & Friesen, W. V. (1969). The repertoire of nonverbal behavior: Categories, origins, usage, and coding. *Semiotica, 1,* 49–98.

Ekman, P., & Friesen, W. V. (1975). *Unmasking the face: A guide to recognizing emotions from facial cues.* Englewood Cliffs, NJ: Prentice-Hall.

Gerbner, G., Gross, L., Morgan, M., & Signorielli, N. (1986). Living with television: The dynamics of the cultivation process. In J. Bryant & D. Zillman (Eds.), *Perspectives on media effects* (pp. 17–40). Hillsdale, NJ: Lawrence Erlbaum.

Giles, H., Coupland, N., & Coupland, J. (1991). Accommodation theory: Communication, context, and consequences. In H. Giles, J. Coupland, & N. Coupland (Eds.), *Contexts of accommodation: Developments in applied sociolinguistics* (pp. 1–68). Cambridge: Cambridge University Press.

Goffman, E. (1959). *Presentation of self in everyday life.* Garden City, NY: Doubleday.

Hoover, K. R. (1984). *The elements of social scientific thinking* (3rd ed). New York: St. Martin's Press.

Janis, I. L. (1982). *Groupthink* (2nd ed). Boston: Houghton Mifflin.

Katz, N. H., & Lawyer, J. W. (1985). *Communication and conflict resolution skills.* Dubuque, IA: Kendall/Hunt.

Knapp, M. L., & Vangelisti, A. L. (2000). *Interpersonal communication and human relationships* (4th ed.). Boston: Allyn and Bacon.

Knapp, M. L. (1978). *Social intercourse: From greeting to goodbye.* Boston: Allyn and Bacon.

Kramarae, C. (1981). *Women and men speaking: Frameworks for analysis.* Rowley, MA: Newbury House.

Marwell, G., & Schmitt, D. R. (1967). Dimensions of compliance-gaining behavior: An empirical analysis. *Sociometry, 30,* 350–364.

Miller, K. (2002). *Communication theories: Perspectives, processes, and contexts.* Boston: McGraw-Hill.

Metts, S. (1992). The language of disengagement: A face management perspective. In T. L. Orbuch (Ed.), *Close relationship loss: Theoretical approaches* (pp. 111–127). New York: Springer-Verlag.

Motley, M. T. (1990). On whether one can(not) communicate: An examination via traditional communication postulates. *Western Journal of Speech Communication, 54,* 1–20.

Motley, M. T. (1991). How one may not communicate: A reply to Andersen. *Communication Studies, 42,* 326–339.

Noelle-Neumann, E. (1993). *The spiral of silence* (2nd ed.). Chicago: University of Chicago Press.

Thibaut, J. W., & Kelley, J. J. (1959). *The psychology of groups.* New York: Wiley.

Tuckman, B. (1965). Developmental sequence in small groups. *Psychological Bulletin, 63,* 384–399.

Turner, J. (1986). *The structure of sociological theory* (4th ed.). Chicago: Dorsey Press.

Wood, J. T. (1996). *Gendered relationships.* Mountain View, CA: Mayfield.

2

Assumptions behind Communication Theories: Reality, Knowledge, and Values

John R. Baldwin

In the previous chapter you learned the definition of a theory and how to decide whether theories are good or bad. This chapter addresses some of the assumptions we make that underlie the construction of various types of communication theories. As a student of communication theory you need to appreciate that each theorist approaches the study of communication based on a unique worldview. Each of us has a worldview, but we often take it for granted and assume that everyone else sees the world much as we do. When researchers study communication, their view of the world is the foundation upon which they build theory. Researchers build theoretical constructions based on differing foundations. In this chapter you will explore some of the dominant worldviews that support the discipline.

In this chapter, you will read about the following concepts:

- Metatheory
- Underlying assumptions behind theories
  - Ontology
  - Epistemology
  - Axiology
- Revolutions in paradigms and theories
- Two major debates
  - Laws/Rules/Systems
  - Scientific/Humanistic/Critical
- Classifications of theories
  - Scientific
  - Humanistic
  - Critical

"Beauty is in the eye of the beholder"—or at least that is what we have heard. Still, as we get ready for our date with that person to whom we are really attracted, we all engage in the same sort of beauty ritual (see Figure 2.1). We comb our hair, brush our teeth, and choose that right outfit for the occasion. We might even bathe. As we go on the date, we tell stories, maybe try to joke around, ask questions about the other person, and look for things we have in common. What is interesting is that, even though we want to believe that each person sees beauty differently and that each person prefers different dating partners, when we are actually on the date, we use strategies we think will work with the average person. So, in fact, do we really think that people are mostly the same? I mean, how do I *know* my date will like men to wear fancy cologne or not to pick their teeth or not to talk too much?

Our **lay theories,** as we discussed in Chapter 1, guide our behavior in this and many other situations. Perhaps as lay theorists we sometimes ask even deeper questions—questions about the nature of human choice, questions about what is real and what we can know and whether there is a truth that exists for everyone. I know my wife, our children, and I talk about such things all the time over dinner! While you may not do this, our society's interest in alternate reality movies like *The Matrix* and *The Truman Show* evidence that such questions intrigue us—at least occasionally.

Communication theorists have wrestled long with this underlying debate: Are we really alike, or are we really different? In the first chapter, we considered definitions of communication and of theory. In this chapter, we will expand our understanding of theory to look at contrasting views of theory and the underlying assumptions that drive those views. What we will see is that theorists, like everyone else, approach the world with different views of what that world is like and what theory should try to do in explaining that world. In this chapter, we hope to lay down a foundation that will help you understand the rest of this book and, perhaps, the rest of your time as a communication student.

FIGURE 2.1   Naïve theories guide us as we prepare for our next date.

©RubberBall Productions

How Should I Understand the World around Me?

Someone discovered long ago that it is easier to carry a pile of dirty laundry by putting it in a container with handles, and it is easier to break something open to look at it if we can first find a crack in the surface. Terms in theory work in the same way—they work like handles in allowing us to better understand abstract and complex ideas. A set of terms that help us to crack open a text to look inside it for meaning, or to get a handle on the various causes of some communication act, would be part of a theory. However, scholars have also developed a set of terms that allow us to analyze theories themselves.

Scholars have called this idea of theorizing about theory **metatheory.** Stephen Littlejohn (1999) explains: "*Metatheory,* as the prefix *meta-* suggests, is a body of speculation on the nature of inquiry that is *above* or *over* the specific content of theories" (p. 31). Metatheory, then, is not a specific theory or a specific explanation about some aspect of communication, but a way of talking about or analyzing individual theories. It is a sort of "theory" about *how* we theorize. Specifically, metatheory provides a set of terms for understanding the various types of assumptions a theory makes about the communication world. *All* theorists base their theories on their unique and personal underlying assumptions about the world, even though most theorists propose their theories without acknowledging their own assumptions about the world that prompted them. The question is, how can we compare the assumptions of each theorist and how can we understand their influence from theory to theory? Various writers have agreed upon three areas of assumptions that are important to explaining and understanding theory: ontology, epistemology, and axiology.

Ontology: The Nature of Reality and What Humans Are Like

The first area of assumptions that sits beneath the surface of theory deals with **ontology,** or assumptions about the nature of being or reality. It is important to note here that ontology is not a single assumption, but a set of ideas about what is real or what explains human behavior. Whether you have considered the idea of what is real, it is likely that readers differ on what they feel constitutes reality or what defines truth. Ontological questions in communication include: Are your responses—like your ability to empathize with others—best understood in terms of temporary conditions (**states**) or in terms of general, relatively enduring predispositions (**traits**)? Should we think of human experience in terms of personalized, individual meaning or truth, or should we look for the truth or reality of communication in terms of general or universal rules that govern all human communication? Is there a universal Truth (with a capital *T*) such as *predictors* of an effective date that will hold true for most people, even in most cultures, or does each culture (or even each individual) define the dating experience uniquely (truth with a small *t*)? Can you really make choices about your behavior on your date, or do your society and your personality influence your behaviors, even your choices (Littlejohn, 1999)?

Epistemology: What We know and How We Know It

Closely related to questions of what is real are questions of what we can know and how we can know it, or whether an individual or society determines truth. The study of knowledge is known as **epistemology.** Epistemological questions address things such as how certainly we can know what we know, whether we must have observable evidence or are allowed to use our intuition in determining what we know, and how explicitly we must know something before it counts for knowledge. For example, perhaps you have had a gut-level feeling that you could not trust your date, but you could not quite put it into words, even in your head—would that count as knowledge? Other epistemological issues include whether knowledge must be *explicit* (stated in words) or can be *tacit* (not able to be stated), whether it should be gained in parts or holistically, or whether believing something is the same thing as knowing it (Littlejohn, 1999).

Axiology: The Role of Values in Our Research

The final set of questions most commonly found in discussions of metatheory involves the role values should take in our research and theory, an area of philosophy called **axiology.** At one level, these questions include whether we can separate theory or research from the individual interests or values of the one creating the theory or conducting the research. Some argue that we should use steps to remove biases from research and that theory is simply a value-free description of what exists outside of our perceptions. Others say that no theory can be free of the values of the researcher. Still other researchers feel that values in theory are actually desirable. They deliberately bring their values into their research and theory in order to make the world a better place. For example, can or should we openly use theory and research to expose and combat racism or class-based oppression? If we say yes, we accept that it is okay for values to guide our work. Many researchers feel that your values limit what you will be able to see. For example, they suggest, if you are a feminist, you might see male privilege everywhere, even where it may not be a key issue. Or, on the other hand, for others, male power or male privilege over women is presented as a kind of accepted and inevitable "reality" or is simply not looked at. Here we can see that any research—even that which claims to ignore value issues—still supports certain values.

In recent decades many have taken the axiological view that no theorist and no research can be absolutely value-free or a completely objective or neutral picture of reality. This acknowledgment is important for the study of ontology and epistemology. It suggests that the values and worldview of the researcher are always present in research, even if the researcher claims to be totally neutral. They appear as the researcher chooses a topic, selects a method for research, and explains the implications of the findings.

In sum, every theory rests on assumptions about what is real, how we understand the world, what counts as worthwhile evidence, whether we should allow values to guide our theory and research, and so on. We cannot say that one theory is "ontological" and another is "epistemological," for *all* theories make *some* assumption about what is real or what is not. A theory cannot exist without some such assumptions about the world. In the same way, we cannot say that a theory that seeks social change is "axiological." *All* theorists have some axiological position—either their position is that they want to be value-free and simply observe the world, or that they want to change the world, or somewhere in between. Most times, just like in our everyday lives, the assumptions are not clearly stated, but they are still there! We will not discuss the underlying assumptions of each theory we discuss, but we hope you come to recognize the assumptions. Often writers of theory use shorthand words to help them cluster theories with different sets of assumptions. The next section will discuss such attempts at making more sense of the types of theory in communication.

Are There Shortcuts I Can Take to Understand These Assumptions?

Rather than discussing every assumption of every theory, communication scholars often find that certain sets of assumptions go together. For example, if you believe that people respond to internal and external "causes," without thinking about their responses, you will also likely believe that most people are in many ways alike (an ontological assumption), and that we can create explanations that predict their behaviors (an epistemological assumption).

Scholars often cluster theories into groups—based on similar underlying assumptions, a sort of classification system of general ways of seeing the world. Each approach to the world and knowledge may have several types of theories within it, and each type may, again, have many theories (Figure 2.2). Thus, a paradigm is a general approach—a view of the world, with theories being the most specific—an explanation of a particular phenomenon. More formally, a **paradigm** is a *way of seeing the social and natural world, with a set of assumptions or beliefs about what that world is like* (Kuhn, 1996). Thomas Kuhn (1996), who was central in challenging disciplines to think about their underlying assumptions about knowledge, challenged the traditional view of knowledge in the natural sciences by proposing that, instead of simply adding fact to fact endlessly, at times whole revolutions of ideas can occur. Kuhn contended that (scientific) disciplines go through stages of **revolutionary science,** when an old paradigm is suddenly overthrown, and **normal science,** when theory and research follow along within an accepted way of seeing the world. As you read a research article or a theory, the writer might be conducting normal science—not explicitly stating his or her assumptions but simply going along within a consistent and regular development of knowledge. In times of revolutionary science, debate and ferment arise about the very nature of our theoretical assumptions.

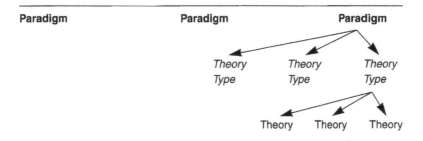

FIGURE 2.2 *Paradigms, Theory Types, Theories.* As this diagram shows, a single paradigm (e.g., scientific) might have several different types of theories (e.g., social-exchange–based theories), and these, in turn, may have specific theories within them (e.g., social penetration theory, Chapter 7).

Kuhn (1996) explains that as a discipline moves into maturity, it lands on a single paradigm for a while (until the next revolution takes place). One could easily say that the communication discipline has, since the 1960s, been searching for that uniform paradigm (see Chapter 4). This search is complicated by the fact that the study of communication bridges the humanities (in terms of examining the art and classic texts of communication), the social sciences (in terms of the effects of media or personality variables), and critical theory positions (in terms of ideology, power, and gender contained in communication). These three influences led to a variety of perspectives in the social sciences. Gibson Burrell and Gareth Morgan (1979) place these perspectives within two dimensions. The first of these is the ontological/epistemological dimension, and the second is the axiological dimension. We will first discuss these two dimensions so that we can return to understand the debates.

The Objective-Subjective Dimension

Burrell and Morgan's (1979) first dimension is between what they call objective and subjective approaches to the world. This distinction is based upon the assumptions of the theorists in terms of ontology and epistemology. First, the **objective approach** tends to believe in "a social world external to individual cognition," that is, "a real world made up of hard, tangible and relatively immutable things" (Burrell and Morgan call this view of the world **realism,** p. 4). Humans are seen to behave largely in patterned, predictable ways, often seen in terms of cause and effect (called **determinism,** as behavior is believed to be determined by internal and external causes). The way one knows this world is by looking for regularities across cases, often through methods that use larger numbers of participants or images, hopefully selected randomly. The researcher controls for personal and other biases in order to be as certain as possible in order to accurately see a reality external to the researcher (**positivism**). Theory and research try to uncover the laws of human behavior—that is, the laws of cause and effect that predict behavior—in a way that could be generalized to as large a population as possible.

This approach has tended to use the **scientific method** of inquiry, which urges objectivity, reliable measures (that test the same thing each time they are used), and the ability to predict larger populations from one's theory or research (generalizability). For this reason, it is often called the **scientific** approach. Within that approach, scientific theories tend to have **variables,** or concepts, that can vary in relationship to one another. **Propositions** state the cause-effect and other relationships between the variables. The theory might suggest how some empirical indicator could measure (**operationalize**)—often quantitatively—the concepts of the theory in a study. Finally, these operationalized concepts (**variables**) can be placed in predictive statements (e.g., "If A goes up, B will go up") in **hypotheses** (Dubin, 1978).

The second approach outlined by Burrell and Morgan (1979) is the **subjective approach.** This view of the world holds that reality and meaning are always personal and always channeled through the society that contains them. For example, love is not something that is external to us, with five dimensions that cover all types of love in all cultures. Rather, each culture defines love and dating its own way. A subjective researcher might even say that your definition of love is different from that of every other person, yet definitions of love still maintain some common threads of meanings given the same culture these persons share. As Burrell and Morgan put it, the subjective approach "revolves around the assumption that the social world external to individual cognition is made up of nothing more than names, concepts and labels which are used to structure reality" (p. 4). That is, things in the social world (including natural objects used by the social world) only exist in human thought because humans have given them names. (Burrell and Morgan call this a **nominalist** view, based on the Latin word for *name*). Thus, the concept of *race*, in reference to a supposed biological differentiation between people groups, only exists because we have created the concept through words.

In the subjective approach, people do not behave on impulse but rather make decisions based on free will (**voluntarism**). Because of people's ability to choose and because of the shifting nature of meanings, any knowledge can be, at best, "relativistic and can only be understood from the point of view of the individuals who are directly involved in the activities which are to be studied" (Burrell & Morgan, 1979, p. 5). Any sort of prediction, which would assume causes for human behavior instead of assuming that people make choices based on individual goals, would be senseless. Rather, theories would seek to explain a specific relationship, organization, individual, or text or perhaps uncover the perception of reality of a specific group. That is, research should be **ideographic** (*ideo,* distinct + *graph,* writing), providing interpretations of specific instances, not predictions of the social world. For this reason, the subjective approach is often called **interpretive** or **humanistic.**

The difference between the two approaches might be understood better if we consider the principle behind the words *objective* and *subjective*. René Descartes was one of the philosophers of modernity who helped frame the modern scientific view by proclaiming that the observer (the subject) was separate and distinct from the observed (the object). Truth was, he suggested, in the *object;* thus, if we remove our personal biases, we will arrive at objective truth.

The objective approach to truth later developed into the scientific method of manipulation and control of variables to see the influence of one variable upon another or the statistical relationship between two variables. In the late 1800s and following, many began to doubt this "Cartesian dualism" (based on Descartes) and said that reality is, to a degree, in the eye of the beholder (the *subject*). As Linda Becker (1992) has suggested, it makes no difference if there is an absolute measurable distance of 18 inches between two people. We relate and respond differently to the 18 inches if they separate us from a lover than if they separate us from a mother-in-law. This new line of research demonstrates more interest in people's perceptions of phenomena (often called **phenomenology**), assuming that those perceptions would be different from person to person. Another type of humanistic research might examine a text (movie, play, public relations campaign) in terms of the history, politics, and other social contexts around it (called a **hermeneutic** approach to a text). To understand the scientific and humanistic approaches, let us consider the date situation mentioned at the beginning of the chapter. The scientific approach would suggest that the same variables will make most dates successful—things like equal turn sharing, nonverbal warmth, and self-disclosure. A humanist might, instead, seek to create a framework of terms that will help you (or the theorist) to understand your particular relationship, your goals and desires in the relationship, and personal meanings you and your partner have developed.

The Social-Change/Status Quo Dimension

Burrell and Morgan propose a second dimension that cuts across the first one, the axiological dimension. This dimension raises questions as to the role of values in research. For example, if you were a traditional ethnographer (someone who studies a culture or organization through observation and interview methods), you might want to leave your values outside the door as you plan to study an organization, just as a scientific researcher would. Others might believe that research cannot be value-free, that one's values influence how topics and methods for research are chosen (Lincoln & Guba, 1985). Still others feel values *must* be brought into research in order to make the world a better place for everyone. Changing the world, in this sense, is not seen in terms of making us better persuaders or even helping us individually in the dating relationship. It is, instead, seen in terms of changing social structures or empowering individuals who are disadvantaged or mistreated by society.

You can see that either subjective or objective theories can seek to change the world. Thus, a subjective theorist might seek to change people's individual view of reality, or might seek to radically alter the social structures believed to be external to the observer. One type of research that seeks to change the world is **critical theory,** which is really a whole range of theories that address social power and power inequalities in society by looking at organizations, relationships, politics, texts, and social norms.

The origins of critical theories have been located in Marxist thought and have been formulated in Europe, primarily in England, France, and Italy, where there is a strong sense of social class (see Chapters 6 and 17 for more detail). Marx believed that the owners of the factories and farms (*capitalists*) maintained and controlled society through their ownership of the means of production. Thus, the capitalists kept the workers (or *proletariat*) in their place through control of the means of production and, in turn, through social relationships. The *bourgeois* were all those persons in the middle class, who were nevertheless often at the mercy or control of the capitalists for their livelihood but who enjoyed more spending power and discretion in their lives than the proletariat class. Marx and his followers felt that schools, religion, the family, and media (the superstructure) were all held in place by the economic system and the interdependence of the social classes of society.

Marx not only recognized that the socioeconomic class of capitalists controlled the means of production and, in turn, controlled financially all the other socioeconomic classes. Marx also recognized that the capitalist, the bourgeois, and the proletarian classes each—because of its respective economic position—held a different ideology. He suggested that a capitalist would see the world differently than a member of the proletariat or the bourgeois would; that is, people according to their respective class positions would live according to a different ideology and, as such, necessarily give different meanings to the world around them.

Many critical theorists today no longer believe in the exclusive power of the economic elite, but do hold that media, family communication, interpersonal communication, and public relations images and messages seek to keep the powerful (in terms of gender, race, class, physical ability, nationality, and so on) in positions of power (**hegemony**). Critical theorists often believe that this is not done intentionally, but blindly, by passing on stock sets of (sexist, racist, and so on) ideas and assumptions about the world (**ideology**). Thus, their goal is to make public the hidden assumptions of media texts and social practices in a way that fights social, gender, or racial oppression. However, there is a wide variety of critical theories, including cultural studies, structuralism, semiotics, feminist analysis, postmodernism, and postcolonialism.

In sum, different scholars approach the same phenomenon, such as relational conflict, with different sets of assumptions (Figure 2.3). [Web site: Types of Critical Theory]

FIGURE 2.3 *Different Paradigms, Different Explanations, and an Argument.* Do we predict conflict styles (scientific), explain how couples create their own communication culture (humanistic), or critique male/female power relationships?

© Tom Prettyman/PhotoEdit/PictureQuest

Why Can't We All Just Get Along?— The Two Dimensions and Two Debates

Two specific debates have arisen that regard the main "paradigms" that we, as communication students, use as we try to understand how and why we study communication. Those can best be understood in terms of the two dimensions above. [Web site: On the Paradigm Debate]

Debate #1, 1977: Laws, Rules, or Systems

First, a special issue of *Communication Quarterly,* in 1977, allowed authors from three different schools of thought to air what they thought communication research should look like. In the introductory essay, W. Barnett Pearce summarizes the field then and now:

> Perhaps the most striking feature which all of the social sciences share is their internal diversity. Various "camps," "schools," and "traditions" ask different questions, use different methodologies, and envision different significances for their labors. (p. 3)

The various authors tended to break camp along three different lines, which are now commonly called the laws approach, the rules approach, and the systems approach.

Laws Approach. First, a *covering law* approach seeks to find explanations for the causes of human behavior, in hopes of arriving at the fullest explanation possible. Specifically, the theory seeks to uncover the *regularities* of human behavior (Berger, 1977). That is, the approach assumes that people act much the same in response to stimuli. If we wanted to understand a communication behavior, say positive reception of a public relations campaign, we would try to isolate those things, such as the visual content of the message, the audience's demographic background, and so on, that would help us to predict the audience's response. Among scientific theorists, debate arose as to whether communication tendencies exist as *traits* or *states.*

Notably, social science as a whole moved away from the hard scientific claims of positivism. Across disciplines, from psychology to sociology to communication, scholars realized that because humans have (at least some) choice, and perhaps based on their symbolic abilities, they simply cannot be predicted like BBs bouncing in a boxcar or pool balls on a billiard table. Thus, the laws researchers with a laws perspective seek are not absolute laws, but rather **probabilistic laws.** Further, many scientific/laws-based writers have come to believe that there are realities that cannot be seen or touched (e.g., friendship, patriotism), but we can try to get close to these with good indicators (e.g., well-constructed surveys). Finally, many have come to suggest that even scientific researchers bring values to their projects in their choices of topic and method. These changes bring these researchers from a positivistic tradition to what is called **post-positivism.** It retains the *positivism* label because while the scholars admit the existence of values and so on, they still seek to reduce their influence, striving for objectivity.

Rules Approach. The rules approach contrasts to the laws approach in that it assumes that people have the ability to make their own decisions. Donald Cushman suggests that people are **teleological;** that is, they behave *toward some end or purpose* rather than *because of some stimulus.* Cushman (1977) outlines several levels at which one might follow rules, either consciously or subconsciously. An important aspect of this perspective is that rules are created through communication among a group of people, and thus will be culturally variable. In sum, we would explain people's behavior in terms of how it follows or breaks the rules of a situation (possibly quite intentionally), and not in terms of abstract variables that may have caused it.

Systems Approach. The third approach popular in the late 1970s was a systems approach. This view of the world, based on the biological approach of Ludwig von Bertalanffy (1968), emphasizes the interconnectedness of the elements in a unit of analysis. Paul Watzlawick, Janet Beavin, and Don Jackson (1967) applied this approach to their counseling of families. They suggested that the appropriate unit of analysis was not the individual member of the family, but rather that one family member's behavior was merely a reaction to that of other members. If one member changed her or his behavior, the rest of the system would change. The world was seen, then, as a set of elements working together, often in unpredictable and mutually influencing ways, as they worked toward a goal.

In sum, a **system** is "the ordered composition of (material or mental) elements into a unified whole" (Simon, Stierlin, & Wynne, 1985, p. 353). Thus, a system can be as small as the mind of an individual (see Kim's theory of cultural adaptation in Chapter 12) or as big as a nation. Peter Monge (1973, 1977) outlined the characteristics of systems as follows (my summary): (1) Systems seek to maintain a comfortable, but not exact, balance (**homeostasis**). (2) Systems vary in level of complexity. (3) The various parts of a system have **interrelatedness**—if one part changes, the others change to adjust. (4) Systems "control and regulate" themselves by sending messages to the different parts of the system either to keep them in line or to get them to change (**feedback**). (5) The different parts of a system send and receive these messages to other parts. (6) Systems both grow and die.

For an example of a system, suppose you are a member of a sorority or fraternity. A member is "hazing" new recruits to your group, which in most schools is now illegal. Either because your organization disapproves of hazing or because someone was injured in the incident, the organization feels your member is "out of line." This disrupts the balance (homeostasis) of your system, so the leaders of the sorority or fraternity must decide what to do. They issue a warning (feedback) intended to bring the system back in line with their goal of being an honorable organization in the Greek system. In recent years, we have not seen many systems theories, though many theories borrow from the terminology.

Debate #2, 1983: Scientific, Humanistic, or Critical

In 1983, the terms of the debate shifted, and, while there are still theories from each of these first three perspectives covered throughout this text, one will more often hear of the "paradigm debate" in terms of new clusters of assumptions. The seminal work in this area was a special issue of the *Journal of Communication*, entitled *Ferment in the Field*.

The chapters in this and later collections of essays point out that the debate on communication theory and research has both narrowed and broadened. The laws approach of 1977 becomes the *scientific* paradigm of 1983; the *rules* approach becomes part of a broader *humanistic* approach that now also includes rhetoric and other forms of research. The *systems* perspective contains elements of both choice (goal) and stimulus response (one part of the system affects all the others) and thus seems to sit between the scientific and humanistic perspective. Finally, the entire new dimension of social change is added, creating a new paradigm, critical theory.

In sum, whether a theory is scientific or humanist is based on its assumptions about reality, meaning, and knowledge. Whether it claims to be critical or value-free depends upon its axiology. Scientific theories seek *to explain, predict, and in some cases control* the communicative world. Typically, they contain variables and connections between abstract ideas (A predicts B, C causes D). Humanistic theories seek, instead, to provide *interpretation and deep understanding* of communication within social formations. For example, they do not try to form generalizations to all dating situations, but rather seek to establish a theory or a process that explains how dating situations can operate. And finally, the purpose of critical theories is to *uncover any problems in the ideology and meaning processes* of social behavior (sex, race, class-based power). Some critical theories are more

subjective and some more objective. The following points summarize my perspective on
the paradigms (scientific, humanistic, critical) in the paradigm debate:

1. We will discuss theories as scientific, humanistic, or critical in this book, because
   these are commonly accepted as paradigms in our discipline today.
2. However, we *should* think of theories as either *more* scientific or *more* humanistic.
   Some theories combine elements of both approaches. For example, cultural studies
   and American interpretativism suggest that we have *shared* social realities. Though
   we create myths like *race* through interaction, they become real in a way, and influence our behavior.
3. Any critical theory also has an ontological and epistemological stance. In the communication discipline, most critical theories are more humanistic. *Critical* usually
   refers to the theory's political agenda to question and identify unequal social power
   structures. (See Figure 2.4 for visualization of the two dimensions, with several of
   the approaches mentioned in this section highlighted.)

Your understanding of these issues will greatly help you as you read this book and
take other communication classes. In some books and articles, you may see a definition of
theory, standards for evaluating theories, and so on. You will now be aware that if you see
words like *predict* and *variable,* that the authors probably have underlying assumptions that

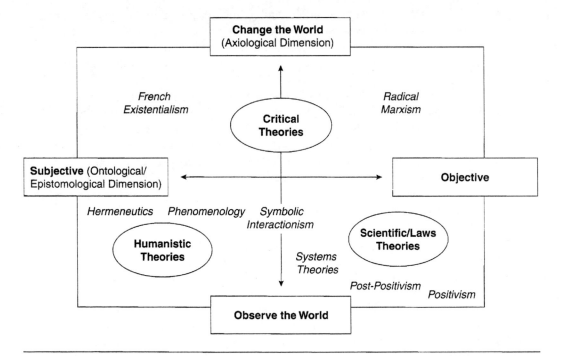

FIGURE 2.4   *Two Dimensions, Three Paradigms.*

Figure adapted from Burrell & Morgan (1979). Reprinted by permission.

lean toward the scientific view. If the authors talk about *interpreting* or *subjective experience,* they are probably writing more from the humanistic side. If the authors mention *empowerment,* the *ideologies* imbedded in the media text, they are operating most likely from a critical perspective. And some writers might sit somewhere among all these perspectives.

Summary

In the end, an understanding of the assumptions of these paradigms regarding reality (ontology), knowledge (epistemology), and the role of values in research (axiology) will help you in two ways. First, as you read definitions of theory and think of how to evaluate theories, you will be better able to tell if the theory meets the objectives of the underlying assumptions, that is, if it is logically consistent with the approach the authors are taking. More importantly, it will help you understand how to apply a theory to real life. If you want to make scientific *predictions* about the communication morale of an organization or the persuasive appeal of a communication campaign, you should call on a scientific theory. If you want a theory that will help you *interpret* the communication in your family or a specific media text, or a culture, a humanistic theory may be more in order. If you want to *challenge inequality* (e.g., sexism or racism), a critical theory will be more helpful.

To return to our opening example, your date has ended, and it was a flop (fortunately not your date with theory!). You might want to understand relationship failure in a way backed up by research that applies to most people (scientific), to interpret the rules and choices you made on your date (humanistic), or to see if power relations, based in societal ideas about gender, sex, race, or class imposed upon your date (critical). In some cases, the type of knowledge you seek to obtain will guide you as you choose the type of theory you want or as you build your own theory. Many of us, at the same time, already tend to gravitate toward one type or another based on our view of the world, of knowledge, and of values.

Interestingly, any one of these general approaches can be used to develop policy for organizations, to instruct how we run a classroom, or to guide us in how we should act in our everyday communication. The difference is in what types of claims each makes, how each one would use research, and how well each one will be accepted by others in the academic community. A look at communication history (Chapter 4) will tell us that our relations have not always been harmonious. We are, hopefully, entering a period of collaboration, where we can learn from one another using different perspectives and methods, as we strive to understand this complex thing we call communication.

Discussion Questions

Use the following case to answer the discussion questions: In 1999, the Mitsubishi Motor plant in Normal, Illinois, had a major scandal involving multiple cases of sexual harassment. The case received national attention and resulted in a multimillion-dollar settlement. Notably, such decisions are made in a trial based on what jurors believe to be a "reasonable standard" of behavior.

1. Is harassment something that exists differently for each person, is it a shared definition in a culture, or is it a notion we can define objectively across all cultures and times (ontological view)? Why would this be important as you plan strategies to address it?

2. How might certain positions or beliefs about the world be related to different ideas about how we can know or understand that world?

3. Describe two or three different stances researchers might take regarding the role of values (axiology) as they study sexual harassment.

4. As Mitsubishi Motor Company mounts a public relations campaign in the attempt to restore its image among the public, how might someone from a "scientific/objective" paradigm approach the study of that campaign differently than someone from a "humanistic/subjective" approach?

5. What are the strengths and limitations of Burrell and Morgan's two-dimension approach?

References

Becker, L. (1992). *Living and relating*. Newbury Park, CA: Sage.

Berger, C. R. (1977). The covering laws perspective as a theoretical basis for the study of human communication. *Communication Quarterly, 25*, 7–18.

Bertalanffy, L. von. (1968). *General systems theory*. New York: George Braziller.

Burrel, G., & Morgan, G. (1979). *Sociological paradigms and organisational analysis*. London: Heinemann.

Cushman, D. P. (1977). The rules perspective as a theoretical basis for the study of human communication. *Communication Quarterly, 25*, 30–45.

Dubin, R. (1978). *Theory building* (2nd ed.). New York: Free Press.

Kuhn, T. (1996). *The nature of scientific revolutions* (3rd ed.). Chicago: University of Chicago Press.

Lincoln, Y. S., & Guba, E. G. (1985). *Naturalistic inquiry*. Newbury Park, CA: Sage.

Littlejohn, S. W. (1999). *Theories of human communication* (6th ed.). Belmont, CA: Wadsworth.

Monge, P. R. (1973). Theory construction in the study of communication: The system paradigm. *Journal of Communication, 23* (1), 5–16.

Monge, P. R. (1977). The systems perspective as a theoretical basis for the study of human communication. *Communication Quarterly, 25*, 19–29.

Pearce, W. B. (1977). Metatheoretical concerns in communication. *Communication Quarterly, 25*, 3–6.

Simon, F. B., Stierlin, H., & Wynne, L. C. (1985). *The language of family therapy: A systemic vocabulary and sourcebook*. New York: Family Process Press.

Watzlawick, P., Beavin, J. H., & Jackson, D. D. (1967). *Pragmatics of human communication*. New York: Norton.

3

Researching Theory in Communication

Mark Comadena

In the previous chapter you read about the types of theories ranging from social scientific to humanistic to critical. We walked carefully through the maze of questions regarding how we know what we know and the various paradigms that undergird the investigations and writings that make up fields of inquiry, including the field of communication. Before that, you were introduced to what theory is, why it is important, and what criteria should be used to evaluate it.

In this chapter, the discussion moves into a more technical phase. You will learn terms and definitions that describe the various components of the research process, especially the components involved in social science research. You've probably had other classes in high school and even in college that have discussed some of these terms, so in some ways this chapter might be a refresher course for you. However, you will probably also travel some new ground as the chapter discusses the various sections of a scholarly report and differentiates between qualitative analysis and quantitative analysis. Whether this is mostly new or mostly review, like the first two chapters, this chapter is foundational for understanding the processes that support the theories to be found in the rest of the text.

In this chapter, you will read about the following concepts:

- A rationale and introduction to communication research
- Terms for understanding theories and theory building
  - Concept/Construct
  - Measurement
  - Conceptual and operational definitions
  - Variable
- The two general research models
  - Inductive
  - Deductive

- Quantitative research
  - Aspects of a quantitative study
  - Some types of quantitative research
- Qualitative research
  - Aspects of a qualitative study
  - Some types of qualitative research

The cartoon that starts off this chapter (Figure 3.1) illustrates the very nature of research. We compare a group in which an event or condition does not occur (the control group) with a group that experiences the event or condition of interest (humorously called the out-of-control group). In following formalized rituals for making such comparisons, we engage in what is known as research, the subject of this chapter.

We research theories that address a wide range of communication phenomena, including interpersonal communication events, group processes, organizational communication, public relations, and the mass media. As noted earlier, a theory is a set of interrelated propositions or claims that explain why events, especially communication events, occur in our social world.

The search for theories is based upon the fundamental assumption that there is indeed order in our social world and that events happen for a reason. The challenge for communication researchers, and social scientists in general, is to discover order to explain those events. But a theory can be incorrect, or one theory might provide a better explanation of an event than another. It is through carefully designed and executed research projects that scientists develop and test their theories and arrive at accurate explanations for the communication activities they study.

CONTROL GROUP   OUT OF CONTROL GROUP

FIGURE 3.1   *Control Group vs. Out-of-Control Group.*
© Pete Mueller, used with permission.

This chapter examines the role of research in the development and testing of communication theories. We begin by exploring the nature of research. We move to a discussion of two general models for developing theories in communication and the characteristics of two methods for conducting communication research. The web site includes a review of how to read the research articles that help build our theories. [Web site: Reading Research Articles]

Why Should I Read (or Do) Research?

When you think of the word *research,* what comes to mind? To many students, the word means library work. And that would be true. Generally speaking, research refers to the process of securing answers to questions. When we use the information available to us at libraries to help generate answers to questions, we are performing research. Library research may reveal, for example, which of the many subcompact cars available today is both the safest and the most economical to operate. In this case, we may use information produced by others, perhaps the National Transportation Safety Board (NTSB), to help us answer our question. But how do the experts at the NTSB know if a certain car is safer or more economical to operate than others are? Again, the answer is research. But here, research means carefully measuring the safety and performance features of all cars in a category under identical circumstances. Such comparative analysis will reveal the safest and most economical cars. Thus, through careful observation or measurement we can come to generate new information about questions of interest. It is this latter definition of research that we adopt and examine in this chapter.

Communication researchers are not typically interested in which cars are the safest or the most fuel-efficient. Instead, communication researchers want to know how people use the mass media, how communication influences the development of interpersonal relationships, and what public relations strategies work for different types of organizational problems. Many college instructors, especially those who teach public speaking courses, want to know what strategies or methods can be used to reduce speech anxiety in their students. In short, communication researchers are interested in knowing how people communicate with one another and what effects those communications have on the parties involved. In addition, researchers what to know *why* people communicate the way they do and *why* messages influence people the way they do. Answers to these "why" questions require the creation of theories. And research is performed to determine if these theories are tenable. After all, what good is a theory if it does not truly explain the phenomenon or event it is supposed to explain? Research, then, is used to discover relationships between events in our social worlds and to test or evaluate the accuracy of the theories developed to explain why those events occur.

In the study of communication, researchers, as noted in Chapter 1, use two general models (**inductive** and **deductive**) for developing and testing communication theories. Methods used can also be categorized into three general categories, somewhat aligned with the three approaches to theory described in Chapter 2. These are quantitative (objective), qualitative (subjective), and critical methods. **Quantitative studies** are almost always "objective" in their approach to the world. **Qualitative studies** might vary in their underlying view of the world from a somewhat objective view to an extremely subjective view, though much qualitative research is used to answer more "humanistic" questions about communication.

Critical methods can incorporate a qualitative or quantitative approach but take a prescriptive stance advocating social change rather than attempting to be unbiased in reporting research observations; thus, what makes the research critical is not the method, but what the writer attempts to do with the method and findings. Researchers who take a quantitative, qualitative, or critical approach to research maintain very different philosophical assumptions about the nature of our social world and utilize very different methods for constructing and testing communication theories. Quantitative, qualitative, and critical researchers hold different perspectives about what constitutes data or findings, and whether those findings need to be generalizable to a larger population.

In this section of the chapter, we explore some of the philosophical assumptions that underlie each model and describe key characteristics of research methods associated with each model. Later we will address the characteristics of quantitative and then qualitative methods. Before we begin our discussion, we need to introduce a few new terms that will enable us to talk about research and the theory construction process.

What Terms Do I Need to Know to Understand Research?

Communication researchers view the world in terms of carefully defined concepts. In fact, the first step in any research project is to identify one or more concepts for investigation. For example, in the study titled "Communication apprehension and learning style preference: Correlations and implications for teachers" (Dwyer, 1998), the concepts of communication apprehension and learning style were investigated. This study was conducted to see if students' fear of public speaking and their capacity for learning in the classroom are related in a meaningful way. This study can demonstrate the various concepts in the research that builds or tests theories. **Concepts** are objects, persons, or events that have something in common. Interactive television, electronic mail, newspaper editorial, stage fright, cartoon violence, and fear appeal are examples of communication concepts. Such concepts and others like them enable us to interact with one another in meaningful ways about our world. Andersen (1989) notes that any concept can be defined by determining its **criterial attributes** (i.e., qualities it must have), **excluding attributes** (i.e., qualities it cannot have), and **irrelevant attributes** (i.e., qualities it may or may not have).

Constructs are special concepts created by scientists to help them explain human behavior (Andersen, 1989). Many constructs refer to things that cannot be observed directly; instead, they are presumed to exist. Some constructs refer to behavioral events, such as speech-time latency (the amount of silence in a conversation between one person's statement and the next person's) and deception (the deliberate attempt to create in a hearer an impression one knows to be false). Thus, we could look at whether people pause longer before responding when they are telling lies. Other constructs refer to various social-psychological phenomena, such as *argumentativeness* and *media credibility*—or, as in our example study, *communication apprehension* and *learning style* (these are concepts, but since they are also used scientifically, they become constructs as well).

A **conceptual definition** is a statement that describes exactly what a concept or construct means. McCroskey (1982) conceptually defines *communication apprehension* as a fear or anxiety associated with either real or anticipated communication with another. Here, McCroskey uses the concepts of fear, anxiety, and anticipated communication to explain what he means by communication apprehension. Conceptual definitions let others know, to use a slang expression, "where one is coming from." Researchers must define their terms because any given concept may have a number of interpretations. For example, in a project on student learning, are we talking about *cognitive learning* (what one knows), *behavioral learning* (what one can do), or *affective learning* (one's attitude about the learning process)? These are issues that need to be addressed in developing a conceptual definition for student learning. Conceptual definitions, then, identify precise events for research.

Clear definitions of central concepts are important in both quantitative and qualitative research. In qualitative research, one often uses the concepts to create a theoretical lens (or **descriptive scheme;** see Chapter 1) by which to analyze a text (music video, organizational image, news coverage, and so on), an organization, or even a culture. In quantitative research, one would seek to find causal or correlational relationships between concepts. A **causal relationship** means that something is understood to influence or create, to increase or decrease something else. For example, increased intimacy of self-disclosure might *make* your relationship with your best friend draw closer. A **correlational relationship** means that as one concept changes, so does another, even if the first does not cause the second. People who drive red sports cars may be more likely to get traffic tickets, even if they do not drive any faster. In this case, the color of the car does not cause traffic tickets. For quantitative studies, especially, additional steps must be taken to *measure* the concepts.

Clear and complete conceptual definitions are also required to develop effective methods for measuring concepts in a study. In scientific studies, we cannot meaningfully investigate the relationship between concepts unless we can measure those concepts in some way. **Measurement** is at the heart of what social scientists do, and we will discuss measurement issues later in this chapter. At this point, we should note that how one measures a concept depends, in part, upon how that concept is defined. The procedure used to measure a concept is called an **operational definition.** Operational definitions describe the exact procedure used to measure a concept in a research project. Good operational definitions utilize procedures that are consistent with or "fit" the concept being measured.

Finally, we should define the term **variable.** In communication research reports, researchers often use the terms *concept* and *variable* in an interchangeable manner. Actually, a variable is a measured concept or construct. When researchers measure a concept, especially in quantitative studies, they systematically assign numbers to indicators of the concept. For example, if we wanted to measure speech anxiety in a group of college students, we would have the students complete a speech anxiety questionnaire. Once completed, we could score the questionnaire and assign total scores to students to represent their levels of speech anxiety (i.e., low scores to represent low anxiety and high scores to represent high speech anxiety). When measured, we would see that students report a range of scores (scores for the concept vary). If scores for a concept do not vary, the concept is a constant. Hopefully, whatever method we employ, the numbers will represent accurately students' levels of speech anxiety (i.e., low scores truly mean low speech anxiety and high scores mean high speech anxiety).

In summary, research projects are undertaken to determine if two (or more) concepts or constructs are related and, if so, why they are related. This is done often, but not always, in order to verify the propositions of a theory. To accomplish this objective, a scientifically focused researcher would systematically measure concepts to determine if his or her measurements reveal relationships between concepts. Through this process, a researcher seeks to discover if particular events (represented by concepts and constructs) are indeed related in our social world. Having defined some key terms, let's now explore two general models researchers use to develop their theories.

How Do We Build Deductive Theory?

As noted above, social researchers are not content simply to discover relationships between two or more events in our social worlds. They hope to explain *why* certain events are related. When we can explain why events are related, we have a theory. In fact, one could argue that the goal of all communication research, especially that research conducted at universities, is to create theories to explain human communication behavior as it occurs in a wide range of settings, from interpersonal relationships to mass-mediated events.

In Chapter 1, we learned that communication researchers may take either a deductive or an inductive approach to developing theories. At this time, let's explore in a little greater detail each approach. In the **deductive** method of theory construction, a researcher begins with a theory, a general explanation for the relationship between two or more concepts or constructs, and seeks to gather information to determine if that theory is accurate. In practice, theory can refer to a formal presentation of assumption, propositions, and axioms that offer an explanation for some event (e.g., uncertainty reduction theory, Chapter 7) or a logical argument that brings together definitions, facts, and assumptions to explain some event. In scientific theory building (as opposed to humanistic), if that explanation for the event is true, then certain predictions, called hypotheses, should follow. These hypotheses are usually tested using quantitative methods.

Hypotheses are declarative statements that predict that two or more concepts are related. The following statement illustrates a simple hypothesis: "Men are more argumentative than women." This hypothesis maintains that two concepts, *speaker sex* and *argumentativeness,* are related. In quantitative research, hypotheses are tested by precisely measuring the concepts and systematically analyzing the measurements. These "predictions" will either be supported or not supported by the measurements. If predictions are supported, the researcher has evidence, although limited, that the theory supporting the prediction appears to be correct. Of course, additional research and replications of the original project are necessary to confirm the original finding. On the other hand, if the predictions for a study were not supported, the data (i.e., the measurements) would suggest that the theory is not correct. In such cases, the researcher would need to revise the theory or discard it all together. Figure 3.2 presents an overview of the relationship between theory and data collection (for both inductive and deductive approaches). [Web site: Examples of Different Research Types]

Research reveals that many people experience a fear of public speaking, also called stage fright, and that many negative consequences are associated with high levels of such fear. You have probably experienced this, at least temporarily, yourself. Given that many suffer from speech anxiety, communication educators are concerned about methods for treating or

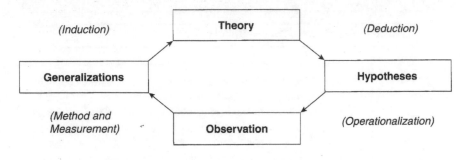

FIGURE 3.2   *The Relationship between Induction and Deduction in Theory Building.*

Adapted from Walter L. Wallace *Sociological theory: An introduction.* (New York: Aldine de Gruyter).
© 1969 by Walter L. Wallace. Used with permission.

reducing this fear. To know how to treat it, we must know why some people experience it. We need a theory. But as one researcher cautions us: "Theory is developed over time, and this theory-building process is repeated many times as different scholars test theoretical propositions in their research. Theories are developed and tested incrementally" (Keyton, 2001, p. 34). Deductive theory building allows a continual testing and refining of theory.

How Do We Build Inductive Theory?

Not all research, however, begins with a theory. Some researchers maintain that it is best to let a theory emerge from the information or data that one has accumulated on a particular communication event. Researchers who take this "bottom-up" approach build theories inductively. Here, a researcher attempts to minimize preconceived ideas about what to expect (no hypotheses) for an outcome. Instead, one or more **research questions** guide the researcher. Research questions are interrogatives that ask what concepts or behaviors mean to people in their everyday lives, how communication processes take place, or whether two or more phenomena (or concepts) are related. They are not declarative statements that predict an outcome for a project. For example, a simple research question might ask: What steps do speakers go through to reduce their speech anxiety? Ultimately, we are interested in whether they use certain tools such as prior experience (concept A) or practice (concept B) in order to reduce their anxiety about speaking (concept C).

To answer this question, a researcher would likely observe speakers if possible, probably interviewing some to find out about behaviors that could not be easily observed. Once these observations are made, the researcher will analyze his or her data to arrive at an answer to the research question. In some cases, the researcher might make enough observations and make them in such a systematic way that the behaviors can be counted and measured. In other cases, the researcher might develop a **grounded theory**—that is, a set of relationships between ideas that are developed through people's lived experience rather than from prior theory and measurement (Strauss & Corbin, 1998). The researcher may choose to turn the

---

Objective Approach to Theory Building

- Quantitative methods used alone (e.g., laboratory observation, quantified field observations)
- Qualitative methods (e.g., observation, interview, open-ended questionnaire) used to develop a quantitative measure (e.g., survey)
- Qualitative methods used to develop the theory, but understood in "objective" terms and seen as sufficient without quantitative "verification"—that is, a theory as a "framework that can be used to explain or predict phenomena" (Strauss & Corbin, 1998, p. 15)
- Qualitative methods used to develop a "theory" as a framework that can be used to interpret individual texts, relationships, or events, but not to predict across cases, such as Philipsen's (1989) speech codes theory. That is, quantitative verification of the theory is not seen as appropriate or necessary.

Subjective Approach to Theory Building

FIGURE 3.3   *A Continuum of Uses of Quantitative and Qualitative Methods in Theory Building.*

observations into a survey to see if the conclusions apply to a larger audience than those observed (Hui & Triandis, 1985). Of course, quantitative and qualitative research can work together. Figure 3.3 presents some possibilities of the way they might work together.

It should be clear that the deductive and inductive methods of theory construction complement one another. For example, a researcher may begin a project by presenting one or more research questions to guide a study (inductive approach) and end her or his project by presenting a theory that may, in turn, suggest one or more hypotheses for testing (deductive approach). A researcher who begins a project with a theory may find that data uncovered to test the theory do not support it. In this case, the researcher will need to modify or create a new theory to explain the data observed (inductive approach).

As mentioned, researchers using the deductive model to develop theory typically use quantitative methods in their projects, while those who take an inductive approach to theory building typically use qualitative methods. In the next sections, we will examine these two general approaches to communication research.

How Do I Conduct (or Understand) Quantitative Research?

The first main method for conducting research that we will discuss is quantitative research. This approach can be used with either deductive or inductive theory building.

Important Terms in Quantitative Research

Earlier we noted that measurement is at the heart of what social scientists do. Scientists measure concepts and constructs to determine if there are meaningful relationships among the concepts examined. The term **quantitative research** refers to a wide range of research designs in which the data take the form of numbers. In quantitative research, **measurement** is defined as the process of assigning numbers to objects, phenomena, and events (i.e., concepts) according to carefully developed rules (Williams & Monge, 2001). By precisely assigning numbers to social processes, researchers may use various statistical techniques to demonstrate the extent to which two or more concepts or constructs under investigation are related to each other.

In quantitative research, concepts must be operationalized. An operational definition explains how a concept will be measured, specifying exactly what will be counted. There are many ways to measure a concept, and different researchers may choose to measure any given concept in different ways. Because of these differences, some quantitative research may appear to provide more support for a theory than does other research testing the same ideas.

A researcher will typically use statistical techniques to analyze and interpret quantitative data. In many projects, a researcher may calculate average or mean scores to compare groups on some concept. Recall our hypothesis that predicted that men are more argumentative than women. Statistically speaking, this hypothesis predicts that, on some measure of argumentativeness, men will have a higher average score than women. To test this hypothesis, a researcher will measure the argumentativeness levels of men and women, calculate an average argumentativeness score for each group, and compare those average scores using an appropriate inferential statistical procedure (e.g., a t-test).

Researchers use inferential statistics to perform powerful tests of their hypotheses. **Inferential statistics,** such as the t-test, estimate the probability a difference in means could have occurred due to sampling error or chance. Let's briefly examine how chance could be responsible for a research finding. To do so, recall our hypothesis regarding a sex difference in argumentativeness. To a quantitative researcher, that statement about our social world is either true or false; it cannot be both true and false. That is, either men and women have different levels of argumentativeness or they do not. To test this hypothesis, a quantitative researcher, because he or she cannot measure every single male and female in our population, will use a technique to obtain random samples of men and women for study. A **random sample** is one that gives all men and women in the population an equal chance of being selected for the project. Now if our hypothesis is correct, we would expect samples of men and women drawn from this population to reveal different levels of argumentativeness; that is, on our measure of argumentativeness, men and women should report different average argumentativeness scores.

Let's assume, however, that contrary to our theory, men and women truly do not differ in their levels of argumentativeness. Furthermore, let's assume that we have drawn samples of men and women for study that displayed different levels of argumentativeness. Is this possible, that men and women in the population truly do not differ in their levels of argumentativeness but samples of men and women drawn from that population revealed a difference? Yes, this could happen; such a difference in scores for two groups could occur purely by "chance." The researcher may have simply drawn two random samples that just happened to include men and women who had extreme scores for their sex. While an unlikely event, the probability of something like this happening in any given study is not zero. This, then, is the purpose of inferential statistics. These tests, in general, estimate the probability that an event, say a difference in mean scores for two groups, could have occurred by chance. If this test reveals that a difference in means had a low probability of occurring by chance, say 5 times out of 100 or less, the researcher will conclude that, in the population from which the samples were drawn, there is a meaningful difference between groups. When a difference has a low probability of occurring by chance, less than a 5 percent chance in most cases, it is said to have **statistical significance,** or to be significant.

Given that measurement is an integral part of the research process, it is very important for the researcher to use good measurement procedures. After all, how can one conduct accurate tests of hypotheses if the measurements are bad? Remember the saying "garbage in equals garbage out." Good measurement means having reliability and validity. Let's briefly illustrate each of these concepts using the "bathroom scale."

Measurement **reliability** refers to consistency in measurement. Suppose you stepped on a bathroom scale this morning, and the scale revealed that you weighed 150 pounds. Now further suppose that you'll measure your weight tomorrow morning with that same scale. If the scale provides a number close to 150 pounds, we can say that the scale appears to be reliable. It is producing consistent scores. If it is a good scale and your weight has not changed overnight, it should produce consistent scores. So, if we were to measure your level of speech anxiety with a questionnaire, you should receive the same score, or pretty close to it, each time you take the test, assuming of course that your true level of speech anxiety does not change.

Measurement **validity,** on the other hand, refers to accuracy in measurement. Are we truly measuring what we claim to be measuring with a questionnaire, interview, or some other measurement procedure? Your bathroom scale is valid if the score it displays truly represents your weight. Likewise, a measure of student learning or speech anxiety is valid if it truly measures what it is supposed to measure. Measurement validity is achieved by demonstrating that a test is thorough and that scores on the test can predict scores on other measures that, in theory, it should be able to predict. Some feel, for example, that the SAT and ACT can predict student success at college and are, thus, valid.

Finally, we should note that reliability does not assume validity. Your bathroom scale may provide consistent scores for your weight, but those scores may be consistently incorrect; your scale may consistently underestimate or consistently overestimate your weight.

Some Methods Used in Quantitative Communication Research

Communication researchers use three common types of quantitative methods—surveys, experiments, and content analyses—to develop and test theories. At this time, let's take a brief look at each of these methods. [Web site: Examples of Research Types]

In a **survey** study, research participants are provided with a standard set of questions designed to measure one or more very specific concepts. The survey instrument (i.e., the actual questionnaire) may be administered in a face-to-face interview, via telephone, or presented along with detailed instructions and self-administered, such as a mail or electronic survey. Respondents must typically choose from among the response options provided on the questionnaire to answer the questionnaire. For example, in a survey on television viewing habits, I might ask respondents the following question: "Which station do you typically watch for local news? (Check one.) __WCIA/Champaign __WEEK/Peoria __WHOI/Peoria __WMBD/Peoria." Survey studies are conducted to describe communication events and/or to demonstrate that two or more events are related. They are expected to be **generalizable** to a broader population. That is, the data gathered should reflect the distribution of data if a census had been taken of the entire population of interest in the study.

An **experiment** is a very special and a very powerful type of quantitative research project. Whereas survey studies are conducted to describe some event or to show that two or more events or phenomena are related, experiments are designed to show that two or more events are causally related. This distinction is not a subtle one. Because experiments are designed to establish **causal relationships** between concepts, they allow for powerful tests of theories given that theories seek to explain why events occur (in other words, what causes them to occur).

In a true experiment, a researcher systematically manipulates a concept and measures the effect that manipulation had on some other concept. In the language of experimental research, the concept manipulated is called the **independent variable.** The concept measured is called the **dependent variable.** In experimental studies, a researcher seeks to control or standardize everything about the study except for the variable that is manipulated to ensure that the manipulation is responsible for any changes in the dependent variable. Experiments allow us to speak of causal relationships because the manipulation is performed before measurements are made, and those measurements are made under controlled, systematic conditions. For example, Teven and Comadena (1996) manipulate office decor of an instructor to see if it influences student perceptions of the instructor's credibility.

A third type of quantitative study is the content analysis. **Content analysis,** as the name implies, is a method for analyzing the content of communications. In the typical content analytic study, a researcher identifies a unit of analysis that is subsequently counted in a message. The unit of analysis could include words or phrases, complete thoughts or sentences, themes, paragraphs or short whole texts, characters or speakers, communication acts, and television programs or scenes (Keyton, 2001). Hence, one can perform a content analysis on virtually any message for which there is a record. For example, one may content analyze speeches, advertisements, memos, music, books, letters, television programs, and cartoons, even graffiti in restrooms. As Stacks and Hocking (1999) note, "While any kind of communication message can be content analyzed, there must be a good reason to do so; that is, the analysis must help us answer an important research question" (p. 164). Content analytic studies may be used to test hypotheses derived from a theory by demonstrating that two or more events are related. As an example, many studies in cultivation theory (Chapter 16) have analyzed television content in terms of acts of violence or gender role stereotypes.

How Do I Conduct (or Understand) Qualitative Research?

Communication researchers may also use a variety of qualitative methods to study the human communication process. To use terminology we learned in Chapter 2, researchers who use qualitative methods to study communication processes typically maintain a number of metatheoretical assumptions that differ from those of quantitative researchers. Perhaps the most obvious difference in these two general methods can be seen in what constitutes knowledge or evidence of some communication process (epistemological assumption).

Important Terms in Qualitative Research

As noted earlier in this chapter, evidence of "covariation" is seen in the statistical analysis of numerical measurements of precisely defined concepts involving large samples of people or messages. In **qualitative research,** on the other hand, data take the form of narratives, people's words or quotes, texts, or other kinds of discourse. In qualitative studies, the researcher seeks to explore the meanings people have for communication events and the extent to which those interpretations are influenced by the larger context in which events are experienced. Qualitative researchers are very sensitive to the context in which communication occurs and believe that the meanings people derive from others' messages are a function of the context in which those messages are sent and received (Lindlof, 1995). Hence, by interacting closely with them, or carefully observing them as they perform the routine activities of their lives, qualitative researchers believe they are well suited to understand how people interpret events in their lives.

Qualitative and quantitative researchers also reflect different axiological assumptions. For example, in most quantitative research, researchers value objectivity; every attempt is made to remove the researcher from the social world he or she is investigating. Quantitative researchers believe that the relationships between concepts and constructs they study are a very real part of our world that can be "witnessed" by anyone who uses their methods. Qualitative researchers, on the other hand, are not interested in removing themselves from the participant. Instead, as Keyton (2001) notes, "The researcher as the primary data collection instrument assumes a more active, fluid, and subjective role. As a result, participation and observation are integrated" (p. 271). To the staunch qualitative researcher, there is no objective reality; what is "real" about the world resides only in our minds. Therefore, while quantitative studies are often conducted in controlled laboratory settings, qualitative projects are more often conducted in field settings with the researcher often interacting in personal ways with the people he or she studies.

Finally, qualitative and quantitative researchers reflect different ontological assumptions. Quantitative researchers search for relationships between concepts that may be generalized to large groups of individuals; they believe that there are universal truths that explain human social behavior. This quest for universal truths leads quantitative researchers to develop what are termed nomothetic causes of social behavior (Schutt, 1999). On the other hand, qualitative researchers typically hold that there are no universal truths and that there are possibly many explanations for why certain events occur. The focus on the individual that many qualitative researchers bring to their investigations leads them to ideograph causes for events. An ideographic explanation is one that focuses on particular actors, at particular times, in specific social settings (Abbott, 1992; Schutt, 1999). According to Schutt (1999), idiographic explanations are "typically concerned with context, with understanding the particular outcome as part of a larger set of circumstances" (p. 151). Researchers who use qualitative methods typically do not enter a project with specific hypotheses to be tested. The research objectives for a qualitative study are not often expressed as formal research questions but as general questions to explore or as problem statements to be examined. Qualitative researchers typically seek to build theories from their data, a process we have already defined as inductive theorizing.

As in quantitative studies, qualitative researchers are also interested in conducting studies that possess measurement reliability and validity. In a qualitative study, measurement validity is achieved when a researcher's account of a communication event accurately captures participants' subjective or personal experiences (Keyton, 2001). Researchers will sometimes ask research participants to read final reports to check on the accuracy of their observations and interpretations. A researcher's interpretation of an event may differ markedly from the research participant's interpretation of that event. When it is the same, however, then measurements have validity. In addition, qualitative researchers will validate their findings through a process known as **triangulation.** Here, a research project will include different methods, or sometimes different researchers to gather data about some phenomenon to determine if similar conclusions can be reached. If different methods produce similar conclusions, the researcher has faith that her or his conclusions are valid.

Measurement reliability concerns the extent to which a researcher interprets communication behavior in a consistent fashion. As we will see, qualitative data often take the form of narratives or extended passages of discourse from one or more individuals. When evaluating these narratives, it is important that similar narratives, from either the same or different people, produce similar interpretations on the part of the researcher. In some projects, a researcher may ask a colleague or two to provide an interpretation to check on the consistency of the researcher. If multiple judges arrive at the same interpretation for a set of narratives, one has additional evidence of measurement reliability (Lincoln & Guba, 1985).

For qualitative research, the principle of generalizability to a larger population, as suggested above, is not usually possible or even desirable. Consider that quantitative data are typically closed-ended, more like answers to multiple-choice questions or, often, numbers. Qualitative data, on the other hand, are people's lengthy responses and discussions to open-ended questions; in qualitative research, respondents are encouraged to elaborate on and explain their answers. In quantitative research, if a research sample of informants or respondents accurately represents the larger population, then findings from the sample can be generalized to the entire population. In qualitative research, on the other hand, findings from a sample of respondents are generalized to the sample only. This does not make the qualitative study weaker; it simply demonstrates that the detailed, human responses and observations that are data for a qualitative study provide in-depth information from some respondents that are taken from a larger group of persons. Indeed, many qualitative researchers feel that to "generalize" beyond the immediate context is to ignore that which makes each situation unique. Thus, they seek a "holistic" view of behavior and messages in their specific context, and disdain the idea that one even could make a "general" explanation of all human behavior. Thus, one purpose for qualitative research is to provide a rich account of meaning or behavior in a specific context.

A second way to use qualitative data and findings is to support or confirm the theoretical framework that guides the qualitative study. Qualitative research is an opportunity to test theories through interviews and observations of individuals. That is, findings drawn from people's responses can be used to measure whether a theory is an accurate explanation of a communication phenomenon or event. In public relations research, for example, qualitative research is invaluable to explore the effectiveness of message design theories and theories of how people develop perceptions of a corporation.

Some Methods Used in Qualitative Communication Research

Common qualitative methods include focus group interviews, in-depth interviews, conversation and discourse analysis, observation (ethnographic) studies, and textual analysis. In a **focus group** interview, a small group of people is brought to a central location for an intensive interview with a moderator. This moderator, using a prepared set of open-ended questions, engages the group in an in-depth discussion of some particular social issue. The group format encourages "brainstorming" to occur. That is, the ideas expressed by one group member may stimulate ideas in other group members. These discussions are often tape recorded to permit the researcher to create verbatim transcripts of the group discussion. These transcripts and other observations are carefully evaluated to identify themes (Lindlof, 1995). In some cases, a researcher may perform a content analysis similar to those performed by quantitative researchers.

Individual interviews operate much the same as focus group interviews. Individual respondents are interviewed at length and given the opportunity to answer in an open-ended way, with freedom to elaborate on any question or answer. In fact, in an interview method, the study's respondents often ask questions of the researcher!

Ethnographic study or **ethnography** seeks to describe people as they interact in naturally occurring groups (Lindlof, 1995). One type of ethnographic study is called participant observation, a method that requires the researcher to become an active member of the group he or she is studying. For example, to investigate employees' reactions to a company's new safety awareness campaign, a researcher may assume the role of a worker, talking to employees from time to time about safety issues and observing the extent to which they show a concern for safety on the job. In many cases, observations are followed up with questions of participants, either in one-on-one interviews or in focus groups, with all methods becoming part of the "ethnography." In sum, ethnography as a qualitative method includes all the personal kinds of methods for gathering people's responses and opinions toward a subject: focus group interviews, individual interviews, and observation studies. In communication, this type of study has evolved into *ethnography of communication,* which focuses specifically on how people use various forms of communication, including silence and nonverbal communication (Philipsen, 1989). For example, Kristine Fitch (1994) observed the way people make requests in Colombia and in Colorado, then did focus groups and interviews to finally describe the cultural differences.

Another very popular kind of qualitative research is **textual analysis.** Rather than collecting data from human subjects, this kind of qualitative research critiques and analyzes any and all kinds of **texts.** Traditionally, the text of analysis would be a speech or written argument, making this the main form of analysis used for the rhetorical theories covered in Chapters 5 and 6. However, a recent line of qualitative research has expanded the concept of text to include any kind of communication event that can be analyzed according to a researcher, based on theoretical principles: television situation comedies, soap operas, romance novels, rock videos, magazine covers, films, and so on. That is, modern textual analysis might focus on speeches or on mediated texts (e.g., Chapter 17). To conduct a textual analysis, a researcher examines a text or a series of texts according to certain identified principles.

For example, given critical theory's interest in identifying power inequities in gender relations or in class relations in society or in the workplace, a researcher might design a study to critique advertisements found in magazines, looking for stereotypical gender portrayals of women. Or a researcher might look at television situation comedies as texts and identify possible racial or class stereotypes imbedded in them. In these kinds of textual analysis methods of research, the data are not a person's words or actions but the themes and meanings that emerge from the content of the texts. The difference between a textual analysis and a content analysis is that the content analysis uses a large number of texts and often seeks some degree of representative statement about a genre of texts (e.g., country and western music videos), whereas a textual analysis is more likely to provide an interpretation of a single text (e.g., the Dixie Chicks' video *Goodbye Earl*).

Textual analysis studies do not have to have a critical theory slant, however. Any document or text can also be examined according to other principles. For example, a rhetorical analysis of texts would bring principles of rhetoric—persuasion, symbols and meanings, historical significance, and so on—to any other kind of text or document. Legal research looks for principles of law and how they are imbedded in certain texts, and historical research entails the examination of the significance of texts as representative of certain periods of history. Once again, the data and findings for these kinds of textual analysis studies would be the rhetorical devices, legal principles, or historical significance and meanings drawn from the examined texts.

While a number of qualitative methods are available to researchers, the choice of method will depend on the nature of the research question to be addressed. In fact, it is not uncommon for qualitative researchers to combine methods in creative ways to obtain the information they need for a given project. Each tool provides a different type of information that adds to what Denzin and Lincoln (1998) term an "emergent construction," a dynamic interpretation or understanding of some social process. Hence, as Denzin and Lincoln note: "If new tools have to be invented or pieced together, then the researcher will do this. The choice of which tools to use, which research practices to employ, is not set in advance" (p. 3). These authors and others note how the face of qualitative research continues to change, being influenced by postmodernism and post-structuralism. [Web site: New Directions: Critical and Postmodern]

Summary

The gathering of observations and their interpretation are central to developing theory. In fact, what makes formal theories of communication different than the everyday (naïve or lay) theories we have in our heads is that formal theories are tested through research. For example, we all have notions in our mind of how to be successful in that job interview—but theories of how people manage their impressions (and what strategies really "work") can actually be tested through observation. As observations accumulate, we can develop explanations of communication processes that can make us better romantic partners, friends, users of media, or organizational members.

In this chapter, we have focused on the research process that sits behind the veil of communication theory. You have read about various types of methods, both qualitative and quantitative, for collecting data and seen how these might be used to develop theory either deductively or inductively. The deductive approach uses research to test predictions (hypotheses), whereas the inductive approach uses observations to derive theoretical statements. You were exposed to key terms that you would need to know to evaluate a research article, such as reliability, validity, and generalizability. We hope that with these tools, you will be more equipped to read and understand the research that serves as the foundation for the theories we build.

Discussion Questions

1. How might you operationalize the concept of TV violence if you wanted to examine its existence in a content analysis? How about self-esteem? Religiosity?

2. Why is replication important in social research?

3. What would make a measurement device, such as a test, unreliable?

4. Assume you have been contracted to develop a safety awareness campaign for a local automobile-manufacturing firm. Prior to developing the actual message campaign, you plan to implement both a survey and an ethnography at the plant to better understand existing safety practices at the plant. Which project would you conduct first? Why? What would you hope to discover? Which project would you conduct second? Why? What would you hope to discover in the latter project?

5. If a researcher is studying how verbal abuse occurs between married or dating couples, would you prefer a quantitative or qualitative approach? Would you prefer a value-neutral approach or a critical approach? Would you prefer a conventional approach or a postmodern approach? Defend each answer.

6. Researchers are ethically obligated to report accurately and completely the methods and results of research projects. Why?

References

Abbott, A. (1992). From causes to events: Notes on narrative positivism. *Sociological Methods and Research, 20,* 428–455.

Andersen, P. A. (1989). Philosophy of science. In P. Emmert & L. L. Barker (Eds.), *Measurement of communication behavior* (pp. 3–17). New York: Longman.

Denzin, N. K., & Lincoln, Y. S. (1998). Introduction: Entering the field of qualitative research. In N. K. Denzin & Y. S. Lincoln (Eds.), *Strategies of qualitative inquiry* (pp. 1–34). Thousand Oaks, CA: Sage.

Dwyer, K. K. (1998). Communication apprehension and learning style preference: Correlations and implications for teaching. *Communication Education, 47,* 137–150.

Fitch, K. L. (1994). A cross-cultural study of directive sequences and some implications for compliance-gaining research. *Communication Monographs, 61,* 185–209.

Hui, C. H., & Triandis, H. C. (1985). Measurement in cross-cultural psychology. *Journal of Cross-Cultural Psychology, 16,* 131–152.

Keyton, J. (2001). *Communication research: Asking questions, finding answers.* Mountain View, CA: Mayfield Publishing Company.

Lincoln, Y. S., & Guba, E. G. (1985). *Naturalistic inquiry.* Newbury Park, CA: Sage.

Lindlof, T. R. (1995). *Qualitative communication research methods.* Thousand Oaks, CA: Sage.

Littlejohn, S. W. (1992). *Theories of human communication* (4th ed.). Belmont, CA: Wadsworth.

McCroskey, J. C. (1982). *Introduction to rhetorical communication* (4th ed.). New Brunswick, NJ: Prentice-Hall.

Philipsen, G. (1989). An ethnographic approach to communication studies. In B. Dervin, L. Grossberg, B. J. O'Keefe, & E. Wartella (Eds.), *Rethinking communication* (pp. 258–268). Newbury Park, CA: Sage.

Schutt, R. K. (1999). *Investigating the social world: The process and practice of research* (2nd ed.). Thousand Oaks, CA: Pine Forge Press.

Stacks, D. W., & Hocking, J. E. (1999). *Communication research* (2nd ed.). New York: Longman.

Strauss, A., & Corbin, J. (1998). *Basics of qualitative research: Techniques and procedures for developing grounded theory* (2nd ed.). Thousand Oaks, CA: Sage.

Teven, J., & Comadena, M. E. (1996). The effects of office aesthetic quality on students' perceptions of teacher credibility and communicator style. *Communication Research Reports, 13,* 101–108.

Wallace, W. L. (Ed.). (1969). *Sociological theory: An introduction.* New York: Aldine de Gruyter.

Williams, F., & Monge, P. (2001). *Reasoning with statistics: How to read quantitative research* (5th ed.). Orlando, FL: Harcourt.

Part II

Communication Studies

In Part I, we introduced the key notions that will guide you as you try to understand and, later, build theory. We began by covering the notions of communication and theory, then we considered the underlying assumptions of theory and how people use research to test or apply theory. In this section, we will introduce our first main branch of practical communication contexts, those dealing with communication studies.

The term *communication studies* here refers to the academic discipline that focuses on one-on-one and/or face-to-face interaction. Its focus on face-to-face interaction includes public speaking, interpersonal communication, intercultural communication, and so on. However, new forms of mediated communication make obsolete old titles such as *speech* or *speech communication*. While *face-to-face* communication ignores mediated interpersonal communication, *one-on-one* communication ignores public speaking, small group, and other contexts.

This section begins with a history of communication studies both as a discipline and in terms of its theoretical roots (Chapter 4). Since the history of communication is wrapped up with the study of media, the authors decided to include some history of mediated communication as well, though this is covered again in a later section (Chapter 12). Chapter 4 then proceeds to introduce several of the models that have been used in communication research, including models of message reception, models of meaning making, and models of social process.

After we introduce the history, we move on to discuss specific content areas of theory. Again, we have chosen this framework because the purpose of the book is to provide theories that both will educate you toward your communication major and will provide you with useful understanding for your everyday life; thus, a content-based approach seemed more useful to us (as opposed to a theoretical roots approach in which a single theory is traced through all possible contexts at the same time). The limitation of this approach is that if a single theory has application in more than one context, you may read coverage of it more than once, though we have tried to limit coverage in later chapters to terms most appropriate to the context that they are discussing.

The first set of contexts focus on *rhetoric,* originally defined as the ways in which people persuade others (in public speech). Chapter 5 covers classical Western rhetoricians

(c. 500 B.C.E. to about 500 C.E.), including Plato, Aristotle, Cicero, and Quintilian. Here you will learn more about argument types and methods of speaking for classical Western speakers. Chapter 6 will introduce you to contemporary (twentieth-century) rhetoricians, including Fisher, Burke, Bormann, and critical rhetoricians Foucault and Habermas. You will see that while all of the rhetoricians focused on delivery and interpretation of messages, there are differences in terms of the focus of rhetorical inquiry and the underlying assumptions. For example, while many classical rhetoricians had a more objective worldview, modern rhetoricians are often more humanistic, with many taking a critical and sometimes postmodern perspective.

The second set of contexts includes four chapters on interpersonal messages. Since much of what happens in small groups, persuasion, and intercultural communication is based on the principles of one-on-one communication, we begin with a look at interpersonal communication. Chapter 7 focuses first on theories of how we receive and understand messages, then turns to how we manage our public image during interaction, finally ending with theories that explain how people develop and maintain relationships. Chapter 8 considers how a small group context of having three to fifteen individuals affects the dynamics of communication. Specifically, it summarizes how small groups grow, create an identity and culture of their own, and communicatively create and recreate their own group structure. Both chapters include theories that explain how you might have better relationships or more effective decisions in small groups.

Chapter 9 introduces an area of communication studies that has received much focus—persuasion. The chapter first considers aspects of the source and the message that might lead to persuasion. It then proceeds to theories that explain the variables that predict effective *persuasion* (changing the attitudes of others) or *compliance-gaining* (changing their behavior). Chapter 10 presents theories of intercultural communication, related specifically to effective communication and effective *intergroup* (e.g., interracial) communication.

Finally, like each of the main theory sections of this book, this section ends with a case study. In Chapter 11, the author considers an extended example—the relationships on MTV's *The Real World*—and shows how various theories from the different chapters might help us interpret or understand what is happening in the show. Remember as you read that the "beyond-the-book" icon (shown at the left) calls your attention to resources and ideas on the text web site. The underlying goal of the chapter—and the section, of course—is to help you make the same applications to the events that occur in your own public speaking, communication, relationships, or small groups, so that you will be a more effective, responsible, and ethical producer and consumer of everyday messages.

4

History of "Speech Communication" Research: Models and Messages

Kevin C. Lee and John R. Baldwin

In the first section of this book, we considered an introduction to communication theory. We first considered definitions of communication and theory (Chapter 1) and then looked at different assumptions that underlie the theorizing process, as well as considering different types of theory (Chapter 2). We will find these different strains of thought in every area of the communication discipline. In this chapter, we will see how different disciplines have influenced the communication field, with a focus on what was once called "speech communication." Now that the field considers much more than speech (e.g., nonverbal communication, mediated communication such as chatrooms and e-mail), many have opted for broader terms, such as "human communication" or simply "communication," though these terms also apply in some senses to the other sections in our book. In this chapter, specifically, we will first consider some of the historical influences on how we study communication and what we study. We will then turn our attention to look at some specific models that have been used to describe the communication process.

In this chapter you will read about the following concepts:

- A brief history of communication
  - Rhetorical theory and the NAATPS
  - Media theory: Lazarsfeld and Lasswell
  - Scientific (persuasion) theory: Lewin and Hovland
  - Cultural theory: Symbolic interactionism and the Chicago School
  - Political theory: Marx and critical theory
- Models and meaning
  - Models of rhetoric and meaning
    - Ogden and Richards's Triangle of Meaning

- Media effects models
  - Lasswell's Model of Mediated Communication
  - McLuhan and Williams
- Models of information processing
  - Newcomb's symmetry model
  - Shannon-Weaver Model of Communication
  - Schramm's Model of Communication
- Cultural and critical approaches
  - Carey's cultural approach
  - Hall's circuit of culture

One thousand miles up the Amazon River of Brazil is a place where the waters meet. This is the Wedding of the Waters. The Wedding of the Waters is interesting because two rivers meet together to form the Amazon. The Rio Negro is warm, full of plant matter, and runs slowly. The Rio Solimões runs from the Andes, is full of sand and silt, runs more quickly, and is cooler. When the Black River and the Solimões meet, they do not immediately flow together—they run side by side, brown and black, in the same riverbed. They begin to merge, patches of brown and patches of black and, only after several kilometers, become one river—the Amazon.

The communication discipline is much like this Wedding of the Waters. As our history shows, we are made up of streams flowing from the headwaters of many different disciplines, each with its own focus and way of doing research. In this chapter, we trace the historical roots of our discipline. Our purpose is first to show the main influences that have shaped our discipline. We suggest that if we understand where we came from in terms of disciplinary focus, we can understand the types of debates outlined in Chapters 1 and 2 and the wide variety of theories that follow this chapter.

Following one of the few major volumes that traces our history as a discipline, Everett Rogers's *A History of Communication Study* (1997) we feel compelled to treat communication broadly in this chapter. We will first consider the *main strands* of history—the origins of specific interest areas of communication. We will then see how the different disciplinary headwaters that feed this ongoing river of the communication discipline have produced different types of models to explain the sending and receiving of messages.

How Did the Study of "Speech Communication" Develop?

The study of communication is thousands of years old, dating, perhaps, to Aristotle and Plato in the fourth century B.C.E. (Wood, 2000). Chapter 5 explores the developments of classical rhetorical theory during this period. However, modern departments of communication are new in the academic field, starting in the early 1900s. The discipline has progressed through layers of influence from different disciplines and, thus, has been influenced by scientific, humanistic, and critical views of the world.

In the Beginning Was . . . Rhetoric

We might be able to say that our discipline began with intercollegiate debate. This debate, founded in the Boston area in the 1890s, soon gave rise to an interest in teaching students to be better public speakers. The training was delivered through English departments, which tended to "assume a proprietary right over all forms of verbal communication in which the English language was used" (Gray, 1964, p. 343).

 From the early roots of English, the National Association of Academic Teachers of Public Speaking (NAATPS) emerged, later becoming the first organization for communication professionals. The earliest focus was very applied—how to deliver more effective public speeches and debate. The focus soon shifted to include scholarly analysis of public address. The first researchers relied on Aristotle and other classical rhetoricians (see Chapter 5), but they soon adopted a wider array of lenses through which to view rhetoric (see Chapter 6). [Web site: History of Beginnings, List of Journals].

Introducing . . . Media Research

In a different corner of the disciplinary world, scholars were growing increasingly interested in mass media research. While Carrier covers this history in some detail in Chapter 13 of this volume, it is necessary to get a quick overview here for two reasons. First, the history of media research and interpersonal research are closely intertwined. Second, later content areas of communication studies, such as mediated (chatroom, e-mail) communication and contemporary rhetoric blend interpersonal and media interests.

The linkages between mass and speech communication can be seen in the work of those who chronicle their histories. For example, Bernard Berelson lamented in 1959 that communication as a field was "withering away." However, he was noting specifically mass communication research. Wilbur Schramm later outlined the founders of the modern communication discipline. Two of these, Harold Lasswell and Paul Lazarsfeld, researched media propaganda and media effects on voting (Chaffee & Rogers, 1997). For a long time, "communication research" was identified in the academic mind with media research, specifically that which focused on determining the effects of media on audiences, even though those in the "communication discipline" were still looking mostly at rhetoric. Some research looked at the use of propaganda by Hitler in Germany and then moved to improving uses of propaganda in American war films. Other research examined influences of newspaper coverage on voter attitude (Griffin, 1997).

Writers have heralded Lasswell, Lippman, and Lazarsfeld as key figures in the development of mass media research and theory. Harold Lasswell examined the communicative activity of **propaganda** and introduced the method of content analysis that is still prominent today in media research. Lasswell and Walter Lippman, another propaganda researcher of the early to mid-twentieth century, laid the groundwork for a strong tradition of agenda-setting research in the communication field (Rogers, 1997; see Chapters 12 and 15 in this book). Paul Lazarsfeld, a Jewish immigrant from Austria, translated his experience doing market analysis to look at how Josef Goebbels's propaganda machine spread Hitler's anti-Jewish propaganda across Europe. He became a leader in studies of radio effects on voters' attitudes, on sources of personal influence, and on the diffusion of medical drugs. Everett Rogers credits Lazarsfeld with creating the model for university research institutes and for beginning the tradition of media effects research (Rogers, 1997).

Jesse Delia (1987) suggests that the "core concern" of much of communication research, as it was commonly understood, was a study of the "processes by which communication messages influence audience members," firmly planting this branch of communication research in the scientific tradition. We also see that media effects research was grounded in sociology and social psychology, running parallel in its time frame to the "speech communication" focus of rhetoric. Wilbur Schramm is largely responsible for bringing a media focus into the communication discipline through his work with others in founding the Institute of Communication Research in 1948 at the University of Illinois. By 1988, this school had produced 205 Ph.D.s in communication.

A Scientific View of Human Interaction

Various writers—Berelson (1959), Schramm (1997), and, most recently, Steven Chaffee and Everett Rogers (1997)—have all included among the founders of the communication discipline two other men, Kurt Lewin, who focused on small group interaction, and Carl Hovland, an early researcher of persuasion. Lewin, a psychologist from Germany, moved to the United States in 1930 when Hitler came to power. Through the course of his work at several institutions, ending at the Center for Group Dynamics at MIT prior to his death in 1947, Lewin conducted a variety of experimental research projects looking at group leadership, gatekeeping, and networks (Rogers, 1997). Carl Hovland examined variables such as source credibility, two-sided messages, and fear appeals, specifically focusing on persuasion through war films. His research served as a "model for many subsequent communication experiments in persuasion" (Rogers, p. 375) and can be seen in the long tradition of persuasion research in the field of communication (see Chapter 9). The influence of persuasion theory grew in communication during the 1970s, and by 1980 persuasion had earned its place as a communication emphasis (Miller & Burgoon, 1978; Roloff & Miller, 1980).

Once again, we see the stream of thought flowing into the communication discipline from another field—social psychology. And, as we would expect, those who look at this type of communication have tended to use the "scientific method" to describe theories in terms of variables, of causes and effects. While the rhetorician was seeking to understand a single speech, the social psychological researcher was determining the variables that, if present in any speech, might lead to persuasion.

A View to Culture: Sociologists and the Chicago School

Some trace the roots of communication to a third tradition, to the Chicago School of the late 1800s and early 1900s. This school included sociologists and social psychologists who researched both media and culture—people such as Robert E. Park (sociology), Charles H. Cooley (social psychology), and James W. Carey and George Herbert Mead (philosophy) (Robinson, 1996; Wartella, 1996). Rogers (1997) calls Robert E. Park the "first academic student of mass communication" (p. 156). What set this school apart was its focus on "pragmatism," an attempt to find workable solutions to real social problems. While students from the school showed diversity of method, it was most noted for the development of a sociological approach to problems—an approach that tried to understand the problem in terms of the "big picture," rather than isolated variables. Some writers in the school (e.g., Mead) were especially interested with how we, as humans, create meaning and society through communication (symbolic interactionism; see Rogers, 1997).

We can see influences of these groups on several strains of communication research. Some of us, for example, research cultural phenomena, like behavior in a concert waiting line, to understand how it is socially created or lived by individuals. Others might use observation to find out how families negotiate the use of the remote control or make media choices.

The Marks of Marx on the Communication Field

Yet another influence on our discipline comes from the sociological and economic theories of Karl Marx. Marx developed a well-known theory of revolution, in which he proposed that societies evolve from feudal through capitalist to socialist and then communist systems. Essentially, he believed that the material conditions—division of labor and resources—dictated everything else that happened in society. For this reason, those who control a society also control the production. The "base" of labor relations—who owns the factories, who merely works there, and the relations between them—is supported through ideas promoted in the "superstructure." The superstructure includes the media, the church, the school, and the family.

Just as with the other theoretical traditions, Marxist thought did not immigrate immediately into the terrain of communication studies. First, in social psychology, writers from what is called the Frankfurt School wrote a 1950 book looking at how capitalism influences prejudice (*The Authoritarian Personality,* by Adorno and his colleagues). Sociological and anthropological structuralists like Pierre Bourdieu and Claude Lévi-Strauss examined how myth in different cultures mirrors the other social structures of the culture and language. Soon, Marxism influenced linguistics, as people looked at how language usage benefits the groups that are in power, and at media, as media images were seen to support dominant ways of thinking.

Marxist thought has evolved so that most researchers who use it today look at various types of oppression—racial, class, gender, and so on, rather than simply economic inequality. Notably, many writers no longer look strictly at class structures, but they are "critical" of any sort of domination by one group of another, either intentional or unintentional. This leads many to call their tradition *critical theory*.

In communication, Marxism has had its strongest influence in media studies, as many scholars abandoned the media effects model to, instead, interpret specific media texts, like the television series "Survivor," or *Rolling Stone*'s treatment of freedom of speech, to determine if these texts challenged power structures in society or passed them on to naïve viewers. Some media researchers today use Freudian psychoanalysis, feminist analysis, semiotics, and other forms of **textual criticism** to media texts. One group, using a variety of these tools, focuses specifically on media and other forms of popular culture, in a research tradition now known as **cultural studies.** However, the influence of Marxist and critical thought is not limited to media. We can also see it in contemporary rhetoricians and philosophers of language, like Foucault (Chapter 6) or Derridá, or in feminist approaches that look at structural inequalities in face-to-face communication and language use.

This approach differs from the early media effects approach in that much (but not all) of the media research in this tradition has focused on interpretation of media texts. We might say this is where "rhetoric meets media." It also differs from the focus on interpersonal communication in the way it looks at power. While interpersonal communication writers might look at power in terms of personal power or the power of an individual group member over others, Marxist-influenced approaches will look at the power someone has in a relationship based on larger societal power. Thus, a man might have certain advantages in a relationship with a woman just because his society privileges his ways of speaking or his relationship agendas over hers.

The "Discipline" of Communication Today

Several of the above influences can be seen when we look specifically at the area of "human communication" or "speech communication." The focus in most schools of communication now is much greater than public speaking; indeed, many of our scholars have little to do with the teaching or practice of public speaking or rhetoric (McCroskey & Richmond, 1996). James McCroskey and Virginia Richmond (1996) conclude, "The study of human communication today is more diversified than ever before in its history" (p. 232). This diversity is reflected in both what is studied and the way that one goes about studying it. The communication discipline, as a whole, also represents the diversity of the approaches mentioned above, each starting from the early 1900s and moving to the present, but each joining the discipline at different times. There is not so much a trajectory of the discipline, but a set of jostling, competing traditions, that sometimes lead to the debates we saw outlined in Chapter 2. [Web site: Diversity of Communication Departments Today]

There are certainly more traditions even than the rhetorical, social scientific (media and persuasion), symbolic interactionist, and Marxist ones mentioned above. Robert Craig (1999), in addition, details the influence of semiotics and linguistic studies (which have led to the postmodern influence in much communication study today); phenomenology (which looks at the interconnectedness between persons, influencing our view of communication ethics); and the cybernetic tradition (which influenced the information theorists such as Shannon and Weaver [1949] mentioned below, and systems theory, detailed in Chapter 3).

The various strains of theory do not simply pass from the scene when a new approach arises. Rather, the waters from each mix together, sometimes more smoothly than others. If you attend an academic conference, you will find each area represented, with many researchers blending elements from various philosophical backgrounds. We can summarize with the words of Gustav Friedrich and Don Boileau (1999): "Communication is best conceived as a practical discipline with the essential purpose of cultivating communication as a practical art through critical study" (p. 8). It is a field that seeks to understand any form of spoken or mediate message, with a focus on the meaning that people give as they send or receive the messages.

How Does Communication Take Place?
Meaning and Models

Many people have tried to describe how the communication process begins, often using either verbal or visual models to describe the process. Models help us to troubleshoot—to pinpoint problems in the communication process. Models also help scholars study communication by breaking down the process into identifiable component parts that can be observed, measured, and analyzed more readily. These are not the type of models you might see at fashion shows in New York or Paris. But whether you find them "super" or not, these kinds of **models** utilize written symbols in an orderly structure to demonstrate a communication process. A good communication model describes how you process the information they receive from a public relations campaign message or helps you identify what went wrong in that last fight you had with your roommate. [Web site: The Strengths and Limitations of Using Models]

Traditionally, scholars ask three series of questions about models (Deutch, 1952):

1. How *original* is the model? Does it provide new *insights* for researchers?
2. How *efficient* is the model? Does it provide a *simple,* clear picture of a process?
3. How *real* is the model? How closely does it *represent* the world in which we live?

Based on our discussion in the first half of this chapter, we suspect that people with different influences and at different times in our discipline might focus on different aspects of the communication process. And models, like theories, suffer this weakness: They must choose to focus on some aspect of the process, but by doing this, they inherently leave out some other part of the process. What unifies the discipline is our focus on symbolic messages and meaning. Thus, all the models in this section focus on the way that messages are sent and received. Just as we could outline the models as they appeared historically, it might make more sense to look at some models from each of the traditions mentioned above. You will note as you read this that some work well for mediated and some for face-to-face communication, with some working well for both.

Consider Jane and Joe, two first-year college students, sitting in the back of Dr. Johnson's 11 A.M. biology class. It's almost 11:45, and the professor is delivering a lecture on classifications of invertebrate animals. Joe is hungry and wants to invite Jane to lunch.

"Psst, Jane. Let's go to a fast food place and get a combo meal after class," Joe whispers.

Jane's eyes light up. She is hungry too. "Good idea," she replies. "We can take my car."

The two students completed a communication event. We could ask, "How successful were the various messages in this scenario?" or "What would communication scholars say about what happened in the biology class that day?" You may recall that theorists early on moved from their initial focus only on the methods of teaching public speaking and debate to a closer examination of the details of public and private human communication.

Jane and Joe's interpersonal exchange, though simple, can help demonstrate **information processing** theories that attempt to explain what takes place when people communicate. But, as we shall see, models that arise at different points in our discipline's history and from different frameworks will focus on different parts of the process.

Theories of Meaning: From the Roots of Rhetoric

It isn't always easy to explain to someone else what you are thinking about in your head. Humans attempt to create *messages* using various kinds of **codes,** which are systems of meaning understandable to both sender and receiver. Verbal communication takes place using languages—codes that communicators share made up of sounds that represent letters and words. Traveling around the world, you can hear people using a variety of language codes, such as English, Arabic, and Mandarin Chinese.

Nonverbal communication also utilizes code. If a friend performs well on the ball field, without saying a word you can give her the "thumbs up" gesture from the stands, indicating approval. Through nonverbal means, you have communicated a "way to go!" message. Codes, though, often differ significantly from one culture to another. In some areas of the Middle East, for example, a "thumbs up" gesture communicates a much different message—one that is obscene. And in Japan, a variation of America's "okay" hand symbol is nonverbal shorthand for "money."

Ogden and Richards's Triangle of Meaning.   One model of communication that seeks to show the nature of how symbols work is Charles Ogden and Ivor Armstrong Richard's (1946) **triangle of meaning.** These authors suggested that a core problem of language use is meaning, and that this, rather than persuasion, should be the focus of communication and rhetorical study. Humans use **symbols,** such as "words, images, gestures . . . drawings, or mimetic sounds" to represent some notion or idea (Ogden & Richards, 1946, p. 23). But since people have unique experiences with the same word, the exact meaning two individuals have for a symbol will differ. Ogden and Richards conclude: "Meaning is in people, not in words" (p. 23). The triangle of meaning (Figure 4.1) suggests that there is a direct link between a symbol and a thought (**reference**); our thought "causes" us to use a certain symbol, or the symbol "causes" us to think of a certain thought. There is also a hard connection between the thought and the **referent,** or the reality with which the thought is associated. But the connection between reality and the symbols we use to represent it is indirect: There is nothing really dog-like in the symbol *dog.* We could just as well call it a *hund* (German), *chien* (French), *perro* (Spanish), or *cachorro* (Portuguese). However, the problem is much more serious when we are dealing with meanings such as *friend, democracy,* or *progress,* or with statements such as "I love you."

This model would make perfect sense of a possible misunderstanding between Jane and Joe. The "combo meal" Jane pictured in her mind did not match Joe's. She began dreaming of a rack of ribs, fries, and a chocolate shake at the famous Juicy Pig restaurant. Joe was pondering a Whopper, fries, and a Diet Coke from Burger King. What happened to their meeting of the minds?

Adding Channel to the Process: Models from Media Research

While rhetoricians have tended to develop models that look at the loss or mismatch of meaning in face-to-face interaction, media scholars from early on have added a new component to the consideration—the channel. That is, the message travels through some

FIGURE 4.1 *Ogden and Richards' Triangle of Meaning.* The same symbol may mean different things to different people.

Illustration by Dylan Simonds.

medium, which may have an added impact to the interaction. Since communication studies writers borrowed terms and ideas from these models, it is useful for us to consider some key media models, after explaining the notion of channels.

Channels and Media.   Sending messages across any distance involves utilization of some carrier, which communication researchers call a **channel.** A channel is something existing *between* communicators that facilitates the transfer of information among them. When Joe spoke to Jane, he used the *air* as a channel. It carried the vibrations of his vocal chords and voice as sound waves. His words were carried by the air channel all the way to Jane's ears. When Jane responded, she used the air channel for her verbal message too. But she also used light for her nonverbal message: nodding her head and raising her eyebrows approvingly. Imagine if the lights had gone out in Dr. Johnson's windowless classroom just moments before she replied. In the pitch black room, Joe would not have seen Jane's nonverbal message because the channel carrying light had been turned off. He only would have heard her voice.

Similarly, when humans choose to communicate by telephone, they isolate their communication to a single channel for voice and other audio signals. In this instance, however, a *mechanical* means of message sending is being used. Such a technology is called a **medium.** When considering more than one medium, we speak not of "mediums" but of **media,** the plural form of *medium.* For example, when people complain about the biased coverage of the *news media,* they mean journalists communicating news stories via newspaper, radio, television, and Internet.

Radio, like telephone, is another medium that carries audible signals for the ear. Radio, though, is a medium of *mass communication* because the senders have the potential of reaching a large (mass) though often diverse audience. The television viewers of the annual Super Bowl include millions of people across the globe. In addition to radio and television, *mass media* include newspapers, magazines, books, film, and the Internet. Video media—including television, film, DVD, and Internet streaming video—utilize two channels: one for audio signals and the other for video, and many Internet web pages add to these the channel of text. Like radio, many visual media do not allow senders direct, immediate access to the human sender. New technologies, however, are moving video in the direction of greater interactivity for preselecting programs, instantaneous feedback (e.g., "chatrooms"), and e-mail.

Currently, the concept of *mass communication* is being reexamined. A number of former mass communication departments and professional organizations have moved to using the term **media communication.** There is talk aplenty of *narrowcasting* for specialized audiences, to reach so-called *niche* groups. The viewers for the Discovery Channel at 3 A.M. and the Cartoon Network at noon and CNN at 8 P.M. are three very different demographic groups, attracting different advertisers, each demanding unique programming.

Researchers are just beginning to assess how the communication innovations mentioned above impact human interaction. Joshua Meyrowitz (1997) explains how **medium theory** can be utilized to compare the particular characteristics of individual media (e.g., e-mail vs. letters) and general types of media (e.g., electronic vs. print). Medium analyses can focus on one instance of differences (micro-level) or differences culturally (macro-level). How, for example, would the lunch invitation from Joe to Jane be different if it was delivered by e-mail or telephone instead of in person? Even if they used the same words, the medium used would shape their interaction, changing the experience for both of them.

Broadly speaking, medium theorists ask: How do the particular characteristics of a medium make it physically, psychologically, and socially different from other media and from face-to-face interaction, regardless of the particular messages that are communicated through it (Meyrowitz, 1997)? Historically, such information-processing models trace their roots to the work of scientists in the 1800s who were attempting to describe the flow of energy among physical objects. These studies were incorporated into a branch of science called *mechanics,* thus such models often are labeled **mechanistic** (Trenholm, 1986).

Lasswell's Model of Mediated Communication.   In 1948, one of the earliest, simplest, and most enduring communication models to include a channel was introduced by Harold Lasswell. He said that when people communicate, scholars can critique the event by asking the following question:

> Who
> says What
> in Which Channel
> to Whom
> with What Effect?

In the case we are analyzing, Joe is the initial *who.* His lunch invitation to Jane was the *what.* The *channel* over which he spoke was air—his vocal chords reverberated to produce sound waves that traveled to Jane's, the *whom's* ears. The *effect* was to elicit a positive response from Jane. Notably, the model works just as well in looking at effects of media communication—in fact, it was in that context that Lasswell developed the model. In this case, the *who* might be the speaker presenting the *lecture;* the *what* would be the classification of invertebrates; the *channel* would be the video; the *whom* would be any audience of that video; the *effect* in this case is lack of attention. It may be that Joe is bored with the class, that the class is running long, or that, like the invertebrates in the lecture, he just doesn't have the backbone to wait until lunch. Gerbner (1956) later modified Lasswell's model by adding the notions of *situation* and *context.*

Marshall McLuhan and Raymond Williams.   Imagine that the president of the United States delivered an important message to the citizens of the nation. Depending on the era in which they lived, the American people's communication experience with their president would be quite different. In Abraham Lincoln's day, people in Washington, D.C., could have witnessed the address in person while others had to read about it later in a newspaper. Franklin D. Roosevelt reached his audiences via radio. John F. Kennedy was the first to deliver regular live news conferences over television. Bill Clinton entertained questions from citizens over the Internet.

Although audiences in each of these eras received messages from presidents, the *means* by which they sent the messages were so different that they helped shape the very cultures in which the communicators lived. Marshall McLuhan (1964) argued that the man-made means used to communicate were in many ways extensions of humanity. These mechanical means for communication play such an extraordinarily powerful role in society, McLuhan argued, that one could say *"the medium is the message."* In other words, precisely because of the prevailing tool of communication, the *print* society of Lincoln's America was vastly different from the *radio* society of Roosevelt's time, and both differed from the *television* society of Kennedy's era. The *Internet* society of today could be contrasted to them all.

Building on the work of Harold Innis (1951) and Lewis Mumford (1963), McLuhan pointed to a world where the predominant means of communication profoundly impacted people groups. The Canadian theorist expanded his contemplations to include the worldwide phenomenon of instantaneous electronic messages that overcome the constraints of time and distance. McLuhan believed lightning-fast media communication drew the world together into one big **"global village"** (McLuhan & Powers, 1989). Another researcher who also theorizes about the importance of technology as determining communication processing is Raymond Williams (1961, 1973, 1974); this British researcher looks at the role of technology, particularly television, and its use and role as a leisure practice within the family setting and within family communication. An American scholar, a student of Williams and close friend of McLuhan, did a landmark study on the telegraph and its role in determining communication in the settling of our country; Carey (1975) argues that the invention of the telegraph, in essence, collapsed time and space and revolutionized how information was sent and processed across broad geographic regions.

Expounding on the work of McLuhan and others, Neil Postman (1986) argued that the fundamental transition from a print-based society to a video-based one generally has had a detrimental impact on American culture (a position that is quite controversial!):

> We have reached, I believe, a critical mass in that our electronic media have decisively and irreversibly changed the character of our symbolic environment. We are now a culture whose information, ideas and epistemology are given form by television, not by the printed word. (p. 28)

Building on the foundations of semantics, epistemology, and history, Postman was instrumental in developing a school of study known as **media ecology.** The characteristics of media ecology include an exploration of the relationship between technology and humanity, the analysis of language as medium and technology, and the need for media education and conservatism (Gencarelli, 2000). Postman argues that the predominant media utilized by a society are so influential that they exert great influence on the direction of a culture, for better or for worse.

Building upon the Scientific Model: Information Processing

As communication as a discipline grew more scientific, with a large impetus from social psychological research, scientific theories began to develop that reflected not just the meaning of words, but the internal processes of making meaning of symbols. These differ from the early rhetorical models in that the rhetorical models sought merely to provide a framework to explain particular misunderstandings. The scientific theories sought to uncover the psychological processes we use when we process information, sometimes with the goal of predicting the level of understanding in a situation. Two models—one of *balance* and one of *information processing*—will illustrate the psychological and scientific approach of the models of this area of our discipline.

Newcomb's Symmetry Model.   Newcomb (1953) created a model that looked a little different than the common ones of his era. His **symmetry model** was triangular in shape, with A representing one communicator, B representing another communicator, and X representing an object or concept to which both A and B relate (see Figure 4.2). In this model, A and B send information to each other. A and B also have some experience with X, with X being something or someone known to both of them. Newcomb believed, therefore, that four different *orientations* or attitudes could be considered in any given communication setting:

1. A's orientation toward X
2. A's orientation toward B
3. B's orientation toward A
4. B's orientation toward X

These orientations can be seen in positive or negative attraction between the persons, A and B, and in favorable or unfavorable attitudes toward X. So if person A (Joe) has positive attraction to B (Jane), and she also admires him, then they will tend to move toward balance or **symmetry** with regard to X (lunch). Newcomb argued that the stronger the orientation of A and B to each other, the greater the strain to move toward agreement on X through acts of communication. In this case, if Joe holds a highly favorable attitude toward Jane, he may quickly be willing to abandon his ideal lunch vision of a quick combo from Burger King and compromise by embracing her desire for a rack of ribs at the Juicy Pig.

Shannon and Weaver's Information Theory.   In 1949 MIT scientist Claude Shannon—working at Bell Telephone Laboratories—developed a classic model for transmitting information. Warren Weaver, a top mathematician-scientist at the Rockefeller Foundation in

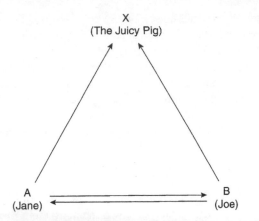

X
(The Juicy Pig)

A
(Jane)

B
(Joe)

FIGURE 4.2 *Newcomb's Symmetry Model.*
From T. M. Newcomb (1953), An approach to the study of communicative acts. *Psychological Review 60*, 393–404. Used with permission.

New York realized that this model could be applied in many fields beyond the engineering project on which Shannon was laboring (Shannon & Weaver, 1949). Indeed, the **Shannon and Weaver Model** (see Figure 4.3) has been used for decades to analyze an array of human exchanges from interpersonal to mass communication.

Applying their model to our example, Joe is the original **information source** as he thought about asking Jane to lunch. Joe's mouth acted as **transmitter** to send words: "Let's go to a fast food place." These spoken symbols constituted an auditory **signal** sent to Jane. Her ears served as **receiver** to take in the sounds. As the **destination,** Jane created a mental image of the lunch message from her friend. Joe's voice, however, was not the only sound in the room. The biology lecture and the droning of the air conditioner

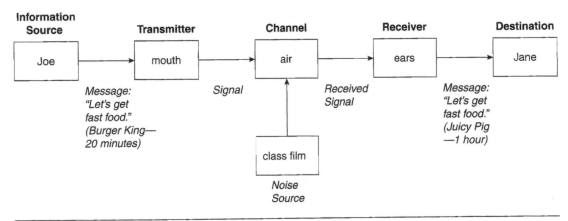

FIGURE 4.3 *Shannon and Weaver's Model of Communication.*   Life in the fast (food) lane: Joe and Jane's communication in Shannon and Weaver's model of communication.

From *The Mathematical Theory of Communication.* © 1949, 1998, by Board of Trustees of the University of Illinois Press. Used with permission of the University of Illinois Press.

added unwanted auditory clutter to the message, distorting it. Even the thoughts of hunger, not to mention Joe's good looks, were clouding accurate interpretation of the message. Shannon and Weaver called these unwanted signals **noise.**

What this model, originally applying to transmission of voices over radio waves, imported into communication was a stress on the encoding and decoding of messages. In our example, the sender, Joe, was **encoding**—turning mental images into words. Joe had a vivid picture in his mind of a Whopper with onion rings and a chocolate shake (rather than the details of Dr. Johnson's lecture). His challenge was to transfer that lunch dream to Jane. He translated the message from his mind into language through the process of encoding. In this case the code was language (American English), which the hearer could understand: "Let's go to a fast food place and get a combo meal after class."

Jane received the sound waves aurally and created neural signals to send to her brain. Through the process of **decoding,** she then created her own mental picture of a "combo meal." The idea was appealing to her, too, and she agreed to a lunch outing with Joe. So the two students completed a successful communication event, wouldn't you say?

Since Shannon and Weaver's model initially was constructed to explain engineering systems, it presented some challenges when applied to human communication. Moving to a more human-centered approach, Charles Osgood's (1954) model posited that each individual person functions as *both speaker and hearer.* This can even happen simultaneously. For example, at the same moment that Joe was animatedly talking about "getting a combo meal," Jane was nodding her head up and down and raising her eyebrows in excited agreement. Jane and Joe both were sending messages and receiving messages in the same moment. Osgood also incorporated such *nonverbal* messaging as Jane's head and eyebrow movement into his model:

> When individual A talks to individual B, for example, his postures, gestures and facial expressions and even manipulations with objects (e.g., laying down a playing card, pushing a bowl of food within reach) may all be part of the message. (pp. 2–3)

Schramm's Model.   Building on Osgood's work, Wilbur Schramm (1954) noted that the persons communicating have a *relational history,* that is, they have talked to each other often in the past and now know a good deal more about how the other person thinks and communicates than when they first met. Schramm created a model that takes into account Jane and Joe's common ground: the overlap of their **fields of experience.** They both have experienced many of Dr. Johnson's classes, for example, and can joke about it together knowingly. More fundamentally, even before they met, both had fields of experience that included firsthand knowledge of the English language, the United States, and the college that they attend.

Schramm (1954) included another important component in his models: **feedback** (see Figure 4.4). When receivers respond verbally and/or nonverbally to a sender's message, they are providing feedback. Speakers often *seek* feedback and will ask listeners if they understand or agree with their statements. Senders ask questions such as "Do you know what I mean?" and "What do you think about *that*?" Or the speaker will pause and wait for a response. These strategies underscore the importance of feedback for clarity in communication.

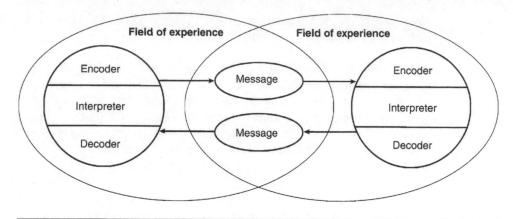

FIGURE 4.4   *Schramm Model (Adapted).*

From *The Process and Effects of Mass Communication.* © 1954 by Board of Trustees of the University of Illinois. Used with permission of the University of Illinois Press.

The Cultural and Critical Approaches

Notably, the scientific approaches of both speech and mediated communication produced more models than the cultural approaches. This is perhaps because cultural approaches, as well as the critical approaches that were often based on them, were more focused on creating sets of terms and categories that explained single cultures, organizations, relationships, or texts. They were less interested in producing a model to describe all communication, especially one limited only to information processing. Still, one cultural and one critical model will serve as examples of how these approaches have looked at communication.

Carey's Cultural Approach.   Conventions of communication are deeply interwoven with the fabric of human society, James Carey believed. He described a **cultural approach** to communication theory that is sensitized to the spiritual and collective values of communities. From a careful observation of human culture, Carey posited a **ritual** definition of communication study:

> A ritual view of communication is not directed toward the extension of messages in space but the maintenance of society in time; not the act of imparting information but the representation of shared beliefs. (Carey, 1975, p. 6)

Based on this view, Carey would not likely be interested at all in how Jane understood Joe's meaning or even whether either of them understood the biology lecture. He would be more interested in how they (along with others in society) have co-created a set of meanings that allows them to speak in the back of the classroom while something else is going on, or how they have developed a set of ideas about what constitutes a good lunch (would it be different in France?) and what constitutes fast food (how fast is "fast"?). Critical scholars often take the same approach to cultural meanings—that they are socially constructed—but also consider social power. For example, are there cultural norms that allow Joe to ask Jane to lunch, but not the other way around?

Hall's Circuit of Culture.   One critical model blends, once again, elements of mediated and interpersonal communication. Paul du Gay, Stuart Hall and colleagues (1997) describe a cyclical process by which cultural artifacts are adopted into personal use through media. Essentially, the **circuit of culture** (Figure 4.5) presents the processes through which a media text or a cultural artifact passes from its initial stages of creation to the time it is reinvented by the producer for further consumption. This model takes our lunch example in a new direction. In the first stage, **representation,** the producer or media maker frames the image of a person, idea, or product with a set of other images and ideas to create a notion for those that "read" the text—for example, the sense of "identity" in Tommy Hilfiger ads.

Spoken communication comes to play in the next stages, thus blending communication studies and mass communication in the same model. In the **identity** stage, people associate themselves with the media image—they link youth and other identities with the purchase of the cologne and the clothes, buying into the messages given about the product. The **production** stage involves how the artifact is manufactured; thus, we would consider the relations of production among the workers and managers, looking at whether wages were fair and whether there was differentiation of labor, say, based on sex. The **consumption** stage involves the actual purchase of the artifact (a behavior), as well as the nonverbal and verbal behaviors that go along with the artifact (e.g., wearing Hilfiger clothes, fighting over the remote control, interacting with others at Gold's Gym). Finally, the **regulation** stage is where governments or organizations step in to institute rules that regulate the representation, production, and consumption of the product, much as many cities outlaw skateboards in many locations.

At first it seems difficult to apply the circuit of culture to our fast food example, but it really fits quite nicely. Different fast food restaurants, such as Burger King, create in their

FIGURE 4.5 *Hall's Circuit of Culture.* Fast food and identity: Fast food is represented, becomes part of an identity, is produced, consumed, and regulated—all in contexts of power relationships.

From P. du Gay, S. Hall, L. Janes, H. MacKay, & K. Negus (1997). *Doing cultural studies: The story of the Sony Walkman.* London: Sage. Used with permission, Sage Publishing.

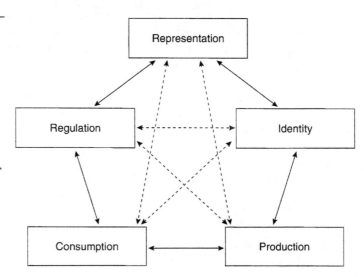

advertisements an image of the clientele as mature (Big Kids' meals), independent ("Have it your way"), and so on. If Joe and others accept this view and want to associate with it (identity), this will create a need. Burger King will need to produce more burgers and more restaurants (and what are the relations and means of production in those restaurants?), and the populace will swarm to find the beef. But we clearly see the Federal Communications Commission regulating the advertisements, the Food and Drug Administration governing the production of the burgers, and so on.

Summary

We realize that different areas of speech communication, such as nonverbal communication or communication education, will have their own histories. But our purpose in this chapter was to trace the main roots of the discipline as a whole and to see where speech communication fits specifically within the larger tradition. Each of several strains of research that have influenced communication studies developed at roughly the same time—in the late 1800s and early 1900s. These included (1) rhetorical theory, which looked at how to deliver and interpret public speeches; (2) media "effects" studies, which originally looked at whether media had a direct influence on users and later grew to include other areas of cause-effect research with media as a variable; (3) social-scientific theory, especially stemming from psychological studies on persuasion; (4) cultural theory, which focused on the interpretation of cultures and was later applied to organizations; and (5) Marxist theory, which grew to challenge any type of oppression and group-based inequality in society.

The media effects and Marxist criticism areas are the strongest in mass media, where rhetoric and the social-psychological study traditions more characterize communication studies. Both areas are influenced by cultural theory. In recent years, however, there is much crossover, with media researchers using rhetoric; speech communication scholars, such as feminists, using variations of Marxist theory; and so on. The various strains of history lead to different views of what constitutes "good" research and what "theory" even looks like! Departments sometimes divide between media and speech communication, but often divide even over which tradition exerts the most influence over the department, based on its founding, its unique history, and so on.

Because of the varying focus on mediated versus face-to-face communication, as well as the scientific, humanistic, and critical influences on the discipline, various writers see the communication process differently. Thus we framed models of communication in this chapter as growing out of the history that defines us. We looked briefly at a number of models based on meaning and semantics, on media effects, on information processing, and, finally, on cultural and critical approaches to communication.

It is difficult to know where the communication discipline will go in the future. We hope that the field will grow in collaboration, as people from different areas (media, PR, face-to-face communication, and other focus areas), as well as those with different underlying sets of assumptions (scientific, humanistic, critical) continue to work together—that our blending and mixing of interests and influences, like the "wedding of the waters" that creates the Amazon, will in the end be a happy and productive one.

Discussion Questions

1. Look over the communication courses in your university's catalog. List courses that you think might relate to the five historical traditions mentioned in this chapter.

2. Consider a misunderstanding that you have had recently. Analyze the misunderstanding using the triangle of meaning and the Shannon and Weaver model. Which works better, and why? Might a different model be more useful in a different type of understanding?

3. What impact do you think that new forms of electronic media will have on interpersonal communication? How are interpersonal and mediated communication alike or different?

4. Reading the models in view of the three paradigms described in Chapter 2, which would you say might appeal more to a scientist? a humanist? a critical researcher? Defend your answer.

References

Berelsen, B. (1959). The state of communication research. *Public Opinion Quarterly, 23,* 1–6.

Carey, J. (1975). A cultural approach to communication. *Communication, 2,* 6.

Chaffee, S. H., & Rogers, E. M. (1997). Wilbur Schramm: The founder. In S. H. Chaffee & E. M. Rogers (Eds.), *The beginnings of communication study in America: A personal memoir* (pp. 125–148). Thousand Oaks, CA: Sage.

Craig, R. T. (1999). Communication theory as a field. *Communication Theory, 9,* 119–161.

Delia, J. G. (1987). Communication research: A history. In C. Berger & S. Chaffee (Eds.), *Handbook of communication science* (pp. 20–98). Newbury Park, CA: Sage.

Deutsch, K. (1952). On communication models in the social sciences. *Public Opinion Quarterly, 16,* 356–380.

du Gay, P., Hall, S., Janes, L., Mackay, H., & Negus, K. (1997). *Doing cultural studies: The story of the Sony Walkman.* London: Sage.

Friedrich, G. W., & Boileau, D. M. (1999). The communication discipline. In *Teaching communication: Theory, research, and methods* (pp. 3–13). Mahwah, NJ: Lawrence Erlbaum.

Gencarelli, T. F. (2000). The intellectual roots of media ecology in the work and thought of Neil Postman. *New Jersey Journal of Communication (8)1,* 91–103.

Gerbner, G. (1956). Toward a general model of communication. *AV Communication Review, 4,* 171–199.

Griffin, E. (1997). *A first look at communication theory* (3rd ed.). New York: McGraw-Hill.

Innis, H. A. (1951). *The bias of communication.* Toronto: University of Toronto Press.

Lasswell, H. D. (1948). The structure and function of communication in society. In L. Bryson (Ed.), *The communication of ideas.* New York: Harper & Row.

McCroskey, J. C., & Richmond. V. P. (1996). Human communication theory and research: Traditions and models. In M. B. Salwen & D. W. Stacks (Eds.), *An integrated approach to communication theory and research* (pp. 233–242). Mahwah, NJ: Lawrence Erlbaum.

McLuhan, M. (1964). *Understanding media: The extensions of man.* New York: McGraw-Hill.

McLuhan, M., & Powers, B. (1989). *The global village: Transformations in world life and media in the 21st century.* New York: Oxford University Press.

Meyrowitz, J. (1997). Shifting worlds of strangers: Medium theory and changes in "them" versus "us." *Sociological Inquiry, 67*(1), 61.

Miller, G. R., & Burgoon, M. (1978). Persuasion research: Review and commentary. In B. D. Ruben (Ed.), *Communication Yearbook 2* (pp. 29–48). New Brunswick, NJ: Transaction Books.

Miller, K. (2002). *Communication theories: Perspectives, processes and contexts.* Boston: McGraw-Hill.

Mumford, L. (1963). *Technics and civilization.* New York: Harcourt, Brace, and World.

Newcomb, T. M. (1953). An approach the study of communicative acts. *Psychological Review, 60,* 393–404.

Ogden, C. K., & Richards, I. A. (1946). *The meaning of meaning.* New York: Harcourt, Brace, and World.

Osgood, C. E. (Ed.). (1954). Psycholinguistics: A survey of theory and research problems. *Journal of Abnormal and Social Psychology, 49* (Oct), suppl., 2–3.

Postman, N. (1986). *Amusing ourselves to death: Public discourse in the age of show business.* New York: Penguin.

Richards, I. A. (1936). *The philosophy of rhetoric.* Oxford: Oxford University Press.

Robinson, G. J. (1996). Constructing a historiography for North American communication studies. In E. E. Dennis & E. Wartella (Eds.), *American communication research: The remembered history* (pp. 157–168). Mahwah, NJ: Lawrence Erlbaum.

Rogers, E. M. (1997). *A history of communication study: A biographical approach (with a new introduction)* (pp. 203–243). New York: Free Press.

Rogers, E. M. (2001). The department of communication at Michigan State University as a seed institution for communication study. *Communication Studies, 32,* 234–248.

Roloff, M. E., & Miller, G. R. (Eds.). (1980). *Persuasion: New directions in theory and research.* Beverly Hills: Sage.

Schramm, W. (1954). How communication works. In W. Schramm (Ed.), *The process and effects of mass communication.* Urbana: University of Illinois.

Schramm, W. (1997). *The beginnings of communication study in America: A personal memoir.* Thousand Oak, CA: Sage.

Shannon, C., & Weaver, W. (1949). *The mathematical theory of communication.* Urbana: University of Illinois Press.

Trenholm, S. (1986). *Human communication theory.* Englewood Cliffs, NJ: Prentice-Hall.

Wartella, E. (1996). The history reconsidered. In E. E. Dennis & E. Wartella (Eds.), *American communication research: The remembered history* (pp. 169–180). Mahwah, NJ: Lawrence Erlbaum.

Weaver, A. T. (1959). Seventeen who made history: The founders of the association. *Quarterly Journal of Speech, 45,* 195–199.

Williams, R. (1961). *The long revolution.* New York: Columbia University Press.

Williams, R. (1973). Base and superstructure in Marxist cultural theory. *New Left Review, 82,* 3–16.

Williams, R. (1974). *Television: Technology and cultural form.* London: Fontana/Collins.

Wood, J. T. (2000). *Communication theories in action* (2nd ed.). Belmont, CA: Wadsworth.

5

Classical (Western) Rhetorical Theory

Craig W. Cutbirth

Having been introduced to the history of research and of theory in personal communication in the previous chapter, you are now ready to proceed with a close examination of each of the contexts that are illustrations of human communication. This chapter provides a look at the earliest kind of formal communication study—classical rhetorical theory. Understanding classical rhetoric is an important starting point for understanding all the various genres of communication that have developed throughout the history of our field. Knowledge of the basic tenets of classical rhetoric will also help you appreciate the essential legacy that classical rhetoric provides for today's study of communication.

Rhetoric is an ancient concept, a traditional label that represents the first systematic study of human communication in the Western world. This chapter will acquaint you with the broad outlines of this initial inquiry into communication. To accomplish this, we must understand what rhetoric meant to those who began studying it thousands of years ago. We will begin by exploring the "classical" time period, then we'll acknowledge the leading figures of this time period, and finally we'll consider the most important principles of rhetoric that emerged from the classical period. In the next chapter, we'll consider more recent approaches to rhetoric.

In this chapter, you will read about the following concepts:

- Where and when classical rhetoric existed
- The prominent classical speakers
  - Sophists
  - Plato
  - Aristotle
  - Cicero
  - Quintilian
- The key assumptions of classical rhetorical theory

- The content of the classical message
  - Argument
  - Proof as logos, ethos, and pathos
- Classical canons of rhetoric
  - Invention
  - Arrangement
  - Style
  - Delivery
  - Memory

For it makes much difference in regard to persuasion . . . that the speaker seem to be a certain kind of person and that his hearers suppose him to be disposed toward them in a certain way.

—Aristotle, Book II, *The Rhetoric* (Kennedy, 1991)

During his two terms as mayor, the crime rate plunged, businesses thrived and tourists felt safer than ever. . . . Giuliani earned acclaim as a tough-talking, no-nonsense leader who tamed the seemingly untamable city.

—New York, December 19, 2001, Reuters Wire Service

If it doesn't fit, you must acquit.

—Defense Attorney Johnnie Cochran, O. J. Simpson murder trial, September 1995

These quotes exemplify several important principles of rhetoric. First, the credibility and respect of the speaker can be inherently persuasive to others around him or her. Aristotle's words and the news excerpt about Giuliani's guidance during the 2001 terrorist attacks in New York all suggest how successful persuasive communication, or rhetoric, can be achieved when speakers or leaders have the respect and high regard of the people around them. Credibility is a central concern of classical rhetorical theory.

The quote from Johnnie Cochran, presented during his closing argument in the O. J. Simpson murder trial, requires some additional discussion. Note first that Cochran does not tell us what "it" is. Reading the quote we know that it does not fit, but to what is the speaker referring? The answer is complex. Those familiar with this trial will quickly recognize the quote as referring to a specific incident during the trial where the prosecution attempted to link Simpson to the crime by having him try on a pair of gloves. Police had discovered a left-handed glove at the scene of the murder and what appeared to be a matching right-handed glove at Simpson's home. The prosecution wanted to show the jury that the gloves belonged to Simpson, thus linking him to the murder. However, when the gloves were tried on, they were found to be too small to fit Simpson's hands. In other words, they did not fit.

Defense attorney Cochran (Figure 5.1) repeated this phrase several times in his closing statement, so that it became a theme of his argument. He used this phrase to refer to the prosecution's overall case, not just to the gloves. In other words, he was telling the jury

FIGURE 5.1   Johnnie Cochran, through multiple trials and press releases, has proven himself a powerful rhetorician.

Photo courtesy of Agence France Press Pool.

to weigh the evidence marshaled against his client and that it didn't fit, it did not add up to a conviction. Classical rhetorical theory equips people to examine and weigh the evidence presented in favor of or against proposed ideas and courses of action and to decide whether the evidence "fits."

These excerpts illustrate rhetoric in action and demonstrate that principles of rhetoric have explanatory power from ancient classical times even to today. By understanding notions of classical rhetoric, you should be better able both to understand others' attempts to persuade you and to create stronger persuasive messages yourself. While this chapter will focus, as did classical rhetoric, on public address, you may also find application of these concepts to written messages and the everyday persuasion that occurs between you and others. The balance of this chapter covers many fundamental rhetorical principles and guidelines to help you understand the contribution of the rhetorical theory of the ancient Greeks and Romans to communication study today.

Rhetoric is a common term. You can likely recall some of the contexts in which you've encountered it. "Mere" rhetoric, "empty" rhetoric, or "let's cut through the rhetoric and get to the facts here" are familiar contemporary uses of this term. These are, however, neither the most useful nor accepted interpretations of rhetoric. Generally speaking, **rhetoric** as it is used today refers to *persuasive communication.* The unflattering references noted here reflect some people's dissatisfaction with the quality of some contemporary persuasive discourse but should not be accepted as the inherent qualities of rhetoric, or persuasion. In order to understand and discern the essential, actual qualities of rhetoric from allegations of false rhetoric, a first look at the rhetoric of the classical age is informative.

Where and When Did Classical Rhetoric Exist?

The **classical period** of rhetorical study began some 500 years before the Common Era and ended some 500 years into the Common Era, therefore encompassing some 1,000 years of time. The beginning of the classical era is linked to the high point of Greek civilization and culture, the so-called golden age of Athens. The end of the classical period is associated with the final fall of the Roman Empire and the onset of the Dark Ages, about 500 C.E. In the middle of this time period, of course, occurred the decline of the Athenian empire, the rise and fall of the Roman Republic, and its subsequent replacement by the Roman Empire. These were momentous events in the ancient world, and they left a clear mark on the development of classical rhetorical theory. [Web site: The Social Contexts of the Classical Period of Rhetoric]

It is impossible to understand classical rhetorical theory without grasping at least the rudiments of the ancient societies that produced it: Classical Greece, the Roman Republic, and Imperial Rome. First, because of the unique decision- and lawmaking structure of the democratic Greek city-states, it was the expectation that citizens would be able both to speak well and to critically evaluate and respond to the speeches of others. The Roman era gave rise to the use of **pleaders** or **patrons**—citizens who addressed the court on behalf of others—and increased government restrictions on public address. We focus here on Western rhetoric since it provides a stronger influence on contemporary mainstream American culture than rhetorical strains from other cultures, and it is the prominent source of the introduction of communication study in this country.

Who Were the Classical Theorists?

Given that classical rhetorical theory spans three distinct cultures, it is no surprise that the prominent contributors to the evolution of thinking about rhetorical communication are quite varied. We will not discuss them in depth here or attempt to identify all who contributed to classical rhetorical theory. It is sufficient for our purposes to gain a simple acquaintance with the most conspicuous individuals of the era. Getting acquainted with these people will help you understand some of the important, and differing, perspectives on rhetoric that emerged during the classical period. Let us look at them in chronological order.

We'll begin not with an individual but with a group of people called **sophists.** The sophists were teachers in ancient Greece who achieved prominence in the fifth century B.C.E. Many of them were not citizens of Athens but traveled from city to city teaching a variety of subjects. The sophists recognized and responded to the need for Greek citizens to be able to speak and listen effectively in public gatherings. Thus, most sophists offered training in rhetoric as the focus of their educational programs.

As a rule the sophists were not interested in teaching people to create their own individual speeches. Instead they stressed the memorization of previously conceived examples of speech content. For example, a sophist teacher might gather a series of paragraph-long examples of things someone might say when considering the usefulness of a trade agreement or the wisdom of signing a mutual defense pact with another city-state. These examples were known as **commonplaces.** Students memorized commonplaces and could string them together to form speeches. The sophists also wrote handbooks of rhetoric, which were the first texts on how to prepare and present persuasive messages. These handbooks discussed the organization of speeches and techniques of presenting them, as well as commenting on the nature of probability, a concept we shall consider shortly.

Many sophists realized that they could increase their income more rapidly by writing speeches for people instead of or in addition to teaching them. Because of this a class of sophists known as **logographers** emerged. Logographers were speechwriters. Their speeches were usually quite generic and were not well adapted to the circumstances under which they would be delivered. Most logographers had compilations of ideas or sections of speeches that they quickly organized for their client, perhaps writing transitions between the sections. The client purchased the speech, memorized it, and then presented it. The sophists frequently took shortcuts in their work, however. They stole from one another, often promised students more than they could deliver, and were not above selling speeches to both parties in a dispute, and reserving the "best" speech for the person who could pay the most money! For these reasons the term "sophist" came to be associated with trickery and deceit instead of its original meaning of "wise man" or "teacher."

It is interesting to note that the sophists produced no major works of rhetorical theory. They were concerned with practice alone, and their interest was fueled not by their desire to know and understand persuasion, but to make money from the activity. In this way, they were concerned with what did work rather than with why it worked. A perfect illustration of this is their use of commonplaces and their emphasis on memorization for their students.

The philosopher **Plato** (428–348 B.C.E.) was an unabashed opponent of the sophists. He believed in the existence of an absolute truth about every subject. He felt that this truth was ultimately knowable by people, and that the sophists' rhetoric was used to obscure the truth by pandering to popular opinion. This view of rhetoric is fully expressed in his famous dialog *Gorgias* (Plato, 1971), in which Plato offers a devastating critique of sophistic practices. Years later Plato wrote *Phaedrus* (1981), in which he conceded that rhetoric need not always follow the sophistic mode but that it could be used to demonstrate the truth to those who could not discover it on their own.

Plato disdained the sophists' focus on practice rather than truth. He was a firm believer that people would inevitably follow the correct or true course of action once they became aware of it. Rather than emphasizing persuasion, Plato urged people to investigate and find the truth and then act in accord with it. Since not all people could discover the truth (a capacity Plato reserved only for philosophers), platonic rhetoric was a tool for those who had learned the truth and could instruct others in its teachings.

Plato's student **Aristotle** (384–322 B.C.E.) offered a middle position between the sophistic standard of "completely relative" and the Platonic view of "absolute, unvarying truth." Aristotle believed that some concepts, such as those associated with physical science, were indeed subject to an absolute, discoverable truth. Other concepts, such as those associated with politics or public policy, fell short of the absolute standard of truth and were instead best treated as objects of probability.

Aristotle expressly rejected the sophists' position that one opinion or probability was as good as another. He did not believe that something was necessarily true if people believed it to be so. He argued instead that people should follow what was the most likely or probably correct position. Thus, probability was itself a variable, with some ideas and courses of action more probably correct than others. The purpose of education (including rhetoric) was to teach people to discover the most probably correct ideas and actions.

At heart, Aristotle was a biologist, but he was interested in a variety of subjects, including rhetoric. He first encountered rhetoric as a student at Plato's famous school, the **Academy.** After an initial acceptance of his teacher's negative view of rhetoric, Aristotle came to appreciate the potential of persuasion in advancing just causes in a democratic society. He lectured on rhetoric both at Plato's Academy and later on in his own school, the **Lyceum.** After his death Aristotle's students assembled his lecture notes and built them into the famous text that is still studied today, *The Rhetoric* (Kennedy, 1991).

Aristotle's *The Rhetoric* is the single most influential work of the classical era. The three books that comprise *The Rhetoric* represent a full, philosophical, practical but definitely not sophistic treatment of the subject matter. Unlike the sophistic handbooks or Plato's dialogs, *The Rhetoric* explores persuasive public speaking in great depth and equips students to create content for their own messages. Rather than promoting memorization of commonplaces, Aristotle offered a system of inquiry that orators could use in analyzing the specific circumstances confronting them in their speaking. While acknowledging and addressing the philosophical foundations of public persuasion, Aristotle offered pragmatic, useful advice for constructing effective presentations. His work was indeed a masterpiece.

Aristotle's death came at approximately the same time as the end of Athens's dominance of the ancient world. Athens did not disappear entirely, of course. It retained its special status as a place of learning and culture, even though its military and political dominance declined. You may recall that the Greeks were ultimately (although not immediately) replaced as masters of the ancient world by the Romans, initially by the Roman Republic. At this juncture our survey of major figures in classical rhetorical theory must move to Rome.

Cicero (106–43 B.C.E.) is a wholly unique figure in classical rhetorical theory. He wrote extensively about rhetoric, but more than this, Cicero is considered the foremost orator of the Roman era. Cicero's status as both an orator and a theorist gives him a unique perspective on rhetorical theory. It almost assures us that his ideas were pragmatic, geared toward the actual production and analysis of persuasive messages. Cicero was a master craftsman writing about his craft. He wrote extensively about rhetoric throughout his life, producing his first work, *De Inventione,* when he was in his teens.

Cicero was experienced as a **pleader,** someone who took cases in the Roman courts, as well as being a noteworthy Roman senator and political leader of the Republic. Interestingly, just as Aristotle's death coincided roughly with the end of the Greek Empire, so Cicero's death coincided roughly with the end of the Roman Republic. The death of the Republic did not end the period of Roman ascendancy, however, as the Republic was followed by the Roman Empire.

The Roman Empire was home to the last person we'll mention in this brief synopsis. **Quintilian** (35–95 C.E.) had a long and distinguished career as a teacher in imperial Rome. In fact, Quintilian was so well regarded that when Emperor Vespasian established a publicly supported "chair" (or endowed teaching position) of rhetoric at Rome in 71 C.E., Quintilian was named as its occupant. Unlike Cicero, Quintilian was no orator himself, and he didn't write extensively about rhetoric throughout his career. Soon after his retirement from teaching in 91 or 92 C.E., Quintilian began work on a monumental volume on rhetoric. His work, *Institutio Oratoria* or *On the Education of the Orator,* is dedicated to the production of an ideal public speaker. The twelve books of *Institutio Oratoria* outline the training and education of an orator from birth onward. In writing *Institutio Oratoria* Quintilian offers the great summary statement of classical rhetorical theory, quoting extensively from theorists and works with which he was familiar but have since been lost. You can see that this review of the important speakers of classical times and the influential teachers of rhetoric confirms the importance that these cultures and historical periods placed on being skillful in rhetoric.

What Were the Key Assumptions of Classical Rhetorical Theory?

Classical rhetorical theory was pragmatic. It addressed vital societal concerns of the Greeks and the Romans and was developed to provide guidance to those who recognized the importance of persuasion. An indication of the utilitarian focus of classical rhetorical theory is found in its focus on the audience. A major weakness in the sophistic approach to rhetoric, which you will recall emphasized the rote memorization of prefabricated commonplaces, was its lack of attention to adapting ideas to listeners.

Aristotle's *Rhetoric,* on the other hand, recognized that every speech addressed a unique situation. The elements of this situation were the speaker, the subject, and the audience. Aristotle recognized that a speech to the Athenian assembly was different in kind from a speech to a jury in the courts and that both were different from a speech prepared for presentation at a festival, celebration, or other ceremonial occasion. Aristotle and those who followed him stressed creating content for specific receivers of the message.

The emphasis on adapting ideas to audiences leads to the key assumption of classical rhetorical theory: *people are rational decision makers.* Let us explore what is meant by rationality here, beginning with what it is *not.* When classical theorists conceived of individuals as rational decision makers, they did not mean that people are logical or devoid of passion. Human beings are not Vulcans! On the contrary, emotion played a significant role in classical rhetorical theory. The classical theorists equated rationality with *conscious decision making,* a process in which individuals identified alternatives, compared and analyzed them, and then deliberately selected the best one, exactly as Johnnie Cochran asked the jury to do in the Simpson trial. Rationality is thus a process that leads people to consider the substance of ideas and proposals. Classical rhetorical theory is aimed at people who follow this rational process of decision making, who respond more to the content of messages than their presentation. This realization leads us naturally to consider the content of messages.

What Was the Content of Classical Messages?

The classical theorists (excepting, of course, the sophists) were concerned with demonstrating to their audiences that a particular belief or course of action was best. They believed as a group that having clear and compelling content in their speeches best accomplished this. The classical theorists embraced the concept of *argument* as the basis of speech content. We will first discuss the nature of argument and then explore the ways in which arguments were and still are constructed and demonstrated to be correct.

Argument, like rhetoric, is a common term. It is easy to conceive of argument as a verb or as an action, as in you and your roommate disagreeing over whose turn it is to do the dishes. You might describe this to a friend as you and your roommate "having an argument." As an activity, argument brings to mind frequently unpleasant images such as anger, insults, or holding grudges. While having an argument as an activity can lead to these things, this is not an inherent aspect of arguing, nor is it the view of argument held by the classical theorists.

For the classical theorists, argument was a noun, a thing rather than an activity. **Argument** was, thus, a unit of content in a speech, so that constructing speeches involved the creation of a series of arguments in favor of a preferred idea or course of action. This conception of argument is still accepted and taught today. You have probably had assignments that required you to take a position in favor of or against a particular point of view or course of action and to marshal justifications for your perspective. These assignments have asked you to make arguments and are very much within the classical rhetorical tradition.

In more technical terms, an **argument** is a claim or conclusion supported by reasons to believe it. It is a statement plus something designed to make us believe that the statement is correct. The classical theorists identified this "something" as a **proof.** An argument is, therefore, a claim or conclusion accompanied by some proof that it is worthy of our belief. You can readily understand that a claim or conclusion without proof, or one with inferior or noncompelling proof, will not be as believable as an opposing statement accompanied by a strong reason or reasons to believe it. The essence of content in the classical rhetorical system was the creation of arguments containing the most powerful proofs available.

At this juncture let us return to Aristotle. I have already explained that for the classical theorists, rhetoric was equated with persuasion and that, given the nature of the ancient Greek and Roman societies, this persuasion typically took the form of public speeches. In Book II of *The Rhetoric,* Aristotle (in Kennedy, 1991) tells us, "Let rhetoric be [defined as] an ability, in each [particular] case, to see the available means of persuasion" (p. 36). It is important to note that in Aristotle's definition, rhetoric was equated with thinking, or the ability to see or discover which means of persuasion were relevant (or available) in a particular set of circumstances. The means of persuasion to which Aristotle refers were known as **pisteis** or proofs.

Led by Aristotle's example, the classical theorists divided proofs into two categories: nonartistic and artistic. Let us take a closer look at these concepts. A **nonartistic proof** refers to something that is not created by the speaker. Nonartistic proofs existed already in law, history, policy, and so on. A contract between two businessmen would be an example of a nonartistic proof, as would the testimony of witnesses in a court proceeding, the precedents set by earlier governments facing circumstances similar to those confronting people today, or a political candidate's public statements about support or opposition to deficit spending. The classical theorists called these proofs nonartistic because they needed only to be discovered, not created by the "art" of the persuader. (See Figure 5.2.)

Artistic proofs thus become somewhat clearer to us; they are proofs created by a persuader and reflect the art or skill of their creator. The artistic proofs were considered the most challenging proofs to master during the classical period, and considerable attention was paid to them by Aristotle and those who followed him. The artistic proofs were divided into three general categories, *logos, ethos,* and *pathos.*

Logos is a term with many meanings. George Kennedy (1994) tells us that "it connotes the content rather than the style [of a message] . . . and often implies logical reasoning" (p. 11). W. Rhys Roberts's translation of Aristotle's *Rhetoric* explains logos as pertaining to when "persuasion is effected through the speech itself when we have proved a truth or an apparent truth by means of the persuasive arguments suitable to the case in question" (in McKeon, 1973, p. 732). Thus, logos generally refers to the content

FIGURE 5.2   *Nonartistic Proofs in the Boardroom.*   We frequently see nonartistic proofs, such as statistical evidence and written laws or regulations, in modern speeches.

© Charles Gupton/Stock (1989), Boston Inc./PictureQuest.

of a persuasive message but more specifically to the logical power or force of the message content. In the Simpson trial, the fact that the gloves did not fit the accused killer undermined the reasoning advanced by the prosecution in trying to link Simpson with the crime.

The classical rhetorical theorists felt that logos was philosophically the most important form of proof. Given their emphasis on probability and their general adoption of Aristotle's view that people in uncertain situations, where the truth was unknown, needed to think rationally and support the most probably correct ideas, it is not surprising that logos was highly valued. As might be expected, they developed a fairly comprehensive theory of logical reasoning to explain their view of logos. In his works on logic and rhetoric, Aristotle, for example, discussed patterns of reasoning (*inductive* and *deductive*), a general model of reasoning (the *syllogism*) and the use of specific techniques of reasoning (*signs, examples, maxims*). It is important to realize that Aristotle and the other classical theorists did not simply identify these things, but they discussed ways of using them effectively. In this manner the classical rhetorical theorists developed rules of logical deliberation that, in some cases, are still endorsed today.

Ethos is a form of proof associated with the character of the speaker, as demonstrated in the quotes opening this chapter. The classical theorists recognized, as do we today, that people do not simply listen to the ideas of a persuader but also consider the source of those ideas, the persuader himself. Book II of Aristotle's *The Rhetoric* begins with a detailed treatment of ethos, observing "that it is necessary not only to look to the argument, that it may be demonstrative and persuasive, but also [for the speaker] to construct a view of himself as a certain kind of person . . . for it makes much difference in regard to persuasion . . . that the speaker seem to be a certain kind of person and that his hearers suppose him to be disposed toward them in a certain way" (in Kennedy, 1991, p. 120).

The classical rhetorical theorists recognized that ethos was, practically speaking, the most powerful of all the artistic proofs. Ethos was studied carefully, as you might expect. The classical theorists analyzed ethos by studying the characteristics of those who possessed high levels of credibility. Their findings led to the recognition of three critical, interrelated qualities of a credible speaker: competence or practical wisdom, good moral character, and exhibiting goodwill toward the audience. The classical theorists understood that these qualities were found in the prior reputation of the speaker and also were subject to development within the speech itself.

Competence (or practical wisdom) was the ability to think clearly and to advocate effective courses of action in pragmatic situations. A practically wise person lived a good life, made good decisions in own life and career, and offered insightful advice to his fellow citizens. A reputation for possessing these qualities would prove invaluable in convincing an audience that the speaker was advocating a judicious course of action in the specific circumstances of the speech. It is axiomatic that a practically wise person would display a thorough, complete knowledge of the subject matter under deliberation. This person would be knowledgeable or even expert in the topic of discussion in the persuasive situation.

Moral character referred to the trustworthiness of the speaker, or the speaker's ability to convince those hearing the speech that he was telling the truth as he understood it. Again, a reputation for truthfulness would be important here, but the classical theorists also recognized that trustworthiness could and needed to be established within the speech itself. As one contemporary writer on persuasion, Charles Larson (1998), notes, "All the evidence in the world, organized perfectly and delivered well, will not persuade if listeners do not trust the persuader" (p. 299).

Goodwill toward the audience was a straightforward concept, referring to whether the audience members believed the speaker shared their interests and concerns. The audience was more likely to believe a speaker if they did not think the person was speaking to satisfy his own desires and interests. Advice offered from an "impartial" person would be valued more highly than advice offered by someone likely to profit if it is accepted.

Just as the classical theorists recognized the importance of ethos in constructing effective persuasive speeches, contemporary researchers have been attracted to the study of this variable. The foremost contemporary researcher into ethos, James C. McCroskey (1997), has noted that "of all the aspects of classical rhetorical theory, the one that has the greatest support from modern empirical research is the theoretical importance of ethos in rhetorical communication. Almost without exception, experimental studies have demonstrated the power of ethos" (p. 87). Interestingly, the first contemporary researchers into ethos, Carl Hovland, Irving Janis, and Harold Kelley (1953), confirmed the classical components of expertness, trustworthiness, and attitude of the source toward the receiver. According to McCroskey (1997), subsequent experimental research into ethos has largely corroborated the classical dimensions of ethos discussed above, so that contemporary persuaders must also consider credibility as a powerful variable in the process of influence.

The final artistic proof, **pathos,** refers to the use of emotions as a technique of persuasion. The classical theorists saw emotion as a powerful and necessary proof but were fearful that emotions could interfere with their ideal of rational decision making. Quintilian, for example, in Book VI of the *Institutio Oratoria,* declares that he is "forced to say something" about emotions. Yet he (1953) also recognized that emotions "demand more than cursory treatment, since it is in their handling that the power of oratory shows itself at its highest" (p. 417). The classical theorists recognized that by learning about emotions, they could also learn about people, and knowing about people was essential to seeing the available means of persuasion in specific cases. In fact, Kennedy refers to Aristotle's treatment of emotions in Book II of *The Rhetoric* as "the earliest systematic discussion of human psychology" (Kennedy, 1991, p. 122).

Aristotle considered emotions in pairs: anger and calmness, friendliness and hostility, fear and confidence, shame and shamelessness, kindliness and unkindness, pity and indignation, and finally envy and emulation in his treatment of emotion (Figure 5.3).

At the same time, Aristotle states, "It is not right to pervert the judge by moving him to anger or envy or pity—one might as well warp a carpenter's rule before using it. Again, the litigant has clearly nothing to do but to show that the alleged fact is so or is not so, that it has happened or has not happened" (Aristotle, in Roberts & Bywater, 1984, p. 20). Thus, while he provided the tools for the effective use of emotion, he did not seem totally sold on the idea!

We have briefly examined the basic elements of classical rhetorical theory. We have reviewed the foremost figures associated with the development of rhetorical theory between 500 B.C.E. and 500 C.E., noting some of their influential works and philosophical concerns. We have identified the basic assumption shared by most of the classical theorists, primarily that people are essentially rational decision makers. We have followed this assumption into the basic focus of classical rhetoric, the construction of effective speech content, and noted the fundamental components of content in the classical system: arguments and their proofs. But of course, this summary, like all summaries, is incomplete. There was far more to classical rhetorical theory than the content of messages. Aristotle and his followers were concerned with discovering *all* of the available means of persuasion, and this led them beyond content.

FIGURE 5.3   Pathos: *Aristotle's Pairs of Emotions.*

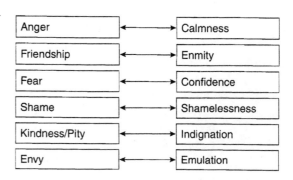

What Were the Classical Canons of Rhetoric?

The Romans examined the works of Aristotle (and several other authors whom we have not mentioned here) with the purpose of discovering how best to train an effective persuasive speaker/receiver. Cicero, in his work *De Inventione,* expressed the belief that the study of rhetoric involved five related concepts. These concepts, known as the *canons,* or principles, of rhetoric, were used to organize classical thinking on rhetoric and formed the basis for education in rhetoric for the next two thousand years.

Cicero identified five concepts as the basic principles or **canons of rhetoric:** invention, arrangement, style, delivery, and memory. He felt that Aristotle treated each of them in his works related to rhetoric, and Cicero's first work on rhetoric, *De Inventione,* was planned originally as a treatise on the first canon, invention, to be followed subsequently by treatments of the next four canons. It may very well be a reflection of Cicero's youth (*De Inventione* was written when he was a teenager) that the other four treatises did not materialize and that *De Inventione* itself went beyond the first canon of invention. We will conclude our treatment of classical rhetorical theory with a synopsis of the five classical canons of rhetoric.

Invention refers to the discovery of the appropriate ideas or content for persuasive messages. It addresses the fundamental question of "what are the best things to say to the audience in this particular situation?" Obviously, invention is closely related to the artistic and nonartistic proofs we have already discussed, but it is not synonymous with proofs. Invention takes us back a step to consider first what it is that we want to prove in this situation. Remember, the classical theorists rejected the old sophistic notion of having students memorize commonplaces and sought to teach their students to "see" or discover their own content. To this end Aristotle and the subsequent theorists advanced a system of *topics* that could be used to invent the appropriate content of a persuasive speech.

The **topics** (often called by the Greek term *topoi*) were a series of fundamental questions that a speaker could ask in order to locate the most appropriate ideas to present in a speech. There were "common topics" which were relevant to any subject under discussion, as well as more specific topics geared to whether the speech was designed for the assembly, the courts, or for a public ceremony or festival. Following Aristotle's observation that persuasion in the assembly was different than persuasion in court or at a ceremony or ritual event, the classical theorists identified three genres, or types, of persuasive speaking: deliberative, forensic, and epideictic. **Deliberative** speeches occurred in the assembly, which deliberated about appropriate policies for the state. **Forensic** speeches were courtroom speeches and involved questions of guilt and innocence. **Epideictic** speeches were speeches given on special occasions and involved questions of praise and blame.

The so-called common topics, those that applied regardless of the genre of the persuasive speech, are worthy of our attention at this time. There were five common topics, and with a bit of imagination, you should be able to see how well they apply to contemporary persuasion. The first common topic was *degree,* sometimes referred to as *more or less.* When you purchase an automobile, you typically want to get the best value for your money, and this is a question of degree. In examining the benefit packages of different firms you are considering working for, you may very well wish to consider which package offers the most utility to you and your family.

The second common topic was *possibility/impossibility.* One may wonder whether peace in the Middle East or Northern Ireland is a possibility or whether we should plan for an ongoing, continuing conflict in those areas of the world. We may also wonder whether it is possible to build a spacecraft capable of traveling faster than the speed of light, whether e-mail will make the U.S. Postal Service obsolete, or whether human cloning is possible.

The third common topic was *past fact.* Did something occur or not occur? Did you tell your boyfriend that you would meet him at a certain time and place? Did your teacher tell you that papers must be typed without errors? Did the Federal Reserve Board raise interest rates last week?

The fourth common topic was, as you can probably anticipate, *future fact,* or how likely it is that something will occur in the future. Will a particular dating relationship last? Will all of your assignments be due at the same time of the semester? Will it be the twenty-second century before the Cubs win another pennant? Will starting a savings program early in your life enable you to retire comfortably at an early age?

The final common topic was *magnitude* or size. How much of our time is spent surfing the web? Too much? How much is too much? Has the development of new communication technology significantly changed the way political campaigns are conducted in this country? How important are the benefits to workers offered by a new labor contract?

The common topics were supplemented, of course, with specific or particular topics related to deliberative, forensic, and epideictic speech situations. The classical theorists developed lengthy lists of specific topics, and we'll simply note their existence at this time without going into great detail on them. Rather, it is important to recall what the topics meant to classical rhetorical theory. They should be understood as an answer to the memorized commonplaces of the sophists. They reflect the classical theorists' interest in teaching people to think for themselves rather than simply memorizing the ideas of others. This was the ultimate purpose of invention.

The classical theorists recognized, of course, that ideas alone were not sufficient to persuade an audience. Those ideas had to be organized into a pattern that the audience would find clear and compelling. Thus, the second canon of rhetoric is **arrangement.** The classical theorists sought to standardize the parts of a persuasive speech and also to understand what could be expected to occur during each section of the message. For this reason, it was difficult to separate arrangement from invention, a difficulty illustrated in the youthful Cicero's *De Inventione.* George Kennedy (1994) notes that most of the classical theorists speculated about the arrangement of forensic or judicial speeches and crystallized the thinking on organization into four basic divisions of a message: the introduction (designed to secure the interest and favorable feeling of the audience), the narration (explanation of the background and relevant factual details of the subject), the proof (the arguments), and the conclusion (recapitulation and final emotional appeal). Different theorists presented different interpretations of this basic pattern of arrangement. Does this effort to organize an oral presentation remind you of your basic public speaking class?

The third canon was **style.** The classical theorists understood the potential of language as a powerful persuasive technique. The stylistic devices you have encountered in your English composition courses probably date back to the classical period during which writing was subordinate to speaking. The well-known figures of speech such as metaphor, simile, and antithesis, for example, date back to the classical period. As with the treatment of topics, we'll simply note that the classical theorists developed an extensive list of figures of speech and that we cannot attempt a comprehensive treatment of them at this time.

The classical theorists' interest in style extended well beyond a compilation of figures of speech, however. Throughout most of the thousand-year classical period there was considerable controversy over the most appropriate style of composing speeches. This concern extended beyond the choice of figures of speech and encompassed the number of stylistic devices used and the overall tone of the message itself. There were three schools of thought concerning style. One school suggested that style should be very prominent in a speech and that the speech style should be quite elevated, almost poetic in tone. The practitioners of this approach to speaking style were uniquely subject to the "empty" rhetoric charges with which we began this chapter, for it was quite easy to subordinate content to presentation when following this exaggerated style of speech.

As might be anticipated, another school of thought was diametrically opposed to the first. This approach to style argued that persuaders should use very little, if any, style in their presentations. This plain style of speaking was nearly devoid of any techniques to elevate it beyond an almost mathematical treatment of its subject matter. Those who accepted this approach to persuasion relied solely on the power of the ideas themselves to be persuasive.

The third school took a middle ground between the high and the plain styles of speaking and was, not surprisingly, known as the middle school of style. Adherents to this approach to style argued that style must be appropriate to the persuasive situation and must be adapted to the subject matter, the audience, and the occasion. The appropriate style would thus be either high or plain depending on the circumstances but, most often, would encompass a middle position between them. The speeches of Cicero, which were studied for thousands of years as models of effective persuasive speaking, utilized this middle level of style.

The fourth classical canon of rhetoric was **delivery.** The classical theorists recognized that even the most logically solid message with the strongest proofs still needed to be presented in a pleasing manner. Included in delivery were concerns about voice and body movement. Voice concerned questions about the appropriate volume to use, the best rhythm to use in speaking, and when and how to be flexible in tone of voice. Body movement involved not just whether to move about or stand still, but how to use one's facial expressions and hand gestures to make ideas more believable to listeners.

The final canon of rhetoric is today referred to as the "lost" canon of rhetoric: **memory.** Remember, the classical period began with the ascendancy of speaking over writing, and, while writing became much more accepted during Roman times, great attention was still devoted to the ability to follow extended arguments in the senate, the Forum, or the courts. The classical theorists thus developed systems of memorization that could be employed to enable orators and citizens alike to recall the key points in their own and in opposing messages.

These five canons were carefully followed by public speakers in ancient Greece and Rome. They were also taught in the schools of this classical era. These five canons represented a formal and consistent way to plan and deliver a speech. Even today, speakers like Ann Richards, Martin Luther King, Jr., or Ronald Reagan become great orators because of their ability to use the canons effectively (Figure 5.4). We do not follow all of these five canons in this exact way today, but this step-by-step way of organizing and presenting a

FIGURE 5.4   Ronald Reagan, known as the "Great Communicator," uses his *ethos* to promote George Bush as President at the 1972 Republican Convention.

Photo courtesy of AP Wideworld.

speech set a foundation and established the principle that we still follow today in teaching and in presenting formal speech presentations—the principle that any oral presentation needs to be carefully thought out and planned before it can be successfully delivered.

Summary

According to the definitions of metatheory and classifications of theory presented in Chapter 2, you can recognize that classical rhetorical theory mixes assumptions of the objective and subjective perspectives. Many of the theorists, such as Plato and Aristotle, treated truth and reality objectively, because they believed that there was, in a given case, only one "truth" (such as a true definition, a true course of action). Rhetoric was a tool provided to acquire knowledge in a way that one could be certain of what one knew. And yet rhetorical theory is humanistic because it deals primarily with understanding communication within the society and as a tool for individual persuasion. Classical rhetorical theory precedes the scientific method and the critical theory movement of modern times. Because of this, those who use classical rhetorical theory today tend to use it to interpret specific messages, rather than making predictions about variables; this makes it more humanistic in the way scholars use it today. Still, many interpersonal communication researchers have picked up the principles of the classical rhetoricians—notions such as credibility and emotional appeals (e.g., fear appeals) and found ways to operationalize them for scientific inquiry. Chapter 9 will consider some of this scientific analysis of persuasion.

The classical period represents the first systematic inquiry into human communication in the Western world. Because the classical theorists studied human communication, they developed considerable insights into what it meant to be human. The classical theorists were limited by the tools available to them for use in studying persuasion, basing their

conclusions primarily upon the observation of persuasive speeches and attempting to catalog the techniques and devices they observed. The "great" classical theorists, Aristotle,
Cicero, and Quintilian, sought not only to discover effective techniques of persuasion but
also to understand why these techniques worked and to develop principles that could be
utilized to govern their use.

    Classical rhetorical theory has much to tell us about contemporary persuasion and is
still studied and used today. At the same time, we must recognize that classical rhetorical
theory was developed for its time, not for ours. For us today it presents a rather parochial
view of a world dominated by males sharing a common culture and educational background. It was oriented exclusively toward public speaking. It is obviously less relevant
to our contemporary, diverse, mediated culture than it was to its own time. Nonetheless,
serious students of persuasion would do well to follow the example of some of the contemporary authors cited in this chapter and begin their investigation of persuasive communication with a thorough study and appreciation of the classical tradition. There is much
there that remains within the realm of "the available means of persuasion."

Discussion Questions

1. During the time of Plato and Aristotle, public speaking was the main forum for lawmaking
   and justice. Some argue today that, with the rise of modern technology, public speaking is
   on the way out. Take a position for or against this statement and defend it.

2. Which of the various principles in this chapter have you seen echoed in your public speaking classes? Which standard of theory evaluation in Chapter 1 might this speak to?

3. Which of the three types of artistic proofs do you feel is most relevant for college-age students today? Explain your answer. Do you believe this has changed since Aristotle's time,
   and if so, why?

References

Cochran, J. (1995, 27–28 September). Closing Argument in O. J. Simpson trial. Available online: http://
www.law.umkc.edu/faculty/projects/ftrials/Simpson/
cochranclose.html

Hovland, C. L., Janis, I. L., & Kelley, H. H. (1953). *Communication and persuasion.* New Haven, CT: Yale
University Press.

Kennedy, G. A. (1991). *Aristotle on Rhetoric: A theory of
civil discourse.* New York: Oxford University
Press.

Kennedy, G. A. (1994). *A new history of classical
rhetoric.* Princeton, NJ: Princeton University
Press.

Larson, C. U. (1998). *Persuasion: Reception and responsibility* (8th ed.). Belmont, CA: Wadsworth.

McCroskey, J. C. (1997) *An introduction to rhetorical
communication* (7th ed.). Boston: Allyn and
Bacon.

McKeon, R. (1973). *Introduction to Aristotle.* Chicago:
University of Chicago Press.

Plato. (1971). *Gorgias* (W. Hamilton, Trans.). New York:
Penguin Books.

Plato. (1981). *Phaedrus* (W. Hamilton, Trans.). New
York: Penguin Books.

Quintilian. (1953). *Institutio Oratoria* (H. E. Butler,
Trans.). Cambridge: Harvard University Press.

Reuters Wire Service, New York, December 19, 2001.

Roberts, W. R., & Bywater, I. (Trans.). (1984). The
Rhetoric *and* The Poetics *of Aristotle.* New York:
Modern Library.

6

Contemporary Rhetorical Theory

Jeffrey L. Courtright, Craig W. Cutbirth, and Stephen K. Hunt

The preceding chapter examined **classical rhetorical theory,** a system of rhetoric that originated in ancient Greece and Rome. Classical rhetorical communication has dominated much of our thinking about persuasion even into the twenty-first century. However, as rhetorical scholar Martin Medhurst (1996) notes, "Aristotle may have written the first systematic treatise on rhetoric, but he did not write the last" (p. xiv). That new theories would emerge to supplement, compete with, and in some cases replace, the classical approach to persuasion is inevitable. Ironically, as communication scholars were picking up "variables" from traditional rhetorical theory to create scientific-approach studies, the new rhetorical approaches remained steadfastly humanistic and interpretive in focus, with later theories introducing critical theory.

From the classical period until today, the study and practice of rhetoric has undergone major shifts. We know from our world history that the classical period of ancient Greece and Rome was followed by about 1,500 years of the relatively "dark" ages or Middle Ages. During this time, medieval rhetoric was necessarily shifted to the hands of the educated and literate, who were the priests and monks. The clergy practiced rhetoric as a religious tool, as a means to write down sermons, letters, and, importantly, to save the Bible and other classical texts in manuscript form. Later, during the Renaissance and the Enlightenment through current times, reflecting the general secularization of culture throughout Europe and the rest of the world, rhetoric emerged as a secular study, once again as a means to understand public and oral communication, as well as the study of literature and the great texts.

This chapter will focus on modern views of rhetoric. We will examine several twentieth-century theories that have produced new and much broader approaches to, and applications of, rhetoric. We will look at a number of theories of contemporary rhetorical persuasion: genre theory, symbolic interaction theories, and critical theories.

In this chapter, you will read about the following concepts:

- How rhetoric has changed focus in modern research
- Genre theory as a transition from classical to contemporary rhetoric

- Symbolic interactionist views of rhetoric
  - Burke's view of rhetoric as motive and identification
  - Bormann's view of rhetoric as symbolic convergence
  - Fisher's view of rhetoric as narrative (storytelling)
- Critical theory views of rhetoric
  - Raymond Williams, cultural studies, and Marxist origins
  - Foucault's view of rhetoric as power
  - Habermas's theory of communicative action

Until the late 1960s, the classical approach served as the paradigm for the study of rhetoric. However, the events of that decade (e.g., the Vietnam War, race riots and the fight for racial equality, student protests) produced public discourse that Aristotle and Cicero's concepts could not explain easily. Scholars thus sought to determine alternative ways to describe and critique contemporary rhetorical practice. This search has produced a variety of alternatives. The great person speaking to the multitude is but one of many situations in which rhetoric occurs, and many theories emerged to explain these diverse situations.

The important thing to appreciate about **contemporary rhetorical theory,** as compared to classical or medieval theory, is that many more models of rhetoric exist in contemporary rhetoric, and scholars have broadened the definition of rhetoric and the type of artifact it can be used to analyze. That is, beyond classical rhetoric's interest in public oral presentations in the realm of politics, contemporary rhetorical theory opens up rhetoric to include any and all kinds of communication—as forms of persuasion, cultural expression, or power—and offers numerous models of rhetoric for analysis of these various forms of communication. A song's lyrics, a printed text such as a web page, a personal speech, a television show, even clothing—any kind of communication that is heard, seen, read, or displayed—is within the scope of contemporary rhetoric and can be considered a **text,** a subject for analysis.

This change in the scope and form of rhetoric is a fun and interesting feature of contemporary rhetorical theory. Today, the field of communication has been enriched—even legitimated to some degree—through the ideas and contributions of several key figures who proposed models of rhetoric that have significant explanatory power. In this chapter we will consider approaches to rhetoric that look at rhetoric humanistically, in terms of how meaning is created through interaction, and approaches that treat rhetoric critically, considering the implications for language in the creation and opposition of power relations. Before these approaches, however, we will present an approach that provides a transition from classical approaches to the contemporary.

When Classical Rhetoric Fails, What Will We Do?

In Chapter 5, you learned that Aristotle observed that speech content varied depending on the situation. Classical theorists argued that some topics and arguments were better for some settings than others. This focus on deliberative, forensic, and epideictic situations—these "**genres**"—naturally match the occasion of "the good man speaking well" in public, to borrow a phrase from Quintilian. But what about war protesters whose discourse was marked by the use of obscenities, strident moral argument, and an ethos counter to the existing hegemony?

According to genre theorists, similar situations that recur over time also generate similar rhetorical styles and strategies (Campbell & Jamieson, 1978). In this vein, Theodore Windt (1972) effectively argued that Vietnam War protesters such as the Yippies were similar to the Cynics in ancient Greece. Finding themselves in an immoral society (situation), the form of discourse they chose, the **diatribe,** served various functions: to shock the audience, to attack societal values through satire and parody, and to critique the ethos of the status quo. Since the diatribe does not rely on traditional argument, its use of logos, pathos, and ethos defy classical understandings of rhetoric.

Because various situations recur, genre theory is useful for understanding everyday rhetorical activity. For example, when a member of the community dies, we feel compelled to address that loss through rhetoric. A scan of a newspaper obituary section demonstrates that death announcements have a particular form that we have come to expect. But a **eulogy** given at a funeral goes even further: we expect the speaker not only to acknowledge the death and console the living, but to offer the audience lessons from the deceased's character that we can emulate. The audience is brought together to mourn, but the loss becomes a means of creating a legacy and unifying the audience.

Genres fulfill a variety of functions and apply to a variety of situations. Although genre theory has tended to focus on the individual speaker (Campbell & Jamieson, 1990), the genre of **apologia,** for example, in which speakers defend attacks against their character, has been applied to public relations crisis situations (Benoit, 1995).

How Does Rhetoric Actually Change My "Reality"?

As illustrated in our discussion of genre theory, scholars who theorize rhetoric today consider it in terms of how individuals relate to others around them, rather than following the classical view of rhetoric as public communication of one person speaking to an immediate, live audience. Contemporary rhetorical critics understand communication among friends, coworkers, or family members, and meanings gained from texts such as television or music, as a process of communicating through the symbols we create and through the meanings we give to these symbols. They suggest that people do not and cannot relate to the world directly through absolute objective reality. That is, as humans, we always experience the world in an indirect way, reacting to the symbols and meanings we create of the world around us rather than through a completely accessible, objective reality of our surroundings. This approach to meaning and communication reflects the idea that interaction creates our social reality. Three contemporary theorists stand out in this school of thought: Kenneth Burke, Ernest Bormann, and Walter Fisher.

Kenneth Burke: Language as Motive and Identification

Kenneth Burke was probably the most influential American rhetorical theorist of the twentieth century. His early work as a literary and music critic for the magazine the *Dial* quickly led his precocious mind from the appeal of art and literature to a lifelong exploration of human beings as "symbol using animals." Burke certainly extended the work of Aristotle but also drew upon a variety of philosophers, critics, and social scientists to arrive at a theory he called **logology,** or "words about words" (Burke, 1961, p. 1). Logology is the study of how we use language in order to know the world around us, work with others, and, eventually, communicate to ourselves.

For Burke, we cannot truly "know" a situation—we can only describe or name it. Through Burke's (1945/1969) system of rhetorical criticism, known as the **pentad,** we can discover the **motives,** or *interpretations,* of speakers. That is, people typically describe situations in ways that fit their orientation to the world around them. For example, think of the many ways in which you can describe an athlete's win or loss. In golf, you could say, "Tiger Woods has natural talent." Here, you are assigning motive to, or interpreting, the **agent** (the actor) as most important to the situation. In contrast, you could frame your view of things in terms of the means or **agency** (how the act is accomplished) at the athlete's disposal: "He should have used a three-wood." Likewise, you might emphasize the end (**purpose**) rather than the means: "Winning isn't everything." Or perhaps the **act** itself best describes the event: "That hole-in-one guaranteed her the trophy." Of course, the **scene** in which things occurred could explain everything: "The sun got in my eyes."

According to Burke, language creates systems of meanings that are shared by groups of people. We treat some words as symbolic or representative of our highest values and aspirations (e.g., freedom, democracy), while others become indicative of the things we most detest (e.g., terrorism, dictatorship). Language systems establish a symbolic hierarchy of our ideals (and opposing hierarchies), and we deal with failure to live up to these ideals through rhetoric (Burke, 1935/1984, 1961, 1966).

We can exemplify this through a rhetorical text including words and images from a web site (Figure 6.1). Voices in the Wilderness (VITW), an antiwar organization, posted images along with some very angry text about how American invasion of foreign countries (even in the supposedly righteous protection of Kuwait during Operation Desert Storm) has done immense damage to foreign countries.

Notice in these drawings some viewpoints toward the United States and Uncle Sam drawn from the viewpoint of suffering Iraqi children following the Gulf War of 1991. These children's drawings are rhetorical because they are persuasive toward a point of view that most of us living in the United States probably do not appreciate. They are symbolic in that they portray the symbolic reality that the Iraqi people feel. The political activism and the symbolic reality felt by the children toward United States foreign invasions is clearly evident here in these drawings featured on the web page. The noble deeds that the United States people attribute to protection of foreign countries clearly do not represent the symbolic reality that many people in foreign countries necessarily feel toward Americans.

This symbol system gives you a sense of right and wrong and, when violated, creates a need in you to resolve the sense of guilt. You may do this through symbolic action. Imagine a situation in which you have a brother or sister who broke an expensive lamp because you were arguing with him or her. **Mortification** is at work when you yourself take responsibility for the violation of ideals (e.g., "I'll pay for the lamp"). Even if you may not be at fault, **victimage** occurs when you rhetorically place the burden of guilt on someone or something else (e.g., "That lamp was too fragile in the first place"). **Transcendence**

Voices in the Wilderness
www.vitw.org

Voices in the Wilderness delegations journey
to Iraq to break the siege and bring
desperately needed medical supplies to
children and families. The U.S. Treasury
Department warns that we risk penalties of
twelve years in prison and $1 million in fines.
As our government puts us on notice, so we
must put our government on notice:
THE CONTINUING ECONOMIC
SANCTIONS CONSTITUTE AN
UNJUSTIFIED AGGRESSION AGAINST
THE CIVILIAN POPULATION OF IRAQ—
A VIOLATION OF INTERNATIONAL LAW
AND A CRIME AGAINST THE HUMAN
FAMILY.

FIGURE 6.1   *A Text-Link from Voices in the Wilderness Web Site.* Iraqi children's pictures
and advocacy group web page makes an argument. We can analyze the rhetorical argument
using Burke's Pentad.

Used with permission, Voices in the Wilderness.

combines opposing symbols or motives (e.g., "Let's clean up the mess together, work to
pay for the lamp, and only roughhouse in the family room"). In this last instance, responsibility (or guilt) is shared between parties.

In presenting Iraqi children's drawings on their web page, Voices in the Wilderness
wants to create mortification in the American people for what they have done in Iraq. They
want to cast the American invasion, or Operation Desert Storm, as the guilty party hurting
the Iraqis. In contrast, official American government rhetoric during the buildup to invasion and the ground war itself continually emphasized that it was not America against the
Arab world, but a coalition of 28 countries allied against Saddam Hussein alone (see Bush,
1991). This unification of seemingly opposed groups *transcends* cultural differences.

From birth until death, the "rhetorical situation" is such that we use symbols to create a sense of belonging with others—a sense of **identification. Consubstantiality,** for
Burke, is a form of complete identification. We use symbols to create a sense of unity with
others (and, as we shall see, to maintain our sense of distinctiveness as well). There are
three types of identification, according to Burke (1973). The first of these, **identification
through similarity,** is achieved by "stressing of sympathies held in common" (p. 268).
Such appeals to joint interest are explicit, and therefore obvious (the coalition of 28 nations against Iraq is a good example). The second of these, **identification through antithesis,** according to Burke, capitalizes on our distinctiveness by emphasizing what we are

opposed to (e.g., none of us likes Saddam Hussein). The third form, the most subtle and perhaps the most powerful, is also the most prevalent, due to the ambiguity of language. It appears in Burke's writings under the label **vicarious identification,** which is a form of **identification through inaccuracy.**

When the president of the United States says, "We won't stand for this," who is the audience? The ambiguity of "we" invites identification. Likewise, when you watch a sporting event, that gratifying feeling you have when your team or individual athlete wins is yet another case of vicarious identification. You live through their success, but you did nothing directly to help them win (especially if you are sitting in front of the television, rather than cheering them on in person). Kenneth Burke's theory of how words work—logology—thus shifts the study of rhetoric from argument to motive, from persuasion to identification. Symbols help us name situations, motivate us to action, and inspire collaboration among other "symbol-using animals" (Burke, 1966).

Ernest Bormann: Language as Symbolic Convergence

Another theory of communication, **symbolic convergence theory (SCT),** also suggests that humans communicate with one another as social actors, but uses a different set of concepts. Developed by Ernest Bormann and his students at the University of Minnesota in the early 1970s, this theory has been used to study a variety of persuasive communication artifacts in an array of situations. Bormann declares that the content of messages is meaning, so let us begin our treatment of SCT by exploring this assertion.

The view that the content of messages is meaning is rooted in the work of Robert Bales of Harvard University, who was interested in the way human beings interacted in a small group setting. Bales (1950) observed that group members would occasionally make comments about people or events not physically present in the group. Bales referred to these comments as **fantasies.** He further observed that group members would sometimes react to one of these comments by getting excited, contributing details about the comment, and even interrupting one another in their eagerness to participate. In other words, the comment energized the group.

Bormann and his students used Bales's observation as the foundation of SCT. We can apply this by thinking about a group of college students sharing a few root beers together, and complaining about their department. One of them makes a comment about the professors ("They must sit and coordinate their exams so they all come at the same time!"), and the group members get excited about it, picking up on it and contributing relevant information about their own experiences with the same or similar situations as the one related by the initial commentator. Bormann referred to this as the creation of a **fantasy theme.** According to Bormann, a fantasy theme is not the same as a fairy tale or a myth. Rather, a fantasy theme is a "creative and imaginative interpretation of events that fulfills a psychological or rhetorical need" (Bormann, 1990, p. 122). Cragan and Shields (1998) note that each fantasy theme we encounter "embodies a dramatizing message depicting characters engaged in action in a setting that accounts for and explains human experience" (pp. 98–99).

The usefulness of fantasy themes is found in the ability of people to relate to them and use them to structure their experience and find meaning in their lives. When a fantasy theme **chains out,** people are said to share the fantasy, which extends beyond simply understanding or accepting the message. When people share a fantasy, they become actively involved in it and contribute to it, sometimes adding details or building on the content of the fantasy. In this manner people *symbolically converge,* or share in the fantasy. When multiple fantasy themes come together, they form a **rhetorical vision,** a large-scale drama that offers people a broad view of things.

For example, Ford (1989) documents how members of Alcoholics Anonymous come to see the world in similar terms through following the 12 principles of the organization's "Big Book." By attending meetings, supporting other members, and following the Big Book's principles, the fantasy themes of Alcoholics Anonymous are reinforced, shared, and communicated into a larger vision of "fetching good out of evil." Likewise, others hold rhetorical visions about human rights, about the role of the United States in world affairs, and about what entails proper behavior by people who identify themselves politically as Liberals or Conservatives. Rhetorical visions can be so large that they might best be understood as worldviews or philosophies of life.

Symbolic convergence theory has proven to be an attractive and useful theory in explaining how communication works to build an identity among a group of people. The fact that such visions are often persuasive makes this theory pertinent to rhetoric, with rhetoric understood as persuasion, or rhetoric focusing on meaning-making of everyday interaction. SCT suggests that persuasion is tied to the creation of meaning in our world and that sharing meaning is a basic function of persuasion. At the same time, its focus on group development also makes it a valuable theory for other contexts of communication; thus, you will find these terms applied elsewhere in this book in relation to small groups (Chapter 8).

Walter Fisher: Language as Narrative

Instead of "identification" or "fantasy," the notion of "story" is central to the next theory of symbolic interaction, Walter Fisher's **narrative paradigm** (1984, 1985a, 1985b). Fisher sought to establish that his conception of drama, which he termed narrative, was the paradigmatic mode of all human communication. Fisher believed that the world was best understood as a series of stories that compete for our attention and adherence. Fisher believed that human beings are, by nature, tellers of stories, and just as we learn to tell stories to one another, so we learn to evaluate them via a process of socialization rather than through training. The **narrative** or "story," for Fisher (1987), is broadly understood as any communicative account that has a beginning, middle, end, and characters. Narratives include conversations, arguments in scientific journals, stories told in public speeches, technical reports, and bedtime stories (Figure 6.2).

In his initial treatments of narrative, Fisher was careful to explain that the narrative paradigm subsumed rather than replaced the Aristotelian view of rationality. In other words, Aristotle's ideas were incomplete more than incorrect. Fisher simply attempted to provide a broader view of rationality than advanced by Aristotle—a view not limited to logical argument but one that embraced values as the center of persuasive discourse.

Fisher advanced an alternative to the Aristotelian system for determining the worth or merit of stories, which he termed **narrative rationality.** He recognized that different

FIGURE 6.2 *Narratives, Narratives Everywhere.* How many forms of narrative can you locate in this picture of an academic advisement appointment?

Photo by Forrest Wisely, Dept. of Communication, Illinois State University.

people would create different stories to explain the same event or events and that these explanatory stories would compete with one another for the attention and support of the public. People evaluate these competing stories by assessing their narrative rationality. Fisher conceived of narrative rationality as including *narrative probability* and *narrative fidelity.* Let us discuss these concepts in turn.

Narrative probability, which has also been termed **narrative coherence,** refers to our tendency to evaluate a narrative as a story. In other words, does the story have all of the elements we expect to find in a story? Can we recognize it as a story? Do the characters in the story act as we would expect them to behave? Does the story explain or account for all of the important details we know about the subject of the story? Clearly, if someone tells us a story that does not "hang together" or "make sense," we will not believe it over a more coherent competitor. It must be internally consistent.

Narrative fidelity refers to the process of evaluating the truthfulness of the story. Fisher refers to this as whether the story *rings true* in the mind of the receiver. Ringing true is a complex process that involves several dimensions of evaluation. One dimension is whether the story we are being told is consistent with other stories we believe. To the extent a new story is compatible with stories we already believe to be correct, we are likely to accept the new story as well. A second dimension of narrative fidelity is how well the story *fits in* with our personal experiences. Most people trust themselves and their personal interpretations of reality. A speaker who tells a story that is consistent with our personal experiences is more likely to be successful than one that is not.

The last dimension of narrative fidelity demonstrates that the narrative paradigm regards the content of persuasive communication to be values. Fisher suggests that all stories contain *good reasons.* They tell us who we should be and how we should behave. These *good reasons* are the most important aspect of message content, and, as we examine the concept more closely, we directly confront values. Speakers will respond differently to a speaker such as Elizabeth Dole (Figure 6.3). However, part of her renowned effectiveness as a speaker may relate to her ability to provide reasons that fit with the character, culture,

FIGURE 6.3 Elizabeth Dole's reputation as a powerful speaker may relate to her ability to tell narratives that relate to her audience's experiences.

© Associated Press, Tribune-Star.

and values of audience members, as she incorporates narratives (not just "stories," as we have noted above) that resonate with her audience's experiences.

Good reasons inherently contain and reflect values. All persuasive communication urges people to accept or reject some idea or course of action; in other words, it tells people what they *should* believe or what actions they *ought* to take. After the terrorist attacks on New York and Washington on September 11, 2001, President George W. Bush (2001) declared:

> Today, our fellow citizens, our way of life, our very freedom came under attack in a series of deliberate and deadly attacks. . . . A great people has been moved to defend a great nation. Terrorist attacks can shake the foundations of our biggest buildings, but they cannot touch the foundation of America. Thus, the attack on the Twin Towers was an attack on freedom itself, and we *should* and *ought* to be willing to defend that freedom.

This provides an excellent example of Fisher's concern with values. The citizens of this country value freedom and value it to the extent of fighting to preserve it. President Bush's statement about freedom being under attack contains the value of freedom and uses it as a means of motivating people to support direct action to defend freedom.

Of course, there are a variety of values that any group of people might share: wisdom, honesty, cleverness, friendliness, good health, and success are a few of the values expressed by many in our culture. In Fisher's view, one or more of these will be embedded in messages, and you and I as receivers of those messages will be able to identify these values and assess their importance to us.

Fisher further develops the concept of narrative fidelity by probing more deeply into the values contained or reflected in messages. Beyond evaluating the importance of the values in a message, Fisher declares *that receivers look at the relevance of those values to the decision the message asks them to make.* After the attacks of September 11th, for example, some people may have felt that capitalism was under attack, or globalization, or modernism. For some, the decision to wage war in the name of freedom may be different than waging war in defense of capitalism, globalization, or modernism.

Narrative fidelity is evaluated further, according to Fisher, as *people assess the consequences of following the relevant values in the message.* Defending freedom after the terrorist attacks involves waging a limited war in which innocent people will inevitably suffer and die. Defending freedom against terrorism means that measures to protect the internal security of the United States must be significantly tightened, which causes inconvenience for citizens and may jeopardize civil liberties. People value convenience and civil liberties, and Fisher might suggest that we consider such values as we ponder a decision of whether to support the president's defense of freedom.

How Can Rhetoric Help Me Challenge Unequal Power Structures?

The theories of Burke, Bormann, and Fisher are primarily humanistic in character, as they primarily *describe* how language creates realities. Axiologically, however, they tend to take a value-neutral stance. Critical rhetorical theories still have a humanistic flavor, but their axiological stance brings values into the research process. Specifically, many of these theorists feel that rhetoric not only does something *for* people, but it can do something *to* them, as it creates and upholds unequal power structures.

Critical theory, as a general approach to the social world (see Chapter 2) is multidisciplinary in focus. As such, we should not be surprised to find that many scholars use critical theory to analyze media texts (See Chapter 17), while others seek to understand the nature of everyday language. This section on critical theory will look at the general characteristics of critical theory as one of the important movements in contemporary rhetorical theory and offer two examples for discussion.

The Origins of Critical Theory: Revised Marxism

The origins and the history of this line of contemporary rhetoric can best define and explain what today is termed critical theory. Only a few decades ago, in the 1940s in England, a prominent professor of English literature, **Raymond Williams,** had an idea to study ordinary people and how they make meaning of their lives. Rather than researching classic literature or other forms of high art that were the typical objects of study in a university, Williams (1973) recognized that the persons who lived outside of London, in the country, lived a different worldview and brought different meanings to their leisure practices and lives in general than the people who lived in London, in the city. He was particularly interested in how technology was used by society and by groups of people in society and, particularly, in the technology and leisure activities of young people. His interest in ordinary leisure activities, or what came to be known as popular culture, became one of the distinguishing characteristics of critical theory.

In order to understand this kind of personal and cultural rhetoric, Williams (1973) privileged the role of class position as an important factor in the meaning process of each individual within a given society, what he called a **social formation.** In contrast to the United States, Europe is much more class oriented and more aware of how socioeconomic level impacts a person's lived experiences and opportunities. Williams, Stuart Hall, and many other critical researchers borrowed from and reworked the basic tenets of **Marxism** to suggest that persons from a lower class, or lower socioeconomic position, process their surroundings and give meanings to their lives in qualitatively different ways than a person from a more privileged, higher socioeconomic level. This appropriation of principles of class position from classical Marxism and reappropriation of class to meaning is termed **cultural Marxism.**

A few more concepts emerge as important to the cultural Marxist position in contemporary rhetorical theory. Looking at class position as a factor impacting personal and social communication and affecting meaning necessarily brings in considerations of *ideology* and *power.* **Ideology** is defined as the worldview of a culture, the fundamental beliefs and myths that most of the members of a culture agree with, sometimes consciously and often unconsciously. For example, dominant ideologies of our culture include our tendency to privilege technological advances as a good thing in society, to believe in the institution of the nuclear family as the ideal family situation, to look at wealthy people as somehow more privileged or better off than others, or to believe that the hardest-working and smartest individuals in a society inherently are the ones who get ahead ("meritocracy").

Further, many critical researchers claim that certain persons, groups of people, or cultural institutions have **power** in society because they are situated in the dominant ideological positions and share in the privileged cultural myths. For example, some might look on the wealthy, or those who own fancy computers or music equipment, or the United States itself with its ability to police countries, as holding positions of cultural power and world power. This does not mean that these individuals or the United States as a world power is better; it implies, rather, that those in the dominant ideological positions tend also to share in the power of the social formation. In other words, cultural Marxism, in its purest sense, would contend that people in the upper, "capitalist" class typically share in the dominant ideology of the culture and share in the power. Conversely, those persons in the lower classes do not—usually—share the ideas of the dominant ideology or share in the power.

From its origins as cultural Marxism, critical theory has experienced the influence of many theoretical positions throughout its development, in the United States and abroad. Throughout its growth, critical theory is distinguished because it has continually brought other theoretical positions and models of meaning into the critical perspective. Theories such as British cultural studies, feminist scholarship, semiotics and structuralism, subculture theory, the power theories of Foucault, and psychoanalytic criticism are just some of the most well-known critical theories that have become the corpus of critical theory. Many of these are used most frequently in media studies and will be covered in Chapter 17. Consistent with the multidisciplinary focus of critical theory and cultural studies, however, all critical theories are, in fact, used for both mediated and face-to-face communication. For our purposes, we will examine the work of two theorists, Michel Foucault and Jürgen Habermas.

Foucault, Rhetoric, and Power

Michel Foucault (1926–1984) was born in Poitiers, France, and educated in Paris. Foucault worked for several years in psychiatric hospitals and even taught psychopathology. In his dissertation, *Madness and Civilization,* Foucault (1965) argues that the source of madness is not within the individual, but in the ways in which societies define madness. In many ways, this work typifies Foucault's approach to rhetoric in that it highlights the power of discourse. Think about this notion: Those who are privileged to define members of society as sane or insane indeed hold a great deal of power! Foucault was interested in the ways that societies use language to create relationships that simultaneously empower and disenfranchise people.

Foucault questions the tendency of Western philosophy to think of discourse as the conveyer of preexisting meaning. Foucault (1965) labels this tendency the **will to truth.** According to Foucault, this tendency is problematic for two reasons. Initially, the will to truth perspective assumes that the speaker is the source of discourse and that the task of the speaker is to bring to life the empty forms of language. In other words, the speaker animates "lifeless" language. This tradition assumes that nature is the source of discourse—that language exists outside of the interaction of humans. Thus, disciplines and societal institutions that operate from this tradition work to reinforce the notion that the rules of discourse are secondary to the expression of thought (Foucault, 1970). Ultimately, the "will to truth" advocates assume that discourse facilitates the exchange of knowledge but does not create it. In short, Foucault *critiques this notion that language use is neutral*—that we merely use language to communicate ideas to each other.

In one of his most famous works, *The Archaeology of Knowledge,* Foucault (1972) critiques the will to truth and examines **discourse** as an event. Foucault argues that meaning and knowledge are a function of discourse. Specifically, Foucault claims that discourse is not simply a vehicle for the transmission of meaning. Instead, it is through the act of discourse—through our communication with others—that we come to an understanding of meaning. Foucault claims that discourse should be viewed as a form of action rather than a reflection of the world.

At this point you may find yourself questioning Foucault's theory of discourse. If meaning does not reside in language, where can it be found? Fortunately, Foucault's theory describes the relationship between language and knowledge, the ways that statements come to have truth, and the uses of discourse to exercise power. Foucault (1972) argues that when we communicate with others, we seek to define and label objects of our communication, and it is through this process that we exercise power. For Foucault, knowledge and meaning reside in the act of communicating with others—not within the object itself.

Foucault analyzes nineteenth-century psychotherapy to explicate his theory of discourse. Foucault claims that mental illness is actually created by the ways we talk about certain behaviors, so that different societies may actually have different ways to be mentally ill (Brummett, 2000). His analysis is couched in three discursive characteristics that contribute to the creation of objects. First, he discusses **surfaces of emergence,** or the contexts of illness. Foucault claims that, in the nineteenth century, mental illness was largely a function of the contexts of family and religion. He advances the argument that mental illness emerged on such surfaces as sexuality. For example, individuals who deviated from established familial and religious sexual norms were likely labeled demented. Second, Foucault describes **authorities of delimitation,** or those individuals who get to say what is mental illness and what is not. In the nineteenth century, medical authorities were afforded this power. Third, Foucault examines **grids of specification,** or types and categories of illness. Interestingly, some illnesses today such as Attention Deficit Disorder (ADD) did not "exist" in the nineteenth century just as some of that era's illnesses, such as hysteria, are not considered "real" diseases today.

The idea of **discursive formations** is central to Foucault's position. Discursive formations are ways of speaking and writing. These formations limit what people can talk about (e.g., who is qualified to diagnose mental illness); they are established by social institutions (e.g., the institution of psychology); and they generate discourse (e.g., the language of psychotherapy). According to Foucault, power flows from these formations—they define both the role and the authority of the speaker. In essence, Foucault is asking us to think critically about several questions as we analyze discourse about knowledge. This can be medical knowledge, the production of communication theory and research, legal opinion, or any other branch of knowledge, including the way you are studying and learning in this course. [Web site: An Extended Foucault Example]

Although Foucault's theories can be difficult to understand, he has contributed significantly to our understanding of the content of communication as power. Foucault's work has served as a foundation for other rhetorical scholars who seek to explain the ways whole societies can be sites where power is created and communicated. Such an understanding of communication is necessary to unmask power imbalances and oppression in society. Importantly, this critique can be applied to any context of communication. The discursive formations mentioned in this chapter can be uncovered in interpersonal, classroom, organizational, public relations, and mass contexts of interaction. Ultimately, Foucault forces us to come to the realization that we all participate in perpetuating the ways that power is organized in our schools, families, business, and nations by the ways that we create and use discourse (Brummett, 2000).

Habermas's Theory of Communicative Action

Likewise, the German philosopher-sociologist Jürgen Habermas has redefined critical theory over the last 30 years. Although his early work sought to explain human action by examining a theory of human interests (Habermas, 1971), his **theory of communicative action** is grounded in language and dialogue. According to this theory, humans act in the world in a strategic or communicative way. In strategic action, people attempt to influence the objective world. In communicative action, humans attempt to come to an understanding with others about something in the objective, social, or subjective world that will allow them to meaningfully coordinate action with others. It is through language that such coordination occurs.

Habermas's theory is built on the foundations established by other scholars such as G. H. Mead's (1934) symbolic interactionism, Austin's (1962) theory of speech acts, Wittgenstein's (1953) language games, and Gadamer's (1975) hermeneutics. In essence, Habermas's theory is grounded in the following two claims: (1) Humans require language in order to pursue goals and to coordinate actions with others, and (2) speech is a form of social action. Importantly, language allows for the creation of a common **lifeworld,** or the shared resources for interpreting objective, social, and subjective worlds (Habermas, 1984).

Habermas argues that language is important because it enables people to acquire and sustain their identities by being initiated in particular traditions that allow them to coordinate social actions, either by pursuing their chosen ends *(strategic orientation)* or by common agreement *(communicative orientation)*. Also, it is through language that people attempt to come to an understanding with one another by making validity claims to truth, rightness, and truthfulness:

according to whether the speaker refers to something in the objective world (as the totality of existing states of affairs), to something in the shared social world (as the totality of the legitimately regulated interpersonal relationships of a social group), or to something in his own subjective world (as the totality of experiences to which one has privileged access) (Habermas, 1990, p. 58).

Discourse about validity claims also forms the basis for Habermas' conception of reason. Habermas (1984) claims that coming to understanding is the inherent reason for human speech. For Habermas then, reason and language are inextricably intertwined. Importantly, he points out that what counts as reason in a particular society varies. Therefore, Habermas's **communication rationality** is grounded universally, but is determined in specific historical and social contexts. In essence, people work out what counts as reason by agreeing to redeem the validity claims they make to truth, rightness, and truthfulness.

Habermas does not focus exclusively on the process of achieving understanding. Indeed, modern societies involve systems and organizations that must coordinate action. This is accomplished through **strategic action.** As we have already noted, communicative action involves actors attempting to understand one another. In strategic action, actors attempt to influence their environment to achieve a desired end.

According to Habermas, the controlling medium for economic and administrative systems is not language (as Foucault might suggest) but money and administrative power. When acting strategically, Habermas contends, we do not treat others as dialogical partners but as assets or barriers to achieving our ends. Applied to the classroom, your teachers act strategically in developing and managing their classrooms and you act strategically in pursuing better grades.

For Habermas, many of the problems of modern society are related to the fact that money and administrative power too often "replace language as the mechanism for coordinating action. They set social action loose from integration through value consensus and switch it over to purposive rationality steered by media" (1984, p. 342). Habermas also points out that this change is often done behind the backs of those affected; that is, we are often unaware of the effects of the steering media. Fortunately, Habermas does offer suggestions, namely in the form of *discourse ethics,* for combating these problems.

Habermas argues that communicative rationality requires a theory of argumentation or discourse. When people debate their assumptions, Habermas (1984) claims that the unforced strength of the better argument should prevail and that such interactions should be free of coercion, manipulation, or any other barriers to rational discussion. For Habermas, discourse presumes *"ideal" speech situations* in which conditions of symmetry and reciprocity rule, including that all people who wish to may initiate and engage in dialogue. Habermas's idea of **communicative orientation** essentially boils down to this tenet: All people should be able to raise, question, and pursue any assertion and they should not repress others in the process.

In evaluating Habermas's assertions, you may find yourself questioning the feasibility of the so-called ideal speech situation. Is it really possible that we could interact with others in such a way as never to repress another's perspective? Can the ideal speech situation ever exist? Is it desirable in all occasions, such as a parent-child or supervisor-subordinate relationship? You can probably think of discussions with your mom and dad where not everyone in the situation was afforded the opportunity to speak! Habermas's answer to this critique is that we should strive for the ideal situation—in the workplace, in the classroom, in our relationships—even if we cannot always achieve it.

Summary

Like critical theories, the American contemporary rhetorical theories reviewed in this chapter also may be used to understand a variety of contexts. Rhetorical genres help us understand recurrent rhetorical situations. Several critical methods derived from Kenneth Burke's theory of logology have been used to understand the rhetorical dimensions of public relations activity, interpersonal and organizational communication, and mass media messages. Bormann's symbolic convergence theory and its methodological counterpart, fantasy theme analysis, have been applied to a wide range of cultural phenomena, from the rhetorical visions of the Puritan colonists to the fantasy themes found in romance novels. Fisher's writings on the narrative paradigm have inspired several communication scholars to apply principles of stories and storytelling to several contexts, including political conventions. Finally, critical rhetorical theories such as those by Foucault and Habermas show how, in addition to creating meaning, language also works to maintain and undermine the exercise of power.

Rhetoric is not the use of questionable communication practices, but the proper study of how human beings use communication to define situations, and to identify with other people through symbols and stories. The theories in this chapter can help understand your group meetings, conversations with your boss, or the interaction you have with your communication theories instructor after your test on this chapter. Rhetoric, you see, is everywhere. We hope that with the theories we have presented here, you be able to recognize how rhetoric shapes the social realities in which you take part and influences the power structures that surround you. More than that, the theories should allow you to become a more active choice maker and more ethical communicator as you realize the power of words and language in your own life.

Discussion Questions

1. Think of an organization that you belong to, and imagine that you have been asked to present an award to a fellow member during an end-of-the-year banquet. Use the assumptions of genre theory to discuss how you would develop a message that would satisfy the expectations of the audience.

2. How are the theories of Kenneth Burke and Ernest Bormann similar? How are they different?

3. What role do values play in Fisher's narrative paradigm and the critical theories of Foucault and Habermas (e.g., what is the axiological stance of each of these theories)?

4. Think of a popular current film and explain its appeal to audiences, using any of the symbolic interactionist theories.

5. Think of a situation you have been a part of, and apply the theories of Foucault or Habermas to understand your actions and those of the other people involved.

References

Austin, J. L. (1962). *How to do things with words*. Oxford: Oxford University Press.

Bales, R. F. (1950). *Interaction process analysis*. Reading, MA: Addison-Wesley.

Benoit, W. L. (1995). *Accounts, excuses, and apologies: A theory of image restoration strategies*. Albany: State University of New York Press.

Bormann, E. (1990). *Small group communication theory and practice* (3rd ed). New York: Harper and Row.

Brummett, B. (2000). *Reading rhetorical theory*. Fort Worth, TX: Harcourt College.

Burke, K. (1961). *The rhetoric of religion: Studies in logology*. Berkeley: University of California Press.

Burke, K. (1966). *Language as symbolic action: Essays on life, literature and method*. Berkeley: University of California Press.

Burke, K. (1969). *A grammar of motives*. Berkeley: University of California Press (Original work published 1945).

Burke, K. (1973). The rhetorical situation. In L. Thayer (Ed.), *Communication: Ethical and moral issues* (pp. 263–275). New York: Gordon and Breach.

Burke, K. (1984). *Permanence and change: An anatomy of purpose*. Berkeley: University of California Press (Original work published 1935).

Bush, G. (1991, January 16). Address to the nation announcing allied military action in the Persian Gulf. *Weekly Compilation of Presidential Documents, 27*, 50–52.

Bush, G. W. (2001, September 11). Statement by the President in his address to the nation [speech transcript]. Available online at http://www.whitehouse.gov/news/releases/2001/09/20010911-16.html.

Campbell, K. K., & Jamieson, K. H. (Eds.). (1978). *Form and genre: Shaping rhetorical action*. Falls Church, VA: Speech Communication Association.

Campbell, K. K., & Jamieson, K. H. (1990). *Deeds done in words: Presidential rhetoric and genres of governance*. Chicago: University of Chicago Press.

Cragan, J., & Shields, D. (1998). *Understanding communication theory*. Needham Heights, MA: Simon and Schuster.

Fisher, W. R. (1984). Narration as a human communication paradigm: The case of public moral argument. *Communication Monographs, 51*, 347–367.

Fisher, W. R. (1985a). The narrative paradigm: An elaboration. *Communication Monographs, 52*, 347–367.

Fisher, W. R. (1985b). The narrative paradigm: In the beginning. *Journal of Communication, 54*, 74–89.

Fisher, W. R. (1987). *Human communication as narration: Toward a philosophy of reason, value, and action*. Columbia: University of South Carolina Press.

Ford, L. A. (1989). "Fetching good out of evil": A Bormannean fantasy theme analysis of the "Big Book" of Alcoholics Anonymous. *Communication Quarterly, 37*, 1–15.

Foucault, M. (1965). *Madness and civilization: A history of insanity in the age of reason* (R. Howard, Trans.). New York: Pantheon Books.

Foucault, M. (1970). *The order of things: An archaeology of the human sciences*. New York: Pantheon Books.

Foucault, M. (1972). *Archaeology of knowledge*. (A. M. S. Smith, Trans.). New York: Routledge.

Gadamer, H. (1975). *Truth and method*. New York: Seabury.

Habermas, J. (1971). *Knowledge and human interests*. (Trans. J. Shapiro). Boston: Beacon.

Habermas, J. (1984). *The theory of communicative action: Vol. I, Reason and the rationalization of society*. (Trans. T. McCarthy). Boston: Beacon.

Habermas, J. (1990). *Moral consciousness and communicative action*. (Trans. C. Lenhardt & S. W. Nicholson). Cambridge, MA: MIT Press.

Hart, R. P. (1977). *The political pulpit*. West Lafayette, IN: Purdue University Press.

Mead, G. H. (1984). *Mind, self and society from the standpoint of a social behaviorist*. Chicago: University of Chicago Press.

Medhurst, M. J. (1996). *Beyond the rhetorical presidency*. College Station: Texas A & M University Press.

Williams, R. (1973). *The country and the city*. London, Eng.: Chatto and Windus.

Windt, T. O., Jr. (1972). The diatribe: Last resort for protest. *Quarterly Journal of Speech, 58*, 1–14.

Wittgenstein, L. (1953). *Philosophical investigations*. Oxford: Basil Blackwell.

7

Theories of Interpersonal Communication

Jodi Hallsten

You have seen in the last two chapters how speech communication theory has been used to address practical questions of how we persuade people through public speeches and other forms of interpersonal communication. As we saw in the history of speech communication chapter (Chapter 4), the communication discipline soon adopted from other disciplines a focus on communication in a wide variety of face-to-face contexts, such as everyday conversation. Writers developed theories to look at how we make sense of others' messages and how we use messages to create meaning in conversations. Scholars eventually turned their attention specifically to how communication is used to develop and maintain relationships.

With this focus also came a shift in methodology. As noted in Chapter 4, the communication discipline received increasing influence from fields such as social psychology, especially in its study of communication in human relationships. Thus, as we move from rhetoric to relationship, we see not only a change in the focal point of what the theory is trying to describe, but also in the underlying assumptions. In this chapter, most, but not all, of the theories are scientific in focus. That is, rather than provide frameworks to understand single relationships or interactions, they are seeking to provide the variables that predict outcomes in relationships in general. This chapter considers theories of how we manage our impressions through communication and then turns to the role of communication in the growth and maintenance of relationships.

In this chapter, you will read about the following concepts:

- Theories of meaning
  - Speech act theory
  - Attribution theory
- Politeness theory/Face management

- Theories of relational development
  - Staircase model of relationship development
  - Uncertainty reduction theory
  - Social penetration theory
  - Dialectical perspective
  - Boundary management theory
- The "dark side": Models of rumor and gossip

We probably have all recently watched some romantic movie, such as *Notting Hill* or *Gone With the Wind.* In each of these movies, we can see relationships played out. In one movie, *Sleepless in Seattle,* Sam Baldwin (played by Tom Hanks) is a widowed father in Seattle, Washington. His son, Jonah, calls a talk show and says his dad needs to start dating. The dad gets on the phone and expresses the love he has for his deceased wife. Annie Reed (played by Meg Ryan) is a reporter in Baltimore. Annie hears the talk show and falls in love with Sam, based on his romantic devotion to his wife's memory. Along with countless others, she sends a letter to him, which Jonah intercepts. Jonah then tries to persuade his father to go meet Annie, while his father, instead, begins dating a local woman, his first relationship since losing his wife. Jonah does not like the woman his father brings home and continues to urge Sam to meet Annie, whom the son finds to be a much more likely candidate for wife and mom.

Within this one movie, we can see a variety of types of symbolic exchange—similar to the ways we communicate every day. We have communication and miscommunication. We meet potential dates (or teachers, or friends) and try to make them think we have certain characteristics. We engage in conflict, persuasion, and relational development. These, along with many other areas, make up the area of human communication known as **interpersonal communication.** Space does not allow us to explore all of these areas or the incredible breadth of interpersonal theory that is developing in the communication field. [Web site: How Can I Make Sense of What She Said? Speech Act and Attribution Theory] However, in this chapter I will discuss some theories of impression management and theories of relational growth. Later chapters in this book will also look at small group communication (Chapter 8), theories of persuasion (Chapter 9), and intercultural (Chapter 10) and organizational communication (Chapter 20), each of which relies on theories of interpersonal communication.

How Can I Look Good to Others?

As we go out on a date, participate in a job interview, or conduct training in an organization, at least in the back of our minds, we are concerned about how we look to others. **Identity management** theories seek to explain this phenomenon, focusing on how we manage our identities in such social contexts.

Some of the most popular theories on this topic have been in the general area of facework and face management. The catalyst for research and theory in this area was work by

Erving Goffman in the 1950s and 1960s, when he sought to explain some aspects of the interaction and experiences that people have in their personal relationships as we manage our identities in contexts with others.

The foundational assumption of **face management** is that face is central to the co-ordinated and continued flow of interaction. **Face** is defined as our public self-image, or the image of ourselves that we portray during interaction; our image can be lost, maintained, or enhanced during any given interaction. Goffman believed that the fundamental organizing principle of social interaction is the alignment of face (Metts & Groskoph, 2002). Thus, while **facework**—the supporting and maintaining of our own and the other's publicly presented self-image—may not be the objective of a conversation, according to Goffman, maintaining face is an underlying motive in all interactions.

Because face can be threatened during an interaction, people use facework to counteract face threats. We engage in *preventative facework* when we try to avoid face loss. When we have lost face, we engage in *corrective facework* to restore it. Preventive facework may involve changing the topic of the conversation to avoid a face-threatening situation or the use of a disclaimer to save face as one enters a potentially face-threatening situation ("This may be a dumb question, but . . . "). Corrective facework can be either defensively or protectively offered. It can take the form of an apology, a joke to make light of another person's transgression and to reduce their subsequent embarrassment, or as an excuse for the transgression. Goffman (1967) contends that as a rule people are supportive and cooperative of each other's face maintenance and of others' attempts to restore face. Sometimes, however, people engage in facework that deliberately attempts to protect or restore their own face at the expense of another person's face. This aggressive facework is often characterized by one-upmanship or the refusal to accept an apology (Metts, 1997).

In summary, face management theory explains one way that we maintain our identities. It explains how we are concerned both with our own face and the face of others. As mentioned before, face management theory has generated a great deal of research. We will find the assumptions of this theory extended into the area of intercultural communication in Chapter 10.

Politeness theory extends Goffman's theory of face. Brown and Levinson (1987) explain, "We believe that ways of putting things are the very stuff that social relationships are made of." They argue that by understanding the principles of language use we can understand "the dimensions by which individuals manage to relate to others" (p. 55). Thus, their theory deals with politeness in interactions as it applies to facework. According to Brown and Levinson (1987), we all have two types of face needs: positive and negative face need. **Positive face need** refers to the desire to be valued and included by others whom we care about, as well as the desire to appear competent. We want to be appreciated and respected by others. **Negative face need** refers to our desire to be free from imposition, constraint, or intrusion. Our positive face is supported when people include us in activities or discussions, communicate concern for us, communicate appreciation for us, and communicate validation of our ideas. Our negative face is supported when people avoid imposing on us, communicate their support for our desired actions, and do not get in the way of our achieving them. They explain that **face-threatening acts (FTAs)** occur when, in an interaction, we fail to meet positive or negative face needs and thereby threaten either our own face or the face of the other. Politeness theory concerns itself primarily with the function of preventive facework.

Metts and Groskoph (2002) review four assumptions that guide politeness theory. First, threats to both positive and negative face need are a natural, daily occurrence in everyday human interaction. Second, FTAs are complex, and speech acts that threaten face may proceed in a variety of ways: some primarily threaten positive face (e.g., insults, embarrassing acts); some primarily threaten negative face (e.g., hints, requests); some threaten both positive and negative face (e.g., demands, conflict). Some acts threaten a speaker's face; some threaten a hearer's face; some threaten both a hearer's and speaker's face at the same time; and some acts that enhance a speaker's positive face inevitably threaten her or his negative face at the same time. The third assumption of the theory presumes that "any rational agent will seek to avoid face threatening acts, or will employ certain strategies to minimize the threat" (Brown & Levinson, 1978, p. 68). That is, as people consider engaging in avoidance of an FTA, consider: (a) the desire to communicate the content of the FTA (wanting terribly to say what you want to say!), (b) the desire to be efficient or urgent in order to achieve something, and (c) wanting to preserve the face of self or other.

As an application of this theory, imagine you want to borrow a friend's car for the evening. This threatens the other's negative face, so it is a face-threatening act. You want to be efficient in being sure the friend knows you need the car and that you need it for the whole evening. But at the same time, you may want to preserve your own and the other person's face. According to Brown and Levinson (1978), you have several options. You can make your request **bald on record,** or directly: "I would like to borrow your car this weekend." A bald request is one "without redress;" it is in the most direct, clear, unambiguous and concise" request possible (p. 68). At the opposite extreme, you could not make the request at all. In between these two extremes, you might make the request **on record.** To go on record is more direct than going off record, but potential face threats can be softened by the use of politeness. On record, your intention is clear to both parties. But you might use communication to buffer the request. That is, to make up for (redress) a threat to face, speakers often engage in positive or negative politeness strategies.

Positive politeness refers to attempts by speakers to minimize face threat (whether it is positive or negative face threat) by assuring the listener that he or she is liked, appreciated, or valued. It frames the threat in such a way that it meets the other person's face needs (e.g., using "we" rather than "you" and "I," or more direct tactics, "You know I love you, man . . . !"). With **negative politeness,** speakers attempt to minimize the imposition on the listener's face (either positive or negative) by minimizing imposition on the other's autonomy ("I know you're really busy right now, and I'll understand if you can't help, but . . . "). This usually involves self-effacement on the actor's part or some other angle that allows the other person an "out" (Metts & Groskoph, 2002). Finally, you might make the request **off record.** Doing an FTA *off record* is stating it in such a way that it is questionable as to whether you intended to commit an FTA and relies heavily on hinting or innuendo. Figure 7.1 illustrates the various strategies.

The final assumption of politeness theory is that whether a FTA is considered to be severe involves consideration of three factors: the *social distance* between the individuals (including status, familiarity, and so on), the *relative power* of the speaker relative to the receiver of the FTA, and the *absolute ranking* of the face threat (how much of a threat the FTA really poses to the individual). According to Metts (1997), "As the severity of a threat increases, the degree of politeness should increase" (p. 387).

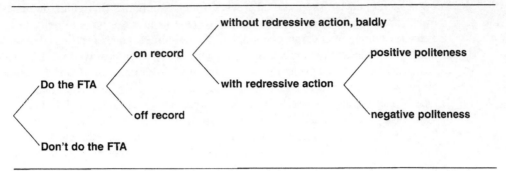

FIGURE 7.1   *Strategies for Redressing Face-Threatening Acts.*

Based on P. Brown, P., S. Levinson (1987), *Politeness: Some universals in language usage.* Cambridge: Cambridge University Press.

In conclusion, one way that people manage their identities is to manage their face. Goffman (1959) originally explained how people engage in facework in their everyday interactions. Brown and Levinson (1978) extended that notion, illustrating the ways people engage in negative and positive politeness as they manage face-threatening acts. These theories are some of the most widely known in the area of interpersonal communication, making them some of the most significant contributions to our field.

How Can I Have Better Relationships?

Though identity management and persuasion consume a large part of our daily communication with others, the core of our communication with others involves our relationships with them. How do relationships develop? The following theories examine some of the communication processes of relationship development, maintenance, and deterioration. Though many theories exist in this area, we will explore only four of the most popular theories. Although I will apply these directly to romantic relationships, we experience uncertainty, self-disclosure, or dialectical needs in work relationships, friendships, and family relationships as well. First, however, it would be good to have a basic idea of how relationships form.

Several writers have explained how relationships grow, plateau, and sometimes break up. One well-known model of relationships is Mark Knapp and Anita Vangelisti's (1996) **staircase model of interaction stages** (see Figure 7.2). These authors suggest that at each stage of the relationship, people—whether they are friends or romantic partners—tend to engage in certain types of information (though some behaviors occur at several of the stages). The first five stages describe the growth of a relationship, and the last five its dissolution. Often, a couple may stay at one stage for a while in a period of "stability" at a single stage.

We can understand these as we apply them to a hypothetical couple, Takisha and Leon. In the **initiating stage,** they meet and draw first impressions of each other. As they move to the **experimenting stage,** they seek information about each other. At the **intensifying stage,** they may adopt nicknames, speak more in terms of "we," develop private symbols or slang, and may show more commitment, such as through limited physical intimacy.

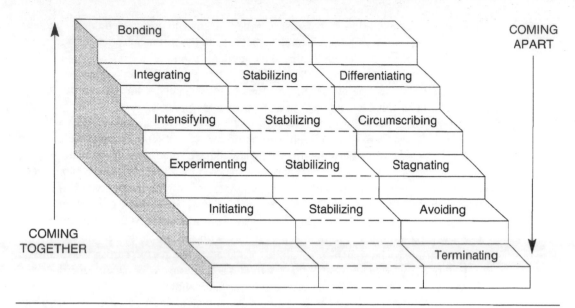

FIGURE 7.2 *Knapp and Vangelisti's Staircase Model of Relational Development.*

From M. L. Knapp & A. L. Vangelisti (1996). *Interpersonal communication and human relationships* (3rd ed.). Boston: Allyn and Bacon, p. 54. Reprinted with permission.

From there, they move to the **integrating stage.** Here, the couple becomes "one," perhaps through finding a common song or joint interests, or perhaps through increased physical intimacy. They may share tokens of commitment (such as a ring.). Finally, at the **bonding stage,** Leon and Takisha may engage in some ritual that announces their commitment to each other to the world or they may form a sort of contract with each other, like marriage. Some call this the "coupling" stage.

Many relationships back out of commitment much as they have moved into it. The first stage down the ladder of relationship is **differentiating.** If Takisha and Leon move to this stage, they may talk less about their joint interests and focus more on "my friends" or "my money." One of the more obvious forms of differentiating is conflict. Next, Leon and Takisha may **circumscribe** or constrict their relationship by controlling the type or content of discussion. They may stop talking about finances or deep feelings; and they may find more periods of "mutual silence, empty gazes, and a general feeling of exhaustion" (Knapp & Vangelisti, 1996, p. 42). At the **stagnating stage,** communication for Takisha and Leon may come to a standstill. They may imagine dialogues that they will have with the other in which they defend themselves, "I know she'll say this . . . but then *I'll* say . . ."). They may move to the **avoiding stage,** in which they may find themselves "too busy" to meet with the other. They may not dislike the other person, but just don't want to spend the energy that the relationship requires. Finally, they may end the relationship (**terminating stage**) in such a way that creates some sort of psychological distance between them and in which each "dissociates" self from the other by imagining a life alone.

Uncertainty reduction theory (URT) explains the initial communication between strangers as it may or may not lead to a relationship. URT asserts that in initial encounters with strangers and in developed relationships when partners do unexpected things, we seek to decrease uncertainty and unpredictability because both are uncomfortable. We reduce this uncertainty and unpredictability through communication.

The theory was developed in 1975 by Charles Berger and Richard Calabrese (Berger & Calabrese, 1975) as one of the first theories to look deeply at actual communication within relationships; it has continued to evolve since then (Berger, 1987, 1995; Berger & Bradac, 1982). The theory assumes that when we first meet someone we are filled with **uncertainty** about that person, which refers to our ability to explain or predict the person's behavior. As you walk into class the first day, you will have some level of uncertainty about most of the people there. But you cannot reduce uncertainty about everyone. So the theory predicts that if we (1) think we will have ongoing interaction with the person, (2) think the person might be able to give us rewards or punishments, or (3) think the person acts in some deviant way, we will be motivated to do something about it. Thus, we could predict that you will be more likely to reduce uncertainty with the people seated closest to you, with the instructor who assigns your grade (or the attractive person across the room you may want to date), or the guy in the back with the aquamarine, cone-shaped hairdo.

Once you have decided to reduce your uncertainty about your classmates or instructor, Berger (1995) explained three basic strategies that we might use to reduce uncertainty and acquire information about someone. One option is a **passive strategy** in which you would simply observe the person from afar. You may want to do this in a situation that is not highly scripted (i.e., is more informal). Thus, you could better reduce uncertainty observing a classmate with friends in the cafeteria than seated during a lecture. Another option you might choose is an **active strategy,** whereby you manipulate the environment (rearrange the chairs to see how the person acts) or actively seek information about the person whom we are curious about (check the professor's web site or talk to prior students). Finally, an **interactive strategy** involves our engaging in direct, face-to-face interaction with the person to acquire information about him or her. The theory proposes that as you get to know others better (can better predict or explain their behavior), your relationships will grow (Berger & Calabrese, 1975).

The authors spend most of their time developing the notion of the interactive strategies, proposing a series of seven **axioms,** or statements about the relationships between variables, that predict the relationships between uncertainty and (1) verbal communication, (2) nonverbal behaviors that show warmth, (3) behaviors that seek information (such as questions), (4) depth or intimacy of communication content, (5) reciprocity, or mutual exchange of information, (6) perceived similarities, and (7) liking. According to the theory, when we talk with someone, show nonverbal warmth, or perceive similarities with another, these will reduce our uncertainty. Reduced uncertainty will lead to more communication and nonverbal warmth, as well as liking. However, higher uncertainty is said to lead us to seek information through questions and reciprocating information.

Social penetration theory (SPT), another theory of relational development, is based on the idea that we try to minimize our costs and maximize our rewards in relationships. This notion is spelled out in more detail in social exchange theory. [Web site: Social Exchange Theory]. SPT, one of the most widely identified theories of relational development, suggests that self-disclosure is what drives relationships closer. However, before we self-disclose to a stranger—or even to our best friend—the theory suggests we mentally weigh over the threat of vulnerability and the discomfort of sharing (and other costs) with the rewards of companionship and intimacy (and other rewards) (see Figure 7.3).

Theorists Irwin Altman and Dalmas Taylor (1973) explain that just like onions have layers of skin, people have layers of personality that are "penetrated" as they self-disclose. The outermost layers of our personalities are identified as more superficial, while the innermost layers are highly personal. As we penetrate through these layers, through the use of self-disclosure, our self-disclosure can vary in terms of both depth and breadth. **Depth** refers to the degree of intimacy involved in the disclosure, while **breadth** refers to the number of topic areas disclosed. In the early stages of a relationship, disclosures frequently have low breadth and depth, but as the relationship progresses, the depth and breadth of the disclosures will increase. We can imagine the process occurring between two people—Kristine and Thad—as they meet at a party. As they meet, they engage in small talk on a limited number of areas. Each makes a decision, perhaps subconsciously, to share more. They might talk about many things (breadth), but without much intimacy (depth)—or they might get involved in a deep conversation on a single topic. The theorists say that both depth and breadth are needed for real relational growth.

As relationships develop, communication moves from the outer to the inner layers of personality through self-disclosure in four stages. Kristine and Thad begin, in the **orientation phase,** to discuss superficial information, such as their basic demographic information and their preferences in music. After time they begin disclosing more personal information, such as their social attitudes and political views. These types of disclosures mark the **exploratory affective exchange phase,** where individuals begin to get a clearer idea of the each other's personality (specifically, they "explore" how each other feels—her or his *affective* orientation—about things). As Kristine and Thad's disclosure becomes more intimate, so does their relationship. Social penetration theory would predict that next they would enter the **[full] affective exchange phase,** where their disclosures become more personal and include such things as their hopes and fears, goals, and spiritual beliefs. In this stage the two might use nicknames for each other and their communication would indicate a stable level of closeness and commitment to one another. Usually only close friendship and intimate partners reach this stage. Finally, disclosure of one's core personality usually only occurs in the **stable exchange phase.** In Kristine and Thad's relationship,

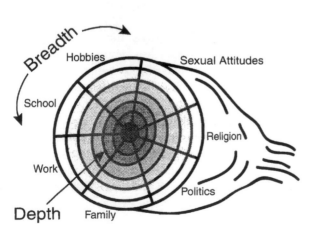

FIGURE 7.3 *A Visual Representation of Social Penetration Theory's Aspects of Self-Disclosure: The Onion Model.* The wedges represent the number of topics discussed (breadth). Any topic can be discussed with varying levels for intimacy (depth).

Illustration by Dylan Simonds.

communication in this stage would be highly intimate and predictable. Altman and Taylor assert that very few people will reach this level of self-disclosure, and very few of our relationships will reach this stage in our lifetimes.

It is important to note first that any given topic can vary in depth. Although some topics (hobbies) tend to be more shallow, and others (religious convictions) more deep, Thad might share only superficially that he is Catholic, and Kristine might go into great detail about why she is so interested in rock climbing. What transports a relationship from one phase to the next is an increase in both *depth* and *breadth* of self-disclosure; and at each stage, the analysis of *costs* and *rewards* is present, as Kristine and Thad ponder issues of trust, vulnerability, and the chance for increased relational intimacy. They can also, the theory suggests, **depenetrate** at any level by reducing either the number of topics of self-disclosure or the level of depth of their self-disclosure. Practically speaking, if Thad wants the relationship to grow, he may need to be willing to open up on more topics or risk being more open about a given topic. If Kristine starts noticing that they are growing apart, it may be that they have intentionally or unintentionally closed off topics of discussion; reopening them may help maintain the relationship.

In sum, SPT suggests that, although intimate relationships such as friendship and romance can move two steps forward and one step back, relational intimacy tends to be progressive, moving from stage to stage. This explanation differs from that of two of our other scientific theories. First, SPT differs from URT in its placement of self-disclosure in the causal mechanism of how relationships grow. In SPT, it is disclosure itself that drives intimacy. In URT, disclosure, among several other variables, allows us to predict others, but it is the predictability that drives intimacy. In comparison to SET, we can see that SET is about all costs and rewards (including those that are not necessarily communicative). SPT, on the other hand, merely uses the cost/reward analogy to predict when and how we might self-disclose. [Web site: Critiquing the Theories]

Where the first three theories we have examined try to predict the outcomes of relationships scientifically, **relational dialectics theory** explores how close relationships are characterized by ongoing, contradictory tensions and how they are reflected in and by interaction within the relationship. Dialectical theorists Leslie Baxter and Barbara Montgomery were greatly influenced in their work by Russian philosopher Mikhail Bakhtin, who conceptualized relationships as constantly in change and partners in relationships as interdependent (Baxter, 1990, 1993; Baxter & Montgomery, 1996). That is, relationships are not static entities that operate in a vacuum; instead, they are constantly in flux as a result of influences from each partner and from the larger context in which they exist. Furthermore, individuals in relationships exist in context with one another, and when something happens to one member of a relationship, inevitably the other person is also affected. This concept, also known as **totality** (Rawlins, 1992), is a central assumption of the theory. Finally, Bakhtin believed that communication creates relational reality, a central idea in this theory.

Dialectical theory suggests that **dialectics,** or tensions between contradictory impulses, are normal, irresolvable characteristics of relationships. Note that dialectics refers to the *tensions* and not the opposing ideas. The notion behind these tensions is that not only does each person in the relationship not feel them alike, but each individual might feel them in different intensities and at differing intervals in the relationship. Therefore, while one person in the relationship may prefer privacy, at the same time the other person may desire a greater amount of disclosure. This becomes complicated as our desires change, and it is possible that one day we might strongly feel one way, but the next we might not feel the same.

Baxter and Montgomery (1996) have identified three main dialectics that exist in relationships. Each dialectic exists both between the individuals in the relationship (**internal**) and also between the relationship itself and the larger context in which the relationship exists (**external**). **Integration and separation** involves the tension between wanting to be connected and wanting to be separate. The internal form of this dialectic is identified as **connection/autonomy.** In a relationship this is when we experience the desire to be close to or connected to one another, and yet we also desire autonomy or independence. Perhaps there has been a time when you have been in a relationship and you have wanted to spend a lot of time with your partner, yet he or she wants independence and time to spend with friends. This has been identified as the primary dialectic experienced in relationships. The external form of integration/separation is **inclusion/seclusion.** This form of the dialectic involves the tension between wanting seclusion as a couple, or wanting to spend time alone together, and wanting to include others, such as friends, in your time spent together.

Expression/privacy involves the tension between wanting to be open and wanting to be closed in a relationship. The internal form of this dialectic is **openness/closedness.** This is the tension between wanting to self-disclose to your partner yet also wanting to remain private. In early stages of relationships many people struggle with this dialectic as they try to balance the needs of self-disclosure to advance the relationship, but also desire to avoid discussion in fear of disclosing too much information and becoming vulnerable (Baxter, 1990). Additionally, there are individual differences in preferences for openness such that sometimes one person will prefer more openness in a relationship while the other person is not comfortable with, and therefore does not desire, to self-disclose. **Revelation/ concealment** is the external form of this dialectic and entails tension to reveal our relationship or details of the relationship to the others outside the relationship, yet wanting to conceal the aspects of the relationship from others. For example, while I feel comfortable discussing fairly intimate details about my relationship to my friends, my husband becomes very upset when he learns that I have disclosed certain things about us to others. This dialectic is commonly experienced in extramarital relationships and in relationships where one partner is abusive toward the other partner.

Stability/change is the final dialectic identified by Baxter and Montgomery (1996). This dialectic involves tension between wanting sameness and wanting variety. The internal form of this dialectic is **predictability/novelty.** Uncertainty reduction theory claims that we desire some degree of predictability in our relationships. However, contrary to uncertainty reduction theory, Baxter and Montgomery contend that too much predictability is boring. Although too much predictability causes a relationship to become uninteresting and may lead to relational dissolution, too much spontaneity and surprise may also lead to dissolution. For example, you may feel that finding your boyfriend on the dance floor closely dancing with another woman is too great a surprise for your relationship to handle! The external form of this dialectic is **conventionality/uniqueness.** This involves our desire for our relationships to conform to social norms, yet also wanting our relationship to be unique. When our relationships are exactly like everyone else's we lack a sense of uniqueness that is crucial to intimacy (Baxter, 1993). Figure 7.4 shows the internal and external tensions.

FIGURE 7.4 *Baxter and Montgomery's Relational Dialectics.*

	Integration/ Separation	Expression/ Privacy	Stability/ Change
Internal Form	Connection/ Autonomy	Openness/ Closedness	Predictability/ Novelty
External Form	Inclusion/ Seclusion	Revelation/ Concealment	Conventionality/ Uniqueness

Based on L. A. Baxter & B. M. Montgomery (1996), *Relating: Dialogues and dialectics.* New York: Guilford.

So what is best for us? What is it that works best in our relationships? Do we need stability or do we need change? Do we need autonomy or do we need connection? We would be tempted to say that we need "balance," but that is too simple. The theory suggests that each person needs both aspects of the various tensions, but in different degrees at different times. Today, you may want more independence, but your best friend wants time together with you; tomorrow, your competing needs will change. This leads Baxter to conclude that relationships are messy and unpredictable. The key is in finding useful strategies for managing the tensions. Over time five basic responses to dialectics have been identified. **Selection** involves selecting and satisfying one opposite while disregarding the other. **Alternation** involves alternating between the opposites, choosing to meet the needs of one opposite at a time. **Segmentation** involves the choice to satisfy one need in one relational situation while satisfying the opposite need in a different situation. In this way both needs are met. **Neutralization** involves compromising and finding a balance or "happy medium" between the opposite tensions that somewhat meets the needs of each. **Reframing** involves a "perceptual transformation" where we change the way we perceive the opposites, reframing them in our mind so that they are no longer opposites (Baxter, 1990).

In *Sleepless in Seattle,* it would be easiest to see the tensions between Sam and his son, Jonah. Jonah wants time together. Sam needs time to grieve the loss of his wife, then to begin dating. As he dates, the son could want time just with his dad, but the dad wants to also have time with the woman he's dating. Jonah develops a relationship with a neighbor girl—how much of what they talk about should he tell his father? How much should his father tell Jonah of his own dating experiences in college? Should Sam provide an environment of stability that is totally predictable, or include times of spontaneity? We would expect the latter, but must realize that Jonah's need for spontaneity will change from day to day, and the dad must be alert to cues to his son's specific dialectical needs from day to day.

In summary, in any relationship tensions exist between conflicting needs. Baxter and Montgomery have identified three main dialectics that summarize these needs. Dialectical theory has been regarded in the field as an exciting way to conceptualize relational dynamics.

One of the dialectic tensions, *expression/privacy* has received much attention as a central aspect of relationships, as disclosure is ultimately about the boundaries between partners themselves and between them and surrounding friends, family, and coworkers. Sandra Petronio (2000) examined the dynamics of these boundaries more closely when she arrived at her theory of **communication boundary management (CBM).** CBM provides a unique understanding of the dialectic of revelation/concealment by providing us with a structure to understand it. CBM defines a boundary as "the border around private information" (Petronio, 2000, p. 38). The theory explains that we deal with the tension of revelation/concealment and of private information about ourselves through our use and management of boundary structures.

We establish **boundary structures** as a way to manage private information. Revealing private information involves the risk of vulnerability. We need to control our threat of vulnerability so we control the boundaries that protect our information. Furthermore, we feel as though we *own* our private information, so boundary structures also help us exercise *control* over that which we feel is ours.

Sometimes we share personal information with others, called *co-owning* information, which expands our privacy boundaries. We then share the responsibility for maintaining boundary structures. If our boundaries are *impermeable* (that is, they allow no information to pass through them) we will likely institute sanctions to motivate others to maintain our desired levels of boundary permeability. When boundaries are impermeable the sanctions tend to be stronger, while *permeable* boundary structures (those that allow the passage of information) tend to elicit weaker sanctions.

We manage our boundary structures by a system of management based on rules that we arrive at individually. The theory identifies four concepts that define this management system. First, **boundary rule formation** explains that we formulate boundary rules to control the flow of information to and from others. These rules are developed based on our culture, our self-esteem, our individual characteristics, and even our individual motivations. For example, a norm of my culture may be that I should not share private information with others. In that case I would formulate rigid rules about what information I share with others and with whom I share it. Or, if I have low self-esteem and I feel threatened, I may formulate rules for my self-disclosure that would protect my self-esteem needs. Boundary rule formation is thus a personal process.

We also use **boundary rules** to manage our boundary structures. Often these rules for information sharing will become so ritualized that they will become a matter of common practice for me in my interactions with others (Petronio, 2000). For example, I may never reveal information about my intimate relations with my partner to others, even when I'm in a situation where I feel pressured to do so because others are disclosing similar information about themselves (locker-room talk). I am using my rules to govern my disclosure about my personal information.

There are some people with whom I choose to share personal information about myself. Because I share different information with various other people, I must **coordinate my boundary rules** with others. Co-owning information requires that I coordinate the revelation and concealment of that information. This explains how I develop rules to manage disclosures and build in sanctions to govern the sharing of the personal information. In this way I am coordinating with others my rules for sharing my information. For example, a family may shun another family member who chooses to discuss a family secret outside of the family unit. In this situation it may be the case that the family member who has disclosed personal information had not understood the implicit rules guiding private disclosures; however, sanctions are there to ensure that such disclosures will not occur regularly.

Clearly it is not always easy to manage boundary structures. Boundary management systems can experience **turbulence** from a variety of situations, including when the boundaries are invaded (e.g., someone asks too many questions, someone uncovers our secrets), when there are difficulties with boundary coordination (e.g., we disagree over how much we should be sharing), or when situations call for boundary rule changes (e.g., someone I trusted revealed one of my secrets). When turbulence occurs, we revisit our boundary rules, modifying them either personally or through interaction with others. In sum, CMB allows us to understand how people manage the dialectical tension of revelation and concealment in relationships. It also helps to explain how we develop and act on rules that manage our privacy boundaries.

Is Communication Always Positive in a Relationship?

We have seen in all discussion so far that communication is a primary tool for enhancing relationships, either through clarifying misunderstanding, through developing relationship by reducing uncertainty or self-disclosing, or through negotiating privacy and other tensions with others. However, we would be remiss in our discussion of interpersonal communication theories if we didn't discuss the dark side of communication, a topic receiving much recent attention by communication scholars (see Cupach & Spitzberg, 1994; Spitzberg & Cupach, 1998). Rumor and gossip, which can affect reputations and relationships, are phenomena that relate closely to the theories we've just discussed, as well as to the areas of mass communication and public relations.

Rumors are speculative statements about other people, about organizations, or about events that are spread from person to person. They can be passed on from person to person in the form of interpersonal communication, or they can be circulated electronically through the media or by way of the Internet. Rosnow (1980, 1988, 1991) identifies four conditions that predict rumor generation and transmission. His model explains that when people feel general, widespread *uncertainty* or doubt about other people or events that are ambiguous to them, rumors may be generated as an attempt to explain the unknown. Second, rumors will often generate when the ambiguous people or events are *important and relevant* to people. Third, people must feel *personal anxiety* as a result of their feelings of apprehension. According to Rosnow (2001), "rumors persist because they play on uncertainty and give expression to emotional tensions" (p. 216). Finally, people must *trust* that the rumor is at least somewhat plausible. For example, **wish rumors** are those that include consequences that people will hope to obtain, while **dread rumors** tell about consequences that people fear or dislike. The bottom line is that social conditions for rumor are ripe when people feel uncertain and/or anxious about someone or something about which they know very little. As we learned from URT, uncertainty is an uncomfortable state that motivates us to reduce it. Rumors, then, help us explain ambiguous people or events and thus reduce that uncertainty.

We can see multiple applications of this model. First, Bordia (1996) explains that rumors on the Internet thrive on uncertainty. It seems that the Internet is an extension of face-to-face communication in this situation, as its users seek out information to support or refute a story. Rosnow's (1991) model also has relevance to public relations professionals as it is applied to the **two-step model** of influence (see Chapters 14 and 20). That is, if opinion leaders in a community discuss rumors, the rumors may be disseminated to larger numbers of people and may be perceived as credible because of the source from whence they came. Finally, this relates to the media because the media often acts as a channel for rumor transmission. For example, in 1969 a story began circulating that Paul McCartney of the Beatles had died. This rumor was fueled by reports found in the media both supporting and refuting the claim. More recently, in the terrorist attacks on the World Trade Center in New York, in the earliest reports of the devastation we heard of a (wish) rumor that some people who were on the top floors of the towers rode down the rubble as the building collapsed, surviving the destruction. In our states of high anxiety and uncertainty, we were looking to explain the events by grasping at any possibility that more people survived the attacks than did.

Close to the notion of rumors is **gossip.** As Rosnow (2001) explains:

> Gossip and rumor might be represented by two slightly overlapping circles, with nebulous forms contained in the overlapping area. That is, gossip is always about people and can involve either fact or supposition; rumors, on the other hand, might or might not involve people, but are always speculative (unlike most urban legends, for example, which are generally presented as "facts" attributed to friends of friends). Some items of communication have a flavor of both rumor and gossip. (p. 211)

An important aspect of interpersonal communication, gossip has been identified as having three main functions (Rosnow, 2001). First, gossip imparts knowledge, fulfilling its *informational function.* Second, gossip has an *influence function,* which explains how it is used to control attitudes and actions. Finally, gossip has an *intimacy function.* We can see this function at work in both social exchange and social penetration theory. In social exchange theory it can be considered as either a cost or reward in a relationship. It can be seen as entertaining, and may be reciprocated, or it may be a violation of privacy, and may be punished. As a reward in a relationship it may be traded for status, power, or intimacy. It may even be perceived as a valued commodity in certain relationships, like, for example, between an informant and the press. The intimacy function also can be applied to self-disclosure in social penetration theory. According to the theory, sharing secrets about oneself is reciprocated (self-disclosure in terms of depth), and as intimacy increases the relationship develops. Disclosures such as secrets are self-gossip, and serve to bring the relationship from one level to the next.

Summary

In this chapter, we have seen two main areas of interpersonal theory that may explain how we live our lives and relate to others around us. First, we considered theories about how people manage their identities in interaction, including the management of positive and negative face. Both theories are more scientifically oriented as they seek to predict the outcomes of face threats and management.

Next, we looked at several explanations of how relationships grow, develop, and fade, and the important role that communication can play in relationships, both positively and negatively. Some approaches simply describe the stages of the relationship. Others suggest that a certain force drives the relationship forward—either our ability to predict and explain the other, our self-disclosure, or our consideration of costs and rewards in the relationship. In this case, URT and SPT are similar in that each posits a central "causal mechanism" that will predict if relationships will grow or remain stable. While elements of one theory might appear in another (e.g., cost/reward analysis in SPT, self-disclosure in URT), each has a different core prediction about relationships.

Moving from relational growth and maintenance, we discussed the tensions that are inherent in all relationships. Relational dialectics theory draws from philosophical roots in philosophy, viewing relationships as something people "do" rather than something they are "in." It is a humanistic theory, or more specifically, a sensitizing theory (see Chapter 1), that seeks to describe the incredible complexity of balancing the linkage between self and others. Boundary management theory, on the other hand, not only describes the specific tension of privacy, but also makes predictions about the dynamics of maintaining privacy, and thus is more squarely scientific.

In conclusion, interpersonal communication theory has made an important contribution to the field of communication. Many people find it to be highly interesting, important, and relevant to everyday life. Although there are no definitive answers to our burning questions about communication in face-to-face situations, clearly there exists a body of theory that explains a great deal of it, providing us with insights that help us understand more clearly what goes on in our daily interactions and why, and piques our curiosity to inquire even further into the area of interpersonal communication.

Discussion Questions _____

1. Think of the last time you presented someone with a big request. Based on Brown and Levinson's taxonomy of politeness (Figure 7.1), what type of request was it? Would another type of request have been more effective? Explain your answer.

2. Discuss your relationship with your best friend in terms of relational dialectics theory. In what ways do you and your friend experience some of the tensions? Have you found yourself using any of the strategies listed for managing the tensions—or other strategies—and if so, how well did your attempts work?

3. Recall a time when you have been the target of rumors or gossip. How might these influence the development of a friendship or romantic relationship (whether the gossip is spread by the person you have the relationship with or the two of you are the target of a third party's gossip)? How might you integrate rumor/gossip into one of the relationship development theories?

References _____

Altman, I., & Taylor, D. A. (1973). *Social penetration: The development of interpersonal relationships.* New York: Holt, Rinehart, & Winston.

Baxter, L. A. (1990). Dialectical contradictions in relationship development. *Journal of Social and Personal Relationships, 7,* 69–88.

Baxter, L. A. (1993). The social side of personal relationships: A dialectical perspective. In S. Duck (Ed.), *Understanding relationship processes, 3: Social context and relationships* (pp. 139–165). Newbury Park, CA: Sage.

Baxter, L. A., & Montgomery, B. M. (1996). *Relating: Dialogues and dialectics.* New York: Guilford.

Berger, C. R. (1987). Communicating under uncertainty. In M. E. Roloff & G. R. Miller (Eds.), *Interpersonal processes: New directions in communication research* (pp. 39–62). Beverly Hills, CA: Sage.

Berger, C. R. (1995). A plan-based approach to strategic communication. In D. E. Hewes (Ed.), *The cognitive bases of interpersonal communication* (pp. 141–179). Hillsdale, NJ: Lawrence Erlbaum.

Berger, C. R. & Bradac, J. J. (1982). *Language and social knowledge: Uncertainty in interpersonal relations.* London: E. Arnold.

Berger, C. R., & Calabrese, R. J. (1975). Some explorations in initial interaction and beyond: Toward a developmental theory of interpersonal communication. *Human Communication Research, 1,* 99–112.

Bordia, P. (1996). Studying verbal interaction on the internet: The case of rumor transmission research. *Behavior research methods, instruments, and computers, 28,* 149–151.

Brown, P., & Levinson, S. (1978). Universals in language usage: Politeness phenomena. In E. Goody (Ed.), *Questions and politeness* (pp. 56–323). Cambridge: Cambridge University Press.

Brown, P., & Levinson, S. (1987). *Politeness: Some universals in language usage.* Cambridge: Cambridge University Press.

Cupach, W. R., & Spitzberg, B. H. (Eds.). (1994). *The dark side of interpersonal communication.* Hillsdale, NJ: Lawrence Erlbaum.

Goffman, E. (1959). *The presentation of self in everyday life.* Garden City, NY: Doubleday.

Goffman, E. (1967). Interaction ritual: Essays in face-to-face behavior. Chicago: Aldine.

Knapp, M. L., & Vangelisti, A. L. (1996). *Interpersonal communication and human relationships* (3rd ed.). Boston: Allyn and Bacon.

Littlejohn, S. W. (2002). *Theories of human communication* (7th ed.). Belmont, CA: Wadsworth.

Metts, S. (1997). Face and facework: Implications for the study of personal relationships. In S. Duck (Ed.), *Handbook of personal relationships* (pp. 373–390). London: Guilford Press.

Metts, S., & Grohskopf, E. (2002). Impression management: Goals, strategies, and skills. In J. Greene, & B. R. Burleson (Eds.), *Handbook of communication skills* (pp. 357–399). Orlando, FL: Academic Press.

Petronio, S. (2000). The boundaries of privacy: Praxis of everyday life. In S. Petronio (Ed.), *Balancing the secrets of private disclosures* (pp. 37–49). Mahwah, NJ: Lawrence Erlbaum.

Rawlins, W. K. (1992). *Friendship matters: Communication, dialectics, and the life course.* New York: Aldine de Gruyter.

Rosnow, R. L. (1980). Psychology of rumor considered. *Psychological Bulletin, 87,* 578–591.

Rosnow, R. L. (1988). Rumor as communication: A contextualist approach. *Journal of Communication, 38,* 12–28.

Rosnow, R. L. (1991). Inside rumor: A personal journey. *American Psychologist, 46,* 484–496.

Rosnow, R. L. (2001). Rumor and gossip in interpersonal interaction and beyond: A social exchange perspective. In R. Kowalski (Ed.), *Behaving badly: Aversive behavior in interpersonal relationships.* (pp. 203–232). Washington, DC: American Psychological Association.

Spitzberg, B. H., & Cupach, W. R. (1998). *The dark side of close relationships.* Mahwah, NJ: Lawrence Erlbaum.

8

Theories of Small Group Communication

Sean Limon

In the last chapter, we examined the kind of communication known as interpersonal communication. We now turn our attention to small group communication. Research on small groups constitutes one of the earliest areas of research done by social scientists in psychology and sociology on communication processes (see Chapter 4).

Small group communication involves many of the aspects of interpersonal communication, such as face management, relational development, negotiation of power, persuasion and conflict management, to name a few (Chapter 7). Additionally, it includes a focus of at least three people working interdependently and sharing a common identity. These aspects make it distinct from interpersonal, or one-on-one, communication. In this chapter, we will consider different theories about how communication takes place in small groups and how communication helps a small group to evolve, creates a sense of "groupness," affects decision making, and allows a group to maintain or change its structure. We hope that by knowing the different theories, you will become a more effective group member.

In this chapter, you will read about the following concepts:

- What is a small group
- How groups grow and form
  - Tuckman's group development theory
- How groups make decisions
  - Functional theory of decision making
  - Groupthink
- How groups create and maintain norms
  - Structuration theory

In the movie *Gladiator,* the son of the Roman emperor Claudius, seeking to preserve his line to the throne, slaughters the family of Maximus, a Roman general. Maximus begins wandering and is captured and sold to a trainer of gladiators. Late in the movie, just before chariots of armed soldiers roll into the Colosseum, Maximus (played by Russell Crowe) tells the other gladiators, "Whatever comes out of these gates, we've got a better chance of survival if we work together." This quote exemplifies one of the assumptions underlying small groups, the assumption that a number of individuals working together toward a common goal will be more successful than individuals working alone. Many aspects of the movie *Gladiator* exemplify what a group of people working interdependently toward a goal can accomplish. Maximus, the leader of the group, not only exhibits strong leadership skills but also understands the value of uniting people (e.g., his speech at the beginning of the movie to the Roman soldiers) and how to unite individuals into a group to work as one.

Other outcomes notwithstanding, the result of the gladiators "working together" led to their victory over the soldiers in the chariots. This outcome was unlikely had all the gladiators worked independently, not interdependently. Although you may never be fighting chariots of armed soldiers with fellow gladiators, it is likely that at some point in time you will be working with others on projects for your class, job, or both. Thus, it behooves you to have an understanding of the many aspects that are associated with working in a group.

Many components and facets explain group dynamics and group communication. In this chapter you will learn about the stages of a group, how a group comes to have a sense of groupness, what makes for good and bad decision making, and how a group's behavior brings structure to the group. The different theories presented in this chapter can help you not only to understand groups better but also to be a better member of the groups to which you belong. Using the knowledge gleaned here, you will have insight into groups that will make your participating in them an easier, more enjoyable, and a more productive experience.

What Is a Small Group?

A small group consists of 3 to around 12 to 15 people. Why at least 3 and why up to around 15? Two people create a dyad. Communication between only two people (dyadic communication) has unique properties, such as a greater level of intimacy and the potential for the development of relationship. Interpersonal scholars focus on these and other aspects of one-on-one communication (Chapter 7). When a group has at least three people, the dynamics change, because you can now have a majority and minority in the group, coalitions can be formed, and so on. However, when a group begins to get too many people (usually around 12 to 15 people), it is difficult for group members to know one another and manage meetings for input from all group members. In other words, after 15 people, the small group becomes a *large* group. In sum, having a minority is unique to groups and differentiates small group communication from interpersonal communication, and having fewer than 15 members differentiates small groups from large groups.

Two other characteristics define a group. The first is that groups have *interdependence*. This means that members of the group are affected by the actions of other group members.

FIGURE 8.1 Small group work can be frustrating or exciting. Could theories help you be a better leader or member of a group?

© Photographers Library LTD (1999)/eStock Photography/PictureQuest.

If one group member does not do his or her job, this may cause the whole group to be unsuccessful. The second characteristic is that group members usually share a *common goal.* Group members recognize and understand that they are all working for the same outcome. What makes small groups different from, say, a group of friends that you spend time with, is that the goal usually has some sort of task focus. In sum, when we talk about a **small group** for this chapter, we refer to 3 to 15 people working interdependently toward a common goal.

How Will My Small Group Form and Grow?

From the birth of a group (forming) to the death of the group (dissolution), groups go through many stages of development. Recall the groups that you have been a part of and how they formed, developed, and disbanded. It is likely that you experienced the stages of group development that we will discuss. One of the most popular descriptions of group development is **Tuckman's group development theory,** a sequential-stage theory proposed by Bruce Tuckman (Tuckman, 1965; Tuckman & Jensen, 1977; see Figure 8.1). Sequential-stage theories purport that groups move through stages or phases as they develop. Tuckman's group development theory proffers five stages: forming, storming, norming, performing, and adjourning. Let us consider these different stages through a concrete example. Most of us have been on a school or work committee that had to plan an event or make a decision on some kind of procedure. Say that a group of persons have been assigned the task to choose a new mascot for their high school because the previous mascot, based on a Native American persona, is now deemed inappropriate and culturally insensitive.

The first stage of group development is the **forming stage** (Tuckman, 1965; Tuckman & Jensen, 1977). During this stage, group members seek information about the other group members, and they seek general information about the group. It is during this time that group members are engaged in an orientation period. Like any other first-time meeting or first date, individuals are careful about what they say and what they disclose. Thus, at this point in the group's development, group members tend to be guarded in what they say in order to avoid embarrassing moments or creating negative perceptions and attributions of themselves. As time passes, group members learn through interaction what is acceptable behavior and what is not. In addition, group members identify how they are going to accomplish the task before them. It is safe to assume, in our hypothetical situation, that during the initial meetings of the newly formed committee, all the participants would be relatively cautious about what they say and how they act, until all the members feel comfortable enough to freely exchange ideas.

The second stage of group development is the **storming stage** (Tuckman, 1965; Tuckman & Jensen, 1977). During this stage, the group addresses different conflicts that emerge. Disagreements within the group can be of an interpersonal nature or related to task issues. Thus, intragroup conflict dominates this stage of group development. Not all group members may get along interpersonally. If you have ever participated in a small group, you know that this is not too hard to imagine! Whether the conflict that arises is between two group members or two subgroups that have splintered into factions, group communication at this stage addresses the different interpersonal idiosyncrasies that are at the root of the conflict between parties.

When the root of the conflict is something related to a task, group members express their disagreement or dissatisfaction with how the group is going about accomplishing their objective. Conflict related to task issues could be anything from how ideas are proposed to how decisions are made. Handling and dealing with the conflict in the group prepares the group for the next stage of group development. For our task committee choosing a new mascot, having passed through the forming and "getting to know you" stage, communication would most probably shift now to the conflict stage. Now the members feel confident enough to disagree with others and put forth their own ideas. Some members might disagree on procedure or might differ on how to identify possible mascots and even on how to make the final decision (for example, shall we vote, or must it be consensus?).

The norming stage is the next stage of group development. The **norming stage** is characterized by high cohesion among group members (Tuckman, 1965; Tuckman & Jensen, 1977). The group feels very united, and there is a sense of "we" as opposed to "I." The group establishes procedures for dealing with the task at hand, and it establishes the different roles group members will perform or fulfill. As a result of the increase in **cohesion,** or increased sense of unity among members, group members participate more and are more satisfied with the group, and there is pressure for individuals not to disagree with the group. For our high school mascot task group, working out disagreements and conflicts about how to proceed in choosing a new mascot now leads to a new sense of cohesion in purpose. They now feel sense of unity that prepares them for the very important, task-oriented stage that follows.

After the norming stage, groups enter into the **performing stage** (Tuckman, 1965; Tuckman & Jensen, 1977). It is now that the group uses established procedures and role structure to handle any tasks and problems. The group is very centered on achieving its objective; thus, members concentrate on performing the necessary functions in order to achieve a high-quality decision. If interpersonal problems arise, the group will revert to already established role structures to solve interpersonal disputes. It is in this stage of performing that the mascot committee can finally get down to work. Now the communication will likely turn to measuring possible mascot choices and working toward the final choice for the best mascot.

Finally, groups reach the **adjourning stage** (Tuckman, 1965; Tuckman & Jensen, 1977), the stage at which the group members terminate the existence of the group and go their separate ways. Groups can disband for different reasons. They may have reached their objective, they may no longer be able to meet, they may not work together very well, and so on. In some cases, an outside force, such as a supervisor or instructor, might disband the group. Whatever the case may be, when the group reaches the adjourning stage, it marks the dissolution of the group. Having chosen their mascot and reached their objective, our committee can now disband. (See a summary of Tuckman's stages of group development, Figure 8.2)

One very important phenomenon most likely occurred during the tenure of this task group, if it is like most groups: The members of the group probably left the conversation about the task concerning the mascot and began talking about another topic like a personal interest or group members may have engaged in talk that strengthens the relationships among group members. At that moment, the group shifted from a **task focus** to a more **social focus.** This is a common occurrence for task groups and a pattern of communication to be expected. When group members are task focused, their communication and behavior concentrates on completing the task. When group members are social focused, their communication and behavior concentrates on the relationships in the group and the climate of the group. Often, groups hard at work discussing or solving a problem will go off topic and discuss casual or personal topics. This is not only expected, but it is often very good for the well-being of the group, as long as the group is able to return to task in a way that fulfills the needs of the organization and the group members.

The stages presented here describe the different stages that groups generally go through. It is not difficult to realize that a group may not follow a straight path from one stage to another. Rather, groups are likely to go in and out of many of the stages. For example, during the storming stage group members address conflict that can be interpersonal or task related. However, during the performing stage one of the types of conflict may manifest, and if this occurs, the group will need to address the issue(s). The result is a going back and forth between different stages. Nonetheless, the stages presented here represent what groups, at least in some point in time, are likely to experience.

FIGURE 8.2   *Tuckman's Stages of Group Development.*

Stage	Behaviors and Perceptions
1. Forming	Group members get to know one another. Careful in what they say and do.
2. Storming	Group members address both interpersonal and task conflict.
3. Norming	A sense of "we" permeates the group.
4. Performing	Procedures and role structures are established and the group concentrates on its objectives.
5. Adjourning	The group disbands.

Based on Tuckman, 1965; Tuckman & Jensen, 1977.

How Can My Group Make Better Decisions?

In contrast to the above theory that recognizes the stages of group formation, the functionalist perspective explains group communication as an occasion when any or all of the members of a group merely step up and perform any task or function that is good for the success of the group. The **functional theory of decision making** evolved from the functional perspective (Gouran, Hirokawa, Julian, & Leatham, 1993). The functional perspective asserts that during the decision-making process, certain criteria or *functional requisites* need to be satisfied in order for a good decision to be made. How well those functional requisites are completed determines the quality of the decision reached. The functionalist view privileges the notion that each group is not only a unique setting of group communication but that each group's members will tend to work toward the success of the group based on the needs of the group.

Investigations into the functional theory have resulted in a number of different **functional requisites** that need to be satisfied to achieve good decision making (Gouran & Hirokawa, 1983; Gouran et al., 1993; Hirokawa, 1985). These might best be understood by application to another hypothetical example. In this case, suppose that a university committee was brought together with the purpose of solving the problem of parking on a college campus. Based on the functional perspective, several things must be addressed at some stage of group discussion for the final group decision to be effective.

One functional requisite that needs to be accomplished is **understanding the problem** (Gouran & Hirokawa, 1983; Gouran et al., 1993; Hirokawa,1985). This functional requisite is often met early and helps to guide the other functional requisites. In accomplishing this criterion, it is important for the group and its members to comprehend the various issues and aspects of the problem(s) that it faces. It is necessary to grasp any and all complexities of the situation and to understand any issues related to the problem at hand. Therefore, if group members clearly understand the problem that they must solve or the situation that they face, they are in a position to make a good decision. The first thing that the university committee in our example would need to do is to get a good understanding of the problem. They analyze the situation and determine that there is a lack of parking on and around campus. Thus, their job is to determine how to increase parking on and around campus.

Another functional requisite is the **establishment of goals and objectives** (Gouran & Hirokawa, 1983; Gouran et al., 1993; Hirokawa, 1985). It is necessary for the group to identify the necessary goals or objectives that need to be met in order to solve the problem it faces; doing so allows the group to identify and lay out what needs to be accomplished in order to make an appropriate or high-quality decision (Figure 8.3). Conversely, if a group fails to propose appropriate goals and objectives, then the decision is likely to be insufficient. By determining the goals and objectives that the group needs to meet in order to solve the problem at hand, the group increases its chances for obtaining a sufficient and adequate solution to the problem. In sum, if the group's goals are consistent with the problem, the solution is likely to be consistent with the problem, but if the group's goals are not consistent with the problem, then the solution is not likely to be consistent with the problem. In our example, the committee then determines a number of goals and objectives that need to be met in order to solve the problem. Along with increasing parking, the committee needs to

FIGURE 8.3   Editors struggle with the author of a book chapter to establish the goals and objectives of the book.

Photo by Forrest Wisely, Department of Communication, Illinois State University.

find a cost-effective alternative, one that satisfies students, faculty, support staff, and the local community, and one that can be implemented within three years.

Identifying alternative realistic proposals is another functional requisite (Gouran & Hirokawa, 1983; Gouran et al., 1993; Hirokawa, 1985). The group carries out this functional requisite by identifying a number of different and feasible solutions. The group can come up with a number of alternative solutions to address a particular problem, but if those solutions are not feasible, appropriate, or realistic, they do nothing to help the group to make a good decision. Determining the best solution or decision from a pool of realistic proposals gives a group a good chance of making a good decision. However, by not having a range of realistic proposals, a group runs the risk of making a poor decision. In our parking-lot scenario, the group has now suggested a number of realistic alternative proposals. Among them are to build a new parking structure, obtain lots off campus and shuttle people onto campus, and reward people for not driving onto campus.

The final decision-making functional requisite is the **evaluation of positive and negative qualities associated with alternative choices** (Gouran & Hirokawa, 1983; Gouran et al., 1993; Hirokawa, 1985). Although a group can propose a number of alternative choices, how they weigh or determine which proposal is to be adopted can have a significant impact on the quality of their decision. Thus, it becomes extremely important for group members to assess each choice based on their positive and negative consequences. It is important for the university committee in our example to identify the positive and negative qualities for each alternative. For example, a positive aspect of the parking structure is that it will supply a lot of parking spaces, but a negative aspect is that it may be too costly. Four errors can occur when addressing the positive and negative consequences of alternative choices: (1) failure to identify positive qualities of available alternatives, (2) failure to identify negative qualities of available alternatives, (3) overestimation of the positive qualities of available alternatives, and (4) overestimation of the negative qualities of available alternatives (Gouran et al., 1993). If a group commits one of these errors, this may cause it to make a decision that is less than suitable.

After going through each functional requisite as enumerated in the functional theory, the university committee in our example is now ready to make a high-quality decision. The goal of the functional theory, as described here, is to assist in good, high-quality decision making. One of the suppositions of this theory is that it does not matter in what order you perform the functional requisites, only that you perform them. However, from the discussion of the functional requisites, it is likely that some of the functional requisites will be performed before others. When making a decision, groups that use the functional theory by paying attention to the functional requisites can avoid making bad decisions, and increase the likelihood of making a good one.

Why Does My Group Sometimes Make Bad Decisions?

One would think that being surrounded by the brightest and best minds in the country would lead to the brightest and best decisions. However, having the brightest and best in a group does not mean they will perform at their brightest or best. Indeed, sometimes group members will engage in behaviors that will impede their ability to produce the best decision. In April 1961, the result of poor decision making led to one of America's worst mistakes—one that cost many people their lives.

With the intent of overthrowing Fidel Castro, the CIA trained and armed Cuban exiles for this purpose. The plan was for the Cuban exiles to land on a part of the coast of Cuba named the Bay of Pigs and overthrow Castro and his government. Within three days of landing, the 1,400 Cuban exiled troops that landed at the Bay of Pigs were either dead or imprisoned. This event was one of the biggest debacles for which our government was responsible. But what led to the Bay of Pigs fiasco when President John F. Kennedy had the brightest and best minds helping him to make the decision about the ill-fated overthrow attempt? One explanation is that Kennedy and his administration engaged in "groupthink" (Janis, 1972, 1982).

Groupthink is "a mode of thinking that people engage in when they are deeply involved in a cohesive in-group, when the members' striving for unanimity overrides their motivation to realistically appraise alternative courses of action" (Janis, 1982, p. 9). Janis's theory explaining this process bears the same name. According to the theory, cohesion is a necessary, but not sufficient, requirement for groupthink to occur (not all cohesive groups practice groupthink!). Groupthink occurs when a group fails to engage in the conflict, or "storming," stage mentioned above because members "don't want to rock the boat" (disrupt the cohesion of the group). Typically, cohesion alone is not enough to lead to groupthink. There must be some other aspects of the structure of the group, such as domineering leadership, short time frame to make a decision, insufficient information resources, or prior group failure that join with cohesion, to lead to groupthink.

The theory is most often discussed, however, in terms several variables related to groupthink. The propositions of the theory suggest that as each of several variables increases, so does the likelihood of groupthink (Janis, 1972, 1982). The nature of these variables leads to a few critiques frequently raised about the theory: first, that the theory is not clear as to whether these are propositions that lead to groupthink or symptoms that demonstrate its existence. Since scholars often hold the second view (e.g., Griffin, 2000), some feel the theory works best to point out problems retrospectively, and does not work well to prevent them. That is, a second critique is that the theory seems to be used more to explain specific (historic) situations then to predict group outcomes. Much recent research, however, contradicts this last notion.

The first proposition regards the **illusion of invulnerability.** Group members believe that the decisions they are making will result in triumph and victory, never defeat. The perception is created that whatever decision the group makes it is the correct one and will not fail. As a result, the group may only devise a few ideas and not consider many alternatives. For example, Kennedy and his administration believed that their plan would be a success and if anything did go wrong, the blame would lie with the Cuban exiles and not the Kennedy administration.

Second is a belief in the group's **unquestioned morality.** Group members believe that their cause is just and that there is no need to question what it is they are proposing. Therefore, group members will not discuss the moral or ethical consequences of their decisions, for in their mind's eye, they are only doing what is best for their just cause. Kennedy and his team of advisors believed overthrowing Castro was a just cause, thus there was no need to discuss the morals or ethics of the idea.

The third indicator of groupthink is **collective rationalization.** Group members convince themselves that their decision is correct, regardless of evidence to the contrary. Rather than discuss and examine contrary information, the group will invent or only discuss information that makes it appear as though they are justified in the actions they are taking. Any information contrary to what they believe as an accurate decision is discounted. Further, any information that suggests the group has made the wrong decision or that they should cease their course of action is also discounted. Thus, collective rationalization involves group members talking themselves into believing that they have made the right decision. Kennedy's advisors asserted that after the attack began, people living in Cuba would fight against Castro with the Cuban exiles because many people did not like Castro. However, experts had presented information to the group that clearly demonstrated that Castro was well liked by many Cubans. Since this information was contrary to what the administration believed, they did not use it for making their decision.

Stereotyping opponents negatively is the fourth indicator of groupthink. Group members portray their rivals or critics as evil, stupid, unjust, or any other negative description they desire. Because of this, the opposition is seen as wrong and/or easily defeatable. As a result, the group ignores or does not actively seek out information that could cause it to revise its decision. Further, the group fails to investigate or discuss any contingency plan. Castro was stereotyped as stupid and his army as weak; both stereotypes were wrong. The fifth indication of groupthink is **self-censorship.** When this occurs, group members keep their criticisms to themselves. Even though a group member might disagree with what is being proposed, he or she does not voice the dissenting opinion to anyone. Arthur Schlesinger, a member of Kennedy's team, had misgivings about the plan the team devised, but he said nothing.

The next symptom is when group members put **direct pressure on dissenters.** When this symptom is present, a group member, often the leader, will pressure any group member that voices disagreement with the proposed plan or decision to conform. Rather than discuss why the group member disagrees or hear his or her arguments, other group members act to quiet that person and get them to agree with the proposal. Kennedy himself would make comments to anyone who had an opposing view to get them to agree with the group's ideas. Kennedy's comments to the dissenters tended to be verbally aggressive.

The presence of what is referred to as **mindguards** is the next symptom of groupthink. Mindguards take on the responsibility of making sure the group does not hear information contrary to the group's proposal. The result of this is that the group makes a decision without all the pertinent and relevant information. In sum, the group makes an uninformed decision. Bobby Kennedy served as a mindguard by not allowing the group to hear certain pieces of important information.

The **illusion of unanimity** is the final indicator of groupthink. The illusion of unanimity follows from the presence of mindguards, the direct pressure on dissenters, and self-censorship. Group members believe that everyone in the group agrees with the decision, when in reality, a number of people disagree with the decision. A number of group members may have had different opinions than what the group was proposing during the group discussion, but they did not voice them. As a result, the absence of voiced disagreement creates the illusion that all the group members are of the same mind. This leads to an important point about groupthink—it is not the same as unanimity! A group can make a unanimous decision with deep and careful discussion (and, thus, no groupthink). It is when unanimity is an illusion that groupthink may be present. A number of people on Kennedy's team disagreed with the plan, but they kept it to themselves, and as a result silence was mistaken for unanimity.

In general, groupthink causes a group to exaggerate and overvalue itself, to be unwilling to critically analyze a problem, and to pressure group members to conform. As a result, the group runs a high risk of making a bad decision. Although it is not a problem if group members agree with one another based on the merits of good arguments and good evidence, the problem arises when concurrence is forced and important information is ignored. Thus, when a number of group members do not want to analyze a problem critically, or when they hide information and force consensus, groupthink is present. A number of steps can be taken to prevent groupthink from occurring (see Figure 8.4). In closing, when you participate in decision making with your group, be aware of the indicators of groupthink and if you identify them, take steps to stop them.

Why Do Groups Function As They Do?

If you were to observe different work groups in the same department of an organization, you would notice that each of those groups is quite different. First, they might differ in their sense of group identity and vision of the world. For this reason organizational researchers often use symbolic convergence theory to explain group identity development. Chapter 6 describes this theory in terms of rhetoric. [Web site: Symbolic Convergence Theory]

In addition, each group probably has a different way of doing things. Even though the work groups might be governed by the same policies, you would most likely notice an

FIGURE 8.4   *Preventing Groupthink.*

1. Critical Evaluator:	Each group member presents his or her objections, doubts, and criticisms.
2. Impartiality:	Group leaders are not biased and do not state their preferences.
3. Subgroups:	Set up subgroups where one creates a plan and one criticizes it or set up two subgroups with each creating a plan and have both subgroups meet to discuss their differences and come to a resolution for one final plan.
4. Consultation:	Group members discuss with "trusted associates" different ideas.
5. Outside Experts:	A qualified person is allowed at meetings to challenge the groups' ideas.
6. Devil's Advocate:	One member of the group scrutinizes the groups' proposals.

entirely different structure within each group. The reason for this lies in how group members create, enact, and utilize different rules and resources. In other words, how a group is structured determines the group's procedures. Why and how a group institutes certain procedures to perform certain tasks is explained by the theory of structuration (Poole, 1983; Poole, Siebold, & McPhee, 1985, 1986).

"Structuration is the process of producing and reproducing social systems through members' application of generative rules and resources (structures)" (Poole et al., 1986, p. 247). **Structuration** attempts to explain people's use of patterns, or structure, while they are participating in, or members of, a social system. In effect, according to structuration theory the group members follow patterns or rules without question, in a natural and comfortable manner, in effect not even realizing that they are following predetermined rules and procedures as structures. Although Giddens's (1984) notion of structuration was not specifically designed to explain small group phenomena, small group communication scholars have adopted the theory and have identified and demonstrated the utility of structuration through its ability to explain various facets of the small group (Poole et al., 1985, 1986). Thinking of groups in terms of structuration allows us to see how groups behave according to rules and to group traditions that members are not even aware of. Structuration—the use of structures—means that group members act according to structures that feel comfortable to them, but they might not ever stop to think about why they follow these procedures, why they behave in the ways they do, or why they follow the rules they do.

A number of concepts are used to explain structuration. To begin explaining structuration, we first need a clear distinction between the terms *structure* and *system*. **Structures** are the "rules and resources" used by people, or group members, when they are interacting. **Rules** are what govern actions and indicate what is and is not appropriate. **Resources** are what the group utilizes to achieve its objectives. Resources may include group members' knowledge, expertise, and skills; the information available to them; and the materials available to them to help them accomplish their task. Group members determine their actions as a result of the rules and resources that are instituted and established in a group, either consciously or unconsciously. A **system** refers to the set of interconnected parts of a group (e.g., the members and their relation to one another, the way materials are used to meet goals, and the decisions the group makes). Systems are the observable outcome of the application of structures. That is, the way people use rules and resources (structures) allows for the development of systems. Put another way, the creation of a system is accomplished through the institution of structures.

A prime example of structuration is demonstrated by how some groups reach a decision. Decision making represents the process of a system; however, different structures can lead to very different decision-making procedures. If a group pursues a democratic style of decision making, that group then, at the very least, utilizes a majority vote procedure for making the final decision (rules) and utilizes the expertise and knowledge (resources) of its group members during open discussion. Conversely, a group where the decisions are made autocratically, most likely by the leader, allows one person to make final decisions (rules). Additionally, the leader might use only people and information from outside of the group, as well as the power invested in him or her by management (resources) to help make the final decision and then inform the group what was decided. The two different groups have different structures guiding the decision-making system. In this way structuration explains why different groups have different instituted procedures.

In structuration, structures take on dual roles. Structures serve as both a medium and an outcome of interaction. On the one hand, rules and resources are used to identify how interaction is to occur among individuals. Rules and resources are used as the medium by which group members understand how to behave, interact, and what to expect. Thus, rules and resources guide behavior and interaction. It is through interaction that rules and resources are created (outcome), and it is the adherence to these rules and resources that guide (medium) subsequent behavior. This circular relationship between interaction and structure has been called the **duality of structure.**

Structuration promotes the idea that reflexive monitoring and rationalization can sometimes guide group members' actions. **Reflexive monitoring** of actions means that in our groups, we consider past actions and analyze the results of those actions. Based on this analysis and conclusion, we can proceed with future plans and actions. The conclusion reached may cause us to change from the original plan of action or, if past action deems it appropriate, proceed as originally planned. Thus, although structures usually guide actions without our conscious reflection, actions within our group can change as a result of consciously monitoring them. Further, when we reflexively monitor, we **rationalize** our actions. In doing so, we describe to ourselves and others, the reasons and purposes for our actions. You can see that any group that questions its unique and respective structures can position itself to improve its behaviors and its success, especially when made aware of the unconscious structures that guide the group.

While this theory could easily be applied to any of the groups we have considered so far, let us consider a new example—a leadership group for a church that is facing a problem of lack of growth. Because the nature of the problem includes the preaching from the pulpit, the minister joins the leadership group to discuss the problem. One of the leaders brings notes from prior meetings, another a laptop, and another opinions he has gathered from the worship and finance committees of the church. The leaders are proposing the introduction of a 12-piece rock band to liven up the worship a little. In this case, the *rules* of the group include the prior decision-making patterns that they use (who speaks when? who assumes leadership? how are decisions made?). The *resources* include both the material items (laptop, pencils, money, written notes) but also the nonmaterial items (the minister's authority, the outside opinions, church doctrine, the leaders' knowledge of their scriptures). These rules and resources inform the decision that the group makes, as the leaders recall prior attempts to change worship both within and outside of their congregation (*reflexive monitoring*). However, as the group communicates, they can reinvent the role of the minister, decide what they do with outside opinions, or even influence the doctrine of the congregation. This mutual relationship between *structure* and interaction illustrates the *duality of structure* (Figure 8.5). Finally, once the leaders make a decision, they will justify this both to themselves and to the congregation (*rationalization*), likely in terms of the rules and resources.

The action group members take is constrained or guided by a number of ideas. The first is *time*. Group members work within certain time frames as well as at certain times. For any action the group takes, there may be a time limit on how long they can perform that action, and the time at which they perform the action is guided by the group's structure. Second, *historical precedents* constrain action. The structures already in place are known to all members and tend to be reified and maintained. Thus, altering already established structures can be difficult. Third, action is a result of *knowledge*. Knowledge is a result of **discursive consciousness,** which is knowledge that can be expressed through language to others, and a result of **practical consciousness,** which is knowledge that cannot be expressed by language. Instead, practical knowledge is implied through actions and behavior. In our example, perhaps the leaders have to make the decision by a certain date, working only on Sunday night meetings. They are influenced by the historical weight of church doctrine, the size of the denomination, and the way prior decisions have been made in their group. And each member brings various types of knowledge (about scripture, prior decisions, denominational events), including unstated intuition.

Another aspect of knowledge that affects action is how the knowledge and resources are distributed. Often, a group member has a particular expertise or has been part of that group for an extended period of time. The resulting effect is an advantage for the expert or

FIGURE 8.5 *Simplified Model of Structuration, Illustrating the Duality of Structure.*

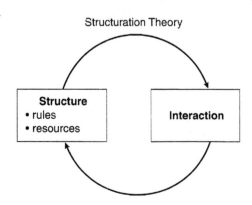

more experienced group member because that person tends to have more control over the structuration process. Finally, actions are the result of *unintended consequences*. Group members may not know how their actions will affect the group or its structures because it is difficult to monitor all that one does.

Recall that groups might have either a democratic or an autocratic decision-making process. Both types of group utilize different rules and resources for making decisions. Let us imagine that the church leadership group in our example has an autocratic style, with the minister exerting strong influence on decisions. But the group is not pleased with how the decisions were being made. Upon analyzing past decisions and the results of those decisions (reflexively monitoring), the group determines that having only the minister make the decision using outside sources is causing the group to perform poorly. As a result, the leader and other group members are perceived negatively by their church. The group decides that procedures need to be changed, or in structuration terms, structures need to be changed. As a result of changing structures, historical precedents are overcome. The group decides that a democratic style of decision making will be used. The resulting effect is that group members now have more say in the final decision. Additionally, the more senior members of the group enjoy more power because many of the younger group members look to them for guidance because of their experience and knowledge.

Although structures guide interaction, structures can be changed as a result of interaction. Rules and resources are not permanent fixtures. If it so chooses, the group is capable of changing structures. A potential consequence of changing structures is changing a system. Thus, if a group dislikes its decision-making procedures, it can change, or at least attempt to change them. The rules and resources are only part of a group's structure if the group applies them. If the group does not use or adhere to certain rules and resources, those rules and resources are no longer part of the group. By understanding structuration, one can then identify how the group functions, or what needs to be changed.

Summary

In this chapter, you first read about a number of theories dealing with small group communication. The first two theories presented perspectives on the role of communication in how groups form, either in terms of specific communication functions or in terms of the creation of a shared vision of a group. Tuckman's group development theory (1965, 1977) demonstrated the different stages a group might encounter, noting how communication varies at each stage of the group's formation (e.g., conflict, cohesion, closing the group).

The next two chapters take more of a functionalist perspective, looking at the factors that lead to good decision making in groups. First, the functional theory of decision making (Gouran & Hirokawa, 1983; Gouran et al., 1993; Hirokawa, 1985) outlines four functional requisites that the group must accomplish when they are making a decision: understanding the problem, establishment of goals and objectives, identifying alternative realistic proposals, and evaluation of positive and negative qualities associated with alternative choices. To the extent that a group accomplishes these requisites, it should arrive at better decisions. Groupthink (Janis, 1972, 1982) discusses what happens when the desire for cohesion in the group shuts down discussion. In terms of Tuckman's (1965) model, we might say that the group moves straight from "forming" to "norming," without the valuable step of "storming." In terms of the functional theory, we would argue that groupthink prevents completion of two, three, or even all four of the necessary functions of decision making.

Structuration theory explains that how a group is structured determines the procedures used by the group. A group's procedures are a result of how structures (rules and resources) are utilized, instituted, and maintained. A system is created as a result of the group's utilization of structures. Group members can change the system by changing how rules and resources are used. However, changing structures causes a change in the system. Thus, a group's procedures can be changed if group members change the group's structures.

We can clearly see in these different perspectives a variety of types of theories and perspectives. First, some of the approaches are more "scientific" in terms of presenting concepts or variables and their relationships to one another than others are. Groupthink is clearly a scientific theory. The functional perspective and Tuckman's approach are also both scientific in focus, assuming that most groups go through the same processes and that the same variables lead to successful outcomes for most or all groups, but are more presented here as "models" of the process rather than as "theories" in the traditional sense of the word. Structuration theory is mostly humanistic—treating the structure of each group as unique—but has an objective aspect as the structure a group creates "influences" communication in a group. In addition, the original theory by Giddens (1984) also contained a critical element, for it provided both a critique of structures of dominance and provided a perspective that allowed for the change of those structures.

There are many components and facets to group life. Groups go through many stages before the group terminates. Groups to which you belong have an identity, and the groups' identity tells us something about you. What can be exciting about group identity is that you might have the opportunity to shape it. If you are responsible for making a decision, you now have the knowledge to help the group to increase the likelihood of making a good, high-quality decision and avoid some of the pitfalls of making a bad decision. You also understand how the underlying structures inherent in groups are produced and reproduced. As a result, you can help to maintain these structures or help to change them. In closing, the theories discussed in this chapter will help you to function as a thriving and productive member of your group.

Discussion Questions

1. What is the importance of the storming stage in group development? Have you ever been part of a group of strangers who were put together for a project where storming was avoided?

2. Which of the functional requisites do you believe is hardest to accomplish and why? Does this change depending on the group you are in and the situation?

3. Describe a situation where you have seen groupthink occurring but felt powerless to stop it. Would knowing the elements of groupthink have changed your response in that situation? How?

References

Giddens, A. (1984). *The constitution of society: Outline of the theory of structuration.* Berkeley: University of California Press.

Gouran, D. S., & Hirokawa, R. Y. (1983). The role of communication in decision-making groups: A functional perspective. In M. S. Mander (Ed.), *Communications in transition* (pp. 168–185). New York: Prager.

Gouran, D. S., Hirokawa, R. Y., Julian, K. M., & Leatham, G. B. (1993). The evolution and current status of the functional perspective on communication in decision-making and problem-solving groups. In S. A. Deetz (Ed.), *Communication yearbook 16* (pp. 573–600). Newbury Park, CA: Sage.

Griffin, E. (2000). *A first look at communication theory* (4th ed.). New York: McGraw-Hill.

Hirokawa, R. Y. (1985). Discussion procedures and decision-making performance: A test of a functional perspective. *Human Communication Research, 12,* 203–224.

Janis, I. L. (1972). *Victims of groupthink.* Boston: Houghton-Mifflin.

Janis, I. L. (1982). *Victims of groupthink* (2nd ed.). Boston: Houghton-Mifflin.

Poole, M. S. (1983). Structural paradigms and the study of group communication. In M. S. Mander (Ed.), *Communications in transition* (pp. 168–185). New York: Prager.

Poole, M. S., Siebold, D. R., & McPhee, R. D. (1985). Group decision-making as a structurational process. *Quarterly Journal of Speech, 71,* 74–102.

Poole, M. S., Siebold, D. R., & McPhee, R. D. (1986). A Structurational approach to theory-building in group decision-making research. In R. Y. Hirokawa & M. S. Poole (Eds.), *Communication and group decision-making* (pp. 219–236). Beverly Hills, CA: Sage.

Tuckman, B. (1965). Developmental sequence in small groups. *Psychological Bulletin, 63,* 384–399.

Tuckman, B., & Jensen, M. (1977). Stages of small group development revisited. *Group and Organizational Studies, 2,* 419–427.

9

Theories of Persuasion

Stephen K. Hunt

As we saw in the last chapter, members of small groups often persuade one another of the correct course of action for a group to take. In the same way, while the interpersonal chapter did not discuss conflict management within small groups, due to limited space, we all know that a key aspect of our relationships with others is persuading them. We could easily say that persuasion is a part of both interpersonal and small group communication. Yet, like small group communication, it has a long history of research—one of the oldest traditions in our discipline. It has received enough attention in theory and research that it merits its own chapter.

Persuasion theories are similar to the rhetoric theories covered in Chapters 5 and 6 in that both seek to explain how people either give or receive persuasive messages. The main difference is that the rhetoric theories take a humanistic focus and tend to concentrate on interpreting single messages. The persuasion theories, influenced more by the field of social psychology, take a scientific approach, seeking to uncover the variables in senders or receivers of messages, or the messages themselves, that will more likely lead to a positive outcome of the persuasion.

In this chapter, you will read about the following concepts:

- Defining social change, persuasion, and compliance gaining
- Characteristics of the persuasive message situation
  - Source characteristics
  - Message characteristics
- Theories of persuasion
  - Theory of reasoned action
  - Social judgment theory
  - Cognitive dissonance theory
- Theories of compliance gaining
  - Compliance-gaining strategies
  - Elaboration likelihood model

If you're like most people, you are bombarded with persuasive messages on a regular basis. From advertising on television to interactions with your friends, people attempt to persuade you constantly. In addition, you might use persuasive techniques to challenge a grade with a teacher, reduce the price of that house or car you are purchasing, convince your parents to send more money for school, get your children to clean their rooms, and so on. These examples illustrate a very important point—persuasion is a central feature of every sphere of human communication. Persuasion is found wherever you find people communicating. In this chapter you'll read about how communication scholars define persuasive communication, the relationships between attitudes and behaviors, components of persuasive transactions, and models of persuasion. In this chapter, you will learn a few theories that can be applied to your everyday interactions with others. You might even learn a few new ways to get that house for less or get more money for school!

Why Should I Even Study Persuasion?

There are several reasons that you should be more aware of theories of persuasion. You have been and will continue to be bombarded with attempts to influence you for the rest of your life. Take a look around your campus, residence, workplace, and classroom for evidence of persuasive communication. As you left your residence for class today you likely encountered people on campus who solicited you for one thing or another. As you sit in the classroom posters for credit cards, apartments, and vacation getaways likely surround you. As you listen to your instructor, you are being persuaded, even if indirectly, to adopt a particular view of the world. As you watch television, you are saturated with advertisement for a whole range of topics. And this is simply a thumbnail sketch of the kinds of ways that others attempt to influence you on a daily basis (Figure 9.1). So a very good

FIGURE 9.1   We routinely have to evaluate persuasive messages.

© Jeff Greenberg (1999)/eStock/ PictureQuest

reason for studying persuasion is to become a more informed and critical consumer of persuasive messages.

You probably have already formed your own personal theories about how to persuade others and to respond to the persuasive attempts of others. You probably test these lay theories in different situations, adapting them as you learn from experience. The problem is that there is a limit to what you can learn from experience alone. In fact, there are times when you should not rely on this learning-from-experience approach. Think about the implications of making a mistake when attempting to buy a car. Such a mistake could cost you hundreds or thousands of dollars. Fortunately, communication scholars have been studying persuasion and have developed a great number of empirically tested persuasive techniques that can help you in every facet of your life—from influencing your friends and family, to buying a new car, to resisting the compliance-gaining attempts of others. These theories of persuasion can be applied to any of the many contexts in which you communicate with others—from interpersonal interactions to the mass media. Here, we apply them specifically to the constructing and consuming of persuasive messages.

What Is Persuasive Communication?

Before we get to specific theories regarding persuasion, it's important to define persuasion and consider some reasons for studying this powerful form of communication.

Persuasive communication is any message that is intended to shape, reinforce, or change the responses of others (Miller, 1980). This definition, as you can see, limits persuasive activity to intentional behavior. Why is such a distinction important? Although many human activities might ultimately affect the responses of others, not all of them are intended to do so. As a result, most persuasion scholars limit their study to the actions that individuals intentionally take to influence others (Bettinghaus & Cody, 1994). A brief description of how messages can shape, reinforce, or change our responses will provide a more complete understanding of the nature and scope of persuasive communication.

We are routinely exposed to new objects, people, and issues that require our evaluation. For example, after the September 11, 2001, attacks on the World Trade Center towers in New York, President George W. Bush used the mass media to mobilize domestic support for military attacks on Afghanistan. President Bush *shaped* the way people perceived Bin Laden by characterizing him as, among other things, an "evildoer." Persuasion can also involve *reinforcing* responses. For example more than 500,000 self-help groups across the United States provide behavioral and psychological reinforcement to people coping with crisis, role transitions, or other problems to find evidence of this persuasive process (Naisbitt, 1982). As another example, most advertising dollars are spent attempting to maintain customer loyalty rather than winning new buyers (Tellis, 1987).

The final component of the definition of persuasive communication involves *changing* responses, as in the extreme case of indoctrination into cults or the more subtle change of a woman slowly persuading her spouse to take up an equal share of the household chores (Stiff, 1994).

Responses can be either internal, such as when we change an attitude, or external, as when we change a behavior. **Social influence** is a term that writers have used to refer to any attempt by one person to influence another; but researchers have specified **persuasion** as the attempt to change the attitudes of others and **compliance-gaining** as the attempt to change their behavior. Our next sections will look at each of these in turn.

What Characteristics Will Help Me Be More Likely to Persuade Someone?

The earliest persuasion theory, as noted in Chapter 5, is thousands of years old and is studied under the area of communication known as **rhetoric.** Aristotle, writing some 300 years B.C.E., discussed different aspects of the message (logos) and the messenger (ethos) that would make a message more persuasive. For example, he felt that speakers must, in their speeches, establish a sense that they know what they are talking about (perceived intelligence), are ethical and moral speakers (perceived character), and have the best interests of the audience at heart (perceived goodwill). Persuasion research, from its early roots in psychology (see Chapter 4) examined these and other characteristics as scientific variables. The general idea is that the more of these that are in place, the more likely one's message is to persuade an audience. Thus, this section will review source and message characteristics of persuasive messages.

Source Characteristics

Source characteristics are often the most important features of persuasion communication. Public hearings, courtroom testimony, and political campaigns are situations in which effective communication skills and personal demeanor are essential for persuasive communication.

Credibility. Imagine for a moment a speaker you've heard recently that you perceived to be highly credible. Is credibility a commodity that the source you're imagining can even possess, or is credibility something that exists in your head, as the hearer of the message? Most researchers argue that assessments of source credibility must focus on the attributions made by receivers of persuasive messages. This receiver-oriented focus has lead persuasion scholars to define **credibility** in terms of the perceptions message recipients hold about a source's expertise and trustworthiness (McCroskey, 1966; O'Keefe, 2002). Therefore, credibility is not a commodity that message sources possess. Rather it is the perception of trustworthiness and expertise that sources are able to engender in a target audience. In general, research suggests that we are more likely to accept the message recommendations of sources that we perceive to be highly credible. This does not mean that we base our decisions on our perceptions of the source alone, but these perceptions do figure into the decision-making process. For example, many Americans perceived Dr. Martin Luther King, Jr. (Figure 9.2), to be a highly credible speaker based on his religious background, the style of his speaking, and the nonaggressive approach he took toward obtaining racial equality.

Similarity. Researchers have found that we are often motivated to comply with the wishes of others based simply on the fact that we like them (Cialdini, 2001), and we like people whom we perceive to be similar to us. Importantly, people often attempt to manipulate similarity to increase liking and compliance. Dressing like us and claiming to have backgrounds that are similar to ours are two ways that people may attempt to manipulate our perception that they are similar to us.

FIGURE 9.2   Aspects of both the speaker and the messages he spoke helped Dr. Martin Luther King, Jr., to be one of the most credible speakers of the 20th century.

© Associated Press, AP

Physical Attraction.   Physical attraction works in much the same way as similarity. Research has shown that we assign favorable traits like talent, kindness, honesty, and intelligence to sources that we perceive to be physically attractive (Chaiken, 1986; Eagly, Ashmore, Makhihani, & Longo, 1991). Why is this important to consider in terms of persuasive communication? The answer is simply that we generally like attractive sources and we tend to comply with those we like.

Message Characteristics

As you might imagine, researchers have devoted significant attention to the role message characteristics play in persuasive communication. Unfortunately, a thorough review of all of this literature is beyond the scope of this chapter. We'll focus our review on the following message characteristics: evidence, one- and two-sided messages, ordering of arguments, and speech style.

Persuasive Evidence.   When you listen to speakers, how much attention do you devote to the evidence utilized? Research suggests that evidence is critically important in our assessments of the persuasiveness of speakers. **Evidence** has been broadly defined as factual statements originating from a source other than the speaker, objects not created by the speaker, and opinions of persons other than the speaker that are offered in support of the speaker's claims (McCroskey, 1969).

Several internal factors influence the overall persuasiveness of evidence: the *credibility of the source of the evidence, evidence quality,* and *novelty.* Evidence is more persuasive when attributed to a highly credible communicator than to a low-credibility source. Evidence is also more likely to change attitudes if it is of high quality, plausible, and is novel rather than something the hearers have already heard several times before.

In addition, external factors also influence the overall effectiveness of evidence: *the credibility of the speaker, message delivery,* and *the subject's familiarity with the evidence.*

The use of evidence enhances attitude change when the communicator is perceived to be moderate or low in credibility (McCroskey, 1969; Reinard, 1988, 1998). On the other hand, evidence has little or no impact when the communicator is believed to be highly credible. However, when the goal of the communicator is to effect long-term changes in attitude, evidence can also benefit the highly credible speaker. As you might imagine, evidence has relatively little impact when it is included in a speech that is delivered poorly, when the audience is familiar with the topic, and when the data presented are inconsistent with individuals' initial attitudes.

One- and Two-Sided Messages.   In what circumstances are **two-sided messages,** those that give arguments for both sides of a controversial issue, more persuasive than **one-sided messages,** those that give arguments only in favor of the persuader's position? Communication scholars used to believe that one-sided messages were more effective than two-sided messages when individuals initially agree with the position advocated in the message (Lumsdaine & Janis, 1953). Scholars reasoned that when addressing an audience of true believers, persuaders are not likely to win many points by acknowledging that there is another position on the issue.

However, more recent research indicates that two-sided messages tend to be more persuasive overall. By giving both sides, the communicator is saying that she or he is aware of the (opposing) information, has taken it into account, and still finds that the weight of the evidence favors her or his position. In a recent meta-analysis, Allen (1998) found that two-sided messages were always more persuasive than one-sided messages, as long as the two-sided messages were refutational. Beyond merely mentioning opposing positions on a given topic, it is critical that communicators strongly refute those counterarguments (Hale, Mongeau, & Thomas, 1991).

Ordering of Persuasive Arguments.   When attempting to persuade others, is it better to give your strongest arguments first? Starting with strong arguments and ending with the weak ones is called an **anticlimax order.** Beginning with weak arguments and ending with the strong ones is called a **climax order.** Putting the strongest arguments in the middle is called a **pyramidal order.** The pyramidal order is least effective—there is no evidence that it facilitates comprehension or attitude change. By contrast, both the anticlimax and climax orders have been shown to facilitate attitude change (Gulley & Berlo, 1956). In courtroom settings, where organization of closing arguments is of particular interest, research has supported the climax ordering (Walker, Thibaut, & Andreoli, 1972). In addition, research indicates that, although the anticlimax and climax patterns are equally effective if information is presented visually, the anticlimax order is most persuasive when information is presented in an auditory manner (Unnava, Burnkrant, & Erevelles, 1994).

Speech Style.   How does your style of speech influence your persuasiveness as a speaker? Researchers have argued that a powerless speaking style reduces communicator credibility (Adkins & Brashers, 1995; Burrell & Koper, 1998). For example, a tendency to hedge and qualify one's statements may suggest that the speaker lacks knowledge, and this may reduce perceptions of expertise. On the other hand, intensifiers ("very surely," "really") and polite forms ("I'd really appreciate," "Thanks for the advice") can accentuate a speaker's credibility. The effects of language forms also depend on the speaker's goals. When the communicator wants to appear sociable, rather than authoritative, polite language forms are likely to create the desired impression (Mulac, 1976).

How Can I Change Other People's Attitudes?

Persuasion scholars have traditionally devoted a great deal of attention to examining the ways in which attitudes can be manipulated to affect behavior. But what is an attitude and how is it changed? What are the conditions that cause people to change their attitudes? In contrast to the **atheoretical** approaches above (i.e., not related to actual theory), several theories have investigated how attitudes are changed.

Though there is not complete agreement among persuasion scholars over the precise definition of an **attitude,** most agree that it consists of an enduring evaluation—positive or negative—of people, objects, and ideas that predispose one to respond in some preferential manner (Eagly & Chaiken, 1993). Attitudes are enduring in the sense that they often persist over time (Ajzen, 2001). A momentary annoyance at something somebody says is not an attitude, but a lasting, negative impression of the person certainly is. Attitudes are evaluative in the sense that they consist of a positive or negative reaction to something (Ajzen, 2001). As you know, people are not passive or neutral observers of the world, but constant evaluators of what they see.

Finding a Match: Theory of Reasoned Action

One of the best-known theories of how attitudes predict behaviors is Martin Fishbein and Icek Ajzen's **theory of reasoned action** (Fishbein & Ajzen, 1980). This theory was designed to predict behavioral intentions toward specific objects or situations. According to this theory, when people have time to contemplate how they are going to behave, the best indicator of their behavior is their intention: Does Sarah intend to go to the movie? Does Marcos intend to get a dog? Does Mel intend to take his dog to the movies? And the best persuasive message contains some match between the elements of the persuasive message and the aspects of the person's current thought and behavior.

In order to determine a person's intentions, we need to know two things: (1) the individual's **attitude** toward performing the behavior (sum of beliefs about performing the behavior and evaluations of those beliefs), and (2) existing **subjective norms** (individual's perceptions of the social appropriateness of performing a particular behavior). These two components combine to predict behavioral intention. As you can see in Figure 9.3, what is important here is not people's general attitude about something but their specific attitude toward the behavior in question.

How might the theory of reasoned action be useful to you? Let's say, hypothetically, that you wanted to organize a campaign on campus to get your fellow students to become organ donors. You decide to start with a survey in which you ask people their attitudes, and from that, predict their behavior. But what question should you ask? You could ask a very general question, such as how much people are willing to help others. Because being an organ donor is one way to help people, this might enable you to predict who will become

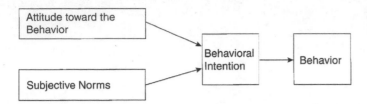

FIGURE 9.3 *The Theory of Reasoned Action.*

Understanding attitudes and predicting social behavior, by Ajzen/Fishbein, © 1980. Reprinted by permission of Pearson Education, Inc., Upper Saddle River, NJ.

organ donors. The problem is that even if people are generally willing to help others, they might fail to become an organ donor because of a host of other factors—they are too busy, they are worried that they will violate their religious beliefs, and so on. To get a better idea of predictability in this situation, it is best to measure people's attitude toward the specific act in question.

In addition to measuring attitudes toward the behavior, however, you also need to measure people's subjective norms. Subjective norms, in this case, might include people's beliefs about the kinds of social pressures they might be influenced by, therefore causing them to perform or not perform the behavior. If you are really interested in determining someone's behavioral intentions, knowing these beliefs is as important as knowing their attitudes. Using the previous example of an organ donation drive, you would want to survey people about their perceptions of their peers on this issue. Even if some individuals hold negative attitudes about organ donations, you might be able to influence them if other people in their peer group hold positive attitudes about organ donation. These subjective norms are important because we often rely on them to interpret ambiguous situations. In addition, people often find themselves performing certain behaviors just to get along with group members and avoid group conflict. In sum, if you know people's attitudes and subjective norms, and can match your message to include elements of those, you are more likely to persuade the audience.

In an attempt to improve the predictive power of this model of the attitude-behavior relationship, Ajzen extended the theory of reasoned action by including **perceived behavioral control,** often called **efficacy.** This refers to the belief that one can perform the behavior in question (Ajzen, 1985). According to Ajzen's **theory of planned behavior,** people's intentions to perform a particular behavior are often stymied by a lack of confidence in their ability to perform the behavior (Ajzen, 1991). For instance, a campaign to influence you to become an organ donor would be ineffective if you perceived you were unable to complete the necessary paperwork to become one (even if you and your peer group held positive attitudes about organ donation). The theory of planned behavior appears in Figure 9.4. Researchers continue to investigate the relationship between attitude and behavior in persuasion. [Web site: The Relationship between Attitude and Behavior]

Taking the Long Road: Social Judgment Theory

The bulk of the persuasion research done on receiver characteristics focuses on message discrepancy. When persuaders attempt to alter attitudes or behaviors, the position advocated in the persuasive message is likely to differ from the position held by message recipients. This difference is generally referred to as **message discrepancy,** that is, the extent to which a persuader's message recommendation is discrepant from the position held by

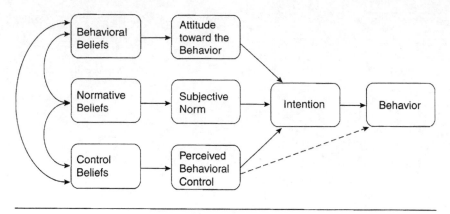

FIGURE 9.4   *The Theory of Planned Behavior.*

Reprinted from *Organizational Behavior and Human Decision Processes, 50,* I. Ajzen, The theory of planned behavior (pp. 179–211). © 1991, with permission from Elsevier Science.

the target person or audience. While several theories deal with messages that are different than one's own belief or behavior, one theory in particular considers the amount of the discrepancy and how we compare messages with our own position.

Social judgment theory classifies attitudes along a continuum, which is divided into latitudes of acceptance and rejection (Sherif & Hovland, 1961). The **latitude of acceptance** represents the positions on the attitude continuum that a person finds acceptable. By definition, a person's ideal or preferred position is centered within this latitude, and is known as the **anchor.** When people perceive that a message recommendation falls within their latitude of acceptance, **assimilation** is hypothesized to occur. That is, receivers judge the message recommendation as being closer to their own position than it actually is. However, when a message recommendation is perceived to fall within the **latitude of rejection, contrast** effects are hypothesized. A contrast effect causes receivers to judge the message as more discrepant from their own position than it actually is. As a result, this theory predicts that a discrepant message will lead you to change your attitude so long as the message falls within your latitude of acceptance, but that the further the message is from your anchor within the latitude of acceptance, the more persuasion will occur.

This theory would have practical implications, especially if you wanted to persuade people to believe something quite different from what they currently believe. For example, imagine that you want to get your social organization to expend a large amount of effort on behalf of a charity cause. Many members may not accept this, preferring to spend their time and money on an exciting club social. Although many of us just "tell it like it is," stating what we want in our persuasive message, the theory would suggest you tailor your message to your audience (perhaps doing some audience research first), to aim the message *within the latitude of acceptance, but as far from their anchor toward your position as possible.* Thus, you might discuss the need to do "some charity work," which most would accept. They would likely assimilate your view as similar to theirs and shift their anchor a degree or two toward your position. Once they accept your position to do some charity, you give a new message, promoting a stronger charity involvement, and so on. The theory suggests that major change will not occur within a single message, but that a campaign of several messages, even over a long period of time, might be more helpful.

Creating Tension: Cognitive Dissonance Theory

See above how attitudes can influence the way we behave. Is it possible that the reverse is also true? Can changes in behavior affect subsequent attitudes? The answer is yes, under certain circumstances. In this portion of the chapter we will examine a theory that explains how our behaviors can affect our attitudes.

Before answering this question directly, let's consider a hypothetical example. Assume that you are a person who loves to jog and that you believe it's important to stretch very carefully prior to running. Let's also assume that one morning, before heading out for your daily jog, you come across a newspaper article by a nationally known and highly respected doctor indicating that recent research suggests that stretching before engaging in physical activity does not do athletes any good—it may in fact do harm. This news is likely not to be very welcome. It will probably make you feel uncomfortable. If you believe the data, then your past behavior is not sensible. Therefore, you will be motivated to try and find a way to dismiss these new findings even to the point of questioning the credibility of the doctor and scientists who conducted the research. The feeling of discomfort caused by information that is discrepant from your notion of yourself as a reasonable person is called **cognitive dissonance** (Festinger, 1957).

In 1957, Leon Festinger described his theory of cognitive dissonance. Evolving from basic consistency principles, **cognitive dissonance theory** posits three basic assumptions about human cognition: (1) people have a need for cognitive consistency; (2) when cognitive inconsistency exists, people experience psychological discomfort; and (3) psychological discomfort motivates people to resolve the inconsistency and restore cognitive balance.

You might find yourself questioning the pervasiveness of dissonance, as Dilbert is doing in Figure 9.5; after all, we have many inconsistent cognitions, yet we do not run around feeling distressed twenty-four hours a day! In truth, all dissonant cognitions are not equal. For example, you might believe that it's desirable to be tidy, but discover one day that you left the cap off the toothpaste tube. Such an inconsistency will probably not be very upsetting to you. However, other kinds of inconsistencies, such as the direct clash between the thoughts "I smoke" and "Smoking can kill me," are likely to cause much greater dissonance. Researchers have found that dissonance is most likely to occur when we do or learn something that threatens our image of ourselves (Thibodeau & Aronson, 1992).

We can see clearly now that some behaviors we engage in may cause us to experience dissonance. So how is dissonance related to attitude change? According to this theory, dissonance always produces discomfort and therefore motivates a person to try to reduce the discomfort. There are three basic ways to reduce dissonance:

- By changing our behavior to bring it in line with the dissonant cognition
- By justifying our behavior through changing one of the cognitions to make it less dissonant (and therefore more consonant) with the behavior
- By justifying our behavior by adding new cognitions that are consonant with the behavior and thus support it

FIGURE 9.5   Dilbert demonstrates the notion of cognitive dissonance.

DILBERT reprinted with permission of United Features Syndicate.

You can see how these methods of reducing dissonance relate back to the opening section for this chapter. If you wanted to persuade someone, for example, to begin to recycle, you would first find ways to raise the dissonance between their cognitions (e.g., between their value system and their behavior). You might find ways to make the environment more important to them, to increase their sense of responsibility for their inactivity, and so on. Or you could give them just enough reward to engage in some small environmentally sound behavior (**minimal justification**)—but not enough to where the reward itself can justify their behavior. They then might change their cognitions to match their new environmentally friendly behavior—thus, their behavior would lead to a change in attitude, rather than the other way around. [Web site: An Example of Cognitive Dissonance—Lowballing]

How Can I Get Others to Do What I Want Them to Do?

Up until now, we've considered several theories that will help you either to persuade others to think in a different way or to recognize when others are trying to so influence you. We've already seen in some of the above examples, however (such as the car-buying example), that the theories also work for trying to get someone to behave in a certain way, an area of social influence known as **compliance-gaining.** In this section, we will consider two final approaches, applying them specifically to compliance-gaining: a compliance-gaining taxonomy and a model of persuasion that could be used to bring about a change in someone's behavior.

Compliance-Gaining Strategies

How do you get your relational partner to do what you want her or him to do? How can you influence your peers? Scholars have examined these questions in detail by exploring the ways in which individuals seek compliance from others. Scholars in the field of communication have produced the most research on the topic of compliance gaining, including many *taxonomies* of persuasive strategies (remember, a **taxonomy** is a list of categories with subcategories). However, it was two sociologists, Gerald Marwell and David Schmitt, who produced one of the first major (and still frequently used) categorization of compliance-gaining strategies, in 1967. Based on the types of power that individuals have at their disposal to influence others, these researchers developed a taxonomy of 16 different tactics that can be used to gain compliance (see Figure 9.6).

Marwell and Schmitt's (1967) research reveals five basic types of compliance-gaining strategies: **rewarding activity** (involves seeking compliance in positive ways, like using promises), **punishing activity** (involves seeking compliance in negative ways, like making threats), **expertise** (involves attempts to make a person think that the persuader has some special knowledge or credibility), **activation of impersonal commitments** (involves attempts to appeal to a person's internalized commitments), and **activation of personal commitments** (relies on appeals to a person's commitment to others). Although this research has been criticized for oversimplifying the process of compliance, it has provided a springboard for more than 100 studies.

These compliance strategies focus on the types of messages that we use to persuade others. Scholars have also examined the sequences of compliance-gaining strategies. For example, if you want to persuade someone to do something for you, should you start with a large request or small request? Does the sequence of requests matter? We'll take a closer look at research regarding two such strategies: the foot-in-the-door (FITD) technique and the door-in-the-face (DITF) technique.

Foot-in-the-Door.   The FITD strategy requires a persuader to send two sequential messages in order to gain compliance. The first message makes a request that is relatively innocuous and sufficiently small that most people will agree to it. The second request, which often occurs several days after the initial request, can be made by another person and is much larger than the initial request. Persuaders using the FITD are interested in gaining compliance with the second, larger request. Presumably, persons agreeing to the initial small request will be more willing to comply with the second larger request (Dillard, 1991). This approach is based in **self-perception theory.** According to this theory, when people comply with an initial small request, they conclude that their attitude toward the issue or source of the compliance request must be favorable. After coming to this determination, they are more likely to comply with the second, larger request.

FIGURE 9.6   *Marwell and Schmitt's (1967) Compliance Tactics.*

1. Promise	If you comply, I will reward you. *Example:* You offer to increase Susan's allowance if she increases her studying.
2. Threat	If you do not comply, I will punish you. *Example:* You forbid Susan to use the car if she does not increase her studying.
3. Expertise (Positive)	If you comply, you will be rewarded because of the nature of things. *Example:* You point out to Susan that if she gets good grades, she will be able to get into a good college.
4. Expertise (Negative)	If you do not comply, you will be punished because of the nature of things. *Example:* You argue to Susan that if she does not get good grades, she will not be able to get into a good college.
5. Liking	Source is friendly and helpful to get receiver in "good frame of mind" before making request. *Example:* You try to be as friendly as possible to get Susan in a good mood before asking her to study.
6. Pregiving	Source rewards receiver before requesting compliance. *Example:* You raise Susan's allowance and tell her you now expect her to study.
7. Aversive Stimulation	Source continuously punishes receiver, making cessation contingent upon compliance. *Example:* You forbid Susan to use the car and tell her she will not be able to drive until she studies more.
8. Debt	You owe me compliance because of past favors. *Example:* You point out that you have sacrificed and saved for Susan's education and that she owes it to you to do well in school.
9. Moral Appeal	You are immoral if you do not comply. *Example:* You tell Susan that it's morally wrong for her not to get good grades and that she should study more.
10. Self-Feeling (Positive)	You will feel better about yourself if you comply. *Example:* You tell Susan that she will feel proud if she studies more.
11. Self-Feeling (Negative)	You will feel worse about yourself if you do not comply. *Example:* You tell Susan that she will feel ashamed of herself if she gets bad grades.
12. Altercasting (Positive)	A person with "good" qualities would comply. *Example:* You tell Susan that since she is a mature and intelligent person, she naturally should want to study more to get good grades.
13. Altercasting (Negative)	Only a person with "bad" qualities would not comply. *Example:* You tell Susan that only someone very immature does not study.
14. Altruism	I need your compliance very badly, so do it for me. *Example:* You tell Susan that you really want her to get into a good college and would like her to study more as a favor to you.
15. Esteem (Positive)	People you value will think better of you if you comply. *Example:* You tell Susan that the whole family will be very proud of her if she gets good grades.
16. Esteem (Negative)	People you value will think worse of you if you do not comply. *Example:* You tell Susan that the whole family will be very disappointed if she gets poor grades.

Door-in-the-Face.   The DITF strategy begins with an initial compliance request that is so large that it is rejected by most targets. After rejection of the initial request, the source proceeds with a second, more moderate request. Presumably, people who refuse an initial large request are more likely to comply with the moderate second request than people who only receive the moderate request (Dillard, Hunter, & Burgoon, 1984). This approach is grounded in a concept known as the **norm of reciprocity** (Gouldner, 1960). This widely accepted cultural norm suggests that you should do things for those who do things for you. In other words, this compliance strategy works because the receiver views the source as giving in on the first request. As a result, the receiver feels compelled to reciprocate by complying with the second request. For example, you get a call from a political candidate's campaign asking you to donate $500.00. You say no, you can't afford it. The caller then says, "Of course, we realize many people cannot afford this, but most can afford $25, $50, or $100. Will you be willing to give one of these smaller amounts?" If the person's strategy works, you at least agree to the $25 amount.

It's important to recognize that we are not defenseless when exposed to the compliance-gaining attempts of others. Indeed, persuasion scholars have explored the ways in which we actively resist the compliance-gaining attempts of others. Some of the strategies we employ in such situations include **identity management** (indirect manipulation of the image of the agent or target), **nonnegotiation** (simple refusal to submit to the agent's request), **negotiation** (engage in mutual talks for the benefit of both parties), and **justifying strategies** (providing reasons, appealing to norms or standards) (McLaughlin, Cody, & Robey, 1980). It is important to recognize that persuasion is an interdependent, transactional process in which both the source and the receiver are active participants in the interaction. As you can see, not only do sources employ strategies to gain compliance, but receivers invoke strategies to resist requests made by sources.

In recent years, communication scholars have taken compliance-gaining research into new areas. For example, Dillard and his associates (Dillard, 1989; Dillard, Segrin, & Harden, 1989) argue that people pursue different types of goals as they attempt to persuade others. These goals are critical as they determine the types of strategies that people use as they attempt to gain compliance. According to Dillard (1989) the primary goal of individuals seeking compliance is to influence the other person. However, other **secondary compliance-gaining goals** also influence people's choices in compliance-gaining situations. Specifically, Dillard (1989) claims that **identity goals** (concerned with maintaining one's moral standards of living), **interaction goals** (concerned with creating a good impression and behaving in appropriate ways), **resource goals** (concerned with maintaining a relationship and increasing personal rewards, and **arousal goals** (concerned with maintaining levels of arousal, such as nervousness, within an acceptable range) all play into a person's decision-making process as they select a particular compliance-gaining strategy. The point here is that people are deliberate in their selection of strategies and they pick strategies that not only help them gain immediate compliance, but that satisfy other goals as well.

Predicting Message Processing: Elaboration Likelihood Model

The **elaboration likelihood model** brings together several of the elements we have looked at above (attitudes, behavior, message compounds). This cognitive model of persuasion emphasizes the thoughts and ideas that occur to people as they attend to persuasive communication (Petty & Cacioppo, 1981). Cognitive responses refer to all the thoughts that pass through a person's mind while she or he anticipates a communication, listens to a communication, or reflects on a communication. The cognitive response approach assumes that receivers play an active part in the communication process.

According to the elaboration likelihood model, you cognitively process persuasive messages that you receive either: (1) centrally, or (2) peripherally. When message receivers engage in **central processing,** characteristics of persuasive messages (argument quality, logical consistency) determine the extent and direction of attitude change. When people engage in **peripheral processing,** persuasive cues that are peripheral to the message itself (source credibility, attractiveness) determine the extent and direction of attitude change. The ELM stipulates that attitude change based on central route processing should show long-term persistence and should be highly resistant to **counterpersuasion.** Opinion changes that result from peripheral cues are expected to show less persistence of persuasion. So, the more deeply you analyze the issues, the more likely that the persuasion will persist. The model further predicts that elaborated messages will most likely lead to persuasive change. In short, if you want to bring the strongest, longest persuasion, you should get your audience to use the central route.

Whether a hearer processes persuasive cues centrally depends on the person's *motivation, ability,* and *need to scrutinize the message* (Petty & Cacioppo, 1981). Thus, if you want to talk your spouse or roommate into purchasing a new big-screen TV for your house, you might use short-processing cues that really do not require thought ("Do this because you love me," "Do this because we've always done it this way") or try to rely on emotion or on your own magnetic personality. All of these would be peripheral routes. Your persuasion will be stronger if your partner logically sees the reasons for the new TV. You will have the best result if you can get your partner to feel the decision is important, if you persuade at a time when there is little distraction (e.g., not 3 A.M. after a night out on the town), and if your audience perceives a need to know more about the message. However, if you are a very credible speaker on the subject, this might lead your partner to consider more your logical arguments. And your partner is very likely to "elaborate" the argument, and if you have a poor argument, this might hurt your cause.

Although the ELM has generated an enormous amount of research by persuasion scholars, some have questioned whether cognitive processing really occurs along two distinguishable lines of thought. This criticism has lead to development of the **heuristic model of persuasion** (HMP) (Chaiken, 1987). The HMP hypothesizes that people engage in parallel processing and simultaneously process **systematically** and **heuristically.** Systematic processing involves a similar level of cognitive effort as central processing in the ELM. Similarly, heuristic processing, like peripheral processing in the ELM, focuses on cues that are peripheral to the message itself.

In sum we can say that elements of the message, of the speaker, and of the hearer can predict your partner's likelihood to reason through your argument. We've pulled full circle to where we began the chapter. The main difference is that while the early approaches merely listed elements of each that would lead to effective persuasion, the ELM and HMP bring several elements together into a more cohesive model.

Summary

We have defined persuasive communication, noting that it refers to messages that are intended to shape, reinforce, or change the responses of others. We also noted that persuasion is not something to be taken for granted. Although we might assume that we are naturally effective communicators, such an assumption can get us into trouble when the persuasive strategy we employ fails. We also noted that it's important to study persuasion in order to become a more critical consumer of persuasive messages (from interpersonal interactions to our consumption of mass media messages).

A significant portion of the research on persuasive communication has focused on the relationships between attitudes and behaviors. According to the theory of reasoned action, the attitude-behavior relationship is best understood in terms of our evaluations of the behavioral request and our perceptions of the social appropriateness of performing the behavior. On the other hand, cognitive dissonance theory highlights the ways in which our behaviors can influence our attitudes. According to this theory, some behaviors we engage in cause us to feel discomfort or dissonance. When this dissonance is related to our self-esteem, we are motivated to do one of three things: (1) change the behavior, (2) justify the behavior by changing one of our existing cognitions, or (3) justify the behavior by adding new cognitions.

We also examined components of persuasive transactions. We noted that characteristics of the source (e.g., credibility, similarity, and physical attraction), characteristics of the message (e.g., evidence, one- and two-sided messages, ordering of persuasive arguments, and speech style), and characteristics of the receiver (how receivers process discrepant messages) all influence our attempts to persuade others.

Finally, we examined different models of the persuasion process. Specifically, we looked at models of cognitive processing and interpersonal compliance. The elaboration likelihood model has utility for those interested in persuasion to the extent that it demonstrates how people process (either centrally or peripherally) the messages they are exposed to. The compliance-gaining literature also has utility in terms of understanding the persuasive tactics we use to influence others.

Discussion Questions

1. How have scholars defined attitudes? What theories have been advanced to explain the attitude-behavior relationship? How could you use the theory of reasoned action to help you construct a communication campaign to change people's attitudes about blood donation?

2. What characteristics of sources influence persuasive communication? According to research, where should you place your strongest argument in a persuasive speech? What role does speech style play in the process of persuasion? How might you use your knowledge of social judgment theory to persuade others?

3. What are the major theoretical assumptions of the elaboration likelihood model? What techniques do you use to influence others interpersonally? Take a look at Figure 9.6. Which of these strategies are likely to be most and least effective? Do these strategies depend on your goals?

References

Adkins, M., & Brashers, D. E. (1995). The power of language in computer-mediated groups. *Management Communication Quarterly, 8*(3), 289–322.

Ajzen, I. (1985). From intentions to actions: A theory of planned behavior. In J. Kuhland & J. Beckman (Eds.), *Action-control: From cognitions to behavior* (pp. 11–39). Heidelberg, Germany: Springer.

Ajzen, I. (1991). The theory of planned behavior. *Organizational Behavior and Human Decision Processes, 50,* 179–211.

Ajzen, I. (2001). Nature and operation of attitudes. *Annual Review of Psychology, 52,* 27–58.

Allen, M. (1998). Comparing the persuasive effectiveness of one- and two-sided message. In M. Allen & R. W. Preiss (Eds.), *Persuasion: Advances through meta-analysis* (pp. 87–98). Cresskill, NJ: Hampton Press.

Bettinghaus, E. P., & Cody, M. J. (1994). *Persuasive communication* (6th ed.). Fort Worth, TX: Harcourt Brace.

Burrell, N. A., & Koper, R. J. (1998). The efficacy of powerful/powerless language on attitudes and source credibility. In M. Allen & R. W. Preiss (Eds.), *Persuasion: Advances through meta-analysis* (pp. 203–215). Cresskill, NJ: Hampton Press.

Chaiken, S. (1986). Physical appearance and social influence. In C. P. Herman, M. P. Zanna, & E. T. Higgins (Eds.), *Physical Appearance, stigma, and social behavior: The Ontario symposium* (pp. 143–177). Hillsdale, NJ: Lawrence Erlbaum.

Chaiken, S. (1987). The heuristic model of persuasion. In M. P. Zanna, J. M. Olson, & C. P. Herman (Eds.), *Social influence: The Ontario symposium* (pp. 3–39). Hillsdale, NJ: Lawrence Erlbaum.

Cialdini, R. B. (2001). *Influence: Science and practice* (4th ed.). Boston: Allyn and Bacon.

Dillard, J. P. (1989). Types of influence goals in personal relationships. *Journal of Social and Personal Relationships, 6,* 293–308.

Dillard, J. P. (1991). The current status of research on sequential-request compliance techniques. *Personality and Social Psychology Bulletin, 17,* 283–288.

Dillard, J. P., Hunter, J. E., & Burgoon, M. (1984). Sequential-request persuasive strategies: Meta-analysis of foot-in-the-door and door-in-the-face. *Human Communication Research, 10,* 461–488.

Dillard, J. P., Segrin, C., & Harden, J. M. (1989). Primary and secondary goals in the production of interpersonal influence messages. *Communication Monographs, 56,* 19–38.

Eagly, A. H., Ashmore, R. D., Makhihani, M. G., & Longo, L. C. (1991). What is beautiful is good, but . . . : A meta-analytic review of research on the physical attractiveness stereotype. *Psychological Bulletin, 110,* 109–128.

Eagly, A. H., & Chaiken, S. (1993). *The psychology of attitudes.* Fort Worth, TX: Harcourt Brace Jovanovich.

Fazio, R. H., & Zanna, M. P. (1981). Direct experience and attitude-behavior consistency. In L. Berkowitz (Ed.), *Advances in experimental social psychology* (vol. 14, pp. 161–202). New York: Academic Press.

Festinger, L. (1957). *A theory of cognitive dissonance.* Stanford, CA: Stanford University Press.

Fishbein, M., & Ajzen, I. (1980). Predicting and understanding consumer behavior: Attitude behavior correspondence. In I. Ajzen & M. Fishbein (Eds.), *Understanding attitudes and predicting social behavior* (pp. 148–172). Englewood Cliffs, NJ: Prentice-Hall.

Gouldner, A. W. (1960). The norm of reciprocity: A preliminary statement. *American Sociological Review, 25,* 161–178.

Gulley, H. E., & Berlo, D. K. (1956). Effect of intercellular and intracellular speech structure on attitude change and learning. *Speech Monographs, 23,* 288–297.

Hale, J., Mongeau, P. A., & Thomas, R. M. (1991). Cognitive processing of one- and two-sided persuasive messages. *Western Journal of Speech Communication, 55,* 380–389.

Lumsdaine, A. A., & Janis, I. L. (1953). Resistance to "counter-propaganda" produced by one-sided and two-sided "propaganda" presentations. *Public Opinion Quarterly, 17,* 311–318.

Marwell, G., & Schmitt, D. R. (1967). Dimensions of compliance-gaining behavior: An empirical analysis. *Sociometry, 30,* 350–364.

McCroskey, J. C. (1966). Scales for the measurement of ethos. *Speech Monographs, 33,* 65–72.

McCroskey, J. C. (1969). A summary of experimental research on the effects of evidence in persuasive communication. *Quarterly Journal of Speech, 55,* 169–176.

McLaughlin, M. L., Cody, M. J., & Robey, C. S. (1980). Situation influences on the selection of strategies to resist compliance gaining attempts. *Human Communication Research, 7,* 14–36.

Miller, G. R. (1980). On being persuaded: Some basic distinctions. In M. E. Roloff & G. R. Miller (Eds.), *Persuasion: New directions in theory and research* (pp. 89–116). Newbury Park, CA: Sage.

Mulac, A. (1976). Effects of obscene language upon three dimensions of listener attitude. *Communication Monographs, 43,* 300–307.

Naisbitt, J. (1982). *Megatrends: Ten new directions transforming our lives.* New York: Warner Books.

O'Keefe, D. J. (2002). *Persuasion: Theory and research* (2nd ed.). Newbury Park, CA: Sage.

Petty, R. E., & Cacioppo, J. T. (1981). *Attitudes and persuasion: Classic and contemporary approaches.* Dubuque, IA: Wm. C. Brown.

Reinard, J. C. (1988). The empirical study of the persuasive effects of evidence: The status after fifty years of research. *Human Communication Research, 15,* 3–59.

Reinard, J. C. (1998). The persuasive effects of testimonial assertion evidence. In M. Allen & R. W. Preiss (Eds.), *Persuasion: Advances through meta-analysis* (pp. 69–86). Cresskill, NJ: Hampton Press.

Sherif, M., & Hovland, C. I. (1961). *Social judgment: Assimilation and contrast effects in communication and attitude change.* New Haven, CT: Yale University Press.

Stiff, J. B. (1994). *Persuasive communication.* New York: Guilford Press.

Tellis, G. J. (1987). *Advertising, exposure, loyalty, and brand purchase; A two-stage model of choice* (Report No. 87–105). Cambridge, MA: Marketing Science Institute.

Thibodeau, R., & Aronson, E. (1992). Taking a closer look: Reasserting the role of the self-concept in dissonance theory. *Personality and Social Psychology Bulletin, 18,* 591–602.

Unnava, H. R., Burnkrant, R. E., & Erevelles, S. (1994). Effects of presentation order and communication modality on recall and attitude. *Journal of Consumer Research, 21,* 1–27.

Walker, L., Thibaut, J., & Andreoli, V. (1972). Order of presentation at trial. *Yale Law Journal, 82,* 216–226.

10

Theories of Culture, Groupness, and Intercultural Communication

John R. Baldwin and Suraj P. Kapoor

As we have considered various contexts of communication, we have seen how interpersonal communication grew as a field of focus (Chapter 4), intertwined with media theory and later public relations. We have seen specific contexts of interpersonal communication, such as interpersonal communication (Chapter 7), persuasion (Chapter 9), and small group communication (Chapter 8). In this chapter, we will consider another area that has received much focus in our discipline, intercultural communication. Indeed, intercultural communication may be one of the fastest growing areas of interest in the field, based on the growth of interest groups in our national associations.

In this chapter, we begin by looking at frameworks that scholars have used to understand cultural differences. We will then consider three areas of theory. The first looks at what happens when people from different cultures, often understood as national cultures, meet one another. The second area considers the notion of "groupness" as co-cultures within a country create their culture and interact with people from other cultures. The final area looks at how power comes to play in intergroup and intercultural communication. Through these areas, we can see how the historical roots described in Chapter 4 come to play in the specific area of intercultural communication.

In this chapter, you will read about the following concepts:

- Definition of culture, intercultural, intergroup, cross-cultural
- Frameworks of cultural difference
  - E. T. Hall's high and low context
  - Hofstede's four dimensions of cultures

- Being a better intercultural communicator
  - Politeness and a face-negotiation theory of conflict
  - Conversational constraint theory
  - Anxiety/uncertainty management theory
- Theories of cultural communication
  - Communicative theory of ethnic identity
  - Communication accommodation theory
- Theories of power and group difference
  - Standpoint theory
  - Muted group theory
  - Co-cultural theory

At the 1998 MTV Video Music Awards, Madonna wore "Vaishnava tilak"—a type of facial marking that is considered sacred among Hindus. However, as she sang, she wore clothing that revealed lots of skin and danced in a highly suggestive manner. The World Vaishnava Association, a Hindu group, immediately sought apologies (*USA Today*, Sept. 14, 1999, cited in BRI, 1999). In a different time and corner of the world, one of your authors sat at a breakfast table in Brazil. As the hostess offered more food, he put his hand horizontally to his neck, as if to say "enough." Unfortunately, the gesture, in Brazil, meant, "This food gags me."

While we may not be pop stars, every day we are involved in some form of intercultural communication. This may seem like an extreme statement, but it makes sense if one takes a very broad view of intercultural communication. At its broadest level, **culture** can be considered a way of life, a system of beliefs, values, attitudes, behaviors, and artifacts that are held by a group of people. [Web site: On Defining Culture] Thus, even different families or social clubs, at least at a small level, have a unique "culture." Usually, such differences do not strongly influence the communication process, so most choose to limit the definition of **intercultural communication** to occasions where "cultural perceptions and symbol systems are distinct enough to alter the communication event" (Samovar & Porter, 1991, p. 70).

You will likely encounter many instances of intercultural communication per week or even per day, depending on where you live, due to increased immigration, international business, and the increased recognition of various co-cultures in the United States (Samovar & Porter, 1997; see Figure 10.1). If not, you will see other cultures in the media. Perhaps you go to chatrooms on the Internet or are on listservs, many of which will include people from around the world. Some even argue that genders, age groups, and social classes develop their own cultures. But is it culture that is influencing your communication in any of these instances, or is it something else?

Why Do We Sometimes Have Problems in Our Intercultural Interactions?

If you have a conflict with your boss who is from a different culture, is the difficulty based on gender differences? On culture? On individual differences? If you experience a tense

FIGURE 10.1   In our diverse world, many of us communicate interculturally every day.

© Dana White (1998)/PhotoEdit/PictureQuest

situation with someone you perceive to be of a different racial group, is it merely a misunderstanding based on personal communication differences, is the difficulty cultural, or is it based at some level on stereotypes and prejudice? Many authors have proposed models to try to understand what is happening in any intercultural interaction. Most of these suggest that even if we consider an interaction to be intercultural, we must realize that people send and receive messages based both in terms of their culture and in terms of individual aspects of their personality. [Web site: Models of Intercultural Interaction] One of your authors (Kapoor) prefers the term *intracultural* to refer to what some have called *co-cultural* or *subcultural* communication—that between people from different groups sharing a dominant culture. Your other author (Baldwin) feels such distinctions are arbitrary, that the differences within such a "culture" can sometimes be greater than the differences between so called dominant cultures.

We feel that, in addition to individual and cultural differences, we should also include the perception of difference, especially when it is perceived in group terms (rich/poor, Latino/Black, Democrat/Republican, Southerner/"Yankee"). In many cases, this second type of communication is riddled more with stereotypes and prejudice than with cultural difference, highlighting group identities rather than differences in communication style. Thus, we call this **intergroup** rather than intercultural communication. We might *perceive* someone to be different because she or he is from a different region, religion, or race, when there are, in fact, not really enough real cultural differences in terms of values, beliefs, or behavior to influence the interaction. Thus, we like to propose a three-dimensional model of communication that considers individual differences (interpersonal communication), real cultural differences (intercultural communication), and perceived differences (intergroup communication). Figure 10.2 illustrates the three dimensions (Baldwin & Hunt, 2002).

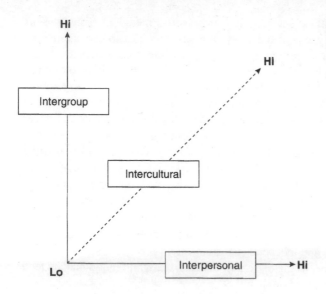

FIGURE 10.2 *Three Dimensions of Communication.* By this three-dimensional model, one can have prejudice although there are no real cultural differences.

We will begin this chapter by looking at situations where cultural is a more important aspect of the interaction—theories of one-on-one interaction and cultural adjustment. We will then present theories where group identity is more important. Finally, we will consider critical theories of intercultural communication that have implication for both media and communication studies. Notably, except for one exception that we will see as we proceed, as we move from culture to groupness to issues of representation, the theories tend to move from scientific to humanistic to critical. Before we look at the theories, however, we need to introduce terms that will help you understand some of the later theories and intercultural communication in general.

Several writers have proposed frameworks to compare cultural differences (i.e., **cross-cultural communication**) that will help us as we consider intercultural explanations of communication. For example, E. T. Hall (1976) suggested that communication is dependent upon the **code** (the words spoken), the **context** (the relationships, rules, and roles present in the interaction), and the **meaning** that communicators ascribe to the event. The notion of meaning is central in intercultural communication, for one of the main intercultural difficulties is when we attribute meaning to others' behavior based on our own cultural frameworks. Hall suggested that some cultures privilege the meaning in the context, and are thus **high-context cultures.** People in other cultures seek meaning in the "explicit code"—the words spoken (**low context cultures**). As Yadong, a Chinese student, has an interaction with his teacher, Dr. Louis, Yadong may base his understandings on his role as a student, his level in his degree, and so on. Dr. Louis, from a low-context culture, will more likely look for meaning in Yadong's exact words. If Yadong also seeks to *give* meaning through context (subtle nonverbal behaviors, nuances of communication), we can guess that the two will have some misunderstanding!

Geert Hofstede (1997), an organizational psychologist in the Netherlands, developed another way to view cultural difference. His framework of four dimensions of cultural difference have become perhaps the most popular in intercultural communication.

Power distance refers to "the extent to which the less powerful members of institutions and organizations within a country expect and accept that power is distributed unequally" (p. 28). One of your authors is from a high power-distance society, in which status difference is expected and even privileged; the other is from a country that claims to be egalitarian (though it values status more than people will admit). **Uncertainty avoidance** distinguishes cultures based on their preference for structure and rules. And **masculinity-femininity** divides cultures based on a preference for direct, goal-oriented communication (masculine) or modest, face-saving communication (feminine).

Hofstede's fourth dimension, **individualism-collectivism,** has received rich treatment by cross-cultural psychologist Harry Triandis. Triandis (1990) states that collectivists pay attention to a certain in-group such as the tribe, the work group, the family, or the nation and behave differently toward members of such groups than toward members of other groups. Individualists do not perceive as sharp a difference between in-groups and out-groups. In individualist cultures, personal goals have primacy over in-group goals. Personal fate, personal achievement, and independence from the in-group are stressed. Thus, collectivists tend to think of groups as the basic unit of analysis, while individualists tend to consider individuals as the basic unit of analysis.

We note that, as a trend, cultures that are more collectivistic also tend to have higher power distance (Figure 10.3), as status becomes more important when one sees oneself in terms of the collective. Also, urbanization, industrialization, and other factors may lead to increased individualism. Thus, Hofstede and others have noted the strong individualism in the United States, with one 1996 study concluding that "the consequences of radical individualism [in the United States] are more strikingly evident than they were even a decade ago" (Bellah, Madsen, Sullivan, Swidler, & Tipton, p. xi). Still, most scholars admit that both ends of any of these dimensions exist in all cultures; our point here is just that cultures tend to have preferences for one value over the other.

How Can I Be a Better Intercultural Communicator?

Many have tried to explain what happens in intercultural interaction and why this is rewarding or difficult. Often these writers lean upon the dimensions of cultural difference listed above, or on other frameworks of variables meant to apply across all cultures. For example, classic and well-supported theories have looked at how we reduce anxiety and uncertainty in intercultural communications, or how we adjust to other cultures. [Web site: Anxiety-Uncertainty Management Theory, Theories of Cultural Adaptation] In this section, however, we consider two theories that extend politeness theory into the area of intercultural communication.

Politeness Theory and Its Extensions

Penelope Brown and Stephen Levinson (1987) suggested that people in all cultures balance the need to fit in, the need to be competent, and the desire not to impose on others in all interactions (see Chapter 7, this text). However, certain cultures have preference for some of these needs over the others. Two writers have extended this theory to explain intercultural interaction.

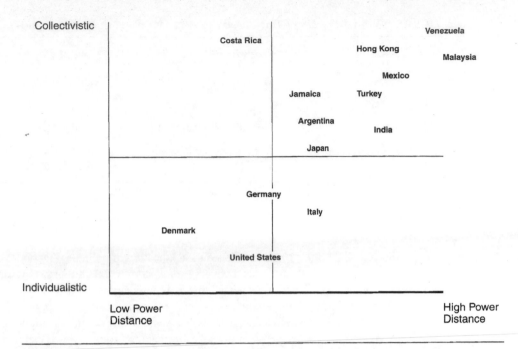

FIGURE 10.3 *Hofstede's Dimensions of Culture: Individualism/Collectivism and Power Distance.* This figure shows placement of some of the 40 nations Hofstede studied on two of his four dimensions.

Adapted from *Cultures and organizations: Software of the mind,* G. Hofstede, New York: McGraw-Hill, © 1997. Used with permission.

First, Stella Ting-Toomey (1988; Ting-Toomey & Kurogi, 1998; Ting-Toomey & Oetzel, 2002) describes what happens in conflict situations in different cultures in her **face-negotiation theory of conflict.** She states that people in low-context cultures tend to be individualistic and those in high-context cultures collectivistic. She relies heavily upon the ideas of **face,** politeness, and face needs (positive and negative) presented in Chapter 7. Ting-Toomey links politeness theory and notions of cultural variation to models of conflict resolution. Such models often present conflict styles in terms of an orientation towards one's own goals and the goals of the other (Rahim, 1983).

In a conflict between Roberto, a South American student, and Dr. Williams, an American professor, if the professor focuses more on her own goals, this would be a **dominating** or competing style (I win, you lose). If she simply gives in, she is **obliging** or yielding (you win, I lose). If she simply shuts down the conversation by not discussing it (e.g., hanging up the phone, walking out), she is **avoiding** the conflict (you lose, I lose). If she seeks a "win-win" situation through discussion, she is **collaborating** (you win, I win). And if she and Roberto seek a midway solution, they are **compromising** (we both win but only in part). Ting-Toomey predicts that individualists prefer direct, self-focused strategies that require confrontation of the conflict (e.g., dominating or compromising), while collectivists prefer face-saving indirectness and minimizing of conflict (avoiding, obliging) or, at best, compromising (Figure 10.4).

FIGURE 10.4   *A Summary of Ting-Toomey's Predictions about Culture and Conflict.*

Aspect of Conflict	Individualistic Cultures	Collectivistic Cultures
Focus of strategy	Own needs	Other's needs
Mode of strategy	Direct communication	Indirect communication
Face needs	Negative face (autonomy)	Positive face (inclusion)
Preferred conflict styles	Dominating, collaborating	Obliging, withdrawing, competing

Adapted from Ting-Toomey, 1988.

Min-Sun Kim (1993, 1995) broadened the application of politeness theory to consider all aspects of communication in her **conversational constraints theory.** Conversational constraints are the "procedural knowledge" that communicators use to "guide the choice of communication tactics and the general assessment of communication competence" (p. 148). Kim proposes that the constraints that dictate what we do in any communication—from persuading someone to conflicting to telling jokes to making requests—originates in certain conversational needs. These include **face support,** including the desire not to impinge upon the other person's free will (negative face) and the desire not to hurt the other person's feelings (one aspect of positive face), and a **need for clarity,** or the desire for conversation to be efficient and explicit. Kim constructs a model that includes both cultural variables, such as individualism-collectivism, and individual variables, such as an individual's need for dominance, **psychological gender** (degree one adopts the traditional gender roles of men or women), and **self-construal** (how an individual sees herself or himself in relation to others).

Although Roberto's culture is classified as more collective, he may have a high need for dominance, stronger "masculine" tendencies (directness, assertiveness), and, based on his focus of needing good grades, an independent self-construal. Professor Williams may be independent, but also may have a need for social approval. In your own interactions, if you need clarity and closure, you may find that you offend people who are more relational (based on both cultural and individual influences) by being too focused on the task at hand instead of paying attention to relationship and "face."

How Should I Communicate within My Group or with People from Other Groups?

Recently theorists have turned the lens of their focus around to look not just at communication between those of different nations but at groups within a single national culture, such as Filipino Americans within the United States. Some have used notions from symbolic interactionism to see how people in a single culture create the identity of that culture through communicating. [Web site: Speech Codes Theory] Others have focused on communication between different people when group identities, rather than culture, are at stake. In this section, we will look at an example of each type of theory.

In the last 25 years, many scholars in communication have begun to treat culture not as a variable that predicts communication, but as something that is created through communication. Hecht, Collier, and their colleagues take such a stance as they look at how groups culturally create an identity through communication in a theory called the **communicative theory of ethnic identity (CTEI)** (Collier & Thomas, 1988; Hecht, Collier, & Ribeau, 1993). This approach to identity assumes that identities have elements that continue to change and elements that remain constant. The CTEI suggests that identities have core symbols, rules, and meanings. For example, core symbols for African American communication seems to be expressiveness, individuality, authenticity, and community (Hecht, Collier, & Ribeau, 1993; Johnson, 2000).

Each of us has multiple, intersecting identities (parent, sibling, male or female, national identity, religious identity, ethnic identity, and so on), and each has its own rules and meanings. These identities vary in **salience** (how aware you are of them at a given moment) and emerge during conversations, and people vary in the **intensity** with which they express or identify. In addition, each identity has both a content and a relationship component. Some identities have a broader **scope,** or number of people who hold the identity. The **content** component is composed of the thoughts we have about what it means to be, for example, a Christian or a Hindu. The **relationship** component consists of the feelings we have for that identity. Thus, identities "are affective, cognitive, behavioral, and spiritual" (Hecht et al., 1993, p. 166). Communication is effective when we see others in the same identity frame (**ascribed identity**) as they claim in a situation (**avowed identity**). Another hypothetical example will help clarify how the theory works.

Shenequa goes into a business meeting feeling apprehensive. She does not like these meetings. First, she feels awkward entering the room because, even after five years in her organization, she is the only African American in the leadership group. More than that, she feels uncomfortable talking with Bob, one of the other division managers. Bob does a couple of things that irritate Shenequa. First, he has a tendency to interrupt her when she is talking and to shift the topic before she is done discussing an issue. These behaviors make her feel that he does not care about what she has to say. Second, when he explains a proposal to the group, he sometimes looks at her and repeats some of the details, slowing down a bit and even choosing simpler words. Despite her masters degree in communication, Shenequa leaves the meetings feeling that Bob thinks she is stupid.

In terms of the communication theory of ethnic identity both Shenequa, an African American woman, and Bob, a Caucasian American man, have ethnic identities. Shenequa's ethnic identity is likely more apparent to her then Bob's, as she enters the meeting and perceives herself to be the only African American in the group. Thus, at this moment, that identity is more salient to her. She has thoughts, feelings, and behaviors that she associates with being African American, just as Bob does with being Caucasian American. Both identities are wider in scope than, say, a Vietnamese Canadian or a Muslim Serb identity. Importantly, as Shenequa walks into the room, she seeks to claim her identity as a business professional. Bob, however, may be behaving on her based on his stereotypes of African Americans. Thus, while she avows a business professional identity, he ascribes her an

African American identity (and, in this case, one that does not really reflect how African Americans see themselves!).

People negotiate multiple identities at different levels. Bob may be thinking not of his racial identity, but of Shenequa as a woman and him as a man. Bob's thoughts and feelings about his masculine identity show the **personal level** of his identity. When he interrupts or changes the topic, he may be enacting his identity through interaction (the **dyadic level**). In his relationships with his close friends at the sports bar or on the golf course, or in the way he acts with his romantic partner(s), he will play out his identity at the **relational level.** Finally, formal and informal rituals and ceremonies can pass on, create, and shape cultural identities at the **communal level;** for example, an awards ceremony might highlight the accomplishments of women in light of "their other duties at home" (something rarely said of men).

Often when we interact with someone whom we perceive to be of a different racial group (or considerably older, or from a different country), we find ourselves changing our behavior to adjust or "accommodate" to our perception of the other group. If you talk to a professor, you might swear less, talk about "academic" things, and even use more precise grammar than you do when you are talking to your friends on the volleyball court. Sometimes this accommodation works quite well—and sometimes it backfires!

Howard Giles, along with Cindy Gallois and others (Giles, Mulac, Bradac, & Johnson, 1987; Gallois, Franklyn-Stokes, Giles, & Coupland, 1988; Gallois, Giles, Jones, Cargile, & Ota 1995) developed the **communication accommodation theory** (CAT) to describe what happens when people from two linguistic groups (dialect, accent, language) meet and interact. When you speak with someone from a different group, you will likely **converge,** or adapt your speech patterns toward the other person, to **diverge,** or make your patterns more distinct, or to simply **maintain** your usual speech patterns. Convergence can be one way (only one person changes) or mutual (both can change). It may be intentional, but is often beyond our awareness. Researchers have looked at several aspects of accommodation, including strategies, factors, and outcomes of convergence.

As you speak, for example, to a "foreigner" you might use a variety of strategies to converge or diverge. These include **interpretability strategies,** such as changing your word choice to words you think the person will understand, slowing down your speech, or speaking more loudly. You might use **discourse management strategies,** such as controlling or yielding control of the topic, sharing turn taking and so on. Or you might engage in **interpersonal control strategies,** such as interruptions, use of commands, use of formal titles (sir, ma'am, Professor, and so on). You might converge in accent, use of slang, expressiveness, or topic selection, among other aspects of verbal, nonverbal, or paralinguistic communication.

Of course, we do not always converge (or diverge). Thus, authors have investigated a wide number of factors to try to predict whether one would converge or diverge. The most important may be your motives. If you want to accomplish a goal such as persuading the other, making the other feel a sense of belonging, or showing you like the other person, this would lead you to converge. But if you want to highlight the differences between your groups, show dislike, or insult the other, you would likely diverge. Other factors that might influence your accommodation to the older person would be your own ability to converge, the norms of the situation (they may require you to converge, say, if you are in a church setting), the strength of the language groups involved, your dependence upon your own language group, perception of threat in the interaction, and so on (Gallois et al., 1988, 1995). For example, if you are a Hmong-speaking Laotian, you might be more likely to accommodate if you live in rural Maine and there are fewer Hmong, more norms for accommodation, fewer outlets to speak a dialect of Hmong, and your interaction goals require it than if you live in Oregon among a community of other Hmong immigrants.

In most cases when we converge, people respond favorably toward us; so in most cases it may be better to accommodate than not. However, convergence can backfire if we are seen as patronizing or if we are stepping on what a group perceives to be the cultural territory of its language. One problem in black-white communication is the tendency of some whites to use **hyperexplanation,** a form of overaccommodation in which whites oversimplify their grammar or word choice, something that makes some blacks feel as if they are condescending or prejudiced (Waters, 1992). We see Bob, in the example above, engaging both in hyperexplanation and in interpersonal control strategies of nonaccommodation at the same time. Similar to hyperexplanation is what has been called *secondary baby talk,* a tendency to talk to the elderly in a higher pitch with first-person plurals and simple language, which many elderly people feel puts them down.

Is It Really Just Ignorance—or Is It Prejudice?

Some writers have taken the ideas of the last theories one step further to look not only at intergender or interethnic discourse or at the understanding of a single culture, but to see how that discourse works against the group with the less power, or how the cultural meaning of a group is one that resists power structures. Early writers, for example, defined prejudice in terms of ignorance of difference or fear of what was different, the solution to which was simply informing one another of cultural difference. But many scholars today have come to the conclusion that racism is not just about ignorance, it is about power. In this section we will consider two groups of critical perspectives, feminist/co-cultural theories and theories of radical difference.

Constructed Difference and Power:
Feminism and Co-Cultural Theory

Gender studies have long focused on differences between men and women; however, feminists have often critiqued these theories because they merely discuss difference without its implication for power. The studies (especially scientific studies), often conflate sex and gender. **Sex** refers to biological difference, whereas **gender** is the social construction of how men and women should behave, what they should value, and so on. Feminist theorists tend to believe that differences found between men and women's communication (for example, in terms of amount and type of interruptions, use of tag questions and hedges by women, assertive versus relational communication, and so on) are socially constructed. Some feel this construction of how men and women are supposed to communicate inherently disadvantages women by socializing them to speak in ways that yield power and authority to men, while others feel that women's styles of communicating have their own power.

Standpoint theory, developed by Sandra Harding (1991), Nancy Harstock (1997), and others, goes beyond language to look at the perception of life itself. The theory suggests that women and men's experiences in life are influenced by their position in the class structure (with men having more economic power and privilege in that structure). Each has a view of the world, a knowledge or understanding. But these group-based views are different; in fact, they mirror each other. Each is only partial and cannot fully understand the others. However, (a) the standpoint of the more powerful typically structures the way both groups live; (b) the standpoint of the more powerful group is harmful for the weaker group; and (c) the less powerful group usually has a better understanding of the more powerful group than the latter has of the former. This is in part because the oppressed group *has to* understand the oppressor, since the rules of the powerful group dictate how interaction and life are accomplished. The oppressing group often does not want to understand the oppressed group, for to do so might demonstrate a need for change. The purpose of the theory is to spark research that presents the standpoint of oppressed groups so that the unjust situation can be seen and changed.

Shenequa will likely have a view unique to women of color that Bob simply cannot understand, part of which is the experience of seeing few other faces like her own in her place of work and of feeling that anything she does may reflect not only on her, but on her racial group. Bob will, of course, have his own standpoint as well. Shenequa will understand Bob's a little more than he understands hers, because it is his way of life and thinking that structures the work environment. Standpoint theory often assumes that all women have the same understanding, which is a limitation of the theory. In fact, Shenequa and Dr. Williams, the professor in our earlier example, will likely have standpoints that are similar in some ways, since they are both women in a men's world, but different due to racial inequalities (Collins, 1991).

A second feminist theory frequently considered by young communication students is **muted group theory.** This theory began with the work of Shirley and Edwin Ardener, who noted that much of the anthropological accounts of cultures relied on men's voices, since the women were not deemed rational or reliable enough to give accounts (E. Ardener, 1975; S. Ardener, 1975). They, along with Cheris Kramarae (1981), who imported the theory into communication studies, argue that women are twice muted. First, men "create" the language and terms of speaking by being the chief dictionary writers, poets, filmmakers, CEOs, music video producers, and news program directors. Second, when women do speak, men do not listen; thus, the women get used to not being heard and become mute.

There is some evidence for such muting. For example, if you go to see a movie that is based on romance and has no gratuitous violence or even sex in it, it is called a "chick flick." All other movies are not called "guy flicks." They are just called movies. A woman walking from the men's dorm in the morning goes on the "walk of shame," while the man returning from the woman's dorm walks the "walk of fame." This language, as well as many of the euphemisms men use for women ("babe," "chick," and so on) reflects either a sexual double standard that allows men sexual freedom but criticizes women if they have the same, or frames women as if they were children or sex objects. One response of critics is that these are just words or that such inequalities in language existed only in days gone by.

Marsha Houston and Cheris Kramarae (1992) argue that women are silenced when men serve as the gatekeepers of knowledge, ridicule women's ways of talking ("nagging," "gossiping," and the like), and engage in sexual harassment. Further, silencing occurs through rituals, such as the wedding ceremony. Because of this silencing, women often cannot find the words to express themselves, especially in terrains normally considered as male (Kramarae, 1981). The theory seeks to help women find new ways of communicating with one another, such as through mentoring, journaling, dialogue, and creating new language. One such example is the creation of the word "sexual harassment." Prior to the 1970s, women had no such word to describe something experienced by between 42 and 92 percent of women in the workplace (Terpstra & Baker, 1989).

Mark Orbe (1998a, 1998b), as noted above, saw the benefit of these two theories in describing not only women's experience, but also that of African Americans and other ethnic groups in the predominantly white United States. In his **co-cultural theory,** he proposes that African Americans, based on their position in a culture that is ambivalent toward them, develop a complex standpoint. He contends that "in each society, a hierarchy exists that privileges certain groups of people; in the United States these groups include men, European Americans, heterosexuals, the able-bodied, and middle and upper class" (1998a, p. 11). Like many cultural studies writers (Chapter 17), Orbe does not feel that those in power always hold their power deliberately. But he does believe the elite hold the positions of power and either directly or indirectly limit the progress of other groups. Thus, he feels, despite differences between co-cultural groups, they will share some similarities in perspective that standpoint and muted group theories explain.

Orbe explains a wide variety of co-cultural communication behaviors through this synthesis theory, including emphasizing commonalities, dissociating, responding in various ways to stereotypes, self-censoring, overcompensating, increasing visibility, and attacking—a total of some 25 different behaviors. He then categorizes different **communication orientations,** which he defines as a stance that co-culture members take when interacting with members of a dominant group. He describes nine stances that vary on two dimensions. The first is whether the co-culture member is nonassertive, assertive, or aggressive. The second is whether the co-culture member adopts **assimilation** (adopting the majority culture's views), **accommodation** (a combination of majority and co-culture views), or **separation** (a maintenance of co-culture views). Figure 10.5 categorizes the communication behaviors in terms of the communication orientations.

If Shenequa is assertive and seeks accommodation, she will seek to educate Bob as to why his behavior offends her. She will communicate her feelings to him and seek liaisons with whites; if there are no African Americans who might mentor her, she might look for wider bases of similarity, such as finding a female or a member of another co-cultural group who might share at least some aspects of her standpoint. If, however, she chooses to be aggressive and separating, she would attack Bob and sabotage his efforts. Most likely, she would combine orientations. Indeed, at times, aggressiveness may be called for; however, depending on her communication goals, her perception of her identity, and her desire to seek social change, she may seek a calmer course instead, at least for now.

Radical Difference: Whiteness, Critical Race Theory, and Postcolonialism

As we saw in the introduction to critical theories in Chapter 2, there is a wide variety of critical theories, and theorists in this area often do not agree with one another. Thus, we see these last three perspectives as even more "radical" than those above. By the term *radical,* we do not mean to judge this set of approaches; rather, they are *radical* in that rather

FIGURE 10.5 *Orbe's Co-Cultural Communication Orientations.*

	Separation	Accommodation	Assimilation
Nonassertive	Avoiding	Increasing visibility	Emphasizing commonalities
	Maintaining interpersonal barriers	Dispelling stereotypes	Developing positive face
			Censoring self
			Averting controversy
Assertive	Communicating self	Communicating self	Extensive preparation
	Intragroup networking	Intragroup networking	Overcompensating
	Exemplifying strengths	Using liaisons	Manipulating stereotypes
	Embracing stereotypes	Educating others	Bargaining
Aggressive	Attacking	Confronting	Dissociating
	Sabotaging others	Gaining advantage	Mirroring
			Strategic distancing
			Ridiculing self

Adapted from Orbe (1998a).

than seeking merely equality for subordinated groups in an otherwise (supposedly) egalitarian system, these perspectives often seek to dismantle the system itself, seeing such things as capitalism, progress, and modernity as ineffective at best and at worst as dangerous for those who live within their grasps as for those who do not. These perspectives share a disdain of modernity and focus on ideology and on meanings created by groups through discourse that collide in conflict.

A critique of **whiteness** began in the late 1980s and early 1990s; two foundational works are Ruth Frankenburg's (1993) interview study of white women, *White Women, Race Matters,* and Richard Dyer's (1997) *White.* Before this time, scholars had migrated from an interest in racial differences as culture to studies of "whiteness, a focus centering on the ways that white domination—as a social and ideological phenomenon—reproduces itself and configures the 'place' of other racial/ethnic groups in 'centering' itself" (Wander, Martin, & Nakayama, 1999, p. 22). White oppression, entangled with homophobia, sexism, and classism, reproduces itself through discrimination, overt and subtle racism toward people of color. But more than that, it reproduces itself by its very intangibility. "Whiteness is a sink" (Wander et al., p. 22), because if it is not nameable it need not even defend its power position.

One study (Nakayama & Krizek, 1995) found that whites often resisted naming their ethnicity, preferring to see nonwhites as "racial," "ethnic," and "other," while they themselves are "American," or sometimes just *are.* Peggy McIntosh (1998) lists 46 invisible aspects of white privilege, such as, "I am never asked to speak for all the people of my group," and "I can take a job with an affirmative action employer without having my co-workers on the job suspect that I got it because of my race" (pp. 98–99).

Critical race theory (CRT) is closely related to whiteness studies; but where the first focuses more on the social and linguistic construction of whiteness, this is the other side of the coin—that looks at how one racial group (predominantly whites) oppresses others. It began in the writings of disenchanted black authors, such as Derrick Bell's (1992) *Faces at the Bottom of the Well,* but was influenced by postmodernism, black feminism (e.g., Collins, 1991), and Marxism (Lynn, 1999). Richard Delgado (1995) lists the key themes of CRT as "the call for context, critique of liberalism, insistence that racism is ordinary not exceptional, and the notion that traditional civil rights law has been more valuable to whites than to blacks" (p. xv). CRT rejects many of the ideals of liberal democracy, such as rationality and universality, and disdains its claims to neutrality and "color blindness" (Lynn, 1999).

CRT has had wide influence on many disciplines, beginning in a strident (and widespread) critique of the legal system (Crenshaw, Gotanda, Peller, & Thomas, 1995). Like Orbe's (1998a) preference for discovering people's experiences situated in their own lives, Lynn (1999) conducted a study of African American female teachers and used the findings to promote an "African American emancipatory pedagogy" (p. 606). In a similar vein, Yosso (2002) raises a critique of American media as a system of exploitation and power to oppress non-whites. In her article, she details how she infuses her teaching with CRT in order to raise the social consciousness of her students.

Postcolonial inquiry goes one step beyond CRT and whiteness studies to see these interlocked systems of gender, class, and race oppression at a global level, intricately tied to the historical processes of colonization. Like the others, it is "interventionist and highly political," with a focus "not just [on] colonial conditions but *why* those conditions are what they are, and how they can be undone" (Shome & Hegde, 2002, p. 250). This approach is impacting the communication field as a whole and intercultural communication specifically. Like CRT and whiteness studies (as well as Orbe's theory and the feminist theories), postcolonial theory explains both mediated and face-to-face communication.

One of the core notions of postcolonial theory is **modernity,** as modernity brought both the rational approaches and hierarchies that many use to justify racial oppression and it brought the industrial, segregated relations that maintain the oppression. The theme of modernity, framed within the relations of the nations that colonized the world and those that were colonized, "constitutes the central investigative impulse of postcolonial studies" (Shome & Hegde, 2002, p. 258). From this springboard, postcolonial studies explore (to use a word perhaps unwelcome in this context!) things such as national power, gendered and sexual politics, globalization (and its negative effects), and politics of immigration (Shome & Hegde, 2002). Colonial relations are marked by an *ambivalence* that the colonized feel toward the colonizers, as they admire them yet resent them; by *appropriation,* as the colonized adopt (and reinvent) the media, artifacts, or ideas of the colonizers; and by **hybridity** (Mahlotra & Crabtree, 2002). This term receives special focus in many studies, referring to the mixture of cultures as the colonized and colonizers rub together within the same social spaces. Finally, linked to immigration and otherness, some focus on **diasporic** groups—those who emigrate from one land to become residents in a number of different cultures. For example, Drzewiecka and Halualani (2002) theorize about the politics and maintenance of the identity of a group that is spread out among cultures, as these exist within structural forces such as governments and economic structures, highlighting differences between two groups—the Polish and Hawaiian diasporas.

These three perspectives all relate to the way we communicate in our intercultural and interracial relationships, suggesting that there may be more than cultural difference when we communicate with others, say with an immigrant or as an immigrant. They also have implications for media studies, such as Raka Shome's (1996) analysis of the way whites and Indians in Calcutta are portrayed in the 1992 film *City of Joy*. Her presentation of the representation of the bodies of the main Indian characters Hasari and Kamla and of the "universality of Whiteness" that allows Max, the white American doctor, to adjust to India with no problems shows the melding in this study of whiteness, critical race studies, and postcolonialism.

Summary

In this chapter, we have explored many branches of intercultural theory. We now admit our triple agenda. On one hand, we traversed areas commonly covered in intercultural research—meeting people from other cultures, creation of cultural and group identities, interacting with those of other group-based identities, and living with the oppression of those group-based identities. At a second level, we have summarized what we feel is a useful way to think about some of the aspects of intercultural interaction. We feel all interaction has, on some level, individual influences (interpersonal), cultural influences (intercultural), and perceptions of group identity (intergroup).

Finally, at a third level, we have introduced theories from all three paradigms mentioned in Chapter 2. Generally, the theories chosen here to describe intercultural interaction were scientific. More theories of identity building and maintenance, because of their roots in phenomenology and symbolic interactionism, tend to be humanistic, as they seek to *interpret* a single culture's norms and meanings, including those for its own identity (CTEI). At the same time, communication accommodation theory is clearly scientific and one of the theories with the longest legacy, "homegrown" in the area of intercultural communication. Orbe (1998) takes ideas from the CTEI and adds how the identity one forms cannot be understood apart from dominant identities that may be oppressive. This argument is extended through the theories of whiteness and critical race theory (though, at least as presented here, these are more perspectives than theories) to postcolonial theory. This last approach critiques not only the racism of a single individual, nor even of the policies of a nation, but sees these as part of a larger system of problematic global politics.

With this set of theories, you can see the diversity both in content areas and also in approaches taken by intercultural theorists. But, most of all, you can see the types of practical issues that intercultural theorists have addressed. You may use these theories as you choose: Perhaps you will focus on the first theories and strive to be a more effective intercultural communicator. You may use the second set of theories to help you better understand the way you maintain with others your different identities (and communicate more respectfully with those with other identitites). Or, from the theories at the end of the chapter, you might decide that there are, indeed, some social inequalities in the world that merit your energies. There is no doubt that intercultural theories can help you to be a "better" communicator, whether you define "better" in terms of your social awareness or simply getting along with your neighbor.

Discussion Questions

1. Recall a time that you were involved in an intercultural interaction. Which differences, verbal or nonverbal, seemed to impact the interaction? How did you feel during that interaction? Be ready to apply Ting-Toomey's or Kim's theories regarding facework or communication accommodation theory to the interaction.

2. Think of a group to which you belong. What are some of the core symbols, meanings, and behaviors that mark membership in that group? How "salient" or important is the group's identity to you (e.g., do you think about it all the time, or only at certain times)? Do others ascribe to you the same identity that you avow? Explain.

3. What are some of the groups (besides any group you belong to) in your university, area of the country, or nation that are targets of prejudice or oppression? How might you see this impacting their communication both within their group and with your group? Which of Orbe's strategies for intergroup communication do you feel will be effective for those in these groups? Support your answer.

References

Ardener, E. (1975). The "problem" revisited. In S. Ardener (Ed.), *Perceiving women* (pp. 19–27). London: Malaby Press.

Ardener, S. (1975). Introduction: The nature of women in society. In S. Ardener (Ed.), *Defining females* (pp. 9–48). New York: Wiley.

Baldwin, J. R., & Hunt, S. K. (2002). Information-seeking behavior in intercultural and intergroup communication. *Human Communication Research, 28,* 272–286.

Bathroom Reader Institute (BRI). (1999). *Uncle John's Absolutely Absorbing Bathroom Reader.* Ashland, OR: Bathroom Readers' Press.

Bell, D. (1992). *Faces at the bottom of the well: The permanence of racism.* New York: Basic Books.

Bellah, R. N., Madsen, R., Sullivan, W. M., Swidler, A., & Tipton, S. M. (1996). *Habits of the heart: Individualism and commitment in American life* (updated). Berkeley: University of California Press.

Brown, P., & Levinson, S. (1987). *Politeness: Some universals in language usage.* Cambridge: Cambridge University Press.

Collier, M. J., & Thomas, M. (1988). Cultural identity: An interpretive perspective. In Y. Y. Kim & W. B. Gudykunst (Eds.), *Theories in intercultural communication* (pp. 99–120). Newbury Park, CA: Sage.

Collins, P. H. (1991). *Black feminist thought: Knowledge, consciousness, and the politics of social empowerment.* Boston: Unwin Hyman.

Crenshaw, K., Gotanda, N., Peller, G., & Thomas, K. (1995). Introduction. In K. Crenshaw, N. Gotanda, G. Peller, & K. Thomas (Eds.), *Critical race theory: The key writings that formed the movement* (pp. xiii–xxxii). New York: New Press.

Delgado, R. (1995). Introduction. In R. Delgado (Ed.), *Critical race theory: The cutting edge* (pp. xiii–xvi). Philadelphia: Temple University Press.

Drzewiecka, J., & Halualani, R. T. (2002). The structural-cultural dialectic of diasporic politics. *Communication Theory, 12,* 340–366.

Dyer, R. (1997). *White.* New York: Routledge.

Frankenburg, R. (1993). *White women, race matters: The social construction of whiteness.* Durham, NC: Duke University Press.

Gallois, C., Franklyn-Stokes, A., Giles, H., & Coupland, N. (1988). Communication accommodation in intercultural encounters. In Y. Y. Kim & W. B. Gudykunst (Eds.), *Theories in intercultural communication* (pp. 157–185). Newbury Park, CA: Sage.

Gallois, C., Giles, H., Jones, E., Cargile, A. C., & Ota, H. (1995). Accommodating intercultural encounters: Elaborations and extensions. In R. L. Wiseman (Ed.), *Intercultural communication theory* (pp. 115–147). Thousand Oaks, CA: Sage.

Giles, H., Mulac, A., Bradac, J. J., & Johnson, P. (1987). Speech accommodation theory: The first decade and beyond. In M. McLaughlin (Ed.), *Communication yearbook 10* (pp. 13–48). Newbury Park, CA: Sage.

Hall, E. T. (1976). *Beyond culture.* New York: Doubleday.

Harding, S. (1991). *Whose science, whose knowledge? Thinking from women's lives.* Ithaca, NY: Cornell University Press.

Harstock, N. (1997). Standpoint theories for the next century. *Women and Politics, 18,* 93–101.

Hecht, M. L., Collier, M. J., & Ribeau, S. A. (1993). *African American communication: Ethnic identity and cultural interpretation.* Newbury Park, CA: Sage.

Hofstede, G. (1997). *Cultures and organizations: Software of the mind.* New York: McGraw-Hill.

Houston, M., & Kramarae, C. (1997). Speaking from silence: Methods of silencing and of resistance. *Discourse and Society, 2,* 387–399.

Johnson, F. L. (2000). *Speaking culturally: Language diversity in the United States.* Thousand Oaks, CA: Sage.

Kim, M.-S. (1993). Culture-based interactive constraints in explaining intercultural strategic competence. In R. L. Wiseman & J. Koester (Eds.), *Intercultural communication competence* (pp. 72–111). Newbury Park, CA: Sage.

Kim, M.-S. (1995). Toward a theory of conversational constraints: Focusing on individual-level dimensions of culture. In R. L. Wiseman (Ed.), *Intercultural communication theory* (pp. 148–169). Thousand Oaks, CA: Sage.

Kim, Y. Y., & Ruben, B. D. (1988). Intercultural transformation: A systems theory. In Y. Y. Kim & W. B. Gudykunst (Eds.), *Theories in intercultural communication* (pp. 299–321). Newbury Park, CA: Sage.

Kramarae, C. (1981). *Women and men speaking: Frameworks and analysis.* Rowley, MA: Newbury House.

Lynn, M. (1999). Toward a critical pedagogy: A research note. *Urban Education, 33,* 606–626.

Malhotra, S., & Crabtree, R. D. (2002). Gender, (inter)national(ization), and culture: Implications of the privatization of television in India. In M. J. Collier (Ed.), *Transforming communication about culture: Critical new directions* (pp. 60–84). Thousand Oaks, CA: Sage.

McIntosh, P. (1998). White privilege and male privilege: A personal account of coming to see correspondences through work in women's studies. In M. L. Andersen & P. H. Collins (Eds.), *Race, class, and gender: An anthology* (3rd ed.). Belmont, CA: Wadsworth (originally published 1988).

Nakayama, T. K., & Krizek, R. (1995). Whiteness: A strategic rhetoric. *Quarterly Journal of Speech, 81,* 291–309.

Orbe, M. P. (1998a). *Constructing co-cultural theory: An explication of culture, power, and communication.* Thousand Oaks, CA: Sage.

Orbe, M. P. (1998b). From the standpoint(s) of traditionally muted groups: Explicating a co-cultural communication theoretical model. *Communication Theory, 8,* 1–26.

Rahim, A. (1983). A measure of styles of handling interpersonal conflict. *Academy of Management Journal, 26,* 368–376.

Samovar, L. A., & Porter, R. E. (1991). *Communicating between cultures.* Belmont, CA: Wadsworth.

Samovar, L. A., & Porter, R. E. (1997). An introduction to intercultural communication: In L. A. Samovar & R. E. Porter (Eds.), *Intercultural communication: A reader* (8th ed., pp. 5–26). Belmont, CA: Wadsworth.

Shome, R. (1996). Race and popular cinema: The rhetorical strategies of Whiteness in *City of Joy. Communication Quarterly, 44,* 502–518.

Shome, R., & Hegde, R. S. (2002). Postcolonial approaches to communication: Charting the terrain, engaging the intersections. *Communication Theory, 12,* 249–270.

Terpstra, D. E., & Baker, D. D. (1989). The identification and classification of reactions to sexual harassment. *Journal of Organizational Behavior, 10,* 1–14.

Ting-Toomey, S. (1988). Intercultural conflict styles: A face-negotiation theory. In Y. Y. Kim & W. G. Gudykunst (Eds.), *Theories in intercultural communication* (pp. 213–235). Newbury Park, CA: Sage.

Ting-Toomey, S., & Kurogi, A. (1998). Facework, competence in intercultural conflict. An updated face-negotiation theory. *International Journal of Intercultural Relations, 22,* 187–225.

Ting-Toomey, S., & Oetzel, J. G. (2002). Cross-cultural face concerns and conflict styles: Current status and future directions. In W. B. Gudykunst & B. Mody (Eds.), *Handbook of international and intercultural communication* (2nd ed., pp. 143–163). Thousand Oaks, CA: Sage.

Triandis, H. (1990). Cross-cultural studies of individualism and collectivism. In J. Berman (Ed.), *Nebraska Symposium on Motivation.* Lincoln: University of Nebraska Press.

Wander, P. C., Martin, J. N., & Nakayama, T. K. (1999). Whiteness and beyond: Sociohistorical foundations of Whiteness and contemporary challenges. In T. K. Nakayama & J. N. Martin (Eds.), *Whiteness: The communication of social identity* (pp. 13–26). Thousand Oaks, CA: Sage.

Waters, H., Jr. (1992). Race, culture, and interpersonal conflict. *International Journal of Intercultural Relations, 16,* 437–454.

Yosso, T. J. (2002). Critical race media literacy: Challenging deficit discourse about Chicanas/os. *Journal of Popular Film & Television, 30*(1), 52–62.

11

The Real World: *A Case Study*

Allison Harthcock

In Chapters 5 through 10 you have been exposed to several overarching areas of theory in the field of human communication. You have been introduced to the origins of the field from the earliest writings on rhetoric by Plato and Aristotle right through the most modern theories in today's more specialized fields of persuasive, small group, interpersonal, and intercultural communication. This chapter uses a setting that is familiar to many modern students, that of the television program *The Real World,* to bring these theories together in a contemporary application. The chapter reminds us of some of the theories used in previous chapters, bringing up a couple of new concepts in the process.

In this chapter, you will read about the following concepts:

- Reducing intergroup (interracial) tensions
  - Orbe's co-cultural theory
  - Fisher's narrative theory
- Understanding a romantic relationship
  - Uncertainty reduction theory
  - Elaboration likelihood model
- Group decision making
  - Compliance gaining
  - Tuchman's group development theory
  - Structuration theory
- Understanding the story of a relationship
  - Burke's motives
  - Social penetration theory
  - Relational dialectics theory

This is the true story of seven strangers picked to live in a house and have their lives taped, but it is a story told in terms of how the people talk to one another, and it is told through the terms of communication theories. We will analyze the lives of these seven people to find out how communication theories can help explain events in our everyday lives. Each season on Music Television (MTV), the program *The Real World* introduces us to a new group of seven strangers who move into a house together. In their time together in the house, the housemates develop new friendships, romances, and conflicts. Even though our lives are not on television for all to see, we are much like the Real World housemates: we meet new people, form friendships and romances, and have conflicts with people around us. In these relationships in our own lives, we can see communication theory in action. Let's take this opportunity to look at the impact communication theory has on our lives by looking at "real" life as it is presented on MTV's *The Real World*.

In 1992, MTV broadcast the first episode of *The Real World*. The program, which is set in a new city with a new cast each season, consists of seven strangers living together for several months, during which time their lives are taped. Also, in more recent seasons, the housemates were given jobs, such as promoters for a record company. Therefore, they are not only living together, but working together also. The program purports to show the audience how people behave when they relax and start getting "real."

During the first season (filmed in New York), approximately 527,000 viewers tuned in for each episode. That number had grown to 2.6 million viewers per episode during the ninth season (2000 in New Orleans; Lu-Lien Tan, 2001). The appeal of the program comes from a variety of things, such as exhibitionism, conflict, and unpredictability (Lu-Lien Tan, 2001). But whether you watch for the cast members, the hook-ups, the fights, or just to see what comes next, *The Real World* offers a place to see communication theory in action. For our purposes, we will look at season ten, "Back to New York."

The housemates for that season were Coral, a 22-year-old woman from the Bay area; Rachel, an 18-year-old woman from Chicago; Kevin, a 22-year-old man from Texas; Lori, a 21-year-old woman from New Jersey; Malik, a 20-year-old man from Berkeley; Nicole, a 22-year-old woman from Atlanta; and Mike, a 19-year-old man from Ohio. We will look the interactions of these housemates and some of their guests from a variety of theoretical approaches. It would be impractical to use all the theories covered in the previous chapters. Therefore, we will use exemplar theories from each section. Also, because various aspects of communication are interrelated and not linear, as the text suggests, we will not treat the theories in the same order as they are presented in the previous chapters.

Can Intercultural Theory Prescribe
Ways to Mend Racial Division?

As the housemates were adjusting to their new life together, Mike, Coral, and Malik went to a pivotal breakfast together (Bunim & Murray, 2001, episode 1). Over the course of the meal, Mike (a white Midwesterner) told his new housemates (both of whom are biracially African/Caucasian American) that his uncle would not hire African Americans because they are less intelligent and reliable than white people. Malik listened to Mike's observations and to Coral's comments when she told Mike to stop talking. Over the following days, Coral had nothing to say to Mike when he attempted to make small talk with her. After two days of the silent treatment by Coral, Mike confronted her and Malik in order to apologize. They both accepted Mike's apology. The relationship between Mike and Malik developed into a friendship, while Coral and Mike continued to experience tension. This tension was expressed through Coral's repeated attacks on Mike on a variety of topics such as his treatment of women and his ignorance regarding African Americans. The conflict between Coral and Mike created tension for the rest of the housemates; most of the housemates expressed their unease with and feelings about the Mike/Coral conflict at some point during the early episodes.

As the housemates moved into February (Black History Month), the tension between Mike and Coral continued to build (Bunim & Murray, 2001, episode 3). Mike's lack of knowledge regarding African American history strengthened Coral's dislike/distrust of him. Coral's attacks and insults continued. On the other hand, when he learned of Mike's ignorance of and interest in learning about African American history, Malik agreed to help by telling Mike about an important figure in African American history each day of the month. Through this process, Mike learned about African American history and his friendship with Malik grew.

While Mike's relationship with the other house members developed, his relationship with Coral continued on an up-and-down trajectory. While Coral responded positively when Mike gave her a personalized bud vase for Valentine's Day (Bunim & Murray, 2001, episode 5), she was still hard on him until other housemates and guests confronted Coral (episode 10). Coral agreed to be more positive and "lighten up" on Mike (episodes 15, 16). Over time, the relationship between Coral and Mike evolved until the two developed a genuine appreciation for each other. Finally, Coral stated she simply had to step into his world and appreciate him. She began to enjoy his sense of humor. Their newfound friendship was displayed during their professional wrestling game and their excursion with Kevin and Lori to Central Park (episodes 15, 16).

Dissecting the Interaction with Orbe's Co-cultural Theory

As you remember from the Chapter 10 discussion of intercultural theories, **Orbe's co-cultural theory** states that cultural groups in a position of power limit the progress of other groups, either directly or indirectly. As a result, how co-culture group members interact with members of the dominant culture depend on two things: (1) whether the co-culture member is *nonassertive, assertive,* or *aggressive,* and (2) the stance the co-culture member adopts (**assimilation, accommodation, separation**).

In the original expression of his preconceived notions about African Americans, Mike expressed the power of the dominant group over others. While Mike's attitude probably developed through a variety of sources, his presentation of it focused around his uncle. Mike's expression, which in part resulted from his uncle's behaviors, exhibited the power the dominant culture has over a co-culture—economically and perceptually. Economically, the power lies in Mike's uncle's hiring practices. Perceptually, the power in Mike's comments lies in the perpetuation of a stereotype. Mike's comment and his lack of knowledge about African American history also demonstrated that the dominant culture knows less about co-cultures than visa versa.

The responses of Malik and Coral to Mike's comments demonstrated different approaches to intercultural communication. Malik's approach to Mike was accommodation that was, at times, both assertive and nonassertive. By agreeing to educate Mike on African

American history and sharing with Mike his personal history, Malik was taking an assertive accommodation approach to the intercultural communication with Mike. Malik at times also took a nonassertive accommodation approach with Mike: He exposed Mike to other co-cultures by inviting Mike to spend time with Malik and his friends. This also worked to dispel stereotypes. As we see, Mike responded positively to these approaches: He learned about African American history (Bunim & Murray, 2001, episode 3); he was appalled by his father's racially biased comments on a later visit to New York (episode 13); and he expressed his pleasure at spending time with such an ethnically diverse group at Malik's birthday party (episode 13). Malik's approach to intercultural communication with Mike had different results than Coral's approach.

Coral's approach to intercultural communication with Mike changed over time. After his original comments, Coral responded with both aggressive and nonassertive separation. Approaching Mike from an aggressive separation position, she attacked Mike on a variety of topics and attempted sabotaging a potential "hook-up" by informing Mike's female friends of his derogatory comments about them prior to their arrival (Bunim & Murray, 2001, episode 4). Coral also responded with nonassertive separation by ignoring Mike's attempts at small talk and humor, along with isolating herself interpersonally from Mike. As time passed, Coral approached Mike from an assertive accommodation position: she offered self-disclosures about her life and thoughts. This resulted in a friendship between the two.

Dissecting Mike's "Story" with the Narrative Paradigm

Another theory that can help us examine the incident with Mike, Malik, and Coral is a modern rhetorical one (Chapter 6): Fisher's **narrative paradigm.** The event that took place involved Mike's story, or interpretation, of the qualities of African Americans. Malik and Coral assessed the **narrative rationality** of Mike's statements. The **narrative probability** was internally consistent; the story has all the expected elements in a story. The **narrative fidelity** of the story is the point at which Mike's narrative paradigm became problematic for Coral and Malik. For Coral and Malik, Mike's story was not consistent with other stories they believed; the story was not consistent with their personal experiences; the story imparted values with which they did not agree.

Have You Ever Really Wanted to Know
What Someone Else Was Thinking?

While Nicole had a date during her time in New York, her heart belonged to a man from her past, Bobby. When a gift arrived from Bobby, Nicole was ecstatic. She became even more elated when Bobby announced that he would be visiting Nicole in New York (Bunim & Murray, 2001, episode 16). Nicole confessed her feelings toward Bobby to her housemates and to the audience. Historically, there had been no physical relationship between the two. Nicole intimated that they had spent a great deal of time together, but they were not dating. She admitted to having "thrown herself" at Bobby with no response from him. Nicole had made herself very available, physically and emotionally, but it had not been reciprocated and she was not clear as to why Bobby did not respond to her advances. She told us that Bobby fills the position of partner in her life, but that he is "still lookin' at applicants" (episode 16). In an effort to move the relationship forward, Nicole developed a plan to pretend to be drunk in order to get Bobby drunk and take advantage of him.

As the evening progressed, Nicole proceeded to get excessively drunk while Bobby did not. Despite her state of drunkenness, Nicole tried to seduce Bobby. When that did not work, she attempted to discuss their relationship with him. He told her the timing was not right. Throughout his visit, Bobby expressed affection for Nicole by giving her a rose and champagne and by engaging in nonsexual physical contact. He occasionally made innuendos about his feelings, but never directly told Nicole, and she never directly asked.

Later, during a housemates' vacation to the Hamptons, Nicole invited Bobby with the intention of directly discussing their relationship (Bunim & Murray, 2001, episode 19). The night before the vacation, Lori asked Nicole to define her relationship with Bobby. Nicole was unable to do so beyond saying that she wants him, but he sends mixed signals to her (this was very clear in their last on-camera meeting).

Understanding Nicole's Tactics through Uncertainty Reduction Theory

As you remember from the Chapter 7 coverage of interpersonal communication theories, **uncertainty reduction theory** states that we seek to decrease uncertainty and unpredictability through communication. We engage in uncertainty reduction when there is an expectation of future communication, rewards are involved, or the person violates our expectations. In an effort to reduce uncertainties or gain knowledge about a person, there are three approaches we can take: **passive, active,** or **interactive.** A passive strategy involves distant observation of a person. An active strategy involves manipulating the environment in order to acquire knowledge about a person or actively seeking information. An interactive strategy involves direct, face-to-face interaction.

Nicole found herself in a relationship in which there was a great deal of uncertainty that she wanted to reduce because she saw the potential for rewards (a relationship with Bobby). She had feelings for Bobby, but was uncertain as to his feelings for her. In an effort to reduce the uncertainty, Nicole used both the active and passive strategies at different times. During Bobby's visit to New York, Nicole's plan to get him drunk was an active strategy to reduce uncertainty. She planned to manipulate the situation (get him drunk) in order to get to know him better by taking advantage of him. Later, during their trip to the Hamptons, Nicole intended to use a more interactive strategy to reduce her uncertainty about Bobby. She planned to ask him directly about their relationship. In both cases, Nicole attempted to develop her relationship with Bobby by reducing the uncertainty she felt in the relationship.

Understanding Bobby's Response through the Elaboration Likelihood Model

We can also look at the relationship between Nicole and Bobby from a persuasive and interpersonal perspective using **elaboration likelihood model** (Chapter 9). Nicole attempted to persuade Bobby that they should be a couple. As seen through their conversations, his affections, and continued relationship with Nicole, Bobby seemed to consider her argument, through both the **central** and **peripheral routes.** We can determine that Bobby was inclined to elaborate Nicole's message: Bobby was *motivated* to listen—the subject was relevant to him. We can assume that Bobby had the *ability to process* the message because Nicole's message was fairly overt. Even when she tried to get him drunk, he retained his ability to process her appeals by not getting drunk (while, ironically, she may have hampered her own ability to create good arguments!). The final factor that determines the likelihood of elaboration is a *need to scrutinize the message.* We cannot tell from what appears on the screen, but if Bobby wanted to know Nicole's feelings for him or her reasons that they should be together, this would indicate a higher need for cognition. This would increase the likelihood that Bobby would not only base his decision on his emotion for Nicole or on her beauty and sex appeal (both peripheral routes), but on the reasons she gives him for developing their relationship (i.e., *parallel processing* from the *heuristic model of persuasion).* In the end, Bobby seemingly elaborated on Nicole's argument. However, he did not seem to be persuaded.

Do You Really Know It All, or Are You Just Acting Like It?

During season ten, the housemates were employed at Arista Records. As part of the job, the housemates were pitted against each other in a record store window-display competition (Bunim & Murray, 2001, episode 15). Lori, Coral, and Kevin were on one team and Malik, Mike, Nicole, and Rachel were the second team. Each team was given a musical artist and a record store in Manhattan. They had to create a window display for their musical artist in their store windows. At the beginning of the episode, Nicole expressed her desire to demonstrate her commitment to the job to her employers. She indicated that she had not given her all up to that point and wanted to change that. Nicole felt the competition offered her that opportunity because she is extremely competitive.

After the initial meeting, Nicole's group developed tension. While the team might have decided on the idea for the window display as a group, Nicole began to take over the project. When they began working with Rebecca, the team coach who works for Arista Records as a window designer (basically, she does for a living what the teams are doing for the competition), Nicole presented the group's idea. While other group members had things to contribute, Nicole ignored or overtly rebuffed their input. At one point, Nicole informed Mike that his opinion was not relevant, that she was seeking the opinion of an expert, Rebecca. The audience learned through the narration that other team members (Rachel and Malik) were disgruntled with Nicole's behavior. Despite that fact, they had to continue to work together as a team in order to win the competition.

As the construction phase of the display began, Nicole's need to control the situation resulted in a 19th Street verbal battle with Mike. When Mike and Malik left to take a portion of the display materials to the window site, Nicole and Rachel were left behind with many other materials for the display. When Malik and Mike returned, Nicole informed Mike that they should have told Rachel and her where they were going; as team members,

FIGURE 11.1 *The Cast of* **The Real World, New York, 2001.** Perhaps communication studies theories can help us better understand communication in "real world" experiences.

Photo courtesy of Bunim-Murray Productions (2001).

Malik and Mike should have informed Rachel and her as to their actions/location. She wanted Mike to admit to her that he and Malik were negligent in their actions and should have left word with her or Rachel of the plans. After a heated discussion (with Nicole doing most of the talking), Mike conceded that they should have told Nicole and Rachel where they were going. The argument continued drawing on previous interactions and conflicts between Mike and Nicole.

When the team was finally putting the finishing touches on the window, another heated discussion erupted when Nicole disagreed with Mike, Rachel, and Malik about the display. Nicole did not want to use a picture in the display that the rest of the team wanted to use. She would not even consider the option offered by Mike of simply testing it out before a decision was made. Nicole told them she had put a lot of effort into the window—she cared about how it looked and would not let them ruin it. Malik, Mike, and Rachel consulted their coach, Rebecca, who agreed with them—the picture should be in the window. When Nicole was informed of Rebecca's advice, she told the group members that the picture looked tacky and if they did not do it her way, they would lose. After their group lost the competition, Nicole informed the other group (Coral, Kevin, and Lori) that she was really glad they won.

Analyzing Detrimental Yet Successful Compliance Gaining

As you remember from the persuasion theory chapter (Chapter 9), **compliance gaining** seeks *compliance* rather than *agreement* with the persuader. The persuader need not convince the persuadee to believe, but simply comply with, the desires of the persuader. Five basic *categories* of compliance gaining strategies are **rewarding activity, punishing activity, expertise, activation of impersonal commitments,** and **activation of personal**

commitments. Nicole employed the strategies of punishing activity and expertise to gain compliance from her group members.

During her discussion with Mike, Nicole attempted to gain compliance using punishment. Nicole felt she and Rachel should have been informed when Mike and Malik left. Nicole's discussion with Mike after the fact involved her effort to make him admit that she and Rachel should have been informed about the actions of Mike and Malik. The aversive stimulation was the lecture Nicole administered to Mike. As is the case in compliance gaining, Nicole was not concerned with whether Mike *agreed* that he should have informed her. Rather she was concerned that he *admit* that he should have informed her (whether he actually believed it or not). In this case, Nicole gained compliance from Mike (the lecture ended) when he said Nicole and Rachel should have been informed.

During their discussion regarding the inclusion of the picture in the window display, Nicole expressed expertise about the negative outcomes of disagreeing with her. Nicole sought to gain compliance from Rachel, Mike, and Malik by telling them that if they went against her wishes, they would lose, implying that hers was a superior idea—if they disagreed, they would incur a loss. This compliance-gaining strategy did not work for Nicole, as the group vetoed her and, as noted above, lost the competition.

Analyzing Small Group Interaction

In addition to compliance gaining techniques, some small group theories (see Chapter 8) also apply to this story. **Tuckman's group development theory** talks about the stages in group formation beginning with **forming,** the point at which Nicole's group was set up. Then comes the **storming** stage when conflicts become apparent. When Nicole began rebuffing and ignoring the input from her teammates, this stage escalated. Eventually some **norming** takes place, simply by Mike giving in to Nicole's demand for an apology and then later when the rest of the group overrode Nicole's demand to include the chosen picture. At this point, **performing** simply had to occur due to the need to finish the display. Finally the group **adjourns,** which was probably the happiest moment for this group.

During the norming and performing stages, we also see some elements of **structuration theory** displayed. **Rules** about the group having to work together to create a display compelled Mike initially to give in to Nicole's authoritarian demands. However, the **resource** available in Rebecca's expertise eventually allowed the rest of the group to justify that a more democratic system be employed to replace Nicole's authoritarian style. The evolution of the structure of the group's decision-making process is explained through structuration theory.

Can This Story Have an Alternate Ending?

At the casting finals, Malik met Jisela, a woman who was cast in the MTV program *Road Rules* (Bunim & Murray, 2001, *Casting Special*). Much later, after a chance meeting in New York, Jisela (along with several other *Road Rules* cast members) spent time with the *Real World* housemates (episode 18). Malik and Jisela spent a great deal of time together holding hands and sharing information about themselves. We learned from Malik that the two were forming a relationship and that he had deep feelings for her. Jisela told Malik that she enjoyed the romance and connection that comes with being involved with someone and that she enjoyed spending time with him, but she did not want a "boyfriend." Malik continued to tell us that they were growing closer and that they were in love.

One evening several housemates and Jisela went out dancing. Although Rachel, the youngest housemate, drank excessively, no mention was made of others drinking excessively. After they returned to the house, the atmosphere became sexually charged leading to lots of kissing among a variety of people. Later in the episode, Malik told us that he and Jisela had sex, and that it happened because they were in love.

On the MTV *Real World* web site, Jisela had an opportunity to respond to the events that took place between Malik and her. In her response, Jisela provided more details for us than the program could provide. While some additional details helped us understand the story better, the story itself was different when it was told from a different perspective. Jisela only hinted at what happened between Malik and her, but she did inform us that she told Malik not to tell anyone. She also told us that the things that happened with Malik occurred as a result of the large quantities of alcohol that all of them consumed on the night the group went out. Both Malik and Jisela had different explanations of the events that occurred between them.

Analyzing the Story through Burke's Lens of Motives

As you remember from Chapter 6, **Burke's concept of motives** provides insight into a speaker's interpretation of an event. The elements of interpretation, the **act** (what was done), **agent** (person or persons who did the act), **agency** (the means by which the act was performed) **scene** (the situation or background to the act), and **purpose** (why the act was performed) can help us understand how a speaker perceives events. The emphasis (or lack thereof) that a speaker places on one of these elements gives the audience insight into the speaker's perception of an event.

In the case of Malik and Jisela (the agents), the act was their sexual encounter. The scene was the sexually charged environment of the house. The agency was the evening at a club and the consumption of excessive amounts of alcohol. The purpose was their feelings for each other (these include feelings of attraction as well as any others). While the elements of the story remained the same in both versions of the story, the order and manner in which they were presented by each of the speakers gives us insight into how they viewed the events. However, Burkean analysis is seldom interested in the actual events, but in how speakers construct the events through language—that is, Jisela and Malik's *statements* about the act, the purpose, and so on. In any given speech or, in this case, dialogue, speakers can weave different stories and events together, often in an effort to deal with negative feelings by accepting them or passing them on.

We can see that Jisela and Malik interpreted the act (the sexual encounter) differently. Malik's emphasis was located in the purpose, or why the act was performed. He told us they had sex because of their feelings for each other. Jisela's version focused on the agency, or the means by which the act was performed. She told us that the alcohol and the sexual tension lead to sex with Malik. While the alcohol and tension (the agency) may have contributed to the act, Malik did not emphasize that information. Likewise, their feelings (another aspect of or interpretation of the purpose) may have contributed to the act, but Jisela did not emphasize that information. By looking at the information Malik and Jisela privilege—their interpretation of events—we can understand how Malik and Jisela viewed the act differently.

Analyzing the Story through the Relational Theories

Two interpersonal theories (Chapter 7) can also be used to examine the relationship between Malik and Jisela: **social penetration theory** and **relational dialectics theory.** From a social penetration theory perspective, when they originally met at the casting special, Malik and Jisela were in the **orientation phase,** during which they shared introductory information about themselves. As they spent time together in New York, Malik and Jisela went through the **exploratory affective exchange phase** and the full **affective exchange phase.** During their time together, they began to share more personal information including hopes, fears, and goals. Jisela and Malik did not reach the most intimate phase of social penetration theory, the **stable exchange phase.**

Relational dialectics theory is a second interpersonal theory that provides insight into the relationship between Malik and Jisela. With the **integration/separation** tension at the **internal** level, Malik wanted **connection** while Jisela wanted **autonomy.** At the **external** level, Jisela wanted **inclusion** of others into the relationship while Malik wanted **seclusion** as a couple. With the **expression/privacy** tension at the external level, Jisela wanted **concealment**—she did not want others to know of their intimacy. On the other hand, Malik wanted **revelation** of their relationship. It is unclear how the **openness/closedness** dialectic manifested in their relationship, but this tension would pertain to how much Jisela and Malik wanted to share with each other in terms of self-disclosure. Also, the **stability/change** dialectic, consisting of **predictability/novelty** at the internal level and **conventionality/uniqueness** at the external level, were unclear in the relationship between Malik and Jisela. Despite this, relational dialectics allow us to see the tensions in the relationship between Malik and Jisela.

Summary

So seven strangers can help us understand communication. MTV's *The Real World* gives us an opportunity to examine communication theory, but these concepts are present in our everyday lives. In this chapter, we first looked at how different theories might explain interracial tensions between people and how those might be overcome. Next we considered how romantic relationships develop. We then saw a group work context and how persuasion and decision making were accomplished. Finally, we compared different stories about a romantic encounter and looked at relationship satisfaction. In each case, different theories, applied to the same situation, lead us to look at different aspects of the interaction. We realize that a theory written to explain one type of communication might also be used to interpret another context. Thus, we used a persuasion theory (elaboration likelihood model) to explain persuasion in relationship development and in theories of storytelling (Burke's motives) along with relationship theories to understand sexual encounters and the stories people later tell about them.

By examining our everyday lives, we can see communication theory in action—in friendships, in romances, in conflicts. In this case study, we applied these to existing communication in *The Real World,* to *explain* past interaction. But once you know how the theories work, you could use them equally as well to *improve your future interaction,* from interracial communication to persuasion, from decision making to building relationships. Understanding communication theory can help us navigate our daily lives. Where can you see communication theory at work in your life?

Discussion Questions

1. Is one approach to intercultural communication more effective than others? Why or why not?

2. How could other theories of relationship development explain the interactions between Nicole and Bobby?

3. Can you think of other strategies that a compliance seeker could use to gain compliance? What strategies have you used to gain compliance from parent, friend, or roommate? Are some strategies more effective than others? Why or why not?

4. If Malik or Jisela interpreted their sexual encounter differently, how might their version of events change?

References

Bunim, M. E., & Murray, J. (Producers). (2001). *The Real World,* episode 1. New York: Music Television.

Bunim, M. E., & Murray, J. (Producers). (2001). *The Real World,* episode 3. New York: Music Television.

Bunim, M. E., & Murray, J. (Producers). (2001). *The Real World,* episode 4. New York: Music Television.

Bunim, M. E., & Murray, J. (Producers). (2001). *The Real World,* episode 5. New York: Music Television.

Bunim, M. E., & Murray, J. (Producers). (2001). *The Real World,* episode 10. New York: Music Television.

Bunim, M. E., & Murray, J. (Producers). (2001). *The Real World,* episode 13. New York: Music Television.

Bunim, M. E., & Murray, J. (Producers). (2001). *The Real World,* episode 15. New York: Music Television.

Bunim, M. E., & Murray, J. (Producers). (2001). *The Real World,* episode 16. New York: Music Television.

Bunim, M. E., & Murray, J. (Producers). (2001). *The Real World,* episode 18. New York: Music Television.

Bunim, M. E., & Murray, J. (Producers). (2001). *The Real World,* episode 19. New York: Music Television.

Bunim, M. E., & Murray, J. (Producers). (2001). *The Real World: Casting Special.* New York: Music Television.

Lu-Lien Tan, C. (2001, July 1). Viewers still get "real" after all these years. *Baltimore Sun,* p. E1.

Part III

Mass Communication

In the previous set of chapters on communication studies, you studied the important theories starting from the earliest origins of communication with classical rhetoric all the way up to theories of how people communicate today. We turn now to the study of communication carried through media channels.

Marshall McLuhan, whom you will read about in Chapter 16 in this section, believed that the channel or medium through which messages are carried hold more influence than the actual message on how individuals interact socially, how institutions function, and how society changes. Whether you agree with the degree to which the medium influences the message, this section holds that there are many effects related to the way messages are presented through various media.

Not all chapters in this section, however, attribute power to the media. Some attribute power to the audience. Members of that audience make choices and are influenced by internal motivations that modify the impact the media may have in their lives.

We start the section in Chapter 12 with an overview of the history of theories of mass communication. This chapter follows the developments from the belief that the media had tremendous persuasive power to the general belief today that the media's influence is strong in limited ways. The next two chapters then look at the audience's ability to modify the media's impact. Chapter 13 then asks how our individual differences, selectivity, and internal beliefs help us nullify many of the attempts to create mass persuasion through media. Chapter 14 looks at how we intentionally use media as a tool to accomplish specific goals in our lives.

Beginning with Chapter 15 the focus returns more to the media's influence on society and individuals. Chapter 15 covers what traditional scientific theories have to say about media effects on our attitudes, beliefs, behaviors, and values. Chapter 16 then opens up new vistas of theory and how they can be applied in the study of new communication technology or computer-mediated communication. Critical and humanistic theories that show how the media serve to further the power of the elites in culture and society are discussed in Chapter 17.

The final chapter uses the events of September 11th's terrorist attacks and shows how the theories from all of the chapters in the section can be brought together to explain various facets of the media coverage. You should be able to think back to your own behaviors and thoughts during the days of those tragic events and compare them with various theories you will study in the first six chapters of this section.

Depending on the course you are taking as you use this book, your instructor may start with theories of mass communication. It would be helpful to review Chapters 1 and 2 before launching into this section if that is the case. Chapter 1 addresses how theories are constructed and how to evaluate if they are good or bad theories. Chapter 2 discusses how different paradigms change the theories that are created, discusses different types of theories, and addresses different dimensions in which theories are debated. Understanding both of these chapters will yield great dividends in helping you think about how the theories you study were created and how they might be applied to your day-to-day life.

Once again there will be additional information on the web site for many of the theories in this section. Look for the "Beyond the Book" icon (as shown at the left) to identify links that apply to your reading.

12

History of Mass Communication

Rebecca Carrier

As we start a new section of the text, we move in a new direction. Instead of looking at how people communicate without—or at least regardless of—technological devices, here we examine the influence of media on and within the communication process. **Mass communication** by definition is the use of technology to enable the dissemination of a message to a large, very diverse, widespread set of recipients. The specific **medium,** the technology through which a message is conveyed, influences the style of the message with pictures and graphics often making up as much or more of the message than the words. Mass communication theories are in some cases extensions or reapplications of those learned in earlier chapters, but are in other cases very unique to the mediated realm. Factors that influence the need for different or modified theories include such elements as the speed or delay of message delivery, the complexity of the media organization behind creating a given message, the vividness of the mediated message, the pervasiveness of media messages, and the profit motive common to mass communication systems.

As you read this chapter, you will be introduced to the question of how media messages influence individuals and society. You will read how the media help create pictures in our minds that guide our understanding of the world. You will learn that our understanding of mass communication effects has evolved over time as the dominant paradigm changed, perhaps coming almost full circle. The original belief that the media were very powerful was abandoned for years, only to be reborn as we shifted our research focus from short-term persuasion effects to long-term cultural effects. This history lesson will serve you well as you proceed through the other chapters in the mass communication section of this textbook. The theories you will be introduced to here serve to illustrate the periods and paradigms of media research. They will be presented in more detail in subsequent chapters.

In this chapter, you will read about the following concepts:

- Role of media in shaping information
- Media as windows to the world
  - How media shape a pseudo-environment
  - Real experience and media experience

187

- Prominent paradigm shifts
  - Powerful effects theories
  - Limited effects theories
  - Limited but powerful effects theories
    - Agenda-setting theory
    - Framing or frame analysis
    - Media system dependency theory
    - Uses and gratifications theory
  - Media as cultivators of culture
    - Cultivation theory
    - Mean world syndrome

With no form of mass media, what would you know about your world? Your knowledge of your friends and family would be basically unchanged because generally you do not rely upon mass media to tell you about these people. But you would know very little about places that you had never traveled, events that you could not attend, new products you had never encountered, people that you had never met, or activities that you had never experienced. With no mass media to gather, organize, make attractive, and dispatch information, you would have to direct much more of your time and money toward getting the information necessary to choose a good college, decide on a profitable career, select a safe and reliable car, or even avoid unhealthy food.

Try to imagine a world without mass media. Understand how people lived long ago, even before the invention of the written word. In that time, thousands of years ago, people depended upon one another to share important information. Without any form of recorded information, people had to live in close-knit tribal communities that facilitated face-to-face exchanges of information. Storytelling, singing, and frequent social gatherings played a central role in preserving a record of these tribal cultures. Additionally, these were the methods of learning about new births (expansion of the tribe), sharing community resources (economics), teaching young members of the society how to behave appropriately (education), and practicing rituals (culture and religion).

As these tribal societies enlarged and civilization arose, it became more difficult to exchange information with everyone in the tribe. Needs of government and religion required the ability to write down and record events, rules, and traditions. Relying on oral techniques was insufficient for their growing information needs. Crude media forms including stone tablets and scrolls began to take the place of the rudimentary oral forms of preservation.

But why is this historical consideration important? Why should we concern ourselves with the time before mass communication?

The answer is twofold. First, this story helps us understand the role of media in our society. Today, we live in a world knit together by many forms of mass media, and it is difficult to imagine how our world might be different if mass communication was impossible. It is far easier to think about a much earlier world, a world where people lived before television, radio, newspapers, or even written language. By thinking about the society represented by tribal cultures and their methods of oral communication, we are better able to consider and appreciate how various forms of mass media influence individual and social behavior in our world today. Thinking about oral cultures helps us ask questions and consider answers to the way that media shape, define, and maintain the culture that we share today.

Second, in studying the history of mass communication (in particular the history of media research) we learn to be more discerning about what we *really* know about our world. By studying the history of media and media research, we force ourselves to think about how we gain information, the reliability of that information, and the differences between those things we experience directly and those things we experience through the media. In short, learning the history of mass communication and media research helps us become more critical of what we know—or what we think we know. Additionally, those who will one day choose a communication profession become more aware of their important responsibilities in shaping society.

How Do Media Serve as Windows to the World?

Walter Lippmann (1922) used an anecdote to emphasize the importance of media in shaping our lives. Lippmann described a small island where a small group of French, English, and German people lived just before World War I. A British mail ship offered the only link between these people and the outside world. The people on this island lived and worked together in friendly and peaceful relations. They were completely unaware that the French and English had gone to war against Germany until the mail ship reported the news—six weeks after the fighting started. For those first six weeks of what would become World War I, these particular islanders lived in peace. Then the ship brought the news of the war, and community relationships changed accordingly. Lippmann's point is that media accounts of the world beyond our experience play an important role in defining our attitudes and actions. The media are our eyes to the world beyond our reach.

Lippmann distinguished between the "world outside" and the pictures that the media help us create in our minds. Lippmann was concerned that media representations inaccurately portrayed events in the *real world*. He pointed out that public relations strategists working for individuals or for corporations make available a one-sided view of the world and thereby influence journalists who lack the time, contacts, and other resources to conduct their own research before reaching their story deadlines. Additionally, Lippmann explained that issues of privacy and the lack of basic access to the point at which news occurs prevent the media from reporting much potential information at all. Thus, because of the very nature of the news process, audiences invariably receive incomplete and distorted information.

For example, in 1988 the *Exxon Valdez* broke apart in Prince William Sound and damaged long stretches of the Alaskan beaches, fishing, and wildlife. After this happened a public relations spokesperson for Exxon was reported in the media as stating that the oil spill had been cleaned up and that soon Alaska would return to its pristine beauty (Exxon Valdez Oil Spill Trustee Council, n.d.). If this press report had not been questioned, perhaps the American public would have accepted this media story as accurate, and the Exxon version would have served as the picture in people's minds. However, when environmentalists and biologists saw the giant water hoses grinding into the beaches to clean up the

FIGURE 12.1   Workers spray high-power hoses along
Quayle Beach, Prince Edward Sound, as part of the
cleanup effort after the Exxon Valdez oil spill.

Photo courtesy EXXON VALDEZ Oil Spill Trustee Council.

oil spill and witnessed firsthand the birds being washed to clean their oil-drenched feathers, they recognized a disconnect between Exxon's portrayal and the actual reality (see Figure 12.1). This more pessimistic picture of the oil spill damage and of the time it would take to resolve the mess came out in media stories answering Exxon's press release. With such a high-profile event, investigative reporting by journalists uncovered more accurate information rather than allowing the public relations message put out by Exxon to dominate the media message. Still, the pictures in people's heads ultimately are bound to be incomplete and distorted due to the lack of knowledge media consumers and journalists had of Prince William Sound. More than this, limited time for journalistic writing and research, the choices made about what information to highlight and what to leave out altogether, and the time people had to actually consume all of this media are other factors that allowed for the pictures in consumers' heads only to approach the real conditions of the oil spill.

And it's not just businesses that use public relations tools to try to present a one-sided version of reality. Politicians, governmental agencies, and political candidates all work to provide information through their media liaisons. The hue and cry for independent counsels and congressional panels to investigate the performance of everyone from the U.S. president to the FBI and CIA occur because even within political circles, politicians don't believe that other politicians are telling the whole truth. If politicians can't get at the inside truth, how likely is it that journalists or the voting public will be able to receive an accurate picture of governmental events?

We Rely on the Media's Version of the World beyond Our Experience

Think about your own communication habits. How much do you rely upon mass media to gather, organize, and present important information? And how much do you rely upon your own experiences?

FIGURE 12.2 This cartoon lambastes the Exxon company for its public relations attempts to gloss over the damage done by the *Valdez* oil spill. It illustrates the difficulty that we, the media consumer, might have in getting a true picture of the things that go on in our world as long as companies and people have agendas that encourage them to promote self-enhancing versions of reality.

© Seppo Leinonen. Used with permission.

Many of us have learned to question some of what we watch on television, hear on the radio, read in the papers, or get from the Internet. And most of us have doubted a particular news report, or we may have disagreed with media coverage that speculates which team will win this weekend's big game.

Still we incorporate our direct (but limited) experiences of the world with mass media reports. Generally, we do not separate the knowledge we have gathered through personal experience from that we have gained through the media. Lippmann was concerned that our blending of real experiences with those experiences delivered to us through the media created a **pseudo-environment** where members of society could not distinguish between what was real and what was manipulated by public relations strategists and packaged by journalists.

This teaches us two important things. First, we should be careful to make a distinction between that which we experience and that which the media present as information or as an experience for us. Importantly, Lippmann is not suggesting that we should avoid media information as we learn about our world. He is arguing, however, that we should analyze where we get our information, and we should be critical of the motives of the sources. Also, we should recognize the power that the media wield in shaping what we think of as real. Remember, Lippmann's example of the French, English, and German islanders illustrates that we often act not upon what is *really* happening but upon mediated reports that have a number of shortcomings.

For a moment, consider what you know about your on- and off-campus housing near your college or university. Some of what you know comes from talking to others or viewing the housing units directly. Some of what you know comes from advertisements or brochures. Are you critical of those ads that start with, "The best college housing—cheap, cheap, cheap"? Do you trust what you experience or hear from your friends about housing more than you trust media reports about the housing?

Now imagine you are planning to study abroad for nine months in a country you have never seen, nor do you know anyone who has been there. How much of your information will come from direct experience or reports from others who have experienced this country? How much of it will come from brochures, magazines, the Internet, television, or other media sources?

Notice that when direct experience of something is readily available (such as experiences with campus housing) we use it and probably trust it more than media information. But when direct experience fails us, we are obligated to depend very heavily upon the media to shape our understanding of reality. Chances are that, should we actually get to the study abroad destination, our experiences will be quite different from our expectations or the picture the media left in our minds.

When Did Mass Communication Theory Get Started?

Lippmann's seminal book *Public Opinion* (1922) was written from a political science perspective, but it is one of the first classic texts that examine in detail the role of the media in shaping opinion, creating stereotypes, and conveying information about day-to-day life. His book reflects the perspective that the media are a powerful force in our lives and in society, a viewpoint shared by many people of his day.

The factors that gave rise to Lippmann's examination of the media and to other research on mass communication are varied. Behavioral sciences were on the rise, new forms of communication had become commonplace, and the need to understand persuasion and propaganda through media channels became paramount because of two world wars (Glander, 2000). Advertising agencies and their clients also desired more knowledge of effective persuasion techniques. Advertisements were becoming more sophisticated, and testing various advertising strategies became more and more common. Radio's effectiveness as a medium for promoting products certainly increased interest in mass communication research from influential scholars like Hadley Cantril in the 1930s (see Cantril & Allport, 1935), as did the advancing propaganda of the Nazi regime that had come to power in Germany (Dennis & Wartella, 1996).

Most of this research gained its foothold in the United States, as might be expected in the nation that fostered media as an industry and commercial outlet. Advertisers, along with those who feared totalitarian government propaganda techniques, played up the power of the media. This perspective, however, would not last long as systematic research using disciplined social science techniques began to show how complex the media communication and persuasion process was (Dennis & Wartella, 1996).

Have Scholars Ever Changed Their Minds about Media Theory?

During the first half of the twentieth century, World War II stirred a flurry of research designed to use the media to rally U.S. citizens behind war efforts—including buying war bonds, donating scrap metal, participating in rationing programs, volunteering for the armed services, and teaching the public to rally against the enemy. Up to this time, researchers generally believed mass media cast magical persuasive effects upon audiences.

In this early period of theorizing about mass media, media's power and influence were largely unknown and misunderstood. Most educators and most citizens on the street believed that the media had great inherent power to persuade an audience. Perhaps this is because the media was looked at macroscopically. **Macroscopic** approaches look at media and audiences as groups. These kinds of studies do not attempt to account for differences across the media or across various audience groups. They attempt to **generalize,** or explain what happens in the majority of cases or on average (even if the general account does not fit any single person in the audience). A macroscopic view paints the world in very large brushstrokes.

As research became more systematic during World War II, scholars found it difficult to prove these powerful effects when they examined a series of individuals. While overall societal chances might have been created, scientists could not account for them at the **microscopic,** or individual, level. By studying well-defined groups of individuals with different psychological, educational, or demographic profiles, researchers began to focus upon what mass media could and, more importantly, could not do. By the early 1960s mass media research emphasized the limited role media play in shaping public opinion. These findings on media influence proclaimed that people were not like sponges who might soak up and believe everything they read or see on the media, but that people had their own power to choose what they accepted and what they didn't, hence the **limited effects perspective** on the media.

The paradigm (the set of assumptions or beliefs that guide how we see the social and natural world as defined in Chapter 2) of limited effects evolved again, since many researchers during the 1970s and 1980s were unsatisfied with the conclusions reached during the 1960s, and they began to look at more specific effects that mass communication might generate. Today, we have a variety of theoretical explanations about how the media are powerful in shaping limited sets of the beliefs that we hold and the decisions we make, a paradigm known as the **limited but powerful effects perspective.** There are those also who today claim substantial media influence again, a belief on par with the powerful effects period though framed quite differently. Rather than examine individual messages, these researchers emphasize the power of the television's systematic themes and its cast of characters.

The remainder of this chapter gives a more detailed historical account of media research and some of the people who have brought us to how scholars think about mass media today. Along with the paradigm shifts you were introduced to above we give special attention to two sets of assumptions—those about how the media can influence people and those about how people actively engage media and their messages.

Powerful Effects—Media Deliver Meanings

Researchers in a variety of other fields in the years just before and the two decades after 1900 began to write about "the manner in which the revolution in communication (had) made a new world for us" (Cooley, 1909/1983, p. 65). One of these was Charles Cooley, who trained in engineering and economics but taught in the area of sociology while considering the importance of the system of communication and its powerful influence on human interaction. Another, Robert Park, was an undergraduate student at the University of Michigan at the same time as Cooley. He also went into sociology, though he served for years as a journalist and human rights activist. He encouraged the quantitative study of public opinion and insisted that such opinion rested on journalism and news (Schramm, Chaffee, & Rogers, 1997). A third was John Dewey, the famous education philosopher. He noted the emergence of an industry for shaping public opinion with the creation of the wire services that could gather and distribute news on a large scale. He seemed to fear that an intellectual paternalism would be at work through the media, a vehicle for propaganda (Dewey, 1918; as cited in Glander, 2000).

The middle 1910s saw the speed and magnitude of structural change in the mass media intensify as a result of the world war. Scholars began to become media experts, though their individual backgrounds were still in other disciplines. Harold Lasswell, whose academic training was from a variety of fields, wrote his first treatise on propaganda. It emphasized the newly pejorative nature of the term, which focused on the attempts of hidden and largely unaccountable people to manipulate the attitudes and thoughts of others (Lasswell, 1927). Paul Lazarsfeld was a mathematician and initially used his skill at data analysis to conduct consumer marketing research. This research eventually migrated in the direction of the new medium of radio in the 1930s. The data from these research endeavors became fodder for studying the social science of mass communication and opinion research (Schramm, Chaffee, & Rogers, 1997). Eventually his research led away from the powerful effects model, but not at first.

In the 1920s researchers in the Payne Fund studies (a series of eleven books published by the MacMillan Publishing Company) tested the effects of motion pictures upon children (among others, Blumer, 1933; Charters, 1933; Dale, 1935; Holaday & Stoddard, 1933). These studies concluded that movies directly and powerfully influenced children's attitudes and behaviors. These studies received a lot of public attention partly because the researchers were very highly qualified and partly because parents in the United States were very concerned about what motion pictures might be doing to degrade the family's role in teaching appropriate moral standards to their children. The high profile of these findings influenced people to believe that media had a commanding effect upon audiences.

Today, we refer to this belief about powerful media effects as the magic bullet theory or sometimes the hypodermic needle theory. In the **magic bullet theory,** media are like a gun firing a message into an audience. In the **hypodermic needle theory,** the analogy uses different imagery suggesting the media are like a needle injecting a message into an audience. Both of these metaphors imply that the media cause individuals to form ideas and take actions according to the messages they receive. Thus, these theories contended that media were so powerful they could directly influence audiences in the way that designers of messages intended. In short, these early researchers assumed that media had the power to tell people what to think and how to behave.

But what do these all-powerful theories of mass communication say about humans and the way our minds work? First, this view presupposes that all humans think the same way. If a message is appropriately written and accurately transmitted, then all who receive that message will interpret it the same way. In this model, differences in age, race, ethnicity, gender, or economic or social status do not affect the way people interpret information received from the media. By assuming that all audience members were essentially the same, it is said that early researchers had a belief in a **mass audience.**

Second, the powerful theories of media effects assume that we will all react the same way to the same message. Not only do our minds work alike, but also given the same instructions from the media, we should behave the same (or nearly the same) way. Importantly, these theories assume there will be no differences between individuals in the way they respond to media messages. Thus, these models expect people to react to mass media messages in the same way they would react to a bullet or an injection—it is something that just hits them. These theories give no power to people to interpret messages differently than the sender intended them. They do not account for the fact that people might react differently to the same message.

Limited Effects: A Tool People Use

Believing the notion that media have all-powerful effects, during World War II the U.S. Army hired Frank Capra, a Hollywood director, to produce films such as *Why We Fight; The Nazis Strike, Divide, and Conquer;* and *Prelude to War.* The military wanted to create messages that would have a direct, positive impact on U.S. soldiers' and citizens' attitudes toward World War II. Given the conclusion of the Payne Fund studies, the military assumed that movies should have the most commanding influence over the U.S. audience's attitudes. But when Carl Hovland and other researchers at Yale tested the effects of these movies upon people, they concluded that the movies largely failed to change people's minds about the war (Hovland, Lumsdaine, & Sheffield, 1949).

At about the same time, Lazarsfeld and his colleagues examined the influence of political messages upon voters in Erie County, Pennsylvania (Lazarsfeld, Berleson, & Gaudet, 1948). They found that the media *did* directly influence a small group of opinion leaders (approximately 20 percent of the population), but generally media only reinforced political attitudes that people held already. This study generated the theory of the **two-step flow,** which gives an account of how media messages are filtered through a small group of people who reshape the messages and pass them on to the less informed masses.

Did the media act like a bullet or a hypodermic needle injecting a message into people? The research was beginning to say *no.*

Although the **limited effects theories** undermined the assumptions about an all-powerful media, they emphasized the influence of social relationships and individual psychological processes. Scholars became more concerned with differences among individuals within an audience, differences such as age, race, ethnicity, and gender. Researchers also began to weigh social influences such as political affiliation, religion, and economic status more heavily.

Researchers began to move away from exclusively assuming that the audience for media messages was largely inactive in the process of media influence. They began to examine how people differed in message interpretation through selective attention, selective perception, and selective retention. This means that researchers began to examine what kinds of messages attracted people, why people had different interpretations of the same message, and why people remembered different things from messages.

Due to the limited effects claims of media scholars, for two generations the texts from fields like economics, political science, history, and sociology—fields that originally gave birth to the new discipline of communication—mostly ignored media's importance.

The passing references to media that can be found reveal naïve understanding of media during the period from the 1940s to the 1980s. Interestingly, and suggestive of things to come, advertisers continued to spend more and more money to reach the diverse segments of the audience that research said would be difficult to persuade (Dennis & Wartella, 1996).

The limited effects tradition, therefore, grew from repeated studies that failed to find the all-powerful effects expected from mass communication. Many researchers agreed with Joseph Klapper's (1960) claim that the media were only one part of the puzzle, and more consideration was given to how individuals interpreted messages and how other kinds of social influence shaped perception. Theories of limited effects will be prominent in Chapter 13, which focuses on how individual differences moderated media messages even in a passive audience.

Limited but Powerful Effects

During the 1970s and 1980s researchers began to again think that media might play a more powerful role. In fact, scholars during this time admitted that the media's effects might be limited, but they were beginning to appear to be very powerful in some narrow areas. Three different approaches show some of the areas in which media were beginning to seem powerful and also offer good illustrations of media research reflecting the limited but powerful effects perspective.

Agenda Setting Function of the Media.   In one of the earliest attempts to prove a direct effect of mass media on audiences, Bernard Cohen (1963) found that media may not be able to tell audiences "what to think," but they could tell them "what to think about." This new idea became known as **agenda setting theory.** This theory said that, at the macroscopic level, the issues people think are important for America to deal with will be correlated with the issues the media most often presents as problems for the society. It quickly became a popular avenue for research on whether media have direct effects upon audience members, even though those effects are limited in scope. McCombs and Shaw (1972) represented the process as the media's ability to place salient issues in the public light, so that the media served as a catalyst for public opinion. Substantial research has shown agenda setting to be a reliable and robust phenomenon that indicates a strong relationship between media agendas and people's beliefs about which issues are important. In fact, the media's emphasis on the economy, while rarely mentioning foreign relations, probably influenced the 1992 election when incumbent president George Bush was defeated. After having enjoyed one of the highest approval ratings only two years earlier while prosecuting the Gulf War, the economy, a perceived Bush weakness, became more important to voters than foreign relations, a Bush strength, due to media coverage during the election cycle. (Agenda setting is covered in more detail in Chapter 15).

Framing or **frame analysis** is another theory about media power in a limited dimension. It describes the set of expectations that we use to make sense of each social situation as a **frame.** This frame is determined through learned **social cues,** or information in our environment that signals the appropriate way to behave or respond. While we may not consciously seek it, we learn many of these social cues through the media. Advertising is especially rife with these cues. [Web site: Framing]

Think about it. If you had just come to America from living in the Artic where the only transportation you had known was a snowmobile or a reindeer and you had seen no advertising messages, what meaning would brand-name tennis shoes or jeans have to you? Or perhaps two cars are side by side, one a Jaguar and the other a Nissan. The drivers exit both cars. What do you think about the drivers? Does one car convey higher status to its driver than the other? The truth is, without advertising and other media to convey status to certain items, these products would carry no social cues.

Cars, shoes, clothes, and hundreds of other objects, however, do mean things to us. We learn to use them as social cues to know how to approach and talk to people. This is especially true in romantic interactions. Media teach us how to interpret (or misinterpret) flirtatious postures, smiles, and subtle eye movements. Men routinely make more sensual meaning of a woman's nonverbal messages than what is intended in part because of media-created expectations (Goffman, 1974, 1979). Many of these cues are unintentionally learned, while others we seek out.

Depending on Media Systems.   A third theory that said the media might have powerful effects in limited situations was developed by Sandra Ball-Rokeach (1976). She developed **media system dependency theory** (see Chapter 13) based on several studies of events during the 1970s. Ball-Rokeach found that media were the most influential when people could not rely upon personal sources of information. In cases such as natural disasters or plane crashes, the media provide the best source of information because few people have direct experience of these kinds of events to share reliable information with their friends and families.

Ball-Rokeach acknowledged the important role that interpersonal relationships played in gathering and interpreting information. When adequate information is available through personal contact, people do not have to rely upon the media as much. These qualifying conditions explain why the media sometimes appear to have very powerful effects, and at other times they appear to have only mild influence on shaping people's opinions.

The limited but powerful effects paradigm accommodates some of the limited effects theories along with some of more powerful models of media effects. Media dependency theory, framing, and agenda setting theory reflect the notion that the effect of the media is limited to only one dimension on a topic and do not attribute sweeping influence to the media. What can be said of limited but powerful effects research is that media sometimes play a very strong role in shaping people's ideas and behaviors, and sometimes media have little influence on audiences.

Do the Media Affect Me, or Am I Affected by My Own Decisions?

Alongside the limited but powerful effects model is a theory that describes how we use the media to satisfy needs and wants based on our own cognitive activity rather than asking how the media affects us. Originally formulated by Elihu Katz, Jay Blumler, and Michael Gurevitch (1974), **uses and gratifications theory** recognized the important role of individuals' motives in selecting media products. This line of research found that people decided which media messages (and media products) interested them. This interest caused individual members of an audience to have different motivations toward processing the same mass media message. Because people come to a media setting with different motives for being there, they naturally receive different results from the same message.

This view focuses upon individual reasoning and goals as a direct influence on how media affects an individual. By examining people's motives for using media messages, researchers have found that many of the weak media findings from the limited effects tradition may be better explained by differences in the media consumption goals of individual audience members.

Along with theories like reception theory and diffusion of innovations (discussed in Chapter 14), uses and gratifications theory assumes that audiences are not targets for the media to hit. Instead, audience members actively select media messages, and they do so with particular goals in mind.

Are Limited Effects Approaches Simply Too Limited?

In the 1970s, George Gerbner (1990, 1998) studied violence in the media, which resulted in his formulation of cultivation theory. This theory directly opposes any notion that media power is limited. While the limited but powerful approach focuses narrowly on one aspect of how or when mass communication has its most powerful influence, **cultivation theory** is a grand theory that assumes media have far-reaching and pervasive effects. But unlike the all-powerful media effects theories, cultivation theory recognizes the audience as active interpreters. In its simplest form, cultivation suggests that media create images that mold society. Media play such an important role in conveying these images that media and culture cannot be separated (Signiorelli & Morgan, 1990). [Web site: Cultivation Theory]

Gerbner came to this conclusion after examining violence in television programming and comparing the attitudes of heavy television viewers to those who seldom watched television. He found that television content overrepresented instances of violence both in the heavy coverage of violence on the news and the use of violence as an audience attraction in entertainment programming. When he compared different levels of television watchers, he discovered heavy viewers were three times more likely to believe that a policeman uses his or her gun more than five times a day. He also found that heavy viewers were more suspicious of others and more fearful of being attacked by another member of society. Gerbner called this unqualified fear and suspicion the **mean world syndrome.** TV's ability to cultivate perceptions of race, sex roles, occupations, religious values, and health practices have verified cultivation theory's importance.

Summary

This chapter has examined the history of mass communication and mass media research so that you can begin to understand the strengths and limitations that media have in shaping our attitudes and actions. We have considered a world before media where people depended upon songs, story telling, and conversations to pass on information necessary to function within the society. We have examined the increasing power of the media as society grew beyond the possibilities of face-to-face exchanges of social information. We looked at the media as a window on the world—a window that helps organize and make information available but, at the same time, distorts it.

Additionally, we have examined a range of research assumptions about the media and their relationships to audiences as a historical approach to media studies. In the earliest of these studies, we found that researchers assumed media had all-powerful effects and that the audience was passive. In failing to prove all-powerful effects, researchers decided that media had limited effects upon audience beliefs and behaviors. Still later, researchers studying agenda setting, framing, media system dependency theory, and uses and gratifications theory agreed that the media had limited influence, but they argued that they were nonetheless powerful. At the same time, media cultivation researchers returned to the all-powerful effects paradigm.

What should be clear from this historical account is that media do play an important role in shaping society, as well as shaping individual beliefs and behaviors. But too, audiences actively select media messages, and this in turn encourages the media to provide some products and not others in order to please the audiences they target. Equally important is the fact that no single perspective or theory completely and accurately captures the media-society-individual relationship, nor does any particular theory or perspective founded on firm evidence deserve to be ignored.

Discussion Questions

1. Why is it important to tell the story about the world before mass communication?

2. Given Lippmann's account of media as a window on the world, how might this change your perspective of the importance of professionalism in the journalistic profession?

3. Describe the theories of agenda setting, media system dependency, and uses and gratifications in terms of microscopic versus macroscopic approaches.

4. Which of your personal characteristics lead you to selectively use media in a different way than some of your friends?

References

Ball-Rokeach, S., & DeFleur, M. (1976). A dependency model of mass media effects. *Communication Research, 3*(1), 3–21.

Blumer, H. (1933). *Movies and conduct.* New York: Macmillan.

Cantril, H., & Allport, G. W. (1935). *The psychology of radio.* New York: Harper and Brothers.

Charters, W. (1933). *Motion pictures and youth.* New York: Macmillan.

Cohen, B. (1963). *The press and foreign policy.* Princeton, NJ: Princeton University Press.

Cooley, C. H. (1983). *Social organization: A study of the large mind.* New Brunswick, NJ: Transaction Books. (Original work published 1909).

Dale, E. (1935). *The content of motion pictures.* New York: Macmillan.

DeFleur, M. (1970). *Theories of mass communication* (2nd ed.). New York: David McKay.

Dennis, E. E., & Wartella, E. (1996). *American communication research: The remembered history.* Mahwah, NJ: Lawrence Erlbaum.

Dewey, J. (1918, December 21). The new paternalism. *The New Republic,* p. 216.

Exxon Valdez Oil Spill Trustee Council. (n.d.). *Oil spill facts.* Retrieved November 21, 2002, from http://www.oilspill.state.ak.us/facts/

Gerbner, G. (1990). "Epilogue: Advancing the path of righteousness (maybe)." In N. Signorielli & M.

Morgan (Eds.), *Cultivation analysis: New directions in media effects research* (pp. 249–262). Newbury Park, CA: Sage.

Gerbner, G. (1998). Cultivation analysis: An overview. *Mass Communication & Society, 1,* 175–194.

Glander, T. (2000). *Origins of mass communications research during the American cold war: Educational effects and contemporary implications.* Mahwah, NJ: Lawrence Erlbaum.

Goffman, E. (1974). *Frame analysis: An essay on the organization of experience.* Cambridge, MA: Harvard University Press.

Goffman, E. (1979). *Gender advertisements.* New York: Harper Colophon.

Holaday, P. W., & Stoddard, G. D. (1933). *Motion pictures and standards of morality.* New York: Macmillan.

Hovland, C. I., Lumsdaine, A. A., & Sheffield, F. D. (1949). *Experiments on mass communication: Studies in social psychology in World War II* (vol. 3). Princeton, NJ: Princeton University Press.

Katz, E., Blumler, J., & Gurevitch, M. (1974). Utilization of mass communication by the individual. In J. Blumler & E. Katz (Eds.), *The uses of mass communication: Current perspectives on gratifications research* (pp. 19–32). Beverly Hills, CA: Sage.

Klapper, J. (1960). *The effects of mass communication.* New York: Free Press.

Lasswell, H. D. (1927). *Propaganda techniques in the World War.* New York: Knopf.

Lazarsfeld, P., Berelson, B., & Gaudet, H. (1948). *The people's choice.* New York: Columbia University Press.

Lippmann, W. (1922). *Public opinion.* New York: Macmillan.

McCombs, M., & Shaw, D. (1972). The agenda-setting function of the mass media. *Public Opinion, 36,* 176–187.

Schramm, W., Chaffee, S. H., & Rogers, E. M. (1997). *The beginnings of communication study in America: A personal memoir.* Thousand Oaks, CA: Sage.

Signiorelli, N., & Morgan, M. (Eds.). (1990). *Cultivation analysis: New directions in media effects research.* Newbury Park, CA: Sage.

13

Media Use and the Selective Individual

Jong G. Kang

In the previous chapter you learned about the various paradigms under which mass media theories have emerged. The powerful effects approach initially assumed that the media were powerful instruments of propaganda and change in society. As research began to try to identify how this happened, findings indicated that many things moderated or limited the influence of the media on individuals. Thus, the powerful effects era gave way to the idea that the media had limited effects. In this chapter you will study the way interpersonal interactions, individual differences, and psychological processes protect us from the outright propaganda effects of mediated content. The theories in this chapter emerged from scientific investigation and are about how the media's societal effects are reduced through our psychological, situational, and social-structural differences. They have a heavy microscopic or individual-level perspective. The way the media will affect us will be largely determined by our own beliefs, the level at which we depend on the media, and the depth of our interpersonal interactions. These theories deal with how information reaches us, how we isolate ourselves against unwanted messages, and how our attitudes are difficult to change through media presentations.

In this chapter, you will read about the following concepts:

- Opinion leaders filter information for followers
  - Two-step flow theory
- The information filtering process is complex
  - Multistep flow theory
- Media is more influential when we must depend on it
  - Media dependency theory
  - Five assertions of dependency theory
- People interpret messages in unique, personal ways
  - Individual differences theory
  - Attitude change theory
  - Selective processes theories
  - Cognitive dissonance theory

If you had been listening to the radio on Halloween Eve in 1938, you might have heard the *Mercury Theater of the Air,* the CBS radio program in which Orson Welles presented the famous "War of the Worlds" broadcast. The program about a Martian invasion of Earth was presented as a series of news bulletins breaking into a program of orchestra music. Listeners who tuned in late missed the setup describing the broadcast as a dramatization of the H. G. Wells book by the same title as the program. Nearly one-sixth of the listening audience of six million is estimated to have panicked when they heard the reports of Martian spacecraft and death rays. People volunteered for the military, packed up their families and headed for the hills, and called their parents to come pick them up from college (see Figure 13.1).

Initially, such responses were seen as evidence of the powerful effects of the media. They were examples of the radio's magic bullet theory (see Chapter 12) in action. But only a couple of years after the broadcasts were aired, some researchers began to ask another question. Why didn't everyone panic if radio had such powers? How come some people enjoyed the event as entertainment while others panicked, believing it to be true? Several theories developed over the next couple of decades to describe why people react differently to the same media message. The previous chapter presented an overview of the important theories that have developed to explain the role and the power of media in our lives. This chapter, as well as the next, will present a more in-depth explanation of some scientific theories that best explain how media have a limited ability to affect everyone in uniform ways. This chapter will look at limited effects theories that allow users to be **passive,** not necessarily making intentional decisions about the media's influence in their lives, but still limit the media's influence. Chapter 14 will then look at limited effects theories that assume the audience is **active,** intentionally trying to use the media as a tool to achieve a certain effect. One of the earliest theories of the media's limited effects came out of research on the use of media for persuasion in presidential campaigns.

FIGURE 13.1   Orson Welles speaks to reporters after the 1938 dramatic radio production of "The War of the Worlds" resulted in panic in nearly a million radio listeners according to some estimates.

AP Wide World Photo.

Who Influences Your Opinions and Decisions?

In the 1940 presidential campaign of Franklin D. Roosevelt versus Wendell Wilkie, media researcher Paul Lazarsfeld and his colleagues attempted to determine the power of the mass media in affecting people's voting decisions. They interviewed more than 3,000 different registered voters from Erie County, Ohio. Nearly 1,000 interviews were conducted every month (a group of 600 was interviewed multiple times) from May to November 1940 to examine what influenced the way these people voted for president. Their findings suggested that media influence on people's voting behavior was limited by **opinion leaders** who initially consumed the mass media content but then passed the information on after adding an interpretation of their own based on their personal values and beliefs. The media, then, influenced the opinion leaders somewhat directly but others only indirectly. In addition, the opinion leaders were not passive sponges parroting the media line. They interpreted the messages themselves before sending them on (Lazarsfeld, Berelson, & Gaudet, 1944).

Media Information Is Filtered for Us

In a follow-up study, Lazarsfeld looked at more than just politics. Everything from purchases at the grocery store to movie choices were analyzed in a study of over 700 women in Decatur, Illinois. Decatur, a city in the agricultural center of the Midwest, was thought to be representative of small cities across the country. His research team asked women what individuals influenced their decisions on purchases and fashions as well as politics. It is important to note that when the interviews were conducted, television had not yet come to Decatur. The resulting research, published with Elihu Katz in 1955, found that neither voting nor product information presented in the mass media had the universal impact on audience members that would have been expected under the old powerful media paradigm and the magic bullet theory. Their book formalized a new inductively reasoned theory of how media content passed through opinion leaders to **opinion followers** as **two-step flow theory** (Katz & Lazarsfeld, 1955). [Web site: Two-Step-Flow link]

Two-step flow theory formally posits that messages are received from the mass media by opinion leaders who pass them along by word-of-mouth transmission to other persons (see Figure 13.2).

The Complexity of the Information Filtering Process

Other research modified two-step-flow theory by illustrating that people receive initial information in one step but are influenced in their beliefs, attitudes, and behaviors through a two-step flow (Troldahl, 1965). Further findings disclosed that opinions on public affairs are reciprocal or that often people share opinions in two directions (Troldahl & Van Dam, 1965). The understanding of the process became more and more complex, revealing that opinion leaders even reciprocally influenced the newspaper editors and broadcast programmers and that sometimes people were receiving their information after being filtered through several other people. This brought about a slight change in the theory. Now, most people talk about the **multistep flow theory** rather than just a two-step flow. It is recognized that the flow of

FIGURE 13.2 *Model of Two-Step Flow of Mass Media Influence.*

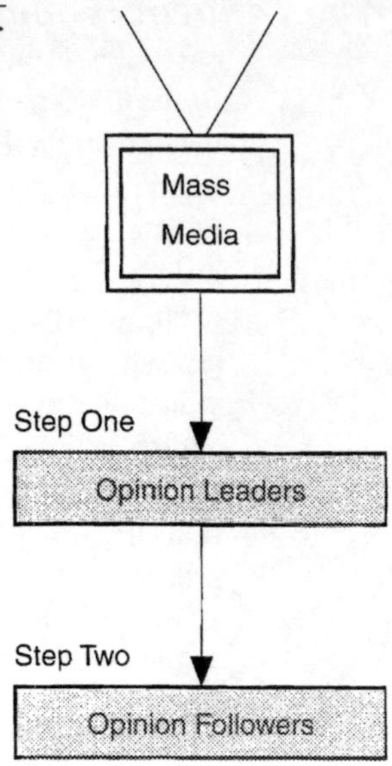

```
        Mass
        Media
          |
Step One  ↓
    [ Opinion Leaders ]

Step Two  ↓
    [ Opinion Followers ]
```

information varies according to the social conditions related to any given issue as well as the type of information being conveyed (Baran & Davis, 2000; Bryant & Thompson, 2002).

Think about how you make political decisions about issues. Are you a member of a campus group dedicated to environmental or human rights causes? Is that campus group part of a national organization? How does information flow down to you as part of that group? Perhaps the media inform the opinion leaders at the national level about an issue. These individuals convey the importance of the issue for the group's cause down to the local chapters. The local chapter leaders may then respond through e-mail or survey on what action they believe the national organization should take in relation to the issue. The national group then organizes the responses into a campaign. The chapter leaders then champion the cause to the local membership, and the local membership then tries to enlist broader public support from the rest of the campus or even from the community. The flow of the information in this case clearly has many steps before the opinion followers in the local chapter and the public decide to join in the cause being promoted.

Variations in the Information Flow Process

The increasing availability of personalized information sources may eliminate the opinion leaders in the flow of the mass communication process from mass media to the receiver. No doubt, opinion leaders still exist. For example, we often ask friends what they have read, heard, or consumed about a medium such as a movie, music, book, CD, or Internet web site, but the centrality of opinion leaders to the larger, societal mass communication process has, according to some accounts, significantly diminished (Baran, 2000).

Theorists have pointed to situations where no opinion leaders could be singled out when studying how people received their information on a particular topic (Williams,

1992). More importantly, later studies have recognized that the flow of information from mass media takes many forms: direct, two-step, and multistep (Westley, 1971). Finally, Melvin DeFleur and Sandra Ball-Rokeach (1989) posit that as a social system becomes more complex and the informal communication channels less reliable, people become increasingly dependent on the mass media. Such media dependency has become more and more important during political campaigns (Jeffres, 1997).

When Do We Really Need the Media?

In an effort to reconcile the idea that the media do have effects on us with the limited-effects model of mass communication illustrated in the two-step/multistep flow theory, DeFleur and Ball-Rokeach (1989) proposed an integrated theoretical perspective of society's dependency on the media. **Media dependency theory** states that the relationship between communication and opinion is not one way but many interactive processes. The theory insists that the more dependent we are on the media for certain functions in our lives, the greater its effect on us will be. This theory stresses the triangular relationships among our society's social system, the media's place in that system, and media's role in the audience's life (DeFleur & Ball-Rokeach, 1982). [Web site: Dependency Theory]

These three interactive factors are related to an audience member's dependency on the media and their content. They operate to increase or decrease the degree of audience members' dependency. Audience members in a modern industrial society, especially in our current information-oriented industries, are increasingly dependent on the media and their content for functioning in the social system. For example, we look to media for information on new products, on the predicted weather for the weekend, and on political or military decisions and activities.

In turn, this dependency leads to a complex web of interactions among media, audiences, and society. Media theorists believe that as our society grows more complex and as the media technology grows more complex, audience members become more dependent on the media and their content. DeFleur and Ball-Rokeach (1989) suggest that the nature of dependencies is different for different individuals, different groups, and different cultures.

The war against Iraq in 2003 serves to help our understanding of this theory. Americans learned of the initial bombing targeting Saddam Hussein and his regime through media reports, and many became glued to their televisions. Public opinion faltered when the advance on Baghdad was reported to have stalled. Days later, reports showed Baghdad fallen into U.S. and British hands and public support was restored to its highest levels. Those with children serving as military troops in Iraq were also dependent on the media for news. Few phones or Internet access points were available to troops, and by the time a letter was written to a soldier and a reply received back home, the war was over. Media was the only avenue for war information.

The use of biological terror following the September 11th terrorist attacks initiated the same response. Few people knew what anthrax was without access to the mediated information. The symptoms of infection, how the germ agent could be encountered, the treatment for cases, and the prevention methods were learned about almost exclusively through the media. Probably only a small percentage of people learned about the disease, treatment,

FIGURE 13.3   A United States postal worker in
Puerto Rico wears gloves and a mask to protect
herself from the possible contamination of mail
by the anthrax virus. Media dependency influenced postal workers even in this territory
outside the 50 states that she might be at risk
of encountering the powdery contaminant.

AP Wide World Photo.

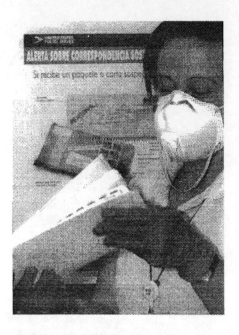

and prevention through their doctors. In fact, it was the dependency on the media and the
constant barrage of stories about anthrax over a period of days and then weeks that led
some people to be initially very cautious, if not fearful, about opening mail or encountering
white powdery substances. Had the information been conveyed through reasonable interpersonal filters, as in the multistep flow theory, perhaps the relative danger of encountering anthrax compared to being struck by lightning, dying in a car accident, or getting heart
disease would have moderated more people's levels of fear about that form of terrorist attack. This is not to suggest that a certain level of caution was not appropriate related to the
anthrax attacks, but only that our dependence and the media's resulting deluge of coverage about the attacks led to levels of fear and caution that were disproportionate to the actual potential danger (see Figure 13.3).

Media dependency theory tends to emphasize the perspective of how great the
media's impact can be. Of course, the opposite of this is that often we are not dependent
on the media for our information. The newspaper doesn't need to tell us what the employment picture is if we lose our jobs or what the price of gas is doing when we fill our car
up at the gas pumps. When we are less dependent on the media, its impact is marginalized
and limited.

Do People's Personal Traits Modify How Media Affect Them?

While the nature of people's dependency on the media varies based on the social system,
the media, and the audience's relationship to the media, many other variables of a more
personal nature can affect how a person responds to media.

As early as the 1930s, social scientists had begun to verify through experimental studies that audience members possessed widely divergent psychological makeups. These studies suggested that audience members selectively attend to messages congruent with their beliefs and supportive of their values. Then, they respond to such messages based on their psychological makeup (DeFleur & Ball-Rokeach, 1982).

This perspective on mass communication is called the **individual differences** theory. Individual differences argues that media influence people differently from person to person, because people vary greatly in their psychological construction. Their psychological makeup is partly related to other aspects of who they are demographically and their past experiences in life. Thus, their different ages, races, education, sex, social status, and an almost infinite list of other characteristics play a role in how people differ in their thought processes and beliefs about the world in response to media (Baran & Davis, 2000). More specifically, media messages have certain attributes that interact differently with the personality characteristics of the various audience members (DeFleur, 1970).

How are you different from even your close friends? Suppose you have a parent who is an emergency room physician who regularly sees people wounded from handgun violence. Compare your likely view of a news report about handgun legislation to the view of someone whose family had been protected from a household intruder who was scared off when he heard the sound of an ammunition clip being inserted into the family's handgun. Every issue provokes different responses from people because of their "individual differences," even when they may eventually come to the same conclusion about how to vote, what legislation should be passed, or what personal behavior to change.

The understanding of how individual differences limit the media's ability to promote change in society served as the catalyst to alter the accepted paradigm about powerful media influence to the view that the media had limited effects. The individual differences perspective reflects a belief that messages cannot be crafted to be widely effective as propaganda since, with only rare exceptions, no one message will affect the bulk of the population in the same way. Combining media dependency theory with individual differences suggests that even when people are very dependent on the media and more widely affected by it, the effects vary from person to person.

How Difficult Is It to Change People's Attitudes?

In an attempt to examine diverse psychological organizations of human beings in the mass communication context, Carl Hovland and some research colleagues (Hovland, Lumsdaine & Sheffield, 1949) explained how audience members' attitudes are formed, shaped, and changed through communication and how those attitudes influence behavior. This idea has become known as **attitude change** research, a broad area of scholarship that serves as an umbrella for several specific theories. Among the most important attitude change theories are a group of three related selective processes and dissonance theories.

We Don't Pay Strict Attention to What the Media Says

The selective processes are highly interrelated with psychological characteristics that influence how audience members confront and cope with the content of mass media. The

selective processes explain that audience members expose themselves to selective communication, interpret messages in line with preexisting attitudes and beliefs, and retain those messages that are consistent with their existing attitudes and beliefs. Social scientists refer to these processes as selective exposure, selective perception, and selective retention.

Avoiding Exposure.   The first selective process, **selective exposure,** emphasizes the difficulty of getting a person to consume a message aimed at changing his or her attitude. Imagine you find live news coverage of a speech being given by a candidate for president. This notion says you are more likely to listen to the speech if it is being given by the candidate you favor but likely to tune to something else if the opposing candidate is speaking. [Web site: Selective Exposure]

Audience members either subconsciously or consciously select from the flow of available communication those ideas that are consistent with their preexisting attitudes, opinions, behaviors, and beliefs about the world. In other words, the individual differences among people influence their likelihood of consuming specific messages. At one time, the fact that newspapers aligned with certain political parties more than others allowed some ease in this selective exposure process. As newspapers have had less and less competition, with only one newspaper serving most cities, and since the broadcast television networks have generally given similar portrayals of the political world, for many years it had become harder and harder to be selective enough to avoid the contrasting points of view on political issues.

Over the past decade, however, it has again become easier to avoid messages that contrast with our personal values and beliefs. Radio talk shows like *The Rush Limbaugh Show* provide a refuge from dissonant messages for the politically conservative. Liberal talk hosts, while none have achieved a ratings success as noteworthy as Limbaugh's, are likely to be avoided by the conservatives but provide a place to tune for the listener on the political left. While the political leanings of cable television news sources are not as openly partisan, the initiation of the Fox News Network has provided a more conservative source of TV news, while CNBC or CNN have been sources seen as more friendly to the left-leaning viewer. Conservatives sometimes even claimed that the Cable News Network's acronym during the late 1990s really stood for the Clinton News Network, in reference to the perception that the network favored President Bill Clinton in its coverage.

Comprehending Selectively.   When audience members interpret media messages in such a way that they are consistent with preexisting attitudes, opinions, beliefs, and behaviors, this is known as **selective perception.** A classical example of selective perception appeared in the late 1980s, when Lt. Col. Oliver North testified at the Congressional Iran-Contra hearings. Millions of television viewers "proclaimed him a national hero and wanted him to run for President, while others were convinced he should be sent to jail for breaking the law and figuratively shredding the Constitution" (Wilson, 1989, p. 13). Similarly, the testimony of Bill Clinton in hearings conducted by special prosecutor Kenneth Starr led many to support his impeachment for perjury and obstruction of justice. Others, however, were convinced that the pursuit of Clinton's impeachment was all about the Republican Party's wanting to grab more political power over what should have been a private sexual matter between Clinton and White House intern Monica Lewinsky. [Web site: Selective Perception]

In selective perception the media consumer is exposed to the information, unlike the avoidance practiced under selective exposure, but the outcome is no different. Audience members recast the message mentally or psychologically so that it matches their preexisting beliefs, values, and attitudes. Thus, they make the information they encounter reinforce their preexisting worldview, even if the source of the information did not intend it that way (Baran & Davis, 2000).

Memory of Convenience.   The third and final selective process says that audience members remember media messages that are consistent with their preexisting attitudes, opinions, beliefs, and behaviors much better and longer than they do contrary messages. Television viewers, for example, are more likely to retain those messages they consciously accepted than those they consciously rejected. This process is called **selective retention.** According to this process, our memory works to conveniently support the things we want to believe.

Someone who supports legislation protecting patients from being treated by an over-tired and overworked doctor will remember the details about malpractice claims against a physician who had been on duty for more than 24 hours before an errant surgery. For others who have no interest or who take a laissez-faire approach to medical safeguards, such an incident will be but a blip on their radar screen. They would recall little, if any, of the story as time went by.

As with selective exposure and selective perception, the selective retention process tends to reinforce existing beliefs. This works against the media's ability to change attitudes, since we just forget things that don't fit our view of the world. Clearly the selective processes explain ways in which we defend ourselves against the power of the media's potential effects.

We Like to Eliminate Psychological Discomfort

Clearly, one of the ways we use selective processes is to shield us from messages—mediated or face-to-face—that will make us feel uncomfortable. Thus, they become important in **cognitive dissonance theory,** a theory developed by Leon Festinger in 1957. This theory is based on the premise that people, when confronted by new information that is not consistent with their preexisting attitudes and beliefs, experience a kind of psychological discomfort. This mental discomfort is called dissonance. According to cognitive dissonance theory, **dissonance** is an unpleasant mental or emotional state caused by conflict between thoughts, feelings, or actions (Williams, 1992). The theory holds that new information that is inconsistent with people's preexisting attitudes and beliefs will create a dissonance that must be resolved. People generally want to keep what they learn about the world and what they themselves think they already know somewhat consistent, and they work at maintaining this. Festinger (1957, 1962) explains, "If a person knows various things that are not psychologically consistent with one another, he will, in a variety of ways, try to make them more consistent." As a result, people consciously and/or subconsciously try to turn dissonance into **consonance,** the existence of consistency between personal beliefs and observations of the world.

If an Israeli citizen believes that most Palestinians are troublemakers, but then is treated graciously by a Palestinian contingent while conducting necessary business, the Israelite must do one of two things to reduce the dissonance between his or her own stereotype of Palestinians at large and the experience of being treated so well in this situation. Modifying his or her beliefs about Palestinians to include more room for friendship with this national group is the first and most desirable option, but the second option, passing the experience off as the exception that proves the rule, is the more likely choice. In other words, the Israelite thinks, "The reason why I noticed these people were so nice to me is that Palestinians never act this way. This just proves that Palestinians are troublemakers."

Mediated experiences with cognitive dissonance are no different. Through selective perception tendencies we can shrug off news information that is inconsistent with our own beliefs, recasting the information so that it falls in line with what we think we know. We may discredit the messenger as untrustworthy, believe the facts to be inaccurate, decide the issue is not that important to us after all, or think that waiting for the full picture of that news event to be revealed will ultimately prove our beliefs right. Fortunately, however, sometimes we might admit that we were wrong and reposition ourselves with a new view of the world.

Summary

In this chapter you have seen many of the barriers that prevent media's influence on people and society from having powerful effects. Theories of media influence contend that media messages flow through society and reach individual receivers in many possible ways. However, barriers inherent in society and in the psychological makeup of individuals safeguard us from being too easily manipulated by media propaganda. People have many of their media messages translated and interpreted by opinion leaders. Because of these opinion leaders, the media's influence on our attitudes, behaviors, and beliefs is minimized.

Research also suggests that when we are especially dependent on the media, their influence can be great. Much of the time, however, we can depend on actual experience or the knowledge of others, thereby minimizing the media's influence.

Individual differences were explained as the largest overarching reason that the media's influence doesn't affect society as a whole to move in predictable directions. Theories of individual differences include, specifically, attitude change theories. Subcategories of attitude change theories showed that three selective processes—exposure, perception, and retention—as well as the theory of cognitive dissonance, affect how we interpret media messages.

Note that even though these "safeguards" make it less likely that the media will powerfully affect us, this is not the final word. Advertisers don't spend billions of dollars annually to pitch cars, drinks, computers, phones, and even brands of bandages at us all for no effect. We are either manipulated and influenced by media messages, or else we use those messages as tools, employing them to show us the best ways to accomplish goals in our lives. More detail on how we use the media personally as a tool in our lived experiences is the subject of Chapter 14.

Discussion Questions

1. Name a few specific sources of mediated information you are very unlikely to consume. What books, newspapers, magazines, radio shows, television networks, or other media sources are unlikely to draw you into the audience? How do these examples reflect your own selectiveness in media exposure?

2. What are some things you depend on the media for? How are you more likely to change your behavior, attitudes, and so on when you depend on the media, compared to when you satisfy your needs apart from the media?

3. Who are the opinion leaders in your life? Are there some you know personally and some you know only through other channels? Are there people for whom you are the opinion leader? Who are they?

References

Baran, S. J. (2000). *Introduction to mass communication.* Mountain View, CA: Mayfield.

Baran, S. J., & Davis, D. K. (2000). *Mass communication theory: Foundations, ferment, and future* (2nd ed.). Belmont, CA: Wadsworth.

Bryant, J., & Thompson, S. (2002). *Fundamentals of media effects.* Boston: McGraw Hill.

DeFleur, M. L. (1970). *Theories of mass communication* (2nd ed.). New York: Longman.

DeFleur, M. L., & Ball-Rokeach, S. (1982). *Theories of mass communication* (4th ed.). New York: Longman.

DeFleur, K. L., & Ball-Rokeach, S. (1989). *Theories of mass communication* (5th ed.). New York: Longman.

Festinger, L. (1957). *Theory of cognitive dissonance.* New York: Harper & Row.

Festinger, L. (1962). Cognitive dissonance. *Scientific American, 207,* 93.

Jeffres, L. E. (1997). *Mass media effects.* Prospect Heights, IL: Waveland Press.

Hovland, C. I., Lumsdaine, A. A., & Sheffield, F. D. (1949). *Experiments on mass communication.* New York: Wiley.

Katz, E. (1957). The two-step flow of communication: An up-to-date report of a hypothesis. *Public Opinion Quarterly, 21,* 61–78.

Katz, E., & Lazarsfeld, P. F. (1955). *Personal influence: The part played by people in the flow of mass communications.* Glencoe, IL: Free Press.

Lazarsfeld, P. F., Berelson, B., & Gaudet, H., (1944). *The people's choice: How the voter makes up his mind in a presidential campaign.* New York: Duell, Sloan and Pearce.

Lazarsfeld, P. F., & Menzel, H. (1963). Mass media and personal influence. In W. Schramm (Ed.), *The science of human communication* (pp. 94–115). New York: Basic Books.

Troldahl, V. (1965). A field test of a modified two-step flow of communication's model. *Public Opinion Quarterly, 30,* 609–623.

Troldahl, V., & Van Dam, R. (1965). Face-to-face communication about major topics in the news. *Public Opinion Quarterly, 29,* 626–634.

Westley, B. (1971). Communication and social change. *American Behavioral Scientist, 14,* 719–742.

Williams, F. (1992). *The new communications.* Belmont, CA: Wadsworth.

Wilson, S. L. (1989). *Mass media/mass culture.* New York: Random House.

14

Media: A Tool to Meet Our Needs

Stephen D. Perry

In the last chapter we examined theories about how the media's influence is limited through the psychological, situational, and social-structural differences of individuals. You read about how selective use of media, having information filtered by others, and our level of dependence on the media all can serve to minimize the media's ability to persuade or change us. Now we turn the focus a little bit. Perhaps when the media successfully influences us it is only because we want to be influenced. Thus, an audience that actively uses media limits the power of the media. In this chapter we look at primarily scientific theories that demonstrate how we actively use the media in our daily lives to meet our own goals.

In this chapter, you will read about the following concepts:

- Four functions of the media
  - Information
  - Explanation
  - Entertainment
  - Transmission of culture
- Audience-centered theories
  - Fraction of selection theory
  - Uses and gratifications theory
  - Mood management theory
- Developmental theories that foster learning
  - Information processing theory
  - Reception theories
  - Diffusion of innovations theory
  - Social learning theory

Robert was an artist. He liked to paint, sculpt, and otherwise get his hands messy making things. His dad was the same way. Neither of them watched the ballgames, shot hoops, or knew the names of last year's Superbowl teams. Now Robert was in college. Living in the all-male freshman dorm, he was feeling like a round peg in a square hole. He wanted to fit in, join campus organizations, and make friends. Where could he turn to help him make sense of this new college culture?

He knew the guys talked about sports a lot. Maybe if he could participate in those conversations, he would be more accepted and find some companions to hang with. The *Sports Illustrated* Robert picked up at the dentist's office first began to explain to him who Shaq and Kobe were. The daily newspaper covered the most recent information telling who won at Daytona or Pebble Beach. He learned some of the history of Wimbledon by going online to Wimbledon.com.

Then there were these things called ESPN's X-Games—crazy stunts on bicycles, skateboards, roller blades, snowboards, and the like. Now he began to understand why signs were posted outside the dorm saying "No skateboards or bicycles on stairs," words that had always seemed ludicrous to him before watching ESPN.

It had been a few weeks since Robert had started trying to understand the world of sports that was so important to many of the guys around him. He now found himself taking sides about who would win the next game and whether Dale Earnhardt, Jr., had a prayer of winning the NASCAR championship. He had been making headway with the guys, but it wasn't until he heard ESPN News coming from a nearby room that he realized he had arrived. He poked his head in the door and found himself laughing at jokes right along with the other guys in the room. As the show ended, Derek patted him on the back and said, "Hey, Rob, want to go in with us on a pizza?"

How had Robert earned the chance to eat pizza with the guys and be nicknamed Rob? What role did mass communication play in his mission to leave the fringes of social acceptance and join in on the fun? This story of Robert, while fictional, illustrates four functions that the media play in our lives. We all use the media to accomplish these functions to varying extents, but each of us—whether consciously or unconsciously—use the media for all four functions: information, explanation, entertainment, and transmission of culture.

In this chapter you will read about how we use the media as a tool to accomplish specific goals in our lives. This is not the question of how the media affect us, but of how we make use of media. Many times we may be unaware we are even doing this. But when we stop and think about it, it becomes clear that the media play a vital role in helping us shape our lives.

What Are the Functions of the Media in Society?

Have you ever been frustrated because you knew there was a concert, movie, parade, or other event going on but you could not find information about it? Or maybe you were looking for inexpensive furniture for your new apartment. Where did you look for that information? Did you listen to the radio, read the newspaper, or watch the local news? Perhaps you searched a local web site instead hoping to find your answer. Each of these media uses illustrates the first function of the media in our lives, that of **information** or **surveillance.**

You might be surprised how often you look for answers about the world in which you live and how many of those answers come from the media. A local radio station probably promotes that concert, and new movies are listed in the entertainment section, on the local cinema web site, or on automated phone sources that list times and titles of movies. Hopefully, the local broadcast and print news sources will give you information about a parade before it happens, but it may be hard to find. A small parade, such as the homecoming parade at a small college, may mainly be promoted by word of mouth or through posters on campus. And that new furniture for your apartment, where else but the classified ads in both print and web form would give you information on such a great source of cheap stuff?

This information function goes far beyond such obvious things though. Weather information, both current and forecasted, is available, as are warnings about dangerous weather. Stores promote their products through the media. The media constantly survey the political landscape and help you know when decisions are pending that might affect your life.

Have you thought about why most people are so choosy about their audio artists but care very little about who created the art that they hang on their walls? Most assuredly, it is the result of information about musicians as received through the media. Pre-1900 recorded music only featured the title of the recorded song with no mention of the singer. The performer did not matter. Recording companies found that they could almost guarantee sales if they created a "star" system for their recordings. Radio became a big part of that system. However, no such system exists for most pop art that college students put up in their apartments and bedrooms. Could you even name an artist that photographs or paints wall art? Most likely you can name far fewer of these than you can of musical artists. You are lacking in information.

Closely related to the information function is the second function of the media, that of **explanation** or **correlation** If you get your news at the top of the hour during a five-minute break in the radio program you are listening to, or if you catch a few headlines in the newspaper or a few minutes of CNN's "Headline News," you might not understand why a given piece of news should be of interest to you. Sometimes, in fact, the information may not be useful to you at all. Many times we fail to seek out the answer to the question of why a piece of information is important. Such seeking often takes energy and time. [Web site: The Explanation Function]

Still, when you want to understand the context and the scope of information you hear, the media often provide that explanation. Go to your favorite news web site. Often there is a short blurb about a news item. Then you can click to "read the whole story," or to "see related items."

Due to its interactivity, the web is the most flexible venue for choosing explanations to accompany your information. Magazines, on the other hand, are the source most noted for regularly providing explanation. *Headline News* might tell you what dress Drew Barrymore wore to the Emmys, but *People* magazine will tell you where she bought it, who designed it, who picked it out for her, how much it costs, and where you can get one.

Satisfying Feelings instead of Reason

Even when a media source is concentrating on information or explanation, rarely does it get an audience that appeals to advertisers if not for some level of the third function of the media. From Rush Limbaugh's radio talk show to Stephen Hawking's book about the universe's origins, their ultimate success in the media marketplace rests on the important need for **entertainment.** [Web site: The Enterteinment Function]

Consumers read *People* magazine's story about Drew Barrymore's dress because it is entertaining, and they want to get behind the scenes in the lives of the stars they follow. People watch ESPN's "SportCenter" not only to get the scores of the day's games but because the hosts regularly deliver puns and humorous plays on words as they analyze the day's contests. The replays show spectacular catches, hard hits, devastating crashes, and unbelievable shots. All these elements not only inform and provide explanation, but they also deliver fun.

Why does the evening news hire attractive anchors for their broadcast? Why do TV stations hire consultants to come in and tell them which graphics to use and how the talent should fix his or her hair? Why do violence and blood, the same elements that are featured in advertisements for action movies, most often open the newscast? The answers to all of these questions demonstrate the desire of the audience for entertainment.

Melding with the Culture

It is probably the fourth function that is least recognized but occurs the most. In the opening story of Robert, his ability to begin to display the knowledge, emotion, and self-identification that his college friends had invested in sports generally and in the X-games specifically helped him become part of their culture. It is in this way that the fourth function of the media, the **transmission of culture,** plays out. [Web site: Transmission of Culture]

One's own culture is, for some people, hard to appreciate and explain. Are you part of the working culture or student culture? Does your race heavily influence your identity, or is that influence minimal? Are you a Southerner, Westerner, from the Northeast, or "at one with the beach"—any beach? Perhaps you have lived in several sections of the United States and feel like you are American but belong to no one region. Your answer to these above questions could influence the way you use TV to absorb culture.

Interestingly, the radio station you choose, the TV networks you watch, and the books you read can all be important for socialization within your culture. If you are a young white male from the rural South, you might find that your friends expect you to listen to the country hits radio station. Or perhaps as a leader in a church you would be embarrassed to admit that you had not read either *The Prayer of Jabez* or any of the *Left Behind* book series, both of which were Christian bestsellers. And what guitar-picking rocker during a late night jam session would dare admit a lack of attention to MTV's music videos?

Why are these specific media culturally important? Many of the shared experiences within a culture come from the media. That's why a bandleader might suggest playing a song in a style similar to R.E.M. or Jimi Hendrix and then expect the other band members to know what that means. The high school student knows what kind of skirt and swimsuit to wear by reading *Seventeen* and by watching the same TV shows her friends watch. The length of shorts, the choice of footwear, the types of fabrics, and the styles of hairdo are each influenced in large part by what is shown on TV and in magazines. For example, Madonna's concert attire influences what stores hang on their clothing racks and what school-age girls are wearing, almost the next day (see Figure 14.1).

FIGURE 14.1   Madonna's plaid skirt was all the rage among teenagers when she appeared in the outfit on the left at the start of her "Drowned World" concert tour in the summer of 2001. At right, concertgoers emphasize Madonna's influence on culture as they wear undergarments as outerwear reminiscent of other costumes Madonna has donned during prior concert tours.

left: AP Photo/Cesar Rangel.
right: AP Photo/Paul Warner.

In more ways than we can cover here, we use the media for these four functions day after day, week after week, and year after year, many times without realizing that is what we are doing (Dominick, 2002; Lasswell, 1948; Wright, 1986). While sometimes these functions affect us without any recognition on our part, in this chapter we focus only on intended uses for which people employ media. We are using the media as a tool to accomplish important goals and for meaningful experiences in our lives (Bryant & Street, 1988).

In the remainder of the chapter we will look at some theories that detail aspects of our intended media uses. These theories ask the question "What do people do with media?" rather than predict what media do to people. Collectively, these theories can be thought of as **audience-centered** theories since they postulate that the audience initiates impacts in media-consumer interactions.

How Do We Make Our Media Selections?

It's seven o'clock. Supper is over and you have some time on your hands. The newspaper still sits in its rubber band, the mail contained two magazines, and the TV guide is next to the remote on the coffee table. As you plop on the sofa you notice the CDs and stereo are underneath the TV in the entertainment center. Which one or two or three of these media will you consume?

One theory of how you will choose your media—or whether you will choose to avoid media—is called the **fraction of selection** (Schramm, 1954; Schramm & Porter, 1982). Your choice will depend on what media function you seek most to have fulfilled. If you want information about business news but you also want to relax and be entertained, you might choose to pick up the newspaper to scan for articles of interest while you listen to a CD. Or perhaps you find the banter on CNBC or FOX News entertaining enough that you will just click on the TV and let the networks dictate the news that you will hear.

The amount of *effort* it takes to scan the newspaper and read is higher than the effort required to watch TV. But you cannot listen to CDs effectively while watching TV. An even greater effort would be required to seek the information on the Internet unless you were already logged on and had signed up for a service that automatically selected your favorite news information for you.

While effort may be greater, *reward* may also be greater in newspapers or on the Internet. With a newspaper you can avoid the news you do not want to read, consuming only that which is of interest to you. With the TV, you might have to wait to get to the information you are curious about while other news items or commercial breaks are playing. On the Internet, you have the widest possible selection of news stories, but searching for them through the maze of web sites and even within web sites can be time consuming and frustrating.

The fraction of selection describes how we balance the *effort required* with the *reward we expect* from our specific media uses. Set up like a math equation, we divide the effort required into the amount of reward we expect in order to determine which media we will consume.

$$\frac{\text{Expected Reward}}{\text{Effort Required}}$$

Did the Media Make Me Do It?

The explanation of media use presented in the fraction of selection theory is developed in other lines of research that are also interested in how the audience uses the media to meet felt needs. From here we move to theories that others have written about at length. We want to see what applications other theories have for our everyday life.

Often when news of horrendous crimes is debated, people look to the media interests of the perpetrator and then blame the crime on the media that had been consumed prior to the violent act. Anecdotal evidence often seems to suggest that the media caused the person to commit the crime.

Uses and gratifications theory, on the other hand, views the person as more influential than the media he or she consumes. This theory contends that the audience actively chooses to consume specific media for a purpose as explained briefly in Chapter 12.

Uses and gratifications (which could possibly be termed "needs and wants") research primarily focuses on the fact that humans have *social* "needs and wants" and *psychological* "needs and wants." These needs lead us to look for ways that the mass media or other sources can provide a solution. We gain experience in using media and come to expect certain media use patterns to provide a remedy for some of our various feelings and needs. This leads us to develop specific patterns of media use that gratify our needs (Katz, Blumler, & Gurevitch, 1974).

If a person desires romance, for example, he or she might turn to a movie in the romance genre of film. Or perhaps interaction in a chatroom on the Internet with a faceless person from across country would better meet that need. The personal ads in the classified section of the newspaper or a romance novel are other options a person might turn to in seeking to satisfy the need for romance. After some trial and error, the person begins to learn what media form best gratifies the need for romance.

It is important to note that while we use the media to help address our needs, other consequences, mostly unintended, can result from such media use patterns (Rubin, 1986; 1994). In searching for romance in an Internet chatroom, a man might find that he is looking for love in all the wrong places only after becoming a victim of a 40-year-old male user pretending to be a 21-year-old female. Watching romance movies may provide the cathartic romance experiences that the viewer desires but may also create unrealistic expectations that actual romantic encounters cannot satisfy in his or her real life.

Therefore, the uses and gratifications explanation of how the media serve as tools is most applicable when the following four qualifications are met: (1) when media use is purposive and intentional; (2) when the purposive media choices are driven by the user's felt needs as the person weighs all possible options to meet those needs; (3) when individuals initiate the media selections they make as opposed to being sucked into an environment where media are forced upon them or when the user has little role in selecting content; and (4) when the individual understands and can articulate his or her reasons for choosing specific media content.

When those conditions exist, uses and gratifications research is able to explain these three things: (1) how the media are used by consumers to satisfy their needs, (2) the motives for media choices and usage patterns, and (3) the media's functions for individuals based on their personal needs, motives, and communication behaviors (Katz, Blumler, & Gurevitch, 1974).

The theories of fraction of selection and uses and gratifications can be applied no matter what our purpose is or what function we would like the media to serve in our lived experiences. Other theories can be applied to only a subset of the potential uses to which we can put the media. These theories explain how the media can be used as a specialized tool to satisfy a specific subset of needs. First we will look at a theory that explains how we use the media to manage our emotions.

How Can I Get Happy?

We all want to be happy or to exist in a state of being that is overall pleasant. Therefore, when we experience unpleasant states, we try to find ways to escape from them. When we find events that increase our pleasure in life, these events leave positive memory traces, leading us to seek out those pleasant events again. Since vast portions of our lives are spent with media, many times it is experiences with media that leave positive memories. So we seek out those media experiences that can replicate earlier positive experiences. The theory explaining this is called **mood management theory.** [Web site: Mood Management Theory]

Unpleasant states can take many forms. These can include boredom, irritation, stress, or even overstimulation, to name a few. Let us assume first that one is bored. A bored person will seek out stimulation and engaging activities. Many nonmedia activities could provide the needed stimulation, but many times media play the crucial role in increasing the stimulation level. Movies, televised sports, a good novel, or some comedy may provide relief from boredom, putting the consumer in a more pleasant mood.

For the movie buff, going out to the cinema, watching HBO, bringing home a video, or ordering a movie on Pay-Per-View may be the answer to boredom. Successfully relieving one's boredom through a movie will increase the likelihood that a movie will be selected on subsequent occasions. The same could be said for any other media experience that relieves boredom.

If instead of boredom, the problem is one of being depressed or sad, perhaps an evening sitcom is the answer. A quick fix of *Everybody Loves Raymond* on CBS or perhaps *Frasier* on NBC would provide the needed pick-me-up.

If the problem is hopelessness or an unclear perspective on the future, the answer might be *American Idol* or one of the series of *Survivor* programs. Your TV surrogates show how a normal person like you could become wealthy over the course of the series. This gives you hope that the future is not as bleak as it seems. In whatever situation or mood you find yourself, a specific medium, genre, and mode of consumption may help elevate your unpleasant mood to become a happy one.

Under uses and gratifications theory's tenets, people must be consciously purposeful in their media selections. Mood management theory suggests that selecting media is purposeful but not necessarily thoughtful. We do not really have to think about what we are choosing because we subconsciously try to shun aversive states of being all the time. Thus, when we want to be happier, we make media choices that have the greatest potential to increase that happiness (Zillmann, 1988).

What Might I Learn?

In addition to emotion and mood alterations through media, people use media as a tool to educate themselves. This begins at the earliest ages. The **developmental perspective** of media use suggests that at different stages of maturity, children understand and use the media differently.

Without even knowing they are doing it, children turn to the media for clues about socialization. They use television, for example, to figure out the roles of moms and dads and other adults. They learn how boys and girls play and how those play schemes are often different between the sexes. Even objects with no gender are sometimes given male and female personas that follow traditional sex role stereotypes. The trains in the children's program *Thomas the Tank Engine* are a perfect example (see Figure 14.2). Such learning, it might be argued, would happen anyway in their real-world interactions. Those who make such arguments prefer to downplay the impact of the media.

Still another area of learning occurs through advertising. Children will often turn to advertisements to learn which toys are most fun and which will be highly esteemed among their peers. Young children, especially those 7 and under, take the portrayed ability of advertised products literally, believing that cars can fly and Barbie can easily stand on her own.

FIGURE 14.2   Thomas the Tank Engine, the main animated character of the educational children's program *Thomas the Tank Engine and Friends,* reflects male leadership while the engine with the female persona is subordinate.

AP Wide World Photo.

Handling Information Overload

Although children might learn such lessons, adults may find television to be a poor tool for information. Other media may serve their needs more effectively. **Information processing theory** says that we can only take in, or even be aware of, a small fraction of the information that bombards us in any given day. According to this theory, we need to recognize and process stimuli we encounter, sorting out and organizing the most useful information. Then we must store the useful information in the right categories in our heads in long-term memory. The problem is, we do not have time to process the first information before new stimuli bombards us in many mediated instances such as when watching television news. [Web site: Information Overload]

Audience Interpretation of Media Content

Reception theory or **reception analysis** looks less bleakly at the ability of adults to learn from media than information processing theory does. Reception theory, which comes out of the humanistic and critical British cultural studies tradition, assumes a very mentally active and able consumer of media information. According to this theory, audience members make sense of the various media content they consume by interpreting the signs and structure of the content (Hall, 1980).

To explain this in its simplest form, we can look at how a person gives meaning to a message. If someone says, "He claimed ignorance of the facts of the case," the meaning changes based on various signs that we decode. If the word "claimed" above is said with a higher or more intense pitch to it, or if the eyebrows rise when the word is spoken, the message receiver should perceive that the claim of ignorance is doubtful. If the word "claimed" is glossed over by the speaker, however, the word may be taken at face value.

Another example can illustrate how complicated the meaning process becomes in that each consumer of the message may interpret the communication event differently based on his or her prior beliefs and experiences. Let us assume that a Democratic legislator, when questioned about the disappearance of a woman with whom he had an extramarital affair, was reported to have "claimed ignorance of the facts in the case." A voter who opposed the congressman in the previous election might read the phrase that he "claimed ignorance" as dubious, no matter how it was delivered. If the reporter intended the audience to believe the claim was dubious, interpreting the statement in the intended manner would be said to be a **preferred** or **dominant reading** of the information. If, however, the voter had donated to the legislator's campaign and was a loyal Democratic Party supporter, the same phrase would be disregarded and carry no special meaning. This rather neutral interpretation, then, resulted from a **negotiated meaning,** one that was personally meaningful to the campaign donor but different in some respects from the intended or preferred reading.

A third potential interpretation might result from an added scenario. Suppose a Republican congressional leader known to oppose this Democrat said the legislator "claimed ignorance of the facts of the case." The Democratic Party supporter and donor mentioned above might then use **oppositional decoding** to interpret what was spoken. In this case, when the Republican speaker raises the pitch of his voice or raises his eyebrows intending to cast doubt on the claim of ignorance, the receiver of the message is likely to consider the claim as absolutely true, believing that the Democrat must be ignorant. This decoding in direct opposition to the message resulted from the viewer's distrust of the message deliverer and his trust of the accused Democrat (Brundson & Morley, 1978).

Reception theory, then, suggests that consumers use the media as a tool to gather information, but that they do so in order to further the messages that they want to hear and the beliefs that they want to perpetuate (Martin-Barbero, 1993). This theory respects the intelligence of media consumers and acknowledges that different people can use the same message to process different meanings.

How Do We Learn about New Things?

A scientific theory that discusses ways that consumers learn through use of the media is diffusion theory, or diffusion of innovation. This theory is about more than just learning, however. It is also about how society adopts a new behavior.

In our rapidly changing society constant innovations enable us to finish our work more quickly, stay healthy, entertain ourselves in new ways, and gather information more effectively. How do we learn about these developments? According to Everett Rogers (1962) and his **diffusion theory** or **diffusion of innovations theory,** several steps or stages allow new knowledge and new products to spread through societies. The mass media play a crucial role at the beginning of this process.

New technologies and processes are first introduced to the public through the media. We become aware of these innovations through television or in newspapers or magazines but may have little idea how they really work or what good they can do for us. Soon, however, a few people are urged to experiment with the new innovation (see Figure 14.3). Perhaps it is a high definition television (HDTV) or satellite-delivered web-browsing technology. These few **early adopters** then begin to show others how their new technology

FIGURE 14.3   The palm pilot has been widely adopted by consumers. Early adopters, opinion leaders, and then opinion followers have jumped on this technological bandwagon, creating a critical mass of users for the industry as described by diffusion theory.

Photo by Forest Wisely.

works. If the technology seems to have promise, some who see it will become its champion, adopt it, and serve as **opinion leaders** who promote the new innovation to others. Do you have high-speed Internet access yet? The opinion leaders sure do.

Once the opinion leaders are on board, they also encourage their friends to adopt the technology. When these **opinion followers** get on the bandwagon, it helps the new technology to reach a stage of **critical mass,** where it is bound to survive until it is displaced by an even better innovation. Reaching critical mass allows the product to be mass-produced at the lowest possible price, making it affordable for the largest possible portion of the population. Finally, after most people have adopted the innovation, a few are left behind. These people, most of whom may still be going without cable TV, are labeled **laggards** or **late adopters.** They are those who bring up the rear in the diffusion of an innovation.

Diffusion theory is foundational for marketing and advertising and public relations campaigns today (Baran & Davis, 2000). Marketing theorists know that advertising is most effective at introducing a new product. Once it is introduced, the advertising reinforces the opinions passed down from opinion leaders or early adopters but is less affective at persuading people to continue to use a product that is not meeting consumer expectations. This is because people use the media as a tool for information about new technologies, products, and innovations. Once they have tried the products, however, the media have little sway in the likelihood that they will continue use of an unattractive product. [Web site: Diffusion Theory and Public Relations]

Diffusion theory is about using media to learn information that leads to adopting new behaviors. These behaviors are complex behavioral systems such as learning a healthy exercise regimen. The next theory deals with learning behaviors on a more minute scale. Rather than the whole exercise plan, perhaps you just want to learn to do sit-ups correctly.

How Much Do You Learn from Observation?

This final theory of the chapter, **social learning theory,** is useful not only for understanding how we interact with persons and realize our identity (as studied in the interpersonal communication chapter), but it is also useful in understanding how the media impact us in ways we might not intend. [Web site: Social Learning Theory]

It says that much of the behavior we learn comes from observing our environment, and this includes television and movies. This theory is very influential in the field of media violence and has traditionally been used to explain effects on a passive audience as you will see in the next chapter. It does have implications for how we use the media to accomplish goals. While this take on social learning theory is not typically addressed, you will recognize how you have consciously employed learning techniques in line with this theory.

Have you ever had someone say, "Watch how I do this, and then you can try?" Stanford psychologist Albert Bandura (1977) described in detail how children and all humans learn from observation. Many things are learned much more quickly through observing than through reading or listening to an explanation. Think about it. When you buy a new product from the store with "some assembly required," it is easier to put the item together if you have seen someone else do it than if you have to decipher the directions that came in the box.

How many of us have never flown a hot air balloon, played golf, gone skydiving, fired a handgun, ascended a rock climbing wall, played laser tag, and on and on? Yet many of us believe we could do these activities with no further instruction if we had to.

Where did we observe these activities? Most of us have only observed skydiving through the lens of the second skydiver who wears a camera. Many have never actually seen a handgun fired in person, but we have seen it several thousand times on television. We have probably seen some of the other activities in real life, but our best views of them are often through the television or film camera's ability to get close to the action.

Social learning theory says that television has become one of our primary tools for **observational learning.** We turn to TV as a tool to teach us how to perform certain activities. How many teenagers have never been instructed how to kiss or what to do on a date? Yet after watching the embraces and kisses of television actors, teenagers will try to duplicate the behavior, first in front of a mirror (perhaps even kissing the mirror), and then in the arms of another person.

The reward or punishment that goes with particular behaviors is also shown and learned. When we observe these through the experience of others this is called **vicarious reinforcement.** Such reinforcement either encourages or discourages the duplication of the behavior.

Summary

In this chapter we have talked about the ways media can be used to accomplish functions in our lives. We use them to gain information, to understand through explanation, to be entertained, and to be able to achieve successful social interaction through understanding culture. We may seek to accomplish multiple functions in a single media exposure experience.

We compare the reward we expect to receive from using a particular media source to the effort we have to expend to select and ultimately consume a media form. Many times we will accept less reward if it takes less effort to consume the media. We may choose activities outside of media and avoid media altogether if that brings the greatest reward in a specific area of interest.

This chapter has explained how the audience uses the media as a tool. It assumes that the audience is somewhat intentional in its media consumption. Uses and gratifications research is the broadest theory using this perspective. Other theories look specifically at how we use media in given areas of our lives.

Mood management theory states that we use the media to alter and regulate our moods. Other research is more interested in how we use media to learn or gain information. The developmental perspective considers the difference in our usage based on age and maturity. Information processing theory says that we have so much information available that using it becomes very difficult. Television news is especially difficult to process.

Reception studies, on the other hand, discuss how we respond to information in such a way as to make it serve our own interests and belief systems. This theory sees the media consumer as very much in control of the information he or she processes.

Diffusion theory and social learning theory are theories that discuss how we use the media to inform not only our minds but also our behaviors. Diffusion theory addresses how people use media when adopting new processes and technological innovations. Social learning theory explains how we learn behaviors through observations and that many of our observations are made mostly through the media.

In the next chapter the question changes from "How do we use the media?" to "How do the media affect us?" In other words, what are the side effects of using media? We may be trying to use them as a tool for one purpose and instead find out they are having effects on us other than those we had hoped for.

Discussion Questions

1. Explain how you might use media to manage your mood if you were feeling depressed. Use the fraction of selection components to explain what options you considered and why you might choose one specific medium.

2. Describe the last time you spent several hours at one sitting with TV, Internet, radio, or some other medium. From a uses and gratifications perspective, what needs and wants were you fulfilling? Were you always using the medium actively and intentionally, or were you a passive receiver of whatever the medium had to offer?

3. Consider any three products or processes that are new in society. Describe your role in the diffusion of this innovation using the terms in the theory.

4. Suppose a reporter wrote, "The president looked away from reporters as he said, 'I knew nothing of the issue.'" Using reception theory, explain what you think the reporter was trying to convey, and then explain how you might give an oppositional reading to the statement.

References

Bandura, A. (1994). Social cognitive theory of mass communication. In J. Bryant and D. Zillmann (Eds.), *Media effects: Advances in theory and research* (pp. 61–90). Hillsdale, NJ: Lawrence Erlbaum.

Baran, S. J., & Davis, D. K. (2000). *Mass communication theory: Foundations, ferment, and future* (2nd ed.). Belmont, CA: Wadsworth.

Brundson, C., & Morley, D. (1978). *Everyday television: "Nationwide."* London: British Film Institute.

Bryant, J., & Street, R. L. (1988). From reactivity to activity and action: An evolving concept and weltanschauung in mass and interpersonal communication. In R. P. Hawkins, J. M. Wiemann, & S. Pingree (Eds.), *Advancing communication science: Merging mass and interpersonal processes* (pp. 162–190). Newbury Park, CA: Sage.

Dominick, J. R. (2002). *The dynamics of mass communication: Media in the digital age* (7th ed.). Boston: McGraw-Hill.

Hall, S. (1980). Encoding and decoding in the television discourse. In S. Hall (Ed.), *Culture, media, language.* London: Hutchinson.

Katz, E., Blumler, J. G., & Gurevitch, M. (1974). Utilization of mass communication by the individual. In J. G. Blumler & E. Katz (Eds.), *The uses of mass communication: Current perspectives on gratifications research* (pp. 19–32). Beverly Hills, CA: Sage.

Lasswell, H. D. (1948). The structure and function of communication in society. In L. Bryson (Ed.), *The communication of ideas.* New York: Harper.

Martin-Barbero, J. (1993). *Communication, culture, and hegemony: From the media to mediations* (E. Fox & R. A. White, Trans.). Newbury Park, CA: Sage.

Robinson, J. P., & Davis, D. K. (1990). Television news and the informed public: Not the main source. *Journal of Communication, 40,* 106–119.

Rogers, E. M. (1962). *Diffusion of innovations.* New York: Free Press.

Rubin, A. M. (1986). Uses, gratifications, and media effects research. In J. Bryant & D. Zillmann (Eds.), *Perspectives on media effects* (pp. 281–301). Hillsdale, NJ: Lawrence Erlbaum.

Rubin, A. M. (1994). Media uses and effects: A uses and gratifications perspective. In J. Bryant & D. Zillmann (Eds.), *Media effects: Advances in theory and research.* Hillsdale, NJ: Lawrence Erlbaum.

Schramm, W. (1954). *The process and effects of mass communication.* Urbana: University of Illinois Press.

Schramm, W., & Porter, W. E. (1982). *Men, women, messages, and media: Understanding human communication* (2nd ed). New York: Harper & Row.

Wright, C. R. (1986). *Mass communication: A sociological perspective* (3rd ed.). New York: Random House.

Zillmann, D. (1988). Mood management: Using entertainment to full advantage. In L. Donohew, H. D. Sypher, & E. T. Higgins (Eds.), *Communication, social cognition, and affect* (pp. 147–171). Hillsdale, NJ: Lawrence Erlbaum.

15

Media (Side) Effects

Stephen D. Perry, Rebecca Carrier, Kevin C. Lee, and Jong G. Kang

In recent chapters you were first introduced to ways in which we prevent the media from powerfully manipulating and persuading us. You also saw how individuals intentionally use the media to accomplish specific goals they are trying to achieve. We recognized how people use media to learn about news, sports, weather, and political information. At other times they use it to relax or find stimulating experiences. In still other instances it provides examples of how to dress, dance, talk, and act in social situations. The fact that people make deliberate choices about their media usage, however, does not mean that the media have no additional effect on us.

In this chapter, you will learn about an area of research normally called media effects. We have given the chapter the title "Media (Side) Effects" because you will study the unintended, and perhaps unwanted, consequences of media exposure—ways that the media influence us without our awareness or at least without any planning on our part to make it happen.

In this chapter, you will read about the following concepts:

- Effects on behavior and perception
  - Uses and effects theory
  - Social learning theory
    - Catharsis hypothesis
    - Aggressive cues theory
  - Cultivation theory (or cultivation analysis)
  - Media addiction
    - Displacement theory
- Effects on political attitudes and voting
  - Agenda-setting function
  - Spiral of silence
  - Exemplar theory
- Positive effects

When Shastri walked into his friend's apartment, he was greeted with a "how-ya-doin'?" spoken in legato fashion with only a slight accent on the "do." He responded with his own "how-ya-doin'?" and then two or three others around the room began to chime in back and forth with him on the same phrase. The rather spontaneous response was not a normal greeting pattern for an international student from India. His English classes preparing him in this second language had said a proper response would have been, "I'm doing fine, thank you."

This behavioral nuance, however, was the product of familiarity with American television and the creation of a cultural fad through an advertising campaign promoting the sale of beer. It isn't just international students who adopt new behaviors through television. Children are also known to be susceptible to adopting many behavioral patterns reinforced through television. Adults may be less susceptible, but they still develop perceptions of what the world is like through the media, and those perceptions influence their voting, attitudes toward strangers, and other behaviors. These behaviors, in turn, may result in either helpful or disruptive influences on a peaceful, democratic society.

Will the Media Affect Me Only If I'm Passive?

As you'll recall, in the last chapter we looked at how the audience purposefully uses media to accomplish specific tasks in their lives. The perspective of media effects theories is often thought to hold that the audience is passive and therefore is susceptible to the media's power. It is true that the audience's activity level (the level of purpose for which they enlist their media consumption) is often left out of research that considers media effects questions. Still, effects research does not specifically rule out the possibility of an active audience. Many times we may be accomplishing our intended purpose, such as finding out whether it will rain, while at the same time we are subconsciously and unintentionally being persuaded that we need to "find a soul mate" by the banner ad for singles running across the top of the web page. Thus, we may both use the media as a tool and be subject to its effects at the same time, resulting in the media-perpetuated "side effects" suggested in the title of this chapter. This notion has been formalized in uses and effects theory.

Consistent with a notion that media effects may be highly individual and subjective is the theory of uses and effects. **Uses and effects** research recognizes that interpersonal decisions shape audience members' motivation to observe and their use of media messages. Additionally, this approach emphasizes that media do affect audience members' behaviors and attitudes. However, uses and effects research also suggests that such effects will vary with the individual motivation, use, and expectation each audience member brings to the media situation.

Uses and effects scholarship combines features of uses and gratifications research with the most common features of the effects domain. Research on the use of media begins with an analysis of the audience and assumes that audience members are active participants with the power to make decisions about what to watch and how to interpret it. On the other hand, effects researchers focus on the media as having the power to influence audiences in particular ways and under certain conditions. Uses and effects research combines both of these approaches by recognizing the active audience component of gratification research while examining the individual and social impact of media effects. While this area of research assumes that the individual's motivation itself may alter the media effect, other theoretical areas promote the idea that the media's effect will be present no matter the motivation of the user. One of these areas is in the study of aggression.

Do the Media Make Us More Aggressive?

Imagine you desire to learn some aspect of the martial arts. You choose to rent a movie or watch a TV show that features karate or kung fu. You intentionally teach yourself to duplicate throws, punches, or kicks you see. Unfortunately, you may unintentionally grasp the attitude that martial arts serve as a good offensive weapon when traditional teachers of the arts would teach you to use them defensively. Such a scenario might fit a uses and effects perspective, but it also leads us to question whether media might have unintended effects, whether in the areas of violence, sexuality, or even in positive behaviors, such as tolerance toward others who are different from us.

A number of court cases in recent years have made parents, clergy, and media scholars question the effects of violent media programming on the behavior of children and even adults in society. In these court cases, attorneys argue that television played an important role by modeling violent or aggressive behaviors that influenced their clients to commit crimes such as murder and rape. Although these defenses have had mixed success, they have raised the issue of television violence to national prominence.

Many studies have counted the number of violent acts on television, and the statistics are staggering. One study reported that children will see 8,000 murders and more than 100,000 acts of violence before they finish elementary school. Other studies have found that a typical day of programming shows an average of 389 serious assaults, 362 uses of guns, 273 punches, and 73 simple assaults (Jeffres, 1997). While there is little doubt that media rely upon violence to sell programming, there is a debate about how violence affects people.

Fueling the Debate: Contrasting Views of Media Effects

There are two competing directions in which hypotheses (or predictions) about the effects of media violence on behavior turn. The **catharsis hypothesis** suggests that angry individuals who watch violent programming will use the programming as an outlet for their anger. Instead of acting aggressively themselves, these people will experience the aggression of television and film characters vicariously. Thus, according to this hypothesis, media offer a safe way of defusing aggressive behaviors and *reducing* violence. Unfortunately, this theory has found little support from science, but lots of support from the media industry that profits from perpetuating what seems to amount to a myth. In addition to the media industry's inside defenders are viewers who are fans of "action flicks." They also like to vigorously defend their right to view violence.

Much more scientific research, however, suggests that media do have some impact on human behavior. Much of this research stems from psychological research on how we learn to act the way we do.

It was during the early 1960s that Albert Bandura was exploring new ways of explaining how children learned behaviors. At the time, most psychologists believed what B. F. Skinner believed—that behavior was learned from direct positive and negative rewards. These psychologists are commonly called **behaviorists.** And behaviorists had good reason to believe that people learned to act in ways that offered rewards or avoided punishments. After all, Skinner and his contemporaries had conducted hundreds of experiments where they offered mice, rats, monkeys, and even humans food (or other) rewards if they pressed the correct buttons.

While these research findings made sense, they could not account for how people's behaviors might be affected by the media because the media did not offer direct rewards or punishments in any way that paralleled behaviorists' experiments where monkeys pressed certain buttons to receive bananas. Instead, Bandura contended that media—particularly television—offered a model of how people should behave. From this perspective and a set of famous experiments with Bobo dolls (weighted blow-up dolls that would bounce back to an upright position if knocked to the floor), Bandura (1977) established social learning theory. **Social learning theory** suggests that people learn some behaviors from observing both real and symbolic behaviors of other people, a process called **observational learning.**

Bandura tested his notion about learning behaviors by examining how different kinds of television presentations would affect the behaviors of children who watched programs with different messages about how to treat a Bobo doll. Bandura showed one group of children a video with violent or aggressive behaviors directed at one of these dolls. Another group of children watched a show where children offered loving and gentle behaviors to the doll. After watching the programs, the children were taken to a room with a Bobo doll. Bandura found that the children who watched the violent program hit and wrestled the doll while the children who watched the gentle program gave the doll hugs.

Unlike the behavioral psychologists, Bandura offered an explanation of how people—especially children—could learn both good and bad behaviors by watching symbolic models on television. His experiments showed that some behaviors can be learned by watching what others do—not just because the behavior earns them a reward or punishment.

Bandura's social learning theory led researchers to ask important questions about what kinds of behaviors television modeled for children. The two most important concerns are about how the media might influence aggressive behaviors and sex because—as we have all heard before—sex and violence sell.

The Televised Modeling of Media Violence

Social learning identified two types of observationally learned behavior from television. The first, **imitation,** is often reported in the news when a person directly mimics actions portrayed in scenes from a movie or television show. The second, identification, is less directly identifiable as a product of television viewing. **Identification** suggests that a person adopts the style of behaviors portrayed by a character on the screen, but adapts them based on his or her own interpretations and situational needs. Thus, a person might take on the role of a tough guy, hate authority, and hold the rebellious attitude portrayed by the likes of Clint Eastwood or Bruce Willis, but might choose to throw stones or swing clubs at an enemy rather than using a semiautomatic weapon. Imitation or identification behaviors do not have to be in the realm of violence. People can adopt romantic behaviors, parenting styles, or a particular work ethic from imitating or identifying with behaviors witnessed in the media. Still, violence is the realm in which the bulk of social learning research has been applied.

A spin-off theory that suggests violent media content increases the incidence of violent behavior is **aggressive cues theory.** This theory claims that elements in portrayed media violence act as *cues* for angry individuals, suggesting that certain types of violent acts carried out against certain kinds of people are acceptable. This theory suggests that when violence is glorified in fictional media toward a certain type of individual, perhaps an African American or a woman or a person who dresses in a certain way, that fictional violence can have a carryover effect in real-life responses against those same categories of people (Berkowitz, 1965; Hansen, 1995; Johnson, Jackson, & Gatto, 1995).

Imagine, for example, that a woman confronts a man about his rude behavior toward his date at the local diner. Now imagine how he might respond to that woman in return if she is wearing a feminine blouse and dress pant ensemble, looking the part of the female professional. Now picture the same scenario with the woman wearing protective leather clothes stereotypically identified with motorcycle riding. Would the man respond differently? Aggressive cues theory suggests that the "biker woman" might absorb more verbal if not physical violence because media images have taught us that people who dress in certain kinds of leather jackets are appropriate targets of aggressive behavior.

Two approaches to violence research make sense here. First, a content analysis of media compared to real-world levels of violence indicate that as media depict greater levels of aggressive behaviors, we see no reduction in the overall amount of violence in society as suggested by the catharsis hypothesis. In fact, some increases in levels of societal and individual aggression have been shown. The second kind of research is very much like the Bobo doll. In controlled environments, angry individuals tend to respond more aggressively when they are exposed to high levels of media violence.

What Will Kids Learn about Sex and Sexuality?

Perhaps the most disturbing finding about aggression and television is the research on media effects related to sex and sexual behaviors. One consistent effect researchers have found is that those who watch sexually explicit media experience increased sexual arousal. Whether you think this is a good thing or a bad thing depends upon your attitudes about sex, but scholars have found that media can trigger sexual arousal in ways that we would all agree are dangerous and unhealthy (Zillmann, Hoyt, & Day, 1974). For example, research shows that media content that shows sex mixed with violence is particularly arousing to sex offenders while it is not very appealing to normal people. Additionally, even normal people experienced arousal while watching sexual violent programming *if* the victim showed any pleasure during the abuse (Diamond & Uchiyama, 1999; Weaver, 1994). These findings fit with the tenets of aggressive cues theory suggesting that it is appropriate to abuse women sexually since they are shown to want such abuse.

So what does a sexually naïve teenager learn when a man is shown physically overpowering a woman to force her to submit to his sexual advances, and the woman's cries of "no" gradually give way to cries of "go" as she gradually begins to experience some fictitious pleasure? Such despicably unrealistic portrayals of a woman's absolute terror changing into pleasure are not uncommon. Aggressive cues theory suggests that male viewers can rationalize that raping a woman is okay since women really mean "go" and want to be forced into submission.

Interestingly, researchers have found that the degree of explicitness does not relate to the degree of arousal. And in some cases, researchers have found that censoring out a sex scene actually makes the program *more* arousing. Generally, research suggests that when sexual acts in the media are vague people tend to imagine these acts consistent with those things that arouse them the most, and arousal tends to be highly individual and subjective.

How Do Media Influence Voters?

While the most visible arenas in which media effects have been studied are those we have looked at initially, there are other important effects of the media. One realm that has been of interest to scholars is that of public opinion, the ways in which the media impact the democratic process.

Media's Effect on What You Think Is Important

Answering a desire to prove a direct effect of mass media on audiences, Bernard Cohen (1963) claimed that media may not be able to tell audiences "what to think," but they can tell them "what to think about." Hence, **agenda setting** research—the formal theory based on Cohen's claim and supported by numerous researchers since—became a popular avenue for establishing that media had a direct effect upon audience members (Rogers & Dearing, 1988). Credited with establishing the traditional metaphor of agenda setting, McCombs and Shaw (1972) represented the process as the media's ability to place salient (meaning important and prominent) issues in the public light, so that the media serve as a catalyst for public opinion. Substantial research has shown agenda setting to be a consistently robust phenomenon that indicates a strong relationship between media agendas and people's beliefs about which issues are important. (See Chapter 12 for more on this theory.)

Rogers, Dearing, and Chan (1991) conducted a classic study that showed how agenda setting might begin and grow, using the issue of the AIDS virus. When the scientific findings of the HIV virus first were reported, they generated little media coverage. But when movie star Rock Hudson and NBA star Ervin "Magic" Johnson of the Los Angeles Lakers were found to have the disease, media coverage expanded exponentially. Polls of public opinion following the increases in media coverage showed that the public suddenly thought this disease was a much more serious problem in America than they had when the media coverage was light. The researchers followed these same kinds of trends over several years as coverage of AIDS and HIV stayed in the news while politicians battled over funding for AIDS research and policies about privacy and children with AIDS attending public schools. Whenever media coverage was high, the public's perception of the seriousness of the problem followed suit. This aspect of setting the public's agenda about what societal problems need solving is at the heart of researchers' agenda-setting concerns.

Agenda setting has two additional components that remain popular in media re-search. The first component, **agenda building,** examines how the media's agenda is set by forces from the president or other head of state to public interest groups to real-world events. The media agenda then influences the public agenda. Thus, the media are the cat-alyst for shifts in the public agenda, but they are often only the mediator of other real-world forces. The second component, **priming,** suggests that the public evaluates political actors, such as the president, based primarily on those issues that have been the focus of the media's agenda (Scheufele, 2000).

Media Influence on Public Policy

Everett Rogers and James Dearing (1988) have tried to expand the domain of agenda set-ting by relating media, the public, and policy making to the above-mentioned concept of agenda building. After reviewing agenda-setting research, Rogers and Dearing (1988) drew these three conclusions:

1. The public agenda, once set by, or reflected by, the media agenda, influences the pol-icy agenda of elite decision makers, and in some cases policy implementation.
2. The media agenda seems to have direct, sometimes strong, influence upon the pol-icy agenda of elite decision makers and, in some cases, upon policy implementation.
3. For some issues, the policy agenda seems to have a direct, sometimes strong, influ-ence upon the media agenda. (p. 579)

These conclusions went beyond the traditional McCombs and Shaw (1972) concept of agenda setting to include media effects upon policy making and vice versa.

Consistent with Rogers and Dearing's analysis of agenda setting and its influence on the political process, McCombs (1981) theorized that media and individuals function di-alectically to influence policy making and voting. In a traditional media audience, specific individuals do not ordinarily influence media agendas, but large groups forming mass opin-ion do influence political decisions and policy making.

Media's Effect on Saying What You Think

There is a saying that advises, "Never discuss two things—politics or religion." But this may be oversimplified. In reality, we do discuss certain political and religious views with different people or audiences at different times. A theory first explained in 1973 called the **spiral of silence** provides some insight into why we might avoid contributing to some po-litical discussions but participate fully in others based on our observations of opinion in the real world and in the world of media.

Some issues are clearly controversial and can get some people in a rage. Certain po-litical beliefs are certainly one area in which this is true, but so are issues of religion. Sports can bring out heated opinions in certain settings as well, with fans of a certain player will-ing to come to blows against others who would malign their sports hero. Issues that be-come quite controversial with people holding definite opinions of right and wrong are said to be **morally loaded** under spiral of silence theory. When issues are of this nature, we become more careful about when and to whom we express our ideas and opinions (Noelle-Neumann, 1973, 1974).

The "Quasi-Statistical Sense."   According to the spiral of silence we are constantly surveying our environment, mostly subconsciously, for trends in public opinion. Some of the sources we might look to as we conduct our unscientific surveys are shown in the left side of Figure 15.1. From the bundle of information we perceive, we make judgments as to what the majority believes on any one issue. Some of our perceptions of public sentiment come from these discussions we hear in class, at work, on the street, and at home, but much of what we hear discussed comes from television.

Television is said to be the most influential medium for this theory since it is (1) **ubiquitous,** or everywhere. Even if we don't own a TV of our own, we see it in stores, dorm lobbies, at McDonalds, and in airports. We *cannot not* see television. Not only is it ubiquitous, but it also has (2) **consonance,** meaning that the messages across various content providers tend to paint similar pictures of trends in public opinion. For example, in a presidential election the story of which candidates are gaining and losing ground tends to

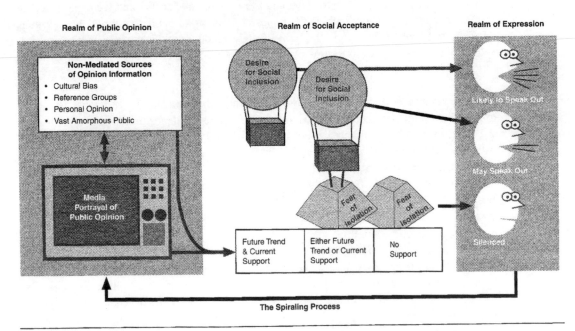

FIGURE 15.1 *Perry's Spiral of Silence Model.*   This figure illustrates the spiral of silence with perceived support from the realm of public opinion (left) leading to a desire for social inclusion, pictured as a balloon. The lack of perceived support results in fear of isolation shown as a weight holding the balloon back when there are mixed signals and sitting at the bottom of the diagram alone when there is no perceived support. The weight leads to silence while the balloon lifts the desire to speak out. The resulting behavior then influences future perceptions in the realm of public opinion through the spiraling process.

Used by permission, © Stephen D. Perry, 1995, 2002.

be uniform, even if the networks present different issue-related stories. Finally, television's impact is (3) **cumulative** in that it builds up over time due to the constant repetition of portrayed public opinion.

Being in the Majority.   Once you have decided where you think the majority stands on a controversial issue, the next step will be to compare your opinion to that of the majority. According to the spiral of silence we all have a desire for social inclusion (shown as a balloon in the accompanying figure) and fear of being ostracized from those around us (shown as a weight). Therefore, if someone believes he or she is in the minority, not only for current opinion, but also according to perceived future opinion trends, then that person will be inhibited from speaking out and expressing the minority viewpoint, feeling the weight of potential isolation (Gonzenbach, 1992; Perry & Gonzenbach, 2000).

Now, it is important to note that the majority we perceive may not be the actual majority. Soon after the AIDS disease was identified by scientists, the media portrayed public attitude to be against allowing children with AIDS to attend public schools even though surveys showed the majority of the public actually supported their public school attendance (Gonzenbach & Stevenson, 1994). Other issues that may have received similarly off-balanced portrayals during the time when they were in the greatest state of flux and were perceived as most controversial probably include the issues of smoking in public buildings, homosexual rights, partial birth abortion, and the right to carry handguns. Still, whether our perception of the majority is accurate or not, we tend to fall silent if we think our viewpoint is in the minority.

More Silence: Changed Society.   So is the adage that you shouldn't discuss issues of politics or religion a good one? Let us look at the nature of silence to discover this answer.

Willingness to speak out can occur at many levels. You can speak out through face-to-face conversation, of course, but what about putting a yard sign in front of your house? Would you wear a T-shirt or put a bumper sticker on your car supporting an unpopular view? You can speak out by writing a letter to the editor, marching in a political rally, or speaking to the news media on camera. In many cases, one's public speech may not disappear completely. It will be diminished, however, as you become less likely to participate in at least some of the potential speaking-out activities.

Is this a problem? The spiral of silence theory says it is. As people become less likely to speak out for their viewpoint on one side of an issue, that side appears to lose ground in the debate faster than before. This causes even more people to fall silent as they perceive the tide of opinion to be turning against them, making the spiraling silence even worse. Those who are undecided on the issue will be more likely to side with the position that is speaking out since that side appears to be winning. This can result in a minority that is vocal gaining support for its side with both legislative leaders and voters in the electorate, ultimately propelling them to majority status and electoral and legislative victory.

Reversing the Spiral of Silence.   Not everyone bows to the fear of being ostracized. For each issue that is morally loaded, there are those who support their position based on internalized values and beliefs rather than based on negotiable facts and traits about an issue. These people may never be silenced. They are called **hardcores.** The hardcores may be thought of as radicals having fringe beliefs, but they stand by their beliefs in good times and bad.

Once an issue has been off the negotiating table for a time, the hardcore believers may seize an unexpected opportunity to bring the issue back into the forefront of public awareness. An incident such as a school shooting, for example, may provide an opportunity for believers in handgun control, while a terrorist attack brought on by foreign nationals in the United States might provide an opportunity for hardcores to renew calls for stricter immigration laws.

Whatever the issue, hardcores reinvigorate their rhetoric, while the "winning" side sees no need to use theirs. For this reason, the minority hardcores may be more effective at getting their voices heard when the issue is thrust back into national prominence. They may then be seen as the side gaining ground in support of their beliefs. This, theoretically at least, could lead to a reversal of the spiral of silence process in favor of the hardcores' viewpoint (Noelle-Neumann, 1993).

The spiral of silence explains, therefore, how we perceive public opinion, what impact those perceptions make on our behaviors, and how the process is self-perpetuating. Because the theory is complex it has been difficult to effectively test this theory scientifically. Still, many scholars believe they have found support for at least some components of the theory, while others remain unconvinced of its accuracy. The spiral of silence theory is not very specific about exactly what characteristics of television content affect our perceptions. However, the next theory is.

Creating Perceptions of Public Opinion

The news media in any form, whether television, newspaper, magazine, radio, or Internet, utilize specific tools to convey information. Textually the media use either facts and figures or they use stories and examples to make their point. **Exemplar theory** claims that it is the distribution of **exemplars,** the stories and examples component, that we use as our main clue to form our perceptions of public opinion and/or problem severity (Zillmann & Brosius, 2000).

It works like this. In a news story about a chemical spill, news reporters interview a dozen people near the scene of the event. They ask these people to tell how the spill is affecting them. Three of the twelve complain of headaches, stomach cramps, and a burning sensation in their throats. The other nine people say something like, "It kind of stinks, but that will go away."

On the television news that night, the anchor begins by saying, "There's been disaster in the city. Citizens are hiding in the aftermath of a poisonous chemical spill. Our reporter on the street has the story."

What do you think the preproduced news package made from those interviews will contain? Will it have all twelve interviews? Of course it won't. The package probably highlights the three worst cases or *exemplars* of sickness, showing those interviews most thoroughly. Then after a transition statement that says, "Others, however, were unaffected," it shows one of the nine interviews with people who still felt fine.

Exemplar theory has shown that the viewers regularly fail to understand that the proportion of exemplars shown is not a scientific measure. Instead viewers come away with the impression that most of the people in the area of the spill are nauseous and otherwise sick. The same happens if the story is portrayed similarly in the newspaper, on radio, or in other forms of media.

While the above example was about a disaster, the same effect is shown to happen in relation to issues pertinent to an election or a legislative action. If activists hit the streets campaigning for bigger garbage cans to be provided by the city sanitation service, those voices become the dominant media exemplars simply because most people don't care enough to say anything either way. Perception of public opinion will then lean more toward the need for bigger garbage cans than toward the silent viewpoint (Perry & Gonzenbach, 1997; Zillmann, 1999).

What about the Gradual Changes TV Brings?

While many of the effects we've covered so far deal with rather immediate influence of television, other theories look at the long-term effects. Even though the television industry has been under continuing attack because of the heavy diet of violence and mayhem it feeds to audiences, it continues to use violence in its programming, because it is an easy, relatively inexpensive way to get audiences to tune in (Berger, 1989).

For thirty years, Gerbner and his associates have been profiling the amount of violence on U.S. network television. In addition to finding that there is an overwhelming amount of violence on television, they have conducted audience surveys to determine whether heavy television viewing results in a distorted and fearful view of society. This is different from the effects of violence raised earlier. Most of those dealt with making people aggressive. Gerbner's questions about the effects of violence deal with perceptions of personal danger (Gerbner, 1970, 1998; Gerbner & Gross, 1976).

The theory of cultivation analysis employs a two-pronged strategy: message system analysis and cultivation analysis. **Message system analysis** is a flexible tool for making systematic, reliable, and cumulative observations about television content. It basically involves a detailed content analysis of types of characters, themes, plots, and settings used on television and includes measures of the amounts and types of violence included in programs (Gerbner & Gross, 1976). The assumption underlying this approach is that certain themes in television content are systematically related to each other and are repeated over and over again. Message system analysis allows researchers to identify almost any aspect of the television world, so that they can then test its contribution to viewers' conceptions of the real world.

Cultivation analysis is designed to assess television's contribution to viewers' beliefs, behaviors, and values based on the delineation of the central and critical facts of life in the world of television (Gross & Morgan, 1985). Thus, the focus of this theory is on how television cultivates a particular way of looking at the world in heavy viewers of television. For example, a question dealing with the amount of violence would have both a "reality" answer alternative and one that is slanted in the direction of the world of television. The assumption is that the more one watches television, the more apt one will be to give an answer that is closer to the television reality than it is to the real world. This holds true for **heavy viewers** (four or more hours of television per day) more than for **light viewers** (two or less hours of television per day), but is also understood to be cumulative. That is, the effect occurs over years of television viewing, making this part of the theory very difficult to prove scientifically. Finally, in cultivation research the content one views is not important. The theory posits that television is homogeneous enough that no matter what one watches—from soap operas to sports, from cartoons to the evening news, one will see the same predominant themes.

Since 1968, a great deal of evidence has supported the cultivation hypothesis: the more time one spends watching television, the more likely one is to report perceptions of social reality that can be traced to television's most persistent representations of life and society. The findings have suggested that heavy viewers of television are more likely to express exaggerated levels of fear about being victims of violence and to overestimate interpersonal mistrust (Gerbner et al., 1979; Gerbner, Gross, Morgan, & Signorielli, 1980). Cultivation researchers have called the perception by heavy viewers that the world is a "mean and scary place" the **mean world syndrome.** However, in addition to violence, cultivation analysis has been used to show how sex roles, racial stereotypes, age stereotypes, and religious perceptions have been influenced by television consumption. Perhaps you are one who has become afraid of your world. Maybe you watch heavy amounts of television. Maybe you have more trouble pushing the off button than the one that says "on."

Can Television Be Addictive?

"I'm addicted!" You might hear this claim from people who love chocolate, from people who can't stop smoking, and from a host of others with syndromes related to many facets of human behavior. Shortly after the rapid adoption of television into the living rooms of most American homes in the mid-1950s, some researchers began to wonder if TV viewing could be addictive.

Inherent in the treatment of many dependence disorders is the realization that the addicts are taking in too much of something that in moderation can be beneficial or simply innocuous. It is in the grand extremes or misuses that behaviors involving alcohol, betting, sexuality, eating, and prescription drugs become self-destructive. When this lens is turned toward television, the question becomes: Can excessive television viewing be harmful? Related questions subsequently deal with an operational definition for "excessive" viewing and the types of harm that might befall those who overindulge. Unlike research on other addictions, however, a great many television effects studies have sought to measure the impact on a particularly vulnerable audience: children.

Defining Addiction

Though the term **addiction** is used casually in conversation and popular culture, clinically it often is associated with habitual patterns of behavior with destructive consequences such as substance abuse, eating disorders, sexual addiction, and gambling. "The term 'TV addiction' is imprecise and laden with value judgments, but it captures the essence of a very real phenomenon" (Kubey & Csikszentmihalyi, 2002, p. 76). Rather than speak of "addiction," some prefer to use the term "dependence." The American Psychiatric Association

(APA) uses the term **dependence** for addictive behaviors involving substances (American Psychiatric Association, 1994). [Web site: Symptoms of Dependence; Identifying Television Addiction; also Solving Television Addiction]

When applied to television and other media claims of addiction or dependence become somewhat hard to establish. Generally, however, four predominant symptom clusters associated with such dependent behaviors emerge from the APA criteria: progression, preoccupation, loss of control, and negative long-term consequences (Walters, 1999).

Progression refers to an enhanced tolerance for the activity, along with the increase in the severity of symptoms. For television watching, some observers note a characteristic malaise during prolonged periods of viewing. Among children, a spaced-out, mouth-ajar state may be accompanied by a delayed response when someone verbally contacts the viewer who is fixated on the set (Healy, 1990). Even adults are conditioned to associate viewing with relaxation, positively reinforcing the viewing behavior, while the disappearance of the image on the screen reinstates stress, a negative association. "Habit-forming drugs work in similar ways" (Kubey & Csikszentmihalyi, 2002, p. 77).

At the conclusion of multihour periods of watching, children reportedly have displayed pent up energy and frustration (Anderson & Collins, 1988). When questioned about their children's post-viewing behavior, parents in one study noted: "They're grouchy and irritable after they watch"; "The moment the set is turned off . . . they whine, they fuss, they absolutely regress"; "nervous, rude, inattentive"; "wild running around and that sort of thing"; "spasmodic, a brief little temper tantrum, blowing up, pushing and shoving" (Winn, 1985, pp. 118–122).

The precise causes for these television-related symptoms are unclear, though neuropsychological functions may account for some. Researchers have little conclusive data regarding the impact of TV on brain activity, but some believe viewer attention may be altered in three realms:

> (1) Some television and videotape programming artificially manipulate the brain into paying attention by violating certain of its natural defenses with frequent visual and auditory changes (known as "saliency"); (2) television induces neural passivity and reduces "stick-to-it-iveness"; (3) television may have a hypnotic, and possibly neurological addictive, effect on the brain by changing the frequency of its electrical impulses in ways that block active mental processing (Healy, 1990, p. 199).

People who spend large quantities of time in a behavior or acts that support it are said to exhibit the second symptom, **preoccupation.** American viewers, on average, spend about four hours a day in front of the tube, though researchers note significant differences among a variety of demographic groups based on race, gender, education level, and marital status. This habitual viewing on a societal level has been cited as a large indication of television preoccupation. Four daily hours add up to about two entire months of viewing every year.

Television's Displacement Effect

Early television researchers, noting that many persons spend more of their waking time watching TV than at any other activity, developed the notion of **displacement.** With the advent of television, they argued, a number of other activities have been displaced in varying amounts (Neuman, 1995).

> Consider what a child misses during the 15,000 hours he spends in front of the TV screen. He is not working in the garage with his father, or in the garden with his mother. He is not doing homework, or reading, or collecting stamps. . . . He is not listening to a discussion about community politics among his parents and their friends. He is not playing baseball or going fishing or painting pictures. Exactly what does television offer that is so valuable it can replace these activities that transform an impulsive, self-absorbed child into a critically thinking adult (Copperman, 1980, p. 166)?

Acting primarily as an entertainment endeavor, TV watching in the 1950s tended to co-opt time spent on activities with **functional similarity.** Television tended to displace earlier entertainment endeavors—particularly movie attendance, radio listening, and comic book reading (Neuman, 1988).

Individuals who indicate they are unable to cease from engaging in a behavior suffer from the third symptom, a perceived **loss of control.** Television viewers demonstrating this symptom would feel that they are unable to turn off the set during prolonged viewing sessions. They also may feel that they cannot keep from turning on the set in the first place, particularly during habitual viewing times: after dinner on weeknights, for sporting events on weekends, for favorite shows (Winn, 1987).

Lastly, addictive behaviors are those that lead to **negative long-term consequences.** Heavy television viewing has been found to correspond with weight gain and decreased cardiovascular health (Miller, 2001) along with the other media effects listed in this chapter.

Many concerns also have been raised regarding the residual impact of excessive viewing on education. Numerous studies note a strong correlation between the increase of viewing hours and the decrease of school performance. "The pattern, based on data representing more than a million young people, is as follows: At every grade level, for every subject, and for every social stratum, there is an inverse association between achievement test scores and amount of television viewing" (Comstock, 1991, p. 119).

How Do Television and Other Media Contribute Positive Effects?

Certainly the effects of media on society are not all gloomy, as evidenced by some of the positive impacts of popular music. Some effects are beneficial. Television provides many models of beneficial social behaviors and sometimes intentionally promotes those behaviors. Without revisiting the beneficial effects of television on learning, we can clearly find evidence that television produces beneficial effects. [Web site: Positive and Negative Effects of Music]

Media and Better Health

Foremost, perhaps, in this area are effects of health campaigns. Televised messages promoting exercise, prevention of heart disease, use of seat belts, kicking the smoking habit, and abstinence from drugs are some campaigns that have promoted positive social change. Information in these campaigns is also carried in print, on radio, and through the Internet. There is not one specific theory of health communication campaigns, but such efforts are developed around communication theories of persuasion to maximize the effectiveness of the campaign. [Web site: Principles for Promoting Health]

Media and Healthier Children

Many of these principles could be restated for efforts to promote prosocial change through children's programming. The most prominent example of efforts in this area come from Children's Television Workshop, the creator of *Sesame Street, The Electric Company, Dragon Tales,* and many other children's educational programs. Other programmers also target children with positive messages. *Barney and Friends, Sagwa, Blue's Clues,* and many other programs come out of these sources (see Figure 15.2).

All of these programs try to do more than help children learn to read, write, and learn their numbers. *Gullah Gullah Island* taught children the value of different cultures, working and playing together, music, and exploring the world. *Dragon Tales* teaches children about persistence, bravery, helping one another, and being kind to others, in addition to giving an appreciation of those who look different and talk differently.

Sesame Street has made special efforts to feature people from all races and ages, people from different nations, people who speak differently, and even people with mental and physical challenges and disabilities in an effort to promote social harmony to children. Research has confirmed the program's success in this effort. The program incorporates music, art, and dress of various cultures in furthering that goal. Research is used heavily to determine the program's effectiveness at delivering its message, and changes are made to further enhance the program's positive impact (Black, Bryant, & Thompson, 1998; Johnston & Ettema, 1986).

FIGURE 15.2   Former host of Nickelodeon TV's program *Blues Clues,* Steve Burns, gives a thumbs-up to Children's Television Workshop's (CTW) *Sesame Street* puppet Oscar the Grouch, during a press conference in 1998. Nickelodeon and CTW announced a joint venture to launch the first-ever educational television network for kids, called Noggin.

AP Photo/Bebeto Matthews

Sesame Street is distributed worldwide in various languages, with different versions of the puppets and characters appearing in many cultures. These variations in the program are made to help the characters promote prosocial values using the native culture rather than through Americanized visions of the world.

Summary

In this chapter we have examined how the media's impact on us can be subconscious and often undesirable. The effects of violence have been addressed in a number of theories from social learning theory to aggressive cues theory to cultivation analysis. Children have been shown to be especially susceptible to becoming more aggressive from watching mediated violence, while fear is cultivated in adults and children alike.

Political opinions are also affected by mediated information, with the press affecting judgments of which issues are important. Building this political agenda is a multifaceted process involving politicians, the press, and the public itself. Additionally, when an issue is controversial, people's perceptions of which side the majority of the public approves of will either free them to speak out on the topic or suppress their voice into silence. The voices that are exemplified in the media are especially potent in their influence on perceptions of public opinion.

You should also have learned about the educational benefits of television, and the potential for becoming addicted or dependent on the media, especially television. The research surrounding the effects of media is ongoing. Regardless, perhaps by being more aware of the unintended (side) effects of media, you can better understand how the media choices you make can result in undesirable effects on you and those around you.

Discussion Questions

1. According to social learning theory, what do movies such as *Mary Poppins, Pocahontas, Beauty and the Beast, The Hunchback of Notre Dame,* and *Mulan* teach children about sex roles for men and women? How might these kinds of movies that we grow up with shape our expectations of what men and women should be like?

2. Do you think pornography is dangerous? How would catharsis theory and social learning theory suggest different things about its effects?

3. Cultivation theory is specifically about the cumulative use of television. But if you studied rock videos, say on MTV or VH1, what view(s) of the world do you think "heavy users" would adopt? Would these views be different than those of "heavy users" viewing NBC's prime-time schedule? Why or why not?

4. From a public relations standpoint, why are agenda-building and priming important in managing corporate and nonprofit industrial images?

5. What do you think are some positive effects of media beyond those mentioned in the chapter? Which of the theories mentioned might best explain those effects?

References

American Psychiatric Association. (1994). *Diagnostic and statistical manual of mental disorders* (4th ed.). Washington, DC: Author.

Anderson, D., & Collins, P. (1988, April). *The impact on children's education: Television's influence on cognitive development.* Office of Educational Research and Improvement, U.S. Department of Education.

Bandura, A. (1977). *Social learning theory.* Englewood Cliffs, NJ: Prentice-Hall.

Berger, G. (1989). *Violence and the media.* New York: Franklin Watts.

Berkowitz, L. (1965). Some aspects of observed aggression. *Journal of Personality & Social Psychology, 2,* 359–369.

Black, J., Bryant, J., & Thompson, S. (1998). *Introduction to media communication* (5th ed.). Boston: McGraw-Hill.

Cohen, B. (1963). *The press and foreign policy.* Princeton, NJ: Princeton University Press.

Comstock, G. (1991). *Television in America* (2nd ed.). Newbury Park, CA: Sage.

Copperman, P. (1980). *The literacy hoax: The decline of reading, writing and learning in public schools and what we can do about it.* New York: Morrow.

Diamond, M., & Uchiyama, A. (1999). Pornography, rape, and sex crimes in Japan. *International Journal of Law & Psychiatry, 22,* 1–22.

Gerbner, G. (1970). Cultural indicators: The case of violence in television drama, *The Annals of the American Academy of Political and Social Science, 388,* 69–81.

Gerbner, G. (1998). Cultivation analysis: An overview. *Mass Communication & Society, 1,* 175–194.

Gerbner, G., & Gross, L. (1976). Living with television: The violence profile. *Journal of Communication, 26,* 173–199.

Gerbner, G., Gross, L., Morgan, M., & Signorielli, N. (1980). The mainstreaming of America: Violence profile no. 11. *Journal of Communication, 30,* 10–29.

Gerbner, G., Gross, L., Morgan, M., Signorielli, N., & Jackson-Beeck, M. (1979). The demonstration of power: Violence profile no. 10. *Journal of Communication, 29,* 177–196.

Gonzenbach, W. J. (1992). The conformity hypothesis: Empirical considerations for the spiral of silence's first link. *Journalism Quarterly, 69,* 633–645.

Gonzenbach, W. J., & Stevenson, R. L. (1994). Children with AIDS attending public school: An analysis of the spiral of silence. *Political Communication and Persuasion, 11,* 3–18.

Gross, L., & Morgan, M. (1985). Television and enculturation. In J. R. Dominick & J. E. Fletcher (Eds.), *Broadcasting research methods* (pp. 221–234). Boston: Allyn and Bacon.

Gunter, B., & McAleer, J. (1997). *Children and television* (2nd ed.). London: Routledge.

Hansen, C. H. (1995). Predicting cognitive and behavioral effects of gangsta rap. *Basic and Applied Social Psychology, 16,* 43–52.

Healy, J. (1990). *Endangered minds: Why our children don't think.* New York: Touchstone.

Jeffres, L. E. (1997). *Mass media effects.* Prospect Height, IL: Waveland Press.

Johnson, J. D., Jackson, L. A., & Gatto, L. (1995). Violent attitudes and deferred academic aspirations: Deleterious effects of exposure to rap music. *Basic and Applied Social Psychology, 16,* 27–41.

Johnston, J., & Ettema, J. S. (1986). Using television to best advantage: Research for prosocial television. In J. Bryant & D. Zillmann (Eds.), *Perspectives on media effects* (pp. 143–164). Hillsdale, NJ: Lawrence Erlbaum.

Kubey, R., & Csikszentmihalyi, M. (2002, February). Television addiction is no mere metaphor. *Scientific American, 286*(2), 76.

McCombs, M. E. (1981). The agenda-setting approach. In D. D. Nimmo & K. R. Sanders (Eds.), *Handbook of Political Communication.* Beverly Hills, CA: Sage.

McCombs, M. E., & Shaw, D. L. (1972). The agenda-setting function of the mass media. *Public Opinion, 36,* 176–187.

Miller, K. E. (2001). Television viewing time increases risk for obesity in children. *American Family Physician, 64,* 1251–1252.

Neuman, S. B. (1988). The displacement effect: Assessing the relation between television viewing and reading performance. *Reading Research Quarterly, 23,* 414–440.

Neuman, S. B. (1995). *Literacy in the television age: The myth of the TV effect* (2nd ed.). Norwood, NJ: Ablex.

Noelle-Neumann, E. (1973). Return to the concept of powerful mass media. *Studies of Broadcasting, 9,* 67–112.

Noelle-Neumann, E. (1974). The spiral of silence: A theory of public opinion. *Journal of Communication, 24,* 43–51.

Noelle-Neumann, E. (1993). *The spiral of silence: Public opinion our social skin* (2nd ed.). Chicago: University of Chicago Press.

Perry, S. D., & Gonzenbach, W. J. (1997). Effects of news exemplification extended: Considerations of controversiality and perceived future opinion. *Journal of Broadcasting & Electronic Media, 41*, 229–244.

Perry, S. D., & Gonzenbach, W. J. (2000). Inhibiting speech through disproportionate exemplar distribution: Can we predict a spiral of silence? *Journal of Broadcasting and Electronic Media, 44*, 268–281.

Rogers, E. M., & Dearing, J. W. (1988). Agenda-setting research: Where has it been, where is it going? In J. A. Anderson (Ed.), *Communication Yearbook, 11,* (555–594). Newbury Park, CA: Sage.

Rogers, E. M., Dearing, J. W., & Chang, S. (1991, April). AIDS in the 1980s: The agenda-setting process for a public issue. *Journalism Monographs, 126*, 1–47.

Scheufele, D. A. (2000). Agenda setting, priming and framing revisited: Another look at cognitive effects of political communication. *Mass Communication & Society, 3*, 297–316.

Walters, G. D. (1999). *The addiction concept.* Boston: Allyn and Bacon.

Weaver, J. B. (1994). Pornography and sexual callousness: Perceptual and behavioral consequences of exposure to pornography. In D. Zillmann, J. Bryant, & A. C. Huston (Eds.), *Media, children and the family: Social scientific, psychodynamic, and clinical perspectives* (pp. 215–228). Hillsdale, NJ: Lawrence Erlbaum.

Winn, M. (1985). *The plug-in drug.* New York: Penguin.

Winn, M. (1987). *Unplugging the plug-in drug.* New York: Viking.

Zillmann, D. (1999). Exemplification theory: Judging the whole by some of its parts. *Media Psychology, 1,* 69–94.

Zillmann, D., & Brosius, H-B. (2000). *Exemplification in communication: The influence of case reports on the perception of issues.* Mahwah, NJ: Lawrence Erlbaum.

Zillmann, D., Hoyt, J. L., & Day, K. D. (1974). Strength and duration of the effect of aggressive, violent, and erotic communications on subsequent aggressive behavior. *Communication Research, 1,* 286–306.

16

Technology and Social Change: The Interactive Media Environment

Kelly Berg Nellis

In the previous chapter we examined theories about traditional media's effects on the consumer. You read about how aggression and fear can be precipitated by media consumption, how media cultivates certain views of the world, and how media influences our political understanding, among other things. In this chapter we look at some of the same theories discussed before in brand new ways—as they can be applied to interactive and synchronous media. In this chapter we look at several theories that demonstrate how new communication technology can either be explained by or else has challenged our old understanding of communication theories.

In this chapter you will read about the following concepts:

- Cues-filtered-out theory
- Media richness hierarchy
- Deindividuation theory
- Technology expectancy image gap theory
- Technological determinism
- Theories of hot and cool media
- Hyperpersonal communication

In 2001, a business started by a teenager became what at first seemed like a struggle between David and the music-industry Goliath. Napster provided file-sharing software on its web site for people who wanted to download popular and even obscure songs off the Internet for free. While millions of college students and other Napster users enjoyed the freedom that the new communication technology brought, the music industry challenged the use of this particular file-sharing software.

Record companies and even some musicians, such as Metallica, felt that Napster infringed on copyright holdings that provide income to composers, songwriters, and publishers, and also coopted industry control over how to distribute music to consumers. Napster and its clients argued that the recordings were a fair way to use the music, just like videotaping something from television for one's own personal use. Artists and the music industry wanted to retain control over how their work was delivered and used, and they felt Napster took away that authority. Napster's more than 28 million users wanted and got used to having more power over access to music they say was for their personal use rather than something from which they profited. As a result of the lawsuits, Napster was court-ordered to protect the rights of musicians and recording companies by reinventing itself. It was eventually purchased by software company Roxio, which reportedly had plans to provide music downloads for a fee rather than for free. The battle between old economic and social structures and the changes that new communication technology brings to society are evident in the battle over Napster's use and even its very existence (see Figure 16.1).

The Napster case embodies a number of challenges facing us in a society in which new technology alters the use and forms of old technology. New communication technology raises questions such as: In what ways do we use new communication technology and for what purpose? What are the similarities and differences between old and new technologies that may tell us what to expect in the future? What new implications do new media have for old media?

In this chapter, you will read about how the characteristics of computer-mediated communication alter the way in which we look at the role of media in interpersonal and mass communication. You also will learn about how the changing media function is likely

FIGURE 16.1 Napster, Inc., founder Shawn Fanning listens to a question during a news conference after the ruling that Napster had to stop allowing the millions of music fans who use its free Internet-based service from sharing copyrighted material.

AP Photo/Paul Sakuma

to have an impact on society more broadly. We will examine which traditional mass media theories may be applied to computer-mediated communication and the implications new media have for old media. As a result, you may see why you use and react to computer-mediated communication and new communication technology as you do.

What Are the Characteristics of New Communication Technology?

New communication technology can be defined broadly to include new methods of storing, delivering, and receiving information. Anything from digital technology, which encodes information in the form of "ones" and "zeros," to the Internet and World Wide Web, to chatrooms and even satellite radio and television, can be thought of as "new communication technology." While you probably will not have the opportunity to engage in digital video editing or satellite distribution of programming anytime soon, you likely have been or soon will be an active participant in sending an e-mail, using a wireless phone or pager, or perhaps even downloading a song by a favorite artist to your computer. Much of the communication you engage in using new communication technology is likely via the computer, what we call **computer-mediated communication,** or CMC. Because CMC spans the spectrum of use from interpersonal to mass communication and alters the function of traditional mass communication, it is particularly intriguing to mass communication researchers. In addition to the four functions of traditional mass media: **information, explanation, entertainment,** and **transmission of culture,** CMC is used primarily for **social interaction.** Thus, the discussion in this chapter focuses primarily on computer-mediated communication and its relationship to interpersonal and traditional forms of mass communication.

Mass versus Interpersonal Communication

CMC has been studied from an organizational, interpersonal, and mass communication perspective. That is because CMC has characteristics of both interpersonal and mass communication and allows one to look at the group and organizational dynamics that result from computer-mediated interaction. Understanding how CMC is changing our understanding of mass communication requires an understanding of how CMC is similar to and different from interpersonal communication.

Face-to-face communication involves two or more people in an interaction in which all parties are together during the communicating event in the same place and at the same time. When communication occurs simultaneously, it is called **synchronous** communication. During face-to-face interaction, communicators can get instant feedback and can see the social cues of each of the communicators in order to adjust and appropriately understand the communication situation.

CMC can be synchronous, too. If you have ever participated in a chatroom discussion, you have been involved in synchronous CMC, because two or more people were discussing a topic in **real-time,** or almost simultaneously. Face-to-face communication and CMC are similar in that you can get instant feedback and adjust your message more quickly based on that feedback.

Impersonal versus Personal Communication

Though a variety of perspectives on defining interpersonal communication exist, a developmental perspective has been applied to determine whether CMC is interpersonal communication. In the developmental perspective, interpersonal communication can be said to rest on a continuum from impersonal to personal. The continuum may be based on the depth of knowledge about your communication partner. During interpersonal interactions, people judge whether to share public and private information, get to know what and why their friends act as they do, and use rules for communicating that fit their relationship. Just as in any new relationship, when you first came to college and met new people, you had to judge whether to share personal information or keep it to yourself until a more appropriate time for sharing that private information (for an example, see social penetration theory in Chapter 7).

At first you probably stuck to more public information, such as your major, your year in school, or your hometown. But as you developed more interpersonal relationships with those people, you felt more comfortable sharing more information about yourself that most people would not know about you, such as your feelings about religion, politics, or your family. Similarly, people who communicate online determine an appropriate time to share public or private information. Often, they do share private information and create interpersonal relationships over time.

But interpersonal relationships also require an understanding of your communication partner's behavior. If you were able to describe only behavior, such as whether the person is funny, motivated, or aggressive, you would have an impersonal relationship. As you become more familiar with someone, you might even be able to predict how that person will act in a variety of situations. You may do this by drawing from your own past experiences with other people, your social expectations of people in a particular situation or culture, and your knowledge of that person. When you can predict behavior, you have moved closer to the interpersonal dimension on the continuum. On the far end of the spectrum, interpersonal relationships require you to be able to explain why that particular person does what he or she does (for example, see uncertainty reduction theory, Chapter 7). People who develop and maintain relationships through CMC also experience interactions that fall into each of these categories.

Each interpersonal relationship also relies on social rules and negotiated rules of conduct. Perhaps in your everyday face-to-face relationships, you joke with friends about common experiences or give them nicknames. You know that with some friends it may be OK to call them every month or so to go out, while with other friends you have to call them every day or they may think something is wrong with the relationship. These unwritten personal communication rules that are specific to your interpersonal relationships are usually negotiated between you and your friend and may not apply to other friends. Likewise, CMC interactions rely on social and negotiated rules for communication.

Is CMC interpersonal communication, then? Studies of interpersonal communication have presented mixed results. There is evidence that people do form relationships that are in the middle to high end on the interpersonal continuum (Walther, 1996). Yet other researchers argue that only face-to-face communication provides the intimacy necessary to develop an interpersonal relationship that is truly personal.

How Can Theories of Interpersonal Communication Inform Our Knowledge of CMC?

Several theories of interpersonal communication are used to point out the differences between face-to-face communication and CMC. In this section, we will look at two theories that have been developed from interpersonal theories and applied to CMC: cues-filtered-out and hyperpersonal communication theories.

Since coming to college, the relationships you once had with people you were close to, such as your parents and some high school or neighborhood friends, likely have changed by the lack of physical closeness. The daily face-to-face interaction you had provided the elements necessary to maintaining your relationship at that personal level. However, since coming to college, you may be keeping in touch with some of those people by telephone, mail, or even e-mail, and occasional visits home. The lack of daily face-to-face contact probably has reduced the level of intimacy you had in some ways. This type of change is the foundation of the **cues-filtered-out perspective** (Culnan & Markus, 1987), which is based on a theory of a **media richness hierarchy.**

Our understanding of how to communicate with other people comes from years of experience in interpersonal interactions. You learn how to read, or decode, people's body language, or nonverbal cues. Based on your interpretation of these cues, you can respond appropriately. You have learned that if your father sits far back in his chair with his arms crossed over his chest, you may need to rethink how open he will be to your message. If your friend is yawning or her eyes glaze over when you talk, you know that perhaps now is not the best time to continue talking. But without those physical, nonverbal cues, you may be uncertain as to how to react to a message. The premise of the cues-filtered-out perspective is that without nonverbal cues (which of course are the ones being filtered out), creating and maintaining strong interpersonal relationships may be more difficult, if not impossible.

The debate about whether CMC is a personal or impersonal medium often comes down to the characteristics of the medium and how much richness of interaction it allows. Those who argue that CMC allows only impersonal interactions argue that interpersonal relationships are only as good as the channels of communication used. The deepest relationships rely on communication channels that provide instant feedback, both verbal and nonverbal, as well as a variety of ways to express one's ideas and feelings. On a hierarchy of rich to lean media, then, face-to-face communication is the richest. It provides physical contact, offers visual and audio cues, and allows a variety of methods for conveying one's ideas and emotions. On that same scale, a flier or bulletin would be considered least personal, or a lean medium, because of its absence of instant feedback, its lack of verbal and nonverbal communication, and its inability to provide for the expression of emotion and ideas in a variety of formats (Trevino, Daft, & Lengel, 1990). In contrast, a telephone call allows you to hear whether the person on the other end of the line is happy or angry by the vocal quality, and brings the communication device close to your body, which provides more variety of richness and intensity than an e-mail. An e-mail is primarily text based and on a display screen several feet away from your body. But the ability for more instant feedback puts it higher than a traditional letter on the media richness scale. In the cues-filtered-out perspective, interpersonal relationships are weaker through CMC than they are face to face.

The explanatory power of the cues-filtered-out theory has its limitations and its doubters. Not all CMC is asynchronous, for example. So, almost instant feedback is possible. Moreover, in studies, CMC participants say they use a variety of communication channels, including face to face, to maintain their long-term relationships (Parks & Floyd, 1996). Additionally, just because you cannot see someone smiling online does not mean you cannot express feeling or know how that person feels. People who communicate through CMC have adapted to the new communication environment and the lack of verbal cues to provide those cues textually and graphically. For example, if you typed, "I am laughing so hard, I fell off my chair," your partner gets an idea of your reaction. As an alternative you might type "ROFL," a now common online acronym for "rolling on the floor laughing." You might *emphasize* your point by placing an * around your words, or you might use symbols called **emoticons** to substitute for nonverbal cues. A simple smile emoticon can be conveyed sideways with a colon and a parenthesis. :) These arguments add up to the possibility that interpersonal relationships can occur online but that they may use different cues than face-to-face relationships. See Figure 16.2 for some common emoticons and Figure 16.3 for acronyms or abbreviations.

FIGURE 16.2   *Common Meanings of CMC Emoticons*

:)	Happy	;)	Winking
:D	Laughing	:(	Unhappy
:/	Skeptical, uncertain	>:(	Angry
:P	Sticking tongue out, so there, disgusted	%-)	Confused
:>	Sarcastic	:,(	Crying
8)	Wears glasses, nearsighted	:*	Kiss
:O	Yelling, shocked	(((insert name)))	Hugging someone

FIGURE 16.3   *Common CMC Acronyms*

LOL	Laughing Out Loud	J/K	Just Kidding
ROFL	Rolling On the Floor Laughing	BTW	By The Way
IMO	In My Opinion	RL	Real Life
IMHO	In My Humble Opinion	VL	Virtual Life
JMHO	Just My Humble Opinion	OOC	Out Of Character
AFAIK	As Far As I Know	OT	Off Topic
OMG	Oh My God	L8R	Later
<g>	Grin	BRB	Be Right Back
<vbg>	Very Big Grin	BFN	Bye For Now
<veg>	Very Evil Grin		

Note: Meanings can vary with specific users.

Some scholars believe that the lack of social cues actually leads to interpersonal relationships that progress more quickly than face-to-face relationships. The lack of cues may make the online interactions we have seem even more attractive to us than face-to-face communication. Without the familiar cues on which to base perceptions of others, we may exaggerate the cues we do have and feel more intimate with our communication partner more quickly. We may attribute better qualities to the person based on the limited information we have obtained in the communication. The result is the theory of **hyperpersonal communication,** the rush to intimate communicating, also called **social deindividuation** (Walther, 1995). Using hyperpersonal communication as the basis for understanding CMC relationships, we can see that interpersonal relationships may be possible but with different characteristics than we typically attribute to face-to-face relationships. [Web site: Hyperpersonal Communication]

How Do CMC and Traditional Mass Media Compare?

In addition to its interpersonal characteristics, CMC also serves as a medium of mass communication. However, as we learned earlier in this chapter, the functions of traditional media do not include that of bringing people together in social interaction. Thus, the characteristics of CMC as a channel of communication are likely have some additional differences from traditional mass media. In the next sections, you will learn about the similarities and differences between CMC and traditional mass media.

Similarities between New and Old Media

CMC and traditional mass media are similar in their reach. Both have the potential to reach millions of people simultaneously with their messages. Television can be broadcast nationwide, reaching tens of millions of people with one program. A web site, too, has the potential to deliver its message to millions of people, globally.

CMC and traditional media also share similar functions in society as providers of information, explanation, entertainment, and transmission of culture. Just as we look to the evening news to find out what has gone on in the world today, we can look to online news sites that provide information and an explanation of how it affects you. You can go to the web site dedicated to your favorite television series to get more information about your favorite characters and performers and, in the process, be entertained by the content of the web site. You might even visit a music or game site for its entertainment function. You can interact with other people from your geographic region or from a country you want to visit and about whose culture you want to gain a clearer understanding. CMC serves the function of transmission of culture when one can use it to better adapt offline.

Just as we learn what to expect and how to react to interpersonal communication situations, we learn from years of interaction with mass media what to expect from them in terms of what we can learn, how we will be entertained and informed, and in what form we can expect our information and entertainment. We expect that a newspaper will present information in a "story" form, giving us information about who, what, when, where, and often why something has occurred. We expect that the information will be chosen for a broad audience of readers and will be presented in the form of a folded paper on newsprint. We expect that we will be unable to provide instant feedback through the same channel to those who created the stories.

New communication technology changes our expectations for communication, because new communication technology brings novel characteristics to the communication situation. For example, the September 11, 2001, terrorist attacks brought a renewed interest in news and information seeking among Americans. Not surprisingly, online news web sites also saw increased audiences (Kelsey, 2001). You may have visited these sites and noticed some differences from the typical newspaper story or television or radio news report. What you probably found at several online news web sites were "stories" that resembled a newspaper in that they were text based with accompanying photos. Perhaps there was something else on those sites, such as the ability to play video and sound clips of the same stories, find additional quotes or speeches, move to other related stories, immediately send feedback to the authors of the news stories through e-mail, and converse with other readers worldwide about their opinions on the news of the moment. Like other web sites sponsored by traditional mass media, the online news sites bring together the characteristics of several communication channels, such as print and broadcast media and interpersonal communication.

Differences between New and Old Media

New communication media also exhibit other characteristics: they allow us to interact with other people synchronously, or asynchronously. When you send someone an e-mail, chances are pretty good that you are *not* both communicating through the computer at the same time. More likely, you send the e-mail, and a few minutes, hours, or days later, that person reads the message and responds to you at a time more suited to her or his schedule. This is known as **asynchronous communication.** In contrast, when you are talking with a friend after class, you are engaging in synchronous, or real-time, communication, as discussed earlier. Synchronous communication occurs through new communication technology, such as online in chatrooms and multi-user dungeons (MUDs) or through teleconferencing. Unlike "old mass media," such as television, radio, or newspapers, which relied solely on asynchronous communication between audiences and the communicators, new communication media incorporate both asynchronous and synchronous interactive communication in one channel.

Old mass media function according to a **one-to-many model** of communication. One source, the television or radio network, sends messages to many people who cannot respond with their own message through the same channel. These media are not considered **interactive media.** Before the introduction of CMC, if you wanted to communicate with an announcer or performer, you likely had to use a telephone or send a letter. If you wanted to send a message to many people at the same time, you would have to rely on the permission of those who controlled access to a channel of mass communication. For example, if you wanted to call in a request to your favorite radio station to have it play a particular song or dedication, or if you wanted to get an opposing view out on the same station, you would have to use a different channel of communication, such as the telephone or face-to-face communication, to request that message be sent.

New communication media offer a **many-to-many model** of communication. Many people have access to the channel and design of the message and can potentially send messages out to millions of people worldwide. Napster and similar file-swapping software and service providers were built on the premise of many-to-many communication. They allow many people to store music and even video files on their personal computers and to search on other personal computers worldwide for content they are interested in acquiring (without paying the legal copyright fees) for themselves. In essence, Napster provided a decentralized method of distributing a message to many people. Traditional mass media use a centralized source from which to send the message to many people.

 CMC also is said to be more "hyper" than traditional mass media. It is hyper because it speeds up access to content and alters the linear flow of traditional message content. If you have ever gone onto the World Wide Web and used a link to a web site, you have experienced **hypertext.** [Web site: Hypertext]

How Do Mass Communication Theories Inform Our Knowledge of CMC?

One of the exciting prospects for the study of CMC is that its blend of interpersonal and mass communication characteristics provides an opportunity to integrate communication theories from various fields of study and provide a more unified understanding of how communication theories overlap. It also provides a fresh perspective on traditional mass communication theories and the potential for revealing better answers to familiar questions. It also raises new challenges and provides the potential for new theories to explain related phenomena. Yet one of the potential difficulties of studying CMC is that explanations associated with new media may vanish as the novelty of the media diminishes and the media change and become more complex (Ruberg & Sherman, 1992). Earlier in this chapter, we looked at how some interpersonal theories have been applied to CMC. In this part of the chapter, we will examine how mass media theories may be and have been applied to the study of CMC.

The potential impacts of the Internet and other information technology on the consumer still are widely speculative. However, we do know that new technology creates new boundaries and hierarchies in communication that are sure to have enormous effects on individuals and society (Jones, 1995). Moreover, new technology alters society's level of alienation, educational requirements, segregation, goal formation, notions of self, productivity, and skill levels, among other impacts (Fulk & Steinfield, 1990). Additionally, regulators already are embroiled in weighing the effects new technology brings to issues of privacy and decentralization of power, as they did with Napster and the music industry. Effects researchers will want to compare the effects of CMC with other media (Morris & Ogan, 1996). They also may examine the effects of CMC content such as pornography, which facilitates even virtual rapes, and addiction to CMC.

A Uses and Gratifications Look at CMC

As a logical extension and complement to media effects research, uses and gratifications looks at the individual's perceived benefits from the use of new communication technology.

Uses and gratifications theory still rests on the assumption that we choose to use the media in order to satisfy some need. The results of numerous studies show that those who engage in CMC report a variety of positive outcomes such as socialization, maintaining relationships, playing games, and receiving emotional support from online contact with others (Parks & Floyd, 1996). Different CMC uses are satisfied through clicking on different icons or bullets on a web site where users can choose streams of dialog about their chosen subject matter.

In choosing CMC, we would have some expectations for our use of that media and the outcomes of that use. Scholars already have begun to examine the relationship between uses and expectations. One question that has been raised is whether the speed and ease of CMC leads people to have unrealistic expectations for immediate responses despite the asynchronous nature of much of the communication (Kiesler, Siegel, & McGuire, 1984).

A newly developing theory in this area is **technology expectancy image gap theory.** This theory suggests that through media discussion of advancing technologies, along with business image promotions that suggest a company has high technological capabilities, people begin to expect more than a company or technology can deliver. The pie-in-the-sky image is so unrealistic that when the consumer pursues the advancing technology or relies on a company that claims to be on the cutting edge, the consumer finds that product quality, reliability, and performance are disappointing. This is bad for word-of-mouth promotion of new technologies but can be financially devastating to companies whose technologically based image creates expectations far above the true performance ability of the developing technologies they employ (Kazoleas & Teigen, in press).

Computer-Mediated Social Learning

Social learning theories, as they relate to mass communication, have centered on how people learn and adopt behaviors. The theories are based on the premise that people learn from their use of the media, as they do in other social interactions. People learn how to behave and react to various situations by modeling others' actions, including people we see on television. CMC, with its mix of interpersonal and mediated characteristics, provides a whole new look at social learning. [Web site: Social Learning through Identity Creation]

CMC changes usual social and situational boundaries. Individuals may engage in synchronous or asynchronous communication. They may become intimate with someone they have never seen and who has never seen them. They must learn to react to people who are in a different location—perhaps in another country—without the usual gestures, facial expressions, and tone of voice that may guide their everyday exchanges. Social learning occurs when CMC participants experience new standards of conduct, moral codes, and values in their online interactions and then shape their own conduct to conform to the online behaviors they see modeled (Jones, 1995).

Communication researchers, as well as psychologists and sociologists, have begun to address some of these socially learned behaviors from CMC. One such behavior is **flaming,** which generally refers to hostile behavior among communicators. The willingness of people to set aside usual social niceties in their interactions online has been attributed to disinhibitions and a lack of social cues that are associated with communicating via computer. But Thompsen suggests the practice of flaming is a more complicated and unique outcome of the medium, as well as a result of social interaction. Media experience and skill, social factors, and situational influences, as well as the features of the medium, work together to indicate whether someone might interpret something as hostile or engage in hostile behavior (Thompsen, 1993).

Understanding CMC as Deterministic

Harold Innis and Marshall McLuhan have had some of the strongest influences on what we think about the role of media in our society today. Both believed in a theory of **technological determinism.** Determinists believe that technology, and particularly mass media, determine or control changes in individuals, social interactions, and institutions. They argue that all new technology is the primary force of social change and that technology is the foundation for how all aspects of our society are structured. [Web site: Determinism]

McLuhan's most well known contribution to communication studies is probably the phrase "the medium is the message." While a number of explanations exist for the meaning of this quote, one basic interpretation is that media restrain and control the content and presentation of the message. For example, one cannot deliver moving pictures in a newspaper or through radio, and television is primarily a visual medium with little text. Since the medium controls the message that can be delivered, McLuhan might argue that the choice of medium to deliver a message is actually more significant than the message itself (Ebersole, 1995).

So if you were to apply determinism to CMC you might ask, "How does new communication technology shape how we communicate with one another?" We might also ask how new communication technology changes our current social institutions or economic and political policies. What biases do communication technologies carry? What is the relationship between new technology and society?

Critics of determinism say that it looks at one factor—technology—and suggests that this is the only cause of change in our culture. They say that the medium is only one of many influences on society. Some people also criticize determinism for assuming that media are independent of society. They argue that, in reality, society's needs and interests also shape the media. By that view, just because a new technology is introduced does not mean it will automatically be accepted and change our society. For example, despite the cable and telephone industries' push to gain acceptance for broadband computer connections in the home, consumers have not adopted the technology wholeheartedly at the pace expected. And though AT&T introduced the first modern videophone in the 1960s, we have yet to see widespread adoption of this technology in society.

The Consequences of New Media Technology for the Old

Just as new forms of communication media change the functions of more established media, they also change the content and design of the old media. When television was introduced in American society, it took popular broadcast radio programs, such as soap operas, and added moving pictures. Radio station owners, fearing the death of the medium because of a likely loss of audience to the television, scrambled to redefine radio as a provider of music programs. When MTV came along, radio programmers were again afraid that the end of radio was likely. Yet MTV provided an unexpected boost to the music industry by elevating musicians to "stars" in a new way.

Among the most recognizable implications of CMC on traditional media such as television, radio, and newspapers are changes in content and design, a shift in the role of the audience in the communication process, considerations about the permanence of the media message, and the use of a fifth function of the medium to create social interaction.

Rethinking Textual Analysis with CMC

Think of your favorite television show as a "text" that can be interpreted, or "read," differently by each viewer. Some texts are designed to create a particular response, or interpretation, in the viewer. Other texts, such as music videos, may leave more room for making a variety of meaningful interpretations. In long-running series, such as *Friends,* there is little room for varying interpretations of the text. You may not like whether Rachel is pregnant, but she is anyway. *Friends* would be what Umberto Eco (1976) called a **closed text** because the possibilities for varying interpretations are closed off to you. In more **open texts,** such as *The X-Files,* other interpretations are acceptable, and even encouraged, for the same episode and series. You may or may not have wanted Mulder and Scully to be in an intimate relationship, and the "text" often was intentionally left relatively open to interpretation by the viewer in order to appeal to viewers with differing interests in the series. [Web site: Textual Analysis]

In CMC, there is a new sense of "open" text available to content creators. Not only is each of us a content creator in CMC, but the possibility of interpretation is more open as well, because of the hypertext characteristic. Hypertext changes the type of content and the presentation of that content for the viewer. When you watch an episode of a television series, you have what essentially are different links to parts of the entire series. Each episode is a link to the next part of the larger story. You might view these links in order as they are broadcast on the television schedule, tape them, or watch them in reruns. When you watch them in the order in which they are broadcast, the text is **linear.** That is, you see the timeline of the series and the development of stories in an order that has a predetermined beginning, middle, and end. However, you might watch them in a **nonlinear** order by randomly choosing your favorite episodes and watching them out of sequence on tape at a later time.

Hypertext is similar to, but more open than, traditional linear texts, which attempt to predetermine what content you will see and the order in which you see it. With a hypertext, the reader can enter the text at virtually any point. There is no set sequence that you must follow; rather, there are multiple sequences available to you. When you visit a web site, you may not enter the site on the main page when you have a link to a different page. You may then link to another web site to get more information on a particular topic mentioned only briefly in the first site, and then return to the first site. While you are going from site to site, you are creating your own episodes. Some of the paths you follow will cohere in your mind as "whole." Some will not. You are in much more control of the text and the interpretation of that text than traditional media allows. Not surprising, then, hypertext writing changes traditional definitions of text, author, and reader. Entrepreneurs are experimenting with hypertext online in the form of "programs," such as soap operas, short cartoons, and science fiction stories. Online soap operas take audience interaction a step further than their television predecessors. Audience involvement is necessary to the online soap opera. For example, in the now-defunct *The Spot,* considered the Internet's first interactive soap opera, viewers had to actively choose to move from one part of the story to the next by selecting several hypertext options. Direct appeals to audience involvement usually were formulated as a character's request for advice on a topic of interest or of trouble to a particular character. For example, one character asked viewers through her journal entry if she was too uptight about another character. Another character directly thanked followers for their e-mail and support and beckoned them to "check out" a new feature on the web site. Audience members even were invited to be guest writers for the series.

There are benefits to the producers of online soap operas and other entertainment web sites that allow interactivity. Opportunities for audience involvement not only build loyalty in the audience, they help producers develop a storyline or interactive experience that interests the viewers. In the example of the soap opera asking the audience to participate in problem solving, the relationship of the viewer is altered from "passive" audience member to active participant in the lives of the characters.

Traditional Media Foster Social Relationships with Their Audiences

The desire to actively engage the audience has led TV program producers to create companion web sites that engage the CMC user in choosing the continuation of future program episodes or in creating various extraneous versions of the lives of the show's characters. These sites provide fans with places to gather and communicate as well as details or statistics on the program. Such activation of the audience points us to McLuhan's theoretical classification of communication channels in terms of **hot** and **cool media.** The categories can be seen as part of a continuum of media so that the classifications may change when compared to other media. The more sensory information provided by the medium, the colder it is. Hot media require less audience involvement since less sensory information is provided by the medium. McLuhan identified radio as a hot medium because it simply provides music in the form of audio that is complete. The audience does not need to fill in the information to make the message complete. Television, on the other hand, was perceived to be a cool medium because of all the sensory information that the audience must actively filter out in order to make sense of the message. Moreover, a television screen is composed of a constantly unfinished picture because of the way in which the image is projected onto the viewing screen. The viewer's eyes and brain must complete the picture. In comparison, movies are warmer than television because the screen is a series of whole photographic images. The viewer does not have to work to fill in any missing parts of the picture. Because of the high level of sensory information, audience activity, and lack of permanence associated with the World Wide Web, it could be considered a very cold medium, even colder than television (Ebersole, 1995).

Could anything be a colder medium than the web? Are there technologies that require more active sensory processing? Virtual reality, the simulation of an actual environment complete with tactile sensory input, might be the extreme in cold media. Since users wear virtual reality goggles, gloves, or even body suits, the whole person is absorbed into a mediated reality complete with interactivity with a computer or other virtual reality participants. This and other cutting edge technologies seem to point to increasingly cold media as we move into the digital communication future.

Summary

In this chapter, you discovered that new communication technology encompasses a wide range of new technology from your personal computer to a pager and even to the new digital editing and storage equipment used at most radio and television stations. We focused on computer-mediated communication because of its implications for interpersonal and mass communication. We explored interpersonal theories that have been adapted and applied to CMC to explain whether people can have interpersonal relationships online. In exploring the levels of knowing as part of a continuum of interpersonal communication, we found that people may share personal and private information; describe, predict, and explain behavior; and use social and negotiated rules in interpersonal relationships. The theory of media richness has informed the cues-filtered-out theory, which argues that online communication cannot be interpersonal in nature because of the lack of richness in the channel of communication necessary to foster and maintain interpersonal relationships.

CMC is similar to mass media in its reach of a critical mass of users. Traditional mass media and CMC differ, though, in a number of ways as well, including a many-to-many communication model and the hypertextual, nonlinear, and synchronous two-way communication that CMC provides but that traditional mass media do not.

Though research in the area of CMC as a mass medium is still relatively new, a few traditional theories can be and have been applied to CMC. One can find research using a media effects perspective, uses and gratifications theory, technology expectancy image gap theory, social learning, and determinism. Media effects theories attempt to explain the effects CMC might have on the users.

Because new media change the function and form of old media, we can expect that our media content and presentation will continue to change. Hypertext changes the form in which the content is presented and interpreted. Hypertext is nonlinear and blurs the boundaries between reader and author. Networks and other businesses have utilized the hypertext and interpersonal functions of CMC to present information and entertainment, as well as build relationships with and among their audiences.

In this chapter, we considered whether new technology shapes our culture by determining our society's structures and the way in which we communicate. In the next chapter, we will explore a variety of other perspectives on how media shape our culture. The chapter looks at critical theories of how our values and our worldviews are molded by our institutions, and particularly the mass media.

Discussion Questions

1. What other media theories do you think might be applied to computer-mediated communication?

2. How would those media theories need to be adapted to accommodate for the unique characteristics of computer-mediated communication channels?

3. Are you more willing or less willing to reveal private information about yourself online than in person? What characteristics of the medium do you think contribute to your choice?

4. What new content and forms have you noticed traditional media utilizing online? What do you think the effects of these changes will be on audiences and on traditional media?

5. What are the impacts of digital and online technology in your everyday life?

6. What other societal effects does the adoption of new communication technology have?

References

Culnan, M. J., & Markus, M. L. (1987). Information technologies. In F. M. Jablin, L. L. Putnam, K. H. Roberts, & L. W. Porter (Eds.), *Handbook of organizational comunication: An interdisciplinary perspective* (pp. 420–443). Newbury Park, CA: Sage.

Ebersole, S. (1995). *Media determinism in cyberspace. Marshall McLuhan (1911–1980).* Retrieved November 17, 2001, from *http://www.regent.edu/acad/schcom/rojc/mdic/mcluhan.html*

Eco, U. (1976). *A theory of semiotics.* Bloomington: Indiana University Press.

Fulk, J., & Steinfield, C. (1990). *Organizations and communication technology.* Newbury Park, CA: Sage.

Jones, S. G. (1995). *CyberSociety: Computer-mediated communication and community.* Thousand Oaks, CA: Sage.

Kazoleas, D., & Teigen, L. G. (In Press). The technology expectancy image gap: A new theory of public relations. In C. Botan & V. Hazelton (Eds.), *Public Relations Theory* (2nd ed.). Hillsdale, NJ: Lawrence Erlbaum.

Kelsey, D. (2001, October 18). Nearly half of people in U.S. get news on net—poll. *Washington Post.* Retrieved November 17, 2001, from http://www.newsbytes.com/news/01/171275.html

Kiesler, S., Siegel, J., & McGuire, T. W. (1984). Social psychological aspects of computer-mediated communication. *American Psychologist, 39,* 1123–1134.

Morris, M., & Ogan, C. (1996). The Internet as mass medium. *Journal of Communication, 46*(1), 39–50.

Parks, M. R., & Floyd, K. (1996). Making friends in cyberspace. *Journal of Communication, 46*(1), 80–97.

Ruberg, L. F., & Sherman, T. M. (1992). *Computer-mediated communication: How does it change the social-psychological aspects of teaching and instruction?* (Report No. IR015885). (ERIC Document Reproduction Service No. ED 352 941).

Thompsen, P. A. (1993, February). *Influence model of flaming in computer-mediated communication.* Paper presented at the annual meeting of the Western States Communication Association, Albuquerque, NM.

Trevino, L. K., Daft, R. L., & Lengel, R. H. (1990). Understanding managers' media choices: A symbolic interactionist perspective. In J. Fulk & C. Steinfeld (Eds.), *Organizations and communication technology* (pp. 71–94). Newbury Park, CA: Sage.

Walther, J. B. (1995). Relational aspects of computer-mediated communication: Experimental and longitudinal observations. *Organization Science, 6,* 186–203.

Walther, J. B. (1996). Computer-mediated communication: Impersonal, interpersonal, and hyperpersonal interaction. *Communication Research, 23*(1), 3–44.

17

Critical Theories of How Media Shape Culture, Values, and Perspectives

Joseph R. Blaney and Arnold S. Wolfe

In other chapters in the mass communication section of this book you have mostly been introduced to scientific theories of the media with only an occasional humanistic or critical theory. In this chapter that emphasis will change. While earlier chapters showed critical theories can pertain to face-to-face communication, here we will look specifically at scholars and research that founded and legitimated the field of critical theory in the area of media.

In doing this we will examine major theories and models of meaning that were brought into the study of critical theory and had profound effects on it. Each approach attempts to account for the creation of social, economic, and political practices in society, as well as the role of media in creating the assumptions by which people live.

What really makes the study of critical theory interesting is that most of the theories covered in this chapter emerged both in Europe and in America at the same time, sometimes in similar and sometimes in different ways, as critical scholars read one another's ideas and studied other subjects like literary criticism, psychology, and anthropology. Latin American, Australian, and other writers picked up the critical ideas, each giving the theories his or her own flavor. For the sake of space, we will focus primarily on the European research and its import to the United States.

In this chapter, you will read about the following concepts:

- Frankfurt School
- Marxism
- Neomarxism
- British cultural studies

- Political economy
- Feminist scholarship
- Structuralism and semiotics
- Postmodernism
- Foucault
- American interpretivism

You can admit it: even you—pragmatic, practical you—have wondered why society is the way that it is. "How did it come to have the social, economic, and political structures that it does?" you might question. Why does our culture embody beliefs in an independent press, a free-market economy, religious freedom, and multiple political parties? And why do other cultures in other parts of the world not have this tolerance?

You may not have known it, but the fact that you speculate about such things might make you a media theorist! Your questions about society's structural arrangements are not bizarre and irrelevant. They proceed from one undeniable fact: social, economic, and political "realities" are social constructs. Moreover, some of the most powerful constructors of this reality are the mass media. This chapter will examine how the mass media not only *shape* cultural beliefs and behaviors but also *reflect* the attitudes and actions that members of a culture come to share.

In this chapter you will learn that culture and values do not inexplicably emerge in a societal vacuum! The following pages will address some of the most notable theories that aim to explain how communication media help shape those social, economic, and political structures you may wonder about and how media also encourage the members of a culture to hold certain values or attitudes. We will look at a very influential line of research and a body of theories that examine these issues of media and culture: **critical theory.** Critical theory is a label given to any theory that examines underlying, cultural forces that shape the media and influence our lives. As noted in Chapter 2, these theories typically have social change as their ultimate goal.

Who Controls the Media, and Whom Do They Benefit? Marx Applied to Media

Karl Marx (1888, 1909), the founder of **Marxist theory,** was a nineteenth-century philosopher and scholar of economic and political theory who wrote that those who own the means of producing goods and services wield the power to shape society. Economic power leads to political power, and subsequently to social and cultural power. Marx believed that there were two primary groups in society. First were those who owned the factories and businesses (the **means of production**). He called these owners the **capitalists,** as they sought the use of goods and production to accumulate more goods (capital)—often for themselves. The working class, who instead of owning their own means of production sold their wages to the capitalists, were the **proletariat.** Marx believed that no social group composed of a few should wield political power over the many. Therefore, he called for the overthrow of the few by the many, who would then collectively own and operate the means of production; this would be, in his terms, **the revolt of the proletariat.**

Researchers have applied this theory to understanding contemporary media. Who controls the means of media production? With some exceptions, the radio and television programs, the movies, and the newspaper and magazine stories you consume are products of a few elite corporations.

Messages produced by these companies will rarely challenge their own legitimacy. Chances are slim that NBC News will break an investigative news report on toxic waste dumps owned by General Electric, NBC's corporate parent, though they might give such a story coverage once the news is out to validate their own journalistic integrity. Marxist theorists insist that the owners of the means of cultural production will produce cultural presentations that express their corporate values and general outlook. And these owners are highly unlikely to make messages that offend their advertisers. Moreover, according to Marx, ordinary people—the many—can be convinced to act and hold beliefs that they are not even aware of, attitudes that might even be against their own interests. Unquestioned assumptions adopted by the populace are what Marx called **ideology.** Ideology, also known as **social myth,** is represented by all those unquestioned rules and beliefs that members of a society follow and live by but, importantly, which they do not even know they are following and acting upon (Barthes, 1981; Fiske, 1990). For example, we in America believe that all persons have a right to an education (a social myth that supports our school systems and colleges and universities); that the close, nuclear family unit is desirable (other cultures live through extended, large families); that having money and possessions indicate a person's success (a social myth that drives many to acquire fancy cars and homes); and a social myth that the ideal physical traits of women in our culture are to be thin and tall with flawless complexions, luxurious hair, and thin thighs! Most persons accept and follow these myths and this ideology without question, but feminists and other critical scholars increasingly fight against them.

For orthodox Marxists, ideology presents itself as knowledge, but it is a form of knowledge that oppresses and represses people as it tries to hide what is true (Sholle, 1988). Convinced that a particular ideology is true, the masses consent to their own exploitation by the elite. For instance, Marxism says the ideology of capitalism works to convince the creators of goods (workers) that they are entitled to only a small portion of the profits derived from those goods. The Marxist doesn't believe that risking one's capital in starting a business venture merits the possibility of reaping a disproportionate share of the profits if that business succeeds—and it may fail.

Consider broadcasting in the United States. The owners of the electromagnetic spectrum (also known as the "airwaves") are presumably all of us, all U.S. citizens. But licenses to broadcast are now bought and sold, starting with a government auction, as though the airwaves were the property of the buyers and sellers. In 1999, the Federal Communication Commission proposed the Low Power FM initiative. The purpose of the proposal was to offer a small portion of the airwaves to nonprofit groups (churches, civic groups, clubs, schools, and the like). However, the National Association of Broadcasters (NAB), which represents the licensees, fought the Low Power FM initiative.

Many felt this diversification was necessary in response to the Telecommunications Act of 1996, which allowed for the rapid consolidation of media ownership. The FCC's engineers determined that the proposed low-power stations posed no significant interference with existing signals. Yet the NAB's opposition was rooted in its assertion that the LPFM initiative would harm existing FM services. Congress agreed and acted to virtually kill the initiative. In short, the representatives of the people bought into the ideology that existing broadcast licenses were private property deserving protection, rather than a public resource to be used in the public's "interest, convenience, and necessity" as envisioned by the Radio Act of 1927.

The optimist may be tempted to ask, "But what about the Internet? Don't online publications, audio, and video create opportunities for alternative cultural productions?" This may be so. But the prospects for a web site that attracts a mass audience are tied to its ability to emulate its commercial media peers. In order to survive, that site will have to attract an audience large enough and desirable enough to advertisers to generate the revenue necessary for its survival. The commercial activity necessary for this could compromise the independence of such web sites. Moreover, what makes one think that successful cyber entities won't be bought up by large corporations, just as "mom and pop" radio and TV stations have been? Of course, the critic of Marxism will note that those who attract the largest audiences might just be doing the best job and, therefore, deserve to dominate the industry. Plus, "mom and pop" could have kept their broadcast station, but money was more important to them than independence, so they sold out.

Hegemony is the Marxist term for this ideological power in the hands of the few to influence the masses. When any person or group of persons enjoy the dominant ideological position in a society, because they might own the media and have control over media content or—in the feminists' view—because they are men, these groups or individuals are said to be in the hegemonic position in society.

Marx's main point is that the ownership of the means of production determines the nature of the messages and values of the owners expressed in cultural presentations. Voices on the economic margins of society will not often pierce the corporate din. We will see the foundation of Marxist theory in each of the critical theories below, though some abandon in part or altogether the notion of **economic determinism** in Marx—that is, the idea that the class structure drives everything else in the culture, including the media.

How the Press Serves the Interest of Big Business Owners

Political economy theory is a media theory that developed from the Marxist approach insofar as it raises concerns about how media hegemony functions to serve the interests of the powerful. What distinguishes political economy theory is its focus on the classical Marxist understandings of the importance of the economic base of the media. Political economists begin by examining how the owners of the means of production manipulate all industries, including media, in order to serve their economic interests. [Web site: Political Economy]

Media political economists assert that an undeniable link exists between the content produced by media and financial interests of media companies. For example, Edward Herman and Noam Chomsky (1988) advanced the idea that news media operate under the following economically driven content filters:

1. Size, concentrated ownership, owner wealth, and profit orientation of media firms
2. Advertising as the primary source of income

3. Reliance on elite news sources (government, business, and experts funded by business)
4. Flak, or economic discipline
5. Ideological anticommunism

Each of these "filters" is a factor that can be reasonably expected to affect the process of providing news. Size, ownership concentration, wealth, and profit orientation of media outlets could facilitate news that is preferential to the wealthy owners. Advertising as a primary source of income could mean audiences with less purchasing power will not be equitably served. Conversely, audiences with more resources would be preferred. The media's reliance on elite news sources might taint the objectivity of the gathering and reporting of facts with the biases of existing elites such as government officials, "experts" from the corporate sector, and representatives of ideological think tanks. The fear of "flak," or the economic retribution that can follow reporting unfavorable to elites, could discourage aggressive, critical reporting on important issues. Finally, American ideological anticommunism might require an unquestioned reaction against socialist policies and governments worldwide.

You probably already know about the mega-media mergers that have been taking place in recent years with companies like Time becoming Time-Warner and now AOL-Time-Warner. The implications for the cultural means of production in this matter are clear enough. However, the political economist sees these mergers as a subcategory of immensely larger mergers, which concentrate private ownership in the hands of fewer and fewer people. Moreover, the political economist is certain that "money talks" more now than ever before.

How Culture Serves the Interests of Big Business Owners

The Marxist and political economy theories point out how ownership of media forms can—intentionally and unintentionally—embody the ideological positions and social myths of the persons who create media messages. This recognition of the power of the media to deliver meanings is one of the distinguishing principles and contributions of critical theory. From the very beginnings of critical theory and continuing until today, a distinctive characteristic of this research is that scholars typically study cultural forms found within media, such as the portrayal of the female body type, rather than a medium such as television itself.

High culture includes those forms of art such as drama, music, and the visual arts that are not mass produced. For example, even a single play is in some way distinct every time it is produced. Some early cultural theorists felt that the level of advancement of a culture was defined by the form of this "high culture." **Popular culture,** however, includes media forms that are frequently seen as "low art," as alternative media, or as ordinary leisure practices. It includes, thus, those activities that we might do for entertainment or pure fun but that would not ordinarily be considered traditional media or classic art forms (Bennett, Mercer, & Woollacott, 1986; Hall, 1982, 1986; Woollacott, 1986). Examples of popular culture research are studies into elements of comic books, romance novel reading, rock and roll music, the Beatles, graffiti, popular dancing, body piercing, and even the McDonald's arches!

Critical scholars have differed in their approach to popular culture. For example, one of the earliest responses to this popular culture was from a group of theorists known as the **Frankfurt School.** These researchers represent a generally negative view toward popular culture. They were not particularly interested in studying the popular or alternative cultural artifacts of all classes of people. Rather, they wanted to keep media research as the study of the more classic forms of art.

The Frankfurt School emerged in the 1930s (concurrent with the rapid growth of radio as a mass medium). They are considered critical scholars because they pointed to the tenets of Marxism to explain ideology in art forms. However, they valued high culture because they believed it was immune from elitist corruption. The inherent integrity of high culture, they believed, represented good in itself. For this reason, they sought to protect high culture by limiting its exposure in mass media. At the same time, they felt that popular culture commodified high culture—that is, it placed a price on culture, making it something that could be bought or sold. Access to "culture" through radio, records, and the local cinema distracted the masses from their real economic division from the elite and got in the way of a revolution of the workers.

As you might expect, some critics found this approach to culture ironically elitist. The intellectual leadership of the Frankfurt School came from Max Horkheimer, Herbert Marcuse, and Theodor Adorno. The ideas of these German critical scholars became even more influential in America as Nazi atrocities forced Jews like Horkheimer to flee Europe, many of them to the United States. Safely abroad, these scholars provided considerable criticism of the German folk culture propagated by the Nazis. Horkheimer eventually affiliated with New York's New School of Social Research. Adorno collaborated with American social scientists on projects about authoritarian attitudes among Americans.

Is Popular Culture Really So Bad? Modifying Marxism for Media Research

The Frankfurt School theorists represent a unique voice within critical theory, a negative position toward studying in an academic, serious way the leisure practices of "ordinary people." Many, however, developed an interest in the "popular" entertainment of the masses. In fact, this interest in studying the popular marks this research as study into all economic classes of people but, particularly, research of the middle and lower economic classes and how they use the media.

Several changes occurred to Marxist theory as scholars picked it up to analyze popular culture. Since it changed from its original "determinist" form, many chose to call this hybrid form of theory **neo-Marxism,** or **cultural Marxism.** As you may infer from the root "neo," this is a somewhat more recent development in Marxist thought, though it has been around since before television. Like traditional Marxism and political economy, neo-Marxism/cultural Marxism is concerned with the relationships between the powerful and the powerless. However, cultural Marxism is much more concerned with issues related to how the audience utilizes media, technology, and leisure practices in general. Whereas political economy questions the way that ideology gets inserted into media messages, cultural Marxism is more interested in how the audience processes and understands these media messages or uses other technological advancements.

Cultural Marxism is the most common theoretical perspective within the broader areas of **cultural studies** or **popular culture studies.** As was noted with cultural Marx-

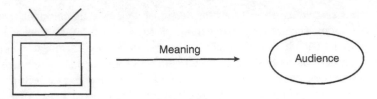

High culture critical research projects meaning from the media to the audience.

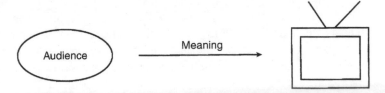

Popular cultural studies looks at how the audience assigns meaning to the mediated messages.

FIGURE 17.1   *Model of High Culture vs. Pop Culture Meaning Study.*

ism, popular culture studies identify two central or fundamental concepts. Along with interests in ideology, power, and the popularity of art of the masses, cultural studies' privileging of audience calls attention to concepts of meaning and text as shown in Figure 17.1.

Popular culture studies researchers are naturally drawn to study the **meaning process** because of their interest in the audience's use of messages. Critical researchers are naturally drawn to study and to problematize the concept of text, since the meaning process inherently needs a text to which meaning can be attributed. Consistent with cultural studies' interest in the leisure pursuits of ordinary people, a **text,** for a critical researcher, is any object of analysis that is a "meaning-full" object for an audience member. That is, cultural studies scholars feel free to study the "meanings" of such unusual or unexpected "texts" as punk music musicians' dress, pornographic films or paperbacks, comic book heroes, tattoos, body piercing, and so on. Let us turn now to some of the individual theoretical positions within the study of critical theory and examine the various ways that each studies cultural artifacts.

Finding Meaning in Media Texts: Structuralism and Semiotics

One of the turns in critical theory was a move to the study of structuralism and of semiotics. These two theories are closely related and operate on similar assumptions—that a kind of language, or structure, is working at an unconscious or deep level of a person or a culture that, nevertheless, causes or prompts language and meaning at the conscious level. Critical scholars turned to structuralism and semiotics theories that were being developed in anthropology and in linguistics and applied them to the understanding of media texts and other popular culture artifacts. [Web site: Structuralism and Semiotics]

First, **structuralism** looks for deep ideological or unconscious structure that affects the conscious, surface level of meaning (Barthes, 1972, 1981). Here is how it works. Anthropologist Claude Levi-Strauss (1963) argued that myth, rituals, or symbols are unconscious or deep structures shared by all cultures. These operate much like an ideology—an unconscious worldview that we follow but do not realize that we follow—that shapes each culture's beliefs, symbols, rituals, and language. We can see an example of this in a simple monetary note—a 500-cruzeiro bill from Brazil used between 1972 and 1980 (see Figure 17.2). On the front of the bill there are five faces, and on the back, five versions of a map of Brazil. The front image is a site of negotiated meanings, with two contradictory readings. One writer (Chiavenato, 1980) interprets the images as proceeding from black to white, a reading clearly in line with Brazil's official policy in the first half of the twentieth century to "whiten" the racial stock of the nation. Another reading, however, is that the images represent the indigenous Brazilian, the explorer, the slave, the merchant, and the modern man. These themes match the maps on the back, which proceed (though from right to left) through five stages of Brazilian history: discovery, commerce, colonization, independence, and integration. Even if this is the reading, it is interesting to note that the truly "integrated" Brazilian is framed as being very white. You can see that critical scholars would be interested in these models of meanings because they provide another system of uncovering meaning and explaining how we use popular culture and other leisure activities.

Semiotics specifically means the study of signs, or things that can represent something other than themselves (Eco, 1976). It developed from linguistics, which names the underlying structures of language as **langue,** that is, a set of rules that the culture—unconsciously—follows to shape the everyday communication of the culture. The term **parole** is the name for this everyday communication, vocabulary, syntax, and grammar that people actually use. In other words, each culture has its own unique langue and manifested parole that characterize that culture and that language. For example, we could study the texts of the nightly news reports carried on network television. Through an analysis of the

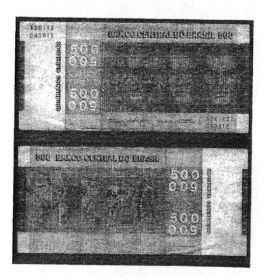

FIGURE 17.2   Racial politics are played out in this example of structuralism, a 500 cruzeiro note from Brazil (1972–1980).

Photo courtesy of Roberto Mollo

stories they choose to cover and the words and visuals they use to report on each (which a semiotician would consider the parole) we could attempt to identify the underlying cultural ideologies and rules (which are the langue) that govern and dictate these messages.

Semiotics provides a specific set of tools that can be used to look in detail at a single text. For example, according to Roland Barthes (1972), a **sign** is a combination of some idea or object that is represented (the **signified**) and an image or word that represents it (the **signifier**). You are probably familiar with Tommy Hilfiger advertisements. In these you can regularly see several signs pulled together—the smooth faces of models representing youth; the colors of patriotism for an American, red, white, and blue; symbols of wealth and class; and the various hues of faces representing diversity. These are linked in a **sign system,** or set of signs working together to transfer meaning with the slogan and icon for Tommy Hilfiger. They present an ideology of what is American (in terms of diversity, youth, and class). The colors and often a flag represent America, but the TH logo, which is also red, white, and blue, then indirectly becomes a part of the larger ideological message. This creates a **mythic system,** by which meaning shifts from sign to sign (an **ideological** or **connotative shift**) to link Tommy Hilfiger in the reader's mind to youth, status, and all things American.

Reading the News, the Romance, and Fashion: British Cultural Studies

The origins of cultural studies occurred in Europe in the early 1970s. Following World War II, England became a hotbed of social theory in what would come to be known as **British cultural studies.** Sharply defined social classes in England made many in the English lower class question assumptions about how their culture operated. The Birmingham School, in London, was most influenced early on by Raymond Williams, who was actually at Cambridge University. Williams questioned the assumption that "high culture" (classical music, canonical literature, and the like) had more intrinsic value than the "folk" culture found among the "commoners." He asserted that the hegemony of high culture was part of a larger domination of the lower class by economic and social elites (Williams, 1961). [Web site: British Cultural Studies]

The British cultural studies movement also spawned scholarship specifically dealing with the production and reception of popular culture. Because Williams and his colleagues lived and taught in and around London, these first critical studies in the early 1970s naturally looked at the popular culture pursuits of those in London and the surrounding countryside. Williams's (1973) work is typical of this kind of research, especially his famous work *The Country and the City,* in which he compares the different ideologies of the city and the rural areas and the different meanings they bring to their leisure pursuits.

Another seminal work that typifies this critical rhetoric is known as the **Nationwide studies** (Brundson & Morley, 1978). Several of these studies looked at the very popular British television documentary show *Nationwide* in order to examine the different leisure practices, the different ideologies embedded in these activities, and the multiple meanings that characterized the entire United Kingdom geographical area. Other critical studies looked into family television viewing and into the affordability of the television set as primary leisure artifact in the home and what it meant to have television as a private source of meaning and entertainment for the family.

Because the 1970s were a time of almost total unemployment for London youth, other critical researchers were drawn to what London youth did in their spare time and how the unemployed youth made meanings of their lives. The scholarship about the meanings these teenagers received from their various leisure practices was termed **subculture theory.** These research interests also led to several studies that looked at the subcultures of London and how each represented its own ideology and symbols of meaning. For example, Dick Hebdige's (1979) famous book *Subcultures* provided detailed examinations of the hairstyles of the punks and their piercing of body parts with safety pins as their way to symbolize resistance and give meaning to their lives. Other subcultures were also studied to reveal the ways that their clothing and their use of Italian motor scooters served as commanding symbols. Can you do some unofficial theorizing of your own about the meanings certain patterns of dress, hair, tattoos, body piercing, wall décor, or perhaps music listening might have for some of your acquaintances?

Deconstructing "Gender": Feminist Scholarship in Media Studies

The success of British cultural studies and subculture theorists to explain the symbolic meaning of British young men brought several female critical theorists to argue that young women's leisure practices were also important to research. **Feminist scholarship** was a significant turn and powerful development in critical theory. Feminists in media studies examined women's leisure pursuits and argued that, within British cultural studies, not only is class a factor in ideology and meaning relative to lived experiences, but gender is an influential factor as well. Examples of this move in critical theory are McRobbie's (1978) studies of the importance of dance in young British women's leisure and Winship's (1987) research into how gender and ideology are represented in magazines.

Feminist scholarship has moved beyond the British setting, of course, since gender is a determining factor in the audience's choice of leisure texts and such leisure is a source of powerful meanings for women everywhere. In the United States, feminist theory developed and gained importance as a critical tool for understanding the ideology of patriarchy and the social role of women. But before we look at critical and cultural studies specific to the United States, there is one more theory to describe, of largely French origins.

Is There Anything New to Say about Reality and Power?

One of the most talked about and often criticized critical theories today is **postmodernism.** This theory has applications in all areas of study, from studies of architecture to literary works to visual art to media texts. Compared to the structural approach, it is both alike and different. It is similar in its critical roots. Postmodern writers began to question whether certain notions such as democracy, illness, or "race" had any real meaning. They came to believe, instead, that each is merely stated or framed together with different words and ideas by different people—that is, an idea exists in different **discourses** and takes a different role in different ideologies. As an example, American news writers at the turn of the twentieth century write on the invasion of territory and ethnic oppression and subsequent heroic acts of resistance to that oppression. But, ideologically, the framing of an Israeli "incident" as a "massacre" or Palestinian response as "terrorism" rather than "resistance" builds an ideological world comfortable to most American readers (Fiske, 1990). Postmodernism tends to reject any linear notion of meaning and objects to accounts that try to frame all men, women, or people of some "race" or nation in a certain light, focusing instead on fragmentation and differences between people in a group. Finally, it rejects any attempt to provide a single explanation of the social world, called a **metanarrative** (Rosenau, 1992).

Grounded in the work of Jean Baudrillard (1983) and as applied to media criticism, this theory suggests that the processing or enjoyment of a media text works as a kind of entrance into the reality of the text. That is, the audience member interacts with a text by accepting the textual experience as a kind of reality—a reality removed from the actual reality that the person is living in. The term for this experience is the **hyper-real** or the **implosion** of reality and hyper-reality (Baudrillard, 1983). [Web site: Postmodernism and Hyper-reality]

Both influencing and yet diverging from the postmodern perspective is critical writer Michel Foucault (1972). You have studied some of Foucault's ideas in the chapter on contemporary rhetoric, but Foucault also has relevance to the study of popular media. In particular, Foucault's ideas on power distribution within a culture, discourses as locations of power, and the knowledge-power relationship imbedded in a discourse all help explain how media can be used by an audience.

It is important to note that the distinctive contribution of Foucault is his theorization of power rather than ideology. He does not deal directly with ideology and its manifestation in a culture or a culture's messages. Instead, he is interested in how power is created and fostered in a culture. For example, he argued through his theory of the **micropolitics of power** that power does not originate from the leaders of a society, or from the top, but, rather, from the bottom of culture and from the lowest and least important persons in a culture. This theory is radically different from all previous theories of social power and political power. In short, Foucault envisions that people who have power have it because the persons in the lower classes give it to them, or let them have the power—hence, the micropolitics of power. [Web site: Micropolitics of Power and Discourses]

Related to this theory are his ideas on discourse. Foucault suggests that throughout any culture **discourses** emerge and sort of "coagulate" around centers of power. For example, he notes the discourse of motherhood in a culture; all the signs of being a mother and the rules and beliefs that any culture has toward a mother and all the attitudes and power we give to motherhood compose a "discourse of motherhood." Another example might be the discourse of physician; most persons in our culture recognize this discourse because we all respect and give power to physicians. Perhaps the most controversial discourse he wrote about was the discourse of heterosexuality. Here he argued that the world's cultures universally privileged heterosexuality over homosexuality and that those in the discourse of heterosexuality enjoyed a more prominent, respected, and powerful position in society than those in the discourse of homosexuality.

In the ideas and insights of Foucault we have a Frenchman who had great influence in critical theory both in Europe and in America. In the following, final section of this chapter, we concentrate on the critical theory that was exclusive to America.

How Does the U.S. Media System Alter the Application of Cultural Theory?

As mentioned above, as the various theories, cultural studies, semiotics, and even post-modernism move from country to country, the scholars in those countries give the theory their own flair, as they tend to rely on one another's readings and focus and also because they are addressing cultural ideologies and media structures unique to each country. Indeed, feminist theories and cultural studies would each expect such changes to occur (McRobbie, 1992). In this final section, we will consider how two of these approaches have changed focus in the United States.

Feminist Theory in the United States

The feminist theory that emerged in the United States had different origins than its British counterpart. Its origins were in women's studies departments and the workplace where concern for equality of pay and employment opportunities was central. This area of scholarship has continued to evolve.

 In recent years in the United States the term "feminist" has taken on various connotations. [Web site: Feminist Theory] To say that one is a feminist could have a variety of meanings. The rhetorical theorist Sonja Foss (1996) asserts that **feminist theory** or feminism can be divided into multiple approaches:

> Liberal-humanist feminists, for example, aim to extend to women the rights already possessed by men; they work for equality within the present system. Radical feminists, in contrast, advocate the revolutionary transformation of society and the development of alternative social arrangements to those currently in place. Marxist or socialist feminists see the capitalistic economic structures as at the root of women's oppression, while lesbian feminists see heterosexuality as a primary cornerstone of male supremacy. Women do not need to define themselves by their relation to a male world, these feminists suggest.

These are diverse approaches, indeed. But, as Foss further asserts, these types of feminism have three commonalities. First, each asserts that women are oppressed by an ideology of patriarchy that serves to put the interests of men before women. Second, women and men experience the world differently. Third, women's points of view are not valued by our culture.

Each of these approaches to feminism can be applied to the study of media. The liberal feminist would be interested in asking questions about inequalities of gender found in media content, ownership, production, and other matters. For instance, are male and female characters represented proportionately as leading characters in sitcoms? Do sports magazines or university press agencies treat male and female athletes equitably? Are there as many women CEOs of movie studios as there are men? Are female voices equally represented on morning radio programs? The liberal feminist is concerned that when women are underrepresented in these ways they are marginalized. Perceptions about women become stereotypical and limiting. The voices of women are excluded from those contributing to the institutions of our culture.

The radical feminist believes that media propagate a dysfunctional and patriarchal model for society. For instance, they view the formulaic casts of situation comedies as agencies of patriarchy. They argue that the families socially constructed by television advance the hegemonic ideas about family that are harmful to women and society in general. From the venerable Ward Cleaver of *Leave It to Beaver* to the omniscient Mr. Drummond of *Diff'rent Strokes* to the irascible title character in *Everybody Loves Raymond,* these family structures have maintained the patriarchal father as the focus of familial organization and power.

The Marxist, or socialist, feminist argues that capitalistic economic structures are the primary source of women's oppression. The patriarchal forces of market economics marginalize women and others who either cannot or will not participate fully in competitive economic activity. Like the Marxists referred to earlier, these feminists believe that the current system for exchanging goods and services functions to advance the interests of the powerful. The Marxist feminist assumes that such power-oriented relationships benefit men to the detriment of women.

Lesbian feminists believe that cultural assumptions about sexuality advanced by the media oppress women (Lederer, 1980; Vance, 1984). Specifically, they believe that the heterosexual reliance of women on men for intimate sexual relationships is at the root of their problems. Only when women free themselves from dependency on men for intimacy can oppression be resisted. They see this problem exacerbated by a "heterosexist" approach to relationships in media artifacts. Media content advances the notion of male/female relationships as proper and normal—even mandatory—with the notion that a woman *must* have a relationship with a man to be complete and happy (**compulsory heterosexuality**). The ideology behind this representation is that homosexual relationships are deviant. Of course, one could point to recent anecdotal relationships to the contrary on shows like *Ellen* and *Will and Grace.*

Like the Marxist, neo-Marxist, and political economic approaches, all of these feminist approaches have implications for social policy. All of the theories make claims about how media unjustly advance existing ideologies and social, political, and economic hierarchies. What distinguishes the feminist approach is its focus on the oppression of women by men and the institutions cultivated by men. The strengths of these feminist approaches lie in the obvious fodder for critique available in statistics that measure women's inequality (lower pay, fewer CEOs, shortage of acting roles for women, and so on).

Cultural Studies in the United States

Just has feminism in the United States faces different issues with different twists than in Europe, so also cultural studies has subtle differences in the United States from that in Britain and other countries. It is important to note that until the Birmingham School recognized the worth of studying the social consequences of "low culture," it was largely ignored by media scholars. However, the work of two Americans, Horace Newcomb (2000) and Lawrence Grossberg (1984, 1986), have ushered in the popular culture studies of these forms of communication.

Horace Newcomb's (2000) scholarship has firmly ensconced the study of popular television programs within the legitimate academy. The ambiguity of meaning found in most television programs is **heuristic,** according to Newcomb, because it allows the viewing audience to assign their own speculative levels of meaning to those texts (Newcomb, 2000). As such, when you are gathered around "the tube" with your friends watching *Buffy the Vampire Slayer,* each of you may assign different motivations to each character's words and actions. The personal experiences that you bring to that viewing experience, combined with the open nature of these media texts, allows for a symbolic exchange between producers and consumers of culture.

Television is one cultural place for scholarship. Perhaps an even more compelling area of inquiry is popular music. In fact, Grossberg (1986) has argued that understanding the appeal of rock music is particularly instructive. Like television, rock music is subject to many differing interpretations. The availability of such interpretations allows consumers to use the music as they see fit. Because of this, Grossberg argued that rock music is potentially subversive. In fact, he pointed to historical attempts to marginalize rock as evidence that elites viewed the music as a place of resistance to cultural norms. Consider the lyrics, "Yackety, yack, don't talk back . . . or you don't get no spending cash." On the surface, those lyrics might appear to express the youthful angst of a young man who resists his parents' attempts to control his behavior through their financial power over him. In this sense, it's slightly rambunctious. However, another listener might interpret the song as a critique of the legitimacy of parental power altogether. Hopefully, you get the point: popular music can be a source of opposition to cultural assumptions.

Several American cultural studies researchers also interpret media texts and other cultural texts. Jan Radway (1984) analyzed romance novels as read by American women. James Lull (1987) analyzed music and its meanings for the fan. Tania Modleski (1982) critiqued the soap opera's influence on the audience, and Todd Gitlin (1986) has been an important critical voice in understanding situation comedies.

The name for cultural studies research conducted by American scholars is commonly referred to as **U.S. cultural studies** or **American interpretivisim** (Livingstone, 1993). In American interpretivisim the focus remains on the audience and on meaning, but there is less emphasis on ideology in messages and more freedom given to the audience member to provide meaning to the text. In other words, in British cultural studies or in structuralism and semiotics, for example, a text is interpreted for how it might embody and deliver the cultural myths in an implied way through the message—the rhetorical analyst makes an argument for certain meanings (ideologies) that are present within the text. But in American interpretivisim the critic privileged the audience member as almost the sole determinant of meaning, rather than the culture. Meaning may be different for different groups of readers, or even for every reader, based on her or his personal experience. This notion of multiple possible meanings is called **polysemy.**

A kind of adjustment to this notion was provided in an important article by Celeste Condit (1989), who took American critical scholars to task for this idea of unlimited meaning in the audience member. She argued that there is, rather, a **limited polysemy** in any audience member and that people can only bring meanings to a text from their own personal lived experiences.

As you can see, critical theory research is very prominent in communication theory and particularly in media research. Critical research has been a strong influence on the media criticism conducted in our country and has also developed independently as a line of research in Europe. Some of the influences and ideas that originated in Europe have been brought to this country and have provided explanatory power in helping us understand our leisure practices and media texts.

Summary

This chapter has presented several theories that demonstrate a unique body of research into the power of the media. This body of theory that we term critical theory embraces several theories and explanations of the media from European scholars as well as American media critics.

Several distinctive characteristics mark the study of media and leisure activities according to critical theory perspectives. From theories of Marx, considerations of ideology and hegemony and socioeconomic class are revealed. These ideas have been extended and developed by other theorists who acknowledge that social class, economic position, and political institutions are embedded in all kinds of media messages.

One group of critical theorists is interested in the production of meaning in texts; this gives us the theories of neo-Marxism and political economy. Other media researchers prefer to study how meaning is consumed and processed by the audience member who relates to a text. Representative theories of the audience perspective are British cultural studies, feminist scholarship, subculture theory, postmodernism, and American interpretivism, to name just a few. Cultural studies re-theorize and problematize concepts such as meaning process, text, and audience.

Further, critical theory privileges the study of ordinary cultural artifacts enjoyed by the ordinary citizen or by the masses. While both mainstream media research and popular cultural studies look at all kinds of broadcast and printed media, popular culture research seeks out the more marginal, popular media such as rock music or romance novels to study and understand. We have seen that while most critical positions view as legitimate the study of all kinds of leisure pursuits, nevertheless the Frankfurt School scholars resisted the study of the art of the masses and emphasized, instead, the study of high or classical art. Throughout critical theory and all the various critical positions that compose it, the emphasis remains on culture and the values and ideologies of culture that end up in all kinds of media messages and all kinds of leisure pursuits.

Discussion Questions

1. When you think of the term "Marxism," what kinds of images race through your head? Do you think that the connotation of "Marxism" has become so negative that people may not be willing to seriously consider Marx's ideas?

2. Likewise, what do you think of when you hear the term "feminist?" This word also has many societal connotations. Do these connotations prevent people from seriously considering feminist perspectives?

3. How does Stuart Hall's approach to hegemony differ from the original Marxist approach? Which, if either, do you feel is more accurate? Defend your answer.

4. Do you feel that meaning lies in the text, in the user of the text, or in some combination? Explain your answer.

5. Do you feel that representations of others in media—from news to billboards—are just and equitable, fair to all involved? Provide examples to justify your position.

6. If you accept critical theory's goal of equality and resistance to traditional power structures, what implications would that have on the media texts (news articles, photographs, web pages, and so on) that you produce?

References

Barthes, R. (1972). *Mythologies*. London: Palodin.

Barthes, R. (1981). *Elements of semiology*. New York: Hill and Wang.

Baudrillard, J. (1983). The ecstasy of communication. In S. Foster & S. Hall (Eds.), *The anti-aesthetic: Essays in postmodern culture* (pp. 126–134). Post Townsend, WA: Bay Press.

Bennett, T., Mercer, C., & Woollacott, J. (Eds.). (1986). *Popular culture and social relations*. London: Open University Press.

Brundson, C., & Morley, D. (1978). *Everyday television: "Nationwide."* London: British Film Institute.

Chiavenato, J. J. (1980). O negro no Brasil: Da senzala à guerra do Paraguai [Blacks in Brazil: From the slave house to the Paraguayan War] (2nd ed.). Sao Paulo: Brasiliense.

Condit, C. M. (1989). The rhetorical limits of polysemy. *Critical Studies in Mass Communication, 6,* 103–122.

Eco, U. (1976). *A theory of semiotics*. Bloomington, IN: Indiana University Press.

Fiske, J. (1990). *Introduction to communication studies* (2nd ed.). London: Routledge.

Foss, S. K. (1996). *Rhetorical criticism: Exploration and practice*. Prospect Heights, IL: Waveland Press.

Foucault, M. (1972). *The archaeology of knowledge*. New York: Pantheon Books.

Gitlin, T. (1986). *Watching television*. New York: Pantheon Books.

Grossberg, L. (1984). Another boring day in paradise. *Popular Music, 4,* 225–258.

Grossberg, L. (1986). Is there rock after punk? *Critical Studies in Mass Communication, 3,* 50–74.

Hall, S. (1982). The rediscovery of "ideology": Return of the repressed in media studies. In M. Gurevitch, T. Bennett, J. Curran, & J. Woollacott (Eds.), *Culture, society, and the media* (pp. 56–90). New York: Methuen.

Hall, S. (1986). Cultural studies: Two paradigms. In R. Collins (Ed.), *Media, culture, and society: A critical reader* (pp. 52–72). London: Sage.

Hebdige, D. (1979). *Subculture: The meaning of style*. London: Methuen.

Herman, E., & Chomsky, N. (1988). *Manufacturing consent: The political economy of mass media*. New York: Pantheon Books.

Lederer, L. (1980). *Take back the night*. New York: William Morrow.

Levi-Strauss, C. (1963). *Structural anthropology*. Translation by C. Jacobson and B. Schoepf. New York: Basic Books.

Livingstone, S. (1993). The rise and fall of audience research: An old story with a new ending. *Journal of Communication, 43,* 5–12.

Lull, J. (Ed.). (1987). *Popular music and communication*. Newbury Park: Sage.

Marx, K. (1909). *Capital*. Chicago: Kerr.

Marx, K. (1888). *The communist manifesto.* London: Reeves.

McRobbee, A. (1978). Working class girls and the culture of femininity. In Women's Study Groups (Eds.), *Women take issue*. London: Hutchinson.

Modleski, T. (1982). *Loving with a vengeance*. New York: Methuen.

Newcomb, H. (Ed.). (2000). *Television: The critical view* (6th ed.). New York: Oxford University Press.

Radway, J. (1984). *Reading the romance*. Chapel Hill: University of North Carolina Press.

Rosenau, P. M. (1992). Post-modernism and the social sciences: Insights, inroads, and intrusions. Princeton, NJ: Princeton University Press.

Sholle, D. J. (1988). Critical studies: From the theory of ideology to power/knowledge. *Critical Studies in Mass Communication, 5,* 16–41.

Vance, C. S. (Ed.). (1984). *Pleasure and danger: Exploring female sexuality*. Boston: Routledge & Kegan Paul.

Williams, R. (1961). *The long revolution*. New York: Columbia.

Williams, R. (1973). *The country and the city*. New York: Oxford.

Winship, J. (1987). *Inside women's magazines*. London & New York: Pandora.

Woollacott, J. (1986). Fictions and Ideologies: The case of situation comedy. In T. Bennett, C. Mercer, & J. Woollacott (Eds.), *Popular Culture and Social Relations* (pp. 196–218). Milton Keynes: Open University Press.

18

Media Coverage of the September 11, 2001, Terrorist Attacks: A Case Study

Jack Glascock

In Chapters 12 through 17, you were exposed to several overarching areas of theory in the field of mass communication. You have been introduced to the origins of the field from the beginning of the twentieth century, when people feared the media's powerful effects, right through to the most modern theories that understand the limitations on the media's effects. This chapter uses the horrific terrorist attacks on the World Trade Center and the Pentagon to bring these theories together in a contemporary application.

In this chapter, you will read about the following concepts:

- Hypodermic needle theory
- Structuralism and semiotics
- Political economy
- Selective processes
- Cognitive dissonance
- Uses and gratifications theory
- Agenda setting theory
- Cultivation theory
- Feminist scholarship
- Social learning theory

At 8:45 A.M. on Tuesday, September 11, 2001, an American Airlines jet, loaded with fuel for a transcontinental flight, slammed into the north tower of New York's World Trade Center (WTC), piercing the building's outer walls and turning its upper floors into a towering inferno. About 20 minutes later, while media cameras rolled, a second jet hit the south tower. In roughly half-hour intervals, yet another jet, also filled with fuel, plunged into the Pentagon in Washington, DC; the south and then the north towers of the WTC collapsed; and finally, a fourth plane slammed into a rural area 80 miles southeast of Pittsburgh. In all, nearly 3,000 people died in what turned out to be a coordinated series of terrorist attacks against the United States. Within hours government officials had identified Osama bin Laden and his Al Qaeda network of terrorists as the chief instigators of the attacks.

Not since the events of the Kennedy assassination, during which Jacqueline Kennedy returned home to the nation's capital in a blood-stained dress and Jack Ruby gunned down suspected assassin Lee Harvey Oswald, had such dramatic events unfolded in front of the camera. The September 11, 2001 (or 9-11), tragedies, complete with identifiable heroes (rescue workers, victims' families) and villains (bin Laden and Al Qaeda), was tailor-made for television. Some viewers reported they initially thought they were seeing scenes from a movie instead of the news that morning. In fact, after the terrorist attacks, military planners were reported to have sought advice from Hollywood producers on possible future terrorist scenarios so they could plan preventive measures (Stanley, 2001). All the major networks stayed on the air nonstop for four days covering the tragedy and its aftermath. Neilsen Media Research estimated that about 80 millions viewers tuned in that Tuesday night to watch TV coverage of the day's events ("Made-for-TV," 2001).

Nearly three weeks after the events in New York and Washington, the United States began bombing Afghanistan, a country suspected of harboring and supporting bin Laden and his terrorist network. Thus began not only the military campaign but also the "propaganda war" with the suspected terrorists. Such propaganda communications are created with a hope of direct effects, as explained in the **hypodermic needle** theory of mass communications (see Chapter 12). This theory, as you may remember, posits that the media's effect is as direct as giving the audience a shot of propaganda in the arm. During war, propaganda is typically used to build support for the war effort at home while painting the enemy as an evil force.

President Bush initially recognized the propaganda war with the terrorists when in his speech to Congress ten days after the tragedy he posed the question, "Why do they (Muslim terrorists) hate us?" ("The hour is coming," 2001). According to many observers the answer was that the government had had no coordinated propaganda strategy to reach the Arab world. As Illinois Congressman Henry Hyde asked, "How is it that the country that invented Hollywood and Madison Avenue has such trouble promoting a positive image of itself overseas?" (Simon, 2001).

The first salvo in the propaganda war was fired by bin Laden, who, in a videotaped speech released within hours after the first wave of U.S. air attacks on Afghanistan, attempted to recast the war on terrorism as one between all of Islam and the West (Poniewozik, 2001b). The following day another videotape, also released by the suspected terrorists, appealed to the world's billion Muslims for Arab unity in the war with the West and promised more terrorists strikes on America. Later, broadcasters were chastised for airing such messages verbatim and, in effect, serving as conduits for a propaganda campaign against the West by the media-savvy bin Laden (see Figure 18.1).

Shortly thereafter the United States began to ratchet up its own propaganda campaign. The military began dropping leaflets on Afghanistan, one showing an American soldier extending his hand to a man in traditional Afghan dress. Another depicted a radio tower and encouraged listeners to tune in to American broadcasts being transmitted from

FIGURE 18.1 In a videotape released to Al Jazeera the day the United States began military attacks on Afghanistan, Osama bin Laden praised God for the September 11th terrorist attacks on New York and Washington and vowed that America would not be safe until its troops left "the land of Muhammad."

AP Photo/Al Jazeera

a flying radio station, known as "Commando Solo" (Marquis, 2001). The radio broadcasts encouraged Afghan soldiers to surrender and offered support to "the innocent people of Afghanistan." The message broadcast to the enemy Taliban troops is an example of fear appeal, a common propagandistic technique:

> Attention Taliban! You are condemned. Did you know that? The instant the terrorists you support took over our planes you sentenced yourselves to death. The Armed Forces of the United States are here to seek justice for our dead. Highly trained soldiers are coming to shut down once and for all Osama bin Laden's ring of terrorism and the Taliban that supports them and their actions. . . .
>
> You have only one choice. . . . Surrender now and we will give you a second chance. We will let you live. If you surrender no harm will come to you. When you decide to surrender, approach United States forces with your hands in the air. Sling your weapon across your back, muzzle towards the ground. Remove your magazine and expel any rounds. Doing this is your only chance of survival. (McIntyre, 2001)

In the aftermath of terrorists attacks, the media, long thought of as an objective, disinterested chronicler of events, was suddenly awash in patriotic symbols, as all the major news networks incorporated images of the American flag on their screens and news anchors took to wearing flag pins. The use of symbols is also characteristic of propagandistic communication, as they tend to evoke positive feelings toward whatever message is also being transmitted. Another example was a *Newsweek* magazine article about the effect of the tragedy on the country's psyche. To illustrate the article, the magazine used Norman Rockwell's "Four Freedoms" paintings (see Figure 18.2), which were originally created for the government during World War II to galvanize public support for the war effort (Gates, 2001). We cannot, of course, see the direct or powerful effects model in the texts themselves, but only if the propaganda has a strong and consistent effect on the chosen audience.

Other theories, rather than looking at the effects of the message, look at the elements of the text. Thus, the study of the symbols and the patriotic ideology that the propaganda messages embody is an example of the critical theory of **structuralism and semiotics** (see

FIGURE 18.2   *One of the "Four Freedoms" Posters Created by Artist Norman Rockwell.* The paintings served as the centerpiece of a massive U.S. war bond drive during World War II and were used to help explain the war's aims.

Printed by permission of the Norman Rockwell Family Agency, Copyright © 1943 the Norman Rockwell Family Entities.

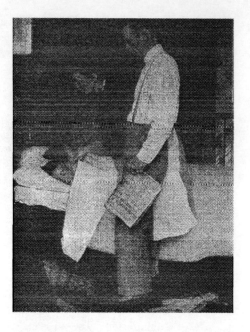

Chapter 17). Recall that according to structuralism and semiotics, a culture communicates its values and traditions through langue and parole. For these media messages, the sudden, revived ideology of patriotism and love of country spurred by the terrorist attacks is the **langue,** or the underlying ideology of our culture. When these ideologies become manifested in such artifacts as media messages, photos, and lapel pins, they are now the **parole,** or concrete communication to the members of the culture. This is an example of meaning as explained by structuralist critics; an underlying structure, or langue, of a particular ideology becomes revealed in a concrete way through the communication, or parole, of that culture.

The U.S. government also assumed a more aggressive role in trying to limit what it considered to be propagandistic messages from bin Laden and the Taliban. When the Voice of America ignored a State Department request not to broadcast an interview with Mullah Mohammad Omar, the Taliban leader, the Bush administration moved quickly to replace the agency's acting director with another, more conservative officer (Barringer, 2001). The White House was also successful in getting the TV networks to refrain from airing verbatim any future broadcasts by bin Laden since the charismatic bin Laden was, in effect, using the airtime to arouse anti-American sentiment (Simon, 2001) and that he could be sending coded messages in such broadcasts. Other U.S. initiatives in the propaganda war included making Secretary of State Colin Powell and National Security Advisor Condoleeza Rice available for interviews on Al Jazeera, the Arab television network that reaches 35 to 40 million people in the Arab World, and establishing 24-hour press centers around the world for the sole purpose of being able to more immediately counter, in any time zone, what White House Press Secretary Ari Fleischer referred to as "Taliban lies" (Crystal, 2001).

The efforts of the government, in particular the Bush administration, to control the messages put out about bin Laden and, similarly, to control the official spokesperson are an example of the critical theory of **political economy** (see Chapter 17). Here is an example of the producers of meaning—government officials—determining the meanings, messages, and *political ideology* that they want delivered. Remember that political economy claims that those with economic and/or political power can control the meanings of a culture.

The direct effects hypothesized by propaganda communication may be mitigated by the selective processes discussed in Chapter 13. For example, people who were hawkish on the war in Afghanistan and believed the United States should bomb and kill enemy forces there would have been more inclined, based on **selective exposure** theory, to tune in to a talk show such as *The Rush Limbaugh Show,* which would support their beliefs. However those opposed to the war would have been more likely to watch a show such as *Donahue* on MSNBC, whose more liberal host and program namesake, Phil Donahue, might have advocated a point of view more in accord with their beliefs.

Another process, **selective perception,** may have played a role in how bin Laden's videos were received by various audience members. To much of the Arab world, bin Laden's list of grievances against the United States—the death of thousands of Iraqi children due to U.S.-sponsored sanctions, U.S. support of Israel, the partition of Arab countries by Europe following World War I, and the continued presence of U.S. troops in Saudi Arabia, home of Muslim holy cities—may have been somewhat convincing (Poniewozik, 2001b). However, for others, the videotapes may have simply represented the rantings of a fanatic obsessed with the downfall of the United States. Applying the theory of **cognitive dissonance,** these latter viewers likely dismissed bin Laden and other high-ranking officials in his terrorist network as liars and the information in the videotapes as inaccurate because their heartfelt beliefs and values ran counter to those of the Taliban leader. Bin Laden was easily discredited in people's minds, making it highly likely that their preexisting support for U.S. sanctions, support of Israel, and/or presence of troops in Saudi Arabia would continue to be maintained while the new information was rejected.

Members of the audience also may have used **selective retention** to remember some images of Arab Muslims and to forget others. For example, those with anti-Arab biases might have remembered the mug shots of the terrorists and their Arab Muslim backgrounds but ignored or forgotten more positive images of Arab Muslims in the United States attending prayer vigils in support of the victims of the terrorist-precipitated tragedies. All of these processes would tend to reinforce beliefs that were already there, as opposed to affecting an actual change in attitudes and beliefs.

How Did the Attacks Alter Your Media Use?

The **uses and gratifications** model (see Chapters 12 and 14) could be used to explain people's media choice during and following the tragedy. For example, if you woke up that morning and turned on your radio, as you might normally do, and heard about the tragedy, your initial usage of the media could be explained by **habituation,** or attending to media out of habit. Further media usage would likely fall under the need for **information** or **surveillance.** For example, once you heard about the events on the radio, you might have switched on your TV to actually see what was going on. The images captured by TV were so dramatic, that, in addition to being informative, you may have found them perversely engrossing, hence also fulfilling a need for **entertainment.** In addition, friends may have contacted you, either by phone or over the Internet through e-mail. These media may have helped fulfill a need for personal interaction or **companionship** during the crisis. If you happened to use e-mail on 9-11 to find out more about the tragedy or just to talk to friends or relatives about it, you were certainly not alone, as America Online reported transmitting a record 1.2 million instant messages that day (Terrell & Perry, 2001). A similar gratification might also explain people congregating around TV sets with friends, or even strangers in public places, to watch continuing TV coverage of the tragedy. The next day you may have picked up a newspaper or logged onto a media web site to read more in depth about what happened, fulfilling the need for **explanation** or **correlation.**

Mood management theory (see Chapter 14), which posits that media are sometimes used to put consumers in a more pleasant mood, might also explain people's media usage following the WTC tragedy. One indication that this might have been the case for at least some consumers after the terrorist attacks was the noticeable increase in comedy rentals reported by video rental stores (Poniewozik, 2001a). Perhaps expecting a more somber audience and a preference for more light-hearted fare, Hollywood studios and network heads postponed movies and programming deemed too violent and/or reminiscent of the events in New York and Washington. For example, Warner Brothers studio delayed indefinitely the premiere of *Collateral Damage* starring Arnold Schwarzenegger and featuring an explosion at a Los Angeles skyscraper. CBS discarded the original pilot for a new show, *The Agency,* because it dealt with terrorism, and Fox reedited a scene in the pilot for another new show, *24,* in which an assassin, out to kill a presidential candidate, blows up an airplane (Poniewozik, 2001a).

How Did the Media Emphasis on the Attacks Influence Our View of the World?

Based on the concept of the **agenda setting function** (see Chapter 15) of the press, we would expect the general public to consider as important the information and issues reported in the media. Here's one example of how this might work. A few days after the tragedy, NBC aired an interview by correspondent Jane Pauley with the family of one of the victims on United Flight 93, Jeremy Glick. Glick was one of the passengers on the airliner who apparently tried to overtake the hijackers, leading the hijackers to crash the plane in Pennsylvania well short of its intended target in Washington, DC. In the interview, Glick's wife, Lyzbeth, described a last, 20-minute telephone conversation she and her husband had just before the crash in which they discussed the situation on the plane and the possible outcome:

"He told me, 'I love Emmy'—who is our daughter—and to take care of her. Then he said, 'whatever decisions you make in your life, I need you to be happy, and I will respect any decisions that you make.' That's what he said and that gives me the most comfort. . . . He didn't sound panicked, very clear-headed. I told him to put a picture of me and Emmy in his head to be strong" (Corvo, 2001).

By airing in prime time such an emotional and compelling interview with the family of one of the victims, NBC focused the attention of many Americans on this aspect of the tragedy. Hence the effect of the tragedy on the victims' families, as well as some of the victims' individual heroism, was made salient by the media's reporting. One possible effect of this type of coverage might have been the enormous outpouring of support in the form of monetary contributions to charitable organizations such as the Red Cross and United Way for the victims' families.

The media's continual coverage of the war on terrorism in the aftermath of the tragedies could provide another example of agenda setting. This reporting—which included special reports on bin Laden, investigations into the hijackers' backgrounds, the recounting of past terrorist acts, and warnings of possible future acts—helped heighten public concern about terrorism. While no doubt much of the public's reaction to terrorism had to do with real-life events, such constant reminders in the media likely served an agenda setting function. Months after the tragedy, airline travel and hotel bookings were down in record numbers and consumer confidence in future travel was still shaken (Sloan, 2001; "Survey," 2001).

Not only does this media coverage have an agenda setting effect, but also it has a cultivating effect on the viewer. One of **cultivation theory**'s (see Chapter 15) postulates is that real-life images of planes slamming into buildings and pedestrians fleeing collapsing skyscrapers contribute to people's perception of the world as a violent place, a process called the **mean world syndrome** in which the violence depicted on TV is theorized to contribute to a more fearful view of the real world among frequent viewers.

Another cultivation effect commonly ascribed to the media is the perpetuation of stereotypes. Here the theory suggests that television can cultivate stereotypical attitudes among frequent viewers by depicting certain categories of people in ways that suggest some uniform characteristics based on the people group with which they are associated. Arabs have often been cast in a negative light on television, and coverage of this incident furthered this notion. [Web site: Cultivating Stereotypes]

Perhaps as a result, the media began offering images to counter such stereotypes (that all Arabs were terrorists). For example, *Time* magazine published a photo of an American Sikh draped in an American flag at a rally for terror victims in New York. And a picture transmitted by the Associated Press showed three American Muslim women wearing *hijads* (head scarves) and singing "God Bless America" at a candlelight memorial service in California. Figure 18.3 shows another Sikh raising the flag outside his Manhattan business in the wake of the attacks.

Another possible cultivating influence of the 9-11 coverage deals with depictions of women. When women are depicted in stereotypical occupations on TV, frequent viewers often come to think of women in real life as being confined to job opportunities that are fewer than those available to men. Analogous to this would be the media's reporting of United Flight 93, in which possible acts of heroism were ascribed primarily to the male passengers, with almost no mention of the role of women on the plane (see for example, Reilly, 2001). In fact, it appears that a number of women may have participated in the attempt to overcome the hijackers. One flight attendant reported that she was boiling water to throw on the hijackers. Another woman, one of the passengers, also called home and talked about a plan to rush the hijackers ("The heroes of United Flight 93," 2001).

Feminist scholars could offer an interpretation of the privileging of male-dominated images according to the critical theory of **feminist scholarship** (see Chapter 17). It is

FIGURE 18.3 Devender Singh, a 1974 Sikh immigrant from India, puts up an American flag outside his Reade Street store in downtown Manhattan ten days after the 9-11 terrorist attacks.

AP Photo/Stephan Savoia.

obvious here in this example that the privileging of males as the primary actors in these incidents inherently reveals the ideology of patriarchy, or messages with meanings that point more toward males than females. [Web site: Discourse of Masculinity and Femininity]

Another media effects perspective, **social learning theory** (see Chapters 14 and 15), might help explain how the 9-11 events could have occurred in the first place. As discussed previously, this theory asserts that viewers can learn and imitate certain behaviors, primarily violence and aggression, depicted on television. In a sense, social learning is a theory that supports the notion that life can sometimes imitate art. Given the preponderance of ever more violent images in the media, one can easily speculate that such imagery might inspire increasingly violent acts in real life. As one commentator noted about the terrorist attacks, life had now imitated the most horrifying Hollywood movie (Seiler & Soriano, 2001).

For many, seeing the video of the second plane hitting the south tower of the WTC was like watching a motion picture, perhaps because the disaster was eerily reminiscent of scenes in such movies as *Independence Day* and *Air Force One* (Seiler & Soriano, 2001). Maybe even more illustrative of social learning theory is the video game *Microsoft Flight Simulator,* which allows users to fly a virtual plane and includes a New York City skyline complete with the World Trade Center towers that players can fly into (Poniewozik, 2001a). Given such representations in the media and their potential influence, it only stands to reason that military strategists have called upon Hollywood producers to help them prepare for future terrorism acts.

This reaction of Hollywood to the reality of the terrorist attacks provides a clear example of the critical theory of **postmodernism** (see Chapter 17). According to postmodernism, reality in our lived experiences and reality as portrayed in media messages can, for some individuals, implode on each other, to the degree that it is difficult to sort out where reality begins and ends and where media reality begins and ends. People's comments that as they watched the planes hit the towers they felt like they were seeing a movie demonstrate the concept of the hyper-real and implosion according to postmodernism's model of how meaning can occur.

Discussion Questions

1. What effect, if any, do you think the events of 9-11 will have on America's appetite for violence? To help prevent future acts of terrorism, should violence in the media be more regulated?

2. What might be some of the prosocial impacts of media coverage of the events in New York and Washington?

3. What should the media's role be in the information/propaganda war between the United States and terrorists such as bin Laden and their supporters such as the Taliban?

4. Think about other theories you have studied in this textbook. Describe how another theory might explain some of the media coverage from the terrorist attack.

References

Barringer, F. (2001, October 8). Voice of America under pressure to toe U.S. line. *New York Times*, p. C1.

Corvo, D. (Executive Producer). (2001, September 13). *Dateline NBC* [Television broadcast]. New York: NBC News.

Crystal, L. (Executive Producer). (2001, November 1). *The NewsHour with Jim Lehrer* [Television broadcast]. New York & Washington, DC: Public Broadcasting Service.

Gates, D. (2001, October 8). Living a new normal. *Newsweek*, *138*(15), 54–59.

The heroes of United Flight 93. (2001, October 4). *The Buffalo News*, p. A1.

The hour is coming when America will act. (2001, September 21). *Boston Globe*, p. A29.

Made-for-TV terrorism. (2001, September 17). *Broadcasting & Cable*, *131*(39), 3.

Marquis, C. (2001, October 16). Propaganda: U.S. steps up leaflets and radio broadcasts to sway Afghans. *New York Times*, p. B4.

McIntyre, J. (2001, October 18). U.S. propaganda to Taliban: "You are condemned." CNN.com. Retrieved November 15, 2001, from http://www.cnn.com/2001/US/10/17/ret.us.propaganda/index.html

Poniewozik, J. (2001a, October 1). What's entertainment now? *Time*, *158*(15), 108–112.

Poniewozik, J. (2001b, October 22). The battle for hearts and minds. *Time*, *158*(18), 68–70.

Reilly, R. (2001, September 24). Four of a kind. *Sports Illustrated*, *95*(12), 94.

Seiler, A., & Soriano, C. G. (2001, September 13). Movie releases are snagged in terror's web. *USA Today*, p. 1D.

Simon, R. (2001, October 22). Waging the spin war. *U.S. News & World Report*, *131*(17), 29–30.

Sloan, G. (2001, October 25). Travel industry braces for 'a long recovery.' *USA Today*. Retrieved November 15, 2001, from http://www.usatoday.com/money/biztravel/2001-10-03-forecast.htm

Stanley, A. (2001, October 21). President is using TV show and the public in combination to combat terrorism. *New York Times*, p. B2.

Survey: Travelers' confidence shaken. (2001, November 15). CNN.com. Retrieved November 15, 2001, from http://www.cnn.com/2001/TRAVEL/NEWS/11/01/rec.travel.survey/index.html

Terrell, K., & Perry, J. (2001, October 8). The day the Web was a lifeline. *U.S. News & World Report*, *131*(15), 67.

Part IV

Organizational Communication and Public Relations

In the previous set of chapters on mass communication, you studied the important theories of mass communication and some of the history of this field within communication theory. We turn now to the study of two additional kinds of communication that are unique subject areas and research interests. Within the body of knowledge known as communication theory, organizational communication and campaign communication emerge as two distinct but related areas of knowledge.

Given these two definitive developments within communication studies—organizational theory and campaign communication theory—this section of the book will present a set of chapters covering both organizational theory and campaign communication theory as specialized kinds of business communication. First, Chapter 19 traces the beginnings and development of theories and research in organizational communication. This chapter examines the history of organizational communication and those theories that explain the operation of an organization as a whole. Conceptualizing and explaining organizations as unique communication settings, this chapter also looks at the many lines of communication manifested within an organization and at the various management styles that an organization can take.

Next, Chapter 20 presents the second body of knowledge and corresponding line of research. This chapter defines all kinds of campaign communication—commercial, political, and social campaigns—but looks especially at the theories of public relations as a unique kind of campaign communication.

Because of communication's rapid and intense interest in all kinds of campaigns, especially public relations, the next three chapters are the application of theory chapters, which will detail the theories and models that have been developed to explain campaign communication and, in particular, public relations campaigns. Chapter 21 presents the theory and research that explains the planning and execution of any kind of campaign.

Chapter 22 focuses on campaign messages, relating the history of campaign messages and pointing out strategies that organizations use to get their images out and strategies that the media consumer can recognize in organizational messages. Chapter 23 examines two major lines of research to emerge in campaign communication: first, that campaign communication is fundamentally relationship communication and, second, that integrated marketing is a unique, and the newest, development in public relations, advertising, and marketing communication. The final chapter in this set of chapters is a case study of campaign communication about the tire recall crisis that affected tire manufacturer Bridgestone/Firestone and automobile manufacturer Ford.

For the discipline of communication, the most striking development in campaign communication is the strong interest in public relations. Even though public relations is taught in some business departments and researched by a number of business scholars, public relations is, to a great degree, the domain of communications. Recent expansion of theory and research into public relations makes this subject area one of the fastest growing topics of study within communication studies. While marketing and advertising are considered primarily business department offerings, public relations has been embraced by communication studies. Even in communication departments with no formal public relations major, usually one or more public relations courses are now offered, introducing public relations as an area of study in most communication departments.

The chapters in this section of the book present research findings that are not typically covered in communication theory textbooks. Most communication theory texts do not typically present research into campaign communication, much less the most current research findings into campaign structure, campaign message design, and campaign communication as relationship building and integrated marketing. So, we want you to appreciate this innovation in this theory text.

Before turning to these chapters in business communication, let us note again some information about theories that was presented in the very first chapters of this book. As you read these chapters about organizational communication and public relations, we are again going to point to information that you learned in Chapters 1 and 2 about theories. Recall from Chapter 1 that theories emerge from social structures such as cultural values, norms, rituals, and so on and that these social and cultural structures tell us what opinions and behaviors are appropriate, inappropriate, rude, or friendly. This is especially true for organizations as social constructs. Corporations are reflections of our society but are also unique social constructions of their own. The public relations chapters will also demonstrate how cultural factors inform theories of campaigns.

Remember also from Chapter 1 that communication is strategic, and it is relational. These two traits will be clearly demonstrated throughout these chapters in campaign communication and in organizational communication.

Finally, Chapter 2 offered a great deal of explanatory power to organizational and public relations communication in its conceptualizations of three kinds of research as systems approach, rules approach, and laws approach. Additionally, the three paradigms of scientific, humanistic, and critical research and the general distinction between objective and subjective research directions are exemplified through the various theories offered to explain campaigns and organizations and will be pointed out to you as we go.

Remember to look for the web site references throughout the following book chapters.

19

Introduction and History of Organizational Communication

Lance R. Lippert and Philip J. Aust

This chapter helps you see the usefulness of understanding the role of communication in an organization, why communication happens the way it does, and what part you play in the communication and message exchange as a member of an organization. We look at how professionals and scholars define organizational communication and why it is beneficial to study communication in an organization. Next, it provides a synopsis of organizational communication's history and its development. Finally, it presents five theoretical approaches with respective theories to help you understand and predict how communication functions in an organization. You will learn that there is not one optimum way or single theory to communicate or manage in an organization (Cummings, Long, & Lewis, 1987).

In this chapter, you will read about the following concepts:

- The history of an academic field
- Definition of an organization
- Why study organizational communication
- Definition of organizational communication
- Organizational communication theories
  - Systems theory
  - Classical or scientific management theories
  - Human relations theory
    - Motivation-hygiene theory
    - Theory X
    - Theory Y
  - Human resources theory
    - Hierarchy of needs theory
    - Theory Z
  - Cultural approach theories

Janice Gooden could hardly believe that her four years of higher education were almost over. Now midway through the final semester of her senior year, Janice was coming to grips with the inevitable; her college career was drawing to a close, and she needed a job—fast. By completing a major in communication and a minor in business, Janice had prepared herself well for obtaining the people-oriented, corporate position that she desired.

After having successfully navigated interviews with several prominent companies in the greater Chicago area, she was in the desirable position of having to select from one of several offers. The pressing question now was, "Which offer do I take?" As she contemplated her prospects, she had a growing sense that each company was unique. "But," she thought to herself, "what makes each company distinct, and what criteria do I use to make my decision?" As Janice mulled over her offers, she had a heightened awareness of how an organizational communication course she had taken provided her insights concerning whether she would like a given job or not.

In this case, Janice recognized that certain things jumped out at her from each company. For instance, she found herself trying to understand the reasoning and motivation behind each organization's values, communication behaviors, hiring practices, management styles, roles and rules, decision making, and performance expectations. It also became clear to her that each corporation reflected one of five main theoretical organizational communication approaches: the systems, classical, human relations, human resources, and cultural approaches. Janice recalled how often one of her favorite professors stated that theory and practice go and in hand. As her professor used to say, "A meaningful understanding of theory provides a foundation for working internally and externally with any organization." Having an awareness of these five approaches increased Janice's confidence that she would not only make the right decision but would have solid footing for cultivating her own effective communication in whichever company she chose.

The remainder of this chapter provides a general understanding of organizational communication theory so that you will more fully understand communication's study of organizational processes as a unique kind of communication research. By understanding all five meta-theoretical approaches, you will have a clearer sense of how each one explains an organization. Ultimately, this information represents an intersection of theory and application that will inform your daily choices, develop your critical eye, and enhance your sense-making abilities as you communicate in any organizational context. The most logical place to begin is to understand how the discipline began.

What Is the History of Organizational Communication as an Academic Field?

Sometimes to gain a better sense of what is currently going on in the world, it is helpful to take a quick look in the rearview mirror. A glimpse of history offers a unique and reflective perspective. In this case, the study of organizational communication reveals progressive insights into organizational processes, theories, structures, and relationships. As our understanding of the various workings of organizational communication grew, so did the overall effectiveness of organizations.

The field of organizational communication has roots in the last century and, depending upon the interpretation, even possibly as far back as Marx and Aristotle. As an academic discipline, organizational communication has its formalized beginnings in this country in the 1940s and 1950s (Redding, 1985). Initially, scholars looked at the organizational behavior of workers but not at the communication (portrayed by the classical approach). Only within the last forty to sixty years have scholars and practitioners started to see the importance of studying communication and the need to investigate the role of communication in organizations. In the 1960s and 1970s, several key studies started to define the field, summarize research, and provide a theoretical footing (Tompkins & Wanca-Thibault, 2001).

Basically, the development of the discipline can best be described by three major periods: (1) The era of preparations (1900–1940) emphasizes communication skills training in regard to certain organizational relationships for the individual in the organization. Theories developed during these decades look at how the member of an organization fits into the organization at large and how the corporate member can communicate effectively within the corporation.

(2) The era of identification and consolidation (1940–1970) signaled the study of the emergence of business communication and business relationships. Theories were shaped that explained and predicted more in depth how the causes and effects of organizational behavior and organizational communication affected the organization itself, other organizations and the surrounding environment, and all the people affected by the organization. The relationships of businesses to other businesses and the study of organizational communication as a unique kind of communication mark this period of theory development. Specific theoretical applications and processes became more consequential, more interested in what events or kinds of communication caused what results.

(3) The era of maturity and innovation (since 1970) sees an effort by researchers to develop the theoretical underpinnings of organizational communication necessary for a changing workplace and workforce (Redding & Tompkins, 1988). Organizational theory today not only explains communication within and among organizations but attempts to use knowledge of communication theory to change the workplace for the better. Contemporary organizational theory acknowledges that multiple kinds of organizational settings exist, each with its own unique qualities and communication demands.

Each period expanded on the previous period's work and focus while privileging new aspects of organization communication and research methodologies. Each of these historical developments is marked by the various organizational approaches and theories that are unique to the era. Early on, the focus was on message transmission and communication skills. Later, the 1960s gave emphasis to formal channels and downward communication between supervisor and subordinates. In the 1970s, Redding's (1972) summary revealed a much more holistic view of the academic field. He provided a unique perspective by emphasizing effective listening, suggesting that organizational climate is more important for communication than skills, stating the importance of shared meaning and receiver-message fidelity, and calling for feedback responsiveness to subordinates. Although interpersonal relations and communication skills are still vital in today's workplace and research agenda, the field has continually expanded its view of communication in organizations to include such phenomena as upward communication, organizational culture, participative decision making, crisis management, power and persuasion, internal and external communication networks, management styles, and teams.

According to the three paradigms of scientific, humanistic, and critical approaches, organizational theory demonstrates that its earliest theorizations were according to the scientific paradigm. Organizations were first studied as objective, material entities that were, additionally, composed of people. The two early theoretical approaches of systems theory and the classical or scientific management theories approach the study of organizations and their members largely through observations and measuring variables, also consistent with the systems kind of research.

The next two theoretical approaches of human relations theory and human resources theory reveal a more humanistic paradigm, where theories are developed to interpret organizations and their personnel through deeper, human interactions and meanings. These more subjective approaches are consistent with the rules and laws kinds of research. The final theoretical model of cultural approach theories shares qualities of the humanistic paradigm but fits mostly with the critical paradigm.

This brief overview of the history of organizational theory development serves to introduce you to the study of organizational communication. But, actually, the history of organizational communication and theory is continued throughout the rest of this chapter. The bulk of this chapter presents the five theoretical approaches that mark the significant developments in organizational theory. But first, some definitions.

What Is an Organization?

An **organization** entails a group of people who have committed themselves to working toward accomplishing a collective number of goals or missions. In doing so, they reflect a distinct structure and hierarchy. Organizations characteristically entail some formal and informal permanent relationships that interact for the purpose of working towards a general end. This effort involves the organization or the planned coordination of "collective activities of people who, functioning on a relatively continuous basis and through division of labor and hierarchy of authority, seek to achieve a common goal or set of goals" (Robbins, 1983, p. 5). Each individual has a specific role or set of responsibilities within a designed hierarchy that determines who is in charge or has control over whom, job and task responsibilities, and the formal channels of communication. Figure 19.1 exemplifies a typical business meeting where jobs and task responsibilities are sorted out; in this meeting of the Biogen Community Laboratory, plans for announcing a new laboratory opening are discussed.

Structure is an inherent part of any organization. Basically, an organization allows a group of individuals in different organizational roles to achieve some common, explicit goal and function as a systemlike collection of interrelated parts. It does this by providing a blueprint of rules and an outline for their coordination that allows for the members of an organization to gain a degree of organizational competency. We organize to get things done. Individuals organize through communication. Not every individual within the organization has to totally agree with the organizational goals, but each individual has to be

FIGURE 19.1 *Meeting of Biogen Community Laboratory.* August 22, 2002: Biogen Community Laboratory's Chairman and CEO James C. Mullen conducts a business meeting announcing the opening of the new laboratory to students.

Courtesy PRNewsFoto, NewsCom.com

willing to participate and commit on some level in order for the organization to function effectively.

Even with specific structure and norms, organizations are not neat packages of procedures but rather bubbling cauldrons of human behaviors, attitudes, communication, agendas, and endeavors that cannot always be predicted, monitored, or controlled. It is important to remember that organizations are more than just containers of communication. Organizations are living entities with permeable boundaries that allow for the integration of internal and external environments involving various stakeholders and their communication. In other words, organizational members and their communication with coworkers as well as with anyone the organization encounters make up an organization and its culture.

Why Should We Study Organizational Communication?

Eventually, each of us comes across some form of a public, private, nonprofit, governmental, or social organization, whether we are functioning as a member, employee, owner, customer, student, or supplier. We come into contact with organizations on a daily basis. You might be returning a purchase, registering for class, applying for a job, or dealing with job stress or burnout. Organizations are everywhere. The pervasiveness of organizations in our professional and personal lives makes having some working knowledge of organizations a useful thing for our self-survival. Learning about the function of communication in an organization is one way to better understand how organizations work and how individuals function in an organization.

Individuals have to learn how to survive and get along in an organization. This can involve something as basic as becoming an effective listener, improving verbal skills, developing interpersonal skills, or learning to manage a meeting. Studying organizational communication assists you in developing as a competent organizational communicator. It is important to recognize the impact communication has on organizational productivity, relationships, longevity, rules, structure, and satisfaction. Organizations are the dominant form of institution in our society (Robbins, 1983).

Every type of communication you are reading about in this book intersects at some point within an organization. By attempting to understand the dynamics of communication in an organization, you can gain valuable insights into organizational structure as you work to become a competent, ethical communicator. The workplace and characteristics of the workforce that you are a part of and that you are encountering are changing. With the start of a new millennium, globalization and technology are reconfiguring the face of traditional organizations; you need to anticipate changing needs and marketplace requirements or demands as you determine where you might want to seek employment or whether you want to establish your own business. As an informed student of today's changing landscape, it is never too early for you to start considering your options and heightening your awareness of organizational communication research.

What Is Organizational Communication?

There are numerous definitions of organizational communication. Ultimately, how practitioners and scholars conceptualize organizational communication depends on their experiences, what they see, and how they view communication. Deetz (2001) sees the process of defining organizational communication as problematic and challenges us to move beyond just a single approach. Ultimately, the question "What is organizational communication?" is misleading. A more interesting question is, "What do we see or what are we able to do if we think of organizational communication in one way versus another?" Unlike a definition, the attempt here is not to get it right, but to understand our choices.

The study of organizational communication puts the focus on the creation, exchange, and movement of messages and the meaning attached to these messages by the persons within the organization. The concept of organizational communication should sound very familiar to you because it includes some of the key variables from some of the basic definitions of communication that you have already read about in this book.

An expanded definition could be that **organizational communication** is the process of creating, sending, and receiving messages in a complex system, which includes a net of integrated internal and external relationships comprising individuals working to manage organizational ambiguity and achieve an outcome or goal. Organizational communication is a process in that it is in constant progression and transformation. The communication in an organization is always changing based upon each person in the organization, his or her interactions, and his or her activities. Messages are at the heart of organizational communication. It is through the creation and exchange of messages that individuals attempt to share meaning and move information with verbal and nonverbal communicative behavior throughout a variety of channels in the organization. A more straightforward definition could refer to **organizational communication** as the sending and receiving of messages in a complex organization. This means that individuals need to be proficient in conveying and interpreting messages or information within a particular hierarchy or structure. The organizational complexity entails workings such as role assignments, organizational entry, socialization, cultural adaptation, performance evaluations, human relations, information management, management, leadership, decision making, conflict management, internal and external communication, communication flow, and communication skills (such as reading, speaking, listening, and writing). Each of these requires the organizational members to display varying degrees of competency and knowledge in order to survive and perform as productive members. Primarily, organizational communication allows individuals to deal with task completion or operation issues, maintain regulations, and develop public, and employ human, relations. [Web site: What Is Organizational Communication?]

Regardless of what definition you feel works best based upon your experiences and perspective, scholars and current organizational texts (Daniels, Spiker, & Papa, 1997; Eisenberg & Goodall, 2001; Miller, 1999; Shockley-Zalabak, 2002; Stohl, 1995) recognize several common features: (1) organizational communication occurs within a complex open system; (2) organizational communication involves internal and external environments concerning multiple stakeholders; (3) organizational communication is an ongoing process; (4) organizational communication involves participants constructing and sharing messages about ideas, objectives, and concepts attempting to make sense of their environment and cope with uncertainties; (5) organizational communication involves messages that flow through formal and informal channels; and (6) organizational communication involves superior and subordinate communication by individuals through their attitudes, feelings, relationships, satisfaction, self-concepts, and skills.

What Are the Most Important Organizational Communication Theoretical Perspectives?

In the upcoming sections, we will discuss five primary schools of thought or theoretical perspectives that will help you understand how communication functions within an organizational structure. Each theoretical perspective or organizational approach contributes new ways of looking at an organization and new ways to understand organizational communication. With each of the five organizational models, we recognize how each approach contributes something to our entire understanding and appreciation of organizational communication. Each approach adds one more spoke to an organizational wheel that displays the progressive development of the discipline and helps us see the interrelated nature of each one to the others (see Figure 19.2).

The Systems Theoretical Approach

The **systems theory approach** represents the earliest kind of organizational communication understanding and represents another example of the systems approach, in this instance in organizational communication research. The systems perspective distinguishes an organization based on the sum of its parts. Essentially, when an organization's parts work together as a unit, the organization may be identified as a system (Rapoport & Horvath, 1968). According to general systems theory, distinguishing an organization as a system allows for its parts to be described, and, furthermore, the relationship between those parts comes into

FIGURE 19.2 *The Five-Spoked Organizational Communication Model.*

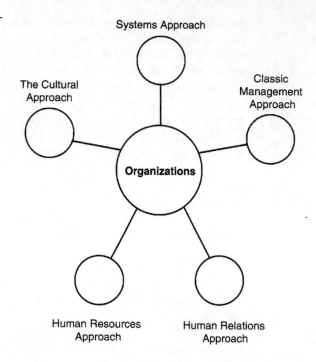

focus. Recognizing how any organization's parts are arranged provides vital clarity for understanding an organization in its entirety.

The human body serves as a nice metaphor for understanding systems theory. Consider the nature of the relationships among all of the body parts that collectively function to produce life. Together the individual organs and parts work together to form a unique system called the human body. Without the physiological interdependence, the sum of all the parts would be quite different.

Although widely used by organizational communication practitioners today, systems theory originated with the work of someone outside the discipline. Specifically, it began with a theoretical biologist named Ludwig von Bertalanffy (Eisenberg & Goodall, 2001). Through the 1920s and 1930s, Bertalanffy's contribution to science came by classifying organisms according to their relationships to one another. Although most biologists initially opposed his ideas, Bertalanffy's persistence and the continual revision of his ideas eventually were met with acceptance, especially after the Society for General Systems Research was founded in the mid 1950s (Littlejohn, 1989). Once established, Bertalanffy encouraged all disciplines to use general systems theory (GST) to further scientific inquiry. The theory's explanatory power made it an ideal tool for clarifying an organization's functions and processes.

Since the inception of GST, many organizational scholars have used and refined the systems approach to make clear the bearing of communication on an organization's processes. For instance, communication researchers have come to recognize that systems have certain basic properties such as holism (i.e., an organization is more than the sum of its parts, or greatest productivity occurs when all parts work together rather than alone), equifinality (i.e., an organization may reach a goal one of several ways), negative entropy (i.e., an organization must remain dynamic or it will falter), and requisite variety (i.e., an organization must be aware of and adjust to its external environment or it will cease to exist) (Miller, 1999). These basic system properties tend to emphasize the interconnectedness of organizational parts and resources.

Karl Weick's theory of organizing, or sense making, is one example of systems theory where the organizational members attempt to make sense of their environment or interpret current and previous organizational happenings through their communication. An organization is more than just a physical entity or object with set structures and hierarchies. Rather, an organization is the dynamic interplay of patterned relationships through which individuals enact or construct their environment through their communication. The ongoing interaction among the organizational members comprises the organization. Communication is the basis for human organizing. It is through communication that workers and management make sense of the place they call the organization.

Making their enacted environment less equivocal or more sensical is the goal for organizational members. The process of organizing involves reducing uncertainty to a manageable level and resolving the unpredictability inherent in any complex information environment. Weick's theory focuses on the verb *organizing* rather than the noun *organization*. This theory highlights the notion of an integrated environment with permeable boundaries and component interdependence. These "networks of self-regulating casual links are realized in a form of coordinated behavior between two or more people" (Weick, 1979, p. 13). Simply put, the theory of organizing says that organizations are more than just containers where communication and message exchanges occur. An organization is the sum of its members' communication and the rationalization of organizational meaning.

Overall, a general understanding of systems theory (see Figure 19.3) allows one to be attuned to the particular organization; moreover, it permits a fuller understanding of how basic internal and external components interact with each other and how organizations relate to one another (e.g., Wal-Mart, its suppliers, and its customers). [Web site: The Systems Theoretical Approach]

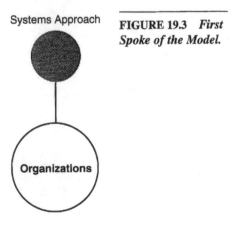

Systems Approach

FIGURE 19.3 *First Spoke of the Model.*

Organizations

Classical or Scientific Management Theory

With the arrival of the Industrial Revolution in Western culture during the late 1800s came a new way to accomplish tasks, produce goods, and organize businesses. Mechanization and manufacturing started to set the pace as the means of production, rather than the individual crafting of goods. Businesses organized workers into assembly lines and started mass-producing products to meet the demands of a rapidly changing culture and society that wanted new and improved merchandise to modernize their lives. This new type of business created new concerns for how owners and managers organized the workplace. Industrialization posed new questions for owners, managers, and workers concerning their understanding of how the company operated and how the company should best operate. At the turn of the century, early studies of organizational behavior did not necessarily focus on communication but rather on problems of productivity and the means to enhance workers' motivation to be more productive. Initially at best, communication was peripheral to the issue of organizational effectiveness and the economics of business profits. Owners wanted to know what they should do in their organizations to maximize profits (see Figure 19.4). They considered workers to be just one spoke in the wheel or one variable in the equation to achieve financial success and efficiently organize their businesses.

Turn-of-the-century researchers Henri Fayol, Frederick Taylor, and Max Weber represent this general school of thought, which focused more on the structure and shape of an organization rather than on the communication. These three men attempted to explain and predict how an organization should work and how management and workers should ideally function. A machine metaphor, characterized by three basic elements, has often been utilized to describe this general approach: specialization, standardization, and predictability (Miller, 1999). This metaphor implies that each employee has a specific task to ac-

FIGURE 19.4 *IBM CEO Plans New Era of Business.* October 30, 2002: IBM CEO Sam Palmisano tells customers of plans for maximizing corporate profits, stating that IBM has committed $10 billion to usher in the "On Demand" era of business. The IBM initative will help companies move information faster and transform key business processes. The $10 billion is funding research and development, acquisitions, advertising, and new IBM On Demand Design Centers around the world.

Courtesy Feature Photo Service, NewsCom.com

complish or job to do in relation to the whole. The quality of the task or the role being filled is more important than the qualities that the person brings to the job. Each individual is re-placeable if they fail to do the job. The role that the person fills becomes standardized to minimize loss. The organization achieves consistent operations through centralized power or control and implementation of rules and standards that supply a fixed rationale for how individuals should do a job or task. If each individual or part does the job the way man-agement expects or predicts, the entire machine or organization will properly function. If not, a breakdown occurs.

We might consider thanking Frederick Taylor, an American businessman with a keen eye and an accurate stopwatch, for our fast food society. The father of scientific manage-ment demonstrated that there is one best way to do a job in certain amount of time. Any deviation from that set standard would impact the running of a well-oiled machine and, ul-timately, organizational efficiency or profit's bottom line. Driven by poor work quality, em-ployee self-interest, and employee manipulation of production, Taylor used time and motion studies to control individuals' work performance. Even though Taylor highlighted organizational role variations between managers and workers, he maintained that a good relationship is crucial. "The mutual interdependence of management and workers, and the necessity of their working together towards the common aim of increased prosperity for all, seemed completely self-evident to Taylor. He was thus driven to ask: why is there so much antagonism and inefficiency?" (Pugh & Hickson, 2000, p. 148). Still, Taylor focused on identifying the right person for the job, the one best way to do the job, and precise and effective training (Taylor, 1911).

Fayol believed that managers alone have the responsibility to determine strategic planning and coordination of task and resources. His main focus is on how management can best perform for optimal organizational outcome through highly structured organiza-tional hierarchies, with centralized control, equitable or fair pay, and clear rules. His prin-ciples of management (Fayol, 1949) include such things as the scalar chain (vertical chain of command), division of labor (specialization), unity of command (one manager), cen-tralization (consolidation of decision making), span of control (number of employees under direct supervision of one manager), and esprit de corps (high satisfaction and morale).

Weber, a German sociologist, introduced the theory of bureaucracy that described the ultimate form an organization should take. Although today we often associate negative things with a bureaucracy, such as red tape, impersonal communication, waiting in lines, and duplication, there are some positive organizational aspects such as explicit rules and exact patterns of acceptable behavior that form predictable organizational expectations. The impersonal nature of some organizational bureaucracies provides an unemotional ra-tionality that could expedite decision making and offer familiar routines for workers and customers. Weber saw this as the most efficient form of organizational functioning. The theory is very similar to what Fayol proposed. However, Weber varies mainly in that he be-lieved certain persons need to be in authority and that this is inherent in the organizational hierarchy. Individuals can earn authority, establish authority through organizational rules and norms, or implement it by legal means (Goldhaber, 1990). With his emphasis on the importance of rules, the division of labor, centralized power, and an established hierarchy, Weber's bureaucracy centered on an impersonal organization driven by knowledge and ra-tional thought rather than emotion and outside influence (Weber, 1947).

One example of an outgrowth of this perspective comes from Douglas McGregor's work in the 1950s and 1960s in which he depicts a wide range of beliefs and assumptions held by managers about individuals and human nature. Theory X and Theory Y of organizational behavior and management style represent opposite views in organizational thinking and perspectives. Certain aspects of the classical school of thought, such as centralized power, controlled decision making, designated authority, and an ascribed hierarchy, motivated McGregor's Theory X (McGregor, 1960). In **Theory X** employees are seen as unmotivated, resistant to change, avoiding responsibility, and apathetic to organizational goals. **Theory Y** is associated with the human relations approach (explained in the next section of this chapter), which attempts to maximize human potential and meet basic needs of the employees. If managers adhere to these assumptions, they might tend to micromanage, making all of the decisions, closely supervising employee behavior, or using reward-punishment influencing tactics. This is an example of a prototypical classical manager (see Figure 19.5). McGregor (1967) made it a point to clarify that Theory X and Theory Y are not representative of managerial styles but rather reflect underlying beliefs that might influence a manager's behavior. While somewhat divergent, these theories are not mutually exclusive. In other words, a manager can hold both X and Y beliefs depending upon the task, the context, or the personalities of the people involved in the interaction. [Web site: Classical or Scientific Management Theory]

The Human Relations Approach

A third major perspective of organizational communication is termed the human relations approach (see Figure 19.6). Human relations theories focus on how organizational members communicate or relate to one another. Their emergence is typically traced to two causes. First, many researchers and pragmatists recognized that the classical approach to communication had shortcomings (Miller, 1999). First, employees who work in an organization embracing the classical approach have a tendency to feel neglected in that they are viewed as parts of a production line rather than as complex entities. Second, the eventual publication and dissemination of the findings of a series of studies conducted from 1927 to 1932 examining worker productivity at an electric plant just outside of Chicago

FIGURE 19.5 *Second Spoke of the Model.*

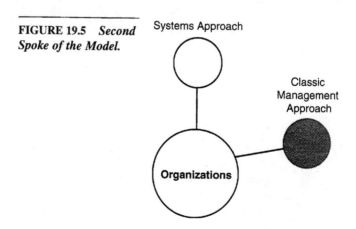

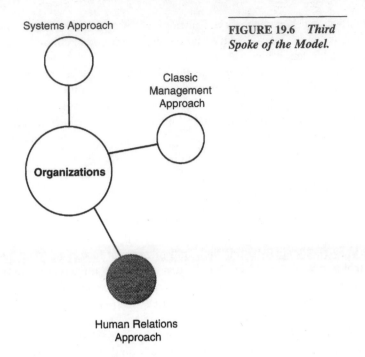

Systems Approach

Classic Management Approach

Organizations

Human Relations Approach

FIGURE 19.6   *Third Spoke of the Model.*

made researchers rethink the importance of social interaction and attention on employee productivity.

At the time, a team of Harvard scientists headed up by Elton Mayo were called in by the plant's manager to determine why employees of the Hawthorne plant were experiencing low employee satisfaction, high job turnover, and poor overall efficiency. After extensive observations, the researchers determined that no matter what changes were made to working conditions (e.g., increased lighting in the room or decreased lighting in the room), the common denominator of increased productivity and job satisfaction was the researchers' presence. Despite the fact that the studies' findings have been called into question, the **Hawthorne studies** resulted in significant interest by organizational scholars and business managers. The result was the advancement of numerous theories explaining the importance of acknowledging employees as beings impacted by social interaction rather than simply as parts of a machine. Two such theories provide a more thorough understanding of this approach: Herzberg's motivation-hygiene theory (Herzberg, 1966), and McGregor's Theory Y (McGregor, 1960). A summary of each theory provides a unique understanding of communication's role in organizational relationships.

Motivation-hygiene theory addresses the role of employee happiness and its bearing on organizational relationships in the workplace. The theory got its unique name from Frederick Herzberg, a researcher with a background in mental health and a familiarity with job satisfaction literature. Based on years of professional observation, Herzberg argued that employees experience happiness as a result of internal and external factors. Those items that impact an employee internally are identified as **motivational factors.** Internal factors include such things as "responsibility, achievement, and recognition" (Miller, 1999, p. 33).

According to motivational-hygiene theory, if an employee has an opportunity to have some level of responsibility on the job, the individual will have a higher likelihood of being satisfied and then work harder.

Herzberg also advanced that those items that impact an employee externally are hygiene factors. **Hygiene factors** include such things as working conditions, salary benefits, and company policy. For instance, if an employee were required to work in an environment that is damp and dark, over time the individual would most likely become dissatisfied with work and as a result become less productive.

In line with organizational literature, Herzberg formally uses the terms satisfaction and dissatisfaction in place of happy and unhappy to describe employee experience, but motivational hygiene theory's description of satisfaction and dissatisfaction makes it unique. Rather than conceive of satisfaction and dissatisfaction as polar opposites, Herzberg argues that satisfaction and dissatisfaction are separate processes affected by independent factors. **Employee satisfaction** is thus the result of internal factors in an organization, and employee dissatisfaction is the result of external factors in an organization. Based on this explanation, an employee can be satisfied (based on internal factors) and indifferent to external factors, satisfied (with internal factors) and dissatisfied (with external factors), indifferent (to internal factors) and dissatisfied (with external factors), or neither satisfied (with internal factors) nor dissatisfied (with external factors). In short, based on motivation-hygiene theory, a manager must be attuned to the factors that promote satisfaction as well as the factors that minimize dissatisfaction so that employee productivity is maximized. The absence or presence of these factors lead to your satisfaction or dissatisfaction with the workplace.

Along with motivation-hygiene theory, Theory Y has been recognized as representative of the human relation's approach. Douglas McGregor, a professor at the Massachusetts Institute of Technology, developed Theory Y in the late 1950s and early 1960s. As McGregor contends, Theory Y is one of two main organizational leadership styles. It is characteristically juxtaposed to its counterpart the classic-management-oriented Theory X, which advances that organizational communication needs to be hierarchical and autocratic because humans are basically lazy, self-centered, and not bright (McGregor, 1960). Conversely, **Theory Y** recognizes humans as easy to motivate (focused especially when clear goals exists) and full of potential. Managers who see their employees in this light stress the importance of employee feedback in attaining organizational goals. As a result, managers applying Theory Y often obtain feedback from employees in order to make more informed decisions. [Web site: The Human Relations Approach]

Human Resources Theories

A fourth major theoretical approach of organizational communication is the human resources perspective. Human resource theories deem humans resources that are to be valued and tapped for organizational development. Human resource theoreticians, reacting to the shortcomings of the human relations perspective, believe that employee satisfaction and organizational goal attainment are not mutually exclusive objectives. Indeed, organizational goals are best structured by keeping employee needs in mind. In this theoretical perspective, employees are an organization's greatest resource and must be used wisely. There are multiple theories representative of the human resources perspective, but this chapter will discuss and then illustrate just two: hierarchy of needs theory and Theory Z.

Hierarchy of needs theory advances that human action is the result of a quest to satisfy needs. If one's base needs are satisfied, an individual will seek to satisfy higher-level needs. The theory was developed by Abraham Maslow and aimed to explain what motivates humans (Maslow, 1943, 1954). Maslow advances that different levels of needs motivate humans. They include physiological needs, or needs for food and clothing; safety needs, or the human need to be free of danger (including shelter and employment); affection needs (a need to be loved and have respect from one's peers); self-esteem needs (such as salary, rank, status, responsibility); and self-actualization needs (such as an ability to creatively pursue one's ultimate potential) (Eisenberg & Goodall, 2001).

Another human relations perspective follows on the heels of McGregor's theories X and Y. **Theory Z** moves away from a leader-follower relational model and instead advocates collaboration as essential to organizational success. Put another way, organizations are most apt to succeed when employees are seen as equals and when all of an organization's members are instrumental in helping the organization adapt to the changing global marketplace. William Ouchi (1981) originated Theory Z and advanced it as a way of explaining why American industry was taking a backseat to Japanese industry through the 1970s. Ouchi felt that the reason Japan experienced such success was based on a difference in cultural values. In his view, America's championing of individual success as opposed to "the Japanese emphasis on the . . . performance and well-being of the collective" prevented the United States industry from competing with its Japanese neighbors (Eisenberg & Goodall, 2001). Ouchi argued that American organizations needed to integrate their current emphasis on individual achievement while giving greater importance to workplace community. Is this a realistic outcome? Not every organization is equipped to achieve this integration. Remember that building relationships and creating team climates takes time and commitment from workers as well as management. Organizations all too often cannot make the transformation because of a lack of follow-through, a competitive workplace, insufficient commitment, and slow cultural change. If an organization can achieve this type of culture, the relationships within American organizations will be tighter, and organizations will have a greater likelihood of meeting the demands of the changing marketplace. [Web site: Human Resources Theories]

Cultural Approach

In this fifth section, we are looking at organizational culture. This approach basically indicates that there is more to an organization than just the structure, roles, or rules. Also important is communication and how the organizational members make sense of their environment through their interactions, shared beliefs, and values. Whether you realize it or not, you continually encounter some form of culture. Sometimes in this country we use the word "culture" to denote high class, sophistication, artistic taste, or style; however, most often we tend to think about culture in a general sense and equate culture with someone's nationality or country of origin. If someone from Japan visits this country, we recognize that they might have certain cultural differences and expectations as compared to our culture, such as language, symbols, diet preferences, traditions, values, practices, or social courtesies that might influence how we communicate and get along.

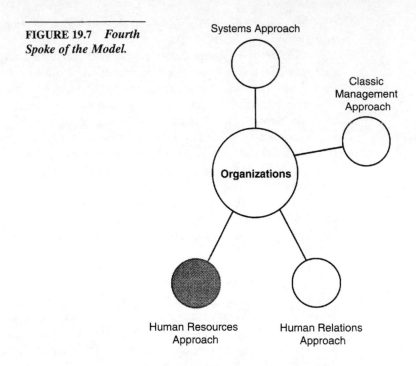

FIGURE 19.7 *Fourth Spoke of the Model.*

Maybe you have visited another country and experienced "culture shock." The culture is new to you and different from what you are familiar with or have been accustomed to for most of your life. Various cultural characteristics comprise each country, while each national culture consists of multiple co-cultures, smaller cultures, or groups. In other words, there is not just one big culture that incorporates everyone. Maybe you are from a small town or rural area and remember your first visit to a big city; you probably noticed some very specific variations between the two locations and the citizens.

Also, refer to your family experiences. Sure, there are some elements that most families have in common, but there are some very distinct aspects about each of our own families that make them unique including: (1) family stories; (2) family traditions and customs such as the family vacation, everyone sitting down at mealtime, and holiday celebrations and rituals; and (3) family rules such as respect for our elders or not wearing our shoes on the carpet. As family members, we learn certain values, appropriate behaviors, and worldviews in order to be a part of the family and to be identified as someone belonging to a particular family in the neighborhood.

With this in mind, we want you to consider that just as the United States or even your family has its own culture laced with its own unique traditions, values, beliefs, behaviors, customs, stories, and norms, so does an organization. Each individual organization has its own distinct culture with "its own way of doing what it does" formed through the organizational members' interactions (Pacanowsky & D'Donnell-Trujillo, 1983). This marks the organization as unique from another organization and individuals as members of a specific organization. Each organization has its own characteristics that represent some particular meaning to individuals in the organization.

Yes, this particular approach is a bit abstract, but we want to make sure that you take into account more than just content, structure, or things when you observe and describe an organization. "Shared values, shared beliefs, shared meanings, shared understandings, and shared sense making are all different ways of describing culture" (Morgan, 1997, p. 138). From a communication perspective, individuals create culture through their interactions and by how they interpret or come to terms with what everything means to them and the organization.

Scott and Hart (1989) tell us that in the 1980's organizational management borrowed some proven anthropological concepts and applied them to organizational performance outcomes. An example of this includes several popular books that turned some heads as they identified key elements of "strong" and "excellent" cultures (Deal & Kennedy, 1982; Peters & Waterman, 1982). If an organization had some of these cultural characteristics exhibited by successful organizations (such as identifiable values, organizational heroes, and a tendency for action), any company would be a healthier place to work. However, theorists and practitioners have a difficult time agreeing on what culture is, let alone trying to plug this concept into organizational life. The intangible qualities of culture and the role culture plays in an organization do not always neatly unpack.

Schein (1992) provides one formal model of organizational culture that highlights the process of socialization, lasting and shared beliefs, and overt behavior. The model has three levels: artifacts, espoused values, and basic assumptions. On the first level, artifacts and behaviors comprise visible organizational components. You might observe written documents, art work, the office design or arrangement, stories, technology, work processes, and personal items as well as patterned communication behavior like greetings, nonverbal characteristics (eye contact), or formal/informal interactions between a boss and worker.

Espoused values comprise Schein's second level of organizational culture. These represent the sought-after or stated strategies, beliefs, and goals of an organization, what an organization would like to accomplish, or what ought to happen in the organization. On the third level, basic assumptions are at the center of what an individual believes, and how they view their world. These underlying assumptions are "unconscious, taken-for-granted" attitudes, thoughts, and feelings (Schein, 1992, p. 17). Miller (1999) suggests an **onion model of organizational culture** that is helpful in understanding the interconnectedness among the three levels (Miller, 1999). Picture Schein's model as an onion with the observable artifacts on the outside layer and the third level of assumptions at the core. In order to get to the values and assumptions, we need to peel off the outer layer or onionskin. In order to truly understand the organizational culture, we need to discover individuals' values and assumptions behind their artifacts or behaviors at the more visible layer. Kotter and Heskett (1992), in *Corporate Culture and Performance,* point out that the more visible parts of culture such group and individual behaviors are easier to change. The invisible aspects such as shared values that tend to shape a person's behaviors are more difficult to alter. Organizational culture is complex and occurs at more than just one level.

A simple example on an individual basis might be on the left hand of a married person. In this culture, the wedding ring is the artifact, while the wedding vows are the communicative behavior marking the two individuals as a couple committed for life. The espoused value is love, with the assumption being that marriage is a positive thing. An organizational example could be encouraging participation through open lines of communication and team building. The value is for the respect of the employees and their contributions, while the assumption could be that everyone has something to offer or that if you feel good about yourself, you will be more productive.

As we look at the cultural approach to organizational communication (see Figure 19.8), we should also realize that organizational cultures carry with them inherent or built-in preferences that privilege and either advantage or disadvantage one group over another. Communication, policies, rules, and structures sometimes contain discriminating elements that deny equal participation or access to opportunities for all organizational members. Also, as individuals, we need to be aware of our cultural biases and predispositions especially when they affect how we communicate or interact with other individuals in the workplace. Understanding the culture of an organization contributes useful insights into the organization's as well as the individual's motivations and expectations. This approach helps us recognize the values and assumptions behind certain organizational behaviors and artifacts.

The **theory of structuration** that you studied in Chapter 8 on small group communication is also relevant here in cultural theories of organizational communication. Recall from the study of group communication that the theory of structuration asserts that persons will follow rules of communication in certain settings—small group settings or organizational settings—without question (Giddens, 1984; Poole, Siebold, & McPhee, 1986). That is, individuals will behave according to the certain rules and traditions (or structures) that have been established and accepted by the members of that setting. Structuration accepts that just as group members will follow rules in a group situation without questioning them, so will members of an organization follow the unconscious structures, or rules, of the organization without a conscious effort. [Web site: Cultural Approach]

FIGURE 19.8 *Fifth Spoke of the Model.*

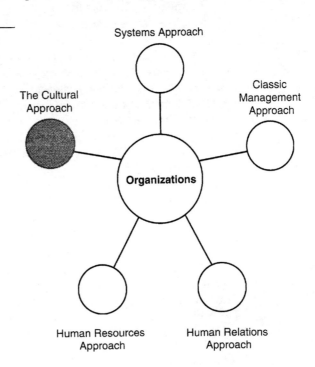

Summary

What does organizational communication entail? Hopefully, these five approaches assisted you in gaining some insights into organizational communication. We are accentuating the importance of improving your communication skills and heightening communication awareness in an organization. It is extremely useful to have working knowledge of how participants create and exchange information as well as interpersonal (relational) and presentation skills. You need to be sensitive to the organization's culture and climate as well as know how internal and external communications function. This should help you in determining if you want to work at a particular organization as well as assist you in packaging yourself as you work to get that job.

The importance of communication cannot be stressed enough. In a recent workplace assessment, managers indicated that skills such as interpersonal relations, critical thinking, and problem solving are more sought after today than ever before (Public Forum Institute, 2002). Communication is a high priority for managers and organizations looking for good employees who are effective communicators and who have good relational skills. [Web site: Summary]

Discussion Questions

1. If you were Janice Gooden, what job would you take? How would you come to this decision? What would be some of your relevant decision points? What additional information would you want or need to make this decision?

2. What is organizational communication? What are some of the organizational aspects that might influence communication?

3. Why is it important to study organizational communication? How can you relate this to some of your personal work experiences? What personal and professional experiences have you had with an organization?

4. Identify an organization that you have encountered that exhibits one of the approaches. Name the organization and describe how it depicts the particular organizational approach.

5. If you are currently an owner of a classically motivated organization, and your desire is to move more toward a human resources type of organization, what would you need to do and consider to accomplish this transformation?

6. Given the five theoretical approaches, where do you think the future of organizational communication research and practice is headed?

References

Cummings, H. W., Long, L. W., & Lewis, M. L. (1987). *Managing communication in organizations: An introduction.* Scottsdale, AZ: Gorsuch Scarisbrick.

Daniels, T. D., Spiker, B. K., & Papa, M. J. (1997). *Perspectives on organizational communication.* Boston: McGraw-Hill.

Deal, T., & Kennedy, A. (1982). *Corporate cultures: The rites and rituals of corporate life.* Reading, MA: Addison-Wesley.

Deetz, S. (2001). Conceptual foundations. In F. M. Jablin & L. L. Putnam (Eds.), *The new handbook of organizational communication: Advances in theory, research, and methods* (pp. 3–46). Thousand Oaks, CA: Sage.

Eisenberg, E. M., & Goodall, H. L. (2001). *Organizational communication: Balancing creativity and constraint.* New York: Bedford/St. Martin's.

Fayol, H. (1949). *General and industrial management* (Storrs, Trans.). London: Pitman.

Giddens, A. (1984). *The constitution of society: Outline of the theory of structuration.* Berkeley: University of California Press.

Goldhaber, G. (1990). *Organizational communication* (5th ed.). Dubuque, IA: Wm. C. Brown.

Herzberg, F. (1966). *Work and the nature of man.* Cleveland, OH: World.

Kotter, J. P., & Heskett, J. L. (1992). *Corporate cultures and performance.* New York: Free Press.

Littlejohn, S. W. (1989). *Theory of human communication* (3rd ed.). Belmont, CA: Wadsworth.

Maslow, A. H. (1943). A theory of human motivation. *Psychology Review, 50,* 370–396.

Maslow, A. H. (1954). *Motivation and personality.* New York: Harper & Row.

McGregor, D. (1960). *The human side of enterprise.* New York: McGraw-Hill.

McGregor, D. (1967). *Professional manager.* New York: McGraw-Hill.

Miller, K. (1999). *Organizational communication: Approaches and processes.* Belmont, CA: Wadsworth.

Morgan, G. (1997). *Images of organization.* (2nd ed.). Thousand Oaks, CA: Sage.

Ouchi, W. G. (1981). *Theory Z.* New York: Avon Books.

Pacanowsky, M., & D'Donnell-Trujillo, N. (1983). Organizational communication as cultural performance. *Communication Monographs, 50,* 126–147.

Peters, T. J., & Waterman, R. H. (1982). *In search of excellence: Lessons from America's best-run companies.* New York: Harper & Row.

Poole, M. S., Siebold, D. R., & McPhee, R. D. (1985). Group decision-making as a structurational process. *Quarterly Journal of Speech, 71,* 74–102.

Public Forum Institute. (2002, January). *Workforce development and the new economy.* Retrieved 9/4/02 from http://www.publicforuminstitute.org

Pugh, D. S., & Hickson, D. J. (2000). *Great writers on organizations.* Burlington, VT: Ashgate.

Rapoport, A., & Horvath, W. J. (1968). Thoughts on organization theory. In W. Buckley (Ed.), *Modern systems research for the behavioral scientist.* Chicago: Aldine.

Redding, W. C. (1972). *Communication within the organization.* New York: Industrial Communication Council; Lafayette, IN: Purdue Research Foundation.

Redding, W. C., & Tompkins, P. K. (1988). Organizational communication: Past and present tenses. In G. Goldhaber & G. Barnett (Eds.), *Handbook of organizational communication* (pp. 5–34). Norwood, NJ: Ablex.

Robbins, S. P. (1983). *Organization theory: The structure and design of organizations.* Englewood Cliffs, NJ: Prentice-Hall.

Schein, E. H. (1992). *Organizational culture and leadership.* (2nd ed.). San Francisco: Jossey-Bass.

Scott, W. G., & Hart, D. K. (1989). *Organizational values in America.* New Brunswick, NJ: Transaction Publishers.

Shockley-Zalabak, P. (2002). *Fundamentals of organizational communication: Knowledge, sensitivity, skills, values.* Boston: Allyn and Bacon.

Stohl, C. (1995). *Organizational communication: Connectedness in action.* Thousand Oaks, CA: Sage.

Taylor, F. W. (1911). *The principles of scientific management.* New York: Harper and Row.

Tompkins, P. K., & Wanca-Thibault, M. (2001). Organizational communication: Prelude and prospects. In F. Jablin & L. Putnam (Eds.), *The new handbook of organizational communication: Advances in theory, research and methods* (pp. xvii–xxxi). Thousand Oaks: Sage.

Weber, M. (1947). *Max Weber: The theory of social and economic organization* (T. Parsons & A. M. Henderson, Trans. and Eds.). New York: Free Press.

Weick, K. E. (1979). *The social psychology of organizing.* Reading, MA: Addison-Wesley.

20

Introduction and History of Public Relations

Mary Anne Moffitt

This chapter initiates the examination of public relations as a distinctive kind of communication by looking at the history of public relations and the definitive theories that explain its development. This chapter features public relations but comments on all kinds of campaign communication and defines all the commercial campaigns of marketing, advertising, and public relations and looks, as well, at political and social issue campaigns. In order to begin to understand and appreciate public relations and the various kinds of campaign communication as unique and distinctive areas of study, this chapter will briefly trace the history of public relations as a specialized area of study within communication theory, present some fundamental definitions of public relations and related business fields, and, importantly, note the important models and theories that define public relations.

In this chapter, you will read about the following concepts:

- Normative public relations
- History of public relations: A profession grows into an academic field
- Definition and conceptualization of a campaign
- Kinds of campaigns
  - Commercial: Marketing, advertising, public relations
  - Political
  - Social issue
- Fundamental theories and models
  - Role theory
  - Collaborative advocacy/Cooperative antagonism
  - Contingency theory
  - Chaos theory
  - Complexity theory

- Systems theory
- Planned behavior theory
- Diffusion of innovations and change agent theories
- Critical theories
  - Collapse theory of corporate image
  - Feminist scholarship
  - Structuralism and semiotics

Even in social life, you will never make a good impression on other people until you stop thinking about what sort of impression you are making. Even in literature and art, no [person] who bothers about originality will ever be original: whereas if you simply try to tell the truth (without caring twopence how often it has been told before) you will, nine times out of ten, become original without ever having noticed it. The principle runs through all life from top to bottom.

—C. S. Lewis (1980)
Mere Christianity

This statement by C. S. Lewis captures the essence of his ideas and his writings, both in his stories for children and in his books on theories of religion. This excerpt from one of his most well-known books advocates the power of telling the truth in all kinds of literature and art—in all kinds of communication. Communicating "your" *truth* to others, a truth that is not self-reflective or self-serving, leads inevitably to a message of originality and honesty.

This chapter opens with a call to "truth" because questions about what is truth and what is the importance of communicating honestly identify a concept central to the practice, the scholarship, and the reputation of public relations itself. Certain individuals who communicate untruths in the name of public relations hurt the reputation of public relations as an important and necessary kind of communication. Since the very birth of the nation, public relations has developed as a kind of communication that corporations, political figures, and social advocates use to tell their stories to the masses. Throughout history, however, instances of individuals and corporate spokespersons presenting falsehoods or "bending the truth to privilege their position" demonstrate negative public relations.

The lessons learned today from the past by all those who engage in public relations is that the only way to conduct excellent and accurate public relations communication is through telling the truth to all affected and interested audiences. Correct public relations, good public relations—or, in other words, **normative public relations**—is relating honestly to all groups of people, even if bad news *momentarily* weakens a political stance, hurts a corporation's image, or affects a business's profits. The good news for public relations professionals is that in the long run, truthful and accurate communication to the public pays off with public confidence and strong images for the corporation, the politician, the consumer advocate, the environmentalist, and so on.

An example of weak public relations is the Clinton response to the Monica Lewinsky scandal. If Clinton had told the truth immediately about his relationship with White House intern Lewinsky, the scandal would probably have been diffused relatively quickly.

But his stonewalling and attempt to hide the truth eventually led to a severe blow to his presidential image.

On the other hand, excellent public relations is demonstrated in two product-tampering crises that occurred in the early 1980s. The product-tampering crises of Tylenol and Girl Scout cookies in Chicago are often referenced as examples of the correct procedure for responding to a corporate crisis. After reports were confirmed that bottles of Tylenol had been tampered with and deaths had occurred, Johnson & Johnson pulled all their acetaminophen products off the shelves to protect the public. A few months later, Girl Scout cookies in the Chicago area were discovered to be embedded with foreign objects. The Girl Scouts acknowledged the tampering and immediately removed all cookie products from public sale. The product tampering "truth" of both crises was immediately communicated to the public, and, in doing so, both organizations saved their corporate images and, more importantly, saved people's suffering and probably many lives.

For sure, Lewis was not referencing the study or practice of campaign communication in his arguments for honest, outgoing communication. But his comments frame this chapter's explanation of how corporations are better off, in the long run, when they tell the truth. Since its very origins all kinds of business communication have come under fire for not telling the truth about their products, for not respecting their customers, and for their disregard for the environment at large.

For decades the tobacco industry told America that no health dangers of smoking existed—when they had evidence of dangers from cancer. The Exxon Corporation used a press conference conducted on the shores of Prince William Sound in Alaska to proclaim that the *Exxon Valdez* oil spill had been totally cleaned up and wildlife returned to the area—when they knew that neither was true. How many political candidates can you name who did not keep election promises once in office? Even social agencies come under attack when it is discovered that money is mismanaged or social benefits not realized as promised. These are only a few examples of corporate blunders and lies imposed on the general public by corporations. It is not surprising that for many people corporate communication or public relations means lies or dishonesty (see Figure 20.1).

WIZARD OF ID

FIGURE 20.1

© By permission of Johnny Hart and Creators Syndicate, Inc.

However, a revolution of sorts is happening in the field of business communication today. Advertising, marketing, and public relations are beginning to recognize their voices of honesty, or truth, for an organization. Business scholars and consultants today find that total honesty of even negative news related by a business to the public pays off in positive images and good will in the long run. Relating corporate reality and facts in a sincere and honest way to everyone in the environment is not only an ethical and moral obligation, but it is good business too (Daugherty, 2001; Day, Dong, & Robins, 2001).

Normative public relations is the focus of this chapter. Examining the history of public relations calls attention to instances of negative public relations tactics and, in turn, attests to proper public relations communication. Later, the presentation of the definitions, theories, and models of public relations will be invaluable in understanding the correct procedures for public relations communication.

What Is the Legacy of Public Relations?
A Profession Finds Its Truth

The examination of the history of public relations reveals that throughout its history, as a particular kind of communication, certain figures have engaged in public relations communication with no real effort to tell the general public the "truth." Unfortunately, given this legacy, even the term "public relations" can mean the communication of falsehoods or the manipulation of information to benefit a person or an organization.

This is a book on communication theory. However, in order to understand the theories that have been brought to the study of public relations and even to all kinds of campaign communication, it is informative to begin with a history of public relations as a profession. Knowing the history of the development of public relations as a kind of communication and eventually a distinct profession will inform, first, how public relations was recognized as a necessary kind of corporate communication and, second, how public relations developed the theories that could explain and predict its successful practice.

Early Roots of Public Relations

A major study of the history of public relations by Scott Cutlip (1995), *Public Relations History: From the 17th to the 20th Century,* marks the beginnings of public relations at the very origins of the nation and notes that, early on, persons were making exaggerated statements to suit their own interests. Cutlip notes that during the 1600s, Sir Walter Raleigh wrote letters to England pleading for colonists for Virginia. Others wrote letters and pamphlets entreating English citizens to settle Maryland, the Carolinas, Georgia, and Florida. Unfortunately, when the British citizens reached the shores of the colonies, they found the promises of a beautiful and bountiful land to be largely unfounded (Cutlip, 1995, pp. 2–10). The first fund-raising efforts were to get the new colonists to donate money for new colleges and universities; sermons, letters, and pamphlets raised money for Harvard, King's College (now Columbia University), and Princeton.

Perhaps the most interesting examples of created myths as public relations surrounds the stories of Daniel Boone (his legend created to sell land in Kentucky) and Davy Crock-

FIGURE 20.2   A study of changing images: the original Samuel Adams staged the Boston Tea Party, but today, he is the image and persona of a beer product.

Courtesy PR Newswire Photo Service and NewsCom.com

ett (stories written by his friends to show him as a great statesman when, in truth, he "spent four years loafing and boasting at the Congressional bar" (Cutlip, 1995, p. 101). "Buffalo Bill" Cody was probably the most publicized showman of the late 1880s, but he never participated in an important Indian war (Cutlip, 1995, p. 176).

Numerous examples of the importance of public relations activities that helped to found the nation are the work of revolutionaries who worked against British loyalties to persuade colonists to support an independent nation. Newspapers, pamphlets, sermons, town meetings, and organized letter-writing campaigns led the attack against British rule (Cutlip, 1995, p. 21). Samuel Adams's Boston Tea Party is credited as the first staged public relations event (see Figure 20.2). Later, various forms of publicity, especially the *Federalist Papers,* mobilized public opinion to adopt the Constitution. Throughout the terms of the earliest presidents, publicists representing political figures and their political parties were not above stretching the truth about their own parties and leaders and exaggerating negatives about the opposition. Public relations also motivated settlers to move to the West and, especially, worked to gain support for establishing the railroads throughout the country.

Professionals Identify the Academic Field

To really understand how public relations has developed into a business profession with its own theories and models and vocabulary, it is necessary to appreciate the political and historical settings that generated the need for a kind of communication known as public relations. [Web site: Big Business Changes Public Relations]

In this climate of struggling industrialization, improper and immoral business practices, and under the watchful eyes of muckrakers, public relations emerged as a necessary kind of corporate communication. Two public relations professionals are acknowledged as the founding fathers of public relations, although in truth each individual engaged in questionable communication, in Lewis's terms "untruthful" behaviors. One very important person led the way in revolutionizing business communication, the father of public relations, Ivy Lee. Lee is one of the central figures in the development of public relations (Hiebert, 1966).

In 1902, Lee was a journalist covering banking and business news in New York City, but he formed his own public relations agency when he saw the value of and need for honest and truthful corporate communication. He made a name for himself in representing coal owners and, in particular, the Rockefellers who owned the Colorado Fuel and Iron Company. Some scholars point to Lee's honesty and upfront press conferences and numerous press releases as averting several damaging coal strikes and protecting the coal owners from ruin (Grunig & Hunt, 1984, pp. 31–35). Other public relations historians, however, claim Lee engaged in blatant propaganda and often manipulated the truth (Olasky, 1987; Pearson, 1990). Olasky (1987) suggests that Lee favored the collaboration and alliances of big businesses and wanted to deny the freedoms of the individual. Some even argue that Lee's inclination to engage in psychological strategy with his audiences stems from the influence of Sigmund Freud. However, perhaps the most controversial contribution of Lee was his open support of Stalin and the Communist experiment in the Soviet Union; he even wrote a book supporting Stalin.

During the 1920s, another key public relations professional stepped up and helped define the field of public relations: Edward Bernays (Baskin & Aronoff, 1992). Bernays distinguished himself through his work on the Committee on Public Information that provided patriotic service to the United States during World War I, as a promoter for the great Italian opera singer Enrico Caruso, and by representing numerous other clients in the arts, building and construction, education, finance, government, and hotels. He also provided services to public interest groups such as the NAACP. Bernays was a public relations professional, but he was also the first teacher of public relations.

In 1922 at New York University, Bernays was the first person to teach a course in public relations and begin the institutionalization of public relations as a legitimate field within academia. He advocated the importance of research as a means to understanding the traits and qualities of audiences in order to communicate effectively to them. Bernays called for the importance of honest communication to an organization's populations and reporting to the corporation what the populations felt toward it. However, it should be noted that during the 1920s Bernays worked for a tobacco client and developed campaigns to persuade women to take up smoking; no doubt many women suffered and some perhaps even died from that campaign. Bernays's important contribution to public relations was his concept of groups of persons as "publics"; he called his strategy for appealing to the targeted populations the "crystallizing of public opinion" and the "engineering of consent" (Grunig & Hunt, 36–47). Like Lee, however, Bernays saw himself as primarily serving the organization's interests.

A realistic assessment of the growth of public relations throughout this century begins with attention to World Wars I and II. During these years of extreme political upheaval, the major use of public relations communication was by the government. Images of Uncle Sam and photos of women working in the factories and people donating their copper pennies for the war effort were all public relations messages delivered to the American populace (Baskin & Aronoff, 1992; Newsom et al., 2000).

Following the war, the huge economic boom and prosperity demanded another kind of public relations. The rapid rise of all kinds of businesses and the move of corporations to communicate their products and their image shifted the emphasis of public relations to communication to customers (see Figure 20.3).

The 1960s and 1970s marked another shift in the use of and need for public relations. During the Vietnam War years and the "me first" 1970s, the phenomenon of activist groups

FIGURE 20.3   This contemporary poster of Uncle Sam differs from the original "I Want You" enlistment poster of World War II. Today, the poster is parodied to encourage people to drink chocolate milk.

Courtesy Business Wire Photos and NewsCom.com

protesting a corporation's product or business practices emerged. This presented a totally new challenge for large and small businesses. A new threat to their livelihood was now possible and, importantly, was largely out of their control. Now businesses had to monitor their own products' safety, the satisfaction of their consumers, the satisfaction of their employees, or their potential damage to the environment.

You can see how this made the role of public relations a necessity for many businesses that regularly faced these new and demanding issues. One of the first examples of a public relations protest that challenged a company's very existence was a consumer boycott toward Dow Chemical Company; customers protested the purchase of Saran Wrap because Dow Chemical manufactured napalm for the Vietnam War. Another example is the protests that the Greenpeace organization continues to set up around the world, protesting whale kills or overfishing or oil tankers' damage to the oceans. Today, various environmental agencies exist to call attention to saving animals, preserving the forests, and cleaning the oceans, to name a few (see Figure 20.4).

The 1980s and 1990s up to today have been marked by a continuous growth in the need for public relations by corporations. Great numbers of corporations are establishing public relations departments within their organizations. Many new public relations agencies have been established, and many advertising and marketing agencies have been adopting public relations components within their agencies. Following in this section of chapters, Chapter 23 will detail the current move to integrating advertising, marketing, and public relations communication into one function of business communication for the corporation.

The 1980s and 1990s also mark a significant interest in offering public relations courses in communication departments. Today, in fact, most communication departments across the nation offer at minimum one or two courses in public relations. A huge increase in majors in public relations offered at the university level also signals the interest in public

FIGURE 20.4   This photo of an Amur tiger in the wild represents the Save the Tiger Fund, Washington, DC.

Courtesy PR Newswire Photo Service and NewsCom.com

relations today. The professional agencies of the Public Relations Society of America and the Public Relations Student Society of America were instituted as organizations that fostered the profession and the ethical performance of public relations. This gradual growth of interest in public relations peaked just ten or fifteen years ago, when an enormous leap of public relations majors and coursework signaled the importance and need for public relations instruction (Benigni et al., 2001). In addition, public relations research and theory has exploded during this period, marked by several journals, specialized conferences, and multiple lines of research exploring all the theoretical issues and applications of the field of public relations. [Web site: What Are the Important Definitions of Public Relations?]

Corporations Communicate via the Campaign

A good place to begin to understand the complexities of business communication is with the conceptualization of a **campaign.** Generally speaking, in the business world today, given all the crisis situations or image considerations that any organization faces, any business—large or small, for-profit or not-for-profit—needs to be prepared for any situation that could face it. Today's businesses can face true or false allegations of pollution of the environment, defective or harmful products, labor issues, contentious media reports, sexual harassment, and even spillover bad press from a negative incident that happens to a competitor!

Given the volatility and dynamics of commerce today, one crucial consideration for any organization is to know how to ready itself for any situation. The central principle guiding corporate communication today is conceptualizing corporate communication principally as a **campaign** (Matera & Artigue, 2001; Moffitt, 1999). Whether it be a routine communication by the corporation or a major communication project—no matter how local or nationwide—it is best to conceptualize any spoken or written communication sponsored by the organization in terms of what kind of campaign will best solve it or address it. The communication specialist working in the corporate world must consider the campaign as the guiding metaphor for doing all kinds of business communication today.

Being absolutely clear as to the definition of a campaign is an all-important place to begin to understand business communication.

> A **campaign** is the strategic and carefully thought-out design of a series of messages sent to one or more targeted populations for a discrete period of time, in response to an identified negative or positive situation affecting the organization. (Moffitt, 1999, p. 3)

Knowing the definition of a campaign is not enough for good campaign communication or good public relations, however. Today's public relations demands that the corporation not only recognize its role in sending out information but also respect and relate effectively to its important audiences. Once again, it is important to note the importance of communicating the corporation's "truth" to all its important audiences. [Web site: Corporations Communicate via the Campaign]

Classifying Kinds of Campaigns

Campaign communication is classified according to three frameworks: commercial campaigns, political campaigns, and social issue campaigns (Pfau & Parrott, 1993). The **commercial campaign** is typically planned on behalf of a for-profit organization and falls into marketing, advertising, or public relations. While marketing and advertising are very close in purpose (sales) and in the populations they communicate to (consumers, potential consumers, retailers), the field of public relations has some important differences.

For **public relations,** many more project-oriented *and* crisis campaign situations plus the obligation to target multiple audiences make it radically different from marketing and advertising campaigns (see Figure 20.5). Outside of marketing's product placement emphasis and advertising's role in sales, the business field of public relations is bigger, with responsibilities to potentially unlimited crisis or image management campaign situations and to potentially every audience that relates to the organization.

The distinctive quality that defines public relations is that of **image management.** In short, public relations creates and manages the images of a corporation and is not concerned directly with sales of the corporation's products (Moffitt, 1999; Pfau & Parrott, 1993). A look at Ryka, a tennis shoe manufacturer for women, can demonstrate. Any advertisements that Ryka places in newspapers or magazines and any shoe boxes or inserts that name Ryka shoes are advertising the product, urging the purchase of the product. At the same time, Ryka sponsors a social issue campaign against domestic violence toward women; they feature this social issue on posters, billboards, stickers, and even as a separate insert placed inside the shoe box. These messages against violence toward women are public relations messages—featuring Ryka's corporate image of concern for women.

In order to manage corporate image, public relations' function is also responsible for any crisis situation that might affect the organization; this specialty is termed **crisis management.** The function of public relations is to research any crisis event and develop messages that can address and hopefully resolve the crisis. If the Ryka tennis shoe manufacturer faces a crisis because news stories are reporting that their shoes are manufactured in Third

FIGURE 20.5 *Comparison of Public Relations, Marketing, Advertising Campaigns, and Respective Audiences.*

Public relations:
Organization communicates to:

Government agencies · Stakeholders · Owners · Industry · Employees · Potential customers · Organization · Customers · Community residents · Media · Activist groups · Retailers · Union officials

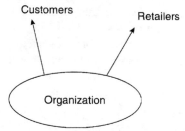

Marketing:
Organization communicates to:

Customers · Retailers · Organization

Advertising:
Organization communicates to:

Customers · Potential customers · Organization

World plants that abuse their workers and don't pay a fair wage (which is not true), then public relations professionals will need to assess the details of these allegations and respond accordingly. Even if a crisis surrounds the product and product sales—reports that the shoes are not good quality and fall apart—the communication that addresses this crisis is public relations, not advertising.

Marketing, as a field of business communication usually taught in business departments, was the first kind of commercial campaign. Its purpose is placing a company's product or service in the marketplace and, hopefully, carving a unique space and creating a singular demand for the product within all the competitive products. In marketing communication, the organization develops strategies for placing the product on the shelves, creating commercial messages about the product that set it off from all other products, and communicating to retailers and distributors about distinctive qualities of the new product. Undeniably, the process of marketing is absolutely critical for the survival of the organization. No profit-oriented business can exist without sales and without accumulated capital from the sales of its products/services.

Advertising grew out of marketing as a more specified, narrower field within marketing. The singular need to sell products led to the more specialized field of business communication known as advertising. This kind of communication is driven more by attention to the campaign messages, to creating an advertising message that will inform the current and potential customer and, hopefully, persuade the customer to try and to buy the product. As with marketing, the purpose of the campaign situation is a project—to promote an organization's product or service. Again, the corporation is usually a profit-driven organization, and the obvious targeted audiences are the customers, potential customers, and retail outlets.

A political campaign is generally conducted to get a candidate elected or a piece of legislation passed. A political campaign obviously targets voters or constituencies and necessarily the media as primary audiences. Any political candidate running for office conducts a political campaign. Any group campaigning to pass a law or revise the Constitution, such as movements to revoke abortion or to pass the Equal Rights Amendment for women, are also examples of political campaigns.

A **social issue campaign** is designed to benefit society in some way, to benefit a social/charitable cause. These kinds of campaigns can be waged by not-for-profit agencies such as Save the Oceans or Greenpeace, but are often conducted today by for-profit corporations who take on a social cause to help manage their image. For example, Mothers Against Drunk Driving and Students Against Drunk Driving are supported by State Farm Insurance and Budweiser beer. And, as noted above in the Ryka examples, this women's shoe product supports a women's social issue of stopping domestic violence.

What Are the Important Models and Theories Explaining Public Relations?

The history of public relations presented at the outset of this chapter demonstrates the important role of public relations communication throughout the nation's history. Through time, key political figures and corporate leaders exemplified the role of public relations to their organizations. This information about the growth of the profession offers insights into the research and theory development that also define the field. It is important to note here the difference in how public relations and campaign theories have developed compared to how theory development has occurred in other fields. The bottom line is this: the profession and the practice of public relations preceded any theory about public relations. The beginning of this chapter outlines the growth of public relations as a profession, as an occupation, and as a function of communication in organizations. This grounding, this basic premise, now serves to explain a lot about public relations theory.

Once the need for the profession of public relations is demonstrated, the need to understand and conceptualize how to make it better naturally follows. Interest in teaching public relations to prepare professionals, demonstrated first in Bernays's teaching at New York University in 1922, led to courses offered at the university level. And, as noted above, the institutionalization of public relations courses and majors in just the past ten years documents the remarkable interest in public relations and campaign communication study in higher education.

One more quality of public relations theory should be noted. The theorization of public relations is multidisciplinary. Even though several theories and models of public relations have been identified, many other theories of campaign strategy, campaign design, and communication flow draw on theories from other disciplines in order to apply them to the specific function of public relations. You will see in the following discussion that theories from media criticism, business, interpersonal communication, persuasion, and sociology have been applied to the understanding of public relations.

We turn now to the models and theories that explain public relations research. The theories presented first are consistent with the scientific paradigm. As you examine the models of public relations and the theories that attempt to explain and extend these models, notice how the research perspective is to study the organizational setting more or less as an "object of analysis." Definitions of models, roles, and kinds of communication are considered scientific objects that can be isolated and defined.

A very important, central model of public relations developed by James Grunig (Grunig & Hunt, 1984) about twenty years ago sets out four models for conducting public relations. These four models—also known as Grunig's **situational theory**—ground the research and theory of public relations. We will detail these models, but first an important point needs to be made about them. Over the years much discussion and controversy among scholars centered on these four kinds of public relations and explanations of the "ideal" model, the "most common" model, or a combination of models. Today, the debate still rages over how to model public relations, how to research public relations, how to theorize public relations, and how to improve campaign strategy. In order to look at the range of theories that explain and predict the field today, we need to define these four important models.

The Growth of an Academic Discipline

Another way to grasp the history of public relations and examine the details of situational theory is to examine the **models of public relations** that also serve as a way to identify historical steps in the expansion of public relations (Grunig & Hunt, 1984, pp. 21–27). As you know from your study of how public relations grew as a profession, up until the time of Bernays, any business felt free to say anything about its products, its services, its way of doing business—whether it was completely accurate or not.

We noted above that about a hundred years ago, during the early days of industrialization, businesses felt no pressure to relate the *truth* of their business. If they could get away with sending news releases that presented an untrue situation that favored the corporation and that were believed and accepted by their customers and other audiences, then it was "fair game" to get away with it. This model of practicing public relations by slanting the truth is termed the **publicity model**.

Unfortunately, this model for doing public relations is still around today. Some organizations continue to practice publicity by relating through their campaign messages or through news stories only selected facts, or even direct lies, in order to present a positive corporate image, such as claims by the tobacco industry that smoking was not a health hazard. Another example of publicity would be publicists who work for actors or athletes. These publicists typically present only news that favors their clients. For another example, if you were to examine the speeches and messages of some politicians, you might not be surprised to find that they also actively practice the publicity model of public relations.

Another, follow-up model to publicity is the model of **public information.** In this kind of public relations, an organization relates information about itself, but, importantly, in this model the information about the organization is true. No effort is made to hide the truth of an organization. This model is the most popular model of public relations practiced today.

These two models of publicity and public information are distinctive because they do not utilize any research on targeted audiences before sending out messages. In other words, messages are designed by the organization and communicated to their audiences, with no real consideration for matching the messages to the needs or attitudes of the audience members. This is why the public information model is so common; the majority of organizations today merely creates messages and puts them out randomly, without going to the trouble of researching the campaign situation or the audiences who receive the messages.

The next two models for practicing public relations, on the other hand, involve doing research, or at least enacting some efforts to understand the organization, the campaign situation, the targeted audiences, and other outside factors. These models operate on the principle that formal and informal research is important and that audience research leads to appropriate messages and successful communication. The model of **asymmetry** is public relations communication where corporate messages—truthful and accurate news—are communicated but, nevertheless, generally favor the organization, hence the term "asymmetry."

The final model of public relations practice, **symmetry,** is unique because it practices equal communication between the organization and the audiences. Unlike asymmetry, where the organization still intends to present itself in positive light, symmetrical public relations makes a conscious effort to listen to and respect the audiences enough to adjust their business practices to benefit the audiences as well as the organization. In the symmetrical model, an organization will listen to the audiences that relate to it and work to satisfy these audiences, as well as to benefit the organization. Obvious examples of ideal symmetrical public relations would be not-for-profit agencies or governmental entities that, like the USDA and National Forest and Park Services that depend on goodwill and reciprocation from their key audiences. Many researchers today advocate the symmetrical model as the ideal and optimum model for excellent public relations; following this model leads organizations to enter relationships with their important audiences that lead to better communication and understanding between the company and the audiences.

We need to present another example here of how the four models work. Let us use a case study of a large automobile manufacturing plant to demonstrate each. Consider, for example, that the automotive plant is faced with a crisis: some of the women employees have accused their managers of sexual harassment. The crisis has grown because the women filed a lawsuit and the local newspaper picked up the story.

If the corporation were to follow the publicity model of public relations, their stance would be to deny the allegations, deny that the corporation is facing a lawsuit, and communicate all the good policies they have in place that could not allow harassment (policies that really don't even exist). According to the public information model, the organization would acknowledge that yes, indeed, harassment allegations and the lawsuit are true; they would send out countless press releases, radio spots, letters, and television messages to reach as many of the community residents they could. For the asymmetrical model, however, the plant would conduct some research to identify the relevant populations in the community, gather information on the details of the harassment and the lawsuit, and gather findings on exactly what these groups feel; then the plant would create messages that told the plant's side of the story and target these messages to the concerns of each relevant population. And finally, for the symmetrical model, the plant would do the research as noted above, but it would meet with the accusing women, the accused men, members of the media, community residents, and any other important audiences and through personal and media communication establish a dialogue with the targeted audiences, in hopes that both sides will satisfy their concerns.

These models have explanatory power for understanding the various ways that an organization can respond to a crisis. However, recent public relations research has produced some additional considerations of these models. When first presented, practitioners and scholars generally accepted that an organization followed one of these models. Research findings now suggest that any organization can follow any or all of these models, depending on the campaign situation. For example, an organization can practice different models for different campaign situations and for different audiences: symmetrical communication with employees, asymmetrical model with customers, and public information with community residents. We turn now to a number of theories that cluster around the efforts of scholars to clarify and extend these models.

Theories Surround the Models

Efforts to understand the models of public relations led to scholarly interest in the roles of individuals working within each of these models. One of the earliest theories identified by scholars trying to understand public relations within the organization was **role theory** (Grunig & Hunt, 1984). Several variations of this theory explain the role of public relations professionals. One early recognition was that public relations is situated at two levels: at the technician or production level and at the manager level. That is, public relations operates as a writing or production function, usually the entry level positions in public relations; and as a managerial function, in the person who makes decisions and creates strategy. The person who writes press releases is the technician; the person who tells the writer what to put in the press release and where to send it is the manager.

Another twist on conceptualizing roles is role theory according to Broom and Dozier (1986). Broom suggests four kinds of leadership roles, which are also public relations roles (Ekachai, 1995). **Expert prescribers** are the highest-level managers, the campaign strategists, who determine the research and responses to any corporate issue. **Communication facilitators** are lower-level managers, or the "go-betweens" between the organization and the audiences; this role is more involved with direct communication from the corporation to the relevant audiences. **Problem-solving process facilitators** are mostly technician or production persons who do the research and collect information about any campaign project or campaign crisis; they report to the managers. And finally, **communication technicians** are the writers, the production staff, the photographers, and the graphic designers who create the messages and execute the campaign.

A final interpretation of role theory in public relations is fundamental to explaining the role of public relations for the organization. The public relations professional, as a link between the organization she or he works for and the environment that affects the company, serves as a **boundary role** (Grunig & Hunt, 1984). A public relations professional serves the organization and communicates to the environment while also monitoring the environment and reporting on the environment to the organization (p. 9). Public relations as boundary role, when done correctly and efficiently, demonstrates excellent public relations, or in other words, normative public relations.

Another few theories offer elaborations to the original four-model system of Grunig. In his landmark study, the IABC/Excellence Study, Grunig (1992) suggests that the original term "symmetrical" was probably a misnomer and that a better term is "collaborative advocacy" or "cooperative antagonism." Grunig's current position toward his models is the theory of **collaborative advocacy** or **cooperative antagonism**, which calls for strong dialogue between the organization and the organization's relevant populations. Out of these good relationships come understandings by both parties that can direct future solutions to problems and challenges.

Another theory attempts to more accurately explain the function of the models of public relations. **Contingency theory** (Cancel et al., 1997; Cancel et al., 1999) is a popular theory that explains that one organization can realistically utilize one of the models of public relations for one situation but then use another model for another situation. In other words, contrary to earlier positions that suggested that an organization followed one of the four models, today we acknowledge through contingency theory that organizations freely move from one model to another depending on the situation, the involved audiences, and the organization itself. As exemplified above, contingency theory explains that a company might follow the public information model to present a new park to the city but follow the symmetrical/collaborative advocacy model to get employees to donate to the park.

A few more theories also explain the function of public relations within an organization, but their contrasts to the models takes them in a completely different direction. So far, all this discussion of the four models and the follow-up theories that explain them assume that an organizational setting is relatively stagnant and easy to conceptualize. Some researchers, however, assert that given any situation, an organization can be upset, unorganized, and even chaotic. Murphy (1996) presents the **chaos theory** as an alternative model of organizational communication and public relations. She asserts that the chaos theory emphasizes uncertainty, open-endedness, plurality, and change as "constants" in any organization. Chaos theory accepts issues of diversity, feminism, multidisciplines, and volatility that can hit organizations at any time. This concept of organizations and the matching chaotic communication runs counter to traditional role theory and the relatively static notions of the four models and their supporting theories. For example, given the sexual harassment example presented above, chaos theory would suggest that whatever research is needed to address the issue, whatever is important to say and do for this crisis, and whatever will solve the crisis directs the proper solution.

Another theory similar to this figure of uncertainty is **complexity theory** (Murphy, 2000). This theory also accepts that loss of control, shifting roles, and general uncertainty typify many organizational settings and affects organizational communication. In contrast to absolute chaos, however, complexity theory views an organization as a setting of shifting communication patterns, where the actors adapt to each situation, thereby forming large-scale patterns of communication. That is, complexity theory acknowledges the flux and potential for change, but this theory focuses more on the communication patterns, on the adaptation of the persons within the setting to adjust to a crisis or new project.

Theories from Other Disciplines

Communication scholars have adapted some theories from other disciplines such as psychology and sociology to the understanding of corporate communication. The first group of theories presented here represents another one of the three research paradigms outlined in Chapter 2: the systems approach. You may recall that this research assumption contends that one way to study communication is to look for the interconnectness of elements within a communication setting. Further, the systems approach is associated with the scientific paradigm because it is mostly objective research that explains and predicts phenomena.

   A global, overarching theory that provides a fundamental explanation of public relations and how it works is **systems theory.** Systems theory, explained in more detail in Chapter 19, suggests that any communication setting—interpersonal, group, organizational—can be theorized as a "system." That is, the communication in any setting functions as a relatively autonomous and self-contained entity, with its own parts and with a unique interaction among all its parts. For example, in an interpersonal or group setting, the parties communicate to each other as part of a system that follows the rules set up by the parties, and, importantly, if one of the parts—one of the persons or a rule or an outside influence—changes, then the entire system is affected (Baskin & Aronoff, 1992, pp. 19–23; Grunig & Hunt, 1984, pp. 94–106; Kelly, 2001, pp. 279–289). The same goes for an organization as a system. A corporation or any kind of organization operates as its own system, containing the employees, the physical surroundings, and the rituals and rules set up and followed by the organization. [Web site: Systems Theory: Open and Closed System Theory; Linking the Organization to Audiences]

Campaigns Equal Persuasion

A couple of theories that have already been presented in the book, in particular in Chapter 9 on persuasion, have great significance and application to the practice of public relations. Ajzen and Fishbein's theory of **planned behavior** (Ajzen & Fishbein, 1980; Ajzen, Brown, & Rosenthal, 1996; Reinecke, Schmidt, & Ajzen, 1996, 1997), which was first termed the theory of **reasoned action** (Fishbein & Ajzen, 1975), is applicable to understanding how to affect an audience's attributes, attitudes, intentions, and behaviors. First, in the initial step of the four-part model, a belief is explained as an *attribute* a person makes toward an *object,* that is, something like "I believe that the company manufactures automobiles." The second part of the model is *attitude,* which is defined as a subjective judgment toward the object, such as "I like this company or don't like it." The third part is *intention,* which is the link between attitude and *behavior;* that is, beliefs affect motivation so that "I think I will buy that car."

   This step-by-step of the theory of planned behavior explains the process of how beliefs can eventually lead to actions. Understanding an individual's beliefs, attributes, attitudes, intentions, and behaviors can inform campaign messages that seek to influence attitudes and actions in targeted audiences. Nevertheless, the theory of planned behavior asserts that changing or affecting one attribute or attitude will not persuade a person; the important thing to remember is that an individual possesses sets of attributes *toward any one object*. The theory of planned behavior assumes that people choose their behavior (the rules approach) and also that regularities exist in all persons' behavior (the laws approach).

A couple of other theories of persuasion that you have already encountered are also relevant to understanding public relations. Rogers and Shoemaker's (1971) theory of the **diffusion of innovations** claims that messages can have great effects on an audience when spread in a two-step method. First, news stories or other information are sent through the media, and second, individuals take the media information and spread it to their friends through personal contact. This theory is a good example of the humanistic paradigm that privileges personal, human study of subjects. The diffusion of innovations theory recognizes the power of the media to initiate messages that are then picked up and spread to others through personal, human contact.

This two-step flow of information is what campaign communication is grounded on. An organization, political candidate, or social agency sends out its messages, in hopes that the message will be processed and will generate enough interest that it spreads to other receivers through word of mouth. An advertisement for a new kind of cell phone or a social issue message to support colon cancer research that appeals to audiences enough to get their attention and get discussion going among their friends is the intention of all kinds of campaign communication.

Related to this theory is the theoretical construct of **change agent.** Jackson (1986) recognized that in understanding the dispersal of information throughout society, one very persuasive factor is the role of a change agent. This could be a very respected person whom people listen to or look to for information, such as a news journalist or a financial analyst or a political figure. A change agent, also known as an opinion leader, however, can also simply be a friend or family member or colleague at work who is trusted and respected. Friends who tell each other about the new features of a cell phone are change agents; a physician extolling the benefits of colon cancer detection to a patient is also a change agent.

Informative or persuasive messages advocating knowledge, attitudes, or behaviors are often successfully delivered when delivered through a well-known change agent. You can see the relevance of this theory when conceptualizing a campaign or when designing campaign messages. The public relations professional can choose respected spokespersons or can deliver messages to key persons who will hopefully facilitate the spread of the message.

For example, think how fast a particularly shocking or significant news item presented on a television broadcast—such as the arrest of the Unabomber or an E-coli breakout in a major restaurant chain—is processed by the television viewer and then passed on to friends. You might even get on the phone to call others to tell them about the news you just saw or heard about. How many of you picked up the phone after the World Trade Center was attacked in New York? However, you might also serve as a change agent over less crucial information; your recommendation to a friend of a new shampoo product or a great film you saw over the weekend makes you a change agent for the shampoo manufacturer or for the film company.

Being "Critical" toward Corporate Image

Within the body of public relations research, several researchers have employed a critical theory perspective to help understand certain issues in public relations. Thus, the critical paradigm is also demonstrated in public relations research, which is also consistent with the subjective/interpretive approach. As you have learned in earlier chapters, the critical paradigm is concerned with power relations, with ideology, and with meanings. For the student of public relations, critical theory perspectives conceptualize an organization as expressing its own ideology through its employees, its messages, and the everyday rituals and actions of the setting. Further, issues of power are also studied in organizations; managers might have more power than technicians, or men might have more power than women. And, finally, the concept of meaning is central to critical theory; critical perspectives strive to understand how people *create* meaning and how people *receive* meanings.

One theory that offers explanations of how corporate image, or corporate ideology, is created by the organization and processed in the audience builds on a popular cultural studies model of meaning. The **collapse theory of corporate image** (Moffitt, 1994a, 1994b, 1999) presents an analogy between the elements of meaning understood by popular culture studies and the model of corporate image in public relations. For meanings of media texts, the text is processed by a receiver, which leads to meaning given to a text or leisure pursuit. The collapse theory proposes that, for the understanding of corporate image processes, the text is the organization's message, the receiver is a member of an audience relating to the organization, and the meaning becomes the image that the audience member has of the organization.

Several implications for public relations theory and practice grow out of this theory of corporate image. First, if we accept that every meaning a person has of an organization represents just one image of the organization, then individuals relating to an organization will have many, maybe hundreds, of meanings/images toward an organization, similar to the notion of polysemy in Chapter 18. Further, unlike previous positions that the organization controls its image and that image is more or less a singular construct/idea/image delivered by the company, image is now recognized also as an audience construct. That is, the audience can be seen to control an image but be free to hold numerous, changing positive and negative images toward any one organization (see Figure 20.6).

For example, consider the university you now attend. You have many things you like about the university, many things you dislike about the university, and probably many things you really don't care about or that really don't affect you about the university. According to the collapse model, every one of these pieces of knowledge, opinions, or behaviors is one image. If a public relations campaign were to be planned to communicate to the student body of your university—maybe a campaign to change parking or to institute a new major in journalism or to require all students to live on campus in dormitory housing—the campaign would have to communicate through multiple kinds of messages with multiple pieces of information in order to touch on the numerous and varied images and meanings that the student body possesses. We will go into much more detail on exactly how campaign message design works in Chapter 22 of this section, but you can see here that the collapse model has explanatory power for the theory and practice of public relations.

Another major contribution to public relations research has come from feminist scholarship that looks at issues of power in the workplace. Several public relations schol-

Each person possesses multiple images of each organizational issue that can change moment to moment.

Employees
I think the organization
- is good to employees by providing good benefits
- is negative to employees by requiring strict attention to time
- has good policies for promoting employees from within
- has been accused of gender discrimination

Products
I think the organization
- has a good product for quality
- but the product is too expensive

Community
I think the organization
- is good to community by providing jobs
- is bad for community by driving up real estate prices
- is good to community by providing tax revenue

NOT ➡ Groups of persons share primarily one image toward each organizational image which remains constant and never changes.

 We all believe all the time that the organization is good to its employees.

We all believe all the time that the organization has quality products.

 We all believe all the time that the organization is always good for its community.

FIGURE 20.6
Corporate Images Are Multiple and Changeable, within Each Person, According to the Collapse Theory of Corporate Image.

ars have generated a significant line of research that looks at women in the workplace and tries to understand how issues of power and the ideology of patriarchy continue to be espoused in the workplace (Creedon, 1991; Hon, 1995; Hon, Grunig, & Dozier, 1992; Serini, Toth, Wright, & Emig, 1997; Toth & Grunig, 1993). Termed the velvet ghetto, feminist critical researchers have examined how female public relations professionals are sometimes treated differently than male public relations professionals. Findings from feminist scholars in public relations have not been optimistic. Males often continue to have the power because they continue to be in upper management levels. Women often continue to be disempowered because they most frequently have the lower-level technical and writing jobs (Creedon, 1991).

Other critical theory research is applied to message design and is based on **structuralism and semiotics** (Goldman, 1992; Goldman & Papson, 1996). Scholars who want to look closely at public relations and marketing and advertising messages have created a relatively new line of research. They want to uncover the underlying ideology that is expressed in commercial messages. (Remember concepts of langue and parole in Chapter 17?)

Findings from close textual analysis of campaign messages are very revealing. Findings suggest that campaign messages not only advertise a product or present a corporate image, but they inevitably continue to embody the common, underlying ideologies of the organization and the society at large. Messages can reveal ideologies of culture such as that happiness or beauty can be bought; think of messages that claim you can buy happiness in a bottle of perfume or aftershave and a new identity through clothes purchases!

Much research continues to be done through these kinds of critical approaches. In addition, a strong line of rhetorical research has also emerged where corporations and corporate messages are analyzed for their rhetorical, or persuasive, appeals (Bostdorff & Vibbert, 1994; Crable, 1990; Crable & Vibbert, 1983; Elwood, 1995; Goldzwig & Cheney, 1984; Heath, 1992). Case studies of particular campaigns, such as the tobacco wars or the religious right's messages or campaigns for and against breast implants, have been studied closely and carefully as *texts* to reveal their hidden and obvious rhetorical strategies. Hopefully, having this general familiarity with the many kinds of theories that have emerged for explaining public relations can help you understand and appreciate the history of public relations and its growth as a profession and as an academic field.

Summary

This chapter has introduced you to the important elements that define campaign communication as a profession and an academic subject area. Understanding the history of public relations as a profession together with an introduction to the kinds of campaigns lead to an appreciation and understanding the need for the various theories to explain and predict public relations communication. Public relations models and theories, along with theories adapted from organization communication, psychology, persuasion, and critical theory, make up the body of knowledge explaining public relations practice and research.

The history of the growth of public relations indicates that, even in the demonstration of the need for public relations in society, certain founding figures and many businesses have communicated a "truth" that favors their preferred stories, not a truth to benefit society at large. Nevertheless, today corporations know that to tell the truth—albeit initially negative or hurtful to their images—is good business and good public relations. Ethical public relations demands immediate, honest, and truthful communication between the organization and its audiences.

The kinds of campaigns, the models of public relations, and the role of the public relations practitioner are all theoretical constructs defining the field. Theories of collaborative advocacy or cooperative antagonism and opposing theoretical models of chaos or complexity theories both explain the kind of public relations an organization can follow given various campaign situations. Theories and models from other disciplines also shape public relations as a system of communication, linkages of populations to an organization, planned behavior, and the diffusion of information through change agents. Critical theories recognize the significance of meaning in the corporate image process, the sometimes unequal power distribution according to gender, and the power of ideology imbedded in campaign messages.

This chapter sets the foundation for the next three chapters that examine the procedure for executing a campaign, for designing appropriate campaign messages, and for establishing audience relationships and building integrated marketing communication.

Discussion Questions

1. For each of the three kinds of campaigns, and for each of the three kinds of commercial campaigns, can you identify campaigns currently being waged that match the definition of each?

2. Can you imagine a real or hypothetical campaign situation where both crisis management *and* issues management would be needed in the same campaign? What kind of campaign would it be? What would be the campaign situation and targeted audiences for this campaign?

3. What one or two theories do you think best explain how to begin planning a campaign?

4. What one or two theories do you think best explain how to enhance communication and spread messages to targeted audiences?

5. Why do you think the origins of public relations are in the work of professionals and not in an academic field?

References

Ajzen, I., Brown, T. C., & Rosenthal, L. H. (1996). Information bias in contingent valuation: Effects of personal relevance, quality of information, and motivational orientation. *Journal of Environmental Economics and Management, 30,* 43–57.

Ajzen, I., & Fishbein, M. (1980). *Understanding attitudes and predicting social behavior.* Englewood Cliffs, NJ: Prentice-Hall.

Baskin, O., & Aronoff, C. (1992). *Public relations: The profession and the practice* (3rd ed.). Dubuque, IA: Wm. C. Brown Publishers.

Benigni, V. L., Lariscy, R. A. W., & Tinkham, S. F. (2001). To evolve is to involve: Student choice in introduction to public relations classes. *Journalism and Mass Communication Educator, 56*(4), 6–18.

Bostdorff, D. M., & Vibbert, S. L. (1994). Values advocacy: Enhancing organizational images, deflecting public criticism, and grounding future arguments. *Public Relations Review, 20,* 141–158.

Broom, G. M., & Dozier, D. M. (1986). Advancement for public relations role models. *Public Relations Review, 12*(1), 37–56.

Broom, G. M., Lauzen, M. M., & Tucker, K. (1991). Public relations and marketing: Dividing the conceptual domain and operational turf. *Public Relations Review, 17*(3), 219–225.

Cancel, A. E., Cameron, G. T., Sallot, L. M., & Mitrook, M. A. (1997). It depends: A contingency theory of accommodation in public relations. *Journal of Public Relations Research, 9,* 33.

Cancel, A. E., Mitrook, M. A., & Cameron, G. T. (1999). Testing the contingency theory of accommodation in public relations. *Public Relations Review, 25,* 171–197.

Crable, R. E. (1990). "Organizational rhetoric" as the fourth great system: Theoretical, critical, and pragmatic implications. *Journal of Applied Communication, 18,* 115–128.

Crable, R. E., & Vibbert, S. L. (1983). Mobil's epideictic advocacy: "Observations" of Prometheus-bound. *Communication Monographs, 50,* 380–394.

Creedon, P. J. (1991). Public relations and "women's work": Toward a feminist analysis of public relations roles. In L. A. Grunig & J. E. Grunig

(Eds.), *Public Relations Research Annual, 3,* 67–84.

Cutlip, S. M. (1995). *Public relations history: From the 17th to the 20th century.* Hillsdale, NJ: Lawrence Erlbaum.

Daugherty, E. (2001). Public relations and social responsibility. *Handbook of public relations* (pp. 389–401). Thousand Oaks, CA: Sage.

Day, K. D., Dong, Q., & Robins, C. (2001). Public relations ethics. *Handbook of public relations* (pp. 403–409). Thousand Oaks, CA: Sage.

Ekachai, D. (1995). Applying Broom's role scales to Thai public relations practitioners. *Public Relations Review, 21*(4), 325–336.

Elwood, W. N. (Ed.). (1995). *Public relations inquiry as rhetorical criticism: Case studies of corporate discourse and social influence.* Westport, CT: Praeger.

Fishbein, M., & Ajzen, I. (1975). *Belief, attitude, intention and behavior: An introduction to theory and research.* Reading, MA: Addison-Wesley.

Goldman, R. (1992). *Reading ads socially.* London & New York: Routledge.

Goldman, R., & Papson, S. (1996). *Sign wars: The cluttered landscape of advertising.* New York: Guilford Press.

Goldzwig, S., & Cheney, G. (1984). The U.S. Catholic Bishops on nuclear arms: Corporate advocacy, role definition, and rhetorical adaptation. *Central States Journal, 35,* 8–23.

Grunig, J. E. (Ed.). (1992). Communication, public relations, and effective organizations: An overview. *Excellence in public relations and communication management* (pp. 1–28). Hillsdale, NJ: Lawrence Erlbaum.

Grunig, J. E. & Hunt, T. (1984). *Managing public relations.* New York: Holt, Rinehart and Winston.

Heath, R. L. (1992). The wrangle in the marketplace: A rhetorical perspective of public relations. *Rhetorical and critical approaches to public relations.* Hillsdale, NJ: Lawrence Erlbaum.

Hiebert, R. E. (1966). *Courier to the crowd: The story of Ivy Lee and the development of public relations.* Ames: Iowa State University Press.

Hon, L. C. (1995). Feminism and public relations. *Public Relations Strategist, 1*(2): 20–25.

Hon, L. C., Grunig, L. A., & Dozier, D. M. (1992). Women in public relations: Problems and opportunities. In J. E. Grunig (Ed.), *Excellence in public relations and communication management* (pp. 419–438). Hillsdale, NJ: Lawrence Erlbaum.

Jackson, P. (1986). How to build public relationships that motivate real support. *NASSP Bulletin,* 25–31.

Kelly, K. S. (2001). Stewardship: The fifth step in the public relations process. *Handbook of public relations* (pp. 279–289). Thousand Oaks, CA: Sage.

Lewis, C. E. (1980). *Mere Christianity.* New York: Touchstone.

Matera, F. R., & Artigue, R. J. (2000). *Public relations: Campaigns and techniques.* Boston: Allyn and Bacon.

Moffitt, M. A. (1994a). Collapsing and integrating concepts of "public" and "image" into a new theory. *Public Relations Review, 20*(2), 159–170.

Moffitt, M. A. (1994b). A cultural studies perspective toward understanding corporate image: A case study of State Farm Insurance. *Journal of Public Relations Research, 6*(1), 41–66.

Moffitt, M. A. (1999). *Campaign strategies and message design.* Westport, CN: Praeger.

Murphy, P. (1996). Chaos theory as a model for managing issues and crises. *Public Relations Review, 22*(2), 95–113.

Murphy, P. (2000). Symmetry, contingency, complexity: Accommodating uncertainty in public relations theory. *Public Relations Review, 26*(4), 447–462.

Newsom, D., Turk, J. V., & Kruckeberg, D. (2000). *This is PR.* (7th ed.). Belmont, CA: Wadsworth/Thomson Learning.

Olasky, M. N. (1987). The development of corporate public relations, 1850–1930. *Journalism Monographs,* 102.

Pearson, R. (1990). Perspectives on Public Relations History. *Public Relations Review, 16*(3), 27–37.

Pfau, M., & Parrott, R. (1993). *Persuasive communication campaigns.* Boston: Allyn and Bacon.

Reinecke, J., Schmidt, P., & Ajzen, I. (1996). Application of the theory of planned behavior to adolescents' condom use: A panel study. *Journal of Applied Social Psychology, 26*(9), 749–772.

Reinecke, J., Schmidt, P., & Ajzen, I. (1997). Birth control versus AIDS prevention: A hierarchical model of condom use among young people. *Journal of Applied Social Psychology, 27*(9), 743–759.

Rogers, E. M., & Shoemaker, F. F. (1971). *Communication of innovations: A cross-cultural approach.* New York: Free Press.

Serini, S. A., Toth, E. L., Wright, D. K., & Emig, A. G. (1998). Power, gender, and public relations: Sexual harassment as a threat to the practice. *Journal of Public Relations Research, 10,* 193–218.

Toth, E. L., & Grunig, L. A. (1993). The missing story of women in public relations. *Journal of Public Relations Research, 5,* 153–175.

21

Planning, Implementing, and Evaluating the Campaign

Dean Kazoleas

The purpose of this chapter is to present the planning, implementation, and evaluation of campaigns. To meet this goal the current chapter will present some fundamental theoretical and professional insights into the planning of effective campaigns, as well as describe some of the more widely applied theories that are used in the design and implementation of many public relations, commercial, political, and social issue campaigns. The purpose is not to provide an exhaustive list of theories that can be applied (because that may be impossible) but, rather, to supply a set of theories that explain the success or failure of campaign messages in attaining their goals, especially those that can be easily used to plan, construct, and implement campaign strategies.

In this chapter, you will read about the following concepts:

- Importance of theory and research to campaigns
- Systematic and professional approach to campaigns
- Models for implementing a campaign: RACE and ROPE
- Theories that drive effective campaigns
  - McGuire's Matrix
  - VALS
  - Situational theory
  - Agenda-setting theory
  - Issue-attention cycle theory
  - Law of public opinion

Communication campaign planners, especially public relations professionals, are often described as the masters of "spin" or manipulators of public perception. Moreover, public relations professionals have sometimes been depicted as easily manipulating the hearts, minds, and actions of the American public in movies such as *Wag the Dog*. Unfortunately, these observations build a perception that public opinion and behavior are easy to manipulate and that campaign professionals face little difficulty in achieving campaign goals for their clients. Nothing can be further from the truth, because attitudes, beliefs, behaviors, and images are difficult to create and even more difficult to change! In order to understand the creation of successful campaigns, the first consideration is knowledge of research and of pertinent theories.

How Do Theory and Research Help in Planning a Campaign?

This is a question that exists in the minds of campaign professionals who are interested in creating and managing a campaign. The answer to this question is very simple. Theoretical foundations and primary research on the targeted audiences maximize the probability for success in the campaign. This being said, it is still amazing to see the large number of campaigns that appear to have no clear research-based rationale for success and are often the result of a whim, a "cool idea," or one of those "wouldn't-it-be-great-if" moments. The problem is that when campaigns cost millions of dollars, have far-reaching business and social implications, and can take weeks, months, and perhaps years to execute, there is too much at stake to be "shooting from the hip."

When planning and executing any campaign, the campaign manager should always try to imagine that a lot of money—often millions—is at stake and that the organization's brand-based identity is at risk if the campaign designer creates a highly unsuccessful and/or embarrassing campaign. When time, money, career, and reputation are riding on the success of a campaign, we can assume that the campaign strategist will want to maximize the probability of success and minimize the probability of failure. The use of business and communication theory and research methods allows us to get a picture of whether our strategies will be effective and/or if they can be modified to maximize desired effects.

As you read this chapter, note that information about how to structure an effective campaign is an excellent example of a premise of communication presented in the first chapter of this book, that is, that communication is strategic and relational. You will see in the study of campaign implementation that designing messages with goals in mind, creating and sustaining patterns of communication, and building personal, social, and professional relationships are all fundamental and powerful assumptions of business communication through campaigns (Cutlip, Center, & Broom, 2000; Guth & Marsh, 2000; Newscom, Turk, & Kruckeberg, 2000; Wilcox et al., 1998; McElreath, 1996).

Students who are exposed to the theoretical underpinnings of campaign communication should not be surprised or confused to see the presentation of mass communication, human communication, public opinion, political science, psychological, and sociological theories used to explain and predict processes in planning and implementing all kinds of campaigns. At the core of the public relations campaign, however, is an understanding that the public relations campaign differs from an advertising and marketing campaign in that it will often focus on relationships with key stakeholders, often use uncontrolled message dissemination strategies such as the news or mass media, (which cost less and add credibility as neutral observers), and make use of a wide variety of direct and indirect strategies and tactics.

No More "Shooting from the Hip": What Is a Systematic and Ethical Approach to Campaigns?

One of the most difficult barriers you could encounter in campaign communication is in trying to develop a systematic and professional approach to the planning, execution, and evaluation of a campaign. The obstacle to achieving this goal is simply a tendency of most individuals to try to use an entertaining or shocking approach to developing campaign strategies and campaign planning. What this means is that too often students and inexperienced campaign planners decide to go with that "hot idea" or the newest and trendiest thought of the moment to drive their campaign strategies and messages.

There are a number of problems with this approach, all of which can be strongly related to campaign failure. To put it simply, campaigns take a lot of time, large amounts of money, large amounts of effort, and can have long-term effects on key publics or target audiences. Unfortunately, a poorly planned campaign can waste time, waste money, and can create long-lasting negative effects that run counter to the goals of the campaign *and* the organization.

Campaign planning also carries with it some direct and indirect **ethical responsibilities.** From a direct standpoint, campaigns should target socially responsible goals and use ethically acceptable tactics. However, some campaigns carry an ethical responsibility because the very attempt to use a series of strategic messages or actions can and will impact the receivers, perhaps making them resistant to future campaign strategies and tactics (McElreath, 1996).

Anti-smoking campaigns can be used to demonstrate this ethical dilemma. For example:

> Researchers know quite a lot about smoking behavior and the difficulty involved in getting smokers to try to quit smoking. First, smoking is a behavior that is largely driven by a physical addiction to the substance nicotine that is found in tobacco. Researchers also know that a smoker's perceptions of efficacy (perceptions of their own ability to quit smoking) is highly related to the behavioral intention to quit smoking. The ethical dilemma for the campaign planner lies in the decision to mix information regarding smoking cessation devices in with their anti-smoking message. Research indicates that the use of a cessation assistance device doubles the probability of the success for actually quitting smoking, and we also know that each attempt at quitting reduces perceptions of efficacy regarding the ability of the smoker to actually quit smoking, which means that if a campaign gets the smoker to try and they fail, this hampers future attempts. This means that, ethically, we should include information on cessation assistance systems (nicotine gum, the patch, or inhalers) in our campaigns to maximize the probability of success, because each failure will reduce the probability of success for each subsequent attempt.

This example also underscores the need for adequate background research and planning. The nonprofessional campaign planner might merely decide to communicate the

FIGURE 21.1 *Firefighters Extinguish "Craving Man" to Show That Smokers Can Beat Cigarettes.* FDNY members are encouraging all smokers to make a promise to quit smoking by logging onto www.makeapromise.com. In the summer of 2002, FDNY started a smoking cessation program that combines nicotine replacement therapy with continuous behavior support to encourage the 2,000 New York City firefighters who smoke to quit.

Courtesy of Feature Photo Service and www.newscom.com

dangers of smoking, ignoring the fact that smoking is driven by a physical addiction to nicotine, which can be quite powerful. Taking the time to do research would reveal to the campaign designers that addictions to narcotics and other drugs create physiological drives in individuals that are similar to the drives caused by nicotine. Similarly, human cravings for food (hunger) and sex are also physiological and psychological drives, which can be quite powerful and extremely difficult to resist. Campaign planners in these areas have determined that one of the best ways to help control these drives is by the use of intervention campaigns that involve the use of significant others to help the target audience overcome the drives associated with addictions. The importance of understanding situational, motivational, and underlying processes is a crucial ethical consideration in the context of the campaign planning process, demonstrating, again, how social structures affect and constrain communication.

Precisely How Do You Structure a Campaign?

Acronyms such as RACE and ROPE refer to public relations campaign planning processes that are based on the principle of management by objectives. This management-

FIGURE 21.2 *Basic Campaign Planning Models.*

Marston's RACE Model of Public Relations Planning	Hendrix's ROPE Model of Public Relations Planning
Research	Research
Action Planning	Objectives
Communication	Publics
Evaluation	Evaluation

based approach calls for the use of systematic, sequential, goals-based processes. Regardless of the acronym used by the theorist or professional, both **Marston's RACE model** (Marston, 1963, 1979) and **Hendrix's ROPE model** (Hendrix, 2001) feature generally similar steps in the planning of a campaign, such as background and preliminary research, the setting of key strategic objectives, careful planning, systematic implementation, and evaluation. According to our liberal definition of theories in this book, the RACE and ROPE steps for planning a campaign are models and examples of formal descriptive theories.

Background Research Grounds the Campaign

The first step in the planning process of the RACE and ROPE models is **background research,** which leads to an understanding of the historical factors, campaign situational factors, as well as underlying motivational processes of both the organization and the stakeholders, or targeted audiences (Eagly & Chaiken, 1993; Kazoleas, 1993a, 1993b). Similarly, understanding the different options that are available for success may be key in identifying pivotal **decision makers.** For example, students often believe that all public relations campaigns comprise large-scale media campaigns that target public opinion. However, at times the key decision maker may be a city government, a zoning board, or a jury in a courtroom that can create a powerful legal precedent. For example, euthanasia organizations have funded and backed Dr. Kevorkian and his physician-assisted suicide tactics in order to attempt to force the courts in the United States to create a pro-euthanasia precedent. The recognition of the importance of decision makers in the structuring of a campaign is an example of the diffusion of innovations theory and the theoretical construct of the role of change agents in this diffusion of information that you studied in Chapter 20.

Similarly, a campaign may need to target specific legislators on key committees to sponsor, create, or kill a legislative bill. Similarly, a corporate decision maker may best be targeted by a coordinated letter-writing and e-mail campaign or coordinated "grassroots" activistic efforts, as opposed to a large-scale media advertising campaign. These are all examples of how the campaign planner can begin to explore the history and underlying causes of a problem or issue, as well as potential mechanisms during the research phase of a campaign.

Analyzing the problem and separating it from symptoms is also a key part of the research phase of campaigns. Treating symptoms may help you achieve some short-term goals, but if the root cause of the problem is not addressed, then the symptoms will return. An example of careful problem analysis during the research phase can be found by examining the phenomenon of drunk driving. To the nonresearch-based campaign designer, this problem appears to be an easy one to solve. However, research and analysis of the problem can quickly identify the paradox that the campaign planner will face.

The anti–drinking-and-driving campaign that targets moderation as opposed to abstaining is difficult *because it asks individuals to make a rational decision in an irrational state.* That is to say that once individuals start to drink, they may find it difficult to determine/remember how much they have had to drink and/or the extent to which they may be impaired. To that extent campaign planners who want to significantly reduce the occurrence of drinking and driving will often focus on getting a driver to abstain (e.g., the designated driver program) or getting others to intervene as opposed to trying to focus on educating the drinker to make a decision regarding driving while they are drinking.

Action Planning Sets the Campaign Objectives

Once a complete understanding of the situation is developed, and decision-making mechanisms are clearly identified, goals, objectives, strategies, and tactics can be developed. This second step in the ROPE and the RACE models signifies the actual conceptualization and beginning of the implementation of the campaign. For ROPE (Marsten 1963, 1979) goals and objectives are identified. For RACE (Hendrix, 2001), specific strategies and tactics can be developed based on an in-depth knowledge of the needs, positions, and demands/desires of the target publics. Both of these action plans' second stages identify key publics and audiences and develop strategies and schedules to target those publics given the organizational resources at hand.

Careful action planning is critical because in the "real world" campaign designers often have limited resources and a limited window of opportunity to get the attention of their target publics. Again, to some campaign strategists, the idea of careful scheduling may seem like a waste of time and effort, because "a good idea is a good idea," and some believe that a good idea will always work. However, choosing to gain attention during an election period or trying to buy advertising for an issue during "sweeps" week by the networks can be very difficult and very expensive because the availability of media time and space decreases during these periods, and costs greatly increase. [Web site: Communication to the Targeted Audiences]

Communication to Targeted Publics

Figure 21.3 demonstrates the importance of communicating to the identified traits of the audience, the third step in the RACE and ROPE models. Calvin Klein shifts the emphasis and image of its Eternity fragrance to family, for its consumer population, away from its earlier appeal to personal beauty.

Campaign planners also need to be flexible. If a large-scale event such as a high-profile celebrity trial, natural catastrophe, or large-scale event such as September 11, 2001, occurs, the media and attention of most key publics will be on those issues and not on the issues that we wish to bring to the forefront. If this occurs, we need to quickly move to halt our efforts and to reschedule and/or redefine our campaign.

You can see that a campaign strategist needs to be careful in communicating to targeted audiences. Having utilized research to identify the significant traits of the audiences and planning to identify the campaign objectives, communicating the specially designed messages requires its own considerations: scheduling and timing. An organization cannot just throw out messages to the audiences. How and when to communicate the tailor-made messages is a careful strategic decision.

Campaign Evaluation

Finally, evaluation is also a critical necessity and a phase of the campaign process that is of the utmost importance for the RACE and ROPE models. This phase, while often over-

ETERNITY

love, sweet love

Calvin Klein

FIGURE 21.3 Calvin Klein expands upon Eternity's thirteen-year fragrance tradition and brings the emotions of family love to life with a new advertising campaign.

PRNewsFoto

looked, will determine the overall success or failure of the campaign. This is also the only mechanism that the campaign specialist has to demonstrate the value and ROI (Return On Investment) for their efforts. **Return on Investment** is when the campaign manager demonstrates to the organization (if in-house corporate communication) or to his or her client (if campaign is planned by an agency) that the money it paid for the campaign did, indeed, reach the goals set out in the campaign. These data can be used to promote additional campaign efforts, to gain new clients, or to help build internal perceptions of value.

There are a number of **forms of evaluation** (Atkin, 1981; Atkin & Freimuth, 1989): formative, intermediate, and summative evaluation. **Formative evaluation** is conducted before a campaign begins; this includes the background research step outlined above. **Intermediate** or **interim evaluation** occurs during the campaign, during the planning and communication stages, to measure and test how effective the messages are while the campaign is being conducted. In the final step of campaign evaluation, **summative evaluation** determines what impacts the campaign had, whether campaign goals were met, if there were unintended effects, and why some goals might not have been met.

What most campaign managers miss is the important observation that as campaign planners *we define* success or failure. In the campaign planning stages we have to make careful choices regarding our goals and objectives. We have to remember that experience and research indicates that attitudes are as hard to change as are behavioral patterns. Campaign planners face the difficulty of wanting to promise lofty goals in campaign proposals in order to get the client to use their services, while knowing that small changes in attitude or belief, changes in health-risking habitual behavior, and/or small increases in market shares against market leaders will be hard to attain. That is why campaign planners have both an ethical duty and a pragmatic duty to select reasonable, attainable, and measurable goals and objectives.

During the evaluation phase campaign managers must use key indicators and measurement tools to determine if campaign goals were met. Again, planners who "shoot from the hip" and throw out percentages that sound good at the time usually don't like this part of the process. If a planner promised a 35 percent increase in sales, or a shift of 25 percent in public opinion, anything less is a failure. In other words, while a 34 percent increase in sales may have meant millions of dollars in profits, given that the campaign did not meet the 35 percent target, the campaign by definition was a failure. Remember that to evaluate success necessitates the setting of realistic, obtainable goals and having reasonable mechanisms in place to assess success or failure.

Key to this process is the capacity for open-mindedness in critiquing all aspects of the campaign. The goal is to determine not only what happened but also why it happened and what can be done to improve future efforts. An unsuccessful effort is not easy to explain to a client or an employer. However, repeated failures are often impossible to justify. Therefore, every campaign needs to be analyzed to determine the role of the campaign in obtaining success or meeting failure.

What Theories Drive Effective Campaigns?

Many theories and theoretical concepts can be used to build effective campaigns—so many that it is often difficult to choose which one to apply to a given problem, issue, or situation. However, there is one theoretical framework—**McGuire's Matrix** (1985, 1989)—that integrates a large amount of research from social influence, persuasion, and attitude change research into a model that can be used to develop effective campaigns across a wide variety of contexts. This simplified variation of a matrix has been developed by William McGuire (1989). This matrix is an effective tool in the development of campaigns because it is easy to remember and targets a number of key variables that have been shown to predict the success or failure of campaigns.

McGuire's Matrix

This model clearly identifies a number of processes that must occur for any campaign to have an impact. In particular, this model examines a number of cognitive factors such as attention to the message, comprehension, retention of at least a small part of the message, and some level of yielding or acceptance that underlie the campaign influence process. These are mental processes that *must* occur for any campaign to have an effect. If a campaign does not get the target's attention (for any reason), if its messages are not understood, or if its messages are "tuned" out or not memorable, it has little chance for success.

The use of this matrix or model is particularly effective in planning campaigns in that the campaign planner can manipulate aspects of the source, channel, and message that are tailored to the receivers' needs, wants, beliefs, and media habits. The chosen campaign strategies and tactics should maximize the probability that the receiver will pay *attention* to the message, will *comprehend and/or understand* the message, will *yield or at least consider* the message, and will *retain* part of the message. *All of these components are necessary for awareness, learning, attitude change, belief change, and behavior change to occur.*

FIGURE 21.4 *McGuire's Matrix.*

Independent Factors	Mediating Processes	Outcomes or Consequences
Source	Attention	Awareness
Message	Comprehension	Attitude Change
Channel	Yielding or Acceptance	Belief Change
Receiver	Retention	Behavior Change

McGuire's model operationalizes the steps for planning, implementing, and evaluating a campaign that were presented earlier in this chapter. The use of this model underscores the need for a systematic approach to planning and executing campaign strategies and tactics. In this model, research is the key to determine what type of source, message, and channel would be the most likely to reach, be received, and impact the receiver. Again, given the wide variations in the demographic, psychographic, and perceptual positions of receivers, a wide range of differing organizational information can be used to catch the *attention* and the *awareness* of the targeted stakeholders. This initial step of McGuire's model demonstrates the importance of *source,* or organizational, presentation or sponsorship of audience appeals to get audience attention. The large number of complex choices to be made reinforces the critical need for preliminary research on the organization and on the audiences.

Care and understanding from the receivers' perspectives have to be used to select message content that the receiver may find credible, attractive, or identifiable, which corresponds to the second step in McGuire's Matrix. For example, if the message uses a fear-based or threat-based appeal, the receivers must view the threat as serious and certain. In the case of an adolescent audience, teenaged targets tend to counter-argue against health-based threats and fear-based messages but respond well to threats regarding social rejection. Additionally, a reward or negative consequence must be motivating to this age group. For example, a $10 savings may not motivate teens who have large incomes, and "being grounded" may not be seen as a negative consequence for adolescents who have televisions, stereos, video-game systems, and computers in their bedrooms. These examples of what kind of message content might be effective with teenagers demonstrates the need to use caution when selecting message components that will impact the targets, as included in the *message* factor of McGuire's Matrix. Furthermore, the planner must also choose message components that maximize the effects of the mediating processes, such as *yielding or receptivity,* which in turn maximizes the probability of *attitude/behavioral change.*

Next, according to the third step of *channel,* we can note that some communication channels offer great reach, frequency, and impact with the receiver. For example, in many television network markets, the nightly news obtains high ratings, but teens tend not to watch it. At the same time, radio advertisements and/or radio news coverage do not offer the "glamour" and emotional impact of television news coverage for adults. On the other hand, in America's large cities large percentages of the youth population spend hours a day in their cars listening to their favorite music. Utilizing radio to reach these teenagers should, in this case, be effective. Similarly, given the ever increasing time spent in cars by commuters, radio ads during "drive time" can be much more effective in reaching those driving to and/or from work than television ads run during the same time blocks.

And, the final factor in McGuire's model, checking the *receiver* for *retention* and *behavior change* is also crucial in campaign planning. A close examination of the receivers is also useful as a last-minute quality control check before finalizing campaign plans. It is important to examine the strategies, plans, and tactics that have been prepared and then run through the mediating processes from receivers' perspectives. Is the campaign likely to get the targets' attention, even in the face of other competing media and messages? Are targeted audiences going to understand and comprehend the message in the form in which it is presented? Research indicates that complex issues are not well matched with broadcast media because of their time limits and the receivers' inability to control the pace of message processing. Moreover, in America's urban centers large numbers of individuals may have limited abilities to speak and to understand English. Is the target population going to yield to the message or accept message recommendations? Counterarguments and opposing campaigns must be taken into consideration. Lastly, will the strategies and tactics have a lasting effect, either by promoting retention or modifying cognitive structures such as attitudes and beliefs? If the answer is no to any one of these questions, it is imperative for the campaign planner to modify the campaign or risk wasting time, money, and effort.

Situational Analysis and Target Publics

McGuire's model and all other public relations models require an accurate understanding of all situational and contextual factors as well as the mindsets, abilities, and limitations that exist among stakeholders. In other words, the planner must understand the factors that underlie current beliefs, the players that have contributed to the current situation, and the factors that can drive or inhibit target publics from action (Hovland et al, 1953; Kazoleas, 1993a, 1993b).

Social psychology, public relations, advertising and market researchers have built incredibly accurate theories and models of what drives individual behaviors, or from what perspective audiences will approach an issue. For example, you have studied in earlier chapters of this book **Maslow's hierarchy of needs** (1954), which suggests that physiological needs and safety needs can be used to drive behavioral action. As part of this model we also learn that humans have strong needs for social acceptance and the esteem for others—so strong that they spend billions per year on beauty/appearance-based products and diet plans.

Along these lines, several consumer behavior models have developed from advertising research, such as **VALS (Values and Lifestyle Behaviors)** and **VALS 2** (Moffitt, 1999; Pfau & Parrott, 1993), that focus on key predictive factors. These models often focus both on the consumers' psychological and cognitive abilities, as well as their material resources and priorities. These frameworks examine audience targets by examining where they are in the life-cycle: for example, bachelor stage of life, married without children, married with children, or "empty-nesters" who are older and have children that have left the home. VALS can often significantly predict where they place priorities, how they spend money, and how much disposable income they have. These VALS models also factor psychological factors such as values, because some individuals are driven by certain core value sets (e.g., those that are fairly religious). Similarly, those who are educated may have higher needs for achievement and esteem.

These are all factors that can be used to choose strategies and tactics in the planning of a campaign and, hopefully, affect changes in attitude, beliefs, or behaviors. The next chapter on campaign message design goes into more detail on the VALS relative to message design, but these considerations are also important to the general structuring of a campaign.

Grunig's Situational Theory

Grunig's (Grunig & Hunt, 1984) **situational theory** also focuses on a set of factors that can be used to determine the extent to which publics might become aware of issues and/or act in relation to issue-based developments or campaign messages. The early forms of this theory state that the target public's action on an issue is based on three main factors. The first is knowledge or awareness of the issue, the second is level of involvement, and the third is the perceptions of constraints/constraint behavior. These variables and their possible combinations predict the information-processing and information-seeking activity **level of publics.** Grunig's early versions of this theory suggested four main public groupings: **nonpublics,** which are not affected and would not be aware of an issue; **latent** publics, which are groups of individuals who would be affected but are not aware of the campaign issues yet; **aware** publics, which are groups that have high levels of awareness and attitudes, but have not yet become actively involved; and **active** publics, which are aware, involved, active, and have behavior toward the campaign situation because they either have no constraints or have overcome constraints. Let's look at how the campaign planner might identify these factors and use this information to motivate and activate an audience.

Key to the campaign planner's strategy is the notion that those nonpublic publics who are not aware of an issue will not be seeking information about an issue and thus will not be likely to be reached with campaign messages; similarly, aware publics have not taken action and do not proactively seek information. This means that the campaign planner must carefully target them by having a key understanding of their media use patterns and using that information to place campaign messages within those patterns. Active publics seek information and are willing to act. This means that the campaign planner must do all that is possible to provide in-depth information to mobilize these publics and to provide information that, hopefully, they can use to become activated.

The Internet is a great example of a tool that can be used to provide informational resources to a public considered aware or active. The internet allows for the storage of large amounts of information, information that is easily searched and retrieved, information that is available "24/7," and information that is relatively inexpensive to use, update, and maintain. The use of the Internet as a channel for rich and comprehensive message content can fulfill a key research goal for the campaign planner, that is, to present the information that will drive the aware public to activation or maintain an active public position at that level.

Additionally, Grunig's (1989, 2001) more recent work has analyzed target publics across many issues and suggests that certain publics always exist across situations. For

FIGURE 21.5 Mike McNeilly creates a 9/11 mural as tribute to New York firefighters.

Courtesy PR Newswire Photo Service and www.Newscom.com

example, college students can often be considered an **apathetic public** in that they often do not focus on political issues that occur in the localities around them. **Single-issue publics** are those that will activate and act on a particular issue. The abortion issue serves as an example of this kind of public.

Hot-issue publics are those who tend to become involved on the issues that become "hot" in society and are talked about by the media and in workplaces and living rooms. For example, 9-11 generated a large amount of patriotism and activism among individuals and groups that want to make America safer; some of these individuals have always been active in these issues, while others were motivated by all the devastating acts and the accompanying media attention (see Figure 21.5).

Last but not least are **all-issue publics.** These are individuals or groups of individuals who will get involved and activated across many differing but related issues. These groups are invaluable to campaign planners because they make excellent strategic allies in coordinated efforts at local, state, and national levels. Psychologically, these are the individuals who usually want to make a difference and are willing to expend the time and resources to try to make that difference. It is these individuals who often serve as a foundation for an effective "grassroots" campaign.

Agenda Setting and Issues: Life-Cycle Theories

Public relations campaigns often target the use of the mass media, focusing on news and publicity as tactics. The smart campaign planner has to approach the media in these instances as a critical target for persuasion. This means that the campaign planner has to understand what the media people desire, need, and expect, and how they do their jobs. Who are the media? They are ordinary people, with goals, desires, attitudes, beliefs, agendas, and biases who work for organizations, which generally have one common goal. That goal is to make money. Ratings, circulations, readership, and independent web "hits" mean the ability to sell advertising. The journalist's job is to tell the stories that will generate interest and attention.

The question is, do the media drive issues and discussion in society, or do they merely reflect the discussion and focus of important issues that are of current importance in society? There are two different ways of looking at this question. The first one deals with the issue of agenda setting and asks what effect the media have on individuals. You learned in the mass communication chapters that **agenda-setting theory** (Devine & Hirt, 1989; McCombs, 1977) tells us that the media do not tell us what to think but what to think about. That is to say that the media set the agenda for our daily individual-level and societal-level discussions. The smart campaign planner understands this process and thereby attempts to get the media to focus on their organization's issues and their specific messages (Ewing, 1997; Lippmann, 1927; VanLeuven & Slater, 1991). However, this still does not answer the question of what drives the issues that gain the attention of the media and society.

A second set of theories revolves around **issue and policy life cycles,** sometimes referred to as **issue-attention cycles** (McCombs, Shaw, & Grey, 1976; Dearing & Rogers, 1996). These theories suggest that latent issues always exist in society, and the triggering events, such as natural events, violent acts or attacks, controversial court rulings or other large-scale events, bring these issues to our attention. Once they have our attention, we start to discuss them, develop positions and related solutions, discuss the solutions, and then act on them. Eventually, some other issue will get our attention, and the issue will go back into a state of latency, until another triggering event occurs.

A good example is the issue of gun control. This issue had faded into the background in the late 1970s, until John Hinckley attempted to assassinate President Ronald Reagan in 1981. This act renewed U.S. discussion of gun control and led to much debate, discussion, and finally action in the form of new gun control laws (e.g., the Brady Bill). The issue then faded again until it was renewed when students used guns to murder other students at Columbine High School in Colorado and in a school in Paducah, Kentucky. These triggering events pushed the latent issues back onto the forefront of societal and media discussion and resulted in more changes in law and policy. Similarly, the execution of Timothy McVeigh for the Oklahoma City Bombing brought media coverage to numerous groups that either opposed or advocated use of the death penalty, and the terrorist events of 9-11 have given the stage to many groups that have been focusing their efforts at making America aware of the dangers of lax immigration and entry policies.

Noted experts on public opinion Hadley Cantrill (1972) and Walter Lippmann (1927) discuss this phenomenon in the **laws of public opinion,** noting that significant events can create discussion, create opinions, or quickly swing public opinions. The smart campaign planner watches for these events related to their causes and issues, and if they relate, moves quickly to capitalize on the newfound attention and opportunity. The news media, as well as the talk show producers, will be looking to fill their content with information and opinions on these issues. It is the campaign planner's job to move quickly and help supply them with information, opinions, and representatives who are willing to be interviewed, recorded, or participate on a talk show (Van Leuven & Slater, 1991).

Lastly, there are times when the campaign planner will create the event using a protest, publicity action, court filing, or the release of credible research findings or even the release of an organization-sponsored, objective public opinion poll to gain media attention and drive debate. In sum, the campaign planner at all times should maximize the use of the media, gaining their attention by supplying them the information they need to fill their column inches, their air time, and their web pages. [Web site: How Do Health and Safety Campaigns Exemplify Campaign Communication?]

Summary

This chapter has focused on the development and implementation of theoretically based campaign communication. As indicated at the outset of this chapter, campaigns are systematic and strategically driven efforts that target a clearly identified set of specific goals and objectives. Furthermore, a public relations approach often incorporates key relational linkages (including alliances) and may use a wide variety of direct and indirect strategies and tactics to achieve desired campaign goals. The public relations focus also has a tendency to use both controlled message strategies such as advertising, and uncontrolled message strategies such as the use of news releases, media advocacy, and/or publicity-based tactics. This approach yields advantages in the area of campaign flexibility, costs, reach, and effectiveness.

This chapter has also strongly advocated the use of theory and research-based approaches to designing and implementing campaigns. The use of tested and theoretically sound mechanisms will not guarantee success but will, however, maximize the probability of success and minimize the probability of failure. These models have demonstrated that campaigns must present clear, applicable, motivating consequences, strategies that minimize counterarguments about certainty and efficacy, and a clear set of recommendations that can be used to avoid the negative consequences.

Students and scholars who study campaigns in the classroom often find it difficult to comprehend the difficulty and complexity involved in the planning and execution of small-, medium-, or large-scale campaigns. Humans by nature are creatures of habit, developing patterns of behavior, media usage, and message filtering. To make key individuals or groups of individuals aware of, involved in, and finally activated toward an issue is a difficult process even in the absence of competing campaigns. This chapter has presented a number of theoretically based and research-based models that have been shown to be effective in the planning, construction, and implementation of campaigns. Does the use of these models guarantee success? No, but their use does maximize the probability of success and greatly reduces the chances of failure. In the end, when the issue is an important one and success counts, anything that shifts the odds in favor of success cannot be ignored.

Discussion Questions

1. What would you say are four of the most important decisions or considerations to make while a campaign is being planned?

2. During the execution of a campaign, what theories inform how to follow the success or failure of a campaign?

3. Since health campaigns are a significant kind of public relations campaign conducted in our society, choose a current health issue of interest (not smoking or obesity) and discuss the kind of fear and danger strategies you would include in these campaign messages.

4. Discuss the many ways that research findings gathered from targeted stakeholders have direct links to campaign strategies and campaign messages.

5. What theories in this chapter are useful for analyzing the receivers, what theories serve as mechanisms for gaining media coverage and attention, and what theories are most helpful for the actual construction of a campaign?

References

Atkin, C. (1981). Mass media information campaign effectiveness. In R. Rice & W. Paisely (Eds.), *Public communication campaigns* (pp. 265–280). Beverly Hills, CA: Sage.

Atkin, C., & Freimuth, V. (1989). Formative evaluative research in campaign design. In R. Rice & C. Atkin (Eds.), *Public communication campaigns* (2nd ed., pp. 131–150). Newbury Park, CA: Sage.

Cantrill, H. (1972). *Gauging public opinion.* Princeton, NJ: Princeton University Press.

Cutlip, S., Center, A., & G. Broom. (2000). *Effective Public Relations.* Saddle River, NJ: Prentice-Hall.

Dearing, J. W., Rogers, E. M. (1996) *Agenda-Setting. Communication concepts 6.* London: Sage.

Devine, P. G., & Hirt, E. R. (1989). Message strategies for information campaigns: A social psychological analysis. In C. Salmon (Ed.), *Information campaigns* (pp. 236–248). Newbury Park, CA: Sage.

Eagly, A., & Chaiken, S. (1993). *The Psychology of attitudes.* Orlando, FL: Harcourt, Brace, & Jovanovich.

Ewing, R. P. (1997). Issues management: Managing trends through the issues life cycle. In C. Caywood (Ed.), *The handbook of strategic public relations and integrated communications* (pp. 173–188). New York: McGraw-Hill.

Grunig, J. (1989). Publics, audiences, and market segments: Segmentation principles for campaigns. In C. Salmon (Ed.), *Information campaigns* (pp. 197–226). Newbury Park, CA: Sage.

Grunig, J. (2001). Two way symmetrical public relations: Past, present, and future. In R. L. Heath (Ed.), *Handbook of public relations* (pp. 11–30). Thousand Oaks, CA: Sage.

Grunig, J., & Hunt, T. (1984). *Managing public relations.* New York: Holt, Rinehart, & Winston.

Guth, D. W., & Marsh, C. M. (2000). *Public relations: A values driven approach.* Boston: Allyn and Bacon.

Hendrix, J. A. (2001). *Public relations cases* (5th ed.). Belmont, CA: Wadsworth.

Hovland, C., Janis, I., & Lumsdaine, A. (1953). *Communication and persuasion.* New Haven, CT: Yale University Press.

Kazoleas, D. C. (1993a). A comparison of the persuasive effectiveness of qualitative versus quantitative evidence: A test of explanatory hypotheses. *Communication Quarterly, 41,* 40–50.

Kazoleas, D. C. (1993b). The impact of argumentativeness on cognitive response and resistance to persuasion. *Human Communication Research, 20,* 118–137.

Lippmann, W. (1927). *Public opinion.* New York: Harcourt-Brace.

Marston, J. E. (1963). *Nature of public relations.* New York: McGraw-Hill.

Marston, J. E. (1979). *Modern public relations.* New York: McGraw-Hill.

Maslow, A. (1954). *Motivation and personality.* New York: Harper & Row.

McCombs, M. (1977). Agenda setting function of the mass media. *Public Relations Review* (pp. 89–95).

McCombs, M., Shaw, D. L., & Grey, D. (1976). *Handbook of reporting methods.* Boston: Houghton Mifflin.

McElreath, M. P. (1996). *Managing systematic and ethical public relations campaigns* (2nd ed.). Madison, WI: Brown and Benchmark Publishing.

McGuire, W. J. (1985). Attitudes and attitude change. In G. Lindzey & E. Aronson (Eds.), *Handbook of Social Psychology* (3rd ed.). New York: Random House Publishing.

McGuire, W. J. (1989). Theoretical Foundations of campaigns. In R. Rice & C. Atkin (Ed.), *Public communication campaigns* (2nd ed., pp. 43–66). Newbury Park, CA: Sage.

Moffitt, M. (1999). *Campaign strategies and message design.* Westport, CT: Praeger.

Newsom, D., Turk, J., & Kruckeberg, D. (2000). *This is PR: The realities of public relations* (7th ed.). Belmont, CA: Wadsworth.

Pfau, M., & Parrott, R. (1993). *Persuasive communication campaigns.* Boston: Allyn and Bacon.

Van Leuven, J. K., & Slater, M. D. (1991). How publics, public relations, and the media shape the public opinion process. In J. Grunig & L. Grunig (Eds.), *Public Relations Research Annual* (vol. 3, pp. 165–179). Hillsdale, NJ: Lawrence Erlbaum.

Wilcox, D. L., Ault, P., & Agee, W. K. (1998). *Public relations: Strategies and tactics* (5th ed.). New York: Longman.

22

Campaign Message Design

Mary Anne Moffitt

Hopefully, by now you appreciate that campaigns—marketing, advertising, public relations, political, and social issue campaigns—are a unique kind of communication. All kinds of organizations use campaigns to communicate to multiple audiences that might be made up of thousands or even millions of people. The previous chapter detailed how to strategize and deliver a campaign. But now we turn to another important component integral to campaign communication.

Only recently have public relations researchers become interested in the specific design of campaign messages. This chapter will extend the study of campaign communication by examining how the public relations strategist plans and designs the written and visual format of a campaign message. This information might seem rather technical, but it is actually based on general and basic principles of visual and written communication. Obviously, this knowledge of message design can be valuable for the person interested in campaign communication.

However, another reason to study this relatively recent, ground-breaking research and theory is that it can help anyone recognize and appreciate basic message strategies. Even if you never major in public relations or never see yourself in campaign communication, you can still become an informed consumer of the media through the study of campaign messages.

In this chapter, you will read about the following concepts:

- Design of campaign messages throughout history
- Theories that explain campaign messages
  - AIDA—attention, interest, desire, action
  - MAO—motivation, ability, opportunity
  - Elaboration likelihood model (ELM)
  - Selective perception and cognitive dissonance
  - Matching exercise

- Examples of message strategies
  - Message components: words and visuals
  - Kinds of basic strategies: knowledge, attitude, behavior
  - Appeals: demographic, needs, psychographic, schema

FIGURE 22.1   *Blondie.*

© Reprinted with special permission of King Features Syndicate.

The cartoon presented in Figure 22.1 is meant to be humorous, but it does point out an issue that is crucial to campaigns. Any cartoon—any message—cannot be very effective or persuasive if the audience does not even understand what the message is trying to communicate. This chapter tackles one of the biggest challenges facing campaign communication: how to design messages that both represent the organization's position and are messages people can understand. As noted above, this examination of the design of campaign messages educates the communicator interested in campaigns but also educates you, as a consumer of the media, to better understand all kinds of media messages.

Planning messages that will reach hundreds, thousands, or millions of people and that will draw them to process and interpret these messages may seem like an overwhelming task. After all, an organization cannot know each member of its respective audiences personally. A campaign manager cannot know what distractions might keep an audience from processing the intended campaign messages. This chapter opens with one excellent way to begin to understand campaign message design, that is, by looking at campaign messages and their changes over time. Then the chapter presents key theories that explain this creative process, examine the specific message strategies that are included in any message, and, finally, cover how campaign messages are designed to be successful.

What Is the History of Campaign Message Design?

A brief look at the history of commercial campaign messages reveals what techniques of campaign message design have been effective (and ineffective) in the past and today. You will notice that most of the examples of campaign messages explained here are from advertising campaigns; advertising scholars have always recorded their message trends more than researchers of other kinds of campaign messages. This is not surprising, since research into marketing and public relations messages has not been as common or visible.

First, corporations engaging in marketing communication generally communicate internally through memos or fact sheets or personal contact to their retailers or distributors. Public relations messages, as well, have not been studied as rigorously as advertisements, but this chapter will comment on the silver anvil and bronze anvil awards given by the Public Relations Society of America (PRSA) for successful public relations campaigns. This chapter will also briefly look at some history of political campaign messages.

Notice that the following analyses of messages are consistent with the scientific and humanistic paradigms. That is, research into message design that assumes these texts can be dissected and objectively measured—especially true of the political messages—follows the scientific paradigm. At the same time, other researchers interpret the deep cultural meanings embedded in these commercials, which is more the critical paradigm.

A final reminder on theory—recall from the first chapters that all levels of theories can be understood as products of social structures such as cultural values, norms, rituals, cultural symbols, social roles, and so on. In the following section on the history of campaign messages, you will see how the social and historical period of the time had a direct influence on the campaign messages that corporations decided to use in their campaigns.

Advertising Design of the 1950s

The first widespread use of advertising campaigns was in the 1950s, after World War II, when the postwar economic boom allowed television to be affordable in most households. Although advertising campaigns appeared on radio and in newspapers and magazines, these first attempts at "mass" advertising campaigns were perfect for television airing. These early messages were very simple in design. The message format was to get the audience to remember the name of the product through the use of a cute song or jingle (Goldman, 1992; Goldman & Papson, 1996, p. 105).

You might see a person dressed as a giant pack of cigarettes dancing and singing about their brand of cigarette. Examples of famous jingles designed to get people to remember the product are "See the USA in your Chevrolet" or "You'll wonder where the yellow went, when you brush your teeth with Pepsodent" (Goldman & Papson, 1996, p. 55). The typical style for these advertisements was a visualization of the product and a little jingle repeated over and over to make sure that the audience would remember the song, and hence the product's name. These earliest attempts at commercial messages assumed a homogeneous audience; no efforts to target audience characteristics are in these commercials. These first messages reflected the organization's interests exclusively.

Advertising Design of the 1960s and 1970s

These kinds of cute song-and-dance commercials lasted during the 1950s, but the 1960s and 1970s presented a general shift in advertising strategy and message design. The use of jingles and cute songs gave way to messages that now presented their products with more abstraction, more color and creativity, and with more attention to the product as a commodity that could be purchased to make life better. The product was often presented in an ideal setting, suggesting that the product could provide an ideal solution to life's problems. For example, an advertisement for a washing machine featured an ideal middle-class or upper-class home. Tennis shoes were advertised as worn by young, hip, and in-style individuals. Makeup or beauty products were seen only on the most beautiful and attractive women.

The underlying strategy contained in these 1960s and 1970s advertisements was that you could buy a good way of life or buy beauty and style. Purchase this product and make your life or your body perfect! Cute jingles stimulating name recall for the most part had given way to images of ideal products to make life perfect.

A slight shift in considerations of the audiences or consumers is revealed in these messages. Message design began to reflect an organization's effort to make the commercials a little more relevant to their consumers.

Advertising Design of the 1980s and 1990s

After about three decades of campaign messages that were mostly unreal and only slightly relevant to the average person's life, the 1980s and 1990s marked a real revolution in the design and variety of design of campaign messages. Campaign planners knew that audiences of customers, potential customers, employees, retailers, and so on had grown suspicious of, cynical toward, and even bored with the claims made in advertising campaign messages and other kinds of campaign messages.

Although some messages have retained design formats of cute recall techniques and the portrayal of the ideal, around the early 1980s until today, most advertisement message designers felt that some dramatic shifts in message design were needed for today's more perceptive and cynical consumer. In fact, advertising researchers offered the first model of how to conceptualize messages and make them relevant to consumers. The **AIDA model** is a historical model of advertising design: Attention (get the attention of the receiver), Interest (maintain the interest of the receiver), Desire (stimulate desire in the product), and Action (lead the receiver to buy the product) (www.adglossary.com).

In the past few decades message designers have created many design innovations. One of these innovations is to show negative aspects of our environment, to include scenes from everyday life and with ordinary people living their everyday lives (Goldman & Papson, 1996, pp. 56–57). For example, messages advertising cereal or other breakfast foods show that a family running around a messy house getting ready to go to work and school can still have time for breakfast. Public relations messages advocating a corporation's efforts to help out a community portray their employees as ordinary people coaching Little League.

Other design shifts have been attempted in order to get the attention of the audience member once again. One of the most common strategies in advertising, political, and even social issue messages is to use a celebrity or "expert" to attest to a product or social cause (Goldman & Papson, 1996, pp. 69–70). Who can deny the impact of Michael Jordan as primary spokesperson for Nike or Sting arguing to save the rainforests? Bob Barker signs off his television show *The Price Is Right* advocating the social issue to control the pet population by neutering pets. Figure 22.2 illustrates the use of celebrities Dennis Rodman and Carmen Electra to sell perfume.

FIGURE 22.2 *Rodman and Electra in Candie's Advertisement.* To launch its new fragrances for men and women, Candie's unveils a campaign featuring Dennis Rodman and Carmen Electra.

Courtesy of Feature Photo Service and www.newscom.com

Another popular way to highlight a campaign message is to feature a well-known song in the background (Goldman & Papson, 1996, pp. 69–70), such as Chevy Truck messages' use of Bob Seger's famous song "Like a Rock." Another fashionable trend is to feature a product or issue by calling up the past, like the Smucker's Preserves campaign that visualizes rural scenes and large families: "With a name like Smuckers, it has to be good."

Other examples of varied strategies employed in campaign messages are to utilize sex and humor. Calvin Klein advertisements, Herbal Essence shampoo messages, and Jockey underwear commercials exemplify the use of gratuitous sexual appeals in message designs. The Dodge Neon automobile goes for the cute and the humorous in their simple "hi" message. And we all have seen the repeated Energizer battery messages featuring the humorous pink bunny drumming across the television screen (see Figure 22.3).

FIGURE 22.3 *Bunny Ad.* The Energizer bunny is at it again. As political candidate Bob Fremgen delivers his platform to the camera, he's interrupted by the Energizer bunny.

Courtesy of Feature Photo Service and www.newscom.com

Another example of message content demonstrates just how exaggerated commercial messages have become to get the attention of the audience member. Commercial, political, and social issue campaign messages have incorporated shocking—sometimes even offensive—designs to draw the audience member to their messages by violating social taboos (Goldman, 1992; Goldman & Papson, 1996, p. 105). Calvin Klein's use of children in provocative poses has brought allegations of child pornography. Benetton—an Italian clothing manufacturer that puts out advertising messages on social issues rather than on their products—engenders a lot of notoriety for their attention-grabbing messages of photos of a priest and nun kissing, a man on death row, and black and white children going to the bathroom together. And the World Wildlife Fund has gained attention for its social issue campaigns with photos of dead elephants left to decay in the forest.

Figure 22.4 illustrates a social issue campaign using humor and shock value in its call to get tested for colon cancer.

And finally, the newest, most recent design in all kinds of campaigns is to sell the image of an organization, not the features of the product or service. The intention here is to construct a message that portrays a scene or mood or attitude, often without even mentioning the organization or the organization's products or the social cause. These messages attempt to entertain the receiver, to humor the receiver, to appeal sexually to the receiver, or, in many cases, to puzzle the receiver by presenting a setting or narrative that merely alludes to the product or the purpose of the campaign.

Examples of ads selling an image rather than providing product information are all those advertisements for automobiles that show drivers racing along a curvy road or climbing the rough terrain of a mountain. Virtually no information about the car is presented, only the fun and pleasure of driving—which campaign designers, nevertheless, hope will lead to sales.

FIGURE 22.4 *American Cancer Society Polyp Man "Lineup" Advertisement.*   Part of the national public service advertising campaign created by the Advertising Council and the American Cancer Society, the Polyp Man™ campaign (depicting the pesky Polyp Man character dressed in a large red polyp suit) included television, radio, Internet, and print advertising designed to air primarily during Colon Cancer Awareness Month, March 2003.

Courtesy PR Newswire Photo Service and www.newscom.com

These various designs and message strategies reveal how difficult it is to deliver effective advertising messages today. As all these message designs suggest, advertising agencies are forced to be very creative in their advertising, given the resistance of the audience member today. We are all saturated with media and advertising messages throughout our day. Society's diversity, media cynicism, and resistance to media stimuli force campaign communication to be challenging to the viewer, with all kinds of humorous, shocking, or sexual campaign messages.

Public Relations and Political Messages

Research into public relations messages is not as detailed as advertising campaign messages. However, professionals in public relations are interested in what works and what does not work in public relations campaigns. For decades the PRSA (Public Relations Society of America), the professional organization for public relations practitioners, has studied and awarded the top campaigns and best campaign messages in the field. The *Public Relations Journal* reveals the silver anvil first place and bronze anvil second place awards every June. Many kinds of public relations awards are presented: three awards for community relations, four for institutional programs, six for special events, seven for public service, one for public affairs, fourteen for marketing communication, three for crisis communication, five for internal communication, one for investor relations, one for multicultural public relations, and four for integrated marketing.

For years these awards for public relations campaigns have marked the best in public relations messages and public relations campaigns. Space doesn't allow a summary of all these awards, but the "best of" silver award for 2002 was presented to the campaign for XM Satellite Radio and Andrews Communications, which worked with Paine Public Relations and with the PR Consultants Group and Allyn and Company.

We don't have a lot of findings on political campaigns either, but Benoit and his colleagues have done more research than anyone on political messages. His research on political campaign messages finds many strategies embedded in these kinds of messages. Benoit, Pier, and Blaney (1997) analyzed political advertisements from the Republican and Democratic election campaigns for President from 1980 to 1996. The close textual analysis of these political messages reveals that acclaiming (favoring one's candidate) and attacking (unfavorable to opponent) were common features across all the political messages, and defense strategies were generally avoided, probably because candidates do not want to talk about the opposition. Democrats were more likely to acclaim than attack; Republicans were more like to attack than acclaim. Content of the commercials focused on policy matters twice as much as character of the candidates. Benoit and colleagues (1997) note the interesting finding that incumbents were much more likely to praise than attack the opposition. As to actual content of the messages, they note that what candidates have done in the past, what they promise to do, and the personal qualities of the candidate are the dominant topics across all political messaging.

This discussion of the detailed history of advertising campaign messages and the lesser-known trends in public relations and political messages nevertheless draws attention to how campaign communication reflects the societal and cultural changes throughout history. Messages reflect society, and messages are tied to the people who receive them.

With this in mind, the next consideration becomes how to choose (if you are a message designer) or how to understand (if you are a media consumer) which kinds of message strategies are most effective in communicating to multiple, different audiences.

What Theories Can Best Explain the Influence of Message Design?

Whether you are a campaign professional designing entire campaigns or you are only an individual who receives and processes commercials, knowledge of the theories and models that govern the creation process are informative to everyone. The campaign strategist is obliged to create unique messages that are tailor-made to each of these audiences and, more important, to get the audiences *to pay attention* to these messages and, hopefully, then *be persuaded* to accept their content. Needless to say, this is a hard thing to do when communicating to thousands or millions of people. It is also difficult for the audience to understand all the messages they are bombarded with every day.

Message Design: A Matching Exercise

The process of *designing* campaigns and *interpreting* campaigns is a two-pronged process. As mentioned throughout the study of campaign communication, the organization and the audiences are in a mutual relationship. The organization wants to communicate its desired messages. The targeted audiences attempt to process and understand the organization's messages. For example, an organization might want to persuade the community to accept its new zoning proposal so that they can build more office buildings. Some community residents might process these messages because they are in construction and could get work. Others might process the messages but not accept them because they see their open green spaces full of buildings and their taxes going up.

A few theories can help us understand the dilemma that faces many organizations and their audiences in the course of a campaign. To begin, it is important to appreciate that the organization's task is to create messages that match the interests of the audiences, and the audience's choice is to pay attention to them and perhaps be persuaded to accept them. Recent research on campaign message design confirms that receivers of information will pay attention to messages that are consistent with their already held beliefs and interests. Only recently have public relations researchers begun to study message design at length and teachers present more about the details of message design (Hallahan, 2000; Moffitt, 1990; Morton, 1984).

Hallahan (2000) presents the **M-A-O model—motivation, ability, and opportunity—** as a model that explains how persons pay attention to messages. Based on earlier research this model claims that persons move through four levels of processing messages: preattention, focal attention, comprehension, and elaboration. When exposed to any new message content, a receiver will enter the preattention stage (this information about the new cultural center is interesting), then the focal attention stage (this cultural center might be something I would use), then the comprehension stage (I understand how much this will cost and all the benefits it will have for me and the community), and finally the elaboration stage (I will tell my friends about this cultural center proposal). Notice that this model is similar to the advertising AIDA model—attention, interest, desire, and action (www.adglossary.com).

Hallahan also points to the **elaboration likelihood model (ELM),** that you studied in earlier chapters, as a theoretical construct that explains people will process information that is topic-relevant to them. In essence, the ELM posits that campaign designers have two key challenges in creating messages: *match* the content to the audience's level of processing and *encourage* deeper processing (p. 466). For example, if an organization wants their employees to accept their proposal for flextime, then the organization will need to deliver messages that show how flextime will aid the employees' daily schedules (matching) and then present message content that details exactly how flextime make their lives easier, give them more time with families, make them more money, and so on (encouraging). Hallahan (2000) presents a lengthy, detailed listing of message strategies appropriate for motivating and moving people to process messages, message features such as novel photos, music and color, concrete words and not abstracts, repetition of messages, and so on.

Selective perception is another theory that recognizes the importance of matching message to receiver for successful meaning. You have already studied selective perception relative to interpersonal, group, and mass communication, but it also has much explanatory power relative to campaign communication (Davison, Boylan, & Yu, 1976; Freedman & Sears, 1965). Selective perception theory explains that audiences will pay attention to messages that agree with their knowledge, attitudes, behaviors, needs, and leisure activities and probably be moved to act on them.

Assuming that previous, original research on these targeted populations revealed the unique and dominant knowledge areas, attitudes, behaviors, or images that each member holds toward the business, the task for the campaign manager is the conceptualization of messages that will contain the textual and visual factors that will appeal to these qualities in the audience (Hallahan, 2000; Moffitt, 1999; Schmidt & Hitchon, 1999).

We should also note here that this theory is an example of the laws approach in communication research, that is, that theories can be based on assumptions that regularities exist in all persons' behavior. Because selective perception theory claims that most people will pay attention to messages that contain information that they agree with, this theory is based on a laws approach. However, at the same time, elements of the rules approach in campaign communication are also present since selective perception theory grants that each individual has unique needs, interests, and opinions that might attract her or him to particular messages.

Another theory taken from the study of relationship and group communication, explained in detail in Chapter 8, and also related to selective perception is cognitive dissonance, which can also be used to explain the design of campaign messages (Festinger, 1957). Where selective perception explains that persons, in general, pay attention to messages that agree with their current beliefs (Davison, Boylan, & Yu, 1976; Freedman & Sears, 1965), the theory of **cognitive dissonance** offers the prediction that persons will also be drawn to messages that disagree with their beliefs (Festinger, 1957, 1964). This is to say that in many cases we can also be affected by messages that are inconsistent with what we believe. This works because when we see a message that contradicts our beliefs, the tension we feel between our belief and the alternative information can encourage us to process the message. That is, we either resist the message or we adapt to the message. The important component of cognitive dissonance theory is that we feel so uncomfortable about the contrary message, we are forced to do something about it.

Now, in cases where a person holds a very strong position toward an issue—for example, toward capital punishment, gun control, or euthanasia—an individual can even be drawn to a contradictory message. The attraction happens because then the person feels, "I disagree so much with this that I nevertheless pay attention to it so I can either confirm my resistance to it or change my mind toward it." With some individuals, the contrary message could work like this: "I feel even stronger about my view, which is opposite to this!"

Examples of how both these theories are operationalized can be taken from the abortion social movement in our society. Most persons have a strong set of beliefs and attitudes toward either the pro-life position of protection of the fetus or the pro-choice position that privileges the mother's wishes. According to selective perception, when persons with a pro-life position view or hear a pro-life message, they are drawn to process it because it is consistent with their pro-life stance. The same goes for individuals with a pro-choice position who see a pro-choice message; they would tend to pay attention to the message that agrees with their position.

According to cognitive dissonance, however, when persons with a pro-life position are exposed to a pro-choice message, they could also be drawn to the message because it makes them aware of their pro-life position. Once again, the meaning process would be something like, "I am pro-life, but I am processing this contradictory pro-choice message because it makes me feel even stronger toward my pro-life opinions" or "I am uncomfortable with this message and am forced to resist it."

Matching messages to audience members does not remove the organization's authority to send out its own views and desired corporate images. For sure, an organization can decide information about itself, its history, its products, or its services and communicate these messages to all its important populations. When an organization makes its messages relative to its audiences, the audiences will, hopefully, be more inclined to process them. Once again, we have the concept of relationship-building explaining public relations, in this instance, effective campaign message design.

Recognition of the explanatory and predictive power of the AIDA model, the MAO model, ELM and of theories of selective perception and cognitive dissonance draws attention to one crucial principle of campaign message design. Campaign message design is a **matching exercise.** If persons selectively perceive and process messages they agree with, then the job of the message designer is to come up with messages that present the organization's views with elements that match the audience's feelings. [Web site: Collapse Theory of Corporate Image]

How Can Messages Be Created to Match the Audience?

In the study of campaign messages, a **message strategy** is similar to a model or a formal descriptive theory. In the same way that a descriptive theory or model presents information, a message strategy is defined as a design feature, or information, that can deliver an organization-produced corporate image or match audience characteristics. For example, a point of information in a message can note the *organization's* environmental conscious-ness or its excellent products or services, a political candidate's pledge to lower taxes, or the World Wildlife Fund's call to save the African elephant. Also in these messages should be information that is of interest to the *audience.*

Message strategies are more than just pieces of information, however. Message strategies can be categorized along many lines. Message content can appeal to the needs of the audience, demographics of the audiences, or psychological traits of the audience members (Hallahan, 2000; Moffitt, 1990; Pfau & Parrott, 1993; Schmidt & Hitchon, 1999). Message content can point to the knowledge, attitudes, or behaviors that the organization would like to encourage in its respective populations.

A message strategy reflects a conscious choice to include in a message those pieces of information that will appeal to the audience members. This benefits both the organiza-tion and the intended audience members. The decision to design a message with a certain kind of information because this information will match the lived experiences of the audi-ence members and draw their interest into the message content has qualities of attention-getting, comprehension, elaboration, and explanation (Hallahan, 2000; Moffitt, 1990; Morton, 1984; Schmidt & Hitchon, 1999). According to AIDA, MAO, ELM, selective per-ception, and cognitive dissonance, message strategies embedded in messages based on au-dience traits and based on organizational intent should be successful. We can explain that this is likely to happen. We can reasonably predict that it will happen.

In this final section of this chapter, we get into the details of message strategies as design features, looking at examples of message strategies so that you can understand how various message strategies can be formatted into a message that both matches an audience's images and at the same time delivers information from the organization. Your understand-ing of this process makes you a better consumer of media and campaign messages.

Basic strategies represent the *kind of information* that the campaign message plan-ner thinks should go into the campaign messages. Basic strategies are not the actual words nor the visuals placed in a message but are the suggestions of what kind of information should be incorporated into the campaign messages.

Basic Strategies: Knowledge, Attitude, Behavior

The most fundamental framework of a basic strategy is a piece of information, an attitude, or a behavior placed within a message in order to match a kind of knowledge, attitude, or behavior in the audience members. At the same time, remember that information, attitudes, or behaviors that reflect the organization are also basic strategies that can be placed within messages. Let us now examine these kinds of basic strategies and see how they can be op-erationalized into a campaign message.

Knowledge/attitude/behavior is the most common classification of basic strategies contained in a message. If you think about the various kinds of advertising, public rela-tions, political, or social issue messages that you are constantly exposed to, you can iden-tify within each of these messages pieces of information that serve as simple knowledge: the cost of a service, the ingredients of a product, the community-enriching activities of an organization, or the social causes supported by a social agency. Looking a little closer at

FIGURE 22.5 *Bill Brady Campaign for Illinois State Senate, 44th District.*

some messages, you might find references to attitudes implied in the message: this product is the best on the market, the corporation is good for the community, this political candidate is most sympathetic to the voters, or a charity fundraiser to support cancer research is the most deserving. Also very common are suggestions in messages to enact a behavior: buy a product, vote for a candidate, get your friends to donate money to our social cause.

Figure 22.5 illustrates how knowledge, attitude, and behavior points are contained in a message. For example:

Knowledge points: Bill Brady is Illinois State Senate candidate.
                               Brady is 44th District.
                               Brady is a family man.
                               Brady owns a dog.
                               Message paid for by Citizens for Bill Brady.

Attitude points: Brady is experienced lawmaker.
                               Brady is friend of hardworking families.
                               Brady is successful owner and employer.
                               Brady favors schools.

Brady favors the local economy.
Brady will work for his district.

Behavior points: Use the web site.
Use the phone to reach Brady.
Vote for Brady.

Note that, in this political message, basic strategies of knowledge/attitude/behavior, or these pieces of information, reflect the intentions of the organization/candidate Brady and match the audience's knowledge, attitude, or behaviors.

Basic Strategies: Demographic, Needs, Psychographic, Schema, Public Position Appeals

Demographic appeals are another kind of basic strategy to place in a message (Pfau & Parrott, 1993). Demographic information is relatively fixed information about a person, such as age, gender, level of education, marital status, and so on. While some of the information can change—age, marital status, level of income—it is nevertheless information about individuals that is relatively separate from their knowledge, attitudes, or behaviors.

Needs appeals represent numerous possibilities for message design features (Pfau & Parrott, 1993). You have studied in earlier chapters the Maslow hierarchy of needs model: that each person has physical, safety, social, self-esteem, and self-actualization needs. That is, a message can—again, through the words or the design elements—contain appeals to one or more of these needs: for example, an appeal to a physical need through information on the importance of joining a gym for physical exercise or of donating to St. Jude charities to benefit the physical needs of sick children.

In addition to these basic needs, other needs can be portrayed in messages (Pfau & Parrott, 1993). One set of complementary needs appeals is to identify a social need or a personal need. For example, a public relations message to employees that urges their participation in a race for the cure for breast cancer could contain either kind of need appeal. If the message contains facts about the benefit to society for helping women through a cure for breast cancer, a social need is present. If the message contains facts that urge women to race because it will empower them personally to do something about a killer disease, then the need appeal is a personal one.

Psychographic appeals, explained in the previous chapter as campaign structure strategies, are, within the framework of message design, also theorized as message strategies. Taken primarily from research findings in the marketing and advertising fields (Clark, 1988; Pfau & Parrott, 1993; Schultz, 1990; Schultz & Tannenbaum, 1989; Schultz, Martin, & Brown, 1984), psychographic information refers to the general psychology of the targeted audiences, to their personality types, to their lifestyle practices, to their leisure preferences, to how they want to be regarded by others, and even to their preferences for how they spend their money. If the campaign manager can determine the psychographics of a given population, making up appeal goals to match these psychological leanings can be very effective in catching the attention of the audience members.

A couple of models of psychographic appeals can illustrate personality types. One model classifies four kinds of personality types: need-driven persons are driven primarily to satisfy physical needs; inner-directed persons live to satisfy themselves with little or no thought to those around them; outer-directed persons buy things and live generally to impress others around them; and integrated persons have elements of inner- and outer-directed personality types (Clark, 1988; Pfau & Parrott, 1993).

Schema appeals are another kind of message strategy. Schema are cognitive processes, or cognitive structures, that all persons have learned throughout their lives (Pfau & Parrott, 1993; Salomon, 1979, 1981, 1987; Schmidt & Hitchon, 1999). These experiences are learned from the media, friends, and family, and all other experiences and stimuli surrounding us in the environment. We are not born with schema. They are learned reactions—rules we develop—to handle the environment around us. Building on findings taken from psychology, schema appeals identify another facet of the individual that can be isolated and then appealed to in a campaign message.

Three kinds of schema have been identified. **Event schema** are learned reactions and social rules people develop for how to act in certain settings and situations. We have learned throughout our lives how to act in church, in school, in our own home. **Role schema** are those learned behaviors and expectations of certain occupations. We have learned the social expectations of how a typical professor is supposed to act, how a minister or priest acts, or how a junk dealer might dress or act in his junkyard. And finally, **person schema** are all those expectations and stereotypes we have learned about certain kinds and labels of persons (not toward occupations but toward types of persons). Take, for example, schema we have for "rednecks," "spacey blondes," or "absent-minded professors." Once again, as with all the other kinds of message strategies already mentioned, a campaign manager who can uncover any of these schema in a population has a head start in designing effective messages that might begin to address these schema, without offending anyone, of course (Schmidt & Hitchon, 1999).

The final message appeal relates to **public positions** that the targeted audiences possess. You have studied in the preceding chapters that several kinds of publics and public positions can be identified in audience members. The situational theory presents four kinds of publics—active, aware, latent, and nonpublic—that label the degree of knowledge, attitudes, and behaviors in persons. For example, an active public will possess knowledge, attitudes, and behaviors, and a nonpublic public will possess none. In addition, other publics are labeled as apathetic, hot-issue, or all-issue publics.

Knowledge of these public positions is important for understanding message appeals. It is very simple: If a campaign designer is planning messages to an interested audience (an audience with active, aware, hot-issue, or all-issue public positions), there should be a lot of copy and a lot of information contained in the messages. On the other hand, planning messages to disinterested audiences demands message design that is uncluttered, simple to process, with very little to no copy and more visuals. You can see that whereas other basic appeals target the content of a message, this appeal to public positions concerns the amount of copy and visuals that are appropriate for the targeted audience members.

Summary

After a review of the history of advertising, public relations, and political messages and a look at the bold and varied trends in current message design, this chapter has presented several key theories that can explain and inform exactly how to design messages for mass audiences. First, the AIDA model, the MAO model, ELM, and theories of selective perception and cognitive dissonance explain how persons will process messages that agree with their lived experiences.

Hopefully, you appreciate the complexity of design elements available for the message designer and the intricacy with which these elements can be combined within messages. One dimension of message strategies is basic strategies, which identify the kind and amount of information appropriate for a given audience.

Understanding the theories and models that guide the campaign message designer can also make you a more informed consumer of messages. Given what you now know about various appeals, kinds of information, and message strategies that go into campaign messages, you can now assume what you think the organization thinks about you. For example, a message with certain demographic or schema appeals can suggest to you that the organization is targeting a particular gender or occupation and that the organization considers you an audience member with these traits. This reverse analysis of organizational intent can be interesting when you deconstruct the strategies of a message.

Discussion Questions

1. Can you identify any commercial, political, or social issue campaign messages that are appearing today that have any of the qualities of the campaign messages of the 1950s through the 1990s?

2. Choose a current campaign that is utilizing mostly the same design messages, and from these messages identify any audience appeals or basic strategies—knowledge/attitude/behavior, demographic, needs, psychographics, and schema—that you see embedded in these messages.

3. Consider that a person is exposed to multiple messages created for a political campaign and, further, that this person has strong attitudes or images toward one side, or one candidate. Do you think the theory of selective perception or the theory of cognitive dissonance would affect this person's knowledge, attitude, and behaviors the most toward her or his favorite candidate?

4. Choose a message from a commercial campaign and identify the frame and mortis. Then through your additional identification of the ratio of copy to visuals, note whether the intended audience is believed to be an interested or a disinterested audience by the organization.

References

Benoit, W. L., Pier, P. M., & Blaney, J. R. (1997). A functional approach to televised political spots: Acclaiming, attacking, defending. *Communication Quarterly, 45*(1), 1–20.

Clark, E. (1988). *The want makers: The world of advertising: How they make you buy.* New York: Viking.

Davison, W. P., Boylan, J., & Yu, F. T. C. (1976). *Mass media systems and effects.* New York: Holt, Rinehart, & Winston.

Festinger, L. (1957). *A theory of cognitive dissonance.* Stanford, CA: Stanford University Press.

Festinger, L. (1964). *Conflict, decision, and dissonance.* Stanford, CA: Stanford University Press.

Freedman, J. L. & Sears, D. O. (1965). Selective exposure. In L. Berkowitz (Ed.), *Advances in Social Psychology* (2nd ed.). New York: Academic Press.

Goldman, R. (1992). *Reading ads socially.* London: Routledge.

Goldman, R., & Papson, S. (1996). *Sign wars: The cluttered landscape of advertising.* New York: Guilford Press.

Hallahan, K. (2000). Enhancing motivation, ability, and opportunity to process public relations messages. *Public Relations Review, 26*(4), 463–480.

Moffitt, M. A. (1999). *Campaign strategies and message design.* Westport, CT: Praeger.

Morton, L. P. (1984). Use of photos in public relations messages. *Public Relations Review, 10*(4), 16–22.

Pfau, M., & Parrott, R. (1993). *Persuasive communication campaigns.* Boston: Allyn and Bacon.

Russell, J. T. & Lane, R. (1990). *Kleppner's advertising procedure* (11th ed.). Englewood Cliffs, NJ: Prentice-Hall.

Salomon, G. (1979). *Interaction of media, cognition, and learning.* San Francisco: Jossey-Bass.

Salomon, G. (1981). *Communication and education: Social and psychological interactions.* Beverly Hills: Sage.

Salomon, G. (1987). *Interaction of media, cognition, and learning: An exploration of how symbolic forms cultivate mental skills and affect knowledge acquisition.* San Francisco: Jossey-Bass.

Schmidt, T. L., & Hitchon, J. C. (1999). When advertising and public relations converge: An application of schema theory to the persuasive impact of alignment ads. *Journalism & Mass Communication Quarterly, 76*(3), 433–455.

Schultz, D. E. (1990). *Strategic advertising campaigns* (3rd ed.). Lincolnwood, IL: National Textbook Company.

Schultz, D. E., Martin, D., & Brown, W. P. (1984). *Strategic advertising campaigns* (2nd ed.). Lincolnwood, IL: National Textbook Company.

Schultz, D. E., & Tannenbaum, S. I. (1989). *Essentials of advertising strategy* (2nd ed.). Lincolnwood, IL: National Textbook Company.

Simmons, R. E. (1990). *Communication campaign management.* New York: Longman.

www.adglossary.com

23

Building Organizational Relationships and Integrated Marketing

Yungwook Kim and Dean Kazoleas

> You cannot depend on the product alone to build consumer confidence. It's the rapport, the empathy, the dialogue, the relationship, the communication you establish with the consumer that makes the difference. These separate you from the pack.
>
> Schultz, Tannenbaum, and Lauterborn, *Integrated Marketing Communications,* 1992

Organizational campaign communication rests on the importance of balanced and reciprocal communication between the organization and its populations. This chapter examines two of the most important issues in recent campaign research that address this ideal of symmetry. First, because the symmetrical model of campaign communication is considered by many to be the ideal model of business communication, researchers have developed theories that can explain, predict, and develop good relationship building with audiences. Researchers have turned to business, organizational, and interpersonal communication theory to further analyze and understand an organization's building of relationships. The second issue of integrated marketing is another recent move in business communication that combines, integrates, and aligns the marketing, advertising, and public relations functions of the organization, so that they present a systematic and unified communication function for the organization. This unified and consistent approach helps the organization to maximize and balance the relationships between the organization and its relevant stakeholder publics.

In this chapter, you will read about the following concepts:

- Organizational relationships' similarity to personal relationships
  - Building relationship characteristics through each stage
  - Misunderstandings and mistrust

- Balance of power in organizations and audiences
  - Economic approach
  - Social exchange theory
  - Social penetration theory
  - Uncertainty reduction theory
  - Dialectic theory
- Relationship marketing
  - Relationship formation theory
  - Steps for fostering organizational-audience relationships
- Integrated Marketing Communication (IMC)
  - IMC versus traditional marketing
  - IMC versus public relations
- Advantages to IMC
  - Changing role of public relations

Chris: I saw a spokesperson for Exxon on television the other night giving an interview about the *Valdez* oil spill in Alaska. This guy was describing and promoting all of the environmental efforts of Exxon and said that Exxon was doing fine on cleaning up their oil spill and on all their other environmental projects. . . . Isn't that ridiculous? Nobody in Alaska or in the other 49 states thinks Exxon is doing okay.

Ann: Exxon does not understand what people really think of them. They think they can say anything and that everybody believes what they say. Those Exxon people think that if they give good things and get good news, then people will automatically like them.

These residents of Alaska and customers of Exxon can be seen as representative voices expressing the images that some audiences probably had about the environmental pollution caused by Exxon (see Figure 23.1). This short conversation between Chris and Ann demonstrates an audience's images of a company and how inaccurate the company's perception of their audiences' images might be, especially if they focus on the use of their "talking points" that are carried by the media. The dilemma faced by the public relations professional is how to balance the communications regarding negative consequences that have resulted from either intentional and/or unintentional acts that occur as a result of organizational policy, with the communications that present the organization's point of view, communications that accurately portray the actions undertaken to rectify issues and/or problems, as well as the statements that are intended to reinforce the organization's commitment to its stakeholders.

For example, if an organization's image suffers because they earn a bad reputation about their environmental policies, the company's recognition of these negative images does not improve their current negative image, nor solve problems that may be linked to these image-based issues. Similarly, their image and or reputation does not necessarily improve if the media portray them as taking effective corrective action, or absolve them of blame. Rather, image repair only occurs when the organization's stakeholders change their cognitive images of the organization. That it to say, only the members of its related audi-

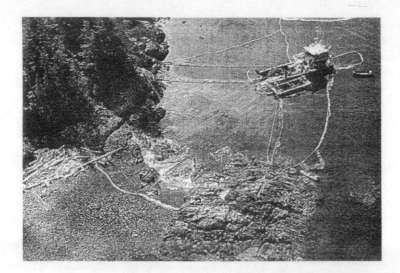

FIGURE 23.1 Aerial photo of a maxi-barge with water tanks and spill workers hosing a beach, Prince William Sound, Alaska.

Photo courtesy of the EXXON VALDEZ Oil Spill Trustee Council

ences can play a critical role in changing the balance and the relationship between the organization and its audiences. Only the audience members' images or perceptions of the issue and the organization can work to change the nature of the relationship between the organization and the populations. Thus, the population's images of an organization (which are often based on the communication efforts of the organization) become the essence of the organization–population relationship (Hon & Grunig, 1999). We begin this chapter with suggestions on how an organization should manage its relationships with all its important, targeted audiences and how the corporation is obliged to communicate its vested images to these multiple audiences.

How Are Organizational Relationships Similar to Personal Relationships?

Recall from the previous chapters that the term "public relations" refers to the process by which an organization creates, monitors, maintains, and manages the relationships it has with all of its relevant internal and external stakeholder groups. Most introductory public relations texts usually illustrate the public relations function through the use of systems theory, whereby an organization exists in an environment where the purpose of the "PR" function is to manage the relationships with key stakeholder groups (such as the media, customers, the community, regulators, industry groups, and so on). In the current chapter, we return to some of the concepts of interpersonal communication but discuss them in the context of how an organization should use communication to cultivate relationships with its multiple audiences. In a number of previous chapters, theories from the disciplines of organizational and interpersonal communication were defined, described, and discussed. The following sections will draw heavily on some of those theories, especially those that deal with relationships.

Before beginning, however, one very important point must be made about organizational communication. A main underlying tenant of effective organizational communication and positive relations with audiences is that organizations should communicate regularly with their audiences, much like two people who are friends would do. So, instead of an organization waiting for a crisis to "explode" or a reactive situation to occur and then be addressed by the organization, organizations should continually communicate with their target audiences and monitor the status of their relationships with all relevant stakeholders. While continual communication and remaining linked with key stakeholder groups seems to make good common sense, and is a relationship that has long been understood by public relations scholars and practitioners, to many in business and industry this seems to be a new and innovative idea.

Relationship marketing is a newer concept in business communication that advocates an ongoing, continual fostering of positive relationships with all the respective and important populations relating to the corporation. What makes this business assumption "radical," however, is the notion that, according to relationship marketing, the audience, the images they hold, and their perceptions are actually more important in the communication process than the organization. That is, the communication to the audience and the images of the audience toward the organization are more important than the organization's images of its audiences. We have a dichotomy here—while many campaign researchers advocate symmetry as the best model of campaign communication, relationship marketing advocates call for more importance and attention on the audience as opposed to the organization. This chapter's exploration of some of the issues of symmetry versus relationship marketing and the privileging of the audiences' images reflects the humanistic paradigm that is based on the deep understanding of communication within the social formation. Further, this discussion reveals features of communication outlined in Chapter 1, that communication reflects social structures and that communication is strategic.

Stages of an Organizational Relationship

All kinds of relationships—those between persons (interpersonal), those within a group, those between audiences and organizations, and, likewise, those between organizations and audiences—have several stages through which they progress. In general, all relationships progress from an initial stage and grow to a final, bonding stage. Once the relationship is initiated, maintaining the relationship becomes critical (Knapp & Vangelisti, 1992).

Research by Stafford and Canary (1991) has identified specific strategies that organizations can follow to establish and maintain positive relationships with key stakeholder and audience groups. This research has also identified a series of stages through which organizations often progress in maintaining relationships with their populations (Stafford & Canary 1991; Canary & Stafford, 1992). Stafford and Canary suggest that **five maintenance strategies** work best when organizations maintain relationships with their publics. First, **positivity,** or good feelings, between both parties enhances the beginning of the relationship. Second, **mutual assurances,** or a building of trust, between the audiences and the corporation build the relationship. Third, **openness** between the organization and its audiences allows the relationship to strengthen. Fourth, cooperation, collaboration, and the **sharing of tasks** increases mutual cooperation and friendliness. Finally, **creating and sharing social networks** brings the organization and its audiences to a strong state of mutual dependence, which in turn can foster increased trust. [Web site: Characteristics of an Organizational Relationship]

Misunderstandings and Mistrust

At this point it should also be clear that just as relationships between individuals can easily be misunderstood, relationships between organizations and audiences can just as easily be misunderstood. The **interpersonal perception theory** identified by Laing, Philipson, and Lee (1966) explains conflict between people and the organization, allowing the theory consequently to explain misperceptions and misunderstandings. This theory calls attention to conflict along three kinds of perception: first, consider **direct perception,** which is person A's perception of an issue; second, consider **meta-perception,** which is person A's perception of person B's perception; third, consider **meta-meta-perception,** which is person A's perception of B's perception about A's perception.

   This complicated tangle of direct, meta, and meta-meta perceptions is revealed in the Exxon conversation that opened this chapter. You might want to think back to what Exxon's *direct perception* of its own environmental policies was, what Ann thought of Exxon's perception of itself, which is *meta-perception,* what Exxon thinks people think of their organization, which is also *meta-perception,* and what Chris thought of other persons' opinions of Exxon, which is *meta-meta-perception.* The **coordination model** (see Figure 23.2) conceptualizes these kinds of perception.

   This figure of the coordination model compares the three kinds of perception and applies this model to the organizational setting. The most agreement is between direct

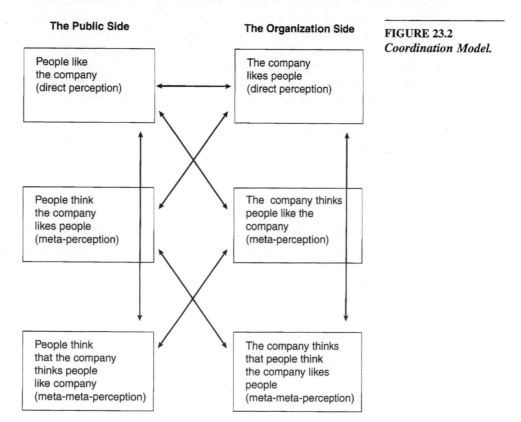

The Public Side

The Organization Side

FIGURE 23.2
Coordination Model.

People like
the company
(direct perception)

The company
likes people
(direct perception)

People think
the company
likes people
(meta-perception)

The company thinks
people like the
company
(meta-perception)

People think
that the company
thinks people
like company
(meta-meta-perception)

The company thinks
that people think
the company likes
people
(meta-meta-perception)

perception of the public side and direct perception of the organization side. The most accuracy is between the direct and meta-perception relationships. Look again at the figure and notice that the most problematic feature in relational conflicts is the difference between direct perception and meta-perception. This is called "misunderstanding" or "inaccuracy" (Broom, 1977; Broom et al., 1991; Broom et al., 1997). Revealed above in the Exxon conversation, this inaccuracy in corporate image in the eyes of the organization and in the eyes of the related populations is a drastic failure in Exxon's corporate image.

Researchers have applied the coordination model and its three kinds of perception identified in the interpersonal perception theory to public relations in an attempt to *understand* the process of *misunderstanding* in corporate image (Broom, 1977; Broom, Casey, & Ritchey, 1997; Grunig & Stamm, 1973; Knodell, 1976). The coordination model reveals the intricacies of the process of agreement, accuracy, and misunderstanding between an organization and its member populations. What this model demonstrates is that organizations can work toward positive images in the eyes of their member audiences only when they hold accurate and realistic images of themselves, only when they have accurate and realistic images of others, and only when they have accurate and realistic images of what others' images are of them.

However, it is important to remember that the relationship of an organization to its multiple audiences is not evenly balanced. The important point that was made at the very beginning of this chapter is critical in understanding this relational perspective—that the audiences' images are more important and more powerful in the organizational relationship than the organization's images of its audiences.

And, finally, one very important way to conduct relationship marketing has been documented through organizational and public relations research and theory. This **relationship formation theory** suggests that good organizational relationships demand a process of adaptation between both parties. The entire relationship between the organization and all its key audiences can be theorized and studied as a separate entity, distinct from the images of either the organization or the audience members. This perspective views all the parties of an organizational relationship as one holistic "unit," which means that we can study the relationship between the organization and its audiences as a separate entity from the organization or any one of its key stakeholder groups. This also means that the whole relationship can be studied to identify factors that impact it, factors and held images influencing each of the parties in the whole unit, and the ongoing interaction of all the parties within the unit (Broom, Casey, & Ritchey, 1997; Grunig & Huang, 2000; Hon & Grunig, 1999; Huang, 1998). Had the Exxon corporation appreciated the complexity of its multiple relationships and its role within the entire organizational relationship it shared with its audiences, Exxon might have done a better job of communicating more truthfully and more effectively to its member audiences.

What Theories Explain the Balance of Power between the Organization and Its Populations?

We see that relationships are initiated and maintained through the interaction of two parties. However, a relationship cannot be understood only in terms of the parties. All kinds of relationship research have demonstrated that relationships themselves can be understood as unique personal and social constructions. That is, the relationship and the communication bound up in the relationship between two parties—two persons or an organization and audience—can be studied as a unique unit of construction. Relationships as single entities can be understood as constructions created within the social network or social system that contains them.

For example, the relationship of any company to its constituencies can be understood as a unique construction of its own that also functions in unique and singular ways within society. Think about this. One company may enjoy a very positive relationship with its audiences, and the audiences may have mostly positive images of this organization; this happens given the unique maintenance strategies and relational characteristics that have fostered this very comfortable and positive relationship. However, another company with a record of damage to the environment and a track record of lies and deceits to its audiences suffers extremely negative images and virtually impossible relationships with its important audiences. Each relationship is a unit, with its own images and communication, which nevertheless has emerged as such given the societal concerns and cultural traits that constrain it.

A broad and profound body of research taken from interpersonal communication, social psychology, and management research provides an understanding of organizational relationships as social constructs and an appreciation of the precise balance of power between the populations and the corporation. Our first consideration here is to look at two theoretical approaches, or paradigms, that explain relationships in a fundamental way and relate them to public relations: the economic and the humanistic perspectives. The **economic approach** explains relationships through costs and benefits between the participants. This approach includes two theories that have been explained above in chapters on interpersonal and group communication. You have already studied a very well-known communication theory, the **social exchange theory,** which explains that a relationship can be built when one party provides something to the other party in exchange for something else, hence as a cost-benefit exchange (Roloff, 1981). For example, the organization provides its audiences and stakeholders with benefits (products and services for customers, salaries for the employees, improvements to the community, and so on), and the audiences in turn provide benefits to the organization (customers' money paid for products, employees' work on producing the product or services, community tax breaks or other amenities provided for the corporation, and so on). Just as in an interpersonal relationship, we could predict whether a customer has a "stable" and "satisfied" relationship with a store or business using these variables.

Another theory that explains how organizations maintain a balance of power with its populations is **social penetration theory** (Taylor & Altman, 1973). You have also reviewed this very popular interpersonal theory in Chapter 7. As it applies to public relations, this theory is consistent with the cost-benefit, or economic, approach because it explains an organizational relationship as the peeling away by both sides of the outer levels of uncertainty to get at the core of real understanding between them. In addition, social penetration theory is consistent with social exchange theory. These two theoretical positions envision more the peeling away of a person or an organization through self-disclosure of other information besides the sales and profits reasons or causes. Applied to an organizational setting, social penetration of the corporation by its related audiences and social penetration of the audiences by the corporation are accomplished both through a cost-benefit or profit-and-needs relationship and through a more indirect, informal approach where business information is simply shared and communicated to both sides. This model is enlightening in that it depicts organizational relationship as a multifaceted process, where audiences seek to uncover the true image of an organization, and at the same time the organization attempts to penetrate the core understanding of its audiences.

In applying social penetration theory to corporations, we would suggest that an organization that seeks a balanced, trustful, and shared power relationship with its audiences will allow the audiences to see inside to its inner core of positive images. An audience who seeks the cooperation and benefits of a strong positive relationship with an organization will give up its reservations and secrets to allow the organization to understand its positions and images. This example demonstrates the give-and-take, the cost and benefits, of the social penetration theory for understanding the power relationships of a company and its populations.

To add further understanding to the complex process whereby organizations build, manage, and maintain relationships, **uncertainty reduction theory** is applied to understanding the earlier stages of a relationship (Berger, 1988). At the onset of a relationship the parties use small talk and safe communication to establish a relationship with the other—hence, uncertainty reduction at the first meetings. Organizations and audience members can also be seen to employ the variables described in this theory, such as methods of reducing uncertainty, information seeking, seeking areas of perceived similarity, or sharing "networks," as they build relationships with each other. In this same way, personal messages and/or media messages serve to reduce uncertainty about the other by providing initial, "safe," or unthreatening, information about the other.

And another relationship theory more often used to conceptualize the later stages of a relationship is the **dialectic theory** (Baxter, 1990). This theory recognizes that audience members *and* organizations often experience the give-and-take, back-and-forth of contrasting positions as they get to know each other in the advanced stages of a relationship. This very human tendency is played out due to tensions and dialectic feelings in personal relationships and in organizational relationships. The pairs of extremes can include, for example, stability (or predictability) versus change (or novelty), autonomy versus connectedness, expression versus privacy, or commonality versus uniqueness. These types of dialectical tensions can be experienced by organizations as they relate to their audiences.

In sum, then, from a cost-benefit standpoint, organizations can enjoy very positive relationships of power with their audiences if they offer results that positively exceed the audiences' expectations of the organization. That is, the organization can offer products or benefits that overcome the expected level of satisfaction.

However, loyalty to an organization can mean more than just costs and benefits. The audiences' decision making and corporate images can include emotional and humanistic images of the corporation, for example, of company products, of positive images toward its charitable works in the community, or of the company's environmental efforts.

As testimony to the danger of losing this loyalty, consider the negative impact a web site such as "MonsantoSucks.com" could have on a corporation. Through this web site dissatisfied stakeholders (including customers, stockholders, community members, and those with environmental concerns) rally against a corporation (see Figure 23.3). Loyalty can represent an audience's long-term, committed, and emotion-oriented relationship to an organization and vice versa. Thus, effective public relations considers both aspects of relationships, which in turn builds favorable relationships with all audiences: offers quality products and benefits to the community beyond the populations' expectations and fosters empathic interactions with the targeted audiences. Organizational relationship management can be defined according to Thomlison (2000) as "the development, maintenance, growth, and nurturing of mutually beneficial relationships between organizations and their significant publics."

A final consideration—even though good organizational relationships are based on equal balances of power and equal relationship goals, the truth is that relationships between organizations and populations are not always based on equality between the parties. An organizational relationship can develop where one party is less truthful or more powerful than the other. As the relationship becomes unequal and asymmetrical, it becomes more difficult for the parties to engage in good communication with the other. [Web site: What Is a Stakeholder?]

An important point cannot be forgotten when studying organizational relationships and organizational image. The simple fact is that it is perceptions that count! When it comes to corporate images as intended by the organization and the corporate images felt by the audience members, according to relationship marketing, the perceptions and images that the audience members hold toward the organization are more important than the intended images of the corporation. When it comes to understanding the corporate image process as an organizational relationship, for relationship marketing, how the audience perceives the organization is more important than how the organization perceives its audiences. Image and perception are everything!

Exxon may give statements and claim no guilt for an oil spill, but the questions and negative images of the audience members interrupt and doom any kind of positive organizational relationship.

Monsanto SUCKS

- Monsanto versus Schmeiser—The Classic David versus Goliath Struggle...Schmeiser back in the fight over Roundup Ready Canola—May 15, 2002
- Monsanto has become the latest example of the biotechnology industry failing to control plants whose genes it has altered—*Wall Street Journal,* May 15, 2002
- Anniston, Alabama—Monsanto Liable for the World's Worst PCB Contamination—February 22, 2002

FIGURE 23.3 MonsantoSucks.com hosts links to a variety of service, labor, and environmental issues posted by disgruntled Monsanto stakeholders.

How Can Relationship Marketing Be Accomplished by an Organization?

All organizations must put forth continuous effort in order to maintain and develop favorable long-term relationships with appropriate audiences. Any organization that is serious about fostering and developing positive relationships and positive images with its audiences needs to consider an organized, conscientious program to enact strong, positive relationships. The development of a relationship management program can help facilitate open communication and positive relationships between organizations and their stakeholders. Such a program emphasizes the audiences' images toward the organization. This audience-oriented new concept has many ramifications for campaign communication. [Web site: Seven Steps for Relationship Marketing Campaign]

The relationship management campaign is more flexible when compared to other campaign strategies. The success of the campaign is evaluated by relational features such as trust, commitment, satisfaction, loyalty, and positivity—not by measures such as increased knowledge, attitudes, behaviors, or other images that are often more clearly evident after the execution of a campaign. Relationship management shifts more emphasis to invisible, long-term assets and their contribution to the organization rather than the typical campaign emphases on stimulating sales, managing corporate images, supporting a political candidate, or engaging a social issue.

Relationship management, as campaign communication, is so new that descriptive theories and prescriptive theories have not yet been tested thoroughly in real situations. Research is ongoing that measures the stages of an organizational relationship, maintenance strategies, and outcomes of these kinds of campaigns, and, importantly, measures an organizational relationship as a separate entity. Many campaign researchers are now beginning to embrace this new way of conducting and evaluating campaigns. The rest of this chapter will discuss another new paradigmatic shift—the move in business communication to integrated marketing—which will offer more information on the recent shift away from short, discrete campaigns to longer, audience-based and relationship-based campaigns.

How Is Integrated Marketing Related to Relationship Management?

Integrated marketing communication (IMC) is essentially the tactical and strategic coordination of all the communication functions that assist the promotion of the organization, its products, and its services to the stakeholder. However, at the core of these definitions the student will always find a number of key principles, such as the integration of all communications with the stakeholder (e.g., public relations, advertising, and marketing), a focus on the customers and information regarding their needs, preferences, and expectations, and a finally a call for a strategic framework where all efforts are made to coordinate and integrate the organization's strategies and tactics that are used to reach and impact its stakeholders. IMC rests on the notion of integration of the business fields of advertising, marketing, and public relations. That is, just as the term *integration* suggests,

IMC is a kind of business communication that consciously and intentionally combines the three commercial fields into order to consolidate all marketing/sales/image communication in messages to stakeholders.

Research utilizing a **systems theory** approach to integrated marketing communication (Sirgy, 1998) offers several excellent definitional examples of exactly how this works:

> IMC is a concept that recognizes the added value in a program that integrates a variety of strategic disciplines—for example, general advertising, direct response, sales promotion, and public relations—and combines these disciplines to provide clarity, consistency, and maximum impact. (p. 4)

Schultz (1996), noted IMC expert, offers this definition:

> The process of managing all sources of information about a product/service to which a customer or prospect is exposed which behaviorally moves the consumer toward a sale and maintains customer loyalty.

These definitions exemplify the integration of communication and the increased customer-based relational focus.

Are You IMC Experienced?

The students who have read the quotation at the beginning of this chapter and the definitions of relationship marketing and integrated marketing communications that were presented above probably believe that they have little knowledge and/or experience with integrated marketing communications models, but in reality they have often been the targets of IMC efforts. For example, when was the last time that you were in the market for some electronic gadget or "toy" like a "walkman" or MP3 player, or wanted to purchase a more expensive product like a computer, and decided to buy a particular brand or model *immediately* after seeing the latest commercial for that product? Probably never! If you are like most of today's students, you probably found a magazine that reviewed the model, looked up a review and/or comparison of models on the Internet, and then you may have asked a friend or two what they thought you should do. If you performed some or all of these prepurchase behaviors, then you are like many of today's critical, value-minded, and quality-oriented consumers. Moreover, if you ever wondered why large stores ask for your phone number when you make purchases, why you are frequently asked to register products, and/or why almost every web site wants you to register (they also track you by the "cookies" that have been placed on your hard drive), it is because they want to gather information about you to better integrate and coordinate their communication with you, making you a part of their integrated marketing communications program. In sum, they do these things to better track your preferences, better communicate, and to better maintain their relationship with you.

Today's consumers (like you) are more critical of products and services than ever and are more likely to pay less attention to advertising, be more critical of ads, and expect more from the products and services that they buy, as well as expect quality customer service and support from manufacturers. These are consumers who make informed purchase decisions, seek information to make decisions, find information including the claims made by ads and by marketing materials, and as such have high expectations.

Responding and perhaps capitalizing on these needs, the media have the provided the critical consumer with reviews, critical comparisons, and an ever-increasing brand of investigative reporting that often takes on an adversarial and/or anti-corporation theme (e.g., NBC's decision to "demonstrate/stage" a gas tank explosion after claims were made regarding fires on some GMC pickup truck models). Finally, the media have become much more fragmented with increasing numbers of both traditional and nontraditional channels (e.g., the Internet) that make targeting audiences difficult because of the increasingly large numbers of media choices (Caywood, 1997; Harris, 1997; Ries & Ries, 2002; Ries & Trout, 1993).

In response to these and other changes in the business and social environment (such as increased regulation and activism), organizations have learned that they have to be better connected to their stakeholders. As noted above, this relational connectivity is needed so that the organizations understand their expectations, understand their media usage patterns, listen to their complaints, and are able to reach them with messages promoting new products and services and that proactively bolster their image. The integrated communication model is the organizational response to the needs of today's organizations that have to compete for attention, dollars, and resources in an ever-changing and more aggressive business and social environment.

Where Is the Theory?

To many students and professionals the concept of IMC does not seem to be research and theory driven. However, this is clearly not the case. *The theory is the integration!* Sirgy (1998) notes that the integrated approach works off of the psychological concepts of contiguity and continuity, which more simply put means distance and association. The idea is to integrate the message strategies so that the associations made to the brand are maximized. In other words, we want to maximize the reach and impact of a well-known brand with a positive corporate image.

Craftsman tools are one such example. Because Craftsman is associated with ruggedness, high quality, and customer responsiveness (a lifetime guarantee on the tool), Sears uses that brand and reputation to market lawnmowers, power tools, and other mechanical implements. The idea is that since the term "craftsman" evokes associations with quality and service, it makes sense to use a wide variety of methods to promote a number of items that carry that positive brand, knowing that the new item will be psychologically linked to the positive feelings. Finally, the marketing, advertising, and public relations efforts work together to maximize the reach of the campaigns. But they all capitalize on the positive brand image of Craftsman.

In order to understand how this move has revolutionalized theory development in these areas of business communication (advertising, marketing, and public relations), let's look at exactly how integrated marketing is different from traditional marketing and from public relations communication.

Integrated Marketing versus Traditional Marketing

There are several characteristics that differentiate an integrated marketing communication approach from traditional marketing strategies. Whereas integrated marketing privileges relationships with stakeholders and integration of marketing/advertising/public relations, **traditional marketing** has always been interested in how to place the product or service on the market, relative to the competition and the consumers. Let's examine more closely the traits of the new trend toward integrated marketing, that is, a customer-and/or consumer-based focus. Schultz, Tannenbaum, and Lauterborn (1993), noted marketing scholars, highlight this recent move to integrated marketing, or customer-based focus, when they note that the four Ps of marketing (product, price, place, promotion) have become the four Cs:

1. Consumer wants and needs—which should drive all parts of the marketing and management process.
2. Consumer cost—this goes beyond the concept of price to include the relative cost to the target market and the degree to which the product provides "value" relative to cost.
3. Convenience—products and services have to be available and convenient to purchase.
4. Communication—two-way communication not only seeks customer input and feedback but also includes mechanisms for the use of that input and feedback into decision-making processes.

This customer focus is one of the ways that IMC models differ from traditional marketing models that focus on developing markets and distribution systems. Some more visible indicators of the integrated marketing communication model will also be the development and/or existence of extensive customer database systems that include tracking and contact management systems, the appearance of a consistent set of looks, feels, "faces" and messages across media and channels, as well as some degree of individualization of message targeting strategies. The more integrated the system, the better the ability to balance a consistent look, feel, and image with the delivery of highly targeted individualized messages (Sirgy, 1998). For example:

> Microsoft Corporation and Microsoft Windows: Microsoft's approach to the development, marketing, and communication of its Windows platform is an incredibly complex set of management and communication processes that integrate and attempt to track customers' needs, desires, and expectations at all times. Microsoft's research and development process includes both direct and indirect customer feedback.
>
> They often release "beta-versions" of new editions to industry experts and innovators in advance of the official release to get feedback that can be used to increase both the usability and the functionability of the product. Microsoft uses data gathered from its extensive web sites, data that are obtained from the "cookies" placed on users' computers, and feedback from registration information and from surveys not only to improve the way the product looks and feels but to build in components to better meet the needs of the customer. Microsoft uses a set of consistent themes in its web presence, its "desk-top" presence, its written communications, and in its advertising and marketing strategies.

Last, because the Microsoft brand is managed on a worldwide basis, it often uses simple catchy phrases that are easily translated into other languages. Microsoft's "Where do you want to go campaign" was projected to generate over one billion gross media impressions and was found everywhere from inside the product packaging of other Microsoft products, to traditional media, on buses, on the Internet, and on banners and other promotional items at industry trade shows. Microsoft also uses registration information to send specific promotional communications to individuals that use a specific product or related services.

Integrated Marketing versus Public Relations

While on the face of it the concept of integrated marketing communication appears to be a new discipline and an evolutionary development within the fields of public relations and marketing, this is not necessarily the case. At the core of the public relations discipline has always been a requirement that organizations promote a consistent and stable image of the organization, an image that demonstrates that all actions of the organization are aligned, or are consistent, with its core set of values, and an image that aims to balance the goals of the organizations with the needs of key stakeholders. This relationship and needs-oriented approach has long been the central focus of the public relations discipline. But in an age of intense market competition, media fragmentation, and rapid changes in the business, legal, and social environments, positive long-term relationships and meeting the needs of the stakeholder have now become a higher priority in the minds of marketers, advertising and public relations professionals, campaign strategists, and business executives.

The mixing of these functions has created controversy, especially among public relations professionals (Ehling, White, & Grunig, 1992; Hutton, 2001; Lauzen, 1995). Not surprising, these strategists see their functions and responsibilities coopted and performed by marketing and advertising communicators. Moreover, marketing practitioners have been much more aggressive in incorporating public relations strategy and practice as one of the integrated marketing activities (Moriarity, 1994). Some public relations practitioners argue that this shift has occurred because traditional marketing and advertising models focused so heavily on short-term gains and ignored long-term relationships that they were destined to fail.

The fear is that these traditionally narrower functions are becoming engaged in communication processes where their expertise is limited and where they pay lip service to the public relations models that work. In short, some argue that the sudden shift toward integration is more profit oriented for advertising and marketing firms, as opposed to a true shift to a relational paradigm, and that the results can cause problems for many organizations. [Web site: Are There Advantages to Integrated Marketing Communication?]

Are There Advantages to Integrated Marketing Communication?

For both the student and the practitioner of campaign communication, the most useful set of distinctions and balance-based formulas for the effective use of public relations, marketing, and the integrated model may lie in allowing the function, goals, and mission of the organization to dictate the degree to which larger emphases are placed on public relations and/or marketing. In other words, a sales-based organization will place greater emphasis and energy on the development of markets, while a health care organization may focus more on identifying the needs of its patients and providing high-quality care at reasonable cost. That is not to say that marketing should ignore focusing on the bigger picture and relationships with a wider variety of publics. Nor should public relations forget that organizations do have to "pay the bills" and are there to make money. Rather, the mission, function, and goals of the organization should be balanced with an effective mix of public relations and marketing.

Even though the move to integrated marketing meets with some resistance with those in public relations, the move toward integrated marketing seems to be an inevitable trend in corporate communication. This move represents an alignment and maximizing of communication resources within an organization. When well managed, an integrated marketing approach can bring with it some large advantages. The first is an increase in communication effectiveness, namely increased reach and increased frequency of organizationally consistent messages, with a higher degree of impact. The integrated model's reliance on research and tracking increases the probability that the right message gets to an interested and informed receiver. The use of nonadvertising strategies also gets attention, which reduces costs, and can help to drive "word of mouth" advertising (Ries & Ries, 2002; Sirgy, 1998). Lastly, the high degree of internal coordination also increases efficiency by reducing the duplication of efforts. Figure 23.4 presents three models for integrated marketing: marketing and public relations as equal but overlapping in importance; marketing communication as more dominant with public relations communication included in the marketing function; and, finally, a model of public relations communication as dominant with marketing a part of public relations function.

Furthermore, the products and services that are the target of those messages are better aligned with the needs and expectations of the customer. This alignment usually leads to increases sales and profits (Harris, 1997; Sirgy, 1998). From a brand management perspective, an integrated strategy incorporates a consistent look and feel, especially one that is built through customer research for increased brand awareness, brand recall, brand recognition, and brand differentiation. The larger focus on stakeholder relationships and social marketing (establishing the organization as a socially responsible member of the community (Fine, 1981; Kotler & Zaltman, 1971; Luck, 1974; Webster, 1992) also helps to build the positive image of the organization with a wider range of stakeholders, which may be helpful in the face of crises or future negative media attention. Integrated marketing adds to the corporation's bottom line by increasing the consistency and persuasiveness of all its messages to all its key stakeholders and by creating a resonant, consistent, and stable brand image (Caywood, 1997; Harris, 1997; Ries & Ries, 1998; Sirgy, 1998).

FIGURE 23.4 *IMC Figure with Interlocking Circles.*

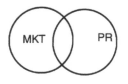
Equal but overlapping

Marketing as dominant

Public relations as dominant

The need for a corporation to integrate its marketing, advertising, and public relations communication makes sense, is logical, and has long been recognized by the public relations field. Hutton (2001) points out that the move toward the integrated model makes sense: first, because the integrated model offers a number of relative advantages over nonintegrated models; second, while the concept of integration appears to be a commonsense "no brainer," the past practices of nonalignment and miscoordination of marketing and public relations efforts are counterintuitive and make little sense.

Hutton further notes that in most instances a lack of integration and coordination of communications efforts are said to be reflective of poor overall communication. Public relations has long recognized the importance of two-way, balanced communication between an organization and its audiences rather than one-way, organization-centered communication to audiences (Grunig, 2001; Grunig & Hunt, 1984). Today, public relations is entering a new era where bottom line integration of all organizational communication has now been recognized as the ideal model of communication for many organizations (Broom et al., 1991; Kim, 2001a, 2001b). More importantly, this need for alignment and integration has now been recognized by public relation's traditional internal competitors such as the advertising and marketing departments and by key decision makers in the upper levels of management.

Furthermore, this trend toward integrated marketing and public relations also has marketers focusing on the long-term relationship, as well as current market opportunities. Kotler (1986) notes:

> Companies are shifting focus from creating a sale to creating a lifetime customer. They are beginning to view the customer as an asset; to retain this asset companies are shifting their thinking from transaction based marketing to relationship based marketing.

Recognized as one of the leading theorists in the area of marketing, Kotler (1986) modified what was considered a "holy mantra" of marketing when he advocated adding public relations as the fifth "P" to the traditional four Ps of marketing (product, price, place, and promotion. Kotler (1991) later stated:

> Marketers are finding it increasingly difficult to reach the minds and hearts of target customers. As mass marketing and even target advertising lose some of their cost effectiveness, message senders are driven to other media. They discover or rediscover the power of news, events, community programs, and other powerful communications modalities. Marketing public relations represents an opportunity for companies to regain a share of voice in a message satiated society. It not only delivers a strong share of voice to deliver a share of mind; it delivers a better, more effective voice in many cases.

In sum, given the changes in the media, social, and business environments, marketing efforts need to increasingly rely on the power of public relations to build reputation, to gain much wanted attention—often through positive media coverage, which is seen as more credible and powerful—and to build long-term relationships (Caywood, 1997; Ries & Trout, 1993; Ries & Ries, 2002). [Web site: The Changing Role of Public Relations]

Summary

Relationship management is an emerging concept in public relations. Its body of knowledge is interdisciplinary but borrows especially from theories of interpersonal communication. This personal, humanistic approach showcases the complexities of interpersonal relationships and applies these dynamics to organizations' relationships with their audiences.

The model of relationship management, very importantly, calls attention to the crucial role of the audience in the organizational relationship, making the organizational relationship an asymmetrical relationship, not a balanced or symmetrical relationship. That is, the populations' images toward the organization are much more critical to the relationship than the organization's images of itself or others.

Public relations research and theory has traditionally advocated a symmetrical, or balanced, relational approach between the organization and its audiences as an ideal communication situation (Grunig, 2001; Grunig & Hunt, 1984). But in the real world today, audiences have gained more control and power over giant corporations. A corporation's audiences can gain control over social phenomena and actively participate in the decision-making process of the organization. The effective use of an aggressive media or regulatory environment by stakeholders can also pressure and/or influence the decision-making process (Mitchell, Agle, & Wood, 1997). [Web site: Summary]

Another significant change in business communication was also presented in this chapter. IMC was presented and defined as the tactical and strategic coordination of all the communication functions that assist the promotion of the organization and its products and services to the stakeholder. IMC is a management system that integrates public relation's relational approach to building positive relationships with key stakeholders with traditional strategic marketing models.

Discussion Questions

1. In addition to the interpersonal theories presented in this chapter that inform campaigns, can you think of any other theories from group theory or organizational theory that might also explain the relationships between organizations and audiences?

2. Think of an organization that you have mostly positive images toward, then one you have very negative images toward. What factors from this chapter could explain why you have these positive images of one and negative images of the other?

3. Choose an organization that has recently suffered a crisis that has resulted in extremely negative press and harmful corporate images, and now explain what you would do, as a campaign manager, to recover its positive images.

4. Of the three commercial fields of marketing, advertising, and public relations, which one do you think is the most important to an organization's communication to its audiences?

5. Think of three campaign messages from one campaign that is currently being conducted and for each of these campaign messages, identify what features of the messages are marketing information, which are advertising, and which are public relations.

6. Think of the e mail you have received in the past two weeks, "snail mail" delivered by the post office, and the interactions you have had while shopping during the same two weeks. Try to identify at least three examples of where you were the target of an integrated marketing campaign.

References

Baxter, L. A. (1990). Dialectical contradictions in relationship development. *Journal of Social and Personal Relationships, 7,* 69–88.

Berger, C. R. (1988). Uncertainty and information exchange in developing relationships. In S. W. Duck (Ed.), *Handbook of personal relationships* (pp. 239–255). New York: Wiley.

Broom, G. M. (1977). Coorientation measurement of public issues. *Public Relations Review, 3,* 110–119.

Broom, G. M., Casey, S., & Ritchey, J. (1997). Toward a concept and theory of organization-public relationships. *Journal of Public Relations Research, 9*(2), 83–98.

Broom, G. M., Lauzen, M. M., & Tucker, K. (1991). Public relations and marketing: Dividing the conceptual domain and operational turf. *Public Relations Review, 17*(3), 219–225.

Canary, D. J., & Stafford, L. (1992). Relational maintenance strategies and equity in marriage. *Communication Monograph, 59,* 243–267.

Caywood, C. (1997). Twenty-first century public relations: The strategic stages of integrated communications. In C. Caywood (Ed.), *The handbook of strategic public relations and integrated communications* (pp. xi–xxvi). New York: McGraw-Hill.

Ehling, W. P., White, J., & Grunig, J. E. (1992). Public relations and marketing practices. In J. Grunig (Ed.), *Excellence in public relations and communications management* (pp. 357–393). Hillsdale, NJ: Lawrence Erlbaum.

Fine, S. H. (1981). *The marketing of ideas and social issues.* New York: Praeger Erlbaum Associates.

Grunig, J. (2001). Two way symmetrical public relations: Past, present, and future. In R. L. Heath (Ed.), *Handbook of public relations* (pp. 11–30). Thousand Oaks, CA: Sage.

Grunig, J. E., & Huang, Y. (2000). From organizational effectiveness to relationship indicators: Antecedents of relationships, public relations strategies, and relationship outcomes. In J. A. Ledingham & S. D. Bruning (Eds.), *Public relations as relationship management: A relational approach to public relations* (pp. 23–54). Hillsdale, NJ: Lawrence Erlbaum.

Grunig, J. E., & Hunt, T. (1984). *Managing public relations.* New York: Holt, Rienhart and Winston.

Grunig, J. E., & Stamm, K. R. (1973). Communication and coorientation of collectivities. *American Behavioral Scientists, 16,* 567–591.

Harris, T. L. (1997). Integrated marketing public relations. In C. Caywood (Ed.), *The handbook of strategic public relations and integrated communications* (pp. 90–105). New York: McGraw-Hill.

Hon, L., & Grunig, J. E. (1999). *Guidelines for measuring relationships in public relations.* Institute for Public Relations, University of Florida, PO Box 118400, Gainesville, FL 32611–8400.

Huang, Y. (1998). *Public relations strategies and organization-public relationships: A path analysis.* Paper presented to the Association for Education in Journalism and Mass Communication Conference, Baltimore, MD.

Hutton, J. G. (2001). Defining the relationship between public relations and marketing: Public relations most important challenge. In R. L. Heath (Ed.), *Handbook of public relations* (pp. 205–214). Thousand Oaks, CA: Sage.

Kim, Y. (2001a). Search for the organization-public relationship: A valid and reliable instrument. *Journalism and Mass Communication Quarterly, 78,* 799–815.

Kim, Y. (2001b). The economic impact of public relations. *Journal of Public Relations Research, 13*(1), 3–26.

Kotler, P. (1986). Megamarketing. *Harvard Business Review, 64*(2), 117–124.

Kotler, P. (1991). *The marketer's guide to public relations.* New York: Wiley.

Kotler, P., & Zaltman, G. (1971). Social marketing: An approach to planned social change. *Journal of Marketing, 35,* 3–12.

Knapp, M. L., & Vangelisti, A. (1992). *Interpersonal communication and human relationships.* Boston: Allyn and Bacon.

Knodell, J. E. (1976). Matching perceptions of food editors, writers, and readers. *Public Relations Review, 2*(3), 37–56.

Laing, R. D., Phillipson, H., and Lee, A. R. (1966). *Interpersonal perception.* Baltimore: Perennial Library.

Lauzen, M. M. (1995). Toward a model of environmental scanning. *Journal of Public Relations Research, 7*(3), 187–203.

Luck, D. (1974). Social marketing: Confusion compounded. *Journal of Marketing, 38,* 70–72.

Mitchell, R. K., Agle, B. R., & Wood, D. J. (1997). Toward a theory of stakeholder identification and salience: Defining the principle of who and what really counts. *Academy of Management Review,* 22(4), 853–886.

Moriarty, S. E. (1994, Fall). PR and IMC: The benefits of integration. *Public Relations Quarterly,* 38–44.

Ries, A., & Ries, L. (2002). *The fall of advertising and the rise of PR.* New York: Harper Business Publishing.

Ries, A., & Trout, J. (1993). *The 22 immutable laws of marketing: Violate them at your own risk.* New York: Harper Business Publishing.

Roloff, M. E. (1981). *Interpersonal communication: A social exchange approach.* Beverly Hills, CA: Sage.

Schultz. D. (1996). The inevitability of integrated communications. *Journal of Business Research, 37,* 139–146.

Schultz, D., Tannenbaum, S. I., & Lauterborn, R. F. (1993). *Integrated marketing communications: Pulling it together and making it work.* Lincolnwood, IL: NTC Books.

Sirgy, M. J. (1998). *Integrated marketing communication: A systems approach.* Upper Saddle River, NJ: Prentice-Hall.

Stafford, L., & Canary, D. J. (1991). Maintenance strategies and romantic relationship type, gender and relational characteristics. *Journal of Social and Personal Relationships, 8,* 217–42.

Taylor, D. A., & Altman, I. (1973). *Social penetration: The development of interpersonal relationships.* New York: Holt, Rinehart and Winston.

Thomlison, T. D. (2000). An interpersonal primer with implications for public relations. In J. A. Ledingham & S. D. Bruning (Eds.), *Public relations as relationships management: A relational approach to public relations* (pp. 177–203). Hillsdale, NJ: Lawrence Erlbaum.

Webster, F. E. (1992). The changing role of marketing in the corporation. *Journal of Marketing, 56,* 1–17.

24

The Bridgestone/Firestone Recall Image Crisis: A Case Study

Kelly Berg Nellis

This case study utilizes the Bridgestone/Firestone tire crisis to demonstrate many of the theories, models, issues, and theoretical constructs that have been presented in the chapters on organizational communication and public relations. The following prescriptive theories and descriptive theories presented in these chapters are demonstrated in this case study.

In this chapter, you will read about the following concepts:

- Asymmetrical model of public relations
- Campaign
- Change agent theory
- Chaos theory/Complexity theory
- Classical/Scientific management
- Cognitive dissonance theory
- Collaborative theory/Cooperation antagonism theory
- Collapse theory of corporate image
- Coordination model
- Decision makers
- Diffusion of innovations theory
- Ethical responsibilities
- Law of public opinion
- Linkage model
  - Diffused linkage
  - Enabling linkage
  - Functional linkage
  - Normative linkage
- Publicity model of public relations
- Relationship marketing

- Selective perception theory
- Symmetrical model of public relations
- Systems theory
- Two-way, symmetrical communication
- Window of opportunity

Dramatic photographs (see Figure 24.1) were not the only, or even primary, factor that led Bridgestone/Firestone, the Japanese-owned tire maker, to recall 6.5 million tires in August 2000. Emotional and dramatic images can have such an impact on the public that opinion can be strongly affected in a short period of time. Additionally, a flurry of media reports surrounding the tire company—combined with lawsuits accusing Bridgestone/Firestone of being responsible for anywhere from 88 to 148 deaths, 1,400 accidents in the United States alone, and some 200 injuries due to the tread separating from its tires—quickly turned public opinion sour. In fact, as in most crises, the company would have had to make the right public relations choices in a 48-hour window of time to maintain control of the situation.

However, the company began its crisis response by shifting blame: first to consumers and then to Ford Motor Company, the auto manufacturer that placed Bridgestone/Firestone tires as standard equipment on many of its sport utility vehicles and light trucks. Utilizing that strategy, the company made what in hindsight may have seemed like the two least palatable public relations choices it could have made.

This is a good place to review the definition of a **campaign** (Chapter 20, 21). The first news stories that came out were not part of any kind of a campaign. They were just a series of news stories. But, when Bridgestone/Firestone began its crisis response messages, an actual campaign began. That is, given that messages were released by the organization and that message content was intentionally prepared to respond to the crisis and to the targeted populations, a campaign was initiated. We are not suggesting here that the campaign

FIGURE 24.1 Edelio and Norma Herrera are seen at Disney World with their 1-year-old grandson, Antonio, on the day of the tire-related accident, Sunday, May 30, 2000. Antonio survived the crash; his grandparents did not.

Courtesy PR NewsFoto, NewsCom.

messages were good campaign communication, only that the Bridgestone/Firestone campaign began with their release of messages.

By the time Bridgestone/Firestone's then-CEO Masatoshi Ono apologized, with head bowed before reporters in a press conference September 2000, the public relations efforts of the company during its tire crisis already had been considered disastrous. Because of that incident alone, the company made the top spot on Jack O'Dwyer's annual list of top 10 biggest public relations blunders. Consistent with the **classical/scientific management style** (Chapter 19), the company "earned the spot because its CEO took a month before making a public appearance to apologize." "Instead, the company tried to blame consumer driving habits and Ford for its tire inflation recommendation," O'Dwyer (2001), of Finneman Associates, wrote in his newsletter.

In this chapter, you will discover more about Bridgestone/Firestone's handling of its **crisis communication** (Chapters 20, 21) situation and how the company and a public relations firm with which it later consulted, New York–based Ketchum, attempted to maintain and rebuild relationships with its publics while simultaneously trying to address a potentially deadly situation. While crisis theories are also applicable to this situation, you will read how a variety of basic communication and public relations theories you have encountered in this text can be applied in a company's public relations efforts both before a crisis and afterward, to rebuild its image.

What Led to the Crisis at Bridgestone/Firestone?

Media reports and Bridgestone/Firestone's own corporate messages show how the crisis unfolded to include both Bridgestone/Firestone and Ford Motor Company. The two companies have had a relationship almost 100 years long. Yet in this situation, only one company seems to be suffering the effects of its public relations efforts: Bridgestone/Firestone. The primary reasons the situation turned into a crisis could be attributed to the company's underestimation of the public's concern, its misreading of the populations with whom it was communicating, and its choice of how to communicate with those populations.

According to effective and ethical public relations models presented by Grunig and Hunt (1984) and the report on what excellent public relations should be (Grunig, 1992), to be effective Bridgestone/Firestone would have had to engage in **two-way, symmetrical communication** (Chapters 20, 21, and 23) with its populations. Such a public relations model might have necessitated that the company report to consumers as soon as a National Highway Transportation Safety Association (NHTSA) investigation began in March 2000, that it was concerned about public safety, and that it would do everything to ensure that its tires were safe, perhaps including the public on some investigation panels and keeping consumers aware of its steps to ensure safety.

Further, the company may have wanted to begin an immediate investigation and **formative evaluation research** (Chapter 21) of its own into the tire tread concerns, letting the public know of its efforts. And, while it may seem an illogical business move to recall tires when it does not make financial sense to do so or to alarm people unnecessarily, there were clear indications of public concern for these issues prior to the August media reports and recall.

Those concerns should have led the company to want to take some action to assure a two-way relationship was maintained between Bridgestone/Firestone and its publics. All these issues should have prompted Bridgestone/Firestone to feel its **ethical responsibilities** (Chapter 21) with all the audiences that related to it during this crisis. Clearly, this case study reveals a general callousness on the part of this corporation toward its audiences and no real efforts to be ethical. Being totally honest at the very outset of the crisis reports and immediately recalling the potentially dangerous tires would have revealed a correct ethical and moral response by this corporation.

Instead, the company seemed to act in what Grunig and Hunt term an **asymmetrical model of public relations,** and at times according to the **publicity model** (Chapters 20, 21), in their attempts to change the behavior of the publics but not the company. In these models, only information that favors the company's position is disseminated. Even if Bridgestone/Firestone did utilize formative research to determine the best messages to convince consumers of its point of view, Grunig and Hunt point out that the two-way asymmetrical model is ineffective when the organization and publics disagree. Because the model looks to change only the populations in the relationship and not the organization itself, the result can be an exacerbation of the conflict and, often, lawsuits. While using an asymmetrical or publicity model of public relations is not a guarantee a company will end up in crisis, it may be one reason the Bridgestone/Firestone crisis escalated as it did.

Where Did the Company Go Wrong in Its Response to the Crisis?

While few would equate the Bridgestone/Firestone crisis situation with the environmental disaster that resulted when the Exxon *Valdez* spilled 10 million gallons of oil onto the Alaskan coastline, the similarities in the mishandling of the **crisis management** (Chapters 20, 21) are evident. James Lukaszewski (1993), a consultant hired by Fortune 500 companies in the 1980s to handle Exxon's crisis response and sensitive communication situations, outlined the public relations mistakes Exxon made at the time of the spill. Among them were a slow reaction to the crisis and slow communication regarding the situation, shifting blame to others, ducking responsibility, showing a lack of concern or arrogance, minimizing the impact, and missing the window of opportunity with the news media and the public (Lukaszewski, 1993). Bridgestone/Firestone's own crisis response seemed to embody all of these elements, according the the classical/scientific management style (Chapter 19).

The company had early indications of concerns over the tires through lawsuits and legal actions in other countries. These, along with the NHTSA investigation into the tires, served as early warnings of the potential for a negative situation (CNN, 2000a). Yet the company's first responses to media reports of concerns regarding tread separation deflected responsibility solely to consumers, who, the company argued, typically neglected their tires. When media attention escalated in August 2000, the company continued to point one finger at consumers while pointing the other finger at Ford, again claiming no responsibility for any problems associated with the tires. Once again, demonstrated here in Bridgestone/Firestone's responses are two models of public relations: the publicity model, where a corporation communicates only favorable information (sometimes even untrue information) to the publics, and the assymetrical model of public relations, where a corporation communicates its version to the publics with little effort to relate accurate information to interested publics.

Additionally, Bridgestone/Firestone spokeswoman Christine Karbowiak's comments that the number of incidents was small compared to the number of tires sold, whether accurate or not, attempted to downplay the impact of the issue and probably portrayed an arrogance that was unlikely to sit well with the interested populations. By the time a formal apology was presented by the company in October 2000, the **window of opportunity** was long past.

Bridgestone/Firestone's delivery of messages to the media, which were then picked up by receivers, discussed among persons, and eventually resulted in negative images and responses, is an example of the **diffusion of innovations theory** (Chapter 20). This media event and dispersal of images demonstrates as well the power of change agents, as explained according to **change agent theory** (Chapter 20); that is, when persons were exposed to Bridgestone/Firestone's messages and spread their negative reactions to these messages to their friends and family, these persons were functioning as change agents.

Whom Did the Crisis Affect?

Any time an organization faces a crisis, the company's fracturing of its **corporate image** (Chapters 20, 21, 22, and 23) is only one result of the crisis. In Chapter 19 on organizational communication, you learned about **systems theory,** which explores how the different parts of an organization are interdependent and affected by the environment around them. Another important part of systems theory describes how important balance is to an organization's success. While an organization naturally undergoes change, it also must learn to identify when it is off balance and work to regain its stability.

Despite the early warnings that lawsuits, regional media reports, and even an NHTSA investigation provided, Bridgestone/Firestone appeared to do little to show it realized that the situation could become a crisis. Media reports suggest the company began creating an **action plan** and **communication plan** (Chapter 21) in regard to the tires in May 2000, yet its responses to the escalation of interest in the issue suggest it made choices that decreased its stability rather than regained the company's equilibrium.

In fact, the Bridgestone/Firestone crisis was not limited to the three models of tires recalled. The crisis extended beyond the company and affected the stability of other populations. For example, additional tires within the company and other companies, as well as Ford vehicles, were called into question. Around the world, other countries began their own criminal investigations into Bridgestone/Firestone tires and Ford vehicles. Even the U.S. government responded by exploring additional safety issues on tires and sport utility vehicles (Winter, 2000).

Esman's **linkage model** (Grunig & Hunt, 1984) can further illuminate all of the potential **populations** (Chapters 20, 21, 22, and 23) affected by and influencing Bridgestone/Firestone during the crisis and show their interrelatedness (see Figure 24.2). Among those in the **enabling linkage** are the populations that allow the corporation to exist, including the chief executive officers (Ono and John T. Lampe), the board of directors for the company, stockholders, and the NHTSA. Clearly the NHTSA was affected in that it was called on to investigate the complaints against the company and to work with both Bridgestone/Firestone and Ford.

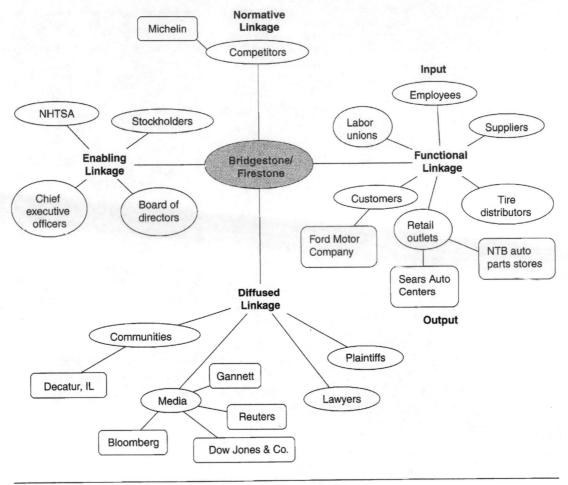

FIGURE 24.2 *Graphic of Linkage Model for Bridgestone/Firestone.*

The stockholders were affected in a number of ways. The recall and its associated costs, estimated at $750 million, along with the dip in consumer confidence, would affect the stock price for the company. In fact, the company's stock dropped 40 percent to a five-year low in the first month of the crisis. Later, the stockholders sued Bridgestone/Firestone, arguing that the company deceived them by inflating its financial status and underreporting the costs of the recall.

Internally, Ono was forced to resign his position to save face for the company and himself after public opinion turned against the company. Lampe was promoted to the vacated presidency and faced the responsibility of pulling the company out of a crisis situation (see Figure 24.3).

The **functional linkage** for Bridgestone/Firestone involves both those populations that provide services and products to the company and those audiences that help put out or purchase the product and services. Labor unions, employees, suppliers, customers, and

FIGURE 24.3   Bridgestone/Firestone CEO John T. Lampe addresses members of the media at a Nashville, TN, news conference October 10, 2000, after being named chairman, CEO, and president of the company.

Courtesy Feature Photo Service, NewsCom Search

tire distributors and retail outlets such as Firestone dealerships and Sears Auto Centers all were clearly affected by the recall and crisis. For example, in the midst of the crisis, the company also was negotiating contracts with labor union employees at its Decatur, Illinois, plant. That particular plant was the focus of the tire company's investigation into the targeted tires. Further, employees at plants in several states were affected by a production stoppage due to lack of demand for the tires.

Among the suppliers and distributors, Firestone and other tire dealerships were affected by the additional paperwork and pressure to comply with the recall requests. Moreover, almost 800 Sears Auto Centers and 350 NTB auto parts stores stopped selling the models of tires involved in the recall, though the impact was minimal because those tires were sold by Sears through special orders only. Perhaps a less obvious impact is that of those involved in providing tires for the tire exchange and assisting in the recall efforts.

Finally, consumers, including Ford Explorer and other sport utility and truck owners, had to take time and, in some cases, money, to replace their tires. Many more were sometimes tragically affected because of accidents related to the tires. More than 200 economic damage, class action, personal injury, and wrongful death lawsuits were filed against the company by February 2001.

Another consumer, Ford Motor Company, also fits into the functional linkage. As one of the largest consumers of Bridgestone/Firestone tires, Ford saw its own costs rise and revenues drop as it dealt with the recall. The estimated cost to Ford for the recall is $500 million.

The **normative linkage** includes other organizations in the tire industry, including competitors, such as Michelin. In fact, Ford announced during the crisis that Bridgestone/Firestone would no longer be the sole provider of tires for the Explorer and that Michelin would be an option on some models. The investigations into the safety of other tire brands brought scrutiny to Bridgestone/Firestone's competitors as well.

The **diffused linkage** includes populations that relate to the organization from an outside perspective. The media certainly were involved in the crisis and had a relationship both with the general public and with Bridgestone/Firestone. Several media corporations, including Bloomberg, Dow Jones & Co., Reuters, and Gannett news agencies, filed motions in existing lawsuits against the company in an attempt to gain access to company documents that the media argued were necessary to public safety.

Also among the outsider relationships were those who spoke out against the company, including lawyers and plaintiffs, and those communities affected by the crisis. For example, Strategic Safety, a research group for attorneys, recommended a tire recall to be extended to tires made as far back as 1991. Another group, headed by the woman who forced Bridgestone/Firestone to recall tires in the 1970s when she was head of the NHTSA, banded together with attorneys to support another recall.

By looking at each of the populations related to an organization, one can see not only those who have been affected by a crisis situation, but how to prepare in advance to meet the needs and concerns of the organization and each of the populations. Each of the populations is affected by and, in turn, affects, the company. A company must be prepared, even before a crisis or positive situation occurs, to continually communicate with all its related populations. This kind of communication would be an excellent example of **relationship marketing** (Chapter 23). This communication process must be ongoing, rather than limited to crisis situations. Failing to engage in a continuous two-way symmetrical relationship with one's publics can have results that extend beyond monetary costs to a change in corporate reputation and an increase in negative images among an organization's publics from which it may never recover.

Theories of **chaos** (Chapter 20) within an organization and **complexity** (Chapter 20) can add to understanding the seeming uncertainty and confusion that Bridgestone/Firestone felt during their crisis campaign. These new theories developed by public relations scholars contend that an organization does not always act in an organized or consistent way to a crisis; rather than assuming that an organization can always be organized and rational, these theories argue chaos can just take over within any organization and campaign planners must admit this and deal with it. As is evident in all the various messages the company released, a measure of confusion and inconsistency in the messages suggests that a unified response or view of correct crisis response was not present. We do not have a privileged window into the crisis room or "war room" at Bridgestone/Firestone, but perhaps chaos theory and complexity theory can explain the multiple, negative, and accusing messages delivered by Bridgestone/Firestone that ultimately hurt their corporate images.

What Public Relations Strategies Could the Company Have Used to Recover from the Crisis?

Whether Bridgestone/Firestone and the Ford Explorer will recover completely from the crisis is unclear. Most agree the image of Ford's Explorer will quickly recover, in part due to its "textbook" handling of the crisis situation, with company CEO Jaques Nassar taking charge immediately after the recall by becoming the company spokesperson, showing concern and sympathy of the company and assuring consumers that the company was committed to resolving the problem, thus exhibiting **symmetrical public relations** (Chapter 20, 21). While consumer confidence and stock prices dropped some for Ford after the recall, vehicle sales were only down slightly, and stock prices on most companies had dropped in the prior eight months. Further, opinion polls suggest that consumers blamed Bridgestone/Firestone more than they did Ford for the situation. This belief may assist the comeback of Ford's Explorer model.

The views on Bridgestone/Firestone are more mixed. A few believe that the company never will rebound. Others believe that the company has weathered worse crises and is likely to survive this one as well. Public opinion polls, exemplifying the **law of public opinion** (Chapter 21), point to a significant drop in consumer confidence in the brand, with half noting that they would turn to another brand when considering buying tires.

Both Bridgestone/Firestone and Ford can take some lessons also as to the lasting impact on their public image this crisis will have from their dual late-1970s crises when Bridgestone/Firestone was accused of hiding safety problems with its tires and Ford's Pinto had a problem fuel tank. While both companies recovered from the crises of 30 years earlier, the public relations personnel in charge of rebuilding relationships with important publics and repairing the companies' images worked for a decade to regain lost ground. In fact, Firestone teetered on the edge of bankruptcy after hiding safety problems with its Firestone 500 tires until Japanese-owned Bridgestone bought the company 10 years later and helped it regain its reputation. [Web site: What Led to Crisis Response for Ford?]

As you can see, both of these companies have experienced a history of communication and miscommunication back and forth between them and their respective consumers, exemplifying the **coordination model** (Chapter 23). Further, both Bridgestone/Firestone and Ford have experienced crisis situations together, leading both companies to accuse and blame the other and to blame their consumers. The **collapse theory of corporate image** (Chapter 20) is demonstrated in these exchanges of information. First, as this theory suggests, image is not only in the corporation's desired images but also in the meanings/images attributed to the corporation by the various audience members relating to the organization. A look at all the images expressed, the allegations of negligence, the lawsuits brought by consumers, and the various explanations offered for the crises demonstrate the collapse theory's positions that images, opinions, or attitudes are not controlled solely by the organization and that they are experienced by both the organization's members and the audience members outside the organization.

Bridgestone/Firestone's recall efforts were to be completed in three stages, focusing first on the southern states, where most of the incidents of tread separation had been reported. However, due to anger expressed by the public over the Bridgestone/Firestone's three-stage recall, Ford announced one day after the recall that all Ford vehicle owners with the recalled tires could come in to have their tires replaced at any time with any brand of tire. Ford CEO Jaques Nassar appeared on television news on August 22, 2000, to say that all of Ford's resources were aimed at resolving the situation. A few days later, Ford revealed that Bridgestone/Firestone would no longer be the sole provider of tires for Explorers in the coming year.

The continued message from the company was that Ford Motor Company employees were working around the clock to resolve the problem. However, on September 6, both companies were reprimanded during a Congressional hearing for failing to notify the public earlier about the tire problem. Ford Motor Company spokespeople blamed Firestone, saying the company had received assurances from Firestone that the tires were safe. Figure 24.4 shows

FIGURE 24.4 *Tire from 1997 Ford Explorer Involved in Herrera Fatal Accident.*
Courtesy PRNewsFoto, NewsCom Search

the damaged tire from the Herrera accident. [Web site: What Was Bridgestone/Firestone's Response?]

What Was Bridgestone/Firestone's Crisis Response?

By the time Bridgestone/Firestone issued a voluntary recall for 6.5 million of its tires on August 9, 2000, the company's ATX, ATX II, and Wilderness AT tires had been under investigation by the National Highway and Transportation Safety Association for more than five months. Yet prior to the August recall, media coverage and public awareness of these events was minimal. The media messages had not yet represented a **diffusion of innovations** (Chapter 20), and media messages had not yet been picked up and circulated by **change agents** (Chapter 20) and **decision makers** (Chapter 21). All this was about to change.

A Texas television station had reported in early February that statewide, the tread on ATX tires found on Ford Explorers reportedly had peeled off their tires. Bridgestone/Firestone was purported to have responded in a printed statement that was posted to the television station's website. In the statement, company spokeswoman Christine Karbowiak defended the quality of its ATX tires and the hard work of the people who make the tires at its plants. The company also claimed that no legal evidence of deficiency in the tire existed and that its investigation of the incidents mentioned in the television report found no evidence that tire separation was the cause of the fatalities, demonstrating the **publicity model** (Chapters 20, 21) of public relations and a misunderstanding of the power of the **collapse theory of corporate image** (Chapter 20).

Regional news coverage was reawakened in July 2000 with the lawsuits of two Florida families who sued both Bridgestone/Firestone and Ford Motor Company for negligence in the deaths of two people. It was not until August that national media outlets begin reporting on the NHTSA investigation and the complaints. By that time, the number of complaints had risen to 193, while the reported death toll had risen to 21. Bridgestone/Firestone's Karbowiak responded initially by saying that the company would inspect tires for damage, wear, and inflation levels and remedy the situation as needed. Five days later, Bridgestone/Firestone called a press conference, during which it voluntarily recalled 6.5 million tires made in its Decatur, Illinois, plant. The company noted that the problems with tread separation may be related to warm weather, since most of the complaints originated in southern states.

All these actions and messages back and forth among Bridgestone/Firestone, Ford, the media, and governmental agencies call to mind **collaborative theory** and **cooperative antagonism theory** (Chapter 20). These theories by Grunig call for any organization to pursue continuous active and mutual communication with all its relevant populations, whether in a crisis situation or not. These theories are different terms, but nevertheless name the same construct of collaborative and cooperative corporate communication. This case study's details about all the miscommunication that occurred in this crisis calls attention for the importance of ongoing, mutual **relationship marketing** (Chapter 23) for every size and kind of corporation. Perhaps positive relationships established by Bridgestone/Firestone before this crisis occurred could have saved this crisis, protected their consumers, and even saved lives.

Finally, the media attention led Bridgestone/Firestone to consider its image in the marketplace. In the whirlwind days to follow, Bridgestone/Firestone made several changes in its plan, in order to meet public concern. In addition to offering reimbursement to consumers who replaced tires with other brands, the company airlifted tires from Japanese plants to meet the demand for replacement tires. Two weeks into the crisis, an ad in newspapers nationwide from Bridgestone/Firestone CEO Masatoshi Ono gave an update on the efforts of the company and its investigation into the problem. The company also announced the beginning of a four-month internal investigation that eventually would encompass an analysis by Ford and Bridgestone/Firestone engineers and other safety experts, as well as an independent expert analysis of the tires.

When NHTSA announced September 1, 2000, that it believed another 1.4 million tires should be included in the recall, Bridgestone/Firestone instead offered free inspection and replacement of the additional tires as necessary. The same day, a blowout of a tire in Texas resulted in the death of a 10-year-old.

After the company was reprimanded, along with Ford Motor Company, at a Congressional hearing into the tire complaints, a new public relations consulting firm, New York–based Ketchum, was hired to assist Bridgestone/Firestone in rebuilding its public image. Within weeks, CEO Ono resigned his position and John T. Lampe, former executive vice president of Bridgestone/Firestone, was named chief executive officer. His first public act was an apology for the tragic accidents.

All this controversy in messages back and forth, first in false allegations and rationalizations and ultimately in the truth about the tires, reveals two theories examined above. **Selective perception theory** (Chapters 20, 22) is demonstrated in how the organization failed to appreciate that targeted audience members are not necessarily going to process and accept the intended messages of the organization. Instead, audiences selectively perceive the content of the messages that match their concerns: tire safety, causes for unsafe tires, the importance of tire pressure, and so on. All the media coverage that eventually came out about all the accidents and even deaths brought the crisis to the persons who drove Ford Explorers or had Bridgestone/Firestone tires. Then, these media stories became very important to the affected consumers, exemplifying selective perception of media messages.

Additionally, **cognitive dissonance theory** (Chapters 20, 22) was probably also at work in the targeted consumers. The messages of the organization most likely made the audience members angry and even polarized in their negative images of the corporations. This reaction to media messages can lead some to process the contrary corporate messages, in order to confirm their opposing images.

Summary

In this chapter, you learned that even the most basic public relations and communication theories can help one understand appropriate public relations responses, especially in a crisis situation. In addressing any public relations situation, two-way symmetrical communication is more effective and more ethical in the long-term for building and maintaining relationships than other models of public relations practice.

This case study suggests that other models of publicity or asymmetry may result in longer, more difficult, and more costly corporate image repair campaigns that will eventually require two-way symmetrical communication for relationships that can withstand future crises. Systems theory also helps in understanding the complexity of communication within and without a corporation experiencing a crisis. A communication practitioner should explore all of the populations that are related to, and interdependent of, an organization. Looking at these linkages according to the linkage model can lay the groundwork for understanding and creating an appropriate and thorough action plan.

And finally, the corporation that escapes a crisis situation through solid and accurate communication will most likely emerge with its desired, positive images intact. The collapse theory suggests that truthful and in-depth information to receivers results in positive images in the various populations that have experienced the crisis situation. The corporation also needs to appreciate the selective process of receiving messages that all their targeted receivers go through.

Discussion Questions

1. What public relations lessons can we take from the Bridgestone/Firestone situation?

2. How does the Bridgestone/Firestone crisis situation illustrate why the asymmetrical model of communication is less effective than a symmetrical model of public relations?

3. What other populations can you think of that may be part of the linkage model for Bridgestone/Firestone? How could that population have been affected by the crisis?

References

CNN. (2000a, August 3). *NHTSA investigating failure of Firestone Brand tires.* Retrieved March 18, 2001, from www.Cnn.com/2000/US/08/03/tire.investigation/

Grunig, J. (Ed.). (1992). *Excellence in public relations and communication management.* Hillsdale, NJ: Lawrence Erlbaum.

Gruning, J. E., & Hunt, T. (1984). *Managing public relations.* New York: Holt, Rinehart and Winston.

Lukaszewski, J. E. (1993). The Exxon *Valdez* paradox. In J. A. Gottschalk (Ed.), *In crisis response: Inside stories on managing image under siege* (pp. 185–213). Detroit: Visible Ink.

O'Dwyer, J. R. (2001, January 10). Bridgestone made No. 1 PR goof. *Jack O'Dwyer's Newsletter, 34*(2), 2.

Winter, D. (2000, October). Together again in the headlines. *Wards Auto World.* New York: Intertec Publishing.

Author Index

Subject Index

Paradigm, 2, 25
Parole, 266, 278
Parsimony, 17
Passive strategy, 112, 177, 202
Pathos, 84
Patrons, 77
Pentad, 93
Pentagon, case study in mass communication,
    275–283
Perceived behavioral control, 145
Perceptual consequences, 7
Performing stage, 125, 180
Peripheral processing, 152
Peripheral routes, 178
Personal level, 164
Person schema, 358
Persuasion, 138–155
    characteristics of the persuasive message,
        141–144
        message characteristics, 142–144
        source characteristics, 141–142
    compliance gaining theories, 148–152
        elaboration likelihood model,
            151–152
        strategies, 149–151
    defining persuasive communication, 140
    reasons for studying, 139–140
    theories of, 144–148
        cognitive dissonance theory,
            147–148
        social judgment theory, 145–147
        theory of reasoned action, 144–145
Persuasive communication, 140–144
    message characteristics, 142–144
        one- and two-sided messages, 143
        persuasive arguments, ordering of,
            143
        persuasive evidence, 142–143
        speech style, 143–144
    source characteristics, 141–142
        credibility, 141
        physical attraction, 142
        similarity, 141
Persuasive evidence, 142–143
Phaedrus (Plato), 78
Phenomenology, 27
Physical attraction, 142
Pisteis (proofs), 81

Planned behavior theory of public relations,
    322
Plato, 78
Pleaders, 77
Politeness theory, 108–110, 160–162
Political campaign, 317
Political economy theory, 262–263,
    279
Political ideology, 279
Political messages, public relations and,
    351–352
Political theory: Marx and critical theory,
    59–60
Polysemy, 272
Popular cultural studies, 264–265
Popular culture, 263
Populations, 384
Positive face need, 108
Positive politeness, 109
Positivism, 26
Positivity, 364
Postcolonial, 169
Postmodernism, 268–269, 282–283
Post-positivism, 30
Power, 100
Power distance, 160
Powerful media effects, 193–195
    hypodermic needle theory, 194
    magic bullet theory, 194
Practical consciousness, 134
The Prayer of Jabez, 215
Predictability, 115, 182
Predictive validity, 16
Preferred reading, 221
Preoccupation, 238
Privacy, 115, 182
Probabilistic laws, 30
Problem-solving process facilitators,
    320
Progression, 238
Proletariat, 260
    revolt of, 261
Proof, 81
Propaganda, 57
Propositions, 10, 26
Pseudo-environment, 191
Psychographic appeals, 357
Psychological gender, 162